Developing Governance and Governing Development

Indigenous Nations and Collaborative Futures

Series Editors: Professor Larissa Behrendt, Dr Simone Bignall, Professor Daryle Rigney and Professor Linda Tuhiwai Smith

Indigenous Nations and Collaborative Futures publishes cutting-edge work by Indigenous and non-Indigenous authors and Indigenous-participant teams, whose inquiry advances post-colonial political thinking. Attending critically to settler-colonialism in the contexts of Australia, Aotearoa-New Zealand and other nations of the Southern Pacific Rim, this series supplements and enriches new scholarship emerging from Indigenous perspectives and experiences in the United States and Canada. It aims to explore and showcase the diverse ways in which Indigenous authorities all around the world are designing and utilising modern political institutions that match with their cultural values and assert a continuing right and responsibility to care for traditional lands and waters. Conceived through the optic of the political, 'Indigenous Nations and Collaborative Futures' will publish innovative and important research that examines the transformative potential of cross-cultural interaction, collaboration and agreement-making to successfully mediate culturally diverse political interests and values in settler-colonial jurisdictions. It contributes new thinking about the reparation of historical injustice and the terms and future conditions of positive coexistence after colonisation.

The Children's Country: Creation of a Goolarabooloo Future in North-West Australia, by Stephen Muecke and Paddy Roe

Trapped by History: The Indigenous-State Relationship in Australia, by Darryl Cronin

Developing Governance and Governing Development: International Case Studies of Indigenous Futures, edited by Diane Smith, Alice Wighton, Stephen Cornell and Adam Vai Delaney

Developing Governance and Governing Development

International Case Studies of Indigenous Futures

Edited by Diane Smith, Alice Wighton, Stephen Cornell and Adam Vai Delaney

ROWMAN & LITTLEFIELD
Lanham • Boulder • New York • London

Published by Rowman & Littlefield
An imprint of The Rowman & Littlefield Publishing Group, Inc.
4501 Forbes Boulevard, Suite 200, Lanham, Maryland 20706
www.rowman.com

Cover Design: The 'Elements of Governance' artwork was created to extend and strengthen the governance story-telling work of the Australian Indigenous Governance Institute and to be widely appropriate to First Nations peoples nationally and internationally. It represents the seven areas of First Nation Governance: Laws and Rules, Meanings, Powers, Values, Knowledge, Ideas and Beliefs. The white circles are the ideas and perspectives that each individual brings to the table. The dots are the practices and solutions that are formed in collaboration. Radiating out from the circle are the positive effects of First Nation Governance which can be felt through all areas of life. The graphic was designed by Jenna Lee from Gilimbaa, https://www.gilimbaa.com.au/

British Library Cataloguing in Publication Information Available

Library of Congress Cataloging-in-Publication Data

Names: Smith, D. E. (Diane E.), 1952- editor. | Wighton, Alice, 1991- editor. | Cornell, Stephen E. (Stephen Ellicott), 1948- editor. | Delaney, Adam, editor.
Title: Developing governance and governing development : international case studies of indigenous futures / ediited by Diane Smith, Alice Wighton, Stephen Cornell and Adam Vai Delaney.
Description: Lanham : Rowman & Littlefield, [2021] | Series: Indigenous nations and collaborative futures | Includes bibliographical references and index. | Summary: "Globally, far too many discussions about Indigenous governance and development are dominated by accounts of disadvantage, deficit and failure. This book paints a different international picture, testifying to Indigenous peoples as agents of governance innovation and successful developers in their own right, telling stories in their words, from their own experiences and countries. From Indigenous voices, we hear alternative concepts and measures of effectiveness, legitimacy, success and sustainability. Indigenous stories and voices are captured as 20 case study chapters, written in lively, clear language about what is happening that is promising and productive in Indigenous self-determined governance for self-determined development in Canada, Australia, Aotearoa/New Zealand and the USA; all English colonial-settler countries"— Provided by publisher.
Identifiers: LCCN 2021014377 (print) | LCCN 2021014378 (ebook) | ISBN 9781538143636 (cloth) | ISBN 9781538143643 (epub)
Subjects: LCSH: Indigenous peoples—Politics and government—Case studies. | Indigenous peoples—Government relations—Case studies. | Indigenous peoples—Economic conditions—Case studies. | Economic development—Case studies.
Classification: LCC GN380 .D48 2021 (print) | LCC GN380 (ebook) | DDC 305.8—dc23
LC record available at https://lccn.loc.gov/2021014377
LC ebook record available at https://lccn.loc.gov/2021014378

Contents

Foreword

In 2012, a group of First Nations leaders and academics from Canada, Australia, New Zealand and the United States gathered in Tucson, Arizona, to share stories of their different pathways to self-determination and self-governance. The meeting kick-started something important—an international conversation that inspired many of us working to rebuild governance and our nations, a conversation that is still going strong today. From that first gathering hosted by the Native Nations Institute at the University of Arizona came the *Common Roots, Common Futures Indigenous Governance Network* (CRCF). Our second network gathering hosted by the Australian Indigenous Governance Institute (AIGI) followed in Brisbane, Australia, in 2017, the third was hosted more recently by the Maori and Indigenous Governance Centre in Aotearoa-New Zealand in 2019.

It is not hard to figure that while the First Nations in the CRCF Network do have marked differences in our respective cultures, histories, politics and laws, we have much more in common. Those commonalities are evident not only in respect to the many similar challenges we face as Indigenous peoples living in settler colonial nations but also in the common ways we go about solving the challenges we face. But, perhaps more importantly, we all share a resilient aspiration for self-determination and a passion to ensure that the future of our First Nations is one to celebrate. It comes as no surprise then that writing and talking about our shared circumstances has generated enduring friendships and commitment to a dialogue across the Pacific rim and wider afield that has at its heart a transformational vision – a movement – to transition from being positioned as the victim fighting for rights, to the victor exercising self-determined governance and putting into place a development agenda that meets our needs.

This publication is a taste of the remarkable stories that First Nations are telling, in their own voices, about the home-based solutions they are designing to rebuild their nations, collective governance and futures. The book captures a rich sample of resilience and resurgence where Indigenous innovation is strengthened, not undermined, by our cultures and identities. Here we see that the issues described in the story of the Yawuru in Australia resonate with the Fond du Lac Band in the United States, the Gitxsan-Wet'suwet'en in Canada and Māori in Aotearoa-New Zealand.

I am sure you will find presented here the honest self-reflections of First Nation authors on their cultures, identities, people, institutions, leadership, capabilities, rules and processes. The authors probe these important foundations, sharing insights into how we might all contribute to rebuilding our Nations, and continue the march forward collectively. We are convinced that building collective self-governance capabilities are essential to delivering the kinds of development outcomes our peoples are demanding. We remain adamant that our sovereignties cannot be and never have been erased by settler colonialism. We also understand that the challenge on the road ahead is not merely to take control over our own affairs, but to govern well and fairly on behalf of our own Nations.

The CRCF Network is part of a wider movement worldwide that is seeing Indigenous people establish their own governance research and training centres, including in Australia, the Australian Indigenous Governance Institute,[1] the Aboriginal Governance and Management Program[2] and the Indigenous Nations and Collaborative Futures Hub;[3] in the United States, the Native Nations Institute[4] and the Native Governance Center[5]; in Canada, the First Nations Information Governance Centre[6] and the Centre for First Nations Governance[7]; and the Maori and Indigenous Governance Centre[8] in Aotearoa-New Zealand. Many of these centres now collaborate on strategic governance advocacy within their own countries, and on cross-country initiatives.

The Australian Indigenous Governance Institute in Australia is a unique, ground-breaking initiative in Australia, committed to ongoing development of resources, expanding the governance knowledge base, creating networks and mentoring opportunities, while taking care not to duplicate existing services. AIGI envisions a future Australia where Indigenous nations can pursue and exercise their right to self-determination and economic development through strong self–governance. We know that practical, effective and culturally legitimate governance is the fundamental building block for delivering real change, and in ongoing collaboration with these and other centres, will continue to provide a platform for Indigenous leaders and researchers via the CRCF Network to promote an international conversation about Indigenous governance, nation-rebuilding and development. The network is testimony to a willingness to move beyond conversations about deficit, marginalisation and recognition, towards a more daring engagement with transforming our collective self-governance and development agenda for nation-building purposes.

This publication is not just a fascinating reading, it is pioneering. The stories in each chapter now belong to everyone – that has been the wish of the authors. I hope they will also contribute to the small but growing body of research and knowledge on governance, government and development from the point of view of First Nations. For these reasons, I find the book inspiring; we should all be proud of, and determined to face, our common roots and our common future together, in solidarity.

Jason Glanville
Chair, Board of Directors
Australian Indigenous Governance Institute

NOTES

1. https://www.aigi.com.au/
2. http://www.amsant.org.au/apont/our-work/nt-aboriginal-governance-management-program-agmp/
3. https://www.uts.edu.au/research-and-teaching/our-research/jumbunna-institute-indigenous-education-and-research/our-research/indigenous-nations-and-collaborative-futures
4. https://nni.arizona.edu/
5. https://nativegov.org/
6. https://fnigc.ca/index.php
7. http://www.fngovernance.org/
8. https://www.waikato.ac.nz/law/research/centre-for-maori-and-indigenous-governance

Acknowledgements

The editors would like to thank all of the governance practitioners and scholars—Indigenous and non-Indigenous—who have participated in the *Common Roots, Common Futures, Indigenous Network* and contributed their insights to the study and exercise of Indigenous governance and nation-rebuilding in Australia, Canada, Aotearoa-New Zealand and the United States. We are especially grateful to the authors of chapters in this book for their patient and generous cooperation during the preparation of the manuscript, and in turn to their Indigenous governments, communities and families for continuing the conversation and hard work of governance resurgence.

This book has been made possible by the ongoing facilitation and substantial funding support of the Australian Indigenous Governance Institute. The international BHP Foundation, which works to address some of the world's most critical sustainable development challenges, supports the AIGI to deliver a program of 'Supporting self-determined governance for Indigenous development outcomes' as part of the Foundation's 'Australia Country Program'. The Annamila Foundation also provides core funding to AIGI, with a focus on Indigenous peoples in Australia taking greater control of their own lives.

Along with AIGI, the Centre for Aboriginal Economic Policy Research and National Centre for Indigenous Studies at The Australian National University, and the Native Nations Institute at the University of Arizona have given much-appreciated salary support to the editors to undertake our work. AIGI, along with the Native Nations Institute in the United States, and the Centre for Maori and Indigenous Governance in New Zealand continue to provide the organisational services for the CRCF Network, which the authors of this book are members of.

We would like to thank Simone Bignall and Daryle Rigney from the editorial board of the 'Indigenous Nations and Collaborative Futures' series, and the committed publishing team at Rowman and Littlefield Ltd for their generous advice and continued encouragement. Margaret McDonnell's work on style formatting and proofing the diverse range of chapters has been greatly appreciated.

Finally, we dedicate this book to Dr Neil Sterritt—Madiigam Gyamk, from the Gitxsan House of Gitluudaahlxw—Gitxsan leader and chief, governance educator, storyteller, mentor and friend, for his lifetime of inspiring work, intellectual generosity, and advocacy for Indigenous First Nations and their governance in all its forms.

Editors: Diane Smith, Adam Delaney, Alice Wighton and Stephen Cornell
2020

Introduction

Indigenous Resurgence for Governing Development

Diane Smith

THE MOTIVATING JOURNEY

Indigenous governance is not only alive and well globally; it is resurgent and flourishing in newly self-determined forms, contributing to the rejuvenation of Indigenous economies and communities, and redefining relationships between Indigenous peoples and settler-colonial states. This resurgence did not happen overnight.[1] Nor is it a fait accompli. The stories by Indigenous authors in this volume testify that the advance of self-governance is the product of decades of Indigenous struggle, internationally and domestically, to secure rights and replace Western-imposed models of governance with institutions that are self-designed by Indigenous peoples. Their stories also demonstrate that Indigenous governance resurgence does not require a disengagement from dialogue or negotiation of decolonisation with settler states (see also Elliott 2018; Lightfoot 2020; Rigney et al. 2015). Rather, building governance has become an innovative force enabling a fundamental repositioning—radically shifting the conditions of collective self-determination itself, and establishing new ground for nation-rebuilding and the negotiation of collaborative futures with settler societies from a position of Indigenous strength. In effect, resurgent self-governance activates a renewal in all manner of relationships—*within* Indigenous communities and local groups, *between* Indigenous nations, and *with* settler societies.

This view of Indigenous self-governance is far removed from the common deficit discourse promoted by settler-colonial society, which is dominated by assertions of failure and dysfunction. The international case studies presented in this collection paint a different picture; one where Indigenous peoples are successful governors, managers, developers, leaders and agents of innovation in their own right. In focusing on the governance solutions that are promising and productive, we do not underestimate the extent of the obstacles. Each author has a tale to tell of adversity and the often-violent suppression of their cultures of governance by colonising regimes. Their accounts are frank and fearless, for not all the obstacles come from externally imposed government controls. Some challenges arise internally within communities, and though derived partly from the bleak legacies of colonisation, they are all the more debilitating, because they are close to home and intergenerational.

Canada, Australia, Aotearoa/New Zealand and the United States—the CANZUS countries—share their status as some of the world's wealthiest countries, yet each includes Indigenous peoples among its poorest citizens. It is not surprising, therefore, that having secured valuable rights and interests in lands, waters, resources, heritage and intellectual property, Indigenous polities—First Nations—in each of these four countries are leveraging their rights to secure resource and development agreements, manage unique cultural and natural endowments, extend their capital bases, establish enterprises and mobilise their systems of knowledge to create new fields of commerce. In doing so, they face a shared challenge: that of rebuilding forms of self-determined governance that will be practically effective in contemporary circumstances and make life better in the ways they want. And if that task is not daunting enough, each case study testifies to the fact that Indigenous nations are also seeking to exercise governance in ways that are culturally meaningful to them.

While self-governance is arguably a key to delivering sustained transformations that will improve peoples' lives in ways they choose, there are gaps in our knowledge about how people actually go about the initial steps of establishing it, and then sustaining and adapting governance arrangements over time. Similarly, there are gaps in our understanding of the kinds of development that will support the work of self-governance by enhancing cultural vitality, community well-being and prosperity rather than undermining it. This volume aims to help bridge those gaps, and speak to the far wider population of Indigenous governance practitioners and theorists throughout the CANZUS countries and further beyond.

The book originated from three small workshops convened by a network of experienced Indigenous governance leaders and researchers from the CANZUS states, who met in 2012 (Tucson, USA), then again in 2017 (Brisbane, Australia), and 2019 (Auckland, New Zealand).[2] Indigenous delegates at the workshops focused on exploring the promising innovations in the field of self-governance and development in each country over recent decades. They understood there are very real differences in their histories, cultures, demographics, political processes and in the extent of their legal rights and Indigenous jurisdictions. But as stories were told, they equally came to recognise that they also shared critical commonalities. For example, that the four countries share fundamentally similar and largely British legal and political heritages and have similar experiences of displacement and marginalisation by European invasion, with familiar catastrophic results.

Additionally, they now experience the same persistent focus by nation-states on implementing interventionist welfare policies that are informed by Western aspirations and standards, with the intent of incorporating Indigenous peoples into national political and legal systems of oversight. In resistance to this, there has been a common Indigenous movement across the CANZUS countries and beyond to regain control of their lands, communities and development—that is, to reassert their status as self-determining, self-governing nations. Consequently, in the four countries, there has been a more recent explosion of new Indigenous institutions of self-governance, as First Nations transition from their fight for rights and recognition to the shared challenge of effectively exercising those rights to deliver long-awaited progress for their citizens. First and foremost, this is a transition away from a focus on external governments and externally imposed solutions to internal creativity and capability. It is a process of governance resurgence that has been incubating for many years and includes Indigenous groups, communities and leaders extending well beyond the CANZUS countries.[3]

The Indigenous authors in this collection hope that by coming together to share their own stories, they could learn from each other's strategies to address what appeared to be some common governance challenges. Canadian Gitxsan leader Neil Sterritt (2001: 9) succinctly summarised these challenges as having 'insufficient power and jurisdiction, excessive government controls, unclear lines of authority and accountability, inadequate funding and training, lack of enforcement mechanisms, confusion about the impact of provincial [government] laws, confusion about leaders' roles and responsibilities, and confusion about governance matters'. In discussing these obstacles in their own nations, the authors describe diverse pathways to creative governance solutions. In common, those solutions do not advocate a simplistic return to an imagined past golden age. Rather, as the authors attest, resurgent Indigenous governance in diverse settler-colonial situations internationally has given rise to locally innovative structures and practices that are winning cultural credibility and mandates in the Indigenous worlds of today.

A key motivation of this collection then is that it aspires to be of general relevance to a far wider population of Indigenous governance practitioners and theorists within and beyond the CANZUS countries. The authors share a sense that their experiences and questions might also resonate with those of Indigenous peoples from North Europe, Africa, Asia and the Pacific, and South America. They hope that some of their hard-won solutions and insights presented as case studies in this collection can contribute to the broader global conversation that is being carried out among Indigenous peoples who are similarly struggling to establish and sustain self-determined ways of self-governing in contemporary contexts.

THE CASE STUDIES AND THEMES

Indigenous peoples around the world have unique ways of telling stories. In this book, a decolonising methodology motivates the style of how case studies are presented. Diverse Indigenous voices, aspirations and insights are heard in chapters that are written in lively, clear language about what is happening that is promising and productive in Indigenous self-governance for nation-building and development in Canada, Australia, Aotearoa/New Zealand and the United States. The storytelling technique sits comfortably alongside each authors' acute analysis and thick description of collective aspirations and obstacles, influential events and strategic action. Each chapter draws on the author's personal experience as a leader, citizen, educator, researcher and governance practitioner. They speak of governance resurgence being mobilised in sectors as diverse as the resource management of lands and waters, treaty and native title negotiations, constitution-building and law-making, community health and well-being, economic development, cultural heritage, data and intellectual property protection, international trade and political advocacy. What emerges are striking similarities in the creative agency and design solutions of First Nations as they move forward in the quest to achieve self-governance on their terms—similarities that are evident, for instance, between the Sioux in the United States, Yawuru in Australia, Huu-ay-aht in Canada and Maori in New Zealand. It could be that the cultural bases of such governance design innovations extend well beyond the geographic scope of the CANZUS countries, to Indigenous groups internationally.

The case-study chapters highlight a shared set of concerns and priorities among First Nations; not only about how to get started and move forward, but about how to then 'test' the success of their efforts and adapt accordingly. This seems to commonly involve coming up with answers to a set of similar questions; many of which call for collective 'future thinking'. For example: What kind of nation or community are people trying to build and govern, not only for themselves but also for future generations? What kind of self-governance arrangements and innovations might be acceptable and consented to now and continue to enhance self-determination into the future? What role should Indigenous culture play in newly designed governing arrangements or development initiatives, and how might that change over time? Who should benefit from a nation's development initiatives, and how will benefits continue to be available for future generations of citizens? How are First Nations choosing to govern their treaties, native title determinations or settlement agreements? And are there lessons from these that might resonate with other Indigenous peoples more widely?

Our approach in this edited volume has been to source a set of interrelated chapters that highlight the locally customised solutions which Indigenous nations are creating to address these future-oriented questions. We place the case studies within a thematic rather than a country framework, to highlight common threads—the common roots—and to draw out the resourceful solutions and innovative thinking Indigenous peoples bring to designing fresh solutions for what turn out to be shared concerns. The themes are as follows:

1. Governing Rights and Interests
2. Governing for Nation-Building
3. Governing Development and Resources
4. Transformative Leadership, Transformative Governance

Many of the chapters easily speak to multiple themes and all tackle big issues emerging in each of the four countries. For each theme, a short Thematic Introduction provides an overview of relevant key concepts, draws out influential issues and commonalities in governance transformations and highlights emerging trends and potentially transferable lessons. To assist readers, two maps provide general locations for the various First Nations mentioned in the chapters.

ABOUT THE CHAPTERS

Theme One: Governing Rights and Interests

S. James Anaya's chapter, 'The UN Declaration on the Rights of Indigenous Peoples: How Far We've Come and the Road Ahead' lays a foundation for the first theme of Governing Rights and Interests and for the book as a whole. The United Nations Declaration on the Rights of Indigenous Peoples, adopted in 2007, is a major accomplishment of decades-long negotiations between Indigenous peoples and member states of the United Nations. However, many of the rights it seeks to assert have not been realised. Anaya presents persuasive insights into the development, adoption and implementation of the Declaration, from the perspective of one closely involved in each phase, including his time in office (2008–2014) as the UN Special Rapporteur on the Rights of Indigenous Peoples. The Declaration offered Anaya in his role as Special Rapporteur a tool to examine how governments entered into negotiations about the issues affecting Indigenous peoples. Examples are presented of how Indigenous groups, in turn, are leveraging the Declaration to secure more substantive governing authority and control over development. Anaya concludes by considering the key obstacles to realisation of the Declaration's goals and suggests ways forward.

The remaining four chapters in this section raise strategic issues around how Indigenous rights and interests are being enabled or disabled in each of the CANZUS states as First Nations move to exercise their hard-won rights. In each context, this transition is linked to the internal challenge of governance readiness, capability and implementation.

Ivan Ingram, a young Aboriginal lawyer, describes first-hand the recent contested landscape of 'Indigenous Governance and Native Title in Australia', outlining the complex native title statutory regime, the governance challenges faced by traditional owners when they engage in native title claims and their strategic solutions to overcome them. Since 1993, there have been close to 500 determinations of native title in Australia, of which 400 are positive determinations allowing for some recognition of native title. This is a statistic worthwhile considering, given—as Ingram explains—that the process of proving native title is long and taxing: financially, emotionally, and culturally.

Despite these very real challenges, the native title regime has also created an opportunity for many Indigenous Australians to begin a resurgence of their collective governance and so exercise more effective control over lands, waters and cultural heritage. Ingram identifies strategic points where internal governance building needs to be prioritised. He then calls on traditional owner groups who have successfully navigated the native title process to advocate for an 'equalising' disruption to the system so as to avoid embedding greater inequalities among Indigenous peoples themselves.

The push for greater governing control by Indigenous nations and their representative organisations over social, political and economic development bears on the way formal negotiations are undertaken, and indeed the willingness of parties to recognise each other's governing legitimacy. In her chapter, 'Reconciling Interests and Rights in Māori Institutions of Governing', Annie Te One, a young Maori political scientist, explores the contemporary relationships between mātaawaka (urban Māori), mana whenua (iwi tribal custodians with authority over land), and British-informed local governments in Wellington, Aotearoa/New Zealand. Colonisation's impacts of dispossession, dispersal and economic marginalisation have generated different Māori residential arrangements: some voluntary, some imposed. Te One describes this phenomenon in Wellington, in part in reference to the Crown's insistence that iwi are the only natural Tiriti/Treaty partners and that partnership should not be extended to mātaawaka groups or urban collectivities through the Treaty process. Te One explains how the complex local layers of contemporary Māori governance are articulating with each other and with New Zealand local government in the city. Her chapter adds to our understanding of the multiple overlapping spheres of Maori governing practice and political engagement and contributes to broader consideration of the collective identities, rights and interests of urbanising Indigenous peoples internationally.

In 'Identifying a Legal Framework for a Treaty Between Australia's First People and Others', Asmi Wood and Christie Gardiner examine the political and legal basis for a treaty with Indigenous Australians, in the context of domestic and international law and the absence of historical or modern treaties in Australia. They consider two possible legal bases: the first being a treaty developed and operating purely under domestic Anglo-Australian law, which the authors argue is unlikely to deliver justice to Indigenous Australians. Their alternative, preferred option is a treaty developed under a domestic Anglo-Australian legal framework but having its operation supervised under a regime that includes relevant international law. Wood and Gardiner then valuably consider the procedural and substantive issues that will determine the process and outcomes of treaty-making, noting that development of a coherent legal framework is simply one of several practical challenges that must be overcome. A pertinent conclusion is that significant work needs to be done concurrently around governance building in order for Indigenous Australians to make fully informed, free choices about treaty-making.

Adam Crepelle's chapter in this theme is a salutary one, reminding us that many First Nations continue to be denied any recognition of their collective rights and ways of governing. In writing about 'Houma Nation Governance: A Reflection on Traditional, Contemporary and Future Rights and Recognition', Crepelle gives a harrowing account as a Houma citizen and lawyer, detailing how the United States continues to perpetuate historical dispossession into contemporary times, with devastating consequences.

At the heart of this chapter is the real-life question of what constitutes Indigenous governance and self-determination for an Indigenous nation living in the stark reality of multiple waves of colonisation and extreme ongoing marginalisation reinforced by the U.S. federal tribal recognition process. Historically, Houma governance and leadership were decentralised and informal. But soon after implementation of the federal recognition process, they adopted a centralised governing structure that proved to be incompatible with their own culture of governance. Crepelle explores the impacts of colonially imposed governing structures and concludes by proposing a systematic agenda for the reform of Houma Nation governance institutions, emphasising the central importance of cultural legitimacy or match. In many ways, this chapter sets out an agenda for governance resurgence that is being undertaken in all the case studies. The Houma are at the beginning of that arduous journey.

Theme Two: Governing for Nation-Building

The tumult and exhilaration of the 'rights era' described by the authors in Theme One opened up opportunities for Indigenous peoples across the globe to re-envision their futures and consider ways to maximise their self-determination. Specifically, a new generation of Indigenous leaders are asking questions such as these: How can valued legal and political rights and recognition be translated into self-determination and self-governance in fact and practice? Why fight tenaciously for rights when the citizens of the nation remain internally divided? What is the point of rights, if governance arrangements are inadequate to the task of exercising them?

One of the powerful ways Indigenous peoples in the CANZUS states and beyond are tackling such questions is through nation-rebuilding, that is, by enhancing their collective abilities to exercise self-governing authority effectively as a polity. The authors show that a nation-building strategy can take many pathways. It can be kick-started through internal conversations about collective identity and relationships, through strategies to revitalise the participation of group members, considering the valued role of culture in future modes of governing, or focusing on rebuilding prioritised institutions (the rules of governing). The consistent feature across these strategies and pathways is that their momentum is uniquely Indigenous-driven. Some of the pathways are detailed in this section.

In their chapter, 'Treating Treaty as a Technique for Indigenous Nation Building', Daryle Rigney, Simone Bignall, Alison Vivian, Steve Hemming, Shaun Berg and Damein Bell consider the potential for volatile treaty negotiations to be used as an opportunity to advance the sovereign political authority claimed by Gunditjmara and Ngarrindjeri leaders in southern Australia. The authors argue that the collection of new treaty negotiations recently initiated by several state governments in Australia should not be considered an end in itself, but are best regarded tactically as a political technology that is successful only to the extent that it supports Indigenous communities to rebuild their nations and reclaim political authority.

From their perspective, treaty-making works best not by imposing a uniform framework upon negotiators, but by establishing principles for enabling the emergence and formalisation of local and culturally distinctive relationships of legal and political pluralism and mutual respect for governing authority. The chapter concludes by outlining the importance of regional treaties in Australia as forerunners to a federal treaty process, with suggestions for future ways to mobilise treaty as a tool for rebuilding Indigenous nations and reclaiming self-governance after colonisation.

Angela Wesley's chapter, 'Ancient Spirit, Modern Mind: The Huu-ay-aht Journey Back to Self-Determination and Self-Reliance', presents a rare insight into how a treaty process has been used to mobilise governance resurgence by the Huu-ay-aht First Nations on Vancouver Island as they negotiated their treaty settlement. This chapter details the history of fifteen years of treaty negotiations up to 2011 and the generations-long struggle for recognition that preceded them, from the perspective of a Huu-ay-aht citizen intimately involved in the process.

Wesley identifies her nation's realisation that the treaty itself did not create the reality of nationhood; rather it contained the tools and resources for identifying and achieving a future collective vision. The second half of the chapter describes how Huu-ay-aht marshalled those assets to rebuild their internal governing arrangements, in particular, their constitution building, re-engaging with their dispersed and disaffected citizenry, making specific laws for the conduct of government, resolution of disputes, use of lands and resources, and identifying roles for traditional leadership in a renewed government.

Several papers address the fundamentally important question of how people actually get started on the road to nation-building when there are no treaties, no negotiations, no legislated right to self-governance, and when self-determination remains contested by the nation-state? There are few stories from the inside about how people have started on the challenging journey to governance resurgence and nation-building. Donna Murray and Debra Evans provide such a valuable account in their chapter, 'Culturally Centred, Community Led: Wiradjuri Nation Rebuilding through Honouring the Wiradjuri Way'. The authors explore the experiences and conversations that provided a new language and concepts by which to articulate the nation transformation they had been working towards for the last twenty years in the Wiradjuri community of western New South Wales, Australia.

Murray and Evans describe a personal journey of working together and being guided by senior Wiradjuri elders, to customise international Indigenous nation-building frameworks for their contemporary Wiradjuri cultural circumstances. The authors reflect on the crucial value of working from the ground up—sharing some of the evolving strategies developed to promote a strong community-based and community-informed framework for getting started. These included having many internal conversations about rebuilding the Wiradjuri Nation, particularly through reclaiming language and leadership, the creation of a tailored Wiradjuri course in collaboration with a regional university, consolidating a cohort of Wiradjuri nation rebuilders, and basing their work on honouring Wiradjuri ways.

The critical role of collaborative engagement and committed individuals is taken up by Joan Timeche in her chapter, 'Nation Rebuilders: An Indigenous Self-Governance Strategy'. An initiative designed to support self-determination and self-governance among the twenty-three American Indian nations who share a common three-state region: Minnesota, North Dakota, and South Dakota was launched in 2009. It was made possible by the Archibald and Edyth Bush Foundation, headquartered in Minnesota, USA, in collaboration with the Native Nations Institute (NNI) at the University of Arizona and in consultation with regional Indigenous leaders. This effort included the ground-breaking establishment of a leadership programme called Native Nation Rebuilders.

Through her senior role at NNI, Timeche was closely involved in establishing and convening the programme from its earliest days, and in this chapter she traces its development, goals and effects. Timeche highlights the idea that the community and economic development success of Native American Nations hinges in part on the quality and capability of their self-determined institutions of governance and on the role of individuals prepared to champion the strengthening and revitalisation of their tribal governments. Programmes such as this one in the United States, and the Wiradjuri Course in Australia, testify to the collaborative engagement and sustained commitment needed to support the success of transformative nation-building.

Still within the United States, Stephanie Russo Carroll, Stephen Cornell and Miriam Jorgensen extend the focus on nation and governance-rebuilding down to the level of jurisdictional responsibility for a specific sector of serve delivery in their chapter, 'Can a Self-determination Strategy Improve Indigenous Healthcare? Evidence from the United States'. The evidence that they present in this chapter suggests that it can. The authors consider why Native American tribes have pursued increased control over healthcare services, describing some of the successes resulting from tribal control and the challenges tribes face. Drawing on a small but diverse assortment of qualitative data, the chapter finds that tribes who have expanded their control have subsequently reorganised healthcare priorities, increased services, diversified funding sources and innovated in care delivery. In doing so, tribes have faced challenges in funding, managing tribal politics, in the complexities of healthcare system administration and in learning from each other. The authors conclude that while tribal self-determination has the potential to improve Indigenous health care, self-determination is not a panacea; tribes have to back it up with capable governance in order to realise that potential.

Theme Three: Governing Development and Resources

The third theme builds upon the previous two, focusing on the intersection of governance with people and their lands, waters and resources. In this section, the authors decentre power away from the nation-state, recentering it onto the agency of Indigenous peoples themselves. Case studies describe efforts to establish capable governance that enables First Nations to translate rights into practice and deliver tangible outcomes to manage their own affairs and assert their agenda for development, and importantly, to do so in ways that prioritise their own cultural values and ways of doing things.

In his chapter, 'Rebuilding the Yawuru Nation: Activating Cultural Rights for Economic Growth and Stability', Peter Yu addresses the strategic agency and capacities required to revitalise communities and First Nations. Yu charts the journey of Yawuru people from systemic oppression by the Australian settler nation-state to their struggles for recognition of native title rights. He poses this within a larger Yawuru philosophical lens—'mabu liyan'—a term describing the interconnectedness between a sense of personal self, the wider community and the natural landscape. Yawuru achieved a successful native title determination in 2006, and then negotiated beneficial agreements with Australian governments. These provided a platform to strengthen social and cultural institutions and establish new structures to support family and community, look after country and create an economic future for Yawuru.

The chapter identifies the core priorities for Yawuru in these efforts: namely, building strong leadership and governance, an ensuring intergenerational transfer of cultural knowledge, re-engaging youth and a redefinition of their relationships with the broader settler community. Yu emphasises that while a key objective is to empower Yawuru through individual and collective wealth creation, importantly, it is being achieved through a set of culturally integrated strategies.

Miriam Jorgensen, Allen Pemberton, Pat Brown and David Conner in their chapter 'The Red Lake Walleye Recovery Project: Tribal Governance for Sustainable Success' explore the role that capable tribal governance can play when natural resources are under threat. Twenty years ago, the Red Lake Tribal Council in Minnesota, USA, passed a resolution banning hook-and-line subsistence fishing for walleye perch, effectively ending all fishing on tribal waters. Recognising that a vital cultural and economic resource was slipping away, the Red Lake Nation took a stand to save the walleye and make the lake healthy again. The tribal government did not know if a recovery effort on a large freshwater lake, which had been overfished for decades, would be possible. Would their own citizens abide by the fishing ban for as long as was necessary? Would the state of Minnesota join them in the fishing moratorium?

In this chapter, the authors give an in-depth account of the governance strategies, practical measures and scientific initiatives developed by the Red Lake Nation that achieved substantial outcomes. Within two decades, fishery recovery was essentially complete, and Red Lake Nation citizens were fishing again under a sustainable catch regime. The positive effects for Red Lake citizens, the environment, the economy and the nation's relationships with neighbouring governments have likewise been sustained and even grown. As the authors explain, in looking back at the fishing recovery project, it is clear that its success has been intimately tied to effective tribal governance.

Several researchers from the National Centre for First Nations Governance (NCFNG) in Canada and NNI in the United States have collaborated with the Listuguj Mi'gmaq Government to report on a similar initiative, this time from the vantage point of 'Making First Nation Law: The Listuguj Mi'gmaq Fishery'. Their chapter describes how, in the mid-1990s, the Listuguj Mi'gmaq First Nation took over the management of the salmon fishery in the Restigouche River where it flows between the provinces of New Brunswick and Quebec. Initially in conflict with Canadian provincial and national governments over fishery rights and responsibilities, the First Nation asserted its jurisdiction to enact and implement under its own tribal authority—the *Listuguj Mi'gmaq First Nation Law on Fisheries and Fishing Act*. Since then, this tribal Act has been the effective law governing salmon fishing on the Restigouche River, displacing provincial and federal authority.

This is the story of a First Nation not only reclaiming inherent jurisdiction over a resource, but reclaiming governance by using law-making and effective enforcement. So effective has this been that, in 2018, the First Nation signed the Listuguj First Nation-Canada Fish Framework Agreement with the Canadian Government.

In his chapter, 'Instilling Good Governance for Community Prosperity: The Canadian Experience', Jamie Sterritt looks to the big picture, considering how Canadian First Nations' understand concepts of 'community' and 'prosperity' and the role governance plays in strengthening them. These concepts have been compromised in Canada, he argues, by the colonial imposition of Western ways of governing, the reserve system, and the *Indian Act 1876*. Jamie Sterritt introduces a much-needed Indigenous corrective to what constitutes 'prosperity', advocating for a balance that encourages the advancement of social, cultural and environmental aspects of community life alongside economic ones. He then explores the characteristics of 'good governance'—again from an Indigenous standpoint—highlighting its critical role in achieving a fuller sense of prosperity.

We are given a frank consideration of the current downsides of poor internal governance, and the positive outcomes that can be enabled when First Nations govern more effectively. Jaimie Sterritt focuses critical attention on the roles of citizens and elected members of tribal governments (chief and councils), arguing persuasively that they need to adopt a renewed 'public-spirited' relationship with each other, which entails preferred kinds of behaviours and abilities. He concludes that a fundamental precondition for achieving a fuller sense of prosperity is for citizens—individually and collectively—to take on a public-spirited responsibility for ensuring effective governance in their organisations and by their leaders.

In considering the challenges of nation-building in Aotearoa/New Zealand, Sacha McMeeking links insights from the ground together with several theoretical frameworks to astutely explore the role social entrepreneurship and social innovation are making within Māori communities and to contemporary self-determination. In her chapter, 'Nation-building through Social Enterprise in Māori Communities', McMeeking presents three social-enterprise case studies to take us beyond the formal institutional view of Maori governance, to explore the value of building localised capabilities for creating community innovation. She examines the growing field of Māori entrepreneurship, revealing it to be led primarily by individuals and families who see opportunities to achieve tangible and meaningful social change that aligns with community priorities. In their hands, entrepreneurship is both a tool for, and embodiment of, community transformation and self-determination that is being put into practice on a daily basis.

Theme Four: Transformative Leadership, Transformative Governance

The contemporary governing arrangements of many Indigenous First Nations—including those with treaties and legislated rights to self-determined governance—bear the legacy of imposed nation-state norms and laws. Inevitably, the latter appear alien to Indigenous traditional modes of governance. Today, Indigenous groups are simultaneously seeking to reclaim their governing authority in ways that are culturally credible to them, while dealing with the ongoing debilitating impacts of settler-colonialism. This is motivating them to design creative ways to decolonise imposed governing structures and institutions. To do this, many Indigenous citizens are looking to their leaders for inspiration and direction. Sadly, some leaders are suffering themselves from the collateral damage and pressures of community dysfunction fuelled by colonisation, caught in internal struggles for power or perpetuating gender practices that marginalise the role of women in governance.

In this final theme, the authors explore the vital need and contemporary contexts for new styles of leadership (collective, individual, face-to-face and digital). They highlight the particularly powerful relationship between leaders and governance outcomes, drawing attention to the transformative agency that can be harnessed by Indigenous leaders and organisations to create a governance environment that positively enables inclusive citizen participation and voice in decision-making. Here, the stories range from the personal to the local community, national and global, describing the 'governance work' of First Nation leaders and organisations to heal social discord, unify disaffected members, mediate internal agreements over land and interests, mentor younger generations of community leaders and break down the politics of invisibility to recognise the vital role of women as governors. This powerful work of social repair and transformation lies at the heart of rebuilding Indigenous nations.

In 'Healing, Decolonisation and Governance', Bhiamie Williamson tackles this issue head on. His chapter suggests decolonisation and healing are both governance processes and inevitably intertwined, providing a deep reflection on the inherently social conditions underlying governance in Indigenous communities. Williamson considers the conceptual roots of healing and its recent emergence in a range of Indigenous discourses. The critical question he asks is how Indigenous leaders and organisations might go about promoting meaningful and sustained healing to bring their own communities together. Here, Williamson argues there is an urgent governing opportunity—indeed responsibility—for leaders and institutions to engage with collective healing, noting how this generates peoples' ability to invest in and trust governing arrangements.

Williamson goes further, suggesting effective Indigenous governance *requires* leaders to decolonise themselves (including the ways they behave, make decisions and demonstrate inclusiveness and accountability) in order to then help decolonise communities and their governance. The author finishes by suggesting that leaders can apply the distinct Indigenous craft practice of weaving in order to bring together decolonisation, healing and governance into a more aligned intersection and resilient vision for the future.

When elected as Chair of the Fond du Lac Band Tribal Government of Lake Superior Chippewa in Minnesota, Karen Diver was the first woman to lead her tribal government. The subsequent learning curve was steep, as vividly described in 'You're Not Just a Leader, You are an Indigenous Leader': Empowering American Indian Women for Governing'. With 4,000 citizens and 1,800 employees, taking up a leadership role in the tribal government entailed being briefed by legal counsel on current issues, developing strategic and work plans, reviewing past financial audits and setting future budgets, engaging daily with tribal citizens, consulting with tribal department managers and external stakeholders, and much more.

After several years, Karen Diver was invited to join President Obama's Task Force on Climate Preparedness and Resilience, to represent tribal interests in the United States. With a leadership role at the national and international level, the learning curve became ever steeper. From these exceptional experiences, Diver gives us her persuasive reflections on the transformative power of Native American women's leadership, their strengths and contributions, and the challenges they face in developing leadership abilities. Importantly, she provides insights born from experience, revealing how such challenges can be addressed in order to further empower the leadership of Indigenous women.

Another arena where Indigenous leadership is transforming the governance conversation is that of social media and digital technology. In her chapter, 'Mana Wāhine: We Care So Much It Exhausts Us!' Mera Penehira presents a colourful narrative in three short case studies depicting how Māori women are reasserting their collective voice as gender and cultural advocates, through social media and networking sites. Penehira considers the digital tactics and strategies used by a group of Māori women, to enact a politics of visibility, which not only unsettles colonial power relations but also cultivates a form of connected solidarity and leadership among women for shaping positive transformation within Māori society. The author suggests that Māori women's engagement in digital activism has the potential to be a powerful decolonising mechanism contributing to systemic change.

The final chapter by Neil Sterritt on 'The Trials and Legacy of Delgamuukw: Transforming Rights into Outcomes for Canadian First Nations Peoples' brings together many of this theme's major issues and takes us back to James Anaya's opening reflection on 'the road ahead'. As an experienced Gitxsan leader, Neil Sterritt deals with three eras that broadly define the historic experience of Indigenous peoples with settler-colonialism and in rebuilding the governance of their Nations: the first being exploration and colonisation, the second the battle for rights recognition, and the third the post-recognition implementation era. Neil Sterritt examines the governance challenges arising from these eras in the context of the life, trials and legacy of an influential leader among the Gitxsan peoples—his elder brother Delgamuukw (Albert Tait)—and the significant Canadian High Court decision in which he and the author were key protagonists: The *Delgamuukw (1997) Case*.

Neil Sterritt suggests that the manifestation of this valuable legacy leaves Gitxsan with what may prove to be an even more important trial; namely, of transforming rights into effective governance and outcomes so that Gitxsan may be self-determining within their homelands once more. As an influential nation leader himself, Sterritt examines the kinds of leadership now necessary to implement this vision. His conclusions have resonance for other First Nations across and beyond the CANZUS states.

THINKING ABOUT SELF-GOVERNANCE AND SELF-DETERMINED DEVELOPMENT

The international Indigenous conversation presented in this volume reveals powerful insights into the state of contemporary Indigenous governance, and has wider implications beyond the four CANZUS countries. From the authors, we hear about the strong connection between capable, credible governance and improved outcomes on the ground for community. We learn about alternative concepts and standards for what constitutes effectiveness, legitimacy, success and sustainability. We see creativity and persistence in experimentation, as leaders and citizens adapt and refine their governance solutions.

In other words, as with Indigenous culture itself, governance is not fixed or static. No single solution will work for all nations. Furthermore, governing institutions evolve over the generations as new priorities, opportunities and threats arise. At the same time, the combined insights from the diverse governing solutions described in this collection point to the powerful importance of each nation developing and maintaining its own shared vision, related cultural values and direction for their governance-rebuilding. It matters not if a First Nation immediately takes up a full suite of self-government jurisdictions, or chooses to rebuild and govern incrementally. What seems to matter most is that the focus of governance remains recentred on the collective 'self', and then is exercised capably and credibly in the service of the whole Nation and its self-determined future.

The work governance resurgence done in a way that has cultural credibility with a First Nation's own citizen's, lies at the core of Indigenous nation-rebuilding and development. However, this Indigenous work is not well supported by the conceptual categories of conventional Western political science or law, which are heavily focused on settler-colonial concepts of democracy, neoliberalism and nationalism. Rather, the case studies that follow suggest a theory of Indigenous governance and nation-rebuilding that directly connects the cultural domain on the one hand, with the political and economic on the other. In other words, Indigenous ideas about the collective 'self' and putting it into practice as a political polity and social identity are directly related to the ways they go about designing the form of governance they regard as most relevant to them today. Indigenous governance is cultural governance with a new face—an ancient spirit in a modern mind. That is governance resurgence.

As a whole, this collection of chapters allows us to propose a theoretical model of Indigenous governance as being relational governance—that is, an ordered form of networked social relationships and political organisation. This seems to be the case across the CANZUS states—where *relationality* lies at the heart of Indigenous governance traditions, jurisdictions and contemporary solutions enabling locally diverse arrangements to be created. Furthermore, Indigenous relationality enables self-governance to be actively rebuilt, remixed and reassessed by Indigenous nations, in order to meet new challenges and opportunities. The lens of 'governance-as-relationality' enables us, in turn, to see Indigenous community prosperity and development as collective spaces of being, thinking and doing that are as much cultural as they are economic ways of operating.

From this standpoint, governance resurgence is about cultural and political reclamation, and vice versa. It is about decolonising and rebuilding Indigenous networked relationships from the inside out. Nation-building is thus a form of future-thinking. The objective of this conceptual and theoretical reframing is fourfold. It directs attention away from impoverished settler-colonial notions of Indigenous governance, to the following:

1. Indigenous evidence base of purposeful Indigenous agency in creating effective solutions to the challenges of governing for self-determined development and prosperity;
2. Repertoire of Indigenous capabilities, expertise, creativity and endowments that empower collective governing agency and choice;
3. Subtle Indigenous understandings and strategic pathways for community healing and nation-rebuilding through renewed forms of governance and transformative leadership; and
4. Implications of all these for sustaining collaborative Indigenous futures and self-determination at the cultural interface.

The interconnections between themes and emerging trends highlighted by the authors allow Indigenous governance innovation to be understood as being the process of creating, gaining support for, and implementing novel ideas of relational forms of collective order, which are deemed by citizens to be culturally legitimate and are also practically capable of achieving a nation's goals for the future. This leads to an understanding of Indigenous determined development as a socially instituted process of adaptive change in which culturally plausible innovation is a necessary foundation, and perhaps even *the* core component. From this vantage point, development might be considered 'sustainable' by Indigenous citizens not only because it delivers desired outcomes, but because it maximises governance resurgence and ongoing self-determination for the nation as a whole. The motivation of authors contributing to this volume is that the Indigenous insights and solutions for governance resurgence described here may hold equal value for Indigenous nations globally.

NOTES

1. There is a growing international Indigenous literature on various circumstances in which Indigenous resurgence has been occurring. More recently there has been a growing Indigenous focus internationally on the role played by governance rebuilding in the cultural and political resurgence of Indigenous Nations. See, for example, Alfred & Corntassel 2005; Broderstad 2011; Corntassel 2012; Gustafson 2009; Hunt et al. 2008; Jorgensen 2005; Kalt et al. 2008; Nikolakis et al. 2019; Rigney et al. 2015; von der Porten 2012.

2. A report from the first meeting in Tucson at which the network was formed is available at https://ncis.anu.edu.au/_lib/doc/common_roots_conf_report.pdf. The group subsequently adopted as its name, *The Common Roots, Common Futures Indigenous Network* taken from the title of the Tucson workshop. A recommendation of delegates at the second workshop in Brisbane 2017 was that their stories be collated into a publication, to make them more widely available to other Indigenous nations. The result is this book. Another recommendation was that each country undertake an audit of the kinds of governance education and training available to Indigenous nations and communities. In response, AIGI developed a template and conducted a preliminary audit in Australia, producing the 'Preliminary Report into Indigenous Governance Education and Training', A. Wighton & D. Smith 2018. Available at https://www.aigi.com.au/wp-content/uploads/2019/08/Preliminary-Report-into-Indigenous-Governance-Education-and-Training-in-Australia.pdf. See also Fodder (n.d.) for a review of programs in New Zealand and the USA.

3. For example, in Latin America, Indigenous peoples in countries such as Panama, Nicaragua, Colombia, Peru and Bolivia have won significant territorial self-governance; though their gains remain vulnerable (see ECLAC 2014, Postero & Fabricant 2019, and also https://www.iwgia.org/en/focus/land-rights/2482-indigenous-peoples-in-latin-america-claim-territor.html and also https://repositorio.cepal.org/bitstream/handle/11362/37051/4/S1420782_en.pdf). In Japan, Ainu were finally recognised by the Japanese Government and are making progress in rebuilding their internal governance (Larson et al. 2008). Sami peoples in Norway have a representative parliament established in 2014 which supports their ongoing cultural autonomy and self-determined development (Broderstad 2014), and Inuit in Greenland effectively have self-government (Dahl 2001). There are also long-established movements among several Indigenous nations of Melanesian countries to gain independence and re-establish more robust forms of self-governance (White 2006). The governance and nation-rebuilding taking place among Indigenous peoples in the CANZUS countries is thus part of a much bigger global movement of Indigenous resurgence.

GREENLAND
ALASKA
BRITISH COLUMBIA
CANADA
NEWFOUNDLAND
QUEBEC
Gitxsan-Wets'uwet'en
Vancouver Island
Huu-ay-aht
Fond du Lac Band Tribal Government
ONTARIO
Listuguj Mi'gmaq
Red Lake Nation
Akwesasne
N. DAKOTA
SOUTH DAKOTA
MINNESOTA
NEW BRUNSWICK
Pacific Ocean
Mississippi R.
UNITED STATES
Atlantic Ocean
ARIZONA
International boundary
Province/state/territory boundary
0 kilometres 1000
Houma
LOUISIANA
MEXICO
© Australian National University CC BY SA 4.0
CartoGIS CAP 19-235a_KP

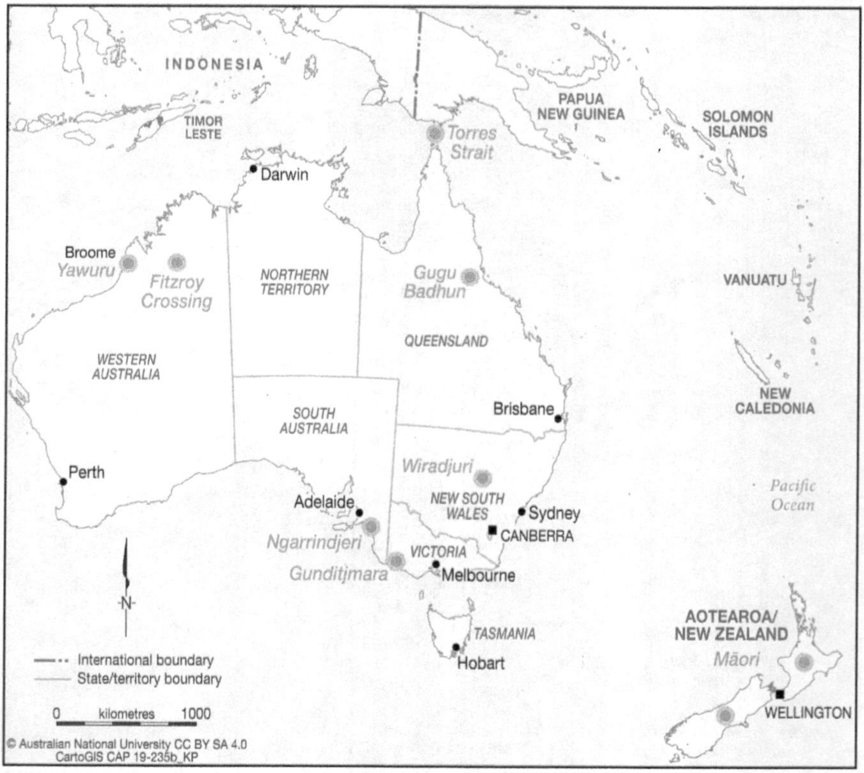

INDONESIA
TIMOR LESTE
PAPUA NEW GUINEA
SOLOMON ISLANDS
Torres Strait
Darwin
Broome
Yawuru
Fitzroy Crossing
NORTHERN TERRITORY
Gugu Badhun
VANUATU
QUEENSLAND
WESTERN AUSTRALIA
NEW CALEDONIA
Brisbane
SOUTH AUSTRALIA
Wiradjuri
Perth
Pacific Ocean
Adelaide
NEW SOUTH WALES
Sydney
CANBERRA
Ngarrindjeri
VICTORIA
Melbourne
Gunditjmara
N
AOTEAROA/ NEW ZEALAND
TASMANIA
Hobart
Māori
International boundary
State/territory boundary
WELLINGTON
0 kilometres 1000
© Australian National University CC BY SA 4.0
CartoGIS CAP 19-235b_KP

Theme One

GOVERNING RIGHTS AND INTERESTS

Thematic Introduction

Concepts, Issues and Trends

Diane Smith

It has been thirty years since the International Labor Organisation adopted 'Convention 169 on Indigenous and Tribal Peoples' in 1989, recognising the aspirations of Indigenous peoples to exercise governing control over their own institutions, ways of life and development within the nation-states in which they live. S. James Anaya notes in his opening chapter in Theme One that the convention has been a double-edged sword—representing significant progress towards the recognition and protection of Indigenous rights—but also demonstrating the limitations and vulnerability of that progress.

Eighteen years later, in 2007, the United Nations (UN) General Assembly adopted the UN Declaration on the Rights of Indigenous Peoples by an overwhelming majority of member-states. Anaya (1999: 257) describes it as the 'mother of all group rights' and 'a necessary foundation for Indigenous peoples' enjoyment of all the other rights they claim'. In his chapter, he gives us an insider's view of just how arduous the drafting process was, spanning more than two decades, and only realised with unprecedented participation by Indigenous representatives. With its unequivocal recognition of Indigenous peoples' right to self-determination, including the right to retain and develop Indigenous systems of self-governance that are born of Indigenous cultural systems, many authors in this volume refer to the Declaration's inspiring influence amongst their own nations and communities.

As of 2020, Australia, Canada, Aotearoa-New Zealand and the United States, who all initially voted against the Declaration, have reversed their positions and expressed support for its principles (though they have not achieved its implementation). A more substantive step was then taken in 2019 by the Provincial Government of British Columbia (BC), which became the first jurisdiction in Canada and internationally to pass specific legislation (Bill 41) to implement the Declaration. The Bill requires the BC Government, among other things, to take all necessary measures to ensure provincial laws are consistent with UNDRIP, and establishes an annual action plan and reporting on progress (Residential School History and Dialogue Center 2020; Sing et al. 2019).

However, the international achievement and promise of the Declaration has to be seen in the broader context of the suite of other rights and interests that Indigenous peoples have been fighting for, and sometimes winning, in their own countries in the decades before and after ILO169 and the Declaration. And as with ILO169, the Declaration represents a substantial promise of Indigenous rights recognition in the context of their ongoing restriction and vulnerability.

This first theme sets the foundation for the book, with the Indigenous authors examining both the promise and practical realisation of their varied rights and interests through the lens of negotiating and rebuilding self-determined governance for their nations and communities. They recount stories of Indigenous peoples' continuing perseverance—in all its starkness and urgency—and critically reflect on the limits and opportunities to be found in contemporary treaty and land claims mechanisms. Over the last thirty years, in each of the four CANZUS jurisdictions, the game has changed or at least is changing. A transition is occurring from the 'rights battle' to the 'implementation' battle. In that context, the important question being considered by all the authors is: How can self-determination be put into effect today, as a daily-lived reality? And specifically, how do you govern the rights and interests—however meagre—in a self-determined way?

Those questions raise a host of formidable issues. The history of settler colonialism in the CANZUS countries, and more widely, for many Indigenous peoples suggests the answers will not come from the nation-state. Rather, the following chapters show that the solutions lie primarily in Indigenous hands. In their accounts, we hear of Indigenous ingenuity, resilience and strategic behaviour that aim to carve out spaces for autonomous action in the tough nitty-gritty of government negotiations, courtroom hearings, international law courts, mediation of intra-Indigenous rifts and wider public opposition—spaces where opportunities for self-determination and self-governance can nevertheless be created in real time.

THE RIGHTS AND RECOGNITION ERA

Reflecting on his long international experience, S. James Anaya identifies three eras in the Indigenous fight for self-determination: the pre-recognition era of colonisation with its denial of Indigeneity; the battle for rights and recognition; and the post-UNDRIP implementation era (see also Cornell 2019; and Neil Sterritt this volume). Elements of all three eras can be seen operating concurrently across many countries, so that the changes and challenges encountered in one era flow (and sometimes collide) into the next. Furthermore, there is now an entire generation of young Indigenous people whose careers and involvement in Indigenous issues have occurred in the third era—where they have witnessed significant rights being won, settlements being finalised and, in some instances, modern treaties being signed. Not only does this give them a different viewpoint on history and what is possible, but they are impatient to see effective practical implementation by their own governing organisations that will deliver reliable outcomes and prosperity for their nations.

There are several reasons for the relative difference in progress made towards self-governance in each of the CANZUS countries: the substantial differences in court decisions and legislative recognition being simply one factor. Another is the considerable diversity in the relative size of the Indigenous land estate and access to resources, not only across countries but within them. Also, Canada, Aotearoa-New Zealand and the United States all have a history of treaty-making encompassing varied rights to lands, waters and resources. A large number of American Indian Nations have exercised at least some legal jurisdiction as tribal governments over reserved lands for decades, and some of their reserved lands are extensive. Although Adam Crepelle's chapter reminds us that other Native Nations in the United States have been sorely marginalised by the very same legal recognition processes, when those have been denied to them. Similar detrimental impacts of 'non-recognition' of rights are raised by Ingram in this Theme, and by Rigney et al. in Theme Two.

Many First Nations in Canada have some measure of legislated and treaty control over reserved lands, but for nearly all, their lands are fragmented (see Jamie Sterritt this volume). The traditional lands to which they have some rights may be more extensive, but their level of control is much reduced. Māori in Aotearoa-New Zealand, having suffered massive land losses over the years, have been engaged in a major effort in recent decades to regain significant lands and other resources—with some significant successes in self-governance and self-determined development (see, for example, Joseph et al. and McMeeking this volume). In Australia, treaty-making has been entirely absent until the last five years or so and, as Wood and Gardiner and Rigney et al. remind us, these initiatives are preliminary and precarious. Varied land rights have been secured across the Australian continent under a range of legislation, with the high point undoubtedly being the recognition of a specific form of inalienable Aboriginal freehold property right in the Northern Territory that resulted in the transfer of large tracts of land to exclusive traditional Aboriginal ownership. However, Indigenous Australians have been hard pressed to secure any jurisdictional rights comparable to those of North

American First Nations. Ivan Ingram reports in his chapter that recognition of native title rights in Australia is still only three decades old and remains hotly contested in the courts.

But these differences in rights recognition only partly explain the diversity of governance outcomes across the four countries. For instance, it appears that the lack of substantive rights has led some Indigenous groups to even greater efforts to exercise whatever areas of self-determination they can, causing them to create more innovative solutions than if they were tethered to state-centric mechanisms. In other words, legislated or court recognition of rights is not a fail-safe precondition for them being able to effectively exercise self-governance (Smith 2019; Neil Sterritt this volume).

Yet despite the evident diversity, in all four countries, Indigenous peoples have succeeded in increasing, to one degree or another, their control over at least some of the decisions that affect their daily lives. And in at least three of the four (the USA may be the exception) Indigenous peoples have activated common initiatives for reconciliation and recompense with the wider mainstream populations of their countries, as well as for addressing discriminatory historical issue. One such common area of advocacy is the 'stolen generations' of Indigenous children who were forcibly taken from their families and communities under racially motivated state policies of assimilation and placed in institutions such as residential schools and 'homes' (see, for example, the 'Bringing them Home Report' 1997 in Australia and the Canadian 'Royal Commission on Aboriginal Peoples, Final Report', 1998).

Another common issue considered by Indigenous leaders and governance practitioners in all four countries, though not entirely resolved in any, has been the Indigenous consideration of how they might govern themselves in ways that are locally meaningful, aligned with their cultural and collective priorities, and enable them to shape their future direction (internally and externally); in short, to practically exercise their right to self-determination. While the right to self-determination has been variously challenged, ignored, undermined, acknowledged or modestly supported over the years by settler-colonial governments in each of these countries, it remains at the very heart of Indigenous self-governance priorities in each.

THE RIGHT TO SELF-DETERMINATION

There are many definitions and views of self-determination. For the purposes of this volume, we take self-determination to refer to Indigenous peoples' right to take control and responsibility for their own affairs (social, economic, political and cultural) through genuine decision-making powers, meaningful participation and freedom from discrimination. At its core, it is about the 'power to exercise power'. It does not refer simply to the self-administration or self-management of programmes or services that are actually controlled by outside authorities. And in the context of self-governance, it has a collective signifier—it is about Indigenous nations, groups, tribes, clans, families and communities.

For many Indigenous peoples, the word contains its own history and promised future. A deconstructed sequencing[1] speaks to the intersecting ideas and experiences involved:

- Self-determi*nation* – Prior to colonisation, there were Indigenous *Nations*. The question of who constituted the 'self' in self-determination was answered: the nation as a collective and culturally based polity.
- Self-de*termination* – With colonisation came efforts to *terminate* Indigenous Nations. Settler-colonial states attempted to extinguish the collective identity of groups and remove their links with country; to reduce the 'collective self' to 'selfish' (individualistic) determination.
- Self-*determin*ation – Then followed an era where Indigenous Nations fought for rights and recognition to be able to *determine* their own collective identities and futures.
- Self-determi*nation* – Now is an era when First Nations are working to implement the rights they have won and to rebuild and exercise collective decision-making authority; to self-govern as nations again.

A powerful motivation driving Indigenous people has been to put the 'nation-as-self' back into self-determination. The chapters in this theme by Wood and Gardiner, Te One, Ingram and Creppelle speak to a paramount challenge this poses for Indigenous people; namely, that of first considering the diverse and sometimes contested Indigenous identities that have been produced under, and imposed by settler colonialism, and second, coming to an agreed internal understanding of 'who' should be the bases of the 'collective self' for their self-governance into the future. In each case study, the solutions are diverse and innovative, designed to suit local realities, cultural norms and needs.

PUTTING COLLECTIVE SELF-DETERMINATION INTO PRACTICE

There have been striking developments in each of the four CANZUS countries with regard to self-determination, relying on a multitude of pathways to securing varied rights and interests, and often resulting in very different outcomes. Its implementation frequently has been compromised by a lack of clarity around goals, insufficient human capability, inadequate resources, constitutional discouragement, political opposition from external governments and internal discord that has fragmented collective resolve. The authors recognise these limitations all too well, suggesting that in fact self-determination is more a *process* of action, an ever-evolving means to an end rather than a fixed end-point somewhere in the future. It is as much about collectively identifying shared goals and devising agreed ways to proceed. And most importantly, it is about doing those things in Indigenous ways, grounded in Indigenous ideas.

The authors consistently link self-determination to the needs of future Indigenous generations. The implication being that the exercise and implementation of rights and interests itself need to be carried out in a sustainable manner. Governance decisions and actions taken now—for example, to negotiate a treaty, establish relations with local government, prove native title, enter into economic development ventures, or write a constitution that embraces traditional ways and asserts capability and relevance in the contemporary world—should not only help make self-determination a reality today but also build its future exercise.

This has important implications for internal issues such as protecting the rights and interests of all a nation's citizens, and gender and age equality. Self-determination is not achieved by means of some individuals or groups asserting modes of exclusive control that act to the detriment of others in a nation. In the first chapter of this section of the book, Anaya advocates a conceptual shift away from the usual division between internal and external self-determination, to focus instead on its substance and remedy. Other authors in Theme One then provide us with contemporary re-imaginings of self-determination that give it practical content, describing how remedies are being shaped (and reshaped) to be more inclusive and responsive to the unique experiences and aspirations of all citizens.

Some Indigenous groups have spent so much time and energy fighting for recognition and rights, and dealing with internal disagreements generated along the way, that they have shortcut building their own governance foundations. As a result, when they do emerge from the maelstrom of the rights era, they then face the challenge of having to implement and sustain hard won rights, but with ill-suited or under-developed governing arrangements. The insight here is that what worked as governance for people to get them through rights negotiations may not necessarily work to implement those rights. It is not surprising then that we are seeing increased attention being given by First Nations to reinvigorating their community memberships and culturally based relationships—rebuilding the 'self'—as the foundation stone for confidently reasserting their collective identity as a polity. Indeed, some nations are engaging in contemporary treaty (see Rigney et al.) and agreement making with other First Nations (see Te One) and the state (see Ingram), specifically as a strategic tool for their internal governance resurgence. They are finding that the process of negotiating a treaty or native title claim (regardless of its success) often affords people a space in which to restructure their existing governance arrangements. In other words, self-determination of governance can be exercised *during* the rights negotiation process.

GOVERNING SELF-DETERMINED RIGHTS AND INTERESTS

The parameters and promise of self-determination are not bounded by time, scale or limited interpretations of sovereignty. Many Indigenous peoples continue to suffer from the complete absence of rights and impoverished forms of 'self-determination' handed out begrudgingly by settler nation-states. The earlier rights movement generally has been directed at national governments and involved broad demands for Indigenous recognition. The case studies in this theme show Indigenous peoples today re-imagining the substance of self-determination through processes of internal governance-rebuilding. This strategic approach is less concerned with a state-centric agenda, instead focusing Indigenous attention back into their own nations and communities: to identifying their governing priorities for action, developing their available capabilities and leadership to programmes of internal institution building (policies, laws, regulations and rules), and creating a collective vision for the future.

In the chapters under this theme, we travel from the international arena of landmark rights initiatives, to domestic treaty negotiations, to witnessing how local aspirations for rebuilding governing rights and interests are translated into practice. The message is clear. Self-determination can be 'done' now, through such diverse acts as constitutional and organisational reform, resetting internal relationships between groups who hold different rights and interests, mediating internal disputes, recognising the rights of women to govern and renewing leadership. Through these internal practices of self-determination, Indigenous Nations are also designing robust frameworks for re-engaging with the nation-state, based on maximising their control, authority and jurisdiction. As several of the authors note, this opens up potential for the future development of political conditions, protocols and frameworks that acknowledge and respect Indigenous sovereign authority and political pluralism, as is required in the international law of treaty and the Declaration.

NOTE

1. See, for example, the exploration of the concept's component meanings by Aboriginal people in the Northern Territory, Australia, at the Central Land Council's 'Strong Aboriginal Governance Summit in Tennant Creek' (CLC 2013, 11), available at https://www.clc.org.au/files/pdf/APONT_Governance_Summit_2013_report.pdf.

Chapter 1

The UN Declaration on the Rights of Indigenous Peoples

How Far We've Come and the Road Ahead

S. James Anaya

On September 13, 2007, the United Nations General Assembly adopted the Declaration on the Rights of Indigenous Peoples with an overwhelming majority of affirmative votes: 143 member-states voted in favour of the declaration, 4 voted against, 11 abstained (other members were absent from the vote). The declaration is a major international achievement, the product of decades-long, intense negotiations involving Indigenous peoples around the world and UN member-states.[1] The declaration delineates and defines the individual and collective rights of Indigenous peoples, including rights to cultural and ceremonial expression and to maintain and strengthen their own identity, language, employment, health and education, as well as addressing other issues. It also emphasises the rights of Indigenous peoples to pursue development in keeping with their own needs and aspirations. However, more than a decade has passed since the adoption of the declaration, the rights it asserts are far from being fully realised. The declaration is a first step. It outlines central features of a destination, but getting there will involve a lot more work. There is a long road ahead.

In this chapter, I first present a broad overview of the mandate of the Special Rapporteur on the rights of indigenous peoples as backdrop to my engagement with efforts to implement the declaration as the holder of that mandate for several years. Next I discuss the development, adoption and implementation of the declaration and then give examples of how Indigenous groups around the world have been working to convert rights asserted in the declaration into substantive outcomes. Finally, I consider some of the key obstacles to the practical realisation of the goals in the declaration, suggest some possible ways forward and argue that getting to the destination set out for us in the declaration will require continuing work to build effective, self-determined, Indigenous governance at both domestic and international levels.

Each of these sections contains personal reflections and insights from the vantage point of my experience as someone involved in the discussions leading to adoption of the declaration and as a former UN special rapporteur on the rights of indigenous peoples from 2008 to 2014. The promulgation and implementation of the declaration have played a major part in my own professional work on Indigenous rights, having worked from the mid-1980s advocating Indigenous issues in United Nations forums and then taking up the role of special rapporteur. I commenced as special rapporteur the year immediately following the passage of the Declaration by the General Assembly of the United Nations, and it immediately provided an influential yet untested framework for my work. Not surprisingly then, this chapter weaves the story of the declaration with that of the role I undertook as special rapporteur, and so I begin with an account of that institution.

THE UNITED NATIONS SPECIAL RAPPORTEUR ON THE RIGHTS OF INDIGENOUS PEOPLES

'Special Rapporteurs' and other independent experts are appointed by the United Nations Human Rights Council (successor to the Commission on Human Rights)[2] with the mandate to monitor, advise and publicly report on human rights situations in specific countries (country mandates) or on human rights situations worldwide in relation to certain themes (thematic mandates). In recognition of the need to address human rights issues facing Indigenous peoples, in 2001 the specific mandate of the special rapporteur on the situation of human rights and fundamental freedoms of Indigenous peoples (renamed, after adoption of the declaration, the special rapporteur on the rights of indigenous peoples) was established.

The special rapporteur on the rights of indigenous peoples is one of three United Nations mechanisms specifically related to Indigenous peoples. The second is the Permanent Forum on Indigenous Issues, established in 2000 as an advisory body of the UN's Economic and Social Council. It is composed of sixteen members—eight appointed by the president of the council in consultation with Indigenous organizations and eight nominated by member-states and elected by the council. Its mandate is to consider Indigenous issues related to economic and social development, culture and the environment, education, health and human rights. An important function of the permanent forum is to orient UN discussions on issues related to Indigenous peoples, raise awareness and promote the integration and coordination of activities related to Indigenous peoples throughout the UN system. The permanent forum holds its annual session each year in New York, attended by thousands of Indigenous people from around the world.

The third mechanism is the Expert Mechanism on the Rights of Indigenous Peoples, established by the Human Rights Council in 2007 to provide it with expertise and advice on the rights set out in the declaration and to assist member-states, upon request, in achieving the goals of the declaration. It is a smaller body, now composed of seven independent experts. The creation of each of these three mechanisms reflects distinct historical and political contexts and the demands of the Indigenous peoples' movement. As a result, their functions overlap somewhat, but together they constitute the UN's institutional environment within which the Indigenous rights special rapporteur operates.

I was the second person elected by the Human Rights Council as the special rapporteur on the rights of indigenous peoples.[3] During my two terms over six years as special rapporteur, I engaged in a range of activities to monitor and promote steps to improve the human rights conditions of Indigenous peoples worldwide and couched that work within the normative framework of the declaration. The scope of my functions fell within four principle spheres: promoting good practices, producing country reports, dealing with cases of allegations of human rights violations and investigating thematic issues,[4] some of which I describe briefly below. I also undertook efforts to follow-up on the recommendations included in my predecessor's reports in relation to the foregoing areas of work. My various reports and recommendations[5] were advanced in the immediate post-declaration-adoption environment but called upon my longer experience as a lawyer working on Indigenous issues in the United States and in the UN and inter-American human rights systems. Later in this chapter, I offer examples as I consider the significance and impact of the declaration.

THE ROLE OF THE WORKING GROUP ON INDIGENOUS POPULATIONS

Efforts to draft an international instrument to promote and protect the rights of Indigenous peoples worldwide took place over several decades.[6] During that time, Indigenous leaders from around the world who became involved in the process quickly became adept, if they were not already, at strategic negotiations and robust advocacy in the labyrinthine corridors of the UN and with their home-nation governments.

Negotiations were launched within the framework of the UN Working Group on Indigenous Populations. In 1982, pursuant to a resolution of the Economic and Social Council and, in response to Indigenous peoples who wanted their concerns discussed and their rights-related efforts recognised at the international level, the Council approved establishment of the working group. At the time, this was one of the largest UN forums in the field of human rights, one of six working groups under the Commission on Human Rights Sub-Commission on Promotion and Protection of Minorities (originally, the Sub-Commission on the Prevention of Discrimination and Protection of Minorities).[7] The sub-commission working group's two-fold mandate was to review developments pertaining to the promotion and protection of human rights and fundamental freedoms of Indigenous peoples and to give attention to the evolution of international standards concerning those rights. It was composed of independent experts and members of the sub-commission—one from each of the geopolitical regions of the world—who served under the impressive leadership of the late Professor Erica-Irene Daes of Greece and subsequently the late Miguel Alfonso Martínez of Cuba.

The Working Group on Indigenous Populations was open to all representatives of Indigenous peoples and their communities and organizations. In other words, the strict member-state or accredited NGO rules of participation that applied to Commission on Human Rights and its sub-commission did not apply to this working group. The open character of the way the group met, which included the participation of Indigenous delegates from across the world alongside representatives of governments, non-governmental organisations and UN agencies, substantially strengthened the working group's position as a focal point of international action by Indigenous peoples. Over time, it became an important vehicle enabling diverse Indigenous groups to forge a global Indigenous rights network around their common experiences and cultural solidarity.

The working group was one of the first international forums in which I engaged. In 1984, long prior to my eventual role as UN Special Rapporteur, I had started to attend annual meetings of the working group in my capacity as a staff attorney at the National Indian Youth Council in Albuquerque, New Mexico. This early working group experience gave me invaluable insights into the international arena and the Indigenous rights movement and into the subtleties and manoeuvrings of multilateral negotiations.

The working group began drafting text for a declaration in 1986, with Indigenous peoples' representation at the forefront of the associated deliberations. In 1993, the working group sent a draft Declaration on the Rights of Indigenous Peoples for consideration by its parent body, the UN Sub-Commission on the Promotion and Protection of Human Rights. The sub-commission endorsed the 1994 draft and forwarded it up the chain to the Commission on Human Rights for consideration. In 1995, the commission established its own inter-sessional working group for the sole purpose of elaborating and continuing negotiations on the draft declaration. Because of the complexities of the issues and processes involved, and with States now fully engaged in negotiations on the draft, it would be more than another decade before a revised text was adopted as the Declaration on the Rights of Indigenous Peoples by the UN General Assembly.

MOVEMENT AND CHALLENGES IN NEGOTIATING THE DECLARATION

Meanwhile, these complex processes of deliberation and negotiation towards adoption of the declaration were having another effect. As more and more delegations of Indigenous peoples from around the world began to participate in the various annual meetings and negotiation mechanisms involved in the drafting process, a common set of aspirations emerged among Indigenous peoples about their place and status in the world. In effect, the drafting of the declaration helped to coalesce a growing, worldwide Indigenous movement that increasingly reflected a sense of shared purpose and a growing optimism among the Indigenous peoples involved. But it had been evident from the start that the effort to better articulate the aspirations of Indigenous peoples within a global dialogue among nations and to negotiate a normative instrument that would be adopted by the UN General Assembly faced formidable political and legal challenges.

One such challenge was for Indigenous peoples to gain meaningful access to the UN system and a level of recognition by UN member-states so that they could advance protection of their rights within the system. Among other things, Indigenous peoples were testing the legitimacy and authority of member-states and the related state institutions that had been constructed around them. Yet they were doing so within the ambit of the UN, an organisation composed of and created by the very member-states that often resist changes in the status quo, especially changes of such a fundamental character. The challenges involved were particularly evident in the occasional statements made by representatives of member-states at the sessions of the sub-commission's working group on Indigenous populations. I felt that many of these states had rejected the notion that the Indigenous peoples' representatives could share space, on equal footing, within a UN-sanctioned process. Many were simply sitting back and observing the deliberations of the working group with what some might describe as cynical amusement. In effect, they were waiting to have their own say in deliberations at the higher levels to prevent things from going too far beyond the domestic policies of their own governments.

In this complex operating environment, both the sub-commission's working group and, eventually, the council's inter-sessional working group persisted in addressing and seeking resolutions for a set of difficult questions that began to emerge. These included the following:

- How could Indigenous peoples' claims of self-determination be affirmed in the face of deep resistance by influential member-states, resistance often couched in terms of international legal arguments on state sovereignty and territorial integrity?
- How could the collective rights of Indigenous peoples be recognised in an international instrument when international law had a primary focus on the rights of nation-states and the rights of individuals as citizens within those states?
- Were the collective rights that were being asserted by Indigenous peoples akin to human rights or were human rights by definition only inferred as individual rights?
- Were Indigenous peoples claiming special rights that other segments of humanity did not have? If so, how could that be reconciled with the presumed universality of human rights?
- Should Indigenous governments be constrained by international or universal human rights norms?

Indigenous delegates themselves spent many years debating these issues within their own ranks so that they might better articulate a cohesive position of solidarity in wider negotiations. There are several intersections in my involvement with these processes, but there is a particular juncture that was significant in my own thinking about how to forge a position for negotiating within the delicate balance of persuasion and compromise. In the summer (Northern Hemisphere) of 1989, Professor Robert Williams, an expert on Indigenous rights from the University of Arizona College of Law, and I met in Geneva, Switzerland, for the annual meeting of the subcommission working group. Our discussions, deepened by Rob's intellect and wry humour, turned to critical thinking on several of the core issues just mentioned. Of course there was no way we could resolve them all—and many remain difficult and unresolved today—but a few key points arising from that early conversation were influential in my own thinking about how to press forward.

First, we were of the shared opinion that the global Indigenous movement could not be limited by the entrenched and often contradictory legal concepts and terminology that kept being put before us through a discourse wedded to state-centric or individualistic understanding of the law, including international law. It would be necessary to go back to first principles of human rights and peaceful co-existence that underpin the foundation of the post–World War II UN system and build consensus from there.

Second, and related to the first, the articulation of international standards concerning Indigenous peoples would have to be built on a broader human rights foundation rather than on the conceptualisation of Indigenous peoples as state-like sovereigns advanced by some advocates. States were, and remain, especially strongly resistant to competing assertions of state sovereignty at the international level. We concluded instead that the discussion and the eventual adoption of international standards concerning Indigenous peoples had to focus more on the concepts of fundamental human rights instead of being grounded in assertions of Indigenous sovereignty (an approach rejected by States under the guise of being the exclusive sovereign arbiters of such rights at the international level). Our argument stressed that the human rights framework invites discussion of issues and standards on the basis of moral and ethical precepts, and that even at the international level the operation of such precepts can prevail over the strictures of existing legal parameters and configurations of state sovereignty. Both Rob and I were convinced that adopting a contemporary human rights discourse was crucial to the success of the Indigenous rights movement, at least within formal international institutions.

The third point we discussed was the need to keep at the forefront of our advocacy the original Indigenous motivation for having an international declaration as a benchmark. The goal was not simply to articulate a set of lofty principles in a written document but to respond to the real-world needs, aspirations and claims of Indigenous peoples in a way that could improve the conditions of their everyday lives. For this to eventuate, and faced with resistance from a number of UN member-states, we believed the Indigenous rights movement had to be pragmatic and tactical. It required an unflinching adherence to the core principles of human rights in conjunction with identifying the means for translating those principles into reality, including creation of institutionalised mechanisms for Indigenous participation and ways to hold states accountable.

In subsequent years, during the long and hard deliberations on what became the UN Declaration on the Rights of Indigenous Peoples, many of us involved in the process did what we could to insert these principles and positions into the mix of negotiations. As with any initiative involving multiple, diverse and powerful actors, each defending their interests while searching for workable solutions that all could support, the end result includes both deeply held aspirations and difficult compromises.

BREAKTHROUGH TO THE FINAL DRAFT

After several years of deliberations, the Working Group on Indigenous Populations produced a draft of the declaration based substantially on proposals advanced by Indigenous representatives. As explained above, that draft was subsequently endorsed by the working group's parent body, the Sub-Commission on the Promotion and Protection of Human Rights, which then, in 1995, submitted it to the Commission on Human Rights for its consideration. It was in the deliberations at that higher, intergovernmental level that negotiations stalled, with some Indigenous advocates insisting on adoption of the sub-commission working group draft without any change, and almost all states participating in the deliberations insisting on modification of one sort or another. Influential member-states, especially Canada, Australia, New Zealand and the United States (the CANZUS States) were uncompromising in their opposition to adoption of the draft without change. They raised concerns over self-determination, access to lands, territories and resources and the definition of the term 'Indigenous'. Other states were more open to compromise.

This impasse persisted for a number of years in the discussions of the inter-sessional working group established by the Commission on Human Rights to consider the sub-commission working group's draft. Indigenous advocates and their supporters persevered, but some sort of breakthrough was needed.

To their credit, in successive efforts the governments of Norway and Mexico took the lead in attempting to move things forward. At one point, Norway's delegation included John Henricksen, a highly respected Sami[8] lawyer employed by the Norwegian Ministry of Foreign Affairs. He was instrumental in drafting alternative language on some key points of the text and in forming a coalition of member-states to back those alternatives. The new language preserved the articulation of essential rights being advanced by Indigenous representatives while at the same time addressing the main concerns of several member-states.

The Mexican Government organised a series of 'off-the-record' informal meetings that were attended by representatives of member-state governments and Indigenous peoples and organisations, along with invited experts. The meetings were convened primarily to discuss certain outstanding issues in candid settings outside the public eye and outside the strictures of UN rules and formalities. The most significant of these informal meetings was held in Patzuaro, Mexico, from 26 to 30 September 2005, in the traditional territory of the Purepecha people, who are part of my own ancestry. The workshop was organised around three themes: Indigenous self-determination; land, territories and natural resources; and general provisions of the declaration. It was opened by Ms. Xóchitl Gálvez, General Director of the National Commission for the Development of Indigenous Peoples. Welcoming statements were also made by an Indigenous representative, the officer of the state governor of Michoacán, and the mayor of Patzcuaro. I felt honoured to attend and be part of these initiatives which bought people together informally for more open conversations and to develop points of consensus.

The diplomatic efforts of Norway and Mexico created a new dynamic in the negotiations. By 2005, the process began to show progress, gaining momentum from key global events such as the 2005 UN World Summit where the high-level Plenary Session of the UN General Assembly recognised the term 'Indigenous peoples' and made a commitment to uphold the 'human rights of Indigenous peoples'. While the negotiations on the text remained difficult and continued to absorb a great deal of time, in 2006 a revised draft of the declaration emerged, reflecting substantial consensus among Indigenous representatives and the UN member-states. Having replaced the Commission on Human Rights in 2006, the Human Rights Council in one of its first substantive acts approved the text and submitted it to the general assembly for consideration. At the general assembly, delegates of African States, which had remained largely silent in previous deliberations, raised concerns that led to amendments to the text to highlight regional differences in the application of the declaration and to affirm the long-standing principle of territorial integrity and political unity of member-states. Even so, the declaration still lacked unanimous support among states. It became apparent that the international community had exhausted its efforts and that, under the circumstances, the likelihood of complete consensus on the text was slim to nil. Hence, on 13 September 2007, the declaration was finally put to a vote in the plenary of the UN General Assembly in New York.

I remember sitting in the hall of the General Assembly that day, watching the vote tally appear on the large electronic screen above the podium. Of the 158 member-states present, 143 voted in favour, 4 voted against and 11 abstained.[9] It was an overwhelming endorsement in favour of a broad constellation of rights deemed to inhere in the world's Indigenous peoples. It also was a moment of intense emotion, the culmination of years of dedicated effort and thinking by many people, some of whom never lived to see their work come to fruition.

Several states took the opportunity to explain their votes, including states that had decided to abstain or vote against the resolution. For example, Australia's representative noted that his government had long expressed its dissatisfaction with the references to 'self-determination' in the text, a concept that Australia felt could be construed as encouraging action that would impair, even in part, the territorial and political integrity of a nation-state with a system of democratic representative government. Notably, however, at the same time Australia expressed its support for the core principles in the declaration.

The adoption of the declaration demonstrated the momentum Indigenous peoples had gained over two decades at the global level for greater recognition of their rights. That momentum continued. Eventually each of the four states that had voted against the declaration—Australia, Canada, New Zealand and the United States—reversed positions and affirmed their endorsement or support for it.

CONVERTING RIGHTS INTO OUTCOMES: THE DECLARATION AND THE SPECIAL RAPPORTEUR

Reflecting now on this highly charged and momentous process, it is clear that after the declaration was passed, we also passed into another era in the Indigenous fight for self-determination; one that took us from the battle for affirmation of rights and recognition to an era of implementation. In that era, the challenge would become how to translate rights into practice.

During my six-year tenure as special rapporteur on the rights of indigenous peoples, starting the year after the declaration was adopted, I made implementation of the rights affirmed in the declaration the central focus of my work. I deliberately made constant reference to it as the benchmark for addressing Indigenous concerns in my pursuance of the UN mandate to monitor the human rights conditions of Indigenous peoples around the world and, in doing so, to identify obstacles and make recommendations on how to remedy those problems. It became a principal normative frame of reference for my role, a basis against which I could measure situations and identify violations. While some governments failed to respond to my findings and recommendations, most of those I worked with eventually engaged with me in genuine dialogue.

More broadly, it soon became apparent that no government could simply ignore the declaration without taking the risk of attracting adverse global attention to its reputation and practice in human rights. And many—having voted in a global, public forum to endorse the declaration and its conception of Indigenous rights—have on their own initiative taken positive actions. I do not wish to assert that the declaration has everywhere paved the way towards adoption of new laws or recognition of Indigenous rights—far from it. However, it did and still does provide an internationally accepted framework for discussion, and it can influence governments and other parties to take domestic action.

A substantial area of my activity as special rapporteur followed from the directive given to me by the Human Rights Council to identify and promote best practices in Indigenous affairs. In this connection, I worked to advance legal, administrative and programmatic reforms and to implement the terms of the declaration in multiple countries, sometimes in response to specific requests made by governments for technical and advisory assistance.

Through this work, I was able to promote positive initiatives and identify models of reform that could be applied in diverse contexts.

An example of this work was my engagement in Suriname, a former Dutch colony in South America (Anaya 2011a). The request for me to visit the country came from Suriname's Minister of Regional Development who was charged with implementing the judgement of the Inter-American Court in the case of *Saramaka People v. Suriname*; a case involving the Saramaka Maroon people. Alongside the Indigenous inhabitants of the country are the Maroons—a tribal people made up of descendants of escaped African slaves who formed a culturally distinctive society in the deeply forested interior region of the country. Suriname had requested my technical and advisory services in developing a law to protect the rights of Indigenous and tribal peoples in the country. During my visit there, I met with government representatives and Indigenous and Maroon groups to learn their priorities in advancing protections for Maroon and Indigenous land rights and to understand how they viewed my participation in this effort.

Following my visit, I provided commentary and analysis (Anaya, 2011a) designed to assist with the development of a legal framework in Suriname that would recognise Maroon and Indigenous peoples' communal tenure rights, their right to a juridical personality and their right to effectively participate in decisions that affect them. This initiative also furthered one of my objectives as special rapporteur, namely, to reinforce decisions of other international human rights mechanisms, in this instance, the Inter-American Court of Human Rights. My report was one of several investigations and reports I produced under similar arrangements with governments and for Indigenous peoples in multiple countries (see, for example, Anaya 2009, 2011a, 2011b, 2012, 2013a).[10] My work added to the ongoing work of the Inter-American Court itself to advance implementation of the judgement, which has been slow in coming.

My role also enabled me to apply the declaration to the consideration of principles and practices regarding natural resource and development initiatives on Indigenous lands, including Indigenous-run initiatives. Several of my thematic reports addressed extractive industries, arguing that as part of their right to self-determination, 'Indigenous peoples have the right to determine priorities and strategies for the development or use of their lands and territories' (Anaya 2013b: 5). I argued for a right of Indigenous peoples to pursue their own initiatives for resource extraction within their territories if they so chose and the need for States to protect Indigenous peoples' land and resource rights against invasion by extractive companies.

My visits to several countries confirmed for me that development outcomes are enhanced when Indigenous peoples are free to pursue their own development initiatives backed by adequate capacity and internal governance institutions (Anaya 2013a, 2013b). Towards the end of my mandate as special rapporteur, I drew upon these country experiences to make recommendations and point to new models for resource extraction that would be consistent with the declaration and other international instruments and conducive to the fulfilment of Indigenous peoples' rights (Anaya 2013b). In my report on Indigenous Peoples and Extractive Industries, I recommended the following 'conditions for getting to and sustaining Indigenous peoples' agreement to extractive activities promoted by the State or third party business enterprises' (2013b: 41–78):

- Establishment of state regulatory regimes that adequately protect Indigenous peoples' rights;
- Regulation of extraterritorial activities of companies;
- Participation by Indigenous peoples and respect for their rights in strategic state planning for resource extraction and development;
- Due diligence by extractive companies to respect Indigenous peoples' rights;
- Fair and adequate consultation and negotiation procedures; and
- Rights-centred, equitable agreements and partnership.

I believe elements of this framework for applying the declaration in the context of extractive industries could be more broadly applied in other areas, such as Indigenous treaty-making, resolution of land and other claims, and so on.

THE ONGOING SIGNIFICANCE OF THE DECLARATION

While the full significance of the declaration may only become apparent over the longer term, it already is a monumental achievement. It is a repudiation of laws and policies that have been complicit for generations in the oppression of Indigenous peoples. It represents a political and, to some extent, a legal commitment by the UN and its member-states to the rights and principles that the declaration embodies. These include the right of Indigenous peoples to exercise self-determination in harmonious co-existence with others, within the states in which they live; the right to maintain and develop their own cultures and religious traditions; the right to continue in possession of traditional lands and resources; the right to determine their own future development; and a host of related rights and correlative state duties. The declaration also affirms that states have a duty to take remedial action where those rights are infringed and a duty to take the affirmative steps necessary to give those rights practical effect. It signals a new model for Indigenous–state relations that is different from those that have prevailed in the past. And within this new model, there is no room for archaic legal doctrines rooted in colonial-era premises of *terra nullius* or mendicant dependency.

My UN experience and subsequent professional work have revealed some of the myriad ways in which Indigenous peoples and organisations are now converting the rights asserted in the declaration into substantive, practical outcomes.

Asserting Indigenous Rights in the Political Arena

Around the world, we see instances in which Indigenous peoples are using the declaration in different settings and through diverse non-judicial avenues of advocacy to remind governments of their obligations and to argue their claims for repossession of traditional lands and resources. In some instances, Indigenous groups are using the declaration to resist the incursions by governments and multinational companies such as, for example, against unwanted oil and other natural resource extraction projects affecting Indigenous communities. In addition, we are seeing a number of situations where the declaration has been used to prompt or guide the development of new legislation and inform discussion of new laws to regulate consultations with Indigenous peoples. This has been the case, for example, in several Latin American countries.

Asserting Indigenous Rights in Claims before Judicial Bodies

Increasingly, Indigenous advocates had invoked the declaration in support of claims advanced through the courts. As a result, some judicial decision makers have referred to the declaration to interpret and apply relevant domestic laws. For example, in 2007, the Indigenous Maya in southern Belize, Central America, filed consolidated claims in court to defend their customary land tenure system. The claimant Indigenous group sought to have the court address their claims of alleged violations of sections of the Belize Constitution on recognition, protection and respect of their customary land rights. In this case, the Supreme Court of Belize referred to the declaration to support its finding that the Constitution of Belize protects customary Mayan land tenure in that country (Campbell and Anaya 2008).

Asserting Indigenous Rights in the International Arena

The declaration continues to serve as a guide or foundation for international institutions and procedures concerned with Indigenous issues. The

Inter-American Commission on Human Rights and the Inter-American Court of Human Rights, for example, have increasingly referred to the declaration in their decisions and reports concerning Indigenous peoples. This is similarly the case among various UN bodies and mechanisms that receive and respond to allegations and complaints by Indigenous peoples, or that seek proactively to establish programmes that relate to Indigenous peoples.

CHALLENGES TO REALISATION OF THE DECLARATION

As special rapporteur, I witnessed first-hand and reported on (Anaya 2013c) the substantial obstacles that hinder implementation of the declaration and the practical realisation of the rights it affirms. Three of those obstacles are particularly influential.

State-Imposed Development Agendas That Presumptively Benefit All

In many member-states, development initiatives purported to benefit a state and its citizens as a whole in fact have negative consequences for Indigenous peoples. These initiatives often involve, in addition to extractive projects, massive infrastructure projects such as dams and transportation facilities in Indigenous territories. For example, in my role as special rapporteur I often encountered a lack of adequate state mechanisms for the participation of Indigenous peoples in the consideration, design and implementation of development initiatives. I also observed an absence of mitigation and reparation measures to take into account Indigenous environmental and cultural concerns. Failure to recognise Indigenous property rights in lands and resources and the absence of equitable sharing in the benefits of development projects were also common (Anaya 2010: 5-6).

Misguided State-Imposed Development Agendas That Are Intended to Benefit Indigenous Peoples in Particular

The second obstacle arises in contexts where states have long-standing concerns about the welfare of Indigenous peoples and, often backed by international actors, design and advance development initiatives that are intended to address Indigenous disadvantages in areas such as health, education and access to material needs. While targeting substandard social and economic conditions, such initiatives often disregard or even subvert Indigenous own aspirations for development and self-determination; in particular, the right of

Indigenous peoples to make decisions, manage resources and maintain distinct cultural identities, languages and connections to traditional lands.

Self-determination is a matter of basic human dignity, but it is more than that. Enhancing Indigenous self-determination has been shown to be conducive to successful practical outcomes. Indigenous peoples who make their own decisions about development have been shown to fare better than those who do not. For example, the Harvard Project on American Indian Economic Development (2008) and the several case studies in this edited volume provide credible evidence of the effectiveness of self-determined governance models for rebuilding Indigenous nations and implementing social and economic development goals.

Indigenous-Determined Governance

Which leads me to my final point. The third challenge to the realisation of rights stipulated in the declaration is linked to Indigenous self-governance. Indigenous self-determination will require changes not only in how states deal with Indigenous peoples but also in the strengthening of Indigenous institutions of self-government. The form these governance institutions take and how they are designed and implemented are matters for Indigenous peoples themselves to decide. Rebuilding and exercising practically effective governance will empower Indigenous peoples to take control of their own affairs in all aspects of their lives and to ensure that development initiatives and related processes are aligned with their own cultural values and world views. In this I echo the many statements that, as special rapporteur, I heard from Indigenous leaders around the world who have long recognised the need for Indigenous peoples to strengthen their own governance capacities in ways they choose, in order to meet the development challenges *and* opportunities faced by their communities.

THE DECLARATION: A CRITICAL BEGINNING

This is the work that now lies ahead of us. Much of it is already being undertaken by Indigenous peoples in various parts of the world and, in some cases, by states. It has been thirty-one years since the International Labor Organisation adopted Convention 169 on Indigenous and Tribal Peoples recognising the aspirations of Indigenous peoples to exercise control over their own institutions, ways of life and economic development, and to maintain and develop their identities, languages and religions, within the framework of the states in which they live. The convention represented progress towards the recognition and protection of Indigenous rights at the international level.

However, it also demonstrated the limitations of that progress as it failed to fully satisfy the demands being pressed by Indigenous peoples.

The UN Declaration on the Rights of Indigenous Peoples has significantly built on this and other previous global steps. While still only a beginning, it is a critical beginning, and its importance will continue to grow. It has much to offer not only for Indigenous peoples but also to humanity more generally. Among other things, the declaration offers a framework for more collaborative and productive relationships between states and Indigenous peoples. It advances the idea that diverse peoples can come together in just and peaceful co-existence. It animates futures in that spirit of 'linking arms together' (Williams 1999) that some Indigenous North Americans imagined and had hoped for in their early relationships with settler Europeans. It embraces the idea that there can indeed be justice for Indigenous peoples in the contemporary world.

NOTES

1. The term 'member-state' has a technical definition in accordance with the Charter of the United Nations and refers to a sovereign state or government that has been admitted to membership of the organization by decision of the General Assembly upon recommendation of the Security Council. See https://www.un.org/en/sections/member-states/about-un-membership/index/.html (accessed 2 August 2019).

2. The Human Rights Council, established by the UN General Assembly on 15 March 2006 and made up of 47 UN member-states, is now the main human rights body of the United Nations. It replaced the Commission on Human Rights which itself was established in 1946 in the aftermath of World War II.

3. The first was Professor Rodolfo Stavenhagen from Mexico who held the position from 2001 to 2008.

4. See https://www.ohchr.org/en/issues/ipeoples/srindigenouspeoples/pages/sripeoplesindex.aspx, accessed 4 June 2019.

5. For a list of documents I produced as special rapporteur see: http://unsr.jamesanaya.org/, accessed 5 June 2019.

6. Accounts of the complex institutional and negotiation arrangements required for the completion of a draft declaration can be found in several publications. See for example, Charters and Stavenhagen 2009; Ciupa 2017; Pulitano 2012.

7. The Working Group ceased to exist in 2006 when the UN's Commission on Human Rights became the Human Rights Council.

8. The Sami people traditionally inhabit a territory known as Sápmi, which spans the northern parts of Norway, Sweden and Finland, and the Russian Kola Peninsula. Although the Sami are divided by the formal boundaries of these four states, they continue to exist as one people, united by cultural and linguistic bonds and a common identity (see Anaya 2011b).

9. Canada, Australia, New Zealand and the United States of America persisted in their opposition and voted against the declaration. Azerbaijan, Bangladesh, Bhutan, Burundi, Colombia, Georgia, Kenya, Nigeria, Russian Federation, Samoa and Ukraine abstained.

10. For a full list of the papers, presentations, annual, special and thematic reports and cases produced during my time as special rapporteur, May 2008 to May 2014, see the website archive at http://unsr.jamesanaya.org/.

Chapter 2

Indigenous Governance and Native Title in Australia

Ivan Ingram

Since the colonisation of what we now know as Australia in 1788[1] Aboriginal and Torres Strait Islander peoples[2] have been the subject of intense race-relations management and regulation. Thus began the pervasive degree of control exercised by successive governments, from the Imperial British Government to the Commonwealth Government of Australia and the various state and territory governments. This control, particularly in the dispossession of Aboriginal people's traditional lands and waters, resulted in them becoming 'the most disadvantaged in Australian society',[3] where such disenfranchisement is seen today across social, economic, health and education outcomes. This deficit has now faced calls for a change in the way Australia, comprising both Indigenous and non-Indigenous peoples, approaches matters affecting the lives of Indigenous peoples. In particular, there is a growing focus on enabling Indigenous Australians to seek opportunities to increase their autonomy, independence and capacity to deal with matters themselves—fundamentally, to enable Indigenous governance.

In the current Australian legal and political landscape, one such opportunity that is an enabling 'space' for the development of Indigenous governance is through the statutory regime of 'native title'.[4] By engaging in the native title process, Indigenous Australians can seek to rectify the disenfranchisement of speaking for, caring for, and managing their traditional country, from which some peoples have been dispossessed since colonisation. Native title provides a platform and seat at the 'negotiation table',[5] which arguably increases Indigenous Australians' ability to assert and exercise governance in managing their internal and external affairs. There is a strong aspiration among Indigenous Australians to have greater autonomy and control over the policies and laws that regulate and govern their lives. Historically, there have been institutions that provided a form of self-governance, such as the now disassembled Commonwealth statutory body known as the Aboriginal and Torres Strait Islander Commission (ATSIC) that operated across Australia (see Jonas 2004; Agreements, Treaties and Negotiated Settlements Project 2011) and the various state-based regimes, such as the system of Aboriginal Land Councils in New South Wales[6] and Land Councils in the Northern Territory.[7] There are also several thousand Indigenous organisations incorporated in Australia under Commonwealth legislation, which represent the rights and interest of Indigenous groups and communities, invariably in respect to service delivery and programmes. This chapter will not examine those institutional regimes in detail; rather, the aim here is to examine how Aboriginal and Torres Strait Islander peoples are using the legislative regime and processes of native title to pursue other modes of self-governance and nation-building. These include leveraging native title to take up opportunities of economic development, cultural heritage protection and preservation, community development, caring for country practices, access to education and health, and other capacity-building exercises to ensure sustainability as a culture and peoples into the future.

With native title being legislated as a body of Australian law and regulatory regime only for the past period extending a little over twenty-five years, there have been substantial inroads pursuing land justice and self-determination made by Aboriginal and Torres Strait Islander peoples. People who have been engaged in the native title regime can identify the numerous deficiencies and inadequacies that hinder the realisation of self-determination and nation-building at their highest forms,[8] because—fundamentally—it is a regime that has been developed and prepared by mostly non-Indigenous proponents in governments and heavily influenced by powerful industry sector interests. Despite the hurdles, Indigenous Australians have had to adapt and push innovation, through the exercise of their native title rights, when dealing with this system. This chapter outlines the native title regime and the regulatory framework that Indigenous people operate within, paying particular attention to the framework of governance of, and within, the native title regime and the issues and challenges faced by Indigenous Australians when developing their governance models through native title.

HISTORICAL CONTEXT

The history of Indigenous affairs in Australia has developed through several phases. Since time immemorial, Aboriginal and Torres Strait Islander peoples have lived and thrived in an environment where the people and land exist in a symbiotic relationship and are not severable concepts. Indigenous Australians are intrinsically connected to the land, and the land is intrinsically connected to its custodians. This intimate connection, developed over at least 60,000 years, has been violently and forcibly disrupted in a little under 250 years, first by the Indigenous inhabitants being viewed as a people who were not capable of being 'civilised' or having any mode of government and, thus, the continent itself being declared 'terra nullius' (land belonging to no one), and therefore ripe for possession by the British Empire.

As the settler-colonial frontier penetrated further into the Australian outback, it resulted in the displacement of Aboriginal people, with violent clashes ensuing. This dispossession went hand in hand with Australian and state governments' efforts to categorise and control Aboriginal people, whether through law or through force. Prior to the Federation of the Australian States in 1901, a system of 'protection' laws was already well-established[9] and continued to operate once federation occurred, and Indigenous Australians were not included in Australia's Constitution. As a result, they were left to be dealt with by each of the state governments. Ironically, these 'protection' laws were not about protecting Indigenous Australians; rather, they provided broad powers for governments to have control over nearly all aspects of their lives, including the ability to remove Aboriginal groups (often *en masse*) to missions and government-managed reserves.[10] This led to generations of children stolen from their families, severing their connections to culture, country and kin (see Human Rights and Equal Opportunity Commission 1997); these children are known as the 'stolen generation'.

Over the many decades following federation, and despite successive stolen generations, relations between Indigenous and non-Indigenous Australians slowly improved, culminating in the 1967 Referendum to amend the Australian Constitution to allow the Australian Government to make laws for Aboriginal Australians and thereby having them counted as Australian citizens. This marked the commencement of a number of policy platforms that governments developed in respect of Indigenous Australians. The shift towards the policy platform of Aboriginal self-determination was launched by the then-prime minister, Gough Whitlam, and was short-lived after being dismantled and diluted by successive Liberal governments. The period of reconciliation emerged in the mid-1990s, with the view towards remedying the divisive relations of the past (Reconciliation Australia 2017). Since the High Court's *Mabo* decision in 1992, the enactment of the *Native Title Act 1993* (Cth) by subsequent Australian governments' has seen the development of native title as a field of Australian law and regulatory oversight. While this chapter is not able to canvass the entire history of Australian Indigenous and non-Indigenous race relations, this background serves to illustrate the origins of many of the challenges beyond any control of Aboriginal and Torres Strait Islander peoples, which they now have to face through the native title regime.

The experience of Indigenous Australians is similar in its violence and usurpation of rights and lands to the history of other Indigenous First Nations internationally. However, in contrast to other Indigenous peoples/First Nations of New Zealand, Canada, and the United States of America, a core difference is the genesis upon which fundamental rights were initially recognised. Notwithstanding the violent histories, in each of those countries there exists a system of treaty-making which provided for certain rights and recognition of those Indigenous peoples as 'First Nations' having their own modes of self-government and some rights to traditional lands and territories. In Australia, the declaration by the British of *terra nullius* presented a different inception, one that was void of any recognition of Indigenous Australians as 'peoples' *ab initio* (from the beginning). This impoverished historical context in Australia accentuates some of the present-day difficulties under native title. However, it has also generated present-day innovations that Aboriginal and Torres Strait Islander peoples have developed in order to progress towards fuller ownership and control of the systems within which they operate.

As an Indigenous Australian lawyer, I have been privileged to work with many Indigenous groups in Australia who are seeking to secure recognition of their native title and creating innovative ways of rebuilding their governing authority and cohesion. Before describing examples of the issues and challenges, I wish to briefly outline the main characteristics of the native title regime.

NATIVE TITLE IN AUSTRALIA

In 1992, following a decade of litigation in the Australian courts, the High Court of Australia handed down the landmark decision *Mabo v Queensland (No 2)*.[11] The High Court held for the Meriam peoples of Murray Island in the Torres Strait region of Australia, that their traditional laws and customs that gave rights and interests in their traditional lands and waters, had 'survived' the assertion of sovereignty by the British Crown and so were capable of recognition by the Australian common law.[12] The orders of the High Court recognised that the Meriam peoples were 'entitled as against the whole world to possession, occupation, use and enjoyment of the lands of the Murray Islands'. Importantly, the Mabo decision did not address the question of the 'mode or validity of the acquisition of sovereignty' (Strelein 2009: 3) over Australia, rather it held that the common law can recognise the traditional land-tenure systems of Indigenous people to their traditional territories.[13] Such recognition was linked to the proviso that certain crucial elements are satisfied. These can be generalised as being requirements to provide proof: first, of the existence of an identifiable Indigenous community or group;

second, that there is traditional connection with or occupation of the land under the traditional laws and customs of the group; and third, that the community or group has substantially maintained connection with the traditional lands.[14]

This decision marked a paradigm shift in Australia's history because it challenged the foundation of the nation's inception and immediately shifted the way in which Indigenous and non-Indigenous relations are viewed. Following the precedent laid down by the High Court, then-prime minister, the Hon. Paul Keating, moved to enact the *Native Title Act 1993* (Cth) by parliament. Notwithstanding the political challenges and negative perceptions of much of the broader Australian community, this law opened the opportunity for all Indigenous Australians to have their native title recognised. However, it also immediately raised these questions: What exactly is 'native title'? Who holds it? And what proofs are required to substantiate claims to native title?

The content of native title and the identity of those groups who hold such title is a legal determination made by the Australian Federal Court, by way of reference to proof of the traditional laws and customs acknowledged and observed by the Indigenous inhabitants of the territory.[15] Native title is the phrase used to describe Indigenous Australians' traditional laws and customs that relate to lands and waters, thereby giving them co-existing rights to the land and waters; these traditional laws and customs are then capable of being recognised by the common law of Australia.[16] Consequently, the only means of them validly extinguishing native title is in accordance with the *Native Title Act*.[17]

The content of native title itself, while determined by way of reference to the traditional laws and customs of that particular group of peoples,[18] also raises the question of what kind of rights are actually conferred upon the group seeking or holding native title. It has to be noted that native title is not a proprietary right in Western property law sense (i.e., a real property right legally asserted against the rest of the world). It is a right that can be recognised as 'co-existing' with the radical title of the Crown. In its strongest expression, the High Court in *Mabo* determined that the Meriam Peoples held native title that conferred exclusive possession, occupation, use and enjoyment to the exclusion of all others; this is referred to as 'exclusive' native title.

However, the way in which the content of Indigenous title would be determined will vary with the nature of the Indigenous relationship to the land itself.[19] For instance, the High Court declared in *Western Australia v Ward*[20] that if exclusive native title could not be recognised because the evidence of the Indigenous relationship to the land itself was not of a calibre so as to confer exclusive possession, then it was 'preferable to express the rights by reference to the activities that may be conducted, as of right, or in relation to the land or waters'.[21] In this manner, it is expressed as a 'bundle of rights' that are non-exclusive (meaning, they are co-existing with other rights and interests in the land). This form of right, whether exclusive or non-exclusive, does not give jurisdiction of any kind to the Aboriginal people or Torres Strait Islanders determined to have native title. In addition, all other laws and regulations will still apply to the native title holders. Herein lies a curve in the inroads that native title was presumed to have made in post-*Mabo* Australia.

Through the *Native Title Act*, national infrastructure and statutory procedures were created, including the establishment of the National Native Title Tribunal, the role and functions of the Federal Court, and the creation of representative Aboriginal and Torres Strait Islander bodies to cover the entire continent. This new institutional system has been developed and, as at November 2019, there have been 478 determinations of native title, 398 of which were positive determinations (native title has been recognised) and 80 have been negative determinations (native title has not been recognised). There are currently 208 native title determination applications (claims) lodged by various Indigenous groups referred to as 'native title claimants' (National Native Title Tribunal 2019).

For Indigenous groups to have their native title recognised, the only legal and administrative avenue available is to make an application and commence legal proceedings in the Federal Court of Australia. This initiates a negotiation and mediation process, often litigious, where the group must prove their native title and have their 'native title' validated by way of a positive determination of native title in a judgement made *in rem* (a judgement that determines rights in the land and waters as against the rest of the world).

The process of proving native title is long and expensive. It is financially, emotionally, and culturally taxing. The burden of proof rests on the Indigenous claimants to 'prove' who they say they are by disclosing cultural knowledge, sacred stories, sites, traditional and cultural business, details about ceremony, and the content of their laws and customs that govern their lives as Aboriginal or Torres Strait Islander peoples. Those laws and customs must show how they have 'rights and interests' that are understandable to Western standards of a proprietary nature, to the lands and waters they say are their traditional lands and waters.

The process also requires them to trace back as far as their oral histories are recollected to show they have a 'continuing connection' with and have maintained those laws and customs and have practised their culture. In this legal context, there has been minimal and confined legal tolerance by the courts for cultural adaptation and evolution of such laws, let alone recognition of the adverse impacts of colonisation on being able to sustain continuous connection.[22] Native title claimants are legally required to have substantially maintained real observance and real acknowledgement of those laws and customs. That is to say, they must be able to prove there has been a transmission from each successive generation of the traditional laws and customs of their particular group members and that the practices of that group have been practised since time immemorial and continue to be practised today. These include, for example, conducting ceremony, knowledge of song and dance, and other distinctive features of their collective identity.

This account is illustrative. I introduce the core legal concept that native title necessarily has its basis in the content of traditional laws and customs of a particular group. The sad irony is that, on one hand, Indigenous peoples have suffered turmoil in the 250 years of Australia's history since the arrival of the 'First Fleet', and, on the other, despite the perils of colonisation, Indigenous claimant groups are required to have sustained their culture, notwithstanding forcible removals and policies of cultural suppression and destruction.

GOVERNANCE OF (AND IN) NATIVE TITLE

Aboriginal and Torres Strait Islander peoples have been collectively self-organising through traditional laws and traditional customs that outline the responsibilities that each individual has to their family, community, and the Indigenous nation of which they are members. However, these structures were disrupted by colonisation, and there are new governance ways that Indigenous peoples must design to achieve the goals and aspirations of their community.

How people in the contemporary sense define 'good' or 'effective' governance, including in the context of Indigenous governance, has been examined and discussed by academics throughout the world (Dodson & Smith 2003; Centre for First Nations Governance 2008; Australian Human Rights Commission 2012; Cornell, Curtis & Jorgensen 2004; Harvard Project n.d.). But having effective governance within a native title process is not just about effective communication, accurate records, clean audits, close scrutiny and economic development. It is about upholding a peoples' collective identity and native title rights and interests against the Western colonial law and custom. Hence, the navigation of the native title process by Indigenous groups and their academic and legal representatives highlights the difficulties and cultural incompetence and/or institutionalised racism which compounds and complicates both the claim process and the post-determination space once a group has had their native title recognised in law.

Legal participation in a native title journey involves several phases where governance is required, and the form of that governance may be developed by the various Indigenous people engaged in the process. For instance, there are governance models being exercised during the native title determination application process of the claims stage. Indeed, arguably Indigenous governance was also involved prior to that stage when groups met together to decide whether to lodge a claim application. Furthermore, governance is also at work after a successful determination of native title in the post-determination stage. The modes of governance required during those different phases are not necessarily the same, but the former phase of governance during the claim can and has significantly influenced the latter stage.

Successfully carrying out a native title application through to a positive determination cannot be achieved without the people first bonding as their own nation, community, group or society and being able to unite strategically in the common goal of pursuing land justice. Furthermore, the procedural and proof challenge involved in the claim process cannot be easily done without the assistance of non-Indigenous expertise, primarily within the legal and anthropological disciplines. The governance challenge, however, is an internal one—a matter for members of a group to work through as they jump through the various legal hoops of the native title regime. Generally speaking, the more effectively groups are able to discuss, agree on, and manage their own internal governance, the more effectively they are able to enter into negotiations with registered parties in the wider native title arena. Compounding these complexities are the Western systems of administration of lands and resources and state-based cultural heritage regimes and other legislation which intersect with native title processes and which inevitably must be navigated by Indigenous claimants and counter-claimants. This regulatory burden does not ease as the groups progress from the claim stage to the post-determination stage.

In practice, the genesis of native title determination applications is brought about either proactively by an Indigenous group or reactively (usually in response to non-Indigenous interests seeking access to land and who legally must 'address' and first deal with native title before being able to proceed). This triggers the need to bring together the Indigenous people who may potentially hold native title and discuss options for having native title considered—particularly the lodging of a claim to gain certain rights under the *Native Title Act,* consequent upon having commenced a native title determination application in the Federal Court of Australia.

In the context of a proactive application of a native title claim, an Indigenous group will make a request for assistance to their Native Title Representative Body (NTRB). These bodies have functions mandated by the *Native Title Act* and are required to assist such groups in the making and prosecution of the native title claim, including provision of legal representation as well as assistance in research in fields such as anthropology.

Reactive lodgement of claims can sometimes suffer from the hurried nature of the initial process of ascertaining membership of a potential claimant group. By comparison, an application that has had the benefit of a research and incubation period, developing a foundation and basis to commence a legal or mediation proceeding including extensive community engagement and consultation, will inevitably result in the particular group acquiring more experience around native title governance processes. They will have had more time for internal conversations about working together, understanding complex legislation and interpretation and how to manage their future claim. However, on occasions a traditional-owner group is identified or asked to file a native title application in response to external factors, with the consequence that the application process is expedited. This may be premature, with Indigenous internal relationship and ways of making collective decisions not yet adequately resolved before the application is underway.

Through the process of a native title application, the *Native Title Act* requires traditional owners to authorise the way in which their claim will be prosecuted and who they will authorise to be the 'applicant'. Groups can make those decisions in two ways. The first is by incorporating and using their traditional decision-making processes, or in the absence of a traditional decision-making process, one that is agreed and adopted by the group (i.e. majority vote, consensus, etc.). Arguably, the authorisation process is one of the more culturally responsive parts of the *Native Title Act* where it requires all decisions about lands, resources and any agreement about royalties to be agreed upon by the members of the claim group.

Under this process, there is a nominated person or a number of persons who are appointed to represent the whole of their group to lodge the native title application in the Federal Court; these people are referred to as the 'applicant'. The applicant is mandated and has the responsibility of dutifully progressing the claim. While there is procedurally a way in which the applicant is appointed in accordance with the *Native Title Act*, the claim group has ownership in varying ways in which members of the applicant are selected. For instance, the native title claim group can nominate representatives based on criteria such as age, gender balance, family group representation (e.g., based on family descent groups from certain ancestors) or other particular qualities they prefer (e.g., by appointing elders or leaders with specific skills and cultural knowledge).

As claims can take anywhere from five to more than fifteen years to successfully prosecute, a significant long-term responsibility is imparted to an individual or group of persons when they take on the role of 'applicant'. This presents substantial challenges of finding a suitable composition of people for the 'applicant', which can result in the perpetuation or exacerbation of internal politics, disparity in representativeness, and a lack of fairness, whether actual or perceived. This issue is common throughout the entire country. However, it can be managed effectively through active community engagement, regular communication, and the consultation and partnership in the design of processes that the claim group wishes to use to progress the claim. Internal conflicts and stress can be managed by careful consideration of, and agreement to the level, scope, and authority that the claim group imparts to the applicant, for example, in respect to the kinds of decisions the applicant can make on behalf of the group, as opposed to those that require specific consultation with and authorisation by the whole of group.

Upon a successful determination of native title, the role of the applicant is complete and legally ends upon the handing down of a determination. It is at this point that a newly formed corporate governing body for the group is created under regulation, known as a prescribed body corporate (PBC).[23] This legal point of change in native title roles and responsibilities can perversely create a new period of uncertainty and anxiety for the native title group. Effectively, it constitutes a complete change in their governance arrangements and, for some, has constituted a period of sudden disputation and internal turmoil.

As the institutional native title holder for the group, the PBC can leverage native title to seek greater levels of self-determination and autonomy over land, resource, development and community matters. For some claim groups, the formulation and composition of the PBC starts well before the determination of native title. More often, however, the legal work required for incorporation of the entity and the consultation process with community is only done when needed for establishment of the PBC. The challenges in doing this are multifaceted. While the claims are progressing towards a determination, native title claim groups are also under pressure to concurrently engage in a level of strategic 'future planning'—looking towards the post-determination setting, undertaking additional levels of community consultation, and acquiring adequate legal advice about the future roles, responsibilities and governance arrangements needed for a PBC. They are under additional pressure to learn how to operate in another future regulatory environment and to fully inform and involve the community in designing a representative PBC. But the reality is that claimants are often pressed for time and under considerable pressure simply to deal with the native title claim process itself.

Also, the laws of the lands still apply, particularly in relation to regulatory compliance. Indigenous autonomy in respect to their self-governance and decision-making is limited by various state and federal legislation associated with land, the environment and resources. The complexities and colonial nature of the native title processes create conflict within most, if not every, traditional owner group who have been through it. The need to devise and uphold culturally legitimate governance structures and processes is crucial. However, again, unlike the native title process which is overseen by the Federal Court, the governance of native title in the post-determination phase, according to the *Native Title Act*, occurs under the surveillance of the Australian Government's regulatory body of PBCs, being the Office of the Registrar of Indigenous Corporations (ORIC).

ISSUES AND CHALLENGES IN GOVERNANCE-BUILDING

The challenges that native title brings to Indigenous groups and communities are many. For the purposes of this chapter, I focus on the specific challenges that influence the self-governance options and capabilities of Indigenous peoples in the process. These can be divided into two categories. The first set of challenges relate to the legal prosecution of a native title application. The second relate to the socio-political context that constrains Indigenous and non-Indigenous proponents and opponents of native title.

Indigenous groups undertake an arduous application process through the Federal Court of Australia for the recognition of their native title as the 'right people' for the 'right country', a process which is arbitrated by non-Indigenous institutions, values and standards. The internal accountability of the applicant in prosecuting the claim, the effectiveness and regularity of their communication with the broader claim group, and the mechanisms they access and use for dispute resolution all need to be clearly set out and well-implemented. In particular, expectations of the claim group and applicant in processing the native title claim need to be carefully articulated, managed and governed. If contentious internal issues are allowed to incubate and remain unaddressed during the claims phase, they will continue to persist—and indeed sometimes expand—in the post-determination stage(s). Moreover, after proving that they have maintained and preserved their laws and customs, native title holders are then expected to operate and engage in governing sophisticated corporate bodies and engage with diverse bodies of Western law and regulation and the complex political, economic and jurisdictional environments of the modern Australian nation state.

Many of the challenges confronting native title claimants and holders arise from complexities in the Australian law itself. The native title regime involves labyrinthine legal processes under the *Native Title Act*, which are further compounded by other legislation that impacts on native title at all levels of government. The burden of regulation, laws and local government ordinances that influence what can be done on their traditional lands and waters comes to the fore in native title, often on a daily or weekly basis.

Legal advisers have a role to play in such contexts, to ensure that the whole of the relevant native title group whom the applicant represents are fully informed, when required to make decisions. Communication on the part of the legal representatives, and by extension the applicant, must be cognisant of all the layers of cultural rights and interest involved within the group itself and the varied degrees of understanding and capacity. It is impossible, when representing Indigenous groups in native title applications, to expect an entire community of people to be operating and thinking at the same level of understanding, expectation and engagement. Even being agreeable to the strategy, direction and decisions, and even given effective communication about the process and the content of what is to be decided, there always remain factions of peoples who hold contrary views and, in some instances, strong opposition to the majority. In this situation, the applicant and their legal representatives must remember that even those who oppose the majority are still part of the community whom they are appointed to represent.

All members of the group are entitled to the benefits and opportunities that native title provides. The challenges presented by the external complexity of the native title law and process, coupled with the internal complexity of community politics, forces a group of people to either unite in order to make common decisions about their common future or dissolve into further factionalism and disputation. If given time and support, many native title groups are able to weather this stormy process and come out the other side with great resolve and unity. A critical factor leading to outcomes that are more positive is giving attention to building strong internal Indigenous governance at all phases of the native title process.

In the native title regime, Indigenous peoples have to operate within two distinct, often incommensurable, worlds of law and legal regulation. This is a real and difficult proposition. On one hand, they are required to understand and comply with non-Indigenous systems of law, and, on the other, to live by and maintain their traditional laws and customs (and often to be able to negotiate across several different groups engaging in a native title claim). Furthermore, Indigenous rights and interests are considerably less powerful legally and less well-resourced when compared with government and industry legislation and institutions. For example, the ability to exercise independence and autonomy in making decisions for country (such as its use, development, access and management) are arguably constrained under the native title regime.

Whether it be the highest form of native title recognised (referred to as 'exclusive native title') or the lesser and more common form of 'non-exclusive native title', native title constitutes a level of rights recognition that remains vulnerable to many other powerful interests in the same areas of land and water. Native title rights and interests are not regarded as land ownership in the same sense as 'freehold title' and private property are understood in the Western system of property law. An additional burden is that there is no accepted and consistent approach by the state and territory governments of Australia to how native title rights can actually be exercised in different jurisdictions.

Once recognised, native title provides a solid foundation for strategic engagement with the 'outside world' and opportunities for economic development, traditional resource management and for joint management of national/conservation parks and marine parks. Inevitably, this means that the governance of native title in the post-determination setting focuses on the governance of agreements and external relationships with government, NGOs and the private sector. Consequently, native title holders are often left with little time to engage in the governance rebuilding needed for their newly established PBCs. Furthermore, they can be quickly caught up in a reactive response mode to agendas set for them by others.

The dichotomy between actively governing their native title and negotiating opportunities with governments is codified in the various Indigenous land use agreements (ILUAs) in relation to mining and other natural resource interests. In such circumstances, Indigenous peoples appear to have an opportunity to engage with conditions that promise to deliver them greater economic prosperity, for example through employment, caring for country programmes, environmental programme, other monetary and non-monetary benefits such as financial benefits trusts for education and health, and other charitable purposes for their community. However, the *quid-pro-quo* is that they must consent, in writing, to a portion of their traditional estate being exploited by an extractive industry or developed by government. Investors often seek to fulfil such agreements through mechanisms such as access, explore or mine or establish other resource development projects on native title land. In such circumstances, the processes created for decision-making and community engagement can meet head-on and collide with the aspirations and objectives of the native title claimants. Some in the community may support entering into such arrangements, seeing the short- and long-term benefits to be secured, while others may oppose such agreements because of concerns about adverse impacts upon their traditional lands and waters.

Native title processes for communication, provision of advice and decision-making operate under immense pressure—especially in such contexts as ILUAs when fundamental core values are challenged. Again, this is a matter for governance—where there is a need to consider the diverse expectations and needs of a community, against the core values that guide their community, whether those be traditional law and cultural in origin or more contemporary, adopted principles. Native title holders can become locked into opportunistic reactionary behaviour, at the behest of external stakeholders and the perceived opportunities they prioritise. Thus, they may fail to give sufficient time and attention to building robust governance during the claims process, let alone later within their PBCs. Indeed, if governance-building is not put at the heart of the native title claim process, arguably it becomes even harder to undertake during the post-native title PBC phase.

For the PBCs, the regulatory burden only increases after native title is determined and the accompanying challenges of demands for transparency and the highly skilled capabilities required to operate effectively, autonomously and independently, whereas during a native title claim, the guidance of most traditional owner groups is provided for by the various representative Aboriginal or Torres Strait Islander bodies.[24] In a post-determination setting, PBCs are left largely to their own devices.[25] This situation poses real and substantive challenges to effective governance. Research on the influential components of effective Indigenous governance, as well as the key factors in establishing successful Indigenous governance models, point to similar fundamentals.[26] Developing a robust governance structure and workable policies, procedures and measures that support native title holders to address the many matters facing them cannot be achieved without the right leadership, practical skill-set, future planning and guidance. It is a long-term process, which is why preparatory work needs to be done on governance-building *during* the native title phase—not afterwards, when a PBC is established.

The reality on the ground for Aboriginal and Torres Strait Islander peoples in Australia in navigating the native title regime is that governing their native title is in its infancy—as a body of law and system. The practical considerations facing many groups today include the fundamental components of operating and governing as a cohesive community—building capacity in terms of human capital and leadership, corporate management and knowledge, administrative capability, financial management skills and negotiation skills. I recognise that there are many members of communities who are able to fill such roles and support their PBCs. Indeed, they are often also called upon to take up senior positions across many other facets of life within their community. However, longer term planning for skills development, leadership and succession planning for governing native title is urgently required. Such planning needs to start at the *beginning* of every native title process. The role of the next generation of Aboriginal and Torres Strait Islander youth will be to take on these existing challenges and the new ones that will inevitably arise as the native title law and development matures over time.

CONCLUSION

While the issues raised in this chapter may continue to recur in various forms, the next era of progress will come about by native title holders engaging in spaces that have yet to materialise in the phase of Indigenous relations in the post-native title determination regime. For example, a major concern is that not all Aboriginal and Torres Strait Islander peoples will achieve recognition of native title. Rather, as is already evident, there will be an increase in the asymmetry of peoples—between those who have native title and those who do not. This disparity will cause a divide between those groups who can successfully leverage their native title rights and interests for the benefit of their peoples and those who do not have access to such rights and opportunities. Thus, there is in native title the potential for further inequality among Indigenous peoples. We need a multifaceted approach to develop strategies to ensure that such disparity does not petrify and acerbate for future generations the disadvantaged plight of Indigenous Australians emanating from Australia's historical race relations.

It is incumbent on native title holder groups who have successfully navigated the native title regime and are in a position of economic and social success to advocate for an 'equalising' disruption to the system that has caused such perceived inequalities. Navigating the native title process does not extinguish the impact of colonisation upon traditional owner groups. It makes nothing right by being an acceptable and modified method of colonisation. However, it is what the late Eddie Mabo and many others fought for: namely, the right of traditional owner groups to hold native title to their land and seas, and with such a legal basis, the opportunity to exercise greater governing control and self-determination over them into the future. It is not the panacea 'to bridging the gap that has to be narrowed between Indigenous and non-Indigenous Australians' but it opens pathways to establish a socioeconomic base and a renewed beginning.

NOTES

1. Although Lieutenant James Cook landed on the shores of Botany Bay in what we now know as Sydney in 1770 and made the declaration of *terra nullius* over the continent of Australia, the colonisation with the arrival of the First Fleet of convicts did not commence until 26 January 1788.

2. In Australia, there are two groups of Indigenous people who are recognised—Aboriginal people and Torres Strait Islanders. In this chapter, I refer to Indigenous Australians and Aboriginal and Torres Strait Islander peoples interchangeably. Aboriginal people are the peoples who occupy the Australian mainland, and at colonisation there were over 500 different nations (language groups or cultural blocks). Torres Strait Islanders are those Indigenous peoples who occupy the Islands in the Torres Strait, which are the islands in the waters between Australia and Papua New Guinea (Australian Government n.d.).

3. *Native Title Act 1993* (Cth) Preamble.

4. See *Native Title Act 1993* (Cth) s 223, and *Mabo v Queensland* (No 2) (1992) 175 CLR 1.

5. For instance, Aboriginal and Torres Strait Islander peoples have the opportunity to be notified and consulted with, and enter into negotiations, in relation to proposed acts and works to be done by other parties including governments, industry or the public on their traditional lands and waters. The native title regime provides for a legislative process by which governments and proponents (non-government organisations, the private-sector businesses dealing with lands such as mines, gas, electricity, water) may be required to notify and consult with traditional owners prior to works being done.

6. *Aboriginal Land Rights Act 1983* (NSW); see New South Wales Government, Aboriginal Affairs n.d.

7. *Aboriginal Land Rights (Northern Territory) Act 1976* (Cth); see Northern Territory Government 2019.

8. For example, native title does not provide for legislated self-determination, sovereignty or rights to self-government. This by way of contrast to Indigenous land rights regimes in other countries where there are treaty-based rights which provide for higher legal status of recognition in respect of land rights; for example, in New Zealand, Canada and the United States of America. Furthermore, the articulation of rights in the United Nations Declaration on the Rights of Indigenous Peoples (UNDRIP) provides for the highest form of articulation in particular rights, including land (see UN n.d.: articles 25, 26, 27).

9. See for example, the Queensland *Aboriginal Protection and Restrictions of the Sale of Opium Act 1897 (Qld)* Preamble noted 'it is desirable to make provision for the better protection and care of the aboriginal and half-caste inhabitants of the Colony'; available at https://www.foundingdocs.gov.au/resources/transcripts/qld5_doc_1897.pdf.

10. See e.g. records of the Legislative Assembly, New South Wales 1883.

11. (1992) 175 CLR 1.

12. *Mabo v Queensland (No 2)* (1992) 175 CLR 1, 57, 69 (Brennan J, Mason CJ, McHugh J agreeing); 100-01 (Deane and Gaudron JJ); and 184 (Toohey J).

13. *Mabo v Queensland (No 2) (1992)* 175 CLR 1, 41-2, in which his Honour Brennan J, noted that: 'it is imperative in today's world that the common law should neither be or be seen to be frozen in an age of racial discrimination . . . The fiction by which the rights and interests in indigenous inhabitants in land were treated as non-existent was justified by a policy which has no place in the contemporary law of this country'.

14. Elements of native title have had extensive judicial comment; see e.g. *Mabo v Queensland (No 2) (1992)* 175 CLR 1; *Members of the Yorta Yorta Aboriginal Community v State of Victoria and Others (2002)* 214 CLR 422; *Western Australia v Ward (2002)* 213 CLR 1; *De Rose v South Australia (2003)* 133 FCR 325; *Alyawarr v Northern Territory (2005)* 145 FCR 422; *Risk v Northern Territory (2007)* 240 ALR 75; *Griffiths v Northern Territory* [2007] 165 FCR 391; *Bodney v Bennell (2008)* 167 FCR 84; *State of Western Australia v Sebastian (2008)* 173 FCR 1.

15. *Mabo v Queensland (No 2)* (1992) 175 CLR 1, 58, 110, 187.

16. This chapter will not go into the nuances of the evidentiary and legal requirements of proving native title. Refer to notes 14 through 18, for cases relevant to the legal elements of native title.

17. The initial *Native Title Act 1993* (Cth) was further amended in the 1998 Amendments, providing for more means of extinguishment and greater certainty for non-native title interests.

18. See *Mabo v Queensland (No 2)* (1992) 175 CLR 1.

19. *Mabo v Queensland (No 2)* (1992) 175 CLR 1, 49, and 88.

20. (2002) 213 CLR 1.

21. *Western Australia v Ward* (2002) 213 CLR 1; 191 ALR 1, [51]-[52].

22. See *Members of the Yorta Yorta Aboriginal Community v State of Victoria and Others (2002)* 214 CLR 422; 194 ALR 538, [44] 'the only rights or interests in relation to land or waters, originating otherwise than in the new sovereign order, which will be recognised after the assertion of that new sovereignty are those that find their origin in the pre-sovereignty law and custom', as per Gleeson CJ, Gummow and Hayne JJ.

23. It is referred to as 'prescribed' as it has specific roles and functions it must perform in accordance with the *Native Title Act*, and the *Corporations (Aboriginal and Torres Strait Islander) Act 2006* (Cth); PBCs are appointed as an Agent or Trustee of the determined native title common law holders. The PBC's details are place on the National Native Title Tribunal's Registry and it is formally made the Registered Native Title Bodies Corporate (RNTBC).

24. There are 15 nationally recognised Representative Aboriginal and Torres Strait Islander Bodies exercising statutory duties under Part 11 of the *Native Title Act 1993* (Cth).

25. It is, however, incumbent on these Representative Bodies to assist in facilitating a transition to independence through capacity-building and continued facilitation and assistance functions in accordance with the *Native Title Act 1993* (Cth).

26. See e.g. Australian Human Rights Commission 2012; Harvard Project on American Indian Economic Development n.d.; Australian Indigenous Governance Institute 2019; and the Indigenous Community Governance Project findings produced by the Centre for Aboriginal Economic Policy Research, Australian National University (see https://caepr.cass.anu.edu.au/).

Chapter 3

Reconciling Interests and Rights in Māori Institutions of Governing

Annie Te One

Research into the diversity of Māori and local government relationships in Aotearoa-New Zealand is a growing field, but still contains significant gaps in our understanding of the breadth of Māori political engagement. For example, Māori and advocacy groups continue to pressure for increased action and awareness about Māori inclusion in the representative structures and decision-making of local government, but we know little about how Māori in their diverse iwi, hapū and mātaawaka collectivities participate in governance and politics at the local government level (Bargh 2013; Te One 2018). This knowledge gap is also indicative of the hesitancy, and in some instances resistance, that local governments themselves have displayed in developing policy to engage with Māori generally (Te One 2019).

Despite the tendency to homogenise Māori as a monolith group, as in other colonial-settler states, they are internally diverse with respect to their ties to Māori identity, culture and traditions (Kukutai 2011). Māori social organisation, land affiliation and internal governance centre on relationships between iwi (the largest tribal nations and political groupings) and their constituent hapū (the several interrelated extended family descent groups). Together, iwi and hapū tend to have affiliation to a shared territory of lands for which they are regarded as having mana whenua rights (i.e., rights of authority based on their long-held occupancy of a particular area of land). But colonisation's impacts of dispossession, dispersal and economy transformations also have generated different forms of Māori residential arrangements: some voluntary, some imposed. Hence today, mātaawaka is a term used to refer to Māori who have migrated away from their own iwi and hapū territories where they have mana whenua rights, to live in other parts of the country. The term is often used interchangeably with 'urban Māori' and can refer to individuals or groups.

Although mātaawaka can encompass numerous individual Māori identities linked to a multiplicity of iwi, it is also a term which can refer to a Māori collective residing in the same urban location (but who do not have mana whenua ties to the lands on which that city has been built). Over time, some of these urban collectivities have positioned themselves strongly as localised polities—groups who assert they have particular rights and interests under the Treaty of Waitangi/Te Tiriti o Waitangi (Treaty/Tiriti), and accordingly are organising themselves in respect to their internal governance. This chapter explores how these complex contemporary layers of Māori governance are articulating with each other at the local government level in Aotearoa, by describing how one particular mātaawaka group in the city of Wellington—as the Mōkai Kāinga Māori Centre—understands its Treaty/Tiriti rights in relation to local government. Wellington is the capital city of Aotearoa and home to the fourth largest Māori population per region in Aotearoa (Statistics New Zealand 2013). This includes both mātaawaka as well as a number of local iwi. In the Wellington City area, the iwi are Taranaki Whānui, which is a conglomerate of iwi including Te Ātiawa; Taranaki; Ngāti Ruanui; Ngāti Tama; Ngāti Mutunga; and other iwi from the Taranaki area.

I locate this discussion amongst wider conversations and debates occurring throughout Aotearoa which show, generally, an uncertainty about how to engage with mātaawaka in substantive and productive ways. I suggest that, for local governments, this uncertainty stems from their failing to look beyond their own Westernised governing preferences to those that exist within Māori communities. I make this argument through two points. The first is that local governments are challenged by the strategic positioning of a non-traditional Māori polity such as mātaawaka as being a rightful Tiriti/Treaty partner, and are therefore reluctant to extend their own consideration of what contemporary Māori collective governance looks like. Second, I further argue that local governments fail to understand the continuity of Māori governing rules and relationships, in particular the ways in which Māori engage with one another—in this case, as iwi and mātaawaka.

I begin with some of the wider debates surrounding mātaawaka rights under Te Tiriti/Treaty, before locating those arguments within developments at the local government level. I then focus on a case study in Wellington Aotearoa, which draws on my doctoral research conducted in 2016–2018.[1] The chapter highlights how Māori continue to challenge ongoing colonial control by strategically positioning themselves as key political actors and governing collectivities within contemporary urban spaces, which often continue to be dominated by Western-informed political structures. Hopefully, the issues raised will resonate with and contribute to the growing consideration of the collective identities, rights and interests of urbanising Indigenous peoples internationally.

DEBATES AND JUSTIFICATIONS: UNDERSTANDING MĀTAAWAKA TIRITI/TREATY CLAIMS

The question of mātaawaka rights under Te Tiriti/Treaty within the local government context has received very little attention in terms of policies, practice and relationships. Partnerships between Māori and local government have, except for a small number of areas, been focused almost exclusively on those drawn from the overlapping rights and interests that iwi have with local governments. Even then, the extent of local government recognition of iwi rights and interests is itself still heavily contested and frequently fails to sufficiently uphold Te Tiriti/Treaty responsibilities (see for example, work by Bargh 2016; Hayward 2003a, 2003b; Te One 2019).

Actions taken by Te Whānau o Waipareira, a mātaawaka group in Auckland, provide important foregrounding and insight into the challenges confronting mātaawaka relationships with local government in Aotearoa more broadly and are evidenced in the Waitangi Tribunal's 1998 Te Whānau o Waipareira Report (Wai 414). Wai 414 diverges from other Tiriti/Treaty claims as it proposes that Te Whānau o Waipareira has the right to a Tiriti/Treaty partnership despite not necessarily having either mana whenua rights of authority based on continued occupancy in Auckland nor kinship ties to one another as does an iwi. Wai 414 claimed that the New Zealand Crown had failed to uphold its responsibilities to protect Māori rangatiratanga (self-determination) under Te Tiriti/Treaty and, as a result, the social welfare role and cultural support network that Te Whānau o Waipareira had developed was unable to function in a way that protected the rights and interests of urban Māori and their position as tāngata whenua (Indigenous people of the land) (Levine 2001).

In the summary of the argument made in the report, John Tamihere, the past Chief Executive of Te Whānau o Waipareira, stated:

> The claim is essentially about fairness, due process and equality of opportunity. It is about our right as a pan-tribal whānau [extended family] in the urban area to be acknowledged as a Treaty partner and our right as urban Māori to organise ourselves in accordance with our own tikanga [customs] to address our own problems our way. (pers. com. 1998: xxiii)

Effectively this claim pursued two possible strategic avenues. One was that urban Māori authorities like Te Whānau o Waipareira could be recognised in a similar fashion as an iwi. The other was that the indicators, which formed the basis of Māori collective identity—such as whakapapa (genealogy) and ahi kaa (continued occupation)—should not be the central determinants for developing Tiriti/Treaty partnerships with the Crown. Te

Whānau o Waipareira argued that, despite the fact that Te Tiriti/the Treaty was signed by rangatira (leaders) representing the interests of different iwi and hapū in 1840, the intention behind those signatories was to support future generations in whatever identity or collective form of polity they held. That included, according to the basis of the Te Whānau o Waipareira Report, urban mātaawaka groups (Waitangi Tribunal 1998).

Within the report, three central principles underpinned the mātaawaka claim: rangatiratanga, protection and partnership, which were summarised as follows:

> If a power imbalance lies heavily in favour of the Crown, it should be offset by the weight of the Crown's duty to protect Māori rangatiratanga [self-determination]. But most of all, the concept of partnership serves to answer questions about the extent to which the Crown should provide for Māori autonomy in the management of Māori affairs, and more particularly how Māori and the Crown should relate to each other that such issues might be resolved. (Waitangi Tribunal 1998: xxvi)

In essence, the mātaawaka claim put forward the case that the Crown has obligations to protect the rangatiratanga of *all* Māori and that this should be encompassed through efforts to develop partnerships with Māori based on their position as tāngata whenua (Indigenous to the land), as opposed to only with iwi as mana whenua.

The report was not accepted by the Crown, who maintained that iwi are the only natural Tiriti/Treaty partners and that partnership would not be extended to other mātaawaka groups through the Treaty settlements process (Levine 2001). However, this case and the realities it speaks to have persisted as a cause for mātaawaka in Auckland and further afield to other urban Māori mātaawaka groups in Aotearoa-New Zealand. While the claim sets out the basis for broadening the understanding of Crown partnerships beyond iwi, traces of this challenge have found initial footing in some local government legislative changes, ensuring that the question of mātaawaka Tiriti/Treaty rights continues to be asked of the local government.

MĀTAAWAKA TIRITI/TREATY RIGHTS IN LOCAL GOVERNMENT

In 2002, amendments were made to the *Local Government Act 1974*, a piece of legislation that guides the most significant aspects of local government duties and powers in Aotearoa. The 1974 Act made no reference to Māori nor Te Tiriti/the Treaty, which led to the 2002 amendments and reference to the principles of the Treaty of Waitangi, stating that: 'In order to recognise and respect the Crown's responsibility to take appropriate account of the principles of the Treaty of Waitangi and to maintain and improve opportunities for Māori to contribute to local government decision-making processes' (section 4).

Prior to this amendment being passed, the New Zealand Local Government and Environment Committee (2002) produced a report on the proposed amendments and made note of the use of the term 'Māori' as a way to include the different Māori identities within local government communities. The report noted that the use of more specific terms, like 'mana whenua', 'tāngata whenua', 'taura here',[2] or 'iwi' and 'hapū', could potentially be exclusive and limit relationships between local governments and the wider Māori community, the risk being that different Māori individuals and groups could be left out if legislation was too specific. Under the section of the report titled 'Who should be consulted under the Treaty?' the Committee noted that: 'We decided that the term "Māori" would allow each authority to determine which were the appropriate groups in each district and that this was consistent with the principle of local decision-making' (2002: 19).

The wording of the legislation, therefore, requires local governments to develop relationships inclusively with Māori individuals and groups, based on local government's obligations to make decisions on behalf of the entire community. On the one hand, the use of the term 'Māori' gives local government the flexibility to develop wide-ranging relationships with the Māori community. On the other hand, it also clearly places the responsibility on local government to appropriately interpret Te Tiriti/Treaty in a way that is relevant to both iwi and mātaawaka. This responsibility has proven challenging since the amendments were made because, despite the inclusive intention behind the use of the term 'Māori', of the seventy-eight local governments throughout Aotearoa, the Auckland Council is the only council yet to undertake any substantial investigation into how mātaawaka Tiriti/Treaty rights might develop in relation to local government.

The 2009 Royal Commission on Auckland Governance ('the Royal Commission') confirmed that local government Te Tiriti/Treaty responsibilities extended to the wider community through their recommendations for future representation arrangements at the point of the amalgamation of Auckland local governments into a single unitary authority (Auckland Governance Royal Commission 2009).[3] First, the Royal Commission argued that designated Māori seats would be an appropriate measure to recognise that Te Tiriti/Treaty extends to all Māori whether they are living in their iwi areas or not. It was proposed that there should be three seats; one held for iwi mana whenua and the other two for any person who might represent the interests of Māori, which could include either iwi or mātaawaka representatives. Although this particular recommendation was not accepted, the current structure for Māori representation on the Auckland Council—the Independent Māori Statutory Board (IMSB)—includes two mātaawaka representatives alongside seven iwi representatives from across the wider Auckland region. Furthermore, the legislation pertaining to the restructure of the Auckland Council led to a legal definition of mātaawaka, confirming the relevance of mātaawaka to the Auckland Council. *The Local Government (Auckland Council) Act 2009*, section 4(1), defines mātaawaka as Māori who (a) live in Auckland and (b) are not in a mana whenua group.

This definition is an important symbol of the legal responsibility that local governments have to mātaawaka by acknowledging mātaawaka as a defined identity in Auckland. This has since been supported by efforts to identify areas of focus for developing mātaawaka engagement with local government, including recognition of 'mātaawaka Treaty rights' and the continued development of 'strong relationships with mana whenua (iwi)' (IMSB 2011: 60). These two values point to the fact that mātaawaka rights within local government, from the perspective of the IMSB, need to be considered within the context of Te Tiriti/Treaty, as well as the nature of the relationships between mātaawaka and mana whenua.

These debates and justifications illustrate some of the contentious issues regarding mātaawaka Te Tiriti/Treaty rights and, in particular, the challenges that arise around a 'non-traditional' form of Māori collective identity and related governance. However, slow inroads are being made within local government, which suggests that the question of how mātaawaka engage with local government will continue to be an area requiring attention and innovative thinking. The case study below illustrates some of the challenges associated with one mātaawaka group in Wellington.

MŌKAI KĀINGA MĀTAAWAKA CASE STUDY

In 2016, as part of my PhD research, I met with a Wellington-based mātaawaka group organising themselves as the Mōkai Kāinga Māori Centre (Te One 2019). Mōkai Kāinga was established in 1982 as a cultural support and advocacy group for all Māori living in Wellington. Mōkai Kāinga does significant work supporting Māori who have been released from prison and offers temporary housing to those individuals. The group also runs a large garden which is used as both a source of food and work, but also an education facility for local schools to learn about gardening. As a mātaawaka group, Mōkai Kāinga has, over the years, developed strong relationships with the Wellington City Council. Importantly, these relationships are in large part due to Mōkai Kāinga consistently positioning itself as a Tiriti/Treaty partner to the Crown.

In my group interview with Mōkai Kāinga members, they spoke candidly about how they understand their position in relation to local governments as Tiriti/Treaty partner. They noted that,

> we were a Treaty (partner) to the Crown and to local body (local government) that's the main reason that we thought here is an opportunity for us . . . because we're a Treaty partner. (Mōkai Kāinga, pers com., 15 September 2016)

The opportunity to pressure local government to recognise Mōkai Kāinga as a Tiriti/Treaty partner was an important strategic decision that, for the group, was part of supporting their position as a collective political entity. The group noted that it was,

> a partnership that gave us mana [authority] and ihi [power] to negotiate with Council on what we required to provide the beginnings of a quality service to Māori by Māori. (Mōkai Kāinga, pers com., 15 September 2016)

In the same way that Te Whānau o Waipareira in Auckland had sought protection from the Crown over their autonomy as a social welfare service, Mōkai Kāinga positions itself in relation to the Wellington Local Government as a partner that has an obligation to recognise its Te Tiriti/Treaty rights. For example, Mōkai Kāinga noted that Te Tiriti/Treaty recognition from local government was dependent on it being able to hold the local government accountable to its promises and obligations:

> We think that they (local government) had to come to the party and see us as a Treaty partner because they had it in their annual plan; that's what we used in the annual plan that if we are your Treaty partner then show us that you help us as a partner. (Mōkai Kāinga, pers com., 15 September 2016)

This understanding of the Wellington City Council's annual plans that specifically mentioned obligations to Māori throughout Wellington (Wellington City Council 2017) meant that the group has been able to point to policy and insist that it related to them because of their status as Māori under Te Tiriti/ Treaty. The group argued that this knowledge of local government plans was further increased by their own personal relationships with local councillors, with one member noting:

> What I do is I just go directly to the council, to the mayor, myself now to talk something over, like we're wanting things for the garden like a portacom

> [portable room]; that is one thing that I have fought for with her and we have got. You see that's coming soon. Even though it's a portacom she wants to have an opening! An opening for it! (Mōkai Kāinga, pers com., 15 September 2016)

Access to councillors and knowledge of council annual plans have been important strategies utilised by Mōkai Kāinga to strengthen its relationship with local government. While fruitful for this particular group, it has been noted by Cheyne and Tawhai (2007) that such a strategy is not a reliable option for all Māori. In their report on Māori engagement in local government, Cheyne and Tawhai noted that, while Māori generally wanted to engage with local government on different issues, they found local government processes difficult and frustrating to navigate, especially when the onus was on Māori to engage with local government and understand how plans and policies applied to them, and not the other way around (Cheyne & Tawhai 2007: ix). In my interviews with Wellington City Council employees of the Treaty Relations Unit, the team charged with engaging with Māori, one past staff member confirmed this concern and stated that,

> Unless tauiwi[4] themselves make that conscious effort and get tipped over and actually know to come and consult us, and know how to consult us, and know when to consult us, we're going to keep revisiting that table and saying, 'Hang on a sec, I don't see any Māori voice in this, why isn't there a Māori person here, or why isn't there representation or consultation?' (M. Ormsby, pers com., 18 April 2016)

Other staff went on to explain how the nature of local government engagement with mātaawaka relied on *ad hoc* measures, saying that,

> based on kaupapa (issues), we have got quite an active group of individuals that belong to a lot of groups, so often those individuals will bang on our door quite a bit . . . We don't have a group who wants to get involved in local politics in the same sense that a council is involved in all of this stuff that a council does. They're issues based and they're location based . . . We don't hear from many people who have at heart and their only concern is the wellbeing of the city and want to be political opponents to our elected members; it's always about an issue. (Wellington City Council, pers com., 11 April 2016)

This reliance by local government on *ad hoc* engagements, which elicited the belief that mātaawaka did not want engagement with councillors, meant that it also rested upon personal relationships in order to ensure any sustained engagement. This meant engagement was vulnerable to the comings and goings of key individuals and had no substantive institutional foundations.

This in itself was contrary to the positioning of Mōkai Kāinga which was explicit about its relationship being based on Te Tiriti/Treaty partnerships. Indeed, if the Te Whānau o Waipareira report is used as a measurement of standards for mātaawaka engagement, then the principles of rangatiratanga, protection and partnership are not present in a reliance on *ad hoc* personal relationships. Certainly, one of the key elements of mātaawaka pressure in Auckland was an expectation that arrangements would become structural in nature, whether through pressure for Māori seats or through the current establishment of the Independent Māori Statutory Board.

The reliance on *ad hoc* engagement provides insight into the form of collective identities that local government is prepared, and not prepared, to engage and seek a governance relationship with. This exclusionary behaviour is a well-known challenge within Māori and New Zealand Government relationships with particular regard to hapū (sub-tribes) in which the Crown has preferred to engage with what it refers to as the 'largest natural grouping' (the iwi) that has, at times, superseded and marginalised the concerns of smaller and more diverse hapū groups (Office of Treaty Settlements 2018).

This same challenge is evident again when it comes to mātaawaka, who represent a significant range of individual identities through whom cultural connection exists as 'Māori' generally. The significant diversity which culminates in the outward appearance of lack of a central identifiable community are factors that contribute to the hesitant approach by local governments in their dealings and commitments to mātaawaka. It illustrates the Crown's preference to engage with Māori based on large collective identities that—according to groups such as Te Whānau o Waipareira—are actually frozen in a time period linked to the initial signing of Te Tiriti/Treaty in 1840. Indeed, the unwillingness of the Crown to accept claims put forward by Te Whānau o Waipereira speaks towards the Crown's desire to control the form of political, governing and cultural organisation being designed by Māori and, as a result, the types of relationships that governments are willing to engage in.

Mōkai Kāinga, as a mātaawaka group, challenge this positioning by being very clear about their understanding of themselves as Te Tiriti/Treaty partners. In doing so, they are also very clear in the assertion of their right to self-determine the contemporary forms of internal governance they build in order to represent their unique rights and interests in urban environments. In terms of relationship-building at the local government level, the standpoint of Mōkai Kāinga requires local government to consider much broader terms and options by which to engage with all Māori. This challenge is made even more important when considered in the context of the way that relationships work between iwi and mātaawaka and local government.

RELATIONSHIPS BETWEEN IWI MANA WHENUA AND MĀTAAWAKA

Relationship between iwi mana whenua and mātaawaka was a further important consideration that was raised during my meetings with Mōkai Kāinga. Although Mōkai Kāinga positioned themselves as a Te Tiriti/Treaty partner in relation to local government, they were careful to make clear that relationships with local government were only one part of the partnerships that were necessary in order for mātaawaka engagement in local politics. In our group interview, they noted:

> We set up as a group that was made up of different iwi; we weren't of one iwi, we were of all different iwi. We wanted to see ourselves as a roopu Māori (Māori group), but more in the sense of taura here Māori, because we knew we were not mana whenua. At the same time, we had a good affiliation with mana whenua; anything we wanted to do in the way of setting up a social service we went to mana whenua. (Mōkai Kāinga, pers com., 15 September 2015)

As a mātaawaka group, they operated on the basis that relationships with mana whenua were essential to being a group with governance 'by and for Māori'. Even if mana whenua were not involved directly in the work done by Mōkai Kāinga, the fact that they, the latter, were operating and making decisions on iwi land meant that, from their perspective, relationships with iwi were necessary. They stated in their acquisition of land for the garden that:

> This land that we are leasing off council; I was saying we need to go to mana whenua and say to mana whenua to give us that land and we will look after that land for mana whenua. We can never own it because we're not mana whenua but we can look after it. (Mōkai Kāinga, pers com., 15 September 2016)

In other words, despite needing to receive local government permission to lease the land, for a Māori group operating under Māori governing values and processes, local government permission was only one part of gaining the use rights over the land. And—in some ways—not necessarily the most important component. Rather, Mōkai Kāinga considered that it was vital to gain permission from mana whenua iwi and to properly acknowledge that the land had once been owned by the iwi (which had never ceded its sovereignty). This intra-Māori process demonstrates a form of negotiation and decision-making that occurs outside of local government and constitutes a fundamental internal recognition of Māori governance relationship rules and institutions. Mōkai Kāinga concluded that in order to achieve that proper internal Māori permission: 'We met with the mayor and councillors . . . the whānau [family] of Mōkai Kāinga and our kaumātua [elders] to mana whenua' (Mōkai Kāinga, pers com., 15 September 2016).

The permission sought was to look after the land, acknowledging mana whenua authority. Although there was no Western legal incentive to request permission from mana whenua, the recognition and exercise of Māori local governing rules and institutions was deemed necessary by Mōkai Kāinga in order for them to use the land. While British-informed local government operates in Wellington, there is a Māori mode of local governance that also continues to operate. Furthermore, that local iwi governance articulates with other Māori residents who, as mātaawaka, are keen to build forms of internal self-governance in the urban setting that are credible within Māori intergroup relationships and world view. Recognising this dynamic is essential for broadening our understandings of the scope of Māori political engagement at the local level. Indeed, a discussion by the late Sir Hugh Kawharu (1968) elaborated on how Māori have been required to creatively develop their own governing modes in relation to an increase in mātaawaka. Pre-colonisation, there was no precedent for Māori living permanently in other iwi or hapū lands, and Kawharu noted how the residency of Māori who were not mana whenua in other iwi lands was not a usual practice:

> Tradition offers no precedent for this, no system by which such 'foreigners' can be incorporated permanently into social activities. Yet, out of self-interest the tāngata whenua must appear not to exclude them, for fear of being thought inhospitable and morally irresponsible. (Kawharu 1968: 175)

Kawharu alludes to the fact that mana whenua caring for 'foreigners', as he puts it—or in this context, mātaawaka—are guided by Māori rules and institutions associated with mana whenua, and the responsibility to care for guests who come to their own territory. This responsibility has its foundations in the authority that iwi have over their lands as a necessary part of maintaining mana. The mana of a rangatira (leader) was determined by the wealth of the community, in the same way that the mana of an iwi or hapū was determined by the outcomes of engagement with other iwi and hapū. An iwi could gain mana by either triumphing over another iwi or hapū in warfare, for example, or by catering for and supporting another iwi or hapū (Mead 2016).

In an interview, a chairperson from the local iwi in Wellington gave an example of how this could work in Wellington, the seat of parliament, where protests often occurred:

> I'll give you a classic example—the foreshore and seabed hikoi [protest]. Whether we liked it or not we had all the iwi coming in to our rohe [region]. There was a cultural responsibility we had in supporting manuhiri [guests] when

> they're coming in on a take [cause] to the Crown. So, we had to feed them. That's the first thing. The second thing is we had to take care of the manuhiri coming through onto our land, which is the land—the Atea [front area] at Parliament. (pers com., 3 April 2016)

This example provides insight into how iwi responsibilities as mana whenua to care for visitors are important for Māori 'visiting' an area. Unlike the relationships between local government and mātaawaka, relationships between mana whenua and mātaawaka are formalised through shared rules, values and institutions deeply embedded in Māori society. Yet the example also demonstrates the clear ability and propensity for Māori to adapt and finesse these cultural ways of governing in order to deal with changing times and identities that are the ongoing products of colonial-settler life. Although there have been changes in the precedents that Kawharu (1968) described, the framework for Māori collective interaction and inter-group governance remains: mana whenua have a responsibility to care for mātaawaka and mātaawaka have a responsibility to recognise that by asking permission to live and work on the lands of mana whenua. The two governing mechanisms are inextricably linked. The chairperson quoted above elaborated further by stating,

> we have to get very clear about who we are and what our role is. It goes back to kaitiakitanga [guardianship]; we have to take care of them (mātaawaka) and enable them to look after their own people. (pers com., 3 April 2016)

While the first instance refers to temporary Māori visitors, the impetus for showing support for mātaawaka who live permanently in the area is understood through the same cultural lens of Māori governance at the local level. To maintain their own authority and respect the rights of other Māori, mana whenua have a responsibility to support Māori who have moved into their tribal areas. Mōkai Kāinga, too, recognised these rules and institutions and, as a result, engaged mana whenua in discussing its use rights over the land. Mōkai Kāinga understood itself as needing to engage in rules pertaining to mana whenua, but also recognised its position as a Te Tiriti/Treaty partner in relation to local government. Indeed, it is arguable that, by approaching mana whenua in this way, it was in effect asserting the right behaviour as a polity, to act in a self-determining way.

To some extent, the Wellington City Council recognised this relationship between mana whenua and mātaawaka, resulting in policies which ascribed to mana whenua a role in assisting to mediate the local government's own relationships with mātaawaka. For example, the Wellington Reorganisation Proposal[5] offered this solution for possible future arrangements with Māori emphasising that,

> the non-mana whenua Māori community could seek the support of mana whenua groups on issues they may wish to raise at council . . . at least twice a year, council should formally meet with mātaawaka groups with agenda matters raised by both Māori and council. (Local Government Commission 2014: 167)

This proposal suggested that mana whenua would act as the mediator between mātaawaka and local government, not only recognised the governing status of mana whenua with respect to local government but also in respect to Māori intra-group relationships. It further acknowledged that the formal relationships between mātaawaka and local government would be dependent on those relationships, presumably facilitated through mana whenua responsibilities.

Although there is some suggestion that relationships between mātaawaka and mana whenua could help in forming and/or mediating relationships with local government, these statements by local government—as they currently stand—obfuscate the responsibilities held by mana whenua and the responsibilities held by local government. For example, during the processes for the Wellington Reorganisation, the Wellington City Council, Hutt City Council, Upper Hutt City Council and the Greater Wellington Regional Council requested advice from three iwi trusts in Wellington Region regarding how local government could manage its relationships with mātaawaka. The three Taranaki Whānui iwi Trusts[6] responded by stating:

> We understand advice is being sought from us in relation to Taurahere[7] and local government engagement in terms of the proposed reform. We are primarily concerned with our duties as Tāngata Whenua of our rohe (region) and therefore do not have a view of how local government may engage with Taurahere. Our own relationship with Taurahere has been established through Whakapapa and observance of our Tikanga (customs) and Kawa (protocols) by Taurahere. We suggest decision makers engage directly with Taurahere on this matter, recognising their status. (Mellish 2013: 6)

Taranaki Whānui were laying out a lesson in Māori intra-group governance for the local government. While mana whenua engage with mātaawaka based on Māori customs and governance protocols, the iwi made it clear that these relationships between Māori were not transposable across to the local government and cannot be seen as the substitute for local government directly developing its own appropriate arrangements with mātaawaka. While mana whenua have responsibilities to support mātaawaka, these are not the same as the responsibility to talk on their behalf or to broker their relationship with local governments under Te Tiriti/Treaty.

Māori engage with other Māori based on systems of relationship-building and culturally based modes of contemporary governance that have adapted to changing times. However, while this constitutes a significant and active local governance process amongst Māori, local governments need to better understand how these parallel forms of Māori decision-making take place and continue to develop informed appropriate means of engagement with mātaawaka.

UNSETTLING LOCAL GOVERNANCE STRUCTURES

Mōkai Kāinga demonstrate how, through its very existence, it poses a political challenge to local government through organising and purporting to be a Te Tiriti/Treaty partner. This is one example of how the strategic building of a polity and internal governance by mātaawaka in Wellington acts to disrupt the monopoly on Western modes of local government power and can 'create fissures in the dominant power structures' (Bargh 2016: 454) by offering an alternative shape to collective organisation and self-governance in an urban setting. Mōkai Kāinga, through its assertion of being a Te Tiriti/Treaty partner, disrupts the preferred exclusionary relationships with Māori that local government agencies have sought to impose. The case study and related discussion have shown that the uncertainty surrounding relationships with mātaawaka is a political disposition developed by local governments, as opposed to how mātaawaka understand themselves in relation to Te Tiriti/Treaty and other traditional Māori polities such as mana whenua.

Although Mōkai Kāinga are only one mātaawaka group, their understanding of how they fit within the local political environment is contrary to the hesitancy and uncertainty that informs local government's engagement with mātaawaka, in particular as evident in its reliance on *ad hoc* processes. The development of personal relationships with council leadership and making direct reference to local government policy and legislative commitments are used as tools by Mōkai Kāinga to pressure local government into engaging with them.

Mōkai Kāinga also valuably demonstrates how parallel sites of Māori self-governance rules and institutions can work at the local level to inform internal Māori collaboration for a single decision. From the Māori perspective, local government is still expected to meet its legislative responsibilities and engage with Mōkai Kāinga as Te Tiriti/Treaty partners, but at the same time mātaawaka relationships with mana whenua are given a centrality, and seeking permission to use and look after the land is equally as important to the development of that land. This is both a challenge to local government power structures, while simultaneously supporting the continuity of Māori relationships and governance, and in particular the ability to adapt to changing times and circumstance in a way that local governments have failed to do.

The report on Te Whānau o Waipareira mentioned earlier in this chapter pointed to the fact that rangatira signed Te Tiriti/Treaty with the future of all Māori in mind. Therefore, while Mōkai Kāinga in Wellington acknowledged that they were neither mana whenua, nor related through kinship, they argued they were entitled to be treated in a way which protected their autonomy as Māori. Mōkai Kāinga provide an example of how local government legislative requirements were, for this Māori representative organisation, only one part of seeking rights and then exercising them to pursue land and social welfare developments. It was mana whenua whom they sought permission from to settle on the land, and local government who were recognised as a Te Tiriti/Treaty partner with the responsibility to help resource their initiatives to support the broader urban Māori community in Wellington. This variation in understandings of local authorities simultaneously confirms mana whenua as a basis for local governing decision-making, as well as demonstrating how Mōkai Kāinga as a Māori organisation is able to challenge the monopoly of power assumed by local government.

Mōkai Kāinga, through its insistence on gaining use rights from mana whenua, poses ongoing resistance to British-informed political structures and their assumed dominance over Māori decision-making. Mōkai Kāinga navigates two parallel sites of authority in its efforts to situate itself as a mātaawaka organisation with Te Tiriti/Treaty rights as well as a Māori group engaging in a culturally credible way with other Māori. As a mātaawaka group that represents a non-traditional collective Māori identity and urban polity, the presence of and actions taken by Mōkai Kāinga disrupt the mainstream political climate which has sought to displace Māori values and relationships as being irrelevant to local political and governing authority in Wellington.

CONCLUSION

Understanding how mātaawaka position themselves as Tiriti/Treaty partners in relation to local government is a field of research that will benefit from having significantly more grounded data and analysis. The debates and case study discussed in this chapter demonstrate that there are strong Tiriti/Treaty justifications and positions held by mātaawaka, but these are yet to be sufficiently understood to enable them to inform the default approach to relationship and distribution of governing power held by local governments.

However, despite this challenge, this chapter has shown how Māori, both iwi and mātaawaka, continue to utilise culturally informed practice and understandings to develop governing relationships with one another, irrespective of how local governments view their Tiriti/Treaty responsibilities to all Māori. Further analysis of how these internal Māori relationships take place and in turn with local governments could contribute to the development of a more informed and equitable understanding of the nature of Tiriti/Treaty partnerships, and how they might differ between iwi and mātaawaka.

NOTES

1. My research examined relationships between my own iwi in Wellington—Taranaki Whānui—and local governments and mātaawaka (Te One 2018).
2. In this instance, 'taura here' has a similar meaning to mātaawaka.
3. Local governments throughout the Auckland region amalgamated to form a unitary authority, which opened the question of how Māori would be included in this new structure.
4. Here used to refer to mātaawaka.
5. In 2014, a proposal was put forward for local governments in the wider Wellington Region to amalgamate to form unitary authority. The proposal was not approved, but it required region-wide submissions, including how Māori would be engaged should the changes occur.
6. Iwi trusts are the governance structures for iwi. The three trusts referred to here are all Taranaki Whānui trusts—Wellington Tenths Trust, Palmerston North Māori Reserve, and Port Nicholson Block Settlement Trust.
7. In this instance, 'Taurahere' has the same meaning as mātaawaka.

Chapter 4

Identifying a Legal Framework for a Treaty between Australia's First Peoples and the State

Asmi Wood and Christie Gardiner

For several decades, Australia has made various political commitments to develop a legal apparatus that recognises the agency of Indigenous peoples[1] which facilitates their autonomy and self-determination. These commitments have rarely yielded outcomes that sustainably advance the interests of Indigenous peoples, and often fail to address the inherent injustice that exists in the relationship between Indigenous peoples and the Australian Government. For instance, in June 1988, then Australian Prime Minister R.J. Hawke promised[2] an historic treaty with the Aboriginal people at the Barunga Festival in the Northern Territory of Australia (Read, Myers & Reece 2013). The resulting Barunga Statement called for a 'Treaty recognising our [Indigenous] prior ownership, continued occupation and sovereignty and affirming our human rights and freedom'.[3] The statement hangs prominently in the Parliament House of Australia in Canberra. Despite this commitment, a treaty was not forthcoming, yet it remains an aspiration of Indigenous peoples, both for its content and for the symbolic significance of this necessary gesture that recognises historical injustices and offers a pathway forward for Indigenous Australians.

In principle, the concept of a treaty (and not excluding the possibility of a series of treaties) represents an opportunity for Indigenous people to formalise relations with the state.[4] As a legal instrument, a well-drafted treaty can provide clarity, certainty and—importantly—accountability in the relationship between the parties. It provides Indigenous Australians with a national framework through which to rebuild internal governance structures. It also supports the development aspirations of Indigenous Australians through facilitating a formal self-determinative process, as currently provided for in international instruments. However, there are fundamental issues that need to be resolved at law, in order to bind the parties to an agreement that ensures the progress of further productive relations between all peoples. Unfortunately, the political environment surrounding the current debate on constitutional recognition of Indigenous people has been 'toxic' (Tucker 2013). This description is likely to apply equally to treaty negotiations given domestic opposition to the notion of a treaty, which is dealt with in the latter part of the chapter.[5] The issue of constitutional recognition, its form, and implications have been examined by the Australian Parliament and others (Expert Panel on Constitutional Recognition of Indigenous Australians 2012; Joint Select Committee on Constitutional Recognition 2014, 2015; Wood 2016a, 2016b). The broad concept of a treaty is also popular among Indigenous peoples, even popularised in a song called 'Treaty' in 1991,[6] and has been an issue that has been raised by many people on many occasions over the years.

The parties to a treaty of the sort proposed in this chapter, and while subject to the exigencies of the time, are likely to be the descendants of the British colonial occupiers of the Australian continent (and others who have come to Australia under their laws and referred collectively to here to as 'settlers') and Indigenous peoples. The 'ethnic' or 'racial'[7] compositions of the key stakeholders are complex in terms of law, language, culture and custom, but for convenience, this chapter refers to the parties broadly as 'the two groups' or the 'the two main parties' to negotiations as appropriate. The treaty promised by then Prime Minister Hawke, which in principle purportedly enjoys the support of other leaders of government and left-leaning political parties, has yet to be given form or substantive content. That is, what is currently being discussed in public is largely the *concept* of the two main parties entering into a treaty, through an as-yet-unspecified process, in some as-yet-unspecified manner, form and content.

Thus, the development of a framework for agreement making/treaty negotiations as an essential prerequisite can, and should, proceed in spite of the politics of the debate. The decision to enter into a treaty is clearly political, but one that in its execution touches on significant legal issues (*Mabo v. State of Queensland (No 2)* (1992) 175 CLR 1). The current discussions on the need or otherwise for a treaty, in what could be described as an almost clean slate in terms of legal policy, can therefore become confused. This chapter explores some of the procedural and substantive issues that will determine the outcome of a treaty in Australia. While important legal issues are raised, they are not examined in a strict, technical legal manner on the basis that the development of a coherent conceptual legal framework is the first barrier these two parties must overcome.

The idea of a treaty has caused angst among some in the Australian settler community. Many believe that the 'Aboriginal problem' has already been solved and do not recognise that further steps are required to repair relations between the parties.[8] Such preconceptions can result in emotive claims and counterclaims by people on all sides of politics. Such opinions are often ill-informed and created in a vacuum, but should not stand in the way of robustly exploring the issues. Thus, the discussions and creation of a legal framework for the free, informed and transparent development of a treaty should be viewed as a useful—and hopefully relatively uncontentious—step in the process.

While the list of issues discussed here is not exhaustive, we seek to move beyond the question of the suitability of a treaty to highlight the complexities involved and identify some steps that will need to be taken in order to effectively negotiate, draft and formalise a treaty. These processes and steps will need to be undertaken with due diligence and care if a resulting treaty is to have a chance of receiving the necessary support of, and acceptance by, the Australian voters. The outcome of this process is also of significant interest to the international community, including the United Nations Human Rights Council and the Special Rapporteur on the Rights of Indigenous Peoples, that closely monitors and often condemns Australia's relations with, and treatment of, Indigenous people.[9] A relevant but salient issue is that Indigenous people do not yet enjoy recognition or legal equality under the Australian Constitution (Wood 2016a).[10] Mutual recognition of the sovereign authority exercised by parties to a treaty is an important legal prerequisite, as it vests agency in the parties to enter into binding negotiations. Importantly, entering into treaty negotiations with Indigenous Australians demonstrates the state's recognition that they have the capacity for self-governance.

Formal negotiations, when they begin, are likely to be a long, costly and complex process and, as proposed here, would be based ideally on internationally recognised principles. A treaty's substantive content should enjoy the imprimatur of the free, prior and informed consent of Indigenous peoples and be framed at a sufficiently high level of abstraction, cognisant of the past but with its direction and vision firmly into the future. That is, Indigenous people in Australia will need to be wary and ensure that a treaty is not reduced by the state to being a mere mechanism for service delivery (or to remedial survival issues): matters that are the intrinsic responsibility of government towards all its citizens. Treaty arrangements consented to by a self-determined people must provide for substantive control over its affairs—that is, for agreed jurisdictions of self-governance—but need not be conflated with political independence.[11]

Two possible but distinct legal bases for the development of a treaty are identified and examined in this chapter and a structured approach is proposed as a productive, non-prescriptive contribution to the debate. The first basis examined is a treaty that is developed and operates purely under domestic Anglo-Australian law. It is argued that such a treaty is unlikely to deliver justice to Indigenous people. An alternative and preferred option is then considered and includes a treaty developed under a domestic Anglo-Australian legal framework, but whose operation is supervised under a legal regime that includes relevant international law as self-effecting and, where appropriate, binding. The chapter is accordingly structured in four parts. The first explores a political and legal environment for the development of a treaty. The second examines treaty in a purely domestic framework. The third examines a framework that includes international law as an integral part of the operative law. Finally, the chapter ends with some concluding remarks.

A FRAMEWORK FOR THE DEVELOPMENT OF A TREATY

The power to *enter into* treaties is an executive power within s.61 of the Australian Constitution, whereas the power to *implement* treaties, in domestic law, that Australia has entered into in the international arena falls within the external affairs power in s.51(xxix) of the Australian Constitution (Senate Legal and Constitutional References Committee 1995: 3). Treaty developments in other so-called CANZUS countries (Canada, Australia, Aotearoa-New Zealand and the United States) provide a useful point of comparison. CANZUS is a useful reference group with which Australia shares a similar colonial history, common law tradition and political challenges that have been self-evaluated by Indigenous peoples to also share many features in common (Cornell 2002, 2015; Smith 2012; Introduction, this volume). Treaty-making processes in CANZUS countries other than Australia intrinsically and necessarily provided Indigenous peoples with a legal personality as a prerequisite to treaty-making (Fletcher 2006). However, for the historical reasons discussed above, this chapter supports explicit constitutional recognition as the better option in Australia. Furthermore, and *inter alia* for the disparity in power relations,[12] without external supervision, domestic law alone will allow treaty provisions to be interpreted very favourably to the benefit of settlers (French 1992: 180, 185; *Kartinyeri v. Commonwealth* (1998) 195 CLR 337).

There is clearly a history and range of views on treaty (Read et al. 2013; Brennan et al. 2005; Davis 2006). In the contemporary Australian and international political and legal context, self-determination for Indigenous people in Australia, rather than full political independence, appears to be the most practical and feasible, achievable and arguably even desirable option (Anthony 2010). As a starting point, self-determination (as opposed to decolonisation that leads to political independence, for example) forms the backdrop for a treaty discussed here. Furthermore, it is crucial that future generations of Indigenous Australians should not be tied to or unduly limited by their weak negotiating position. This position was most recently described by the Uluru Statement as 'the torment of our powerlessness'.[13] This asymmetrical power relationship in law is further highlighted by the lack of constitutional recognition of Indigenous peoples in Australia (National Constitutional Convention 2017). One means of mitigating, if not overcoming, this problem is suggested below through the creation of a form of Indigenous constitutionalism.

Self-determination as a legal right is also most likely to be achieved in the international arena. Support for this assertion lies in the dualistic nature of Anglo-Australian law which creates a clear separation between municipal law and international law. Norms of self-determination are defined in binding international human rights instruments and universally agreed meanings, and these could be adopted in their full meaning in a treaty.[14] It is argued here that procedural and substantive fairness could better be achieved by adopting internationally accepted and understood notions of what constitutes important human rights norms, including notions such as equality, human dignity, self-determination, and free and prior informed consent—concepts that the Australian Parliament should not have the power unilaterally or lawfully to narrow or redefine. On the other hand, while a treaty—as with all similar legal instruments—should be considered binding, it should not be entrenched or considered eternally binding. Rather, it should be subject to evolving conditions such as, for example, the norms with respect to treaty modification as provided for in the Vienna Convention on the Law of Treaties (United Nations 1969). A treaty should thus contemplate changes (according to say the Vienna Convention 1969), but for fairness also enable stability and predictability, which are governed by such applicable customary international norms.[15]

In Australia, there are to date no formal agreements between Indigenous peoples and the settler British and their heirs and successors (Brennan et al. 2005: 1). In fact, the notion of a *terra-nullius* Australia *must*, in the minds of the British, have precluded the possibility of there being anyone here to cede territory or engage in warfare or from whom the British could acquire territory through conquest or with whom they could negotiate an agreement.[16] Furthermore, and with respect to the Crown's claim of sovereignty over the continent, there is not a common multi-party understanding or agreement between the various political parties in Australia of the consequences of the High Court's rejection of *terra nullius* in 1992, or the parliament's subsequent codification in the Commonwealth's *Native Title Act 1993* (Dodson, Bailey & Wood 2016; Wood 2016a). A more detailed discussion of the history of *terra nullius* and its impact are presented elsewhere (Borch 2001).

While this process has its challenges, particularly in securing multi-party support, the recognition of Indigenous peoples in the Australian Constitution (which is currently being considered by the Australian Parliament)[17] would finally and completely expunge the myth of *terra nullius* from Anglo-Australian law.[18] It would also then become possible to reject the historical validity of the notion and begin to reverse or unwind the impacts of its operation throughout the history of the operation of Anglo-Australian law. For Indigenous People in Australia, constitutional recognition undoubtedly creates a legal personality, which is recognised in the international arena. It sets the scene for treaty negotiations between the relevant 'peoples' in the meaning of the United Nations (UN) Charter (https://www.un.org/en/charter-united-nations/index.html.) The resulting instrument or treaty should fairly and honourably reset the relationship between the two main parties. Consequently, these negotiations, which are an opportunity in a sense to begin (almost) afresh, should be conducted on a fair and equitable basis, informed by an historically accurate set of agreed facts.

The next part of this chapter examines the development of a purely domestic treaty. There are some common preliminary legal issues, including matters such as legal personality, competence to represent parties, identification of stakeholders, and so forth, that are in principle necessary for treaty formation and will be discussed further in the second part of this chapter. As similar issues arise in the third part, for convenience and readability only matters that differ significantly in principle are explicitly addressed separately.

ISSUES TOUCHING ON THE DEVELOPMENT OF A TREATY SOLELY UNDER DOMESTIC AUSTRALIAN LAW

In 2006, former Prime Minister Tony Abbott said that he never supported the notion of a treaty while another former Prime Minister, John Howard, stated that he was opposed to the idea of a nation entering into a treaty with itself (Henderson & Borrello 2016). There are, consequently, significant social, cultural, economic and political complexities involved in creating a treaty at present. On the other hand, the current opposition, the Australian Labor Party, said it was open to 'a treaty, potentially along the lines of agreements struck between Indigenous peoples and governments in New Zealand and Canada' (Henderson & Borrello 2016). The desirability of this model is examined below. Left-leaning political parties would arguably support a treaty that includes most Indigenous aspirations, the right-leaning parties are perhaps much less supportive.

Treaties between Indigenous people and the colonial powers in the other CANZUS countries generally began their existence as 'international' instruments, that is, as treaties entered into between then sovereign powers or, in the case of Indigenous peoples, as 'nations' under the international law existing at the time. The idea of 'nationhood' in the Westphalian sense, broadly speaking, is constitutive and in this context merely required the mutual recognition by the sovereign parties concerned. From the Western perspective, however, treaties were entered into with Indigenous peoples as a means to gain comparative advantage over other European colonisers, particularly for military, economic and strategic reasons. Once the coloniser gained the upper hand in the military sense, undertakings to protect the interests of the colonised Indigenous populations were abandoned and the British and their successors in the CANZUS countries had little incentive to honour the original terms of their agreements and undertakings.

The rejection by the Labor Party of the treaties between Native Americans and the British (and later with the USA) as a legal precedent and as a potential model is significant. This is because First Nations in the United States have been described as 'domestic dependent nations' under U.S. Federal law. The two-treaty partners in the United States are not equal sovereigns because any disputes between them are finally determined by the U.S. Supreme Court and not subject to independent review under international law as would be the case if they were true sovereign equals. Under Anglo-American law, Native Americans are not sovereign equals but are subjects and litigants, thus having significantly less power to give meaning or force to treaty terms. Some have argued that this treaty processes has, therefore, led to an 'inferior' form of sovereignty, described as 'domestic sovereignty' in the remaining lands of the tribal nations (Kalt & Singer 2004).

In Australia, the British King George III commanded Governor Phillip to 'establish friendly relations with the natives'.[19] This initial 'recognition' of Indigenous peoples in the law by the King gradually diminished to nothingness in the late 1800s when the Privy Council held, in effect, in *Cooper v Stuart* ((1889) 14 App Cas 286, 291), that Australia was *terra nullius* (Wood 2016a). While there were exceptions, 'friendly relations' between the two parties in Australia generally did not exist in practice.[20] Once the land was secure from other competing colonisers, the internal struggle became one of competition for control over the most valued and productive land. Dispossessing Indigenous peoples was clearly in the interests of the coloniser. This competition led to the so-called—but then often unacknowledged—'frontier wars' (Reynolds 2013) or other conflicts now only dimly visible through the reports of some of the few civil and criminal cases of the times (*R v Murrell* (1836) 1 Legge 72; *R v Bonjon* (1841), *Port Phillip Patriot*, 20 September 1841). In the other CANZUS countries, the British unilaterally determined the content and scope of their treaties and did so almost always to their advantage.[21]

From experience, we consider that a treaty devised under purely domestic Australian law is not likely to fare much better. We have consequently argued for a treaty concluded under international law. Furthermore, the treaty relationship between Indigenous peoples and the colonial powers in both New Zealand (Stenson 2012) and Canada (Asch 1998; Miller 2009) have not been without their own individual problems. These issues have been examined in much greater detail in the literature (Miller 2009). Thus, including the reasons examined below, caution and careful scrutiny must be exercised before using these treaties as a model in Australia.

In practice, and notwithstanding the existence of treaty relations in Canada, First Nation Canadians were subject to the removal of children in a manner not dissimilar in principle to the Stolen Generations in a 'no-treaty' *terra nullius* Australia. Furthermore, in Aotearoa-New Zealand, the legal system privileges the English (over the Māori) version of the Treaty of Waitangi that, many have argued, was originally misinterpreted based on Western epistemologies of which the courts continue to give expression (Smith 1999). The dominant power of the Pākehā (people in Aotearoa/ New Zealand who are of British or European descent) has again meant that the treaty is interpreted largely in favour of Pākehā, to the detriment of Māori.

On the other hand, in Canada, there have also been significant benefits that have accrued to Aboriginal peoples, often negotiated under a settlement agreement based on treaty (Regan 2010). However, it is not always clear in the Canadian context whether it was treaty or the goodwill of contemporary political leanings of individual leaders which makes the more significant difference (Zillio & Stueck 2017). For example, a treaty did not prevent Aboriginal Canadians from being subjected to residential boarding schools, a situation that may be compared to the Stolen Generations in Australia. In Aotearoa, there has been a broad popular recognition by Pākehā of Māori as a distinct 'people', and the commemoration of the Treaty of Waitangi is both symbolically very significant and holds substantial benefits. On balance and by analogy, while treaties may afford diverse recognitions and benefits, the intrinsic political, social and legal barriers that face the development of a fair and equal domestic treaty in Australia are not insignificant and should not be underestimated.

Legal Personality

The Barunga Statement identifies the Australian Federal Parliament as one party that will, in this instance, represent the settlers (AIATSIS n.d.). This much is likely to be uncontentious and the representative democratic nature of the parliament is unlikely to be challenged as not representing the rights, aspirations and views of the settlers. For the settler community, the parliament is well-resourced and legally competent to ascertain its position on central issues over time. As the much stronger party, however, there must be some agreed measures to help 'level' the playing field to ensure Indigenous people can also participate as closely as practical as equals in the process. Critiquing the agreement-making processes and outcomes between Indigenous People and the Australian Government in other areas, such as land rights and native title, would be instructive for this process. Consequently, the issue of funding for Indigenous groups for equity is a preliminary issue which parliament *should* address to ensure a free and fair process that is representative and reflective of Indigenous aspirations.[22]

Treaties in the other CANZUS jurisdictions implicitly recognise the legal personality of Indigenous people, but this often came at a very significant cost, including the *de facto* loss or at least the diminution of Indigenous sovereignty as argued above. That is, legal personality gained through a treaty and as part of the common law alone appears to be of little intrinsic value in subsequently enforcing the terms of a treaty. History shows that domestic treaties have not yielded justice for Indigenous peoples. For the reasons discussed, therefore, a constitutionally entrenched Australian Indigenous legal personality is symbolic and legally significant for international negotiations between the parties.

Constitutional Issues

A domestic treaty may also face other constitutional hurdles. At present, the Australian states retain plenary power, and thus power over treaty formation within their jurisdictions (see e.g. Blackshield and Williams 2010: 426). In Victoria and the Northern Territory, the parties are at a very early stage in their (state-government based) treaty negotiations. There was a treaty process in South Australia but it appears to have stalled ('SA Government decides not to go ahead' 2018). These treaties, when in force, would include the state government and local Indigenous nation groups, and this process of treaty-making is likely to provide important lessons and insights into helping establish the framework for a nationwide treaty process.[23]

Arguably, a domestic treaty would not be an instrument that falls within the meaning of the external affairs power of the Federal Constitution. Therefore, the cooperation of the state jurisdictions is an important preliminary issue for the Australian Government, perhaps through the referral of powers by all state jurisdictions (*Commonwealth of Australia Constitution Act 1900* s.51 (xxxvii)).[24]

There are also critical matters related to process and the scope and substantive content of a treaty. Indigenous People in Australia have largely been invisible to the law other than as legal subjects. They have been displaced from society, segregated and shunned and, accordingly, there are some key legal issues that Indigenous people will need to ascertain among themselves before engaging in negotiations with each other and/or the Australian Government. Three legal developments that may help Indigenous people to crystallise and articulate their own positions on key fundamental issues before treaty negotiations can begin are examined below.

AN EQUITABLE TREATY FORMED IN A DOMESTIC LEGAL SETTING: SOME PRELIMINARY STEPS

An Indigenous Constitution

Each new period of time and new generation brings with it its own unique challenges. British law over time has established constitutionalism (written or otherwise) as its custom for preserving its civilisation in law. Constitutionalism is arguably a reasonable way of capturing and maintaining the collective memory, history, custom, law and wisdom of a people in a formal, slowly evolving but not overly rigid way. Indigenous society has been seriously dislocated by colonisation and needs the time and resources to rebuild internal governance structures. This British constitutional model (which includes both written and unwritten conventions) would arguably benefit Indigenous people to help formally reclaim their cultural inheritance,[25] including through Indigenous elders, among whom there is a vast accretion of knowledge of the human condition bequeathed to them from over the generations (Cornell & Kalt 1995). Wiradjuri constitutional lawyer, Mark McMillan has noted, Indigenous peoples decide how, when and in which order or priority they can 'operationalise these aspirations.' (2018). Provided Indigenous peoples are legally empowered and resourced to make these decisions for themselves, we agree with this statement. We concede that following a coloniser's precedent might not be acceptable to many Indigenous leaders, but this option might serve as a starting point.

Some attempt to capture and, where permissible, codify some of this knowledge (as identified by each self-determined group) in a form of constitutionalism is arguably suited to Indigenous peoples' knowledge and epistemology. An appropriate group of elders and lawyers could perhaps help develop an Indigenous constitution that is in part written and captures common and important values and principles.[26] Various Indigenous nation groups could augment and complement this document with their oral histories, customs and law as appropriate. There are also organisations and institutions, such as the Australian Institute of Aboriginal and Torres Strait Islander Studies and various universities, that hold significant bodies of useful works on Indigenous people, which could form part of this collective memory. Indigenous people could then self-determine how their knowledges are deployed.

An Indigenous constitution could also reflect in principle the unique significance to Indigenous peoples of land, caring for country, language and spirituality, as well as more prosaic but central issues of primary education, bilingual and bicultural education, and the concomitant right to maintain culture—particularly cultural responsibilities tied to land. These are some among a range of important issues normally captured in a constitution. There are also issues with significant financial implications such as the sharing of natural resources including sub-surface, seabed, continental shelf, water and water column resources generally. These are currently exclusively claimed to be regulated solely by the Crown (in some cases subject to international treaties),[27] but cognisant of the importance of avoiding a service-delivery model, we argue that, nonetheless, it is vital to note important issues of principle relevant for securing human well-being and Indigenous cultural survival.

Contemporary issues should arguably not completely dominate a long and rich culture that has lasted millennia. On the other hand, the inclusion of the lessons delivered in some seminal reports that have documented the collective experience of Indigenous peoples in the more recent traumatic years could be a useful repository of knowledge. This is particularly important to ensure that a colonial history that sought to annihilate Indigenous people will not be repeated. There is also a significant collation of Indigenous and broader human rights norms in the international sphere. Instruments such as the UN Charter, the Universal Declaration of Human Rights, United Nations Declaration on the Rights of Indigenous Peoples (UNDRIP), and other human rights, cultural and political declarations and conventions from the UN and the International Labour organisation (ILO),[28] among others, can also provide a useful body of norms from which Indigenous people can draw as culturally relevant.

Some of the broad substantive issues that would need to be examined in careful detail include questions of sovereignty,[29] self-determination, self-governance and Indigenous laws (and how they may operate and evolve within a new legally pluralistic common law framework), and mechanisms dealing with an extended notion of the conflict of laws. At present, Anglo-Australian law manages conflicts within its several jurisdictions, but one would have to contemplate how this model could be extended to include Indigenous jurisdictions (a notion that needs to be further explored and better defined in time).

A First Nations Assembly (FNA)

The second important step would be determining how a collective agreement could be ascertained and identifying a suitable forum for this purpose. The next suggested step is the creation of a FNA, which may look like a 'parliament' but that is a term avoided in this paper and also by the government, the parliamentary committee and many Indigenous groups. This is because the former Australian Prime Minister, Malcolm Turnbull, rejected the possibility of working with an Indigenous body (elected or otherwise) that—in his view—resembled a 'third chamber' to parliament and, consequently, to which he attributes the privileges of a Westminster-style parliamentary chamber.[30]

A FNA could help establish agreed processes to select or elect a representative subgroup of Indigenous people with the requisite knowledge and experience to help articulate Indigenous aspirations and concerns, such as, but not limited to, the creation of an Indigenous Constitution, identifying suitably qualified and representative negotiators for a treaty processes, and the mode of decision-making under which such Indigenous representatives would be expected by their own Indigenous members to operate. A broad, representative forum for decision-making among Indigenous people is an important piece of governance infrastructure that is crucial for self-determination, even in the absence of the issue of a treaty. Such a body or voice is supported in principle by the majority of Indigenous people.

While this is not a new idea and there have been several manifestations of governance mechanisms, such as those created through legislation (the now defunct Aboriginal and Torres Strait Islander Commission, see Parliament of Australia 2003), or under the corporations law (e.g. National Congress of Australia's First Peoples 2019), an over-reliance on government funding has limited their sustainability. However, if Indigenous Australians can become less reliant on government—though the government has an inherent moral obligation to provide assistance—this will overcome many barriers that impact upon their agency and independence (United Nations 2008).

Importantly, financial independence would prevent the settler state from controlling the selection of, or demanding unreasonable accountability for, representatives of such a body. It is crucial that the Australian Government should not be able to cherry-pick its preferred candidates to represent Indigenous people at the negotiations and thus skew the processes and outcomes. Such a forum, appropriately adapted to account for geography, size of the First Nation, and other relevant factors such as local customs with respect to representation, could then provide a familiar, robust, democratic and representative institution that is acceptable to all groups.

There are also likely to be significant differences between an FNA and a purely 'elected body'. The FNA, by analogy, is more akin to the UN General Assembly representing a range of peoples of varying population sizes and distribution. Thus, some compromise set-up between the FNA and the elected body would be better suited for the purpose. An agreement on a fair process for how representatives will be selected or elected, and providing for equitable representation of all Indigenous peoples, is an important preliminary step, as is determining how and by whom each of the First Nations is represented.

We concede that the establishment of an FNA is likely to be a complex and expensive exercise. However, this process fits within the undertakings given in the international arena by Australia to promote self-determination among Indigenous peoples and to which Australia is yet to give effect.[31]

Treaty Negotiations

For practicality, it seems unlikely that every First Nation group can be represented at the treaty negotiations, though efforts should be made to facilitate this wherever possible. On the other hand, it is crucial that adequate, broad and collective representation at the negotiations that is acceptable to Indigenous people be established.

Furthermore, Indigenous people could use the FNA to discuss and achieve a level of consensus in principle on both key procedural and substantive issues touching on treaty formation. A FNA (or, as mentioned in the Uluru Statement, an Indigenous Voice to the Australia Parliament) could generally help establish consensus on central issues and do so as part of its own self-determined process. It may seem to be a contradiction that the 'parliament' provides self-determination when we speak of using treaty to achieve this end. The rules and manner in which the negotiations under domestic law will lead to a treaty, and how the treaty may be amended in the future, should also be set out with a degree of flexibility to help everyone navigate what will be, in large part, a *sui generis* process. Suffice to say, the entire process should be viewed as an organic and iterative evolution of a solution rather than a linear process with specific predetermined milestones.

These and other preliminary steps that can be identified by Indigenous people, followed by a series of good-faith negotiations, would need to take place before the content of a treaty can be finalised in principle. Negotiations should not be rushed for pragmatic or instrumental reasons or for convenience.

A DOMESTIC TREATY: SOME CONCLUSIONS

A domestic treaty will largely be negotiated, concluded, signed and ratified in Australia. There are legal issues of how one would (*in specie)* distinguish a 'domestic treaty' from a mere contract that was concluded between the same parties.[32] It is likely that the High Court of Australia would resolve disputes and be the final arbitrator of legal disputes between the parties based on domestic law alone. This is not an ideal arrangement given the deference paid by the High Court to the notion of parliament's supreme position in the Anglo-Australian version of the Westminster system, which disproportionately favours the coloniser.

This problem was highlighted in the exchange between Justice Kirby and the solicitor general when the latter confirmed that the constitution would permit the parliament to validly make laws that were akin to those promulgated by the Nazis (Kirby J. in Blackshield and Williams 2010: 985). The race power is still part of the Australian Constitution in 2020 and clearly permits the detrimental treatment of Indigenous people (*Commonwealth of Australia Constitution Act 1900* s.51(xxvi); *Kartinyeri v Commonwealth* (1998) 195 CLR 337). (French, R., *The Race Power: A Constitutional Chimera*, in Lee, H. and Winterton, G. (eds) *Australian Constitutional Perspectives*, Lawbook, 1992, 180, 180.)

While service delivery has been an important part of the relationship between Indigenous people and the Australian state, the final treaty should not in substance reflect this past relationship (Anthony 2010). Rather, a treaty should represent a visionary, strategic and high-level document setting out the future relationship between peoples, laws and civilisations. Indigenous Australians should be given, and should insist on, the opportunity to exercise free, prior informed consent at every important stage of the negotiation, and finalisation of the instrument should perhaps occur through a process akin to the Westminster 'Committee System'.

However, many Indigenous people would concede that a free and fair treaty outcome is not likely to be achieved in the domestic arena alone. For the reasons explored above, it would therefore appear best not to follow a domestic treaty as the sole means of reflecting the aspirations of the parties.

This chapter now focuses on some key complementary aspects that can, broadly speaking, be concluded in the international arena. What is proposed here is a combination of both domestic and international laws as forming the policy and legal frameworks for a treaty. The representative structures and other important legal prerequisites necessary to obtain input and consensus-building for a domestic treaty largely remain primarily the same, for the purposes of the next part of the chapter.

A FRAMEWORK FOR A TREATY UNDER INTERNATIONAL LAW

In creating a treaty between the parties, we argue that Indigenous people will be better served by using international law as the operative law. This would include a judicial body where appropriate jurisdiction over the subject matter and disputes would vest (but which does not exclude the High Court of Australia). Some key issues are now briefly examined. This list is not exhaustive but aims to show that there are few legal impediments to treaty formation in international law terms. Whether there is a political will to do so is a separate but relevant question. The resetting of race relations between the two main parties is, however, a fundamental question of justice. Treaty formation in the international arena will make it difficult for racist domestic politicians and their core constituencies to use domestic law and prejudices to frustrate the process under the cover of nationalism and populism.

As a member of the UN, and in conjunction with Indigenous peoples (although this is *not* a legal prerequisite for negotiations to commence), Australia might be able to seek the assistance of the UN Special Committee on Decolonisation (see United Nations n.d.) and/or the International Court of Justice under the UN Charter Article 96(1) (see United Nations 1969) in securing an advisory opinion of the court to explore the question of how a tract of land wrongfully declared *terra nullius* could now be decolonised fairly.

The starting point for a legal framework provided for in the Vienna Convention is a tried and tested internationally acceptable framework for treaty negotiations (United Nations 1969). For the purpose of treaty formation, English legal conventions that are appropriately adapted for use in the international context are also likely to be acceptable to the majority. These include conventions relating to treaty negotiation, amendment, interpretation and dispute resolution. However, as mentioned, the applicable body of law should encompass common law notions but also incorporate relevant international law as self-effecting for purposes of litigation, interpretation and dispute resolution, generally to prevent the parliament from using the Australian Constitution and domestic law as unfair obstacles.

The parties can, by consensus, agree to negotiate a treaty under international law (Trindade 1976). Most Indigenous people in Australia accept or support the proposition that sovereignty has never been ceded, a position that can be supported in law and fact (Wood 2016a). This arguably means that sovereign Indigenous people are a 'people' in the meaning of the UN Charter and can seek to be decolonised under the rules and processes available under the UN umbrella. However, parties may have to ensure that any preliminary procedural matters are satisfied, which is now broadly considered (Trindade 1976).

The Exhaustion of Domestic Remedies

The exhaustion of domestic remedies before seeking international human rights remedies is an established international law principle (Trindade 1976). What exactly 'exhaustion' might mean is arguably unclear for the purposes of a treaty in Australia. In any event, the High Court of Australia has stated that adjudication on this issue of sovereignty is outside the competence of a municipal court (*Mabo v. State of Queensland (No 2)* (1992) 175 CLR 1, 31 (per Brennan J)) and is authority for the proposition that the relevant domestic legal avenues have been exhausted. Nonetheless, it is possible for parties to unjustly try to use this option as an opportunity to increase costs, introduce delays or frustrate the treaty process. On the other hand, parliament could in good faith preclude this possibility by passing appropriate legislation.

A remaining question in this context is whether the Australian Parliament has the authority to pursue this question internationally. It is argued here that both the external affairs power and, arguably, the so-called nationhood power will provide the parliament with a lawful head of power to engage in negotiations with sovereign Indigenous peoples in the international arena (Blackshield & Williams 2010).

Legal Personality and Equality Before the Law

The issue of the Australian Parliament representing settlers has been discussed. With the appropriate legislation in place, the agreement of the state governments is not a prerequisite, as the external affairs power of the constitution permits the parliament to enter into a treaty in the international arena (*Commonwealth of Australia Constitution Act 1900* s.51(xxix)).

Constitutional recognition would create both domestic and international legal personality for Indigenous people, which is an important legal prerequisite for treaty formation outside a purely domestic context (Dodson et al., 2016). Alternatively, as discussed above, the treaty itself can implicitly recognise Indigenous legal personhood. The question of how the content and expression of Indigenous personality is given practical effect and represented in treaty negotiations with the Australian Government are also crucial issues which will have to be resolved during the process. It is important for Indigenous people that, given the power disparity, Indigenous delegates are seen to be free from any form of coercion or undue influence by the Australian Government. Strict adherence to the Vienna Convention would help in this regard, as the International Court of Justice should, as agreed by the parties, have supervisory jurisdiction over a treaty formed under international law.

Indigenous peoples in Australia do not enjoy legal equality under the Australian Constitution (Wood 2016a). Internationally, however, and under customary law, equality is axiomatic, and it is proposed here as a *jus cogens* norm; that is, a norm from which no derogation is permitted. It is noted here that, if Australia honours its international obligations, it will consider itself bound to not use domestic law (*Commonwealth of Australia Constitution Act 1900* s. 51(xxvi); *Kartinyeri v Commonwealth* (1998) 195 CLR 337) to defeat this (*jus cogens*) norm (United Nations 1969: Article 64). The key issue is to prevent the parliament from using the race power in the constitution to the detriment of Indigenous peoples.

Terra Nullius and International Law

Internationally, it is unlikely that Australia will be able to sustain its past claims that the continent was *terra nullius* (International Court of Justice 2019). On the other hand, Indigenous people could seek an international declaration that Australia was never *terra nullius*; a claim that is most likely to succeed (International Court of Justice 2019). The implication for Indigenous people is that they may be able to seek reparations. For good-faith negotiations, however, Indigenous people could agree not to pursue matters such as claims of genocide, in return for a fair and equitable treaty that is negotiated in good faith and that results in an honourable self-determination regime for Indigenous people, but which also recognises historical facts.

Adopting the International Court of Justice's official language versions (in English and French) of a treaty as equally authoritative is not likely to be contentious. However, in addition, each Indigenous group should have the right to have the treaty translated into its own language but, for practicality, the issue of authoritativeness should be left open for negotiation, cognisant of practicality and opposability. Due to the possibility of disputes arising based on linguistic interpretation, the creation of extrinsic statements concerning the accepted meanings of such terms could be included as part of the *travaux preparatoires* (the official records of negotiation).

The notion of self-determination is vital to Indigenous people and is a notion that has been well explored internationally. The scope and meaning of self-determination is included in several human rights instruments that have been developed in the post-colonial era. Consequently, the internationally settled notions of self-determination are much more likely to be fair to Indigenous people, particularly when opposable in the international dispute resolution framework.

The identification of the Indigenous parties to the final content of a treaty and how, by whom, and where a final treaty between the parties will be signed and ratified could also be developed by consensus through the FNA.

The forum for treaty negotiations is likely to be in Australia. The final signing and ratification process could perhaps be carried out simultaneously in Geneva, Canberra or other important Indigenous places in order to represent both practical and symbolic elements of the process. A degree of transparency and international oversight would likely benefit Indigenous people due to the power disparity between the parties, which is otherwise significant. The processes for how Indigenous nations will express their assent for ratification must also be settled.

CONCLUSION

Relations between Indigenous peoples in Australia and the state have been difficult over the years. The alienation, segregation and forced assimilation of Indigenous people have comprised a history that is difficult, but one that must not be ignored for political or pragmatic reasons. Many leaders in Australia have accepted—arguably most eloquently by former Prime Minister Paul Keating—that historical injustices need to be addressed and that this should be done fairly (Keating 1992). For their part, Indigenous people are recovering from the harsh policies of the past and, importantly, they are seeking to reset relations with a firm eye on the future.

The High Court of Australia has accepted that the normative systems of Indigenous people predate British arrival, and this creates a new paradigm for relations that were denied to Indigenous people in the days of *terra nullius* when mere survival was the best one could hope for (*Mabo v State of Queensland (No 2)* (1992) 175 CLR 1). The High Court of Australia has also conceded that determining questions such as sovereignty of the continent are outside the scope of its jurisdiction. This creates an opportunity for the parties to seek initial resolution, such as through a treaty, and to do this in an international environment where the ghosts of the past will not inhibit or frustrate the establishment of a genuinely equitable framework for future relations between the parties. One of the main purposes of a treaty is to create a legal framework which ensures the sustainable and transparent self-governance of Indigenous nations. Governance mechanisms, while determined by each First Nation, should develop a common understanding as to what constitutes good governance with reference to international standards.

Indigenous notions of what constitutes sovereignty appear to be significantly different to the meaning of the term at international law, and its full expression under Indigenous notions of the term is likely to create futures that might pleasantly surprise many non-Indigenous people. Disadvantages of the past mean that there needs to be a significant period of governance-building among Indigenous peoples so that they are in a position to make fully informed and free choices that will benefit their people and set them on the road to recovery of their cultures and civilisations in the fullest meaning of these terms. This is likely to be a fairly expensive exercise but one which a wealthy nation, such as Australia, can, and must, fund if it is true to its word that it seeks to reconcile and make amends for its past cruel and dishonourable treatment of Indigenous peoples.

We have argued in this chapter that achieving a framework for justice is likely to be difficult, but is nevertheless possible. The conduct of negotiations in the international arena is more likely to alleviate the problems caused by the distrust rife within the domestic sphere of law and politics and to help the two main parties to bring their collective aspirations together in a visionary, strategic and high-level document setting out the future relationship between peoples and societies. The process should be viewed as organic and incremental rather than as plainly linear.

Concluding a treaty that broadly sets out the aspirations of all people sharing this continent is likely to help ease the injuries of the past, to benefit from the interaction of great civilisations and to help build a brighter future for all our children. The former Prime Minister, Malcolm Turnbull, said he was committed to doing things with, and not to, Indigenous peoples ('Turnbull: We Are Committed to Doing Things . . .' 2018). This means that Indigenous people can determine their own priorities and solutions (i.e. self-determination in practice). This is what the vast majority of Indigenous people want: namely, a people determining their destiny in a form of self-determination that is free and fair. Mr Turnbull is not the first to make this commitment. The current Prime Minister, Scott Morrison, has been silent on many key issues of relevance to Indigenous people but has broadly committed to take Indigenous views into consideration and has followed this up by appointing an Indigenous person into cabinet for the first time. Will he, however, be the first to do as he says? The signs are not promising, but it is not too late for him to be remembered in history as one who spoke with a straight tongue.

NOTES

1. 'Aboriginal and Torres Strait Islander' peoples is the commonly used term in Australia to describe its First/Indigenous peoples. These are clearly colonial terms (i.e. terminology variously used by the settler state collectively to refer to a range of tribes and peoples, often who each identify separately) and their use is not uncontentious. This paper generally, but not exclusively, employs the phrase 'Indigenous people/s' for this purpose, as it is the term preferred in international instruments, including by consensus in the United Nations Declaration on the Rights of Indigenous Peoples (United Nations 2008).

2. For the purposes of this paper, and in concert with international law, a formal statement by a current head of government is taken as being indicative of the position of that nation (United Nations 1969). Consequently, the fact that then Prime Minister, R.J. Hawke, proposed a treaty during Australia's Bicentenary in 1988—an idea that has survived for 30 years or so—must mean that Indigenous people can reasonably expect that legal or political obstacles (if any) to a treaty can be overcome.

3. (https://aiatsis.gov.au/collections/collections-online/digitised-collections/treaty/barunga-statement).

4. In this chapter, the 'state' means the Australian Federation, made up of its States and Territories.

5. For a discussion of the legal environment, see Wood 2016b, 2017.

6. Composed by members of Yothu Yindi, 'Treaty' was released in 1991 on the *Tribal Voice* album. The original version can be found here: https://www.youtube.com/watch?v=Jf-jHCdafZY.

7. Race is a socially constructed notion. Prichard (2011: 44, 50) notes that 'the dominant view among biological scientists, anthropologists and social theorists is that the concept of "race" is socially constructed, imprecise, arbitrary and incapable of definition or scientific demonstration'. However, the term is used here as it is part of the Australian legal diction. The legal test for indigeneity in Australia also has a racial component (see *Shaw & Anor v. Wolf & Ors* (1999) 163 ALR 205).

8. John Gardiner-Garden, 'The 1967 referendum: history and myths' (Australian Parliamentary Library Research Brief No 11, 2006-7) 4.

9. See United Nations Convention on Elimination of All Forms of Racial discrimination (UNCERD). (https://www.ohchr.org/en/hrbodies/cerd/pages/cerdindex.aspx).

10. Constitutional recognition is, in the view of this paper, highly desirable but not absolutely essential, particularly if a treaty is concluded in the international arena. If constitutional recognition does not come to pass, there is an international law-based alternative which is discussed later in this paper, though it is less ideal.

11. It is an established position among most Indigenous Australians that sovereignty has not been conceded. However, the inclusion of this within a treaty as a preambular matter is something the two parties will need to decide upon.

12. See below for the comparison by the High Court of Australia of the constitutional powers with that of the Nazis. Refer to Blackshield and Williams Constitutional law text (5th ed).

13. The Uluru Statement refers to the 'powerless' position of Indigenous people. While the authors acknowledge the disparity in power, they reject the characterisation of Indigenous people as powerless. The Uluru Statement can be found at https://www.referendumcouncil.org.au/sites/default/files/2017 05/Uluru_Statement_From_The_Heart_0.PDF.

14. Some of these norms are reflected in the instruments referred to in the United Nations Declaration of the Rights of Indigenous Peoples (UNDRIP), endorsed by Australia in 2009, which acknowledges that the Charter of the United Nations, the International Covenant on Economic, Social and Cultural Rights, the International Covenant on Civil and Political Rights, and the Vienna Declaration and Programme of Action affirm the fundamental importance of the right to self-determination of all peoples, by virtue of which they freely determine their political status and freely pursue their economic, social and cultural development (United Nations 2008).

15. Article 39 of the Vienna Convention holds that a treaty may be amended by agreement between the parties. (United Nations 1969).

16. These were the other legal bases for the acquisition of territory in 1788 (*Mabo v State of Queensland (No 2)* (1992) 175 CLR 1, 32 (per Brennan J)).

17. See, for example, the Interim Report of the Joint Select Committee on Constitutional Recognition relating to Aboriginal and Torres Strait Islander Peoples (Parliament of the Commonwealth of Australia 2018).

18. An alternative view is that international law forms part of the common law and consequently the legal personhood and equality of Indigenous people in Australia

already has the force of international law. The dualistic nature of Anglo-Australian law arguably means that Indigenous people would be safer with explicit recognition in the constitution.

19. See Governor Phillip's Instructions 25 April 1787 (Museum of Australia. n.d.).

20. It is noted that the denial of the frontier wars by Anglo-Australian law also denies the claim that the British acquired territory and sovereignty by conquest.

21. While much of the brutality of the British remains undocumented in Anglo-Australian law, the treatment of other colonised peoples is better documented. For example, in Bengal, India, the fingers of weavers were cut off so that their work would not compete with the inferior textiles from Manchester, UK. This gives us some insight into how Aboriginal people (who were barely recognised as human by their invaders) were treated in Australia in creating time for the British to gain the upper hand with their colonisation (Jack 2014).

22. UNDRIP, which was endorsed by Australia in 2009, acknowledges: 'that the Charter of the United Nations, the International Covenant on Economic, Social and Cultural Rights, and the International Covenant on Civil and Political Rights, as well as the Vienna Declaration and Programme of Action, affirm the fundamental importance of the right to self-determination of all peoples, by virtue of which they freely determine their political status and freely pursue their economic, social and cultural development' (United Nations 2008).

23. Canada has also been involved in some post-colonial treaty-making and might provide some lessons for Australia (Davis 2006: 127).

24. According to the Constitution s.122, the Commonwealth or the Federal Parliament in Australia retains plenary powers over the Territories, which are the Northern Territory and the Australian Capital Territory.

25. For further information on the state's plenary powers, see Blackshield and Williams 2010: 3.

26. For a discussion on the issue of multiple voices, see, Parliament of the Commonwealth of Australia 2018: 118–23.

27. Sections 42 to 47 of the *Aboriginal Land Rights (Northern Territory) Act 1976* (Cth) give Aboriginal traditional owners in the Northern Territory an effective right to some inalienable freehold land ownership and a power of veto in limited circumstances. This compares with much weaker rights under the *Native Title Act 1993*. While negotiations are likely to be contested and difficult, free and fair negotiations are likely to produce better and fairer outcomes for Indigenous people. This paper does not, however, seek to paint an overly positive picture of internationally based negotiations. The dispute between Timor Leste and Australia over oil resources in the Timor Gap, the subject of an international agreement, is an example of an iniquitous outcome, including allegations of bad faith in the course of the negotiations between unequal parties. (https://www.legislation.gov.au/Details/C2016C00111)

28. See, for example, for further information on the state's plenary powers, Blackshield and Williams 2010.

29. Please note that, to this point in the paper, reference to sovereignty has been used in the international law meaning of the term, from the time of the Treaty of Westphalia or the notion that the 'sovereign' has the divine right to rule. Sovereignty

used in the particular treaty context discussed here arguably carries a very different meaning, one that will be defined by Indigenous people over time but which will, through necessity, have to intersect at some points with the Westphalian meanings of the term. Sovereignty in an Indigenous sense carries implications of a duty to care for country and its citizens and to hold its care as a trust on behalf of our children, to be delivered intact, taking from country only what we need to live according to our own laws (See also Reynolds 1996: xiv–xvii).

30. The authors concede that there is some resistance to the idea of an Indigenous 'parliament', particularly among the right-of-centre political leaders, but more importantly among the leaders of the larger parties. While dispelling the perception of an FNA *ipso facto* as being 'problematic' is important in practice, such perceptions are largely political and not a legal impediment. We cite the existence of the Sami Parliament in the Nordic states as an example of a legal model of an Indigenous parliament that would work within a parliamentary democracy. Whether such a model is acceptable to, and among, Indigenous peoples in Australian is also something that would have to be ascertained through consensus.

31. Funding the treaty program is a relevant issue not examined in any detail here. While Australia is obliged by international law to help fund self-determination for Indigenous people, a mix of government, private and philanthropic, etc. funds could be used to achieve this. See United Nations 2008.

32. A domestic treaty, if viewed as a contract, raises issues such as the rule against perpetuities in Anglo-Australian law. These are technical issues that will need to be settled if a domestic treaty becomes the key instrument in this matter.

Chapter 5

The United Houma Nation

Whose Governance? By Whom? For Whom?

Adam Crepelle

In April 2010, the United Houma Nation (UHN) living along their coastal territories of the southern United States experienced a man-made disaster over which the nation had no control and no form of redress, but which had devastating impacts on all Houma—the British Petroleum (BP) Deep-water Horizon oil spill.[1] Caused by an explosion on an offshore oil rig platform in the Gulf of Mexico, the volume of oil escaping the damaged well—originally estimated by BP to be about 1,000 barrels per day—was thought by United States (US) Government officials to have peaked at more than 60,000 barrels per day, amounting to an estimated 4.9 million barrels of oil discharged overall. As oil began to contaminate Louisiana beaches in May, attempts were made to manually remove it using dispersants and skimmers. More difficult to clean were the state's marshes and estuaries, where the topography was knitted together by a delicate ecosystem. By June, oil and tar balls had made landfall on the beaches of Mississippi, Alabama and Florida. In all, an estimated 1,770 kilometres of shoreline were polluted, with long-term environmental, resource, health, economic and social consequences. More than a third of federal waters in the gulf were closed to fishing at the peak of the spill, due to fears of contamination.

In news media commentary about what was acknowledged to be the largest marine oil spill in history, several Houma Nation citizens spelled out the specific and wide-ranging consequences for them:[2]

> . . . The native Houma people, who have long relied on fishing and trapping in the marshlands of Louisiana, have been through a lot as a tribe . . . They have been robbed of their lands, subjected to segregation, witnessed the steady erosion of marshlands and been displaced by hurricanes. Now, some fear the oil

slick that threatens to invade the bayou could be the final blow to their culture and traditions.

. . . We still could make a living here. But now, with the oil coming, I don't know. The tribe, which has about 17,000 members, has lived off the marsh for hundreds of years, and until recently many members made their living entirely off the marsh resources—moving from one harvest to another, season by season.

. . . My biggest concern is the future of our people. We have lived off the land, we have lived in our traditional homeland for generation after generation. I have great concern of what the oil spill is going to do to our communities. You know, we grow up learning how to deal with hurricanes. We have experienced four devastating hurricanes in the last three years. Our people are resilient. We know how to gut out our homes, rebuild, repair our fishing vessels and move on. But this [the oil spill] is totally different. The impact that this has could be totally devastating to our tribal citizens and it's quite frightening.

Joseph Goodman, writing in the *Miami Herald*, 1 June 2010 summed it up, saying that the oil spill 'has the potential to destroy the village and cultural identity of the United Houma Nation' (Goodman 2010).

Although various sources, including the US Government, verified that BP was responsible for the oil spill on the Houma Nation's traditional lands and waters, the company denied the UHN's claim for restitution, by hypocritically asserting that:

While BP indeed processes claims from federally recognized Indian Tribes, through this process, our review of your submission indicates that the United Houma Nation is not a federally recognized Indian Tribe entitled to assert claims pursuant to the *Oil Pollution Act of 1990* (OPA). Therefore, we are closing your file with regard to this matter.[3]

The oil spill was one of the most flagrant reminders to the Houma Nation of the on-going negative impacts of their failure, over many decades, to secure federal recognition as a Native American tribe—a reminder of their powerlessness and lack of recognised self-government. Indeed, some Houma and others have asserted that the interests of the oil industry have been the primary reason why the UHN did not successfully pass the federal recognition process. In the 1930s, American cultural anthropologist Frank Speck wrote that the oil companies staunchly opposed any action that might give the Houma rights to land (quoted in Moberg & Moberg 2005: 99).[4] More recently, Professor Mark Edwin Miller (2004, 2006: 201) noted that multinational oil companies had lobbied against the Houma because 'tribal acknowledgement would give the Houmas standing in court to press claims under federal Indian laws.' How did the UHN come to find themselves in this precarious position?

At the heart of this chapter is the real-life question of what constitutes self-governance and self-determination for an Indigenous nation living with the deeply embedded consequences of multiple waves of colonisation, extreme dispossession and powerlessness in the face of disasters, such as the BP oil spill. The tribal lands and peoples of the United Houma Nation along the great Mississippi River of Louisiana have been subject to invasion and warfare from multiple quarters since the late 1680s, leading to depopulation, forced dispersal, racial discrimination and segregation, and the suppression of Houma cultural ways of governing—indeed, leading to the denial of our very right to be recognised as a Native American Nation. This chapter presents an account of this dire history in order to critically consider the implications for the Houma Nation today.

The operation and impacts of the US Federal Recognition Process are given close attention as an insidious driver of our continued colonisation. Historically, Houma governance and leadership was decentralised and informal. In an effort to achieve U.S. Federal government recognition, the tribe adopted a formal governance structure, the UHN government, which served to centralise power in the tribe's council, something at odds with Houma culture. By overviewing Houma history, the chapter explores the conditions and tensions generated by having a colonially imposed governing structure. However, the wider aim of the chapter is to draw attention to the persistent fight over many decades—indeed centuries—by Houma for recognition of our *own ways* of governing. To support that goal, by way of conclusion, I suggest an action agenda for how we, as the Houma Nation, might make a start on reconsidering and revitalising our traditional, more decentralised governance practices, for contemporary purposes. In doing so, I propose ways the current UHN Government could play a central role in the greater engagement and mobilisation of Houma citizens in a governance-rebuilding process.

THE 'BRAVEST SAVAGES ON THE RIVER': COLONISING THE HOUMA

At the time of first colonial contact, the Houma Nation occupied their traditional lands in the area where the Red River met the Mississippi River. The Houma population was likely less than 1,500 when the tribe first encountered Europeans in 1686 when Italian-born expeditioner Henri de Tonti, in service to France, voyaged down the Mississippi River. According to Swanton (2010: 139), Tonti proclaimed the Houma, 'the bravest savages on the river' and formed the first alliance between the Houma and France. In 1699, Pierre

Le Moyne and Sieur d'lberville led the next French expedition into Houma territory. At that time, the tribe marked its territorial border with a red stick, so d'lberville named their land Baton Rouge—the name which Louisiana's capital still bears. Though early relations between the French and the Houma Nation were amicable, diseases introduced by Europeans had reportedly killed about half the tribe within a few years of d'lberville's arrival (Swanton 2010).[5]

Weakened by disease and caught in the midst of Euro-colonial politics,[6] the Houma began to migrate south in 1706. Migration caused the tribe to fracture, with villages being established on the east and west banks of the Mississippi River. During this period of dislocation, the surrounding Bayougoula, Acolapissa, and other tribes began, by necessity of survival, to merge with the Houma.

Later still, France's fear of Great Britain acquiring Louisiana was a factor in the transfer of Louisiana to Spain through the Treaty of Fontainebleau in 1762 (Library of Congress n.d.). According to Kniffen, Gregory and Stokes (1994: 88), Spain entreated with the Houma in 1769, and thereby provided the Houma with land grants and generally treated the Houma favourably, allowing them to remain largely autonomous and respecting Houma land (at least in comparison to France and Great Britain).[7] By the 1770s, the Houma had splintered into three bands, each with its own leader. Spain attempted to unify the three bands of Houma in Lafourche, but the effort failed because the Houma were distrustful of the Spanish commandant who had suggested the reunification. Sadly, what happened to the two northern bands remains a mystery to this day. However, around 1780, the southern band pushed further south to 'Chufuhouma'—known today as the city of Houma (Duthu 1997: 422–23).

Under their alliance, the Houma joined Spain (at the behest of the then Spanish Governor of Louisiana Bernardo de Galvez) to battle against Britain during the American Revolution, and Spain subsequently transferred Louisiana back to France in 1800. France continued Spain's Indian policy of generally respecting the Houma's independence. When France sold Louisiana to the United States in 1803, it sought to protect the territory's Indigenous inhabitants' rights, including those of the Houma. As a result of France's efforts, Article VI of the Louisiana Purchase required the United States to honour agreements between Spain and the Natives.[8]

The Houma made efforts to secure their treaty guaranteed rights. Two Houma Chiefs (one of whom was Chac-Chouma while the other's name was not reported, though Houma tradition holds that it was Louis Le Sauvage) (Duthu 1997) met with the U.S. Governor of New Orleans William Claiborne, in 1806 and 1811. Governor Claiborne recognised the Houma and presented them with coats—a means employed by colonial powers at the time to formalise relations with Indian Nations. Moreover, the Houma Nation helped the United States defeat the British at the Battle of New Orleans. Nevertheless, the U.S. government still refused to acknowledge the Houma's rights to their land, stating that '[w]e know of no law of the United States by which a tribe of Indians have a right to claim lands as a donation' (Office of Indian Affairs 2008).[9]

The US Government's denial of the Houma's land claim prompted the tribe to migrate farther south in the 1820s. The bayou wetlands offered isolation from whites; nevertheless, the Houma Nation's location must have been well-known among other tribes (Bowman & Curry-Roper 1982), for refugees from various other tribes assimilated into the Houma during this period. Furthermore, the Choctaw, who had been removed by the US Government to Oklahoma, invited the Houma to join them on the Choctaw reservation as they shared a similar culture and spoke the Mobilian trade language (Kniffen et al. 1994: 124).[10] Though some Houma may have accepted the Choctaw's offer, most remained in Louisiana's wetlands.

White settlers began migrating to Chufuhouma in south-central Louisiana and chose to name the site Houma, after the tribe, in 1834. Relations between the settlers and the Houma quickly deteriorated. After whites burned down the home of the Houma's renowned leader, Rosalie Courteaux, the Houma again moved farther south, deeper into the swamp. Finding themselves at what may have seemed like the ends of the earth, however, did not mean the Houma were entirely isolated. Houma communities were dispersed across 80 kilometres east to west and 160 kilometres north. Additionally, there is evidence that the Houma had direct relationships with Mexico, the Caribbean and perhaps further afield to South America. For example, the Houma are thought to be the only tribe in North America to make composite blowguns similar to the design used by many of South America's Indigenous peoples (Curry-Roper 1982; Jett 1983).

The next major event to occur in the Houma's history was anthropologist John Swanton's visit. To this day, Swanton is considered the foremost expert on Indians in the south-eastern United States. His interaction with the Houma in 1907 inspired him to write, 'It is plain that remnants of all sorts of tribes joined the Houma before and at this period, though it is certain that most of these were Muskhogean, and that the Houma was always the dominating element' (Swanton 1946: 292). Culturally, the Houma were a relatively open society, enabling them to accept citizens of other Indian tribes as well as people of other racial backgrounds such as Acadians, French, Spanish, English, African Americans and others (Ng-A-Fook 2006).[11] This very openness to the in-migration of different ethnicities and races would eventually be to the Houma's own considerable detriment for they began to be characterised by the majority white population in Terrebonne and

Lafourche Parishes (holding to their white supremacist ideology) as 'sabines', a pejorative term equated with being 'mixed breed' Indians (Gaudet & McDonald 2003: 85). The term was used to degrade the Houma as not being 'real' or 'authentic' Indians, thus impugning the Houma's Indian identity (Minchew 2017). Indeed, the Houma did not fit neatly into Louisiana's binary system of racial segregation. For example, H.L. Bourgeois, the Terrebonne Parish school superintendent from 1914 to 1955, wrote of the Houma:

> They call themselves Indians, and claim a social status comparable to that of the white man. But, as a matter of fact, they are not Indians. They are the descendants of that union of the Indian and the free *gens de couleur* of many generations back, with large infusions of white blood. They are pariahs. (Quoted in Minchew 2017: 12–13)

Indeed such was the dominance of this racialised, denigratory categorisation of Houma that the Louisiana Supreme Court in 1918 ruled the Houma were 'coloured' for the purposes of segregation.[12]

However, Frank Speck, an anthropologist visiting the Houma in the late 1930s–early 1940s wrote differently, that '[i]n my judgment, as based upon comparisons with Indians of the south-eastern tribes over a number of years, I should rate the Houma as a people possessing Indian blood and cultural characters to a degree about equal to that of the Creek, Choctaw, Catawbe, and Seminoles' (quoted in Fischer 1965: 150–51). Speck procured a federal grant to have an Indian school built in Terrebonne Parish in the 1940s, and Lafourche Parish established an Indian school a few years later. The three-way racial segregation—white, black and Indian—extended to all facets of life in these two parishes. Slowly but steadily, Houma self-determination of its own collective identity was being usurped and reshaped by settler-colonial governments and officials.

For nearly a century, the swampy land on which the Houma resided in Terrebonne and Lafourche was not desired by whites, allowing Houma some respite from the onslaught of colonial takeover of lands. This changed drastically with the discovery of oil in the 1930s. Suddenly whites began moving into the area and resorting to ignominious tactics to obtain Houma land. Many, perhaps most, Houma could not speak English during the first half of the twentieth century; consequently, crooked oilmen were able to cheat the Houma using dubious land contracts. For example, during this period, Speck wrote that oil companies would use their political power to prevent the Houma from exercising any rights that would interfere with oil interests. Violence, deceit and tax sales were highly effective tools used to steal Houma land. Tribal historian Michael Dardar recollects that,

> . . . after oil was discovered in the marsh area, the Houma suffered another land grab . . . The Houma were mostly illiterate, and spoke only the Houma-French language. A lot of people came in and (acquired) their property through a variety of methods . . . Many Houma people signed documents they were told were leases by the oil interests and others, but the papers turned out to be quit-claim deeds. Later, hundreds of the documents held by the parishes mysteriously disappeared. (Quoted in Huus n.d.)

Louisiana's inheritance laws were directed towards the same goal of land alienation. The Houma often married pursuant to tribal custom; that is, they did not venture out of the bayou to get an official marriage licence from the State of Louisiana. Accordingly, children born from customary Houma unions were regarded as illegitimate under Louisiana law, and so not entitled to inherit land (Crepelle 2018a: 161; Williams 2009: 101).[13] Steadily, Houma were being fully dispossessed of their lands.

Progress, however, was making its way down the bayou by the 1960s. Building on the Supreme Court's landmark 1954 decision in *Brown v. Board of Education*,[14] a Houma Indian brought a lawsuit to end Terrebonne Parish's 'separate but equal' Indian school system and prevailed in 1963. Nevertheless, Houma children remained in segregated Indian schools until 1969—five years after the *Civil Rights Act, 1964* officially outlawed discrimination and ended segregation throughout the United States. Lack of educational opportunities has resulted in employment obstacles for Houma as most work as fishermen, in the oil industry, or perform other manual labour occupations. Many Houma families left Terrebonne and Lafourche Parishes in order that their children might try to 'pass' as white in order to obtain an education.

During the 1970s, the Civil Rights Movement and national American Indian political rights events inspired the Houma to formalise a government, as an institutionalised structure in order to gain access to federal programmes and advocate for the tribe (Miller 2004: 188–89). The Houma also hoped by doing so to gain recognition as a tribe. Although the contemporary federal recognition process was not yet created, federal recognition was possible through other pathways including a federal court decision, as an executive order or a congressional act. Unfortunately for Houma, the recognition process that was established and controlled by the U.S. government became simply another mechanism for undermining Houma identity and self-governance.

THE FEDERAL RECOGNITION PROCESS

The so-called 'federal recognition process' that exists today in the United States is the result of a radical federal government policy change from the 1970s onwards. Following World War II, the US official policy towards tribes was one of assimilation. Accordingly, the U.S. legislatively terminated its relationship with over 100 tribes during what is referred to as the Termination Era. Also during the Termination Era, the United States relocated Indians from their rural reservations to big cities in an effort to destroy tribal culture and assimilate Indians into the US mainstream. However, President Richard Nixon formally rebuked the U.S. tribal termination policy and ushered in an era of tribal self-determination in 1970 (Nixon 1970). Pursuant to this shift in American Indian policy, in 1975 the US Government created the American Indian Policy Review Commission.[15] The commission studied several areas of American Indian policy, one of its focal points being the concept of 'federal recognition'. The commission's consideration and recommendations were to have momentous consequences for Houma, which the nation is still confronting today.

The commission concluded that the United States had committed a grave injustice by denying federal recognition to several legitimate Indian tribes; that is, by denying the official acknowledgement and implementation of a government-to-government relationship between the United States and an Indian tribe. The commission concluded that the US Government's tribal recognition decisions, up to that date, were not based upon any legal, historical or anthropological factors. Sadly, but unsurprisingly, the commission confirmed that some tribes were denied federal recognition 'solely on the grounds that there was only enough money for already recognized tribes' (American Indian Policy Review Commission Final Report 1977: 457).

The Houma were a victim of this administrative cost-cutting and policy fallacy, as the Bureau of Indian Education had indeed refused to provide the Houma with services in the 1930s, not because it questioned the Houma's legitimacy as an Indian tribe but because extending services to the Houma would have been costly. The Houma's home state of Louisiana was also one of the contentious places in the United States for the so-called 'unrecognised' tribes. For instance, the state of Louisiana placed Indians in mental institutions for speaking their Indigenous languages, on the grounds that the speakers were not *real Indians*, simply because their tribes did not have federal recognition—so according to the government, those 'talking Indian' must have had psychiatric issues. The experiences of the Houma and citizens of other unrecognised Native American Indian tribes led the commission to recommend that an objective process for federal recognition be created.

Once established, the resulting process quickly became embroiled in complicated considerations within U.S. federal and state governments, many of which added further complications to the Houma situation. One such example involved government attempts to create an objective definition of what constitutes a 'tribe'. This has a long history in the United States and was a common process by which colonial settler states categorised and classified

Indigenous peoples (Scott 1998). One of the first legal attempts by the United States occurred in the 1901 Supreme Court case of *Montoya v. United States* where the court defined a 'tribe' as a 'body of Indians of the same or a similar race, united in a community under one leadership or government, and inhabiting a particular though sometimes ill-defined territory'.[16]

The Bureau of Indian Affairs (BIA)—the federal agency that was originally located in the Department of War, yet remains in charge of the federal government's fiduciary relationship to tribes—subsequently attempted to develop criteria to define such a 'tribe' as part of the 1930s 'Indian New Deal',[17] though the criteria were never developed. Although Congress did not act on the commission's recommendation, the BIA responded and promulgated criteria for an administrative federal recognition process in 1978. Minor revisions have been made to the criteria over the years, most recently in 2016; however, the criteria remain essentially the same. They require that 'the petitioner/petitioning group' must:

1. be identified as Indian on a substantially continuous basis since 1900
2. demonstrate that it has existed as a distinct community from 1900 to the present day
3. demonstrate that it has exercised political authority over its members from 1900 to present
4. submit a governing document or written statement setting forth the tribe's membership criteria and governing procedures
5. prove that it descends from a historical Indian tribe or a combination of Indian tribes that merged and acted as a single entity
6. prove that the majority of individuals enrolled in it are not enrolled in a federally recognised tribe
7. prove that Congress has enacted no legislation preventing it from achieving federal recognition. (Legal Information Institute n.d.)

Noble intentions motivated the creation of the federal recognition process, but there is universal agreement among Indian Nations that it is a failure. In fact, 'it has been estimated that approximately 70% of the currently recognised tribes could not successfully pass the administrative recognition process today' (Crepelle 2018a: 153). Among its problems, the process can require daunting levels of documentation, costs millions of dollars—which most petitioning tribes do not have—and takes an average of thirty years to complete. For example, Senator Jon Tester has stated that 'the Little Shell started their process in 1978. And the process continues on. They are in the appeals process right now in 2012, some 34 years later, $2 million in legal fees, and 70,000 pages of documents' (Tester 2012: 2–3). Requiring strong documentary evidence may appear reasonable; nonetheless, this criterion presents problems for many tribes. For instance, the remaining 'unrecognised' tribes often kept their distance from white populations and concealed their Indian identity due to anti-Indian sentiments, so records of their existence will necessarily be sparse.

Regarding the criteria themselves, the BIA's definition of political authority or governance is a major obstacle, in that the criteria are invariably foreign to many Native American modes of governance. For example, historically most tribes did not have centralised leadership figures or institutions that exercised meaningful political authority over their citizens. Describing the tribes located in present-day Washington, a federal district court observed that 'No formal political structure had been created by the Indians living in the Puget Sound area at the time of initial contact with the United States Government'.[18] Likewise, the Hopi had no centralised government until the BIA used unscrupulous tactics to create such a form of government among them (Wilkinson 1996). Historically, leaders among the Choctaw 'did not have to be obeyed' (Klopotek 2011: 179). Political leadership and governance in most tribes was more informally organised and governing structures more aptly could be described as decentralised and networked. American Indians typically enjoyed tremendous personal autonomy compared to their European counterparts.

HOUMA GOVERNANCE AND ESTABLISHMENT OF THE UNITED HOUMA NATION

Written records are not clear on the exact structure of the Houma government prior to and during the early years of European contact, though they do reveal the tribe had a hereditary male chief (Swanton 1946: 286–88). Records from early contact also indicate that women occupied leadership roles among the Houma. In fact, a female chief was the most revered of all the Houma leaders circa 1700. Though her name has been lost, she earned her position by leading war parties and her prowess in combat. Houma chiefs, nonetheless, likely possessed no binding authority over other Houma, as the earliest accounts of the Houma state, 'The [Houma] chiefs are no more masters of their people than are the chiefs of the other nations in the direction of Canada. I have only noticed among them more civility' (Swanton 1946: 287).

As the Houma began to migrate during the early 1700s and split into separate villages on separate sides of the Mississippi River, their separate communities continued to adapt and reshape their own informal governing structures to suit their changing circumstances. Upon moving into the Louisiana swamps, the Houma again adopted more of a localised family or clan-like structure (Michael Dardar, Houma historian, pers com., 6 September 2019).

However, as is common among many Native American tribal groups, Houma leaders would not have had any unilateral decision-making or coercive powers over other Houma. Houma leaders could only lead by convincing others to follow—by their prowess, knowledge and experience. Houma citizens, in turn, chose to follow those whom they believed to be wise and honourable. The primary method of tribal leaders' influence was moral and cultural force.

The result is that, today, few historical Houma leaders are known by name—the most well-known and respected is undoubtedly Rosalie Courteaux. Though she was real, the surviving stories of her are more myth than fact. Her date of birth is unknown, but she died in 1885. During her life, Houma legend states that she was a medicine woman, a warrior (*couteau* means 'knife' in French), with a reputation for being ornery, yet generous. She led those in her community and was esteemed well beyond it. Despite the debilitating racial dynamics of her era, she treated all people with respect. For example, Houma folklore states that she donated food to hungry blacks and adopted an orphaned white boy. The greatest indicator of her legend is that nearly all of the roughly 20,000 contemporary Houma claim descent from her.

But Rosalie was not a 'chief'. The Houma never had such a figure in the sense that the term is used today. She is more aptly described, using the French words, as a 'super-Tante'—a female leader within a Houma community. Tantes, as well as their male counterparts, 'Noncs', did not campaign for their titles nor was there any formal selection process. Rather, Tantes and Noncs obtained their status organically through their actions and ways of behaving—Houma just knew whom to turn to. Tantes and Noncs were typically middle-aged to elderly individuals who possessed strong character, integrity, expertise, and wisdom. They offered guidance to their community when dealing with external affairs, but their primary role was in resolving inter-community matters. Many Tantes and Noncs would not have spoken English until the 1940s (Ng-A-Fook 2006: 140–41).

Up until the 1970s and until the commencement of the BIA recognition process, there had been dramatic and debilitating impacts on Houma governance. But many traditional modes of leadership and intra-group ways of making decisions continued. In order to gain access to federal programmes and better advocate for Houma people, influential citizens, such as Helen Gindrant, Frank Naquin and others, believed the Houma needed an official government. Accordingly, the Houma in Lafourche formed the Houma Tribe in 1972 and elected Frank Naquin as its chief. The Houma in Terrebonne in turn formalised their own government, the Houma Alliance, in 1974 (Miller 2004: 188–89). The Terrebonne and Lafourche Houma both desired federal recognition and were advised that the Houma could not achieve federal recognition as two distinct entities, since the Houma in both parishes and beyond were the same people. Accordingly, the Houma merged in 1979, creating the contemporary United Houma Nation, selecting Kirby Verret as its chairman. This new unified governing institution was to have long-lasting major ramifications for Houma.

Prior to the 1970s, the Houma never had a constitution nor any other written rules for governance or otherwise. However, under a constitution newly written at the time, the newly formed UHN Government claimed to represent all Houma. The Tantes and Noncs remained; however, their internal influence was diminished. After all, the tribe now had *real* leaders. The early leaders of the UHN advocated that the tribe should proceed into the recently created administrative federal recognition process in 1979, in hopes of validating their collective identity and acquiring services for tribal citizens.

Although the UHN adopted its government model specifically to meet the BIA's requirements, the BIA submitted a letter of 'obvious deficiency' to the UHN in 1986 stating that the last leader of the tribe was Rosalie Courteaux and questioning the tribe's leadership structure. The BIA letter also noted that Frank Speck had earlier said that the tribe had no 'headmen and council'.[19] The BIA clearly had problems with the Houma's lack of centralised political authority over its members. In fact, the BIA's assessment of Houma historical leadership is not wrong, but its postulation completely ignores the fact the Houma never had a centralised political authority. More importantly, the BIA was unable to understand the more dispersed, networked mode of governance that Houma *did* have. In effect, by adopting a centralised, formal governance model as a tool to secure federal recognition, the Houma became less Houma in the traditional sense.

It is therefore not surprising that the UHN's strategy did not work. The BIA issued a proposed finding against recognising the UHN in 1994. Though the BIA had decided not to recognise the Houma, it nevertheless concluded (frustratingly) that 'Indian ancestry can be verified for the petitioner without doubt or question' (Office of Federal Acknowledgement 1994: 25). The rest of the BIA's finding has been widely criticised due to its failure to accept basic documented facts (Crepelle 2018a: 167). For example, the BIA could not verify that the City of Houma—where the Houma have been a documented presence for over 200 years—was named for the Houma Indians. The BIA admitted that foremost anthropologists, such as John Swanton and Frank Speck, had identified the Houma as a tribe. Nevertheless, the BIA argued that all of these highly regarded anthropologists were wrong. Furthermore, in the 1850s and 1930s, the BIA itself had also identified the Houma as an Indian community. However, in the BIA's finding against extending the Houma federal recognition, it stated that the Houma had not been *consistently* identified as an Indian community. The very dislocation and marginalisation of Houma generated *by* colonisation was further used against them.

The BIA's failure to recognise the Houma has had grave consequences for the UHN, and the creation of the UHN has in turn had grave impacts on Houma governance. For instance, without federal recognition, the tribe has not been able to legally exercise its sovereignty as a government to protect its land, waters and culture. This has meant, for instance, that the UHN has been unable to prevent the graves of its ancestors from being defiled because it lacks federal recognition (see Seidemann 2009). The Houma's ancestral lands continue to be rapidly eroded—now in a very literal sense—through devastating hurricanes, floods and climate change. However, the lack of federal recognition means the tribe does not have the legal authority to take measures to protect its own coastline areas. Furthermore, when levees were built in the region to protect against rising sea levels and flooding, Houma communities were left outside of the levee, because the federal government thought extending the levee to Houma communities would be too expensive.[20] Former Principal Chief of the UHN Brenda Dardar-Robichaux confirmed the dire consequences for Houma:

> The lack of recognition has hindered us on many levels. When it came time to recovery with the devastating four hurricanes in the last three years, we were left on our own. We did not receive direct assistance from FEMA as a tribe or as an indigenous nation. We did not receive assistance that other federally recognized tribes did. (Quoted in National Public Radio 2010)

UHN GOVERNANCE: PARTICIPATION AND PERFORMANCE

Since the UHN is not a federally recognised tribe in the United States, it lacks the ability to assert legal sovereignty over its territory. Accordingly, the UHN is organised under Louisiana state law as a non-profit corporation (see Secretary of State, Louisiana 2019). Despite being a non-profit corporation, the UHN's governing document is a constitution (United Houma Nation 2001). The constitution was most recently updated in May of 2001 and begins with a preamble declaring that the UHN are a 'sovereign native people' who have adopted a constitution:

> in order to organize for the common good, to protect our inherent right to govern ourselves under our own laws and customs, to maintain and foster our tribal culture, to protect our homeland, to conserve and develop our natural resources, to promote the social and economic well-being of our people, and to govern, protect, and advance the common good of the United Houma Nation and the members of this Nation. (United Houma Nation 2001: Preamble)

The UHN Government now operates in eleven districts and is comprised of a twelve-member UHN Tribal Council (United Houma Nation 2019). The tribal council possesses 'the power to make and to enforce laws' (United Houma Nation 2001: 5). Eleven members of the tribal council are selected to represent their particular geographical district for a four-year period. Each district encompasses one of the primary UHN population areas, stretching along Louisiana's coast from St. Mary Parish to Plaquemines Parish (United Houma Nation 2019). Tribal council members must be at least 25 years of age, reside in the district they wish to represent and possess a high school diploma or its equivalent (United Houma Nation 2001: 6). Additionally, the council is responsible for overseeing committees and boards, such as the budget and finance committee, the HR personnel committee and election board. The council also selects a vice principal, chief, secretary, treasurer and parliamentarian from among its ranks (United Houma Nation 2001: 7).

The principal chief of the UHN serves as the twelfth member of the tribal council and is elected by majority vote from among all of the UHN registered voters (United Houma Nation 2001: 6). In order to be eligible to serve as principal chief, an individual must meet the requirements to serve on the tribal council, as well as have previously served at least one full term on the tribal council and be at least 35 years of age (United Houma Nation 2001: 6). The principal chief is limited to two consecutive four-year terms in office (United Houma Nation 2001: 6–7) and his/her duties include presiding over tribal council meetings, serving as the official spokesperson for the UHN, acting as the tie-breaking vote in the event the council is deadlocked and performing 'the usual duties of a principal chief' (United Houma Nation 2001: 7). The principal chief is also responsible for overseeing the operation of the UHN administrative staff (United Houma Nation 2019).

While talking to multiple Houma citizens including former elected representatives of the UHN about this chapter, there was an absolute consensus that the UHN governance system is in dire need of reform. Indeed, there are several troublesome aspects with the current UHN Government. The government is not effective at seizing opportunities; in fact, the tribal council seldom appears to accomplish substantive project outcomes. According to UHN citizens, the tribal council's modus operandi seems to be wait, delay and 'do nothing'. Consequently, many UHN citizens have come to believe that not everyone on the tribal council has the best interests of the Houma Nation at heart. Citizens have expressed serious concerns about the tribe's financial management, conflicts of interest and a general lack of transparency.

These concerns have led to a debilitating low level of civic engagement among the UHN citizens, of whom there are approximately 20,000 (Encyclopedia.com 2019). A particularly telling point is that the nation is seldom able to fill the entire tribal council with elected representatives. (At the time of writing in September 2019, three tribal council seats are vacant.) Similarly, failure to achieve a quorum is a common occurrence at tribal council meetings. As a result, tribal council meeting attendance is low and, from observation and discussions with citizens, attendance seldom reaches thirty people.

This low level of citizen engagement is directly linked to having a governance structure that is incompatible with Houma culture and ways of making decisions. Constitutions, holding elections and electing leaders for four-year terms may work in other contexts, but are not the Houma way. Adopting a constitution was a well-meaning step in the tribe's effort to achieve federal recognition. Unfortunately, this construct has backfired, creating unintended consequences as the constitution has not enabled the tribe to achieve federal recognition and the model of corporate governance it continues to reinforce does not align with Houma traditions and practices.

The use of the term 'United Houma Nation' is also problematic. Houma have always existed as a closely interconnected society, but at no point in the tribe's history was it ever 'united' as in the English definition of the word. Rather it operated more as a loose confederation. The Houma people were always free to move beyond their traditional borders and return. By the mid-1700s, reports of separate Houma villages exist. When the Houma migrated into the swamp, communities necessarily became more isolated due to the terrain. Nevertheless, the Houma maintained close contact with each other, and they dug canals to facilitate communication and commerce between Houma communities (Miller 2006: 174; Crepelle 2018a: 167). The first early effort to produce an official Houma Government resulted in the immediate formation of two separate tribal governments. The only reason the Houma subsequently 'united' was because the Houma could not achieve federal recognition as two separate entities (Kirby Verret, Houma citizen, pers com., 7 September 2019).

Indications of the challenges facing the UHN's governance begin in the preamble of its constitution, wherein it uses the phrase 'sovereign native people'. While sovereignty is now a commonly shared political goal for many Native American Nations seeking recognition of their collective jurisdictions, at no time in recorded history did the Houma try to assert sovereignty or control *over other Houma*. Indeed, it is possible that the Houma never thought of themselves in this sense. 'Free', 'independent', 'autonomous' or 'self-governing' would be more culturally relevant terms for the Houma. Moreover, 'native people' is not terminology that most Houma use to refer to themselves. While local whites attempted to classify the Houma as 'coloured' and disparage them as 'sabines', the Houma fought—often literally—to be called 'Indian'. These subtleties of meaning and usage suggest the constitution is out of touch with lived Houma culture and were not generated out of a widely inclusive engagement with all Houma, wherever they live.

Aside from the preamble, the UHN constitution contains several provisions that appear to be contrary to the tribe's culture. One such provision is the constitution's requirements for election procedures (United Houma Nations 2001: 3–5). No Houma leader was elected until the 1970s. The constitutional requirement for tribal council members to have a high school diploma might be reasonable, but not in the context of Houma struggles over many decades to obtain an education. Even after Houma were allowed into high schools, discrimination remained rampant. Many Houma dropped out of school due to the atrocious treatment they received in integrated schools (Ng-A-Fook 2006).[21] In addition, many Houma parents encouraged their children to work in traditional Houma activities, such as trapping and fishing, to help support their families (Ng-A-Fook 2006).[22] Hence, many Houma did not graduate from high school. To insist on having a high school diploma or its equivalent as an eligibility requirement to serve on the UHN Tribal Council shows a stark disconnect from the realities of Houma experience and history.

The constitution grants the tribal council the power to make laws on behalf of all Houma. Of course, the Houma had a code of conduct prior to written laws, but the rules would not have been formally promulgated. There seems to be little connection between the values and practices of Houma traditional laws and the more corporate governance laws enshrined in the UHN constitution. As a result, the two forms of law often appear to be at odds with each other. Also antithetical to Houma culture, the principal chief can only serve two consecutive terms. Early European records suggest Houma leaders held their position for life. When the Houma migrated to the swamps, Tantes and Noncs often held their position for years, and often for life.

Given the mismatch between the Houma lived experience, traditionally based ways of governing and the UHN government model, it should be no surprise that the Houma Nation is not functioning effectively and struggles financially, partially due to missed opportunities as a result of ineffective governance. Without a strong financial base, the tribe is largely forced to fund itself by grants and small-scale fundraisers. Arguably, the UHN government is currently ineffective because it was designed in the context of expectations by external federal bureaucrats rather than to culturally resonate with the Houma people's customs, history or geography.

GOVERNANCE REFORM: A WAY FORWARD

The current governance and constitutional structure is not working for Houma people. Many citizens have lost faith in the UHN Government, which has suffered from having a culturally incompatible governance structure. The recent history of many Native American Nations and of Indigenous peoples internationally tells us that this does not need to continue to be the case. The UHN government must and can change, and the Houma citizenry can drive that change.

All cultures evolve—including Indigenous cultures. That includes Indigenous ways of governing, which have always adapted to changing circumstances. As Professor Gavin Clarkson notes:

> Tribes have adapted to their environments for millennia, and the arrival of Europeans did not diminish that adaptiveness. Many tribes pride themselves on their ability to adapt: the Navajos developed a thriving weaving industry using wool from sheep brought over by Europeans; the Plains Indians incorporated European horses into their culture; and the Choctaw claim that if the Europeans had brought aluminium foil with them, Choctaws would have been cooking with it while the other tribes were still regarding it with suspicion. (Clarkson 2006: 20)

The same is true of the Houma. When Europeans arrived near present-day Baton Rouge, the Houma were primarily agricultural peoples. The Houma also spoke their own language as well as other Indigenous languages for commercial purposes, prior to European contact. However, the Houma became fluent in the French language almost immediately after contact because they saw an alliance with France as means to bolster their military and economic status.[23] The Houma lost their hereditary leaders as the tribe migrated down the bayou and shifted to a more clan or family-based leadership style. The Houma economic practices also shifted from agriculture to predominantly hunting and fishing while in the swamp.

The Houma are now living in the twenty-first century and the world is changing rapidly around them. The land that has supported Houma culture for over two centuries is rapidly vanishing and, with it, many of the Houma's sacred places and medicinal plants. The economy is changing as well. Houma families are having a harder and harder time supporting themselves in the seafood industry. Likewise, the oil industry jobs that employ many Houma will likely become less lucrative in the coming years. Ecological and economic changes will force more and more Houma away from Terrebonne and Lafourche Parishes. The UHN governance system needs to evolve to better meet such diverse contemporary needs of its citizens.

Similarly, it is arguable that the UHN constitution should be reformed to better reflect the nation's current legal challenges and opportunities. Importantly, this should be done in such a way that gains support from Houma, through their being fully engaged in developing a new constitution that supports the rebuilding of their own culture and a shared vision for the future. Indeed, it may well be that, in order to move forward, the Houma

Nation needs to disconnect the form of its future governance (and its constitution) from external federal recognition requirements that have not led to effective, culturally compatible governance in the past. Rather, the Houma citizenry, through the UHN, could begin working together to adopt a new government structure that accounts for the characteristics of its land, the tribe's demographics and socioeconomic opportunities.

Amending the UHN constitution is possible but difficult. Thirty per cent of the tribe's registered voters must vote in the election, and a majority must vote in favour of amendment (United Houma Nation 2010: 18). Electronic processes can facilitate voting (United Houma Nation 2010: 4). Theoretically, the voting period could be open for an entire year or longer. This would provide Houma citizens with ample opportunity to amend the UHN constitution. If the amendment process were successful, UHN citizens would have the opportunity to reshape their government through an internal process of constitution-building.

In the meantime, the UHN's most pressing governance issue is to create a governance institution and processes that are more effective at engaging the UHN's citizens. Altering how the UHN Tribal Council meetings are scheduled can increase citizen participation. The UHN constitution currently requires quarterly meetings of the entire tribal council (United Houma Nation 2010: 11). At present, the council meets ten times per year at varied locations. The purpose of alternating meeting locations is to provide access to each UHN community but, ironically, meeting monthly in different communities reduces overall citizen turnout. The reason for this is that people often do not know where tribal council meetings are being held. Moreover, it takes about three hours to drive from one end of the UHN region to the other. People do not want to spend their entire Saturday travelling to and from tribal council meetings.

Reducing the number of tribal council meetings each year may increase community engagement. In place of monthly tribal council meetings, each UHN district representative could host district meetings every two months. During these meetings, the district representative would be able to update the community on the tribe's finances, tribal events, progress towards federal recognition and other information pertinent to the community. Members of the community could relay their concerns to the council member who in turn would relay the concerns to the entire tribal council. On the third month, the UHN Council could meet as a whole, at a set location in Terrebonne or Lafourche Parishes. These two parishes are in the middle of the UHN territory where the bulk of Houma reside. This makes the location convenient and such a meeting scheme will likely increase citizen turnout.

Additionally, the tribe needs to explore the use of information technology to broadcast its tribal council meetings and issues of general importance to all

Houma. Many UHN citizens live outside of UHN council districts and may have any number of reasons why they cannot be physically present at meetings. Livestreaming meetings would allow a greater number of citizens to see what occurs at UHN council meetings. Citizens could participate from a distance as well as by emailing questions or calling in. As more Houma have the opportunity to participate in tribal council meetings, more Houma will become energised about the UHN and invest in its governance.

Finally, there is a persuasive argument to be made based on the history detailed in this chapter, that UHN governance can be substantially improved, for the benefit of all Houma, by rebuilding a more traditional or culturally compatible governance model and, in the process of rebuilding, by clearly articulating and formalising a shared tribal vision for the future. As part of a strategic rebuilding, the Houma could collectively consider ways in which they can embrace and reinvest in valued traditional governance practices. For example, what might be the internal roles of the Nonc and Tante system? No rules need to be drafted for the selection or powers of Tantes and Noncs. Houma people know how the system works.

This internal work of reconsidering and rebuilding Houma self-governance needs to be given priority. Then, a revitalised UHN Tribal Council or some other newly created government institution can progress to the pursuit of federal recognition, with a renewed citizen mandate. Though federal recognition comes with its own problems,[24] it will enable the Houma Nation collectively to protect their land and culture and provide the tribe with access to numerous opportunities. Federal recognition is something every Houma citizen desires; in fact, Houma elders still feel the unjust irony that they suffered through racial discrimination, because they are Houma at the same time as having the United States refuse to consider them 'real Indians'.

By rebuilding governance framed around the traditional Tante and Nonc governance system, Houma internal relations will improve. Improved internal relations will lead to greater citizen participation and enable the UHN to focus on issues that matter to the UHN community. Focusing on issues of importance to the Houma people will reinvigorate the UHN. Positive goal-oriented energy will enable the UHN to come together as a community, share history, transmit culture and fight for the rights of the tribe with a single voice. Coming together as Houma people will enable the UHN to exist as a nation forever—even if the United States continues to refuse to recognise it.

NOTES

1. On the night of 20 April 2010, a surge of natural gas blasted through a concrete core recently installed by contractor Halliburton in order to seal the BP oil well for

later use. It later emerged that a similar incident had occurred on a BP-owned rig in the Caspian Sea in September 2008. Once released by the fracture of the core, the natural gas travelled up the Deep-water rig's riser to the platform, where it ignited, killing eleven workers and injuring seventeen. The rig capsized and sank on the morning of 22 April, rupturing the riser. Without any opposing force, oil began to discharge into the gulf. For more detailed timeline and accounts of the oil spill, see Encyclopaedia Britannica (n.d.); National Commission on the BP Deep-water Horizon Oil Spill and Offshore Drilling (2011).

2. See interview comments by Houma citizens: Huus (n.d.) and NPR (2010).

3. Letter from Geir Robinson, Director of Claims, BP Gulf Coast Restoration Organization, to Lanor Curole & Thomas Dardar, Jr., on Claim Filed on Behalf of United Houma Nation, dated 18 November 2010.

4. Moberg and Moberg state that, '[d]uring the late 1930s and early 1940s, Speck explained in his communications to federal authorities, Houma efforts to win federal recognition were strenuously opposed by oil and gas companies that were then laying claim to the region's energy resources' (2005: 99).

5. On 4 March 1700, lberville reached the Houma landing place and found that half of the tribe had been destroyed by what he calls 'an abdominal flux' (Swanton 2010: 285–87).

6. European settlement in the Americas resulted in many Indian nations forming alliances with different European nations, and negotiating new alliances with other Indian nations. Battles, diseases, new trade and other consequences of European contact resulted in major tribal migrations.

7. Kniffen et al. note that, 'Spanish laws had treated Indians generously, a circumstance they found fortunate as empires changed. *Las Recopilaciones de los Indios* had given Indians the right to settle the king's lands and had guaranteed them a square league around their villages for tribal use. The Spanish also had recognized tribal policy and the rights of chiefs to rule over their tribes' (1994: 88).

8. In return for fifteen million dollars, or approximately eighteen dollars per square mile, the United States acquired 2,140,000 sq. kms. The Louisiana Purchase extended US sovereignty across the Mississippi River, nearly doubling the size of the country. At the time of the purchase, the territory of Louisiana's non-native population was around 60,000 inhabitants, of whom half were African slaves. See Burgan (2002).

9. The records (Office of Indian Affairs 2008: 95) state that '[a] claim of the "Homas" tribe of Indians to 12 sections of land was submitted to the U.S. General Land Office (GLO) sometime between 1813 and 1816. The register and receiver of the land district for the Eastern District of Louisiana in New Orleans recommended against confirmation of such a claim in a report prepared in November 1816. These officials submitted this report to the Commissioner of the General Land Office who, in turn, forwarded it to the US Congress in January 1817 (GLO 1/16/1817, claim #625 at p. 265). This report was prepared and submitted to Congress in accordance with legislation of February 27, 1813 (2 Stat. 807), which extended the time period for the submission of land claims in the State of Louisiana; a process which originally had been authorised for the Territory of Orleans by the Act of March 2, 1805 (2 Stat. 324).

The Federal Land Office officials thereupon categorised the "Homas" claim as one "not embraced by existing laws" (GLO 1/16/1817, 264). They reasoned that, "[w]e know of no law of the United States by which a tribe of Indians have a right to claim lands as a donation"' (GLO 1/16/1817, 265).

10. Mobilian was the trade language used by tribes in the south-eastern United States. The vocabulary was primarily derived from Choctaw and Chickasaw, but included words from other Native American Indigenous languages. Eventually European words were incorporated as well. See Mufwene. n.d.

11. Ng-A-Fook (2006: 121) notes that, due to the effects of continent-wide migration after the colonisation of North America, the reality of identities within the United Houma Nation became multiple and complex.

12. *Henry Billiot vs. Terrebonne Parish School Board,* 143 La. 623 (1918) involved the refusal by the Supreme Court to reverse the lower court's ruling that the Houma are 'colored', on procedural grounds.

13. Williams (2009: 101) cites the Bureau of Indian Affairs anthropologist Ruth Underhill, who wrote in 1938 that, '[m]y present opinion is that the Indians have been robbed of their property but by entirely legal procedure . . . The means are Louisiana law which forbids "bastards" to inherit, even if their father makes a will in their favour. The Indians, who do not go in for white marriage procedure are all technically "adulterous bastards", with no rights to their father's lands.'

14. *Brown v. Board of Education* 347 US 483 (1954).

15. See the 'American Indian Policy Review Commission Final Report', produced by the American Indian Policy Review Commission, 1997: 442. Available at: http://files.eric.ed.gov/fulltext/ED164229.pdf.

16. *Montoya v. United States* 180 U.S. 261, 266 (1901).

17. *The Indian Reorganization Act*, colloquially known as the 'Indian New Deal', was a major shift in federal Indian policy. The Act is the first piece of legislation in U.S. history designed from the premise that tribes should exist. The Act did many positive things, including securing tribal land bases. Nevertheless, it has been widely critiqued for being overly paternalistic. The Act remains a cornerstone of contemporary U.S. Indian policy.

18. See *US v. Washington*, 384 F. Supp. 312, 355 (W.D. Wash. 1974).

19. See https://www.bia.gov/sites/bia.gov/files/assets/as-ia/ofa/petition/056_uhouma_LA/056_ta_letter3.pdf?

20. South Louisiana is losing land rapidly due to sea level rise, as well as 50 years of unregulated oil drilling in Louisiana's wetlands. Historically, Louisiana's coast was replenished by the Mississippi River; however, damming of the river in the 1920s to prevent it from changing course and flooding has deprived Louisiana's coast of sediment. Making matters worse, unregulated oil drilling has allowed salt-water to penetrate the freshwater marsh. This kills the freshwater vegetation that holds the marsh together. For a detailed discussion of how coastal erosion and federal recognition have impacted the UHN, see Crepelle (2018b).

In the early 1990s, the U.S. Congress decided to do something, and tasked the U.S. Army Corps of Engineers with a project known as 'Morganza to the Gulf'. Still in progress, the project will one day line the Louisiana coast with 100 miles of levees, keeping hurricane waves from breaking across the land. Nevertheless, it will not protect Houma residences on Isle de Jean Charles. The Corps determined that to do so would require building across open water, on soft soils, at a cost of $190 million. It would be far cheaper, they decided—approximately $8 million in total—to simply move everyone elsewhere.

21. Ng-A-Fook reported that, '[h]owever, the newly acquired "equality" which desegregation provided, came at a violent psychological cost. Many Houma students were pushed out of high school due to the constant teasing that took place on the bus, in PE classes, and out on the schoolyard. "A lot of the girls that were in school," Helen said, "quit school because they could not take the strain." "And the students," she continued, "would raise their hand, but the teacher would always call somebody else. You had to study and fight everyday." "Everyday," Laura repeated. "So a lot of them dropped out of school," Helen concluded' (2006: 165).

22. Helen, a Houma citizen interviewed by Ng-A-Fook, explained that '[w]e had trapping season and the kids had to go with their parents. So they were out of school during the season, for however long it lasted' (Ng-A-Fook 2006: 144).

23. Ng-A-Fook (2006: 8) notes that '[d]ue to the community's initial contact and close international trade relationships with France, for the most part, the Houma people learned how to speak French'.

24. Federal recognition comes with tremendous federal oversight. This is certainly a negative, but no federally recognised tribe is asking to relinquish its federal status. Moreover, tribes that have had their federal recognition terminated have sought to have it restored.

Theme Two

GOVERNING FOR NATION-BUILDING

Thematic Introduction

Concepts, Issues and Trends

Diane Smith

> There will be no magic leap from 'rights recognition' in the courts to self-government or self-determination on the ground. We need to be practical and we need to begin with effective governance. But even that won't be easy, given . . . the size and remoteness of our communities . . . retaining experienced, educated Aboriginal people with capacity and skills, of being able to build organisations with economies of scale, and of having access to economic opportunities, which all present a significant challenge. Nevertheless, we have to find innovative ways to meet this challenge, and perhaps, eventually, we will have to make some difficult decisions.
>
> —Neil Sterritt, Gitxsan Leader (2012)

The tumult and the exhilaration of the 'rights era' described by the authors in Theme One opened up many opportunities for Indigenous peoples across the globe to re-envision their futures and consider ways to maximise their self-governance—to turn rights recognition as a legal and political matter into self-determination and sovereignty in practice. Bolstered by The United Nations Declaration on the Rights of Indigenous Peoples (UNDRIP) and their own shared experiences, Indigenous peoples today are engaging, with zeal, in a massive effort to regain control of their lands, resources and futures, to escape colonial legacies of powerlessness and re-establish their ways of governing. But in doing so, they are confronted by the obstacles and internal dilemmas that Gitxsan leader Neil Sterritt alludes to above, and which Adam Crepelle and Angela Wesley discuss at length in their chapters.

NATION-REBUILDING MATTERS

As several authors in this theme remind us, there is now an entire Indigenous generation of young people who are impatient to replace deficit colonial discourses with real governance success and practical outcomes. This younger generation are asking frank questions of their own nations and leaders, such as these: Why fight tenaciously for rights when our citizens are scattered and internally divided, our families broken and treasured cultural ways are being eroded? What is the point of rights, if our governance arrangements are not up to the task of implementing them or our collective capacity to actually exercise jurisdictional authority is weak or entirely absent?

One of the potent ways Indigenous peoples are tackling these questions and the often-painful challenges involved is through nation-rebuilding: that is, by strengthening their ability to act in solidarity as a polity; that is, to act as an organised political entity with a collective identity, and so give shape to a form of collective self-governance that will enable them to wield contemporary power and authority for their own determined purposes. It was this capacity collective agency—to act as a polity—that was one of the first foundations of Indigenous jurisdiction that suffered under the onslaught of settler colonisation across the globe.

Prior to colonisation, Indigenous nations were sovereign entities. Today, they continue to assert that they have never ceded their sovereignty to the modern nation-states in which they now reside. Many are finding new ways to come together, to rebuild and reassert their nationhood and autonomy. As the authors in this theme demonstrate, that process of nation-rebuilding inevitably includes a deliberate resurgence of governance, often involving a deliberate fusion of cultural ways of doing things with new strategies, tools, institutions and structures of self-governance. In fact governance resurgence is itself a motivator and process of nation-building. The momentum is uniquely Indigenous driven, and some of their struggles, diverse pathways and innovative solutions are detailed in this theme of 'Governing for Nation Building.'

THE 'NATION' IN SELF-DETERMI*NATION*

There are many views and a considerable international literature about what constitutes a 'nation', and we see from the case studies in this theme that the practice of acting as an Indigenous nation is not simply the product of the more recent Westphalian system and its modern 'nation-states'. Indeed, Indigenous nations arguably predate the formation of modern nation-states. In this book, we follow Marshall (in *Worcester v. Georgia* 31 US (6 Pet.) 515

(1832)) who found Indian nations to be 'distinct independent political communities' . . . 'a people distinct from others' and argue that is applicable in Canada, New Zealand, Australia and likely further afield. This sense of nation recognises the conditions not only of political solidarity but also of collective 'grouphood' where a people share a common language, culture, ethnicity, descent or history.

Today, the concept of 'nation' is part and parcel of an international Indigenous discourse referencing a wide suite of Indigenous concepts that commonly express the foundational idea of a group or society with deep affiliations to, and custodianship of, a territory of land and waters. In other words, the Indigenous nation is embedded as a form of relational sociality as much as it is a political formation. This culturally infused notion of 'nation-as-polity' forms the bedrock for the Indigenous nation-building initiatives described by the authors in their chapters for this theme.

The case studies reveal another fundamental point. There is an influential diversity in the type and scale of Indigenous nations across the CANZUS countries, ranging from tribes, clans, extended family networks, communities, hapu, iwi, houses, alliances, confederations and so on. These Indigenous nations existed prior to their colonisation at different times and do not rely on legislated rights or treaty recognition from settler states for their internal cultural legitimacy—although today rights and recognition can strengthen a nation's self-determination and decision-making powers. Hence, an Indigenous nation may share a single common territory with physical boundaries or jurisdiction or it may be a dispersed nation (with dispersed territories) within another larger nation. This means Indigenous nation-rebuilding takes a comparable diversity of forms and content. There is no single nation-building formula. In fact, adaptation and remixing of the old and the new to create culturally legitimate governance innovation is a long-standing hallmark of the creative Indigenous responses to resolving problems and taking up novel opportunities.

While acknowledging the heterogeneity of First Nations and their self-governance solutions, it is also clear from the case studies that a common set of factors has given life to Indigenous nation-rebuilding across the CANZUS countries. Particularly important has been the relative success over recent decades of the rights agenda, reinforced by UNDRIP and a global momentum toward self-determination. We emphasise 'relative', because any account that describes the fight for Indigenous rights as successful must acknowledge the continued vulnerability of those rights in each context—not least because another condition shared in common by the CANZUS states, and highlighted by each author, is that Indigenous rights remain susceptible to legislative overturn and the political agendas of their colonial-settler governments.

Perhaps more to the point, the chapters in this section make clear that nation-rebuilding does not require a treaty, a devolved jurisdiction or a legislated right. On the contrary, some groups proceed more urgently and decisively in their nation-building precisely because those are absent. Sir Mason Durie (2012) succinctly identified a powerful motivation when discussing Maori pathways to self-determination: 'We are in a transition from victim to victor'. The challenge in this era is to transform hard-won rights into tangibly improved outcomes for people: for individuals, families, communities and for nations as a whole.

WRITING ABOUT NATION-BUILDING

In the hands of the Indigenous authors in this theme, writing about nation-building becomes an act of resurgence in itself. The authors provide first-hand personal accounts, repositioning Indigenous ways of governing at the centre, interweaving those with probing analyses of what is working and what is not working so well in their communities.

The authors consistently emphasise that the solutions will be found not in the adversarial, outward-gazing politics of the rights era. Certain part of the nation-building mind-set involves a critical reassessment of the governmental forms imposed by colonialism, which are notably ineffective for Indigenous self-determination and self-governance. Rather, the authors argue for a necessary redirection of energy and investment to within, to each other as citizens, kin and governors. They write frankly and inspiringly about the risk-taking involved and the personal courage required to undertake that momentous internal task of nation-building.

THE WORK OF NATION-REBUILDING

Not surprisingly then, the work of nation-rebuilding rests upon a different way of thinking, talking, acting and even writing. What worked for people to get them through a claim or treaty negotiation process is not necessarily what will work to implement the rights and recognition they have secured. Success in gaining rights propels people from thinking about past grievances to 'future thinking'—to the needs of their children and great-grandchildren. Rather than focusing on leadership tactics for external negotiations or competing for scarce government funding, a nation-building standpoint privileges an internal focusing of energies and expertise on critical issues such as collective identity and relationships, group membership, maximising participation and voice, and the role of culture in modes of governing. And as Rigney et al.

persuasively demonstrate in their chapter, by adopting that standpoint, even external negotiations become grist for the work of internal nation-rebuilding.

This internal work requires different skills from leaders and from citizens. Under a nation-building framework, leadership becomes more about prioritising inclusion, working to create a credible balance between the sometimes competing demands of juxtaposing what Angela Wesley eloquently refers to as an 'ancient spirit' with 'modern minds'. Donna Murray and Deb Evans share the view of citizen members of a nation, finding themselves in perhaps unaccustomed advocacy roles, championing conversations within their own families and communities, and taking up the critical role of being 'nation rebuilders' which is described so well by Joan Timeche.

Several decades ago, Professors Stephen Cornell and Joseph Kalt, founders of the Harvard Project on American Indian Economic Development, set out a ground-breaking framework for understanding nation-rebuilding that was derived from their long-term applied research with Native American Indian Nations across the United States (Cornell & Kalt 1992). The Harvard researchers proposed that the significant factor in successful nation-building as a political collective is having practically effective governing institutions, with genuine decision-making authority, and implementing those in ways that match Indigenous political culture (a 'cultural match') and so win the support of the nation's citizens. The project's early work emphasised self-determination as a starting point among Native American tribes as they strategically mobilised their substantial legislative, treaty, jurisdictional and financial powers to revitalise their nation governance.

The Harvard Project research continues to valuably inform practice and produce evidence-based insights from their expanding work with Native Americans and internationally with other Indigenous people and research projects (see, for example; Fodder et al. 2014; Hemming et al. 2019; Hunt et al. 2008; Jorgensen 2007; Nikolakis 2019). Joan Timeche's chapter in this theme describes some of the impressive contributions that project has been making for many years through the Native Nations Institute's programmes to support nation rebuilders in the United States. However, we are still short of personal Indigenous accounts of the first steps—of exactly *how* people actually go about getting started, on a day-to-day basis, and *how* they go about sustaining motivation in times of adversity.

An important consideration for this volume is whether the Harvard project framework is appropriate or replicable outside Northern America, with its particular historical, political, legal and treaty circumstances. The case studies in this section indicate that for collective Indigenous polities, the Harvard framework of building institutions and capable governance as a pathway for self-determination and economic development remains highly relevant. The added contribution of the authors' accounts in this volume is that they persuasively extend that framework by describing the broad range of practical and personal strategies and tools being used 'on the ground' in other countries, by Indigenous people who are at the beginning of a journey; for example, entering into entirely new treaty discussions (Rigney et al.); engaging with digital platforms (Penehera); starting their first conversations about nation-rebuilding (Murray & Evans), or how they might reconnect with their disaffected citizens (Crepelle and Wesley).

The accumulating wider international research evidence—including that presented by authors in the following chapters—suggests no single governance or nation-rebuilding framework can simply be inserted out of its cultural context, as a 'package deal' solution. Research-based frameworks are useful precisely because they can give inspiration, be further tested in diverse conditions and adapted as suits. They provide a disruptive lens, which First Nations internationally can deploy to shake up their own thinking, experiment with and customise to suit local cultures, priorities and circumstances. Donna Murray and Deb Evans, in their chapter, show how that enables a dynamic remix and growing motivation for getting started on locally relevant governance resurgence.

The case studies in this theme depict diverse Indigenous visions for, and pathways into, nation-building; several of which do not necessarily start with institution-building but all of which do involve rethinking internal *relationships* as a foundation for reasserting self-determination. For many small, fragmented Indigenous nations, or those who have been driven off their homelands under colonial regimes, there is considerable work in rebuilding internal relationship that needs to happen prior to institution-building, and in order for that to then be commenced. What also appears to be consistent and necessary for the work of nation-building across all four countries is that whatever form local strategies and models take, they are being discussed, designed, chosen and implemented by Indigenous peoples themselves. In other words, self-determination is not an end product of nation-building or governance resurgence. Rather, it is being activated as a necessary foundation for those; as Cornell et al. clearly demonstrate in their chapter is occurring with Native American tribal health care in the United States. Self-determination comes to life as soon as people collectively begin to think about the kind of nation they want to rebuild for their future and how they are going to govern to get there.

WE THE PEOPLE: THE 'SELF' IN *SELF*-DETERMINATION

The case-study chapters point to something fundamental at the heart of the Indigenous nation-building project; namely, the desire to engage in a deep conversation among citizen members about the shared and ancient roots of their self-governance. For this step, institution-building may be vital, but is not sufficient. In fact, as Wesley, Murray and Evans, and Rigney et al. show us, the Indigenous creation of revitalised governance institutions (such as systems of law, rules, regulations, constitutions, policy checks and balances, guidelines and charters) is only made possible *because* other preliminary work has commenced. Here, the authors reveal that a striking commonality in the resurgence of self-determined action is the emphasis on people and relationships, not structures or institutions. People are the real starting point for rebuilding—specifically, the citizens of the nation and their relationships to each other and their leaders, to their culture, lands and waters.

If human relationships are the bedrock of the nation-building process, then what follows is starting a different kind of conversation, one that is about the kind of nation that people wish to build for themselves and future generations. Here we see the Indigenous authors consistently asking themselves and their fellow citizens the same compelling questions: Who is or should be the collective 'self' in our *self*-determination? Who and where are our members? Who is the nation in self-determi*nation*? And who *determines* the answers and the ways forward? These questions and the solutions described by the authors lead us to appreciate that Indigenous self-governance for nation-building is, first and foremost, embodied as a shared way of being (i.e. it is ontological) and a shared way of knowing (i.e. it is epistemological), which is realised through a shared way of doing (i.e. a culturally based praxis). The case studies speak directly to this Indigenous worldview and its primary role in producing an embodied sovereignty that forms the bones of nation-rebuilding and self-governance.

One challenge in moving into a nation-building conversation is that it inevitably activates embedded fears, old resentments and deficit mentalities borne from the colonial cauldron of intergenerational dispossession and trauma. Several chapters in the book and this theme tackle this difficult issue. They show how deliberately focusing conversations onto identifying internal strengths and shared values can spark a renewed sense of solidarity and lead to the design of culturally credible solutions for healing and managing internal cleavages, internal peace-making, reconnecting with dispersed family members, rebuilding relationships and trust among citizens and leaders, and strengthening political action. This core work of internal reunification appears to be the way that many people get started on the road to nation-building.

A particularly important component of this foundation work is to give shape to an enduring collective vision for the future, one that will bring people together to turn the promise of self-determination into a practical reality for their families. To do this, many communities return to their own knowledge systems, undertake research on their country and lands (mapping territories, sites and resources), investigate their governance history and its impacts, document their membership (recording genealogies, stories, expertise) and reflect on valued cultural beliefs, practices and norms. This internal research enhances people's consideration of the things that remain important to them and their role in strengthening the governance of the nation. It is through such internal considerations and dialogue that we can see a critical transition—where institutions (both new and old) are able to be designed for nation-building, based on ways of governing that are collectively valued and deemed credible. As consensus emerges among citizens and with leaders, it can be mobilised and enshrined within institutions and structures for self-governing and directly improve the outcomes of Indigenous-led services and development initiatives.

GOVERNANCE RESURGENCE AND NATION-REBUILDING

The stories of nation-building described in the chapters in this theme reveal Indigenous people as agents of change, particularly, as agents of culturally constructed innovation. Resetting a self-determined vision for the future can generate cultural and governance resurgence. The chapters commonly report that this involves leaders and citizens together asking: What kinds of governance arrangements might be acceptable and consented to now by citizens, and also enhance self-determination into the future? Who should have the authority to speak about and for the nation, to whom and when? What role should collective culture and traditional institutions of leadership play in contemporary governance arrangements, and how might that change over time?

The authors keep returning to the fundamental importance of inclusive, regular communication with *all* citizens, providing them with accurate, clear information and listening to their stories. Better-informed citizens are motivated to have a voice and invest in decision-making about new governance institutions and alternative development options. Several case studies describe the value of investing in the full repertoire of governance capabilities of the nation's people, to further empower choice and action.

Finally, the case studies testify, not only to the diversity of models of governing for nation-building but also to the realisation that there is no fast track or perfect end-state. As Rigney et al. show, Indigenous peoples need not wait for a treaty or settlement with settler-colonial states to start their journey to self-governance. Some Indigenous groups are beginning by prioritising their efforts around a priority governance institution—such as developing a new nation constitution, rules for collective decision-making and leadership accountability or regulations that promote a preferred alternative approach to development.

Given that nation-building—with its weighty undertaking of governance and cultural resurgence—is an intergenerational project, the incremental adaptive approach adopted in several cases is eminently sensible. Current generations have particular needs that may change in the future. Some governance foundations need building now, to enable others to be added later. Governing one area of jurisdiction well reinforces the nation's collective capabilities and confidence to take on others at a later date. Such incrementalism works for Indigenous peoples regardless of whether they have treaty or legislated rights.

Whatever the strategic pace adopted, the chapters in this theme emphasise that the central principle and practice for nation-building is to place decision-making choice and voice into the hands of the nation and its people. Importantly, in each of the pathways described here, redesigning governance *is* nation-building. Remaking trust and unity *is* nation-building. Treaty-making *is* a tool for nation-building. Developing a constitution *is* a nation-building exercise. They are all examples of sovereign decision-making—of 'self-determination in action'.

Chapter 6

Treating Treaty as a Technology for Indigenous Nation-Building

Daryle Rigney, Simone Bignall, Alison Vivian, Steve Hemming, Shaun Berg and Damein Bell[1]

The increasing number of jurisdictions engaging in debates about the prospect and nature of treaty indicate Australia is poised to enter into a new era of potential agreement and reconciliation between settler states and Indigenous authorities. The future of participating Indigenous nations, as well as the social potential of Australia, rests significantly on the objectives and the success of the negotiation processes currently being developed. There is, however, little local guidance for treaty-making, which entails an agreement reached between mutually recognised sovereign powers. Australia is a colonial society with a unique political history: it does not recognise the original sovereignty of Aboriginal and Torres Strait Islander peoples as First Nations within its jurisdictional boundaries, and therefore has never realised a genuine treaty or accord with Aboriginal authorities.

This situation means Australian polities have no clear precedent or proven process for the negotiation of political settlements of this nature. Consequently, a significant stream of Australian research has been devoted to questions of treaty-making (see e.g. Aboriginal and Torres Strait Islander Commission and Australian Institute for Aboriginal & Torres Strait Islander Studies 2003; Attwood 2009; Behrendt 2004; Brennan et al. 2005; Mansell 2016). At times, it points to past opportunities for engaging in treaty that were presented at the first colonial encounter but never adequately realised. It typically argues the case for treaty as a matter of principle and a pragmatic necessity for post-colonial reconciliation. In some instances, it draws from international Indigenous experiences to examine possible models for an Australian treaty and the mechanisms to give it legal effect, also considering options for pursuing the path forward.

A related focus of enquiry concerns a new culture of partnership agreement emerging in Australia, especially in relation to land and natural resource management. Indeed, a relatively recent history of contract law agreements, native title settlements and other negotiated land-use arrangements have opened up potential for the future development of political conditions that acknowledge and respect Indigenous sovereign authority, as is required in the international law of treaty (e.g. Langton et al. 2008; Hemming, Rigney & Berg 2011; Cosens & Chaffin 2016). While this body of work provides a crucial framework for understanding the necessary components, activities and social benefits of a more formal treaty process, the academic discussion of this topic remains largely speculative and polemic. This is largely a consequence of the so-far hypothetical nature of treaty in Australia, which results from the ongoing refusal of Australian governments to properly recognise Indigenous sovereign authority as a prerequisite condition for political negotiation and settlement.

There was, therefore, a landmark shift in Australian political society when, in 2016, the states of Victoria and South Australia (SA) each expressed their commitment to treaty-making with Indigenous peoples. While other Australian states and territories have since announced their intentions to open conversations about treaty, the processes of treaty-making actually begun and underway in southern Australia provide a vital opportunity for advancing empirical knowledge of effective treaty principles in an Australian context. Community discussions are ongoing in Victoria as the Indigenous nations, individuals and groups occupying this region attempt to form a unified and representative body under the umbrella category of 'Aboriginal Victoria', able to enter into an intergovernmental agreement. By contrast, the former South Australian Labor government, led by Jay Wetherill, formally recognised the self-determining powers of Aboriginal regional authorities for the first time in Australian history since colonisation and began developing various distinct accords co-signed with the individual Indigenous governing authorities residing in this jurisdiction.

While the current South Australian Liberal government headed by Premier Steven Marshall has retreated from a treaty process and from the recognition of Aboriginal sovereignty, the Labor opposition party so far remains committed to the recognition and support of Aboriginal regional authorities with a capacity for self-determination. Indigenous nations in South Australia continue to advance treaty discussions whenever there is a change in government. Although many Indigenous leaders remain sceptical about the willingness of governments to act in good faith to support political changes that accommodate Aboriginal sovereignty and enhance Indigenous self-determination, these developments in Victoria and South Australia sit alongside the Uluru

Declaration from the Heart, the constitutional recognition of Australia's First Nations, and the prospect of a federal government treaty process, as subjects of escalating public and research interest (see Davis & Langton 2016; M. Dodson 2012).

This chapter identifies key principles for advancing sovereign political authority, identified by Aboriginal leaders in Victoria and South Australia in concrete situations of treaty discussion and negotiation. The chapter argues that treaty should not be considered an end in itself, to be pursued for its own sake, but is best regarded strategically as a political technology that is successful only to the extent that it supports Indigenous communities to rebuild their nations and reclaim their political authority. Accordingly, treaty works best not by imposing a uniform legal framework upon negotiators but by establishing protocols for enabling the emergence and formalisation of local and culturally distinctive relationships of legal and political pluralism, expressing the mutual recognition of rightful governing authority. The chapter concludes by outlining the importance of regional treaties as forerunners to a federal treaty process and suggests some future directions for mobilising treaty as a tool for rebuilding Indigenous nations and reclaiming self-governance after colonisation in Australia.

TREATY IN VICTORIA

In February 2016, approximately 500 Aboriginal people gathered in Melbourne to consider the Victorian government's self-determination policy, announced the previous December (Hutchins 2015). Discussion and debate turned to the federal government's proposal for constitutional recognition, which the group soundly rejected (Toscano 2016). One Aboriginal elder described it as a distraction from the 'main game' of Indigenous sovereignty and reparations for injustice (Fitzsimmons 2016). Instead, the meeting passed a motion requiring the state government to provide the resources for treaty negotiations. The Victorian government responded positively, and consultations to create a negotiation process were initiated. At the time of writing, the most recent development has been the enactment of the *Advancing the Treaty Process with Aboriginal Victorians Act 2018* (Treaty Process Act), which provides for the election of Aboriginal Victorians to constitute a state-wide representative body.

The preamble to the Treaty Process Act outlines the goals of the treaty process. These are to embark on a 'renewed and mature relationship' of 'equal partnership' that is 'founded on mutual respect and a commitment to justice and equality for Aboriginal Victorians' and that will also promote 'reconciliation between Aboriginal and non-Aboriginal Victorians' (State of Victoria 2018: Preamble). These are laudable ambitions, but Aboriginal people have expressed mixed feelings about treaties and the process. On the one hand, some people are optimistic and there is hope that, at long last, an Australian government might be serious about reforming the relationship between Aboriginal and non-Aboriginal people. Jill Gallagher, the Victorian Treaty Commissioner, argues that 'Treaty provides a real hope of addressing our powerlessness. Treaty requires government to sit down and engage with Aboriginal people as equals—not as a problem to be managed, or as stakeholders to be consulted once and then ignored' (see Gallagher 2019). On the other hand, there is also scepticism from Aboriginal people who have heard governments repeatedly use the language of a 'new relationship' even while introducing neo-colonial policy platforms. There are legitimate concerns about the nature and purpose of the proposed treaty discussions. Some people have raised concerns that the process is government controlled and run by bureaucrats: they claim it is too rushed and worry how it is dominated by Aboriginal community organisations rather than Aboriginal sovereigns (Marks 2018). Others look to the history of treaty breaches, or disregard for treaties, made with Indigenous peoples across the world (Marks 2018). Gunditjmara man, Damein Bell, reminds us that colonisers used treaties to justify their own asserted sovereignty and to 'legally' dispossess Indigenous peoples of their territories and resources. Some critics argue that contemporary treaty-making achieves the same result. Bell claims that a 'new relationship' cannot be created using a tool that had previously been used to secure colonial interests.

It is apparent that the commencement of treaty negotiations almost 250 years after invasion raises numerous questions about the Aboriginal parties who will opt to negotiate, their capacity to negotiate on a level playing field and about the proposed content of the negotiations. However, the fact that the Aboriginal people of Victoria called for a 'treaty', rather than another kind of relationship, means that the recognition and exercise of Aboriginal sovereignty will be at the centre of discussions. Treaties are political agreements made between sovereign entities or representatives of sovereign entities (State of Victoria n.d.).[2] It follows that treaty negotiations have a polity-to-polity, nation-to-nation or government-to-government quality that is absent in other agreements made by state governments with 'stakeholders' or 'interested parties'.

However, Aboriginal sovereignty is itself contested. We note that some Indigenous scholars reject the concept of sovereignty as being too Western, as racist and as not in accordance with Indigenous world views (see e.g. Alfred 2001, 2009; Williams 1986). Damein Bell says the concept of 'sovereignty' is not sophisticated enough to capture the relationship of Indigenous people with their country. Bell explains that Gunditjmara people are tied together by blood, stone and country. Gunditjmara people do not own country but own the obligation to care for country. In a similar way, Ngarrindjeri people describe how they are indivisible from their land, waters and all living things. It is for this reason Bell contends that treaties really should be negotiated with country. In doing so, Bell points to the most fundamental questions of jurisdiction that must be addressed: that is, the continuing obligation of Indigenous peoples to care for their country regardless of what European invaders may have built or done to country over the last 250 years.

While acknowledging its inadequacy, the notion of 'sovereignty' may be the closest term in English able to portray the obligations to country and community that Aboriginal Elders and leaders describe. In that sense, as Behrendt observes, 'the notion of sovereignty goes to the heart of the restructuring of the relationship between Indigenous and non-Indigenous Australians' (Behrendt 2003: 96). Similarly, the Victorian Treaty Advancement Commissioner states, 'Aboriginal people have never wavered in their call for treaty as a recognition of their ancient sovereignty' (Gallagher 2019). But what does Aboriginal sovereignty look like in Victoria in 2018? How is Aboriginal sovereignty manifest today? Where is the locus of its authority? Which sovereign peoples will negotiate with the Victorian state: Aboriginal nations? Aboriginal clans? A mixture of nations and clans? The entire Aboriginal population of Victoria?

Organisations representing traditional owners in Victoria have expressed different views about where sovereignty lies, some arguing that treaties should be negotiated with clans, others arguing that nations, language groups or peoples are more appropriate.[3] Still others contend that the sovereignty of Aboriginal people in Victoria exists at a state-wide level (Marks 2018) or even at the level of the nation-state, arguing that there is only one Aboriginal people in Australia (P. Dodson cited in Mansell 2016: 75). Further complicating the matter, as a consequence of colonial histories of translocation, Victoria now includes Aboriginal inhabitants who are not the traditional owners or first peoples of lands and waters in this territory; these individuals may also seek to resolve their claims with the state through the treaty process.

The critical subject matter in treaty discussions by sovereign peoples is jurisdiction. For treaty negotiations to be considered successful, the parties must agree on how jurisdictional matters are to be shared or allocated between the relevant Aboriginal peoples and the State of Victoria. Conceptually, negotiating jurisdiction should not cause concern since such discussions are at the heart of federal structures such as in Australia (see Vivian et al. 2017). Furthermore, federations are not static. Federal, state and local governments continue to negotiate, allocate and reallocate jurisdiction over time as the expectations of their constituencies evolve. Adding Aboriginal jurisdictional concerns to this fluid jurisdictional mix actually has the potential to strengthen the authority and capacity of the nation-state.

While conceptually possible, there will be significant challenges. First, a challenge for the nation-state is that the sources of authority for Indigenous jurisdiction are not those of the mainstream legal and political systems. Macklem's conception of 'constitutional pluralism' is instructive in describing an environment where there are 'multiple legal norms of different content, multiple sites of legal norm production, multiple legal sources for these sites, and multiple forms of norm enforcement' (Macklem 2017). However, these are matters dealt with in the international system as a matter of course and do not pose insurmountable problems.

Second, the failure to recognise Indigenous peoples' rights to exercise authority from the time of first invasion to the present inevitably complicates the process of separating out and negotiating jurisdiction in Australia. The critical starting point for these negotiations lies in acknowledging that Indigenous peoples' claims that they have never ceded sovereignty also means they continue to have sovereign obligations for the entirety of their country today, regardless of development or impact after invasion. This is not a naïve urge to return to a time before invasion, but is a statement of the reality of genuine pluralism that requires a mature analysis of how jurisdiction might be shared. Shared jurisdiction also has impacts for the operation of existing legislation and policy. For example, how do native title, the Traditional Owners Settlement Act and cultural heritage legislation fit with treaty negotiations?

Third, whichever Aboriginal polities choose to negotiate with the state and the jurisdictional concerns that they choose as the subjects for negotiation are defining of the treaty outcome, since different kinds of Aboriginal polity will have different jurisdictional authority (such as differing responsibilities for issues or country). These are matters to be decided freely by self-defined Aboriginal polities in Victoria, according to the just terms of treaty.[4] Therefore, which polities choose to enter into negotiations will also influence the nature and content of any negotiated agreements, which may differ according to the aspirations, values, norms and governance systems of the Aboriginal peoples concerned. For example, traditional owners and Aboriginal Victorians may have different rights and interests, and it may be appropriate to describe them as having rights to negotiate over different jurisdictional areas. Inevitably, this is a highly sensitive matter and has the potential to be divisive. It follows that the negotiation process, or processes, must have the flexibility and variability to engage with different Aboriginal polities in relation to different jurisdictional areas and could even negotiate different kinds of agreements, while simultaneously ensuring that all Aboriginal Victorians are treated equitably. This may mean that a treaty process will necessarily concentrate on substantive rather than formal equality; a distinction commonly made in international law.[5]

While different jurisdictional areas may be the subject of discussions with different Aboriginal polities, self-determination will necessarily be the platform for all negotiations. Of the rights that are inherent to First Peoples' status, self-determination is arguably the most significant for two reasons. First, the right to self-determination is the most fundamental human right and the basis of all other human rights. It is grounded in the idea that peoples are entitled to control their own destiny through legal and political structures and processes of their own choosing. Second, there is abundant and credible evidence from Australia and North America that collective self-determination is a prerequisite for Indigenous peoples being able to meet their community development and economic, social and cultural aspirations (Cornell & Kalt 2007; Hunt & Smith 2011). The evidence demonstrates that, when communities have control over their own affairs and resources, community development outcomes are significantly better than when external parties make decisions for them.[6]

Over recent years, Indigenous peoples in Australia have begun using a 'nation rebuilding' approach to repair and advance their capacities for self-determination or 'practical sovereignty'. Insofar as having the legal and political structures to support self-determination as a requisite basis for Indigenous participation and success in treaty negotiation, we argue that Indigenous nation-rebuilding has a crucial role to play as treaty situations unfold across Australia. This is especially evident in the South Australian context, where in 2016 the state government took some first steps towards negotiating treaties with a number of individual Indigenous governing authorities in this region. The following section considers the experiences and political aspirations of the Ngarrindjeri Nation in South Australia in this context.

TREATY IN SOUTH AUSTRALIA: A NGARRINDJERI PERSPECTIVE

In December 2016, the South Australian Government announced its intention to pursue a treaty—or treaties—with Indigenous people.[7] The treaty initiative was an outgrowth of a concerted effort made over recent decades on the part of Indigenous communities in this region to rebuild their structures of authority and reclaim their capacity for self-governance, social influence, co-management of resources, and protection of Indigenous lands and waters in the wake of colonisation. For the Ngarrindjeri people, this became even more urgent after the losses and humiliation suffered by the community during the Hindmarsh Island Bridge development and associated litigation.

The South Australian commitment to treaty has been shaped significantly by the nation- rebuilding activities of the Ngarrindjeri people, whose leaders in 2007 formally reconstituted and centralised their traditional political authority (Tendi) in a contemporary governance body named the Ngarrindjeri Regional Authority (NRA). Through this body, Ngarrindjeri leaders were more effectively able to engage with non-Indigenous powers and to advance the interests of the Ngarrindjeri Nation (Ngarrindjeri Nation 2007; Rigney, Bignall & Hemming 2015).[8] Since that time, the NRA has instigated a series of legally binding partnership agreements with local, state and federal governments, as well as with diverse other entities including research and cultural institutions. These accords are known as Kungun Ngarrindjeri Yunnan Agreements (KNYA), which translates approximately as 'Listen to Ngarrindjeri People Speaking'. Initiated by Ngarrindjeri in 2002, these formal legal compacts, and the new partnership collaborations they describe, over time expanded into a South Australian treaty process not only involving the NRA but also extending to other regional Indigenous governing agencies.

In recognition of the significant positive impact and general public benefit of formally expressed Indigenous nationhood as a basis for political partnership and socioeconomic development, the South Australian Government in 2015 announced its nationally innovative Aboriginal Regional Authorities policy. This established a basis for 'Leader to Leader relationships between the state government and Aboriginal leaders' and supported 'a network of Aboriginal governing bodies charged with representing and advocating for their communities, and driving regional priorities and economic growth' (South Australian Government 2016: 3). Interested Indigenous governance agencies were invited to apply for recognition as an Aboriginal Regional Authority (ARA), which confers mutually agreed recognition of the self-governance right and capacity of their Indigenous Nation or community. An ARA Recognition Agreement also acknowledges that an Indigenous governing body has the requisite legal status and political capacity needed for entering into an intergovernmental treaty with the South Australian Government. The criteria for this were identified in 2017 by the South Australian Treaty Commissioner through a process of consultation with Aboriginal communities (Thomas 2017).

Unlike in Victoria then, the South Australian treaty process recognises a clear locus of Aboriginal sovereignty in the governing structures of Indigenous authorities. Because each Indigenous Nation will have its own governing authority stemming from its traditional obligations to protect and care for a particular stretch of country, the South Australian government understands it must negotiate a series of individual treaties with the Indigenous authorities responsible for the various Indigenous lands, waters and local ecologies that comprise the area now known as South Australia.

As a consequence of significant advancements in their individual processes of nation-rebuilding and the reconsolidation of their governing authority, leaders of three Aboriginal nation groups in South Australia—Ngarrindjeri, Adnyamathanha and Narungga—began negotiating landmark treaties in 2017, with the expectation that the first agreements would be reached in 2018. Although the new Marshall Liberal state government has since retreated from the standing commitment to treaty negotiation, Ngarrindjeri continue to use the formal legal process of Kungun Ngarrindjeri Yunnan Agreement-making as a platform for political negotiation, especially because such agreements are binding upon the Crown and not simply upon a particular government for the provisional duration of its term in office.

In the period 2002 to 2018 when the Labor government held office in South Australia, Ngarrindjeri made significant progress towards defining their position with respect to the treaty process and identifying the most crucial issues and terms of negotiation required for a future treaty with the state. For Ngarrindjeri, the basis for treaty lies in the original (forsaken) promises of a just settlement in South Australia contained in the Letters Patent 1836 and other founding documents.[9] The Colonial Office in London had developed policies to ensure that people seeking to establish a new colony or province had clear instructions in relation to their dealings with the Aboriginal natives. The policy objective of the Colonial Office was to provide some form of protection to Aboriginal natives and to ensure that, in establishing the new colony or province, the colonists acted in a just manner. It insisted, in the case of South Australia, that the colony could proceed if the land was fairly acquired from the Aboriginal population. It directed that these transactions were to be supervised by a government-appointed protector. To this end, the Letters Patent issued by King William IV on 19 February 1836 created the Province of South Australia, with the proviso:

> that nothing in those our Letters Patent contained shall affect or be construed to affect the rights of any Aboriginal Natives of the said Province to the actual occupation or enjoyment in their own Persons or in the Persons of their Descendants of any Lands therein now actually occupied or enjoyed by such Natives . . .[10]

It is clear in the *South Australia Colonisation Act*, the instructions to the Resident Commissioner and the Letters Patent, that the Colony of South Australia was established at a time when British colonial policy recognised the need to protect the property rights of Aboriginal people and to secure—by way of bargain or treaty—consent and just compensation for any voluntary transfer of property (see Berg 2010, especially chapter 1). The Colonisation

Commissioners were to ensure in their dealings with Aboriginal people that the following objectives were achieved, namely:

> to guard them against personal outrage and violence; to protect them in the undisturbed enjoyment of their proprietary right to the soil, wherever such right may be found to exist; to make it an invariable and cardinal condition in all bargains and treaties made with the natives for the cession of lands possessed by them, in occupation or enjoyment, that permanent subsistence shall be supplied to them from some other source. (quoted in Berg 2010: Appendix)

The Ngarrindjeri position on treaty stems from the 'unfinished business' begun with the Letters Patent. In the words of Ngarrindjeri leaders:

> The legal implications of the Letters Patent and other founding documents of the state has been a burning issue for us. These documents have not been effective in protecting our rights to occupy and enjoy our lands and waters but are explicit in their terms. We know many of our ancestors were forcefully removed from their traditional dwelling areas by demeaning methods thus denying their children their full inherited rights to enjoy occupy or own these areas.
>
> Our Old People, our Elders, and our families have been subjected to oppressive laws for a long time. This law has denied our Elders equal human status: it has taken our land; it has imprisoned some of us on Reserves and Missions; it has placed us in gaols; it has wrecked our communities and our economy. For all of us we need to understand why the law has failed to protect our Rights to land. It makes no sense to us why our native rights to our lands and waters were protected in the Letters Patent but not in reality. We needed to find answers to these questions for ourselves and our brothers and sisters from other Aboriginal communities in South Australia and across Australia. (Trevorrow, Trevorrow & Rigney 2010: vii)

Ngarrindjeri leaders believe a treaty process will be meaningful only if it can discuss the mechanics for a fuller or broader range of Aboriginal sovereign powers being used in the future, to overcome the wrongs of the past and recognise a beneficial and enlivened Indigenous authority in which Ngarrindjeri can take responsibility for their country and their community.

It is intended that a treaty reset and reshape the relationship that has existed between Aboriginal authorities and the settler-colonial government. For this to occur, each of the parties in the treaty discussion must direct their attention to the fundamental principles needed for the creation of a new relationship. In the first treaty negotiation sessions, Ngarrindjeri expressed the view that the concepts of 'dignity' and 'integrity' should drive the treaty discussion. These concepts are central to the key guiding principle of self-determination but have been missing historically from the relationship between Aboriginal people and the state. More specifically, Ngarrindjeri suggested a treaty process should enable:

1. Acknowledgement of the status of Ngarrindjeri People as the original inhabitants and custodians of their traditional lands, waters and sky;
2. Recognition that the Ngarrindjeri People have cultural rights, responsibilities and obligations and that they speak for these matters to ensure their community and country are healthy;
3. Social and economic opportunities germane for the development and fostering of Ngarrindjeri interests, such that Ngarrindjeri can take responsibility for creating its own future;
4. A voice for Ngarrindjeri People in legislation and policy, including a review of all legislation and policy to ensure their agency is included and the enhancement and structuring of communication channels with the Ngarrindjeri People at all levels across government and the community;
5. Accurate social histories of the past and apology for wrongs; and finally,
6. Guarantees of accountability to the treaty principles.

Ngarrindjeri therefore consider that treaty principles should drive a new relationship between Ngarrindjeri and the South Australian state government and that the ancillary agreements are needed to implement the actions that follow, from a principled commitment to the conditions of an improved relationship. To this end, legislation should be introduced in state parliament providing authority and consent of the legislature for the Treaty and Implementation Agreement to be entered into by the state. This legislation could be based upon similar legislation passed in comparative jurisdictions, for example in Canada (see Government of Canada 2016; Government of Canada, British Columbia and First Nations Summit 2016).[11]

Ngarrindjeri do not have a fixed view of the mechanisms that need to be put in place to achieve treaty outcomes but consider those mechanisms need to have practical and real effects in achieving a positive future for their community and provide for a new and better future relationship with non-Aboriginal people. And, because the future is open-ended and the relationship is ongoing and developing, any such agreement should include a potential for revision over time. The ancillary agreements needed to action treaty principles could continue post-treaty in the form and structure of the KNYAs, some of which already exist and others which would need to be created. Kungun Ngarrindjeri Yunnan Agreements specify from the outset that Ngarrindjeri have the sovereign authority necessary to enter responsibly into binding legal contracts. Because it has already entered into a number of such contracts that affirm a measure of Aboriginal sovereignty, the state is familiar with this kind of mechanism of leader-to-leader or nation-to-nation negotiation and understands (from demonstrated experience) the effectiveness of KNYAs in securing practical outcomes. None of these matters appeared to be controversial in the early stages of negotiations, and each appeared to be well accepted.

Ngarrindjeri leaders were, then, disappointed (though not entirely surprised) when, in mid-November 2017, the South Australian Government penned an overbearing letter to the NRA, indicating an intention to use the treaty process to entrench Aboriginal people into a relationship of service provision to the government. Rather than enabling Ngarrindjeri self-determination, this outcome would therefore simply reinforce the colonial role of the government as the sovereign determining agent of the decisions and policies affecting Ngarrindjeri lives and country. The Ngarrindjeri response to this unfortunate development included the following pointed remarks:

> A treaty is not required to further enshrine the errors of the past into the future relationship between Aboriginal People and the State. The State already has a well-tuned system for overpowering Aboriginal People, and it is not necessary, nor should it be presented as necessary, to add to that system a treaty document in which Aboriginal People agree at law to do violence to themselves . . . It would be improper for a *service based agreement* to be labelled as a *treaty document*, and with respect, it would be an act of bad faith by the State if it were to seek to use this forum for such to occur.[12]

For Ngarrindjeri, any treaty worthy of the name must act as a tool for the renegotiation of jurisdiction and the powers of Indigenous self-governance. In other words, treaty must enable and support the sovereign activities of the Aboriginal people party to the agreement and should encourage the future flourishing of their Indigenous nationhood as the fullest expression of the developmental potential contained in the principle of Aboriginal self-determination. Anything less would simply diminish the solemnity of, and significance inherent in, a genuine treaty agreement and Ngarrindjeri would rather walk away from the negotiations.

NATION-BUILDING FOR TREATY AND TREATY FOR NATION-BUILDING

For Indigenous peoples embarking on treaty negotiation, valuable lessons can be learned from international experience. When the scope of a treaty extends to negotiation of jurisdiction or powers of self-government, it demands that signatories have a legitimate authority and recognised representative responsibility for the decisions taken on behalf of the territories and the people who will be subject to the terms of the agreement (see e.g. discussion in Brennan et al. 2005: 124). International research finds that Aboriginal Nations who succeed after colonisation have rebuilt capable organs of self-government that are affirmed by the nation's citizens as legitimate and representative. This happens when the nation's governing institutions achieve a cultural 'match', 'legitimacy' or 'credibility' between their peoples' traditional worldviews and the governance technologies required for political interaction in the contemporary context (see Hunt & Smith 2006; Cornell & Kalt 2007). When exploring why some Indigenous nations had been able to achieve their aspirations whereas others lived in circumstances of profound distress, the Harvard Project on American Indian Economic Development (2008, 2015) found that *stable political governance* is a more important factor to the capacity of Indigenous peoples being able to meet their economic, social, cultural and community development aspirations than any other factor.

Australian and North American research has consistently shown that thriving Indigenous nations demonstrate certain characteristics or principles including decision-making control over their affairs, effective and culturally legitimate institutions of self-government (whether newly created or reinvigorated), strategic direction and community-spirited leadership (Jorgensen 2007). Together these principles or characteristics comprise Indigenous nation-building or perhaps, nation-rebuilding, which has been defined by Miriam Jorgensen as 'the process by which [an Indigenous] nation enhances its own foundational capacity for effective self-governance and for self-determined community and economic development' (2007: xii; see also Vivian et al. 2017).

A nation-building approach to self-governance is well-established in the political systems, institutional practices, environmental policies and socio-economic aspirations of many Native Nations in the United States and Canada and is being used by some iwi in Aotearoa-New Zealand. It is also materialising in Australia as a lens through which some Aboriginal polities are finding it useful to understand, organise and advance their activities (2007: xii; see also Vivian et al. 2017; Gooda 2014: 130–53). By 'identifying, organising and acting' as an Aboriginal Nation (Cornell 2015: 4), governance activities become refocussed around a more holistic vision for the future of citizens.

Beyond building managerial capacity for delivery of services decided and funded by non-Indigenous powers, Indigenous community leaders instead strive to create institutions of governance and decision-making that can support the cultural values and economy of a flourishing community and enable the expansion of jurisdiction over the lands, resources and peoples within the nation's borders. Strategies of nationhood can assist in strengthening cultural identity, civic participation, social cohesion and political efficacy. This suggests that Indigenous nation-rebuilding can play a valuable role in the process of negotiating treaty and, conversely, that treaty negotiation can enhance an Indigenous Nation's capacity for identifying, organising and acting as a governing authority.

This is the perspective that informs Ngarrindjeri thinking about the mandatory issues, rights, responsibilities and aspirations appropriate for representation in a treaty agreement. In effect, Ngarrindjeri leaders have used the treaty situation as an opportunity for strengthening their vision for the future health of the Ngarrindjeri Nation, by identifying the comprehensive policy framework and jurisdictional expansions required to achieve this vision. According to Ngarrindjeri, the holistic nature of self-determination—when this is expressed in the full range of activities defining a nation—suggests that treaty principles must be actionable across all realms shaping the experience of Indigenous life, including the areas of cultural practice, governance, economic development and employment, environmental protection and resource management (caring for, and speaking as, country), health, education, justice, housing, the arts and religion.

There are essentially two aspects to consider for each of these areas: the broader, conceptual matters relating to governance and administration that ensure Ngarrindjeri gain and retain rightful responsibility for the management of their affairs but also the concrete outcomes that the Ngarrindjeri desire from a treaty. Treaty drafters must therefore achieve a balancing act whereby the need to avoid a 'list' orientated document is weighed against the potential for achieving tangible outcomes by identifying specific responsibilities. In each case, the crucial task involves redefining jurisdictional boundaries shared between the two sovereign partners involved in treaty.

For some areas of activity, such as cultural practice, rightful responsibility must be understood as being held under sole control of the Aboriginal party. Ensuring that culture is dealt with appropriately is a crucial part of the treaty process. Simply providing or cementing the 'right' to practice culture does not properly encompass the breadth of what culture is to Ngarrindjeri. A treaty agreement must avoid any restriction of what 'right to practice' means. Ngarrindjeri culture is not and should not be limited to Western assessments of what constitutes 'legitimate' Aboriginal cultural practices and traditions. Frustration is frequently expressed at Australian native title processes which compel proof of cultural ties or practices that, in some cases, do not accurately represent manifestations of self-determined Aboriginal cultural identity. Furthermore, it is fundamental that the disruption caused to Ngarrindjeri culture by European arrival is properly recognised, including the fact that it affected Ngarrindjeri cultural identity in myriad ways. For example, strong Christian beliefs now form part of some aspects of Ngarrindjeri culture. Essentially, the crux of a proposed treaty's dealings with cultural practice or identity must be that it affords informed choice. It must ensure that an

Aboriginal people have the collective right to their contemporary cultural identity in whatever form of expression it takes.

While the expression and practice of Indigenous cultural identity should fall squarely within Ngarrindjeri jurisdiction, other areas relevant to a treaty, such as the provision, to and by Ngarrindjeri, of services and benefits including health, education, employment opportunities and justice will involve mapping and managing overlapping responsibilities properly shared between the NRA and the South Australian Government. Much of the impetus for Ngarrindjeri in going through a treaty process is the desire to be able to control their own affairs. This is often expressed as a desire to take responsibility for the resources within their country, both to ensure that proper cultural requirements are fulfilled in relation to them and that significant development opportunities can be taken advantage of in a way that is appropriate for Ngarrindjeri.

Provided that the Ngarrindjeri have the infrastructure to manage these resources, the opportunities opened up for them are enormous. Not only is it well-established that Aboriginal outcomes are far more beneficial when Aboriginal-run, but being able to take responsibility for their future development fuels and fulfils the Ngarrindjeri desire to attain that control. Further cementing this will be the concrete outcomes pertaining to the regulation and administration of resources on Ngarrindjeri country. This could be obtained in a number of different ways, for example, delegating or passing regulatory authority over the resources to the Ngarrindjeri from the state government body in which it currently vests.

However, expanded scope for Ngarrindjeri self-governance does not absolve the state from responsibility for, or commitment to, concrete outcomes that need to be achieved as part of the objective of overcoming the systematic disadvantage faced by Aboriginal people generally or ensuring equality of opportunity in the general enjoyment of human and socio-economic rights available to all Australians. It is the view of Ngarrindjeri leaders that a treaty should outline the revisable ways in which a complex and sometimes overlapping set of responsibilities can be appropriately divided between the two powers: that is, between the state government and the NRA.

Furthermore, Ngarrindjeri believe a treaty provides an opportunity for a clearer expression of responsibilities accruing solely to the state as a consequence of colonial histories of dispossession and other kinds of damage causing severe social trauma to Ngarrindjeri, among other Aboriginal people. For example, a truthful approach to the past involves the acknowledgement that Aboriginal land was taken without consent of the Aboriginal owners and occupiers. The earlier discussion of the Letters Patent and other colonial writings, laws and issuances makes clear that Aboriginal land was knowingly taken without consent by colonial authorities in 1836 and after (Rigney, Hemming

& Berg 2008: 161). Not only was the land taken without consent, but without consideration. The requirement to provide recompense for Aboriginal people who voluntarily transferred land was clearly outlined in the Letters Patent. The unjust removal of land has done untold damage to the Aboriginal population as a whole. The Royal Commission into Aboriginal Deaths in Custody (1991) specifically points to the alienation of Aboriginal land as a driving factor in intergenerational disadvantage and poverty (see e.g. Commonwealth of Australia 1991: xlvii). The depth of the trauma experienced through the severing of extremely important cultural ties to land cannot be overstated. There is no equivalent for that relationship in mainstream Australian culture; it pertains to the very essence of Aboriginal culture, collective and personal identity.

However, this issue now has to be addressed from the contemporary perspective. Part of addressing the topic of land in a treaty means facing the reality that much of traditional Ngarrindjeri land has been alienated to third-party, private-property holders, whose enjoyment of property is legally justiciable and who today would be harmed by the loss of their personal property. The Ngarrindjeri have acknowledged this and recognise that, in order to adhere to the idea of justice which has been so central to the treaty process for them, they must affirm the rights of all other Australians (Ngarrindjeri Nation 2007). As it stands now, the issue of land removal is intertwined with the rights of innocent third parties. Just settlement for past injustice cannot be dealt with by restitution, or at least not by restitution alone. Instead, Ngarrindjeri leaders suggest implementing a system of recompense for the land taken, not in the form of compensation for damages but rather as a rent equivalent paid by the government to the Ngarrindjeri.

In this way, the narrative—although understanding the wrong of the past—can shift into one of beginning a new relationship between the parties, where the exchange is consensual and the shifting of Ngarrindjeri into their rightful position of owner achieves a sense of equality and recognises Ngarrindjeri rights and history. Therefore, Ngarrindjeri propose that any future treaty affecting Ngarrindjeri make use of this concept of the rent equivalent. For example, the government may commit money towards 'buy back' schemes or funding to ensure the Ngarrindjeri can meet their responsibilities under the treaty. Furthermore, the fact of having had land forcibly taken and then having to pay for its return causes much frustration to Ngarrindjeri, as it does for Aboriginal people across Australia. Ngarrindjeri therefore suggest that a second (supplementary) way of addressing this issue may involve the government providing compensation to Ngarrindjeri who have purchased land within the Australian tenure system that falls within traditional land boundaries.

The range of treaty principles and concrete measures proposed by Ngarrindjeri as (part) solutions to colonial injustice and as the basis for a better relationship between Indigenous and settler peoples going forward each stem from a carefully cultivated, contemporary self-awareness that Ngarrindjeri have reiterated over recent decades in the course of their Nation-rebuilding activities. This core strength affords Ngarrindjeri a philosophical, cultural and political literacy that is guided by a set of aspirations for the healthy future of country and people, expressed in terms of a 'national' vision (Ngarrindjeri Nation 2007; Rigney, Bignall & Hemming 2015; Hemming, Rigney & Berg 2011). Indigenous Nation-rebuilding involves developing institutions of self-government that are culturally appropriate to the nation and that are effective in enhancing the nation's capacity to make timely, strategically informed decisions about its affairs and to implement those decisions. These, of course, are also the capacities Indigenous nations must embody in the course of treaty negotiation. Identifying, organising and acting as a political collective, as a self-directed nation that is well-organised with a clear set of objectives in mind, enables Aboriginal peoples to maintain the kind of strategic coherence and discipline necessary to secure lasting beneficial outcomes from treaty negotiations.

For Ngarrindjeri, their participation in treaty discussions, though aborted before an agreement could be reached, at the same time provided valuable political knowledge transferrable to their wider project of sovereign nation-rebuilding. Among other things, their engagement in treaty discussions confirmed some key practice-related lessons of Indigenous nationhood. First, develop and hold your political ground in an appropriately sovereign way; begin by establishing authority in the process itself as a primary sovereign act of political relationship and don't let the state control the relationship, or decide the nature of the process, or determine the limits of the outcomes. Second, keep your organisation disciplined and maintain a firm agenda; plan strategically for the unplanned; know your teams' individual and overall capacities, such as who has the right skills to achieve the desired outcomes; know how to delegate responsibility while maintaining control. Third, remain mindful of the desired end point and know what cannot be left out or negotiated away; know in advance when to compromise, and why—for what gain? Each of these involves the exercise of sovereign decision-making for the strategic purpose of advancing the Nation's long-term interests. For this reason, we suggest nation-rebuilding is a necessary supportive framework for Indigenous peoples involved in treaty and, at the same time, that treaty can be a useful tool for advancing Indigenous nationhood.

CONCLUSION: TREATY FUTURES

The Australian and North American evidence demonstrates that Indigenous nation-building could be crucial to the success of treaty negotiations. Three implications seem self-evident. Those Aboriginal collectives that have begun the work of creating their own governing institutions and mechanisms should continue to do so. Those Aboriginal collectives that have yet to begin organising themselves for self-government should begin to do so. And since the work of Indigenous nation-building is at the level of the self-identified political collective—the nation—the work of identifying the 'self' in self-determination is critical. While building and exercising decision-making capacity is necessarily the prerogative and responsibility of the Aboriginal collective, in view of the colonial depletion of Indigenous resources and the associated diminishment over time of Aboriginal capacities for self-determination or 'practical sovereignty', resources and support from mainstream governments will be needed initially for capacity and institution-building to take place.

Crucially in the Victorian treaty situation, Aboriginal people will need to have resources, capacity and time to decide which collective is appropriate to negotiate over which territory and which issues and to decide the content of the treaties. They will need resources, capacity and time to create their own decision-making structures and governance mechanism that will allow them to be independent in the negotiation process. Finally, they will need culturally legitimate dispute resolution processes for inter- and intra-community disputes and conflict.

In considering the case of Ngarrindjeri in the South Australian treaty process, we have shown that treaty can be viewed as a strategy for expanding jurisdiction and governance capacity, and therefore as a useful technology for Indigenous Nation-rebuilding. Treaty benefits Indigenous polities only if it affirms and secures the self-determined governance structures, resources and relations that can help Indigenous nations realise their developmental aspirations into the future. It therefore should not be viewed as a panacea or as something to be pursued for its own sake—especially not if it merely reinforces the terms of a colonial-style relationship in which decision-making and determining authority remain vested in the state and Aboriginal peoples are treated as service providers to government.

In other words, it is important to remember always that treaty is simply a tool for the exercise of sovereignty, and therefore is a variable political technology also available for use by governments seeking to maintain their sovereign grip on power. Indigenous authorities will therefore do well to remain vigilant regarding the strategic use of treaty by governments. It is necessary to question continually: to what end are the terms of treaty being defined, to whose benefit, to whose compromise and to whose detriment?

Nonetheless, when used in good faith, treaties provide Australia with a valuable political technology for resetting the historically conflicted, non-consensual and unjust relationship between First Nations collectives and the governments which usurped their original sovereignty. Treaty discussions should aspire to create peace and prosperity for all persons and include ways to overcome the impacts and effects of dispossession, imposed control and trauma resulting from past acts of the Australian state that have been directed at Aboriginal people. By addressing historic injustices which have undermined trust and co-operation, better and stronger partnerships among Aboriginal people, governments and the private sector can more effectively emerge. In addition to building these partnerships, the understanding and settling of specific historical claims will better support economic development on Aboriginal lands and in their surrounding communities.

In his 2018 Mabo address, former attorney-general the Honourable Michael Lavarch discussed how certain flashpoint events arising in Australia's recent history, such as the *Mabo* decision of 1992 and the Uluru Convention of 2017, 'draw a line in the sand' between past injustice and future societal success based on true and meaningful acknowledgement of unceded Aboriginal sovereignty in the form of a 'Makarrata' or treaty (Lavarch 2018). He noted that treaty discussions tested and proven at the regional state level can be a guide to the way of a shared future where all people in Australia enjoy Australia's benefits. A federal treaty pathway is enabled by the groundwork established at the state level, since this is where actual interactions between plural systems of law first take place: between state governments and sovereign First Nations. Accordingly, across the Australian federation's various levels of political organisation, treaty provides a useful mechanism to enable coexisting authorities with overlapping and shared jurisdictions to develop a common understanding of the issues and consider ways to move into a relationship oriented to the future. In the words of the Uluru Statement from the Heart:

> Makarrata is the culmination of our agenda: *the coming together after a struggle*. It captures our aspirations for a fair and truthful relationship with the people of Australia and a better future for our children based on justice and self-determination. (Aboriginal First Nations 2017, *emphasis in original).*

NOTES

1. This article was produced with support from the Australian Research Council for projects titled "Negotiating a Space in the Nation: The Case of Ngarrindjeri" (DP1094869); "Indigenous Nationhood in the Absence of Recognition: Self- governance Insights and Strategies from Three Aboriginal Communities" (LP140100376); and "Prerequisite conditions for Indigenous nation Self-government" (DP190102060). The authors thank the Ngarrindjeri Regional Authority; the Gunditjmara People; Berg

Lawyers; and other research partners involved in these projects. We are grateful for the assistance provided by the book editors during the writing process.

2. The nature of treaties as agreements between political collectives is clear in the Victorian Government's definition: A treaty is an agreement between states, nations or governments. This can include an agreement between Indigenous peoples and governments. See State of Victoria at https://uat.www.vic.gov.au/aboriginalvictoria/treaty/quarterly-essay-correspondence-commissioner-jill-gallagher-ao.htmlria (n.d.).

3. The Clan Elders Council argues that treaties should be negotiated with the 100 remaining clans of Victorian Aboriginal nations, but the Federation of Victorian Traditional Owner Corporations notes that, while all traditional owners acknowledge the significance of clans, some traditional owners have chosen to organise politically at the higher level of nation, language group or people. See Hocking (2018).

4. We note that the standard chosen by the Victorian Government is that of free, prior and informed consent. Processes to assess compliance with that standard are essential.

5. International law recognises that formal equality, that is, purported equal treatment before the law, can result in disproportionate outcomes. The international system's quest for substantive equality before the law means that people may need to be treated differently, so as to achieve equal outcomes. Therefore, differential treatment can be permissible under international law; one example is positive discrimination designed to address structural inequality.

6. For an overview of the Harvard Project's research findings, see Jorgensen et al. (2007), especially chapter 1.

7. On 14 December 2016, Minister for Aboriginal Affairs Kyam Maher announced in State Parliament a treaty process for South Australia and explained the need for treaty: 'It's a way of formally acknowledging and recognising the cultural authority of our Aboriginal nations. It's a way to formally consider and address some of the devastating consequences of colonisation for Aboriginal South Australians. It is another step towards justice for those who have been subject to dispossession and denigration under the laws of our society and its institutions'. In his Parliamentary response to this announcement, Ngarrindjeri Professor Daryle Rigney acknowledged 'the significance of this historic decision offering both Aboriginal and settler South Australians an opportunity to engage positively and respectfully in a new shared relationship to our mutual advantage and enrichment. The possibility for a healthy respectful relationship was sadly missed during the founding of the State with all the consequences of the historical and contemporary injustices that followed. With today's announcement hope returns. Hopefulness that we can collectively move forwards on a journey towards restorative justice through proper ongoing contemporary Aboriginal practices of sovereignty and nationhood . . . . Treaty actions need to be dynamic, alive with negotiation and life giving. Treaty actions must not be reduced to mere transactions as if simply part of some Aboriginal Affairs policy and dealt with as if they were merely a 'program'. Ngarrindjeri want to secure the future by taking responsibility for their lives as a result of a negotiated treaty'.

8. For a comparable discussion of Native Nations' constitutionalism in the USA, see Tatum et al. (2014).

9. For a discussion of the effects and implications of the founding documents pertaining to the colony of South Australia, see Berg (2010).

10. Letters Patent establishing the Province of South Australia by King William IV dated 19 February 1836.(https://www.foundingdocs.gov.au/resources/transcripts/sa2_doc_1836.pdf).

11. The readiness criteria that has been devised in Canada in the British Columbia Treaty process should assist in determining the criteria to determine whether Aboriginal People are ready to proceed with treaty negotiations. See: http://www.bctreaty.net/six-stages.

12. Letter from Shaun Berg, legal representative for Ngarrindjeri, to the Principal Negotiator, State of South Australia, 29 November 2017.

Chapter 7

Ancient Spirit, Modern Mind

The Huu-ay-aht Journey Back to Self-Determination and Self-Reliance

Angela Wesley

Shortly before midnight on 31 March 2011, citizens of the Huu-ay-aht First Nations[1] gathered around a ceremonial fire on Huu-ay-aht lands on Vancouver Island in the province of British Columbia, Canada. We proceeded to burn, page by page, copies of the infamous *Indian Act* (hereafter 'the Act'),[2] the Canadian legislation that for more than a century had controlled our lives, as many say, 'from cradle to grave'. Following cheers, drumming and tears, we entered the House of Huu-ay-aht, our contemporary gathering place and on that night our house of government, and at 12.00 a.m. on 1 April 2011, the Maa-nulth Treaty, the first modern-day treaty to be concluded on Vancouver Island and the first multi-First Nation[3] treaty concluded under the modern-day British Columbia treaty process, came into effect. Our Tyee Ha'wilth (head hereditary chief), the most recent in a long line to carry the traditional name Tlii'shin, swore in our newly formed Huu-ay-aht legislature. This legislature then proceeded to enact a set of Huu-ay-aht First Nations laws designed to provide a foundation for our future and the generations of Huu-ay-aht citizens[4] to come.

These events were the culmination of fifteen years of negotiations in the modern-day treaty process, preceded by a generations-long struggle for recognition of our territories and jurisdictions. It was a turning point marking our journey back to self-determination and self-reliance. On that early spring morning, the Huu-ay-aht First Nations began once again to exercise our own authority and jurisdiction in relation to the preservation of our culture, the management of our lands and resources, the exercise of our rights and the operation of our own government. But we learned that the treaty itself does not create the reality; it contains the tools and resources for achieving our collective goal and vision. Most importantly, it provides the governing authority that allows us to take back control of our own lives. That reality, however, is only coming to life through hard work.

This chapter tells the story of that long journey and how Huu-ay-aht are rebuilding our self-determined governance. It examines the sometimes hard decisions we made and solutions devised along the way in order to turn the promise of the treaty into tangible outcomes for our people. And it describes some of the tools and strategies which Huu-ay-aht marshalled to rebuild our internal government: in particular, constitution-building; re-engaging with our dispersed citizenry; making specific laws for the conduct of government; resolving disputes and developing our lands and resources; and how we went about identifying the role of traditional leadership in a renewed government. That foundational work has provided a self-determined platform from which the nation can continue the vital work of translating the rights of treaty into practical outcomes for our citizens. Today, our government is guided by our own supreme law: the Huu-ay-aht Constitution, a document that was built in our nation, by our citizens and grounded in our culture and traditions.

OUR HISTORY

The traditional territories of the Huu-ay-aht are located between Bamfield and Port Alberni on Vancouver Island in what is today the province of British Columbia, Canada. The main community, Anacla, is situated on Pachena Beach, at the head of the West Coast Trail, close to the Pacific Rim National Park Reserve. The Huu-ay-aht First Nations, like many other Indigenous peoples around the world, lived within a complex society where oral history and teachings prevailed. Strict laws were not written, but they were deeply understood by all. Our Tyee Ha'wilth, head hereditary chief, was vested with rights to the lands, resources and waters of our territories and had the responsibility to be the guardian of all who was contained in those territories. That responsibility was bestowed upon our Tyee by Naas, the Creator. Within our society, every individual had a role to play and was raised from birth and before to learn the requirements of fulfilling that role. Our beach-keepers, fishermen, whalers, speakers, warriors, artisans, canoe builders, spiritual people, healers, hunters and many others understood that, if they did not fulfil their role, the entire community might suffer. The sacred laws that governed our territories were strictly enforced; consequences for breaking them could be severe. These laws and sacred principles brought us through countless generations and, in one form or another, have survived. We know what they are. In the context of our treaty implementation and especially our renewed self-governance, they now need to be strengthened and used once again.

For Huu-ay-aht, the intimate connections between people, nature and the spiritual world are clearly evident and very strong. The sky, sea, forest, mountains and earth are said to be inhabited by supernatural creatures, such as the Thunderbird, Giant Sharks and the Ya'i spirits of the mountains. Tribal and family histories recount numerous adventures of our ancestors' encounters with such creatures, where they received spirit powers and treasures that have since been passed down through many generations. Over the centuries, our ancestors grew strong and came to number in the several thousands. They learned from keen and patient observation of the natural world. This traditional wisdom was accumulated by our Ha'wiih (hereditary chiefs) who were responsible for the welfare of their people and for the stewardship of the abundant resources under their custodianship.

Unfortunately, a series of diseases brought by British colonisers during the late 1700s and early 1800s killed nearly 90 per cent of the Huu-ay-aht. At one point, we numbered less than 250 people. Since then, the Huu-ay-aht have faced many difficulties and challenges and have struggled to survive and maintain the ancient and proud traditions of our ancestors (Huu-ay-aht First Nations n.d.). Today, we feel the responsibility that comes with survival and having secured important rights and recognition. We feel the weight of countless generations of our ancestors in every square inch of our territories and within our own being. We are aware of the responsibility we bear for our children of today and those of the future. We also are aware of the debilitating legacies of colonialism that we have to overcome. A report of the British Columbia Claims Task Force (1991: 5) starkly describes some of those legacies:

> The colonial society was an immigrant society whose values were very different from those of the aboriginal peoples. The new society distrusted communal values, exalted the enterprising individual, favoured progress over tradition, and believed that the betterment of humankind lay not in harmony with nature but in its conquest and transformation. The British Columbia society saw itself as the successor of European explorers, who believed they had 'discovered' an unknown, even empty, land that was free for the taking. Thousands of years of aboriginal habitation in the area were ignored. First Nations were accorded no place in colonial British Columbia. Individual aboriginal people were denied recognition, respect, dignity, and even the minimal opportunity that was implicit in the policy of assimilation.
>
> When British Columbia joined Canada in 1871, aboriginal people, who were the majority of the population in British Columbia, had no recognized role in political decision-making. The Terms of Union made no mention of aboriginal title, but ensured provincial control over the creation of further Indian reserves. Canada assumed responsibility for 'Indians and lands reserved for Indians'. The

> government of British Columbia considered the 'Indian land question' to have been resolved. Thereafter, it regarded the federal government as responsible for all matters pertaining to the aboriginal peoples. (British Columbia Claims Task Force 1991)

Aboriginal people in British Columbia were restricted by colonial law to 'using and occupying' small portions of their traditional territories, set aside as 'Indian Reserves'. They also became legal wards of the federal government, ruled by a single piece of federal legislation, the Indian Act which came into being in 1876. Under that legislation, still in force today, the lives of Aboriginal people residing on Indian reserve lands are under the control of the Canadian Government 'from birth to death'. Numerous decisions are subject to the approval of the government of Canada through the Federal Minister of Indian Affairs. These include decisions about personal matters, whether you are a citizen (or 'member') of your First Nation, what can be done with your lands and resources, how your money can be spent, how your children can be educated, how your health care will be provided, how your estate will be managed when you pass to the next world—and other personal matters.

That same legislation, at various times and through its history of amendments and related acts, has outlawed cultural practices such as the potlatch (our feasting system that governed our economies and enshrined and affirmed our social and governmental practices). It imposed a system of residential schools that stole our children, separating them from their families, their territories, languages and cultures. That same system of governmental controls then left us reliant on federal support programmes—simply, and sometimes barely, able to survive. In effect, our future collective and cultural development were no longer in our own hands.

We knew that if we were not only to survive but to flourish, we needed to get rid of the Indian Act and the power the Department of Indian Affairs held over our lives. Our citizens, and especially the elders of our nation, found it unacceptable that we were forced to sit back and watch as valuable resources—our forest resources in particular—were removed from our territories, year after year. We were denied any say in what happened to those resources and received no benefit from their removal and use. Of the approximately 80,900 hectares of Huu-ay-aht traditional territories, only about 1,090 hectares (1.4 per cent) had been set aside in the 1870s as 'Indian Reserve Lands' for the 'use and benefit' of our people. But ownership of those lands and jurisdictional authority over them were held by 'the Crown', Her Majesty the Queen, in Right of Canada. Before doing anything on those lands—social, cultural or economic—permission was required from the Minister of Indian Affairs, a person appointed from a changing procession of politicians ignorant of us, our values and our history, and working in an office nearly 4,800 kilometres away in Canada's capital city of Ottawa.

INCREMENTAL STEPS TO A MODERN-DAY TREATY AND SELF-GOVERNMENT

We had resisted these developments as best we could. Archives and our oral histories confirm that, since the time of first European contact and settlement in our territories in the late eighteenth century and the establishment of small Indian reserves in the mid-nineteenth century, our ancestors fought for the return of our lands and other resources and tried to reclaim the authority to govern. In the early 1900s, delegations of First Nations people from across British Columbia travelled to the province's capital city (Victoria) and Canada's national capital city (Ottawa), and even London, England, to protest the intrusion of settlers, the dispossession of First Nations from their territories and their relegation to living on tiny parcels of reserved lands.

In the 1940s and 1950s, First Nations on the west coast of Vancouver Island began actively sharing political strategies and coordinating their actions through provincial organisations such as the Allied Tribes of British Columbia. For example, the Allied Tribes originally formed to represent the interests of sixteen First Nations groups in British Columbia in the early 1900s and continued its land claims advocacy work (sometimes 'underground') despite a 1929 amendment to the Indian Act which made it a criminal action to meet to talk about land claims or to seek resolution of aboriginal rights or title. That law remained in effect until 1951 when this and some of the other atrocities of the Act of the day were repealed. The Native Brotherhood of BC was established in 1932 and is now recognised as Canada's oldest First Nation organisation. Over the years, it was a powerful voice for Indigenous rights in British Columbia, especially concerning fisheries, education, health and welfare, employment and the right to vote.[5]

During those decades, our population in our homelands was also diminishing and citizens who resided in the main Huu-ay-aht settlement of Sarita on Vancouver Island were displaced by the establishment of a logging camp on those lands. With no other settlement available and no funding to build a new community, many Huu-ay-aht moved away from our territories. A number of those who were removed by law from their homes and families as children to be placed in residential schools never returned home. The tragedy and heartache created by the abuse suffered by many in those schools left a population largely lost and suffering. With no housing, jobs, services or opportunity, only a small percentage of citizens were able to remain in the territories and only began to return in the mid-1960s, when a new community was established in the territories at Pachena Bay.

The Huu-ay-aht First Nations today are one of fourteen First Nations on the west coast of Vancouver Island who, in 1958, formed a political alliance known as the West Coast District Council of Chiefs (now called the Nuu-chah-nulth Tribal Council). The alliance was based on family, cultural and historic ties as Nuu-chah-nulth people (formerly known as 'Nootka'). This organisation grew to become one of the most powerful and progressive of its type in the country and began assuming increased jurisdiction in areas such as health, capital and infrastructure, child protection, block funding arrangements and education (Nuu-chah-nulth Tribal Council, 2019). Although these areas of authority were delegated from provincial and federal authorities, the taking on of more and more authority was part of an overall, long-term Tribal Council strategy that saw those delegations as stepping stones towards the eventual return of full self-governance to our own nations and institutions. We had to start somewhere. These steps, taken in alliance with other First Nations, created the solid foundation for Huu-ay-aht to begin to realise our own vision of a future in our homelands. But year by year, it became obvious that even with increased delegated authority, there was little hope of achieving a much improved quality of life for Huu-ay-aht as long as the Indian Act was the rule of the day.

While some First Nations elsewhere in British Columbia have situations or locations that allow them to survive and in some cases even prosper despite the impositions of the Act, we knew that we did not have the economic potential that existed in those other parts of the province. While our location, a small seasonal fishing village on the west coast of Vancouver Island, is one of beauty, it is remote; access to the nearest populated area is via a 96-kilometre gravel logging road.

In the 1990s, only a fraction of Huu-ay-aht citizens (approximately 10 per cent of its 550 citizens at that time) lived 'at home'. The community had few jobs, opportunities or basic services. Our language was approaching extinction, our resources were being over-harvested by others with no benefit to Huu-ay-aht, our lands and environment were threatened, substance abuse and other social problems were growing. We were no longer the strong, independent, free people we once had been. The situation for our people was becoming dire.

The British Columbia Treaty Process which resulted from the 1991 BC Claims Task Force Report offered us an opportunity to negotiate for tools (governance authorities, lands, resources and cash) that we could use to change our world in a positive way and regain some control of our destiny. So we began to move in that direction. It was our chance to begin the work of rebuilding our First Nation and reclaiming and reasserting ourselves in our territories. We knew it was time to govern ourselves again. It was time to finish what our ancestors had begun. It was time to rebuild our nation and its governing capacity from the ground up, beginning with the people and creating a government that reflected who we are, where we come from and what we want to be.

The treaty process required that First Nations citizens provide approval and a mandate to become involved in the negotiation process. Huu-ay-aht leadership called a 'band meeting', as it was then called, so that citizens could discuss the option of pursuing our goals via a modern-day treaty negotiated with the governments of Canada and British Columbia. Overwhelmingly, the decision was to involve ourselves in that process, and a small negotiating committee was formed.[6] Significantly, citizens were the ones who chose the negotiating committee. They named our Tyee Ha'wilth (head hereditary chief) Tlii'shin, who at the time was Arthur Peters, and the next in line for that position Spencer Peters, as standing members of the committee. Arthur and Spencer are respectively the grandfather and father of our current Tyee Ha'wilth Tlii'shin (Derek Peters). Three other citizens were selected to be a part of the treaty negotiation committee, and I was honoured to be one of those named. Robert Dennis Sr, a visionary and Huu-ay-aht historian who had long been involved in administrative and leadership positions in the nation, and who would shortly thereafter become the long-standing elected Chief Councillor for Huu-ay-aht, was also part of the negotiating team. Robert was joined by another of our hereditary chiefs, Tom Happynook. Robert in particular always worked closely with our hereditary chiefs and was a strong force not only in bringing the nation through to a treaty, but as elected Chief Councillor, also in consistently maintaining multi-pronged strategies outside the treaty process. Those broader strategies would keep Huu-ay-aht on a stronger and stronger path towards regaining self-government. The negotiation team was fully committed to engaging and informing citizens throughout the process, so that the end result was shared by all. This ended up being a critical foundation for our ongoing work to rebuild the nation.

One of the first tasks undertaken by the negotiation team was to work with citizens to document the vision of the Huu-ay-aht nation. It was recognised that the vision was not a new one, but one that was passed on to this generation by those who came before us, and one that we would leave for our future generations as well. The vision statement that was developed and endorsed by the citizens of the nation in the early 1990s and which remains our vision today is as follows:

> Huu-ay-aht First Nations envisions a strong, self-governing and self-reliant Nation. Iisaak will guide us as we work together to foster a safe, healthy, and

> sustainable community, where our culture, language, spirituality, and economy flourish for all. (Huu-ay-aht First Nations n.d.b)

It is a simple statement but carries in it all the striving and aspirations of our people for generations past and into the future.

Being unsure of where treaty negotiations would go and how long it might take to reach a final agreement, Huu-ay-aht searched for and took advantage of every opportunity to have a say in what happened in our homelands and to arm ourselves with the knowledge we would need. Among other things, we knew we needed to define our traditional place in our territories, territories we had never abandoned but had been taken from us. That process of researching our own history—the ways we had used our lands and waters, the place names and the family stories—helped us re-learn and enlarge our collective understanding of our relationship with the lands, and especially our own governance history. For our elders, it was both a painful reminder of what had been taken and a joyful celebration of the land itself. For our young people, it was an education in who we are as Huu-ay-aht. They were at the heart of our resurgence.

All of this took years, and none of it was easy. We experimented and made mistakes, and not everything worked as well as we would have liked. But we persevered in a broad set of initiatives, some still underway today in the post-treaty environment. For example, we completed a detailed study of the traditional uses of lands and waters within our territories, identifying close to 1,000 traditional-use sites, traditional place names, historic sites and more. We conducted a comprehensive study of the most valuable resources in our territories: the forests. As of 1996, the time of the study, a conservative estimate of the value of timber that had already been removed from Huu-ay-aht territories was $8.75 billion dollars. This had all been done without our participation, consent or benefit (and forestry was only one of the resources being similarly extracted from our homelands). Furthermore, it was clear that existing harvest plans of the tenure-holders—large international corporations—would result in the loss of much of the remaining timber resource while the treaty negotiations went on.

Supported by decisions from the Supreme Court of Canada (Haida, Taku River, Mikisew Cree),[7] we sought and established new relationships with the government of British Columbia regarding our forest-rich territories, which required forest companies to consult with us prior to harvesting forest resources. This subjected the proposed harvest area to more intense scrutiny where our traditional use was known or still evident. We also began to take back control of some of our forest lands by acquiring tenures and licences directly. Through treaty and such other means, we now in 2019 either control or have a decision-making role in forests and other resources in approximately 30 per cent of our territories. The total is growing—and we will continue to grow it. This is governance at work. We also worked with industry to begin restoration of a major salmon-bearing river in our territories, a river we call 'the heart of the people', and produced two films about the river and its place in our lives.[8]

Recognising that others also have interests in Huu-ay-aht territories, we pursued and achieved (both pre-treaty and post-treaty) several important joint-management arrangements. Importantly, these placed us at the decision-making tables with the provincial government, with industry and with other influential entities, such as Parks Canada, which has a large national park in our territories: The Pacific Rim National Park Reserve. We are not yet where we want to be in some of these new relationships, but we see them as critical steps towards regaining the ability to have a genuine role in decision-making and protect our territories for the benefit of our people. For example, we came to an agreement with Parks Canada for the commemoration of Kiix?in, our ancient capital, as a National Historic Site so that all of Canada and the world can learn of our deep history in our territories.

Using the treaty process and other means, we have worked on several fronts to preserve sacred places and restore the original names of key geographic features in our territories. Recognising the importance of our own cultural spaces and knowledge transmission, we built the 'House of Huu-ay-aht' with welcome figures that replicate those that historically stood at our ancient capital of Kiix?in. We established an immersion 'language nest' where our young pre-school children and their parents can learn our language and our history directly from the elders of our nation. We launched a revival and strengthening of our potlatch and feasting system.[9] We also built a new administration building for our own government. In order to forge a direction for our future self-reliance, we established an economic development corporation to promote business and entrepreneurship within our nation and among our citizens. As part of that process, we are developing long-term plans to house, employ and care for our people, allowing those who wish to do so to return home.

Perhaps most importantly, we undertook the work of setting a foundation for Huu-ay-aht governance—a Huu-ay-aht constitution—that would recognise who we are and where we have come from and would incorporate the values and principles by which we could govern in a way that continues to be meaningful for Huu-ay-aht.

THE HUU-AY-AHT CONSTITUTION: ASSURING MEANINGFUL GOVERNANCE

In the early 2000s, we started work on a written Huu-ay-aht constitution (Huu-ay-aht First Nations 2014). The treaty negotiations in which we were engaged required that each nation under treaty draft and ratify a constitution that would include matters specified in the treaty. While the treaty process required it, each of the five First Nations that are part of the Maa-nulth treaty also realised that a written constitution was something we needed, and that developing our constitution was more than simply a treaty requirement. It was a way of laying out a government structure and a set of self-governing processes that would work for us in the contemporary context. Each nation undertook the work to develop their own constitutions to guide them into the future. The five First Nations negotiated a single treaty together, but negotiations allowed for each to remain autonomous and have its own constitution and governments, lands and resources.

Constitution-Building

For Huu-ay-aht, and indeed among all of the Maa-nulth First Nations, constitution-making was an opportunity for our citizens to rethink how we govern and to envision a way of governing that would make more sense to us culturally and historically. If we were successful in reclaiming, through treaty, the right to rebuild our community and govern ourselves in our own ways, a constitution would give us the practical mechanism we needed to put that right to work. A constitution could articulate our own highest law, based on our own idea of who we are as a nation and on our own view of the world. We could use it to teach and re-establish the governing roles of our Ha'wiih (hereditary chiefs), to define not only the rights but the responsibilities of citizenship, to teach and re-establish our own principles and values, and to take the best of the governance practices that worked for us for thousands of years and translate them into governance tools that could be effective in today's context.

So we set to work. To begin, our elected Chief and Council of the day (led by Robert Dennis Sr.), much to their credit, decided that the process of developing a constitution must not be perceived as Council-driven or as protecting the interests of that or any future Council. It had to be an effort made by citizens on behalf of the nation. The leadership convened a meeting of citizens and invited nominations for a Huu-ay-aht Constitution Committee. A small committee of trusted citizens was appointed. Two appointees, Jeff Cook and Tom Happynook (who are, incidentally, also two of our seven hereditary chiefs, although that was not a specified criterion) were appointed to the committee and one of the members of our Council, Stella Peters, was also appointed. The committee was mandated to draft a document that would reflect how our people wanted to see ourselves governed in years to come. As time went on and at the committee's request, Chief and Council added two additional representatives, an elder—Benson Nookemus—and a youth—John Jack.

The committee started by educating ourselves on all aspects of a constitution. Our legal counsel, Gary Yabsley, a constitutional expert who had spent many years working with First Nations, spent hours helping us understand the 'how and why' of constitutions and then working with us to identify the questions we needed to answer, never trying to answer those questions for us. Armed with some basic information and questions, the committee then drafted a questionnaire as a first step in seeking Huu-ay-aht citizens' thoughts and input.

Contacting and Communicating with Our Citizens

Our very first challenge was to find the many citizens who had not maintained contact with the nation over the years. As mentioned previously, the logging industry had displaced people from our reserve communities in the 1940s and 1950s, and many of those who attended residential schools brought their pain from that experience into urban areas and were temporarily lost or disconnected from our nation and their families. With no other housing available and with the fishery upon which our people depended severely depleted by industry, Huu-ay-aht people had been forced to disperse throughout the region and to distant urban centres. Only in the late 1960s did some people start to move back home, as Huu-ay-aht was able to re-establish a village in our territories at Anacla in Pachena Bay. But the numbers were small: by the 1990s, only about 10 per cent of our citizens resided in our home community. Others had lived away from home for decades, completely losing touch with the nation. Even finding them was challenging and took time.

Furthermore, memories of having been removed from the community, some by industry, some to residential schools, others for personal reasons, remained sharp for many of our people. Some carried a lot of anger towards the nation for things that had happened to them or to their parents or grandparents, or felt let down by a nation that had shown little interest in them in the past. Again, the impacts of being governed by a piece of colonial legislation, the *Indian Act*, was not understood by most citizens, and Chief and Council often found themselves carrying the burden of blame for our circumstances which, in many instances, they had little or no control over. For many, the efforts that were made to reconnect with them to discuss a constitution were the first time the nation had ever tried to reach out to them. As a result, not only was making contact difficult, but our first interactions often were dominated by anger and venting.

We sent one of our young and aspiring leader citizens, Trudy Warner, as our communication worker in search of our citizens. Trudy travelled near and far, armed with our constitution questionnaire. We counselled her not to argue with people or dispute their comments, and our Chief Councillor committed to following up with anyone who wanted to speak with him directly. That young woman deserves huge credit for perseverance, patience, courage and a sympathetic ear. She let people talk, finding that once citizens had said their piece, they became interested in the reason for the visit and the door to two-way communication began to open. This process of listening and then building a conversation in turn began to build a level of trust and connection within our community that had not existed for decades.

Most citizens' first response to the questionnaire was that they 'did not know anything' about constitutional development or the initiatives of our nation and that they had no input to provide. But as the practical nature of the questions emerged, the topic began to seem less intimidating and citizens began to speak out. Once the conversation got going, they turned out to have strongly held opinions about how their government should operate! Among the many topics and questions we discussed were these:

- What does it mean—to you—to be Huu-ay-aht?
- What are our traditional values/practices?
- Should our Hereditary Chiefs play a role in modern-day governance? If so, what should that role be?
- How can we make things work for today and tomorrow based on our own values?
- How can we make things work *better* for today and for tomorrow?
- What are your views on structure and roles: numbers and terms for councillors, gender equality, hereditary chiefs' involvement, decision-making and process, elections, meeting frequency?
- What are your views on finances and budgets—approvals, reporting requirements?
- What are your views on ethical conduct and expectations?
- What restrictions should we have on the use and allocation of our lands and other assets?
- What are your views on collective and individual rights *and responsibilities*?
- What issues should require approval from our government and what should require approval from our citizens?
- If we want to change or amend our constitution later, how should that happen?

The most important question we asked, however, was a very simple one: 'Do you want to be visited again?' The answer, over and over, was a resounding 'yes'.

It is hard to convey just how important this first step of face-to-face contact has been to all of our subsequent governance work. The community engagement and communication process was both immensely time consuming and costly, but it began to build trust and encourage unity in our nation. It was a valuable lesson learned and helped us to understand the necessary level of citizen engagement if we were to meet the high threshold of approval that would be required for ratification of both the constitution and treaty. If we truly wanted to rebuild our community from the ground up, it was critical that citizens be informed and provide their input on a regular basis and that the leadership took notice of their priorities and ideas. Without that trust there would be little hope of strengthening the nation.

As the questionnaire process went on, a number of repeated themes emerged. Citizens desired:

- recognition of our traditional governing system
- a say in decisions affecting the community, no matter where we live
- fairness in our government and community
- governmental accountability
- strong leadership
- a say over membership/citizenship
- fair and informed decision-making
- a shared vision for all of our people.

The Constitution Committee spent six years, off and on, carrying out this communication (there was no consistent funding for this important work, so there was competition with the many other priorities of the nation). It involved gathering and analysing information about what our citizens wanted and how our government should operate, learning about what it might take for us to govern ourselves once again, and talking about how we might reinvigorate and use some of our traditional governance practices that had worked for us and sustained our communities for generations prior to colonial contact. We talked about how our values, principles and the best of our traditional governance practices could be translated in a meaningful way and incorporated into our modern-day government. We talked about how to overcome the impacts of operating for years under the Indian Act: the colonisers' version of governance. We talked not only to each other, but to other First Nations, looking at what they had done in their constitutions. And we had ongoing dialogue with our citizens about all these matters, reporting what we were learning and the progress we were making, and then listening again to their views.

The Role of Our Traditional Leadership in a Renewed Government

One of the issues that kept coming up was the potential role of our Ha'wiih, our hereditary chiefs, in our future government. Huu-ay-aht is an amalgamation of a number of smaller tribes that once occupied the territories. As a result, there was a head chief, which is the highest ranking, as well as sub-chiefs who held responsibilities in different parts of the territory. The head chief was always acknowledged as being the senior one; decisions were ultimately made by the head chief who was expected to take the time to consult with each of the sub-chiefs. Any resources that were extracted from the land or sea were first taken to the head chief, who would ensure that the bounty was shared among all, and that everyone was cared for. This traditional system of government was sophisticated and complex and there were many roles and responsibilities divided among citizens to ensure that both the people and resources were cared for and the history, culture and traditions maintained.

Despite the fact that our community had lived for more than a century under the *Indian Act*, and despite the fact that generations of our people had grown up in residential schools and been denied access to our language, culture and families, many of us still maintained a strong belief in our traditional governing institutions, feeling they could still form the basis of a strong nation and a strong government. On the other hand, many of those who had not lived at home for years, or not at all, saw only the dysfunction in our Indian-Act government and had little faith that either the traditional system or those who currently held hereditary seats could work for us again.

Yet there was still strong support to include an advisory role for our Ha'wiih in the constitution. However, once that was agreed on, we struggled to figure out how to define that role in our highest law, until one day we realised what should have been obvious long before: that it was not up to our committee to tell our Ha'wiih what their role should be nor was it within our role or capacity to tell our citizens that they should once again be governed by a hereditary system. What we did instead was to create a Ha'wiih Council as an arm of our newly constituted government. We put enough responsibility within the constitution, and subsequently within our laws, to provide the hereditary chiefs themselves with the ability to prove to members, through whatever level of involvement they chose to take, that they could be a positive governing force in our community once again. For example, the Huu-ay-aht Constitution provides for the Ha'wiih Council to appoint an individual of their choice from among their ranks or otherwise, to be a standing member to the Council. They are not subject to election or any length of term. It is entirely up to the Ha'wiih Council to choose the person and how long they will serve. In the Council role, the Ha'wiih representative has the same authority as elected Council members. All Huu-ay-aht laws include provisions throughout that require that the Ha'wiih Council be consulted on all matters of government and law. The Ha'wiih Council does not have any veto powers nor are they obliged to provide feedback if they choose not to do so, but they cannot be overlooked in the consultation process.

This approach was accepted by the Ha'wiih at the time. They agreed that it would likely be the next generation of Ha'wiih who would determine just how our hereditary chiefs and our traditional governing system could most meaningfully be incorporated into our modern governance structure. In practice, however, Huu-ay-aht councils both before and after the effective date of the treaty have increasingly involved our hereditary leaders in the activities and decisions of government. During the process of treaty negotiations, the elected Chief Councillor (Robert Dennis Sr) recognised that citizens would need to understand that the involvement of hereditary leadership was not a threat to the nation in any way. In addition, the hereditary leaders themselves would need to be exposed to the kinds of inclusive decision-making required for our modern-day government if they were to become more involved in governing. Having the hereditary chiefs at the table, particularly in discussions and negotiations around the lands and resources for which they held responsibility for future generations, helped not only Huu-ay-aht citizens but also governments and industry to understand the importance we placed on our hereditary system and the sacredness of our territories, which we are bound to protect.

The first elected Huu-ay-aht Council after the effective date of the treaty consisted of seven members: our Tyee Ha'wilth, who holds an automatic voting seat on Council; and six elected Council members, three of whom happen to hold hereditary chief seats within our nation. Today the Ha'wiih Council, led by our Tyee, is becoming increasingly and constructively involved in the governance decisions of the nation.

Approving the Huu-ay-aht Constitution

The preamble to the Huu-ay-aht constitution provided us with an opportunity to clearly set out our self-governing mandate and goal. An excerpt reads:

> As self-determining peoples, we accept the responsibilities inherent in governing ourselves and seek, with the assistance of Naas (the Creator), to govern with wisdom and respect for all people. Through the act of governing, we assume the power to preserve our natural world and enhance our identity. (Huu-ay-aht First Nations 2014: Preamble)

Our draft constitution included declarations of Huu-ay-aht identity and values. It confirmed the rights of the nation, and the individual rights, freedoms and responsibilities of our citizens. It outlined the structure and authorities of our government, including how our hereditary chiefs and citizens could have a voice in government. It specified how our land system would work, and how our government would be required to manage our finances and be accountable to Huu-ay-aht citizens. It specified the conduct our citizens expected of our governing officials and placed limits on conflicts of interest. It required the nation to put in place a process of our own for resolving disputes that would end the expectation that the Department of Indian Affairs would resolve disputes for us—an approach that had often failed in the past, leaving decades of disharmony and resentment in its wake.

Some of what was included in the constitution—especially relating to law-making jurisdiction and authority—was dependent on concluding a treaty. But, to their credit, the Huu-ay-aht councils in place during the long development of our constitution made a commitment that, regardless of what happened in treaty, we would start to govern in the spirit and with the intent of our constitutional work. After all, while the Indian Act might require accountability to the government of Canada, there was nothing in it that would prevent us from being accountable to our own citizens. In other words, we had every intention of acting in a self-determining way.

When the Constitution Committee and the Council of the day felt we had done all we could in drafting a Huu-ay-aht constitution, we turned to the community for ratification of the final document. It was a requirement of the impending treaty that a constitution be approved prior to the treaty coming into effect, and in April 2007, our citizens approved the Huu-ay-aht First Nations constitution. Sixty-five per cent of voters turned out to vote, and of those, 82 per cent voted in favour of the Huu-ay-aht constitution.

PREPARING FOR TREATY: MAKING LAW

With the citizens' approval of the Huu-ay-aht constitution, community attention refocused on the treaty process, bolstered now by the knowledge (at least in outline) of how we intended to govern ourselves.[10] Nonetheless, our citizens still had questions. They were especially concerned about three substantial matters. The first had to do with what protections we could put in place to assure that the nation's present and future assets would be productive in service to our people and, at the same time, protected so as to benefit future generations. This was an issue that would be critical for our ongoing development agenda. The second had to do with leadership selection. How would we ensure that we have capable leaders who would serve the nation's interests and not their own? The third had to do with practical daily matters. How would things like housing, health care, education assistance and family services work under treaty and the new constitution?

Specific answers to these questions would have to wait; this was a large part of the work yet to be done. But it was both daunting and empowering to realise that the answer to all such questions was: 'It's up to us!'

Self-government means that the nation and its citizens now had the power to set our own priorities, to choose our leaders, create our own governing procedures and to generate revenues in ways that both protect our assets and serve our citizens. These things will no longer be dictated by an imposed piece of legislation or by non-Native agencies located thousands of kilometres away and having no concept of our circumstances or priorities.

In July 2007, three months after adoption of the Huu-ay-aht constitution and following an intense community communication process, 80 per cent of eligible voters and 90 per cent of those voting showed their faith in Huu-ay-aht's future by agreeing to move forward with the treaty. This result made Huu-ay-aht the first of the five Maa-nulth First Nations to approve our Final Agreement. The other four Maa-nulth First Nations ratified the Final Agreement in October that year.

For a number of reasons, however, including delays in ratification by the Canadian Government, there was a long gap between the Maa-nulth First Nations' treaty ratification and the treaty's effective date of 1 April 2011. The Huu-ay-aht Nation spent that time preparing ourselves for the shift to self-government and drafting specific Huu-ay-aht laws that would come into force on the effective day of the treaty.

The treaty recognises a broad range of Huu-ay-aht law-making powers in areas ranging from citizenship and the structure and procedures of Huu-ay-aht government, to land management and environment, child protection services, economic development, education, and the protection of culture and language. All five of the nations signing the Maa-nulth Treaty decided to assume their law-making authority in a slow, deliberate and pragmatic way. From our lengthy experience in treaty negotiation and constitution-building, our leadership in each community understood that returning to self-government was a big step. While citizens had high expectations of early benefits, change would not be easy and it would take time. It would be important to lay careful foundations for a government that was accountable to citizens, was fiscally responsible, and could function as an effective steward of our lands, resources and heritage. Based on that thinking, the nations decided that the first laws to be put in place—and to be enacted on the day the treaty became effective—would cover three general categories, including examples of specific laws. These were:

First: Governance: laws that govern our government, including:

- Government Act (including the overall structure of government, roles and responsibilities, meeting requirements, development of laws and regulations)
- Legislature/executive rules of procedure
- Code of conduct

- Financial administration Act
- Government personnel Act
- Dispute resolution law

Second: Citizenship: laws that ensure citizens have a say in government, including:

- Elections Act
- Referendum Act
- Citizenship Act
- Access to information
- Freedom of information and Protection of Privacy Act

Third: Land and Resources: laws about how lands and resources will be protected and accessed:

- Land Act
- Community and land use planning
- Resource harvesting Act
- Environmental protection Act

Other areas of law-making, many involving sensitive social issues, would be addressed once the nation had rebuilt its governing capacity and once citizens had confidence that the new government could be effective at pursuing the nations' goals.

Huu-ay-aht's design of these initial laws used small, issue-specific working groups composed of leadership, staff and citizens. Participants were tasked with understanding the purpose and requirements of each law, considering relevant policy questions and providing input to legal counsel for the formal development of the law. To make Huu-ay-aht laws user-friendly for citizens, the introduction to each law included a plain-language explanation of its purpose and meaning.[11]

This period of intense preparation leading up to the date when the treaty would come into effect also had a downside. The volume of work to be done was high, time was short and the communication effort with citizens accordingly was more limited. Not surprisingly, citizen support started to wane during this period. Some felt that communication only happened when the government needed the votes. We relearned the lesson and have had to correct that impression later by making sure our citizens are routinely involved in the steps we are taking. Accordingly, one of the continuing tasks of Huu-ay-aht government is to sustain a high level of community unity and enthusiasm for this new chapter in our lives. When the Maa-nulth Treaty came into effect on 1 April 2011, the first action of our new government was to enact these foundational laws. At that point, the Huu-ay-aht First Nations realised the dream of our grandparents, our great-grandparents and preceding generations. We became a self-governing nation again.

THE ROAD AHEAD

The Maa-nulth Treaty acknowledges the right of our peoples to govern ourselves and provides additional resources and opportunities we can use to create a new reality for families and for future generations. But the treaty does not create that reality; it is nothing but a document. The reality we have striven for will only come to life through hard work. The treaty is a toolbox. What we build with the tools is up to us.

More than seven years have passed quickly since Huu-ay-aht became self-governing and are using the tools of treaty and our constitution. Though progress has not been as quick as we all would like, there has indeed been progress. In our initial post-treaty years, we had to spend considerable time understanding what kind of contemporary laws we wanted to have and, importantly, how to make them work for us. We have made small but significant changes in how we do business and how we tend to the needs of our citizens. For example, it is safe to say that anyone wishing to further their education or skills is supported by the Huu-ay-aht government to do so. Elders are provided with a generous monthly payment in recognition that they will not see the full benefits of the treaty, though their efforts made such a large contribution to us achieving the milestone. Attention and resources are provided to enhance our language and the revival and practice of our culture and citizen engagement in homelands and in urban areas. Traditional foods are provided on a regular basis to citizens whether they live at home or away from home. A special panel was appointed to review and make recommendations about the high levels of Huu-ay-aht children in care and, as a result, the Canadian government has committed $4 million over three years to act on the recommendations of that panel (Huu-ay-aht First Nations 2017a).

Our nation-owned businesses are experiencing an upward growth trend despite the need to continue to build the economy of the region by bringing more people into the territory. Although we still remain dependent on forestry, the efforts to diversify our economy are constant, and we have added tourism and hospitality enterprises to forestry and other resource-related businesses. We continue to operate and are expanding our successful Pachena Bay campground operation, which is located at the head of the world-renowned West Coast Trail. Three years into treaty, the nation purchased a market/café in the neighbouring village of Bamfield (population approximately 200), which is within our territory. In 2017, the nation purchased eleven additional properties including an airstrip, a motel and pub, a fishing lodge and moorage, and a bed and breakfast facility. For the past two years, the nation has been putting itself on the Indigenous tourism map by offering free guided tours of our ancient village site of Kiix?in and is exploring partnerships in the tourism industry. For example, Huu-ay-aht has a unique partnership with Steelhead LNG (liquefied natural gas) and are working together to develop the Kwispaa LNG facility on Huu-ay-aht lands. Through that partnership, Huu-ay-aht has been able to continue important work in its watershed restoration and fisheries enhancement on one of our most valued river systems, the Sarita River. Development of a clean energy 'run-of-the-river' facility is also underway: a project that will use natural stream flows and natural elevations to generate electricity. I believe that most, if not all, of these initiatives would not have been possible without the tools provided through the treaty and our own constitution, coupled with the determination of our citizens and our leadership.

Years ago, we articulated a collective goal and vision of seeing the Huu-ay-aht people return to our homelands and live in healthy communities where we have access to education and health services, where we have opportunities to be gainfully employed, where we have an economy that can support us and where the practice of our culture and language will once again be a daily part of our lives. In doing this, we have adopted a motto: 'Ancient Spirit, Modern Mind':

> We must look back to how our ancestors walked and it will help us to take the right steps today . . . We have been disconnected from our home, from our resources, from our food, our language, our songs. Everything that distinguishes us as Huu-ay-aht has almost been taken away, but we are now a modern treaty nation and we have the ability to govern and care for ourselves in a way that we see fit in a modern day. For as long as there is a sun in the sky, we believe that there must be Huu-ay-aht in the land. We're always going to have that deep-rooted connection to our home, and now it is going to be up to us to find that balance between our Ancient Spirit and our Modern Mind. (Wish-key (Robert Dennis Jr), Traditional Speaker for Tyee Ha'wilth Tlii'shin, quoted in Huu-ay-aht First Nations 2017b)

That vision drives our story, but that story is unique only in its details. There are many other nations doing what we have been doing: struggling to reclaim self-governing power and protect their homelands and the future of their children. For pragmatic reasons, we chose to use the treaty process as part of our struggle, but we didn't put all our eggs in that one basket. Developing our constitution, for example, may have been occasioned by treaty, but it did not depend on it. Nor did many of the other things we have been doing. We were going to rebuild our governing system and take control of our lives regardless of what happened in treaty. For that reason, we did not sit back and wait for the treaty implementation to begin before being self-governing.

But at every step we tried to do two things. First, we tried to engage the community—as many of our people as we could—in the decisions about how to move forward. We did this better at some points than at others, but it remained a crucial goal. Second, we tried to make sure that our own values stayed at the centre of our plans and actions, guiding us along the way. These being:

- ʔiisaak (respect—for the community and its people, traditional knowledge, the natural world, the metaphysical world, and other peoples and communities)
- ʔuuʔałuk (taking care of not only the land and the natural world but future generations), and
- Hišuk ma c̓awak (everything is one—the physical, social and spiritual interdependencies of people, land, waters and the wider world).

These principles by which our ancestors lived and led their people are the principles that will inform how we as leaders today in the modern day should be engaging with our people. Because this is the tradition by which our leaders led in the past, it informs the expectations of our people. They know when it's there and they know when it's not there. So we have to demonstrate good governance according to those three principles, which are core to the identity of Huu-ay-aht.

Some other nations are taking approaches very different from ours, and we know we can learn not only from our experiences but from theirs as well. In 2019, in our seventh year of self-government, it is reassuring to hear from our friend—the Nisga'a nation from northern British Columbia, now in their eighteenth year—that their work also continues. It has been more than a century since we governed ourselves, and the impacts of colonialism will not be reversed overnight. It is an ongoing task, and each nation has to find its own way, based on who they are, what they value and how they wish to govern. Then each nation can offer what they have learned to the wider Indigenous world. In our constitution, we declare that:

> We, the people of Huu-ay-aht, by this Constitution declare our unique identity as a Nation and claim our rightful place as equal participants in Canadian society.
>
> We have existed from time immemorial and have occupied and used the lands, waters and resources of our traditional territory throughout history, a traditional territory that extends from the mountaintops to the off-shore areas.

> We draw our identity from our relationship to our land and from our rich heritage, culture, language and stories, myths and oral tradition.
>
> We honour our ancestors and our elders and commit ourselves to the values that they have preserved for us, values that provide us dignity and enhance our humanity. We honour our children in our determination to see these values carried into the future.
>
> As self-determining peoples, we accept the responsibilities inherent in governing ourselves and seek, with the assistance of Naas (the Creator), to govern with wisdom and respect for all people. Through the act of governing, we assume the power to preserve our natural world and enhance our identity. (Huu-ay-aht First Nations 2014)

It is now the responsibility of our leadership and of each of our citizens, today and tomorrow, to work together to make this vision come true. Our journey back to self-determination and self-reliance has just begun. We have a long way yet to go before we can claim to have realised our vision. In 2007, when our treaty began its ratification stage in the Legislative Assembly of British Columbia, my uncle and long-time Chief Councillor Robert Dennis said, 'We each need to ask ourselves: What can I do to make our way of life better? We have a lot of catching up to do'. This challenge was posed to all the parties to the treaty: to the citizens and leadership of the five Maa-nulth First Nation signatories, to British Columbia, and to Canada. But the greatest burden of responsibility now rests with us: the First Nations. We have chosen to govern and have forged a means of doing so. Now we have to put it to work on behalf of those who are yet to come.

NOTES

1. 'First Nation' is a term used to identify the diverse Indigenous peoples of Canada who are neither Métis nor Inuit. The term came into common usage in the 1970s to replace the *Indian Act* terminology of 'Indian' and 'Indian Band', which many find offensive. The Huu-ay-aht First Nations changed its name in the early 1980s from the name prescribed by the Canadian Department of Indian Affairs ('Ohiaht Indian Band') to the more traditional pronunciation and reflection of the Nation as an amalgamated group of nations who once occupied our traditional territories.
2. The *Indian Act (An Act respecting Indians.* R.S.C., 1985, c. I-5) is an act of the Canadian Parliament that concerns individuals registered as 'Indians', their 'bands', and the system of 'lands reserved for Indians'. The Act was first passed in 1876 and

is still in force with amendments. First Nations people in Canada often say that we are the only race of people in Canada who are governed on our reserve lands by this single piece of legislation. From 'birth to death' or 'cradle to grave', this Act defines how the government of Canada interacts with the 614 Indian Bands in Canada. For additional background on the Act, readers may wish to refer to the many references on the internet including Henderson (2018 [2006]).

3. The five First Nations signatories to the Maa-nulth First Nations Treaty are: Huu-ay-aht First Nations, Ka:'yu:'k't'h' and Chek'tles7et'h' First Nations, Toquaht Nation, Uchucklesaht Tribe, and Yuułuʔiłʔatḥ. For further information on the Maa-nulth treaty see British Columbia Government (n.d.), and a short video, *Our Journey, Our Choice, Our Future*, of the Maa-nulth treaty accomplishment (New Journey Productions 2011).

4. Leading up to and after the effective date of the treaty, much of our terminology changed. People of our Nation were previously referred to as 'members'; today we commonly use the term 'citizens'. I use the term 'citizens' throughout this paper, as I find it difficult to revert to the use of the term 'member'.

5. Early organisations such as these remain largely under-researched, but achieved major early breakthroughs for the rights and recognition of many BC First Nations. For further information about the Brotherhood refer to McFarlane, P. (1993) 'Brotherhood to nationhood: George Manuel and the making of the modern Indian movement'. Toronto, Between the Lines. Canada. Also see https://nativebrotherhood.ca/.

For further information on the Allied Tribes' activities which had issues of land claims and aboriginal title foremost in their objectives, see https://en.wikipedia.org/wiki/Allied_Tribes_of_British_Columbia and also http://bclearningnetwork.com/LOR/media/fns12/pdf/Module4/The%20Allied%20Indian%20Tribes.pdf.

6. Originally 12 of the 14 First Nation members of the Nuu-chah-nulth Tribal Council negotiated together in the treaty process. However, in 2001, in a vote on the 'Agreement in Principle', six First Nations voted in favour and six were opposed. Unable to reconcile differences, five of the First Nations that voted in favour of the Agreement in Principle agreed to continue negotiations together as the 'Maa-nulth First Nations' ('Maa-nulth' being a selected name for the group of five, simply meaning villages along the coast). Those five Nations still remain as part of the Nuu-chah-nulth Tribal Council for matters outside the treaty.

7. Reasons for decision can be accessed through searching https://scc-csc.lexum.com/scc-csc/scc-csc/en/nav_date.do.

8. See 'Heart of the People' https://www.youtube.com/watch?v=nkan35ifAyI and 'Return of the River' in four parts, beginning at https://www.youtube.com/watch?v=vc5imz0a2qs; and, for example, New Journey Productions. 2011. Maa Nulth Treaty Celebration. Video. Available at http://www.youtube.com/watch?v=EQeCOugKlJg.

9. Recently my mother, the matriarch of her family, held a feast where 75 individuals—four generations of our family—received traditional or tribal names. This was an emotional and treasured moment for us, demonstrating the deep cultural resilience we had all been working to protect and strengthen.

10. Because the Huu-ay-aht Constitution was drafted and approved prior to approval and implementation of the Maa-nulth Treaty, that constitution would have to be 'truthed' with the treaty once it was approved. In the event, only minor changes to the constitution were required after the effective date of the treaty.

11. For a complete list of current Huu-ay-aht legislation see Huu-ay-aht First Nations (2019).

Chapter 8

Culturally Centred, Community Led

Wiradjuri Nation-Rebuilding through Honouring the Wiradjuri Way

Donna Murray and Debra Evans

> We've all been brainwashed by Aboriginalisation, we have to start thinking and doing things in a Wiradjuri way. We have to heal our nation before we can heal our people. By looking after our land and rivers, our land and rivers will look after us.
>
> —Pastor Cecil Grant[1]

> You didn't wait for everyone's permission because you wouldn't have got it, and we'd still all be arguing over it. Now you've got people speaking Wiradjuri everywhere, and all these books and courses . . . you just did it. You just went ahead with rebuilding our language, and if you can rebuild our language, then we can rebuild our nation. We're thankful for what you've done!
>
> —Uncle Jimmy Ingram[2]

> Finally, young people understand what Uncle Jimmy and I have been talking about for years! Before now, they'd think, what are these two Ol' Fullas talking about?
>
> —Uncle Ramsay Freeman[3]

This chapter describes the transformational journey of two friends who have worked together for over twenty years in a bid to shift the focus from Aboriginalisation to Wiradjuriness. Our goal is big—we are aiming to rebuild vibrant communities that have an attitude to freedom and sovereignty that is deeply grounded in the sacredness of Wiradjuri language and culture.[4]

We share our insights so far, the things that have worked and, equally, the things that still challenge us today. We focus on a series of complementary initiatives undertaken across Wiradjuri country with individuals, groups and communities as we continue to find new ways of changing the conversation towards strategic, strength-based and action-orientated processes. We are choosing our own reality rather than being blown off course by outside governments, incrementally rebuilding sustainable and culturally legitimate governance processes. The Wiradjuri language and culture are the philosophical compass for this process of restoring and making healthy, eternal Wiradjuri belonging/identity.

The first part of the chapter briefly outlines our thinking and work since 2013 in our efforts to kick-start Wiradjuri nation-building. We now realise that some elders had been asking us to work on Wiradjuri nation-rebuilding for twenty-plus years, but we had not understood their thinking. We briefly outline the lessons they had *tried* to teach us. In the second part, we describe Indigenous nation-building principles and how we have adapted and embedded them within the Wiradjuri Nation. Then we list the key enablers put in place to engage with Wiradjuri elders, allowing us to begin to grow our cohort of Wiradjuri nation-building champions. Here we also explore the challenges faced. Finally, we share our lessons and insights in the hope they might be more broadly useful to others. There are many ways of rebuilding Indigenous nations, including the Wiradjuri Nation. We do not pretend to speak for others; we merely recount what has worked for us so far.

Wiradjuri country is a resource-rich and vast region of central New South Wales (NSW) in Australia situated on the plains running north and south on the western edges of the Blue Mountains and bounded by at least three major river systems. The declaration of martial law by the British colonists removed any obstacles that might have impeded invasion, which was relentlessly destructive to Wiradjuri language and primordial custodianship. Today, the Wiradjuri Nation is one of the largest in NSW, with an estimated population of approximately 28–30,000 citizens dispersed over several rural towns and discrete communities. There are numerous Wiradjuri organisations for community service delivery and representation, and several claims for land are lodged via local Land Councils under NSW land rights legislation (Grant & Rudder 2010: 40).

OUR THINKING AND OUR WORK

Ours is a story of wanting freedom, justice and sustainable change in Australia and trying to grasp the lessons our elders have been teaching us. We have now changed our thinking and our focus from a deficit lens to an

Indigenous nation-building lens. We have benefited enormously from our experiences and by reflecting on stories of success from elsewhere. As these stories of success fold back into our own stories, they allow us to think more deeply and strategically about potential solutions to our own set of concerns and community priorities. Notably, our greatest successes have come from the work we have done within the Wiradjuri Nation itself. The ancestral language and culture of the Wiradjuri Nation is now central to how we do business. *It has been vital to restore and reposition deep Wiradjuri cultural concepts as the foundation stones upon which to rebuild the nation.* We tell this story in the hope that you can find a common thread to create your own diverse solutions and strategies to support a rebuilding process in the places you live and work. First, our story honours the unwavering wisdom, guidance and sustained efforts of numerous Wiradjuri elders, language teachers and other community-spirited leaders who continue to turn up to teach, cook and make the fire; drive the elders to gatherings; teach culture and participate in our courses and events.

Our focus is now on what *we* do, not on what others (such as state and federal governments) *are not* doing. Our thinking and our work is undertaken within two complementary frames—Indigenous nation-building and the Wiradjuri cultural frame or standpoint stated in the title of this chapter: Bagaraybang burrambin Wiradjuri-giyalang ('to restore and make healthy, eternal, Wiradjuri-belonging and identity'). But this was not always the case. Over twenty years ago when we first started working together, we didn't understand that we would not be able to achieve our aspirations so long as we stayed in the service-delivery realm, as this is described by Miriam Jorgensen (2007). So how did we change our practices? The thirty years of research from elsewhere[5] has been critical in changing our approach to education and development. However, the real transformation began when the wider Indigenous nation-building work became centred in a Wiradjuri paradigm. This community strengthening work is, consequently, a reflection of the wise practices of numerous Wiradjuri elders and other community-spirited leaders who continue to work tirelessly to restore Wiradjuri language and culture as the foundational asset for rebuilding vibrant and culturally legitimate communities in Wiradjuri country.

It was Wiradjuri elders and language teachers Uncle Dr Stan Grant, Letetia Harris and Harry Lambshead who recognised that there was a cultural match between the Indigenous nation-building evidence from the other side of the world and their own Wiradjuri ways of thinking and understanding the world, filling three whiteboards with matching concepts. Our Wiradjuri nation-building team is now in the process of undertaking more rigorous academic research to fully understand what is working in this Wiradjuri space.[6] By employing a Wiradjuri paradigm as opposed to a colonial one, we also hoped we might contribute towards reshaping the world of education and research.

Wiradjuri elder Uncle Stan Grant (Snr) stated, 'Wiradjuri knowledge can teach us many things including how to live Yindyamarra; how to live a respectful, gentle and responsible Wiradjuri life'.

Speaking after a series of Wiradjuri Graduate Certificate 'Indigenous nation-building'[7] classes, he said:

> Right . . . if we are going to rebuild our Wiradjuri nation then it has to be done in a proper Wiradjuri way. Our Wiradjuri language and culture has always existed, it just went *inside* for a bit and now this work we are doing is waking it up and bringing it back into the *outside* world. We have to ensure this rebuilding work will be culturally right for my people, at the end of the day, I want my people to be Wiradjuri giyalang', I want them to belong properly to Wiradjuri, this will keep the dream of my Grandfather alive.

Uncle Stan learnt Wiradjuri language directly from his grandfather, Wilfred Johnson, who was jailed for speaking Wiradjuri to him in public. He told his grandson, 'one day my boy, this could be good for you, you might do good things with this language'. Their legacy is enlivened today as Wiradjuri students learn to think and speak in Wiradjuri, they learn to find their way into profound cultural concepts such as Bagaraybang burrambin Wiradjuri-giyalang. Somehow, the students are revealing a deeper and deeper expression of their inner identity, appearing (anecdotally at this point) to be finding their own ways of transforming their own lives. Individuals tend to shift their focus to the collective as they appear to be changed by engaging deeply with Wiradjuri *inner* cultural knowledge and Wiradjuri ways of understanding the world.

The Indigenous nation-building lens backs up and compliments this Wiradjuri work as we continue to expand our community of Wiradjuri Nation rebuilders. It means using a Wiradjuri paradigm to allow elders, students and community members to begin to find their own Wiradjuri ways of working towards finding their own ways of rebuilding. They are actively involved in this for the long run; they are consciously choosing to rebuild and secure a future of their own design, for their children and for their grandchildren, and—critically—for the generations yet to come. A large number of the Wiradjuri Graduate Certificate alumni continue to turn up to the course intensives after they graduate—they are returning to our extended family of rebuilders to recharge themselves and remain stoic and energised. They know the nation-building approach is both evidenced-based and endorsed by their elders.

Many things won't change overnight as we all face new challenges such as climate change and a world heavily focussed on economics. From our lived experience as co-facilitators and subject coordinator, we know that the Indigenous nation-building approach to development inspires First Nation communities to think and act differently. Generally, current Australian governments tend to lean heavily on the *standard approach*, which often blames our communities for the consistent failures in both policy and practice. This 'blaming default' by governments was evident in the need for the 'Close the Gap Refresh' presented by the Federal Government in December 2018.[8] Now we at least have the foundational Wiradjuri compass right, allowing for further exploration of Wiradjuriness at a deeper inside level, or at the very least the work is co-designed and centred on Wiradjuri-giyalang (belonging to Wiradjuri).

The two co-designed solutions shared in this chapter—the Wiradjuri Graduate Certificate in Nation-Building and the Indigenous Nation-Building Facilitators Training—continue to be reflexively shaped and reshaped by the instructions of the elders. It's their wisdom and their dreams and aspirations that are considered central in the process of this rebuilding work. This approach has led to them becoming Indigenous nation-building champions who strategically work to protect the sacred foundations of Wiradjuri, while meeting the demands of modern times and circumstances. The centrality of these cultural concepts supports everything the team does, as we try to find new ways of providing opportunities for Wiradjuri people to 'restore and make healthy eternal Wiradjuri belonging and identity'. The elders consider this identity a foundational asset for living a good life and being a responsible and honourable citizen of the planet who is responsible to the generations yet to come.

Additionally, this is what it means to live and work within a yindyamarra paradigm:[9] a Wiradjuri concept about how to live a good life by being gentle, respectful, polite and giving honour. It also means to go slowly, to take your time to gather the evidence before proceeding. This kind of wisdom sits *inside* the Wiradjuri language and lies at the philosophical heart of our bid to reverse the impact of Australia's colonial history on the lives of our First Nations communities across the south-eastern part of Wiradjuri country in NSW, Australia. The view of the world from this ancient compass fills the hearts and minds of our team every day, so when we get pushback from the settler-state, we know how to bounce back.

We did not always have such clarity about the direction we should take. Prior to 2013, we spent the first fourteen years of our friendship collaborating on various 'Aboriginalised' education and community development initiatives. We thoroughly enjoyed working with fabulous people, both Indigenous and non-Indigenous. However, we got into the cycle of responding to each new round of state and federal government policies and agendas. We sought funding and diligently implemented settler-state government programmes across our various communities. We wrote reports and acquitted the programme funding before the next funding cycle began. We were pretty busy, and the programmes benefited enormously from our networks, as we travelled and worked tirelessly towards the shared goal of achieving equitable outcomes for all. Maybe we had truly bought into the Australian dream/myth of a 'fair go for all'?

Today, our orientation has changed. Now, in 2019, our goal is big. The question that sits at the heart of our work is, how do we strategically and incrementally keep moving forward to rebuild vibrant Wiradjuri communities that are self-governing and deeply grounded in the sacredness of Wiradjuri culture?

GETTING PAST THE DEFICIT MODEL

One of the reasons that we are friends is that we share a deep commitment to support Wiradjuri communities to promote their cultural, social, spiritual, physical and economic well-being. We knew our aspirations required collective action and that development of the community as a whole was essential to an all-encompassing, collective well-being. We hoped this could be achieved with settler-state government assistance. At that time, we primarily engaged with the communities through issue- and service-specific government priorities and projects with individuals and groups, with the aim of creating solutions for stronger communities.

However, while the rhetoric of government policy and programmes was (and continues to be) about accommodating community-specific needs and circumstances, their very substance tends to be 'one size fits all'. Settler-state governments' language of 'community planning' was the norm, but Wiradjuri communities were inevitably locked into short-term funding cycles and external programme objectives and locked out of decision-making. Settler-state government policies were, and are, based on a homogenising 'pan-Aboriginal identity' that treats Aboriginal communities as interchangeable rather than seeing the unique cultures of communities and nations as providing the foundation for rebuilding through community-led and culturally centred initiatives. For example, rather than being embedded at the heart of policy and programmes, Wiradjuri language and culture were usually tacked on as a 'cultural extra' to be rolled out once a year for Aboriginal events such as during celebrations for NAIDOC Week.[10]

Therefore, despite the commitment, dedication and incredible hard work of Wiradjuri elders, leaders and community members, we rarely saw the significant shifts we hoped for. We came to realise that our aspirations could not be realised by attempting community development through a service-delivery model alone, for at its centre is a fundamentally deficit view of Wiradjuri—emphasising what was absent, weak, deficient, poorly managed and so on. Our mistake had been to attempt to strengthen our communities through alien corporate structures and governance arrangements in ways that prioritised external government policy and programmes over our own cultural, social, economic and political aspirations. We had become lost in an overly bureaucratised, corporate compliance system. What was missing was 'self-governance' as defined, designed and implemented by our communities.

Instead, we needed to think more holistically about the nation and communities in a way that was long term, focused on culture first—not last, and based on the strengths of our ways of working together as Indigenous people. Wiradjuri elders had known this all along.

LEARNING THE WIRADJURI WAY FROM OUR ELDERS

What became clear to us was that not everyone was thinking in this externally imposed, corporatised fashion. There were Wiradjuri elders amongst our network who consistently challenged us to think and work differently and to look for solutions *within* our communities. Back in the1990s, the late Wongamarr (known as Pastor Cec Grant) was renowned for agitating for extensive social and political changes across many sectors including the faith sector, education and health. He lobbied local governments to erect welcome signs acknowledging that modern towns such as Wagga Wagga are located on Wiradjuri Country. He worked with Aunty Aggie Coe to form the Wiradjuri Council of Elders and started the first Wiradjuri language reclamation programme,[11] which he later instructed his younger brother Stan Grant (Snr) to take over. He travelled internationally and met with other First Nations Christian leaders, dined with the Queen of England and met the President of the United States. He brought back numerous ideas and initiatives and worked tirelessly within the national and international faith sectors. He lectured to university staff, students and school groups on reconciliation and caring for the land and its rivers.

Luckily for us, Wongamarr took us under his wing. He saw that we both were committed and hardworking, but he also knew that we really hadn't grasped the dangers of thinking in a heavily 'colonised' way. In particular, he often spoke to us about his vision for a healthy Wiradjuri Nation and its people. While he was a patient man, Wongamarr was frequently frustrated with us for not understanding the task and gift he attempted to give us and for failing to appreciate the fundamental change in thinking we needed to adopt in order to support our communities to achieve their aspirations. Repeatedly he would say, 'You are not hearing me'. We assumed that meant listening, which is what we thought we were doing. However, he was pointing to a deeper cultural meaning and understanding—a deeper cultural way of doing things—that we were missing.

Part of that deeper way of thinking was highlighted for us in one of Wongamarr's main passions: the reclamation of the Wiradjuri language, which he had begun years earlier along with many other visionary members of the Wiradjuri Council of Elders. This group of fearless elders was a self-funded and self-defined collective that could call any government or non-government agency to the table to report on their outcomes for the communities they represented.

The Council of Elders directed the language reclamation work of Uncle/Dr Stan Grant (Snr) and Dr John Rudder and instructed them to build a programme to teach Wiradjuri language across the vast Wiradjuri footprint. The Elders travelled vast distances and partnered with vocational and educational training providers. In 2010, the Council of Elders instructed the late Aunty Flo Grant to invite Charles Sturt University (the regional university with campuses across Wiradjuri country) to partner with them to develop a course, the Graduate Certificate in Wiradjuri Language, Culture and Heritage. This was a ground-breaking initiative for Wiradjuri. The course was to later provide a vital platform for promoting Wiradjuri Nation-rebuilding conversations. The certificate course continues to produce an enthusiastic cohort of Wiradjuri people invested in shifting from the old deficit conversation to a more critically reflective nation-building conversation about our strengths and a united future as a nation. While Wongamarr may have been frustrated with how long it took us to take up his challenge, we did ultimately come to understand what he had been saying.

How did this transformation in our way of understanding, being and doing come about? In the remainder of this chapter, we describe the challenging processes and hard thinking involved and the extraordinary contributions of so many people along the way. The journey is not over, but we have made a start and are doing it on our own terms. A big turning point for our internal conversation occurred in 2013.

A 'LIGHT BULB' MOMENT

We were in Tucson at the University of Arizona's 'January in Tucson' intensive governance programme in January 2013 when, as Donna said,

> a switch went on in my head, it was my light bulb moment . . . it all made perfect sense . . . the course was giving me the language to describe what I'd been trying to say for years. Particularly in community development, I was struggling

> with trying to move people or communities from the standard, service-delivery approach, to a community driven and led agenda . . . I was pinching Deb and saying, 'I told you, this is what I have been trying say!' (Donna Murray, Wiradjuri participant)

We had travelled to Tucson to participate in the programme offered by the Native Nations Institute (NNI) and Indigenous Peoples Law and Policy Program at the University of Arizona. We were members of a group of ten Aboriginal Australian participants from three nations—the Gunditjmara People from south-west Victoria; the Ngarrindjeri Nation from the River Murray, Coorong and Encounter Bay region of what is now South Australia; and five of us representing the Wiradjuri Nation.

It was here we encountered North American tribal leaders and researchers discussing the key principles and framework of Indigenous nation-building and how they were attempting to implement them in their own nations. What we learnt there was life changing. In effect, we had travelled far to rediscover what our ancestors and elders (such as Wongamarr) back home had tried to tell us both, directly and through Wiradjuri language and stories.

Over the last six years, our work as facilitators, mentors and supporters of a Wiradjuri Nation-rebuilding process has been fundamentally informed by the international research coming from the NNI and the Harvard Project on American Indian Economic Development led by Professors Stephen Cornell and Joseph Kalt. Their influential research produced evidence about how Native American Nations were going about their self-government and nation-building in the United States. Cornell, Begay and Kalt described the opportunity for nation-building amongst Native American peoples as being one where they could re-envision their futures and rebuild their governments and their economic strategies to realise those futures. It was a framework that focused attention on laying a sound institutional foundation, on strategic thinking, and on informed action, and was based around five key principles:

1. Practical self-rule (where the nation has genuine authority to 'call the shots')
2. Capable governing institutions (where authority is backed up with competence)
3. Contemporary 'cultural match' (where governing institutions match community beliefs about how authority should be organised and exercised)
4. Strategic orientation (where decisions are made with long-term vision and priorities in mind)
5. Community/Public-spirited leadership (where leaders focus on collective well-being and future direction rather than self-interested politics)

This advocates a different agenda that redirects Indigenous peoples' attention from the work of claiming rights as offered by settler-state governments with its emphasis on individual Aboriginality and remaining focussed on service delivery, to the work of building their collective nations. It suggests a different focus: on us, not them; on what we do, not what they do; on self-government, rather than self-administration or self-management. This requires a different set of governing and leadership skills, ones that are less to do with externally focused protest and litigation and more to do with internal communication, negotiation and acting for nation-building. It also implies a different timeframe. The governing challenge in nation-building happens every day and is for the long term—not just the next funding or programme cycle.

We were initially intimidated to find ourselves undertaking academic studies in a law faculty, sharing classes with other First Nation leaders and non-Indigenous academics. However, the longer term value of the series of short courses was soon to become apparent as the nation-building principles and North American case studies began to resonate strongly with us. In Tucson, we spent hours with fellow students having in-depth discussions and analysing what each course might mean for the Wiradjuri Nation. Every evening we tried to identify a local cultural perspective relevant to the Wiradjuri that applied to the material we had looked at during the day. The classes and experiences were demanding but fascinating. They built our enthusiasm and inspired us to do more and better for our own people back home in Australia.

In particular, the field trips to Native American tribal communities to learn about their governments had enormous impact on us. Seeing the key principles put into practice and talking with tribes about the different strategies they were using to get results that focused on their priorities and values was truly inspiring and motivational. The field trips provided practical examples of sustainable change, where solutions and strategies were coming from within the community and for the whole nation as a collective.

We felt challenged to ask why we couldn't have this as well. Aboriginal and Torres Strait Islander peoples are strong First Nations within our own country, so why can't we have this? We could see similarities between our cultural, spiritual and relational worldviews and began to envisage a different future for the Wiradjuri Nation that Wiradjuri people would design. The Tucson course and conversations also reinforced the questions we had been asking over many years: Why are we always discussing the negative issues? Why don't we focus and act on our collective assets and strengths? What are our strengths? How can we have the discussions in our communities with leaders and elders? Why can't we have our own Indigenous governance structures based on our strengths? Who gets to make such decisions about those things, and for our future?

As we came to better understand the principles, we also understood that the Harvard Project's message of self-determination and self-governance was in fact a restatement of what our Wiradjuri elders' had been teaching us and expressing in their exhortations to gather Wiradjuri people together for collective action. We were finally able to see the cultural gap that Wongamarr had repeatedly instructed us to remedy. He was trying to get us to change the way *we* were thinking about our business, to think in a Wiradjuri way, to decolonise our thinking. He had repeatedly told us that 'when we heal the nation, we heal the people'.

The nation-building framework gave us a tool to begin identifying and describing the aspirations our Wiradjuri elders had been articulating for a very long time. It also encouraged us to think more deeply about Cornell's interconnected processes of Native Nationhood; namely, 'planning, organising and acting' as a nation (Cornell 2015). In particular, it enabled us to challenge 'business as usual' and to critically challenge ourselves. The big question then for us was how we could use those principles in our work back home. What did we need to do to ensure the principles and languages from North America were relevant and appropriate to Australia? How could we get started?

Our goal was to shape the learnings from North America according to our decades of experience in community and to implement our own Wiradjuri Nation-rebuilding principles back on Wiradjuri Country. We decided to start by initiating a new conversation amongst Wiradjuri people when we got back home based on; telling stories of success, identifying the cultural values which we all treasure to ensure this cultural centre shapes the future governance of our nation; and creating a shared vision of that future. Of course, these conversations were difficult. One issue was that we needed to keep training our own brains to think differently. Now that we know more about this experience in reframing how we think, we are contextualising it for other nation-building champions.

GETTING STARTED ON WIRADJURI NATION-BUILDING

We arrived back from Tucson filled with enthusiasm. We told anyone and everyone about what we had experienced and how nation-building principles might apply to rebuilding the Wiradjuri Nation. More importantly, we looked for ways to share our learnings and experiences with our communities and to create ways to put the key principles into practice in our own local cultural context. For this, we looked again to our elders who have the cultural authority (walan.bang.an, in Wiradjuri). At the same time, we were working with the late Aunty Flo Grant and Ros Brennan Kemmis on developing the Wiradjuri Graduate Certificate at Charles Sturt University using the Wiradjuri language work of Dr Uncle Stan Grant (Snr) and his non-Indigenous brother, Dr John Rudder. This language foundation that lives inside our elders alerted us to key Wiradjuri values that would resonate with our communities to rebuild this internal space. We met with elders to talk about how we could adapt what we had learnt at the University of Arizona with Wiradjuri culture and community contexts.

We travelled our region and began exploring Indigenous Nation-Building (INB principles with communities in Narrandera, Tumut-Brungle and Wagga Wagga. We had previously worked with these communities on education and community development issues and could therefore draw on both kinship connections and existing relationships from which to start a new conversation about how to do things differently. We also understood that these were Wiradjuri communities with different histories, different experiences and views of what it is to be Wiradjuri. This was important. It provided a deeper comparative aspect to our understanding of how we might apply the nation-building principles. For example, we knew we would get different feedback that would help us to create credible conversations, and which might then be able to be generalised to other communities interested in rebuilding themselves.

For us, maintaining a relationship with NNI at the University of Arizona was critical. So it was with Professor Miriam Jorgensen that we hosted and facilitated a series of collaborative community conversations with the three communities, by open invitation. We gave nation-building presentations and encouraged conversations in order to find appropriate Wiradjuri language words and concepts and to test ways of contextualising the overall nation-building framework and principles to ensure it would be relevant to Wiradjuri people. These community gatherings were a deliberate attempt to shift the conversation from one focused on disempowerment and deficit to one that emphasised our strengths and the possibilities for the future through self-determined, strategic thinking and leadership.

This community engagement was essential in helping us to translate nation-building from an international idea to a valid local context and was the necessary starting point for changing mind-sets in our communities. Some of the feedback we received from these early gatherings reinforced how embedded the old deficit model has been in shaping our community and personal narratives. It was difficult for many people to 'hear' the research findings because their default narrative was so often an unfavourable comparison between the United States and Australia. People frequently focussed on what they did not have compared to Native Nations in North America: 'we don't have sovereignty', 'we don't have treaties', 'we don't have reservations,' 'we don't have land', or tax-free income from casinos and so on. A number of people also argued that there was nothing to learn from overseas.

This suspicion of international (and indeed Australian) research evidence and practices, and the pessimism about whether alternative futures are possible, is not alien to us as First Nations people. For example, one of us had previously undertaken a great deal of community planning and development work at a national level that was designed to build the capacity of communities to identify their priorities and tell governments what they wanted. Anecdotally speaking, and in our collective lived experiences of working in government for over twenty years, we shifted to the language of community development and engagement but—in the end—it didn't lead to the changes we required. We now understand why the application of our service-delivery, standard approach didn't improve the long-term well-being of our communities.[12] Something was missing.

From our elders and our experience in Tucson, we realised that the missing element was a *genuine* commitment to being self-determined, to being prepared to *self*-govern. Self-government enables communities to assert their values and priorities, to make decisions about the future of their communities, to implement their decision, and to take the responsibilities that go hand-in-hand with governing. In other words, we needed to work on building our own capacity for self-government, not waiting for others to deliver that for us.

The initial community gatherings made it clear that to start Wiradjuri Nation-rebuilding, we needed to focus on the local community contexts, so that people could envision what we were talking about for their own place. In other words, we were challenged with how to 'Wiradjuri-ise' the Harvard Project's nation-building principles, frameworks and process for our people's own local experiences. This is where our local knowledge and relationships were critical. We quickly became convinced that while some Australian Indigenous communities may not have many of the legal rights and resources of some Native Nations internationally, nevertheless there are notable strengths and successes amongst Wiradjuri people that can be called upon to create a self-governing strategy. In particular, we have Wiradjuri identity, culture, language and many stories. These provide the foundation for strength-based approaches that can enliven Wiradjuri Nation-rebuilding. We knew we could not wait for legal recognition or treaties and rights. We would have to do it ourselves.

DEEPENING THE WORK

After hosting several gatherings in community, we expanded our conversational engagements and initiatives in the hope of bringing a wider range of people into the conversation and to recruit other champions. For example, presentations were given to staff and students at Charles State University (CSU) in Wagga Wagga, NSW, which were telecast live to CSU staff at Bathurst, Orange and Albury. Most of CSU's campuses are on Wiradjuri country and so the university has a responsibility and a unique opportunity to support Wiradjuri Nation-rebuilding. We were also conscious of the need to engage with the mainstream local government for the region. We had learnt from the examples of Ngarrindjeri and Gunditjmara elders and leaders who had worked hard to establish relationships with local government that these offered the chance to evolve into government-to-government relations. Therefore, one of our first presentations was with the Wagga Wagga City Council, followed by a public forum. We had a long history of doing great work with the local city council, so we strategically collaborated with their key people early in order to build stronger reciprocal relationships that have proven helpful.

Before we went to 'January in Tucson', the elders had tasked us with starting a Graduate Certificate in Wiradjuri Language, Culture and Heritage at CSU. Discussions about a course had been many years in the making, with our Wiradjuri elders leading the negotiations. Eventually, we were asked to become key members of the governance committee for the Graduate Certificate, as well as members of the team to develop the course. This gave us the opportunity to include nation-building as a core, integral element in our Wiradjuri course. As it developed over the next four years, that component of the course has made an immense contribution to collectively rebuilding Wiradjuri identity and reinvigorating our Wiradjuri ways. It is contributing to strengthening our cultural governance through the revitalisation of the Wiradjuri language work of Uncle/Dr Stan Grant and Dr John Rudder.

Two reviews of the course were undertaken in 2016 and 2018. The preliminary data suggest we are witnessing a course that is enabling a healing process through the reclamation of Wiradjuri identity on an individual and collective basis. Student engagement with Wiradjuri culture and language seems to give them the tools and language to develop confidence in their approaches to influencing and inspiring positive change and starting up dialogue with communities and individuals (who live on and off country). However, our work, wherever possible, happens in Wiradjuri country and is focused on changing the conversation and envisioning a positive future for the Wiradjuri Nation.

The next component of our Wiradjuri nation-rebuilding activities took the form of more intensive workshops and engagement with Aboriginal people across Wiradjuri country and from other nations. These have been influenced strongly by the cultural leadership of Uncle Jimmy Ingram, Uncle Ramsay Freeman, late Aunty Flo Grant and Dr Uncle Stan Grant who insisted that the foundation of our more recent conversations be expressed in the Wiradjuri language and Wiradjuri ways, underpinned by 'yindyamarra'. This leadership direction for Wiradjuri Nation-rebuilding was central to the successful Wiradjuri gatherings from 2014 to 2017 in and around Wagga Wagga and Brungle. At the Inter-Nation Summit at Lake Condah in 2015, the elders suggested to us that the conversation has changed, or perhaps is—at the very least—changing.

This community-led and culturally centred approach to leadership and development has the foundations of 'yindyamarra—that is, to be respectful and to give honour' (as Uncle Stan Grant reminds us) and 'ngurrbul—doing everything with great love' (as Uncle Jimmy Ingram always reminded us). The wisdom of these significant elders provides a culturally responsive framework for action and direction to implement the strategy of: 'Identifying as a nation → Organising as a nation → Acting as a nation' (Cornell 2015).

KEY ENABLERS AND CHALLENGES TO WIRADJURI NATION-REBUILDING

As our future direction becomes clearer (with apologies to Wongamarr and Uncle Jimmy Ingram, who were always very clear), the question for us personally becomes how we might live and breathe INB, not just for the Wiradjuri Nation, but in sharing with other Indigenous nations and our organisations. As we reflect on our six years of working on Wiradjuri Nation-rebuilding, we have identified certain key relationships, events and even particular questions and statements that have had the effect of positively shifting our nation-rebuilding exponentially forward. The scope of this chapter prevents us from discussing these activities in depth. We present a summary list of them here, with a brief description of these key enablers.

Culturally Centred Leadership from Wiradjuri Elders

We have had the privilege of culturally centred leadership from important and highly respected Wiradjuri elders who explain and model yindyamarra in how they live and the values they embody. They also embody self-determination in their actions and in the way they fulfil their responsibilities to Wiradjuri country, culture and community. While we always valued the importance of Uncle Stan Grant's irreplaceable work in reclaiming the Wiradjuri language, we didn't really understand its significance for what we now call nation-building, until we witnessed students uncovering deep cultural concepts as they absorbed his teachings. According to Uncle Stan, the purpose of learning

Wiradjuri is to instil the cultural concepts in your soul and in your heart so that you may think, be, and act in a proper Wiradjuri way.

Elders told us through language and stories how leadership and self-governance is critical to our survival as nations and as custodians of our country. Uncle Jimmy Ingram and Uncle Ramsay Freeman were unequivocal in instructing us that culture, language and Wiradjuri ways of being must be the foundation for our *entire* Wiradjuri Nation-building endeavours. Inspired by what they had seen and heard at the Lake Condah Inter-Nation Summit in October 2015, Uncle Jimmy and Uncle Ramsay hosted weekend nation-building facilitator gatherings at Goobarragandra, near Brungle, and at Borambola, near Wagga Wagga. The aim was to talk about how Wiradjuri people might learn from the strategies and stories shared at the summit and to create the space for nation-building conversations.[13] As Uncle Jimmy stated at one such facilitator gathering at Borambola in 2017: 'Until we bring the Wiradjuri people together, we won't get anywhere.' Resulting from this leadership, we have begun to overlay the lens of cultural leadership on the key Harvard Project's nation-building principles, in a deliberate and strategic way.

Community-led Direction and Engagement

From the outset, we were conscious that we needed to engage broadly and inclusively with Wiradjuri people at the local level. It was crucial to have the wisdom of our local elders shape a shared understanding of the importance of the nation-building approach and to work together to develop a shared vision, so that we could move forward with cultural integrity and legitimacy. This does not mean that we asked elders to do the work but rather to provide leadership, advice and direction allowing us to progress the rebuilding with their blessing and appropriately for local circumstances.

Graduate Certificate in Wiradjuri Language, Culture and Heritage

The Graduate Certificate in Wiradjuri Language, Culture and Heritage (CSU) has been a catalyst for the resurgence of leaders and Wiradjuri citizens keen to champion nation-rebuilding. The course curriculum includes the knowledge and wisdom of the elders and key leaders, positioned respectfully at the centre of the teaching and learning programme. Seven graduates now make up a team teaching the programme, as they continue to be apprenticed to language master, Dr Uncle Stan Grant. Subjects include Wiradjuri language, culture and heritage, nation-rebuilding and community development: all informed by current evidence-based research and made possible by our collaborative partnership with CSU.

Since its inception in 2014, we have become increasingly aware of the programme's enormous potential and its significance. First, it was an act of Wiradjuri sovereignty in and of itself, being an initiative of a group of elders who conceived of the course as one aspect of the university fulfilling its responsibility to promote and enliven the well-being of the Wiradjuri Nation and who persevered with bringing the programme to life. Second, the governance group with oversight of the course consists of Wiradjuri elders, Wiradjuri course graduates, community representatives and university personnel, which means the course is taught through a Wiradjuri lens, ensuring the cultural legitimacy of the course content and pedagogy. Third—and of particular importance—we have witnessed a profound shift in students' own concepts of identity as they get *inside* the Wiradjuri language and culture. The capacity for healing is, we think, enormous. Finally, the programme serves to create a pool of nation rebuilding champions who are keen to act as multipliers for this work within their own families and communities.

Community Gatherings 'On Country'

As described above, we initially hosted community conversations on country about how to share our learnings we had encountered in the Tucson programme, and how we could, in turn, have these conversations in a respectful, culturally legitimate way in our own communities in Australia. What we ultimately became aware of, as Vivian et al. (2017) have observed, is that the very process of talking about appropriate protocols for community engagement, and about who has the authority to direct nation-rebuilding activities, is in fact a nation-building activity in itself.

Holding community gatherings hosted by elders 'on Country' has been highly significant, not just for the concepts shared, the community solidarity, the opportunity for reflection and meditation often absent in our busy lives, but for enabling significant cultural engagement and discussions to be contextualised and practised. It has been astonishing as co-facilitators of the Graduate Certificate and other related training we describe in this chapter and to watch as the international and national research about INB and sovereignty affirms Wiradjuri ways of understanding the world.

Inter-Nation Summits

A pivotal event in our journey was attendance at the Lake Condah Inter-Nation Summit in October 2015, hosted by the Gunditjmara people.[14] Aboriginal delegates attended the summit from eleven Aboriginal nations and four states and the Northern Territory. International speakers also attended, including the former Governor of Laguna Pueblo (New Mexico, USA), Mr

Richard Luarkie, and Speaker of the Huu-ay-aht First Nation's Legislature (British Columbia, Canada), Ms Angela Wesley.

The invitation to attend the Lake Condah Inter-Nation Summit, as a cohort of Wiradjuri delegates, was enormously significant for those Wiradjuri elders who could make the long road trip. Meeting on Gunditjmara country at Lake Condah was also important. We were able to see first-hand what they had achieved and being in such a culturally significant place helped us to focus on our goals and aspirations. Furthermore, we were welcomed to Gunditjmara Country as delegates of collective nations (rather than Aboriginal individuals) and presented with message sticks that represented the language of diplomacy between Aboriginal nations.

Our Wiradjuri elders were inspired by the strategies, learnings and stories shared by delegates of other nations, and by Angela Wesley and Richard Luarkie about how their respective nations in Canada and the United States went about community engagement to create a governing structure and draft a constitution (in the case of the Huu-ay-aht First Nation; see this volume) and to reform the constitution of the Laguna Pueblo. They were determined to take action. A critical conversation occurred between Wiradjuri members at the summit that has been pivotal to our continuing engagement as Wiradjuri Nation rebuilders. Uncle Jimmy Ingram asked the Wiradjuri elders present, 'Are you happy with Wiradjuri, as it is now?' Elders replied that they were not. Uncle Jimmy asked the further question, 'Well, what are *we* going to do about it?' His questions led to a discussion amongst a diverse group from various parts of Wiradjuri country about what is important to Wiradjuri. As a group, we had heard stories about successes, strategies and processes and saw self-governance models from a range of different nations that generated an observable shift away from a focus on what external governments were going to do, to what *we* were going to do. We see this dialogue as creating a crucial shift in our work—and that may be the case for others.

University and Research Collaborations

As First Nations people know only too well, the history of university engagement with our communities is often one of exploitation and reinforcement of the colonial narratives. Therefore, many First Nations, including us, are suspicious about the capacity of universities to reconcile our aspirations to be Western educated *and* culturally educated and centred in our own ways of being in the world.

Despite this trepidation, we have formed important relationships with the NNI at the University of Arizona, Jumbunna Institute of Indigenous Education and Research (which now includes an Indigenous Nations and Collaborative Futures research hub) at University of Technology Sydney and

Charles Sturt University, each of which supports our rebuilding agenda. Our colleagues and mentors Miriam Jorgensen, Steve Cornell and Alison Vivian have been extremely influential in our work,[15] providing significant support, advice and expertise in communicating nation-building practices and working with us in a flexible environment to co-design, develop and implement new tools and dialogue in the Wiradjuri context. Co-facilitating with our colleagues not only in the Wiradjuri Nation but across Australia with settler-state governments, other Aboriginal communities and other universities has been instrumental in our vision of self-governance and economic development. Their relationships with Wiradjuri elders are extremely strong and continue into the future through teaching into the nation-building subject within the Wiradjuri course.

October in Sydney

In October and November 2017, Jumbunna Institute at the University of Technology Sydney and the NNI at the University of Arizona co-delivered a series of short courses based on the Tucson programme. A large cohort of Wiradjuri people attended the Jumbunna workshops, which allowed them to share a learning experience with Aboriginal people from other nations and to explore how the teachings might apply to rebuilding the Wiradjuri Nation. The experience was greatly enriched by the participation of senior elders, Uncle Jimmy Ingram, Uncle Ramsay Freeman, Aunty Cheryl Penrith, Aunty Bronwyn Penrith, Uncle Ray Woods, Uncle Pat Connolly and Uncle Dr Stan Grant. The cultural lens that these elders brought to the discussions provided a depth of insight about the contents of the workshops that was quite remarkable. We were honoured to share our learnings and take participants through the importance of embedding cultural leadership, focussing on self-reflective practices and ways individuals can build their journey together.

Capturing Our Own Stories and Oral Histories

Capturing Wiradjuri stories and oral histories about our nation has become integral to our work. As opportunities for facilitated conversation and workshops are increasing, it seems that elders are seeking to deliver new teachings. In particular, as stories from other nations—whether from Australia, Canada, Aotearoa-New Zealand, the United States or further afield—are shared, our elders are reminded of Wiradjuri stories, which they then share. As part of this Wiradjuri journey we are now working with other community members on the collection and collation of our stories and maintenance of their cultural and intellectual property. We are part of a group that has set up a non-profit publishing company. This is another act of self-determination in ensuring that we respect, identify and support our elders in sharing their knowledge and expertise.

CONCLUSION

Today, across Wiradjuri country and in many different settings, more and more Wiradjuri citizens are honouring Wiradjuri language and culture as the central, foundational asset on which to rebuild vibrant and self-determining futures that meet the demands of contemporary times and circumstances. Their aim is to restore Wiradjuri ways of thinking and understanding the world, and Wiradjuri ways of being Wiradjuri, Wiradjuri ways of relating and doing things in a way that is right and properly Wiradjuri. They are using Wiradjuri Buyaa (Law), to restore a more balanced and responsible system that sustains people, sustains Wiradjuri country and fulfils their Wiradjuri responsibilities and obligations.

Our main driver for continuing this work continues to be the honour and privilege of having our elders actively lead the dialogue around reshaping the future of the Wiradjuri Nation and our citizens. Sovereign Wiradjuri must speak with the freedom of a sovereign and united voice, rebuilding Wiradjuri through 'honouring the Wiradjuri ways', expressed as 'Bagaraybang burrambin Wiradjuri-giyalang (restored and healthy, eternal Wiradjuri belonging/identity)'.

Our team's work continues to be aimed at restoring and rebuilding our communities, using Wiradjuriness as a foundation for living Yindyamarra and to do the work in a way that could be referred to as 'doing things properly in the Wiradjuri space' or 'Wiradjuri giyalang (belonging to Wiradjuri)'. While it's always problematic directly translating deep cultural concepts into English, our best attempt is that this approach to Wiradjuri Nation-rebuilding is: restoring to wholeness, doing the eternal action of deep Wiradjuriness, working as a whole (habitual action). We are now oriented by a different compass from the colonial one we inherited, focussing our lives and our work in a Wiradjuri way, a way that is more committed and informed by the evidence of nation-building.

The final word must belong to our nation-building champion and senior Wiradjuri elder, Uncle Jimmy Ingram (dec). He said, 'Being Wiradjuri is all about love, it's all about Ngurrbul, having love in our hearts'. He left us some really important instructions, which continue to shape and guide our work into the future. Critically, he was a living example of how to be restored and healthy, how to have eternal 'Wiradjuri belonging/identity' and how to use this as a platform for rebuilding.

NOTES

1. Pastor Cecil Grant (Wongamarr/Wungamaa), Wiradjuri elder, 1998.

2. Uncle Jimmy Ingram, Wiradjuri elder, paying tribute to Uncle Stan Grant's 30 years of Wiradjuri language revitalisation work, 2016.

3. Uncle Ramsay Freeman, Wiradjuri elder, October 2017.

4. We acknowledge the quest for sovereign action, self-government and self-determination by Aboriginal and Torres Strait Islander peoples across Australia and other First Nations People across the world. In particular, we acknowledge the wisdom and integrity of our Wiradjuri Elders and leaders, this work exists because of their achievements. The instructions of our Wiradjuri Elders direct and reshape our activities. We especially acknowledge the spirited leadership and guidance of the late Aunty Flo Grant, the late Uncle Jimmy Ingram, Uncle Ramsay Freeman and Uncle/Dr Stan Grant, who remind us to be grounded in Wiradjuri language, and other Wiradjuri ways in all of our community-strengthening work.

We could not have achieved the outcomes that we have without the support and work of our friends and colleagues, Uncle Ray Woods, Aunty Cheryl Penrith, Bernard Sullivan, Miriam Jorgensen, Alison Vivian, Steve Cornell, Daryle Rigney, Damien Bell, and a developing cohort of Wiradjuri nation rebuilders who have undertaken CSU's Graduate Certificate in Wiradjuri Language, Heritage and Culture.

5. Thirty years of research in the USA was led by Stephen Cornell, Professor of Sociology and of Public Administration and Policy and Director of the Udall Centre for Studies in Public Policy at the University of Arizona. His co-researchers included Joseph P. Kalt, the Henry Ford Foundation Professor of International Political Economy at the John F. Kennedy School of Government at Harvard University, and Navajo academic Dr Manley Begay. Together they initiated and co-directed the influential Harvard Project on American Indian Economic Development (hereafter 'the Harvard Project').

6. This consists of Deb Evans's PhD thesis research and its further exploration, which is being carried out by a Wiradjuri nation-building team, Donna Murray, Sue Green, and others.

7. For further information about this course, see Charles Sturt University, n.d.

8. The Closing the Gap (CTG) approach is the dominant Australian policy framework to Indigenous Affairs established by the settler-colonial Australian Government in 2007. From its inception, the policy has been characterised by a standard western approach to policy implementation that is very much based on quantitative measures of so-called 'equity' outcomes and by a 'deficit model' of Indigeneity, which blames Indigenous 'life choices' for the 'gap' in life expectancy (as measured as a distance from non-Indigenous society) . The current 'refresh' by the government aspires to rethink this framework through a policy approach of co-design with Aboriginal and Torres Strait Islander peoples and their established services and organisations.

9. Yindyamarra means 'the wisdom of knowing how to live well in a world worth living in'.

10. During NAIDOC week each July, events take place across Australia to 'celebrate the history, culture and achievements of Aboriginal and Torres Strait Islander

peoples. Local community celebrations during NAIDOC Week are encouraged and often organised by communities, government agencies, local councils, schools and workplaces'. See https://www.naidoc.org.au/about/naidoc-week.

11. We prefer to use the term 'reclamation of language', rather than 'revitalisation of language'.

12. See, for example, the ongoing dismal outcomes from the Australian Government's Close the Gap Refresh policy 2018. Australian Human Rights Commission. 2019. Close the Gap—10 Year Review (2018). Available at https://www.humanrights.gov.au/our-work/aboriginal-and-torres-strait-islander-social-justice/publications/close-gap-10-year-review.

13. Uncle Jimmy and Uncle Ramsay have often spoken about the Lake Condah summit as inspirational and energising and how they had inspired others with their aspirations for the Wiradjuri Nation. As the co-hosts, they asked Miriam Jorgensen from the Native Nations Institute at the University of Arizona and Alison Vivian from Jumbunna Indigenous House of Learning (as it was then) to facilitate the weekend.

14. Undertaken as part of an Australian Research Council Linkage Project, the Lake Condah Inter-Nation Summit was a formal space for dialogues between Indigenous nations as nations, particularly those with proven track records of outstanding strategic and institutional innovation. Summit presentations and workshops provided an opportunity for sharing transferrable lessons and effective strategies for nation building. Such summits can also build nation-to-nation relationships, expand expertise, and strengthen Indigenous nation sovereignty, self-determination, and self-governance.

15. Professor Miriam Jorgensen, research director of the Harvard Project on American Indian Economic Development and the Native Nations Institute at the University of Arizona (see University of Arizona n.d.), was a researcher with the Harvard Project from its beginning. She is also a researcher with the Indigenous Nations and Collaborative Futures (INCF) research hub at Jumbunna Institute for Indigenous Education and Research at the University of Technology Sydney. Dr Alison Vivian is a lawyer undertaking research on Indigenous nation building with the INCF research hub at Jumbunna Institute for Indigenous Education and Research (see UTS 2019).

Chapter 9

Nation Rebuilders

An Indigenous Self-Governance Strategy

Joan Timeche

Extensive research, primarily from the United States (US) but with growing evidence from other contexts, indicates that the community and economic development success of Native American nations hinges in part on political factors and, in particular, on the quality and capability of their self-determined institutions of governance (see e.g. Cornell & Kalt 2000; Trosper 2003; Hunt & Smith 2006; Jorgensen 2007; Hemming, Rigney & Berg 2011; Hotte et al. 2018). For many Indigenous nations globally, this research points to the crucial role of rebuilding or strengthening of their governments so that they can achieve self-determined goals. That body of research also points to the importance of gaining the support of tribal citizens for achieving a strategic, collective and sustained nation-rebuilding effort.

An initiative was launched in 2009, designed to support self-determination and self-governance among the twenty-three American Indian nations that share the geography of the Bush Foundation's three-state region: Minnesota, North Dakota and South Dakota. It was facilitated by the Archibald and Edyth Bush Foundation (Bush Foundation 2019), headquartered in the state of Minnesota, in collaboration with the Native Nations Institute (NNI n.d.) at the University of Arizona at Tucson, and the Harvard Project on American Indian Economic Development at Harvard University at Boston (HPAIED[1] n.d.) and in consultation with regional Indigenous leaders.[2] As part of that effort, the partners developed a leadership programme called Native Nation Rebuilders.[3] That programme has a strong focus on individualised learning with tribal citizens and leaders who have a passion for innovative tribal governance practices and ways to take these ideas and approaches to their own Native nations to make a positive difference. The programme has now been operating for a decade. This chapter is written in the hope that what we have learned so far may have lessons or ideas to offer to others interested in community change and ways to go about revitalising Indigenous nation governance. I was one of those involved in that programme from its earliest days and, in this chapter, I trace its development and some of its effects.

First, it will be helpful to provide some brief background on the American Native Nations of the United States of America. Prior to European entry into North America, these were diverse but self-determining nations with functioning governing systems, some of which are still in place in one form or another today. However, as in other parts of the world, European colonisation and its frequent violence forced these nations to give up not only the vast bulk of their lands but many of their languages, their lifestyles and much of their freedom to govern themselves as they wished. Imposed governance and legal structures and imposed rules left them subject to US authority in numerous aspects of their daily lives and drove them into poverty.

As of November 2019, there are 574 tribes that are recognised by the US federal government; state governments recognise more than sixty tribes.[4] Together they constitute between 2 and 3 per cent of the US population. After long decades of fighting for their rights, many of these nations are moving to rebuild governing systems of their own and develop their communities and remaining lands according to their own visions of the future.

GETTING GOING: A CRITICAL PARTNERSHIP

The partnership which initiated the programme was itself an innovative collaboration between university-based researchers, a Native-nations teaching and governance institution, and the US philanthropic sector with financing coming from the Bush Foundation. The NNI at the University of Arizona is a research, service and outreach organisation supporting the nation-rebuilding efforts of Indigenous peoples in North America and, increasingly, other parts of the world. As an outgrowth of the Harvard Project on American Indian Economic Development at Harvard University in 2001, NNI works with Native nations and organisations to support Indigenous self-determination, strengthen Indigenous governance capacities, and achieve Indigenous community and economic development objectives. It does this through practical research on how some nations are achieving their self-determined goals, hands-on collaboration in strengthening governance and development capabilities, and educational programmes and outreach services designed to assist Indigenous peoples in rebuilding their nations according to their own designs.[5] We refer to this work of NNI and HPAIED as Native Nation-Building (or Rebuilding).

Archibald Bush, from the state of Minnesota, was an executive of the 3M Corporation (Minnesota Mining & Manufacturing). He and his wife Edyth established the Bush Foundation in 1953. Over the years, the Foundation supported the arts, early childhood education, healthcare, community problem-solving and leadership development in the foundation's three-state region. In the mid-2000s, new leadership (Chief Executive Officer and Board of Trustees) at the Foundation turned increased attention to the Indigenous nations that share its three-state geography, asking itself, in effect: How can we be a better resource to these nations in support of their own self-determination and self-government objectives? Some American Indian programmes already had received Bush Foundation funding, but most of it had gone to tribal non-profit organisations and tribal colleges or to the support of individuals involved in Bush's leadership programmes. The Foundation wanted to shift its focus towards self-determination and self-government, but it realised that it didn't know how best to work with Indigenous nations in that broader arena and that it might have to leave its comfort zone. Willing to experiment, in 2008 it began to explore the possibilities, reaching out to a number of the American Indian nations and individuals in the region and to researchers at the Harvard Project and NNI for advice and assistance.

A first major step in this collaboration was a 'design lab' hosted by the Bush Foundation in St. Paul, Minnesota, where Native American leaders from across the region and country, scholars in the field of Indigenous self-determination and governance, and Foundation staff could discuss the challenges facing native nations and possible strategies to address them. The result was the adoption of a 'Native Nation Building' strategy. The Foundation quickly committed a significant budget to the initiative and hired Jaime Pinkham (Nez Perce Tribe) as their lead executive. The lab was followed by extensive on-the-ground consultations by Foundation staff with the tribes in the Bush Foundation service region, testing ideas, soliciting input and refining options.

These efforts eventually led to a four-pronged, multi-year strategy, launched in 2009 by the Bush Native Nation-Building Initiative staff and NNI with Bush Foundation funding, support and participation, which was identified as a 'Goal for the Decade to support the self-determination of the 23 Native Nations in our region.' The initiative included the following:

Education and Peer Engagement introducing nation-building concepts to elected tribal leaders and staff from the twenty-three native nations through tribal seminars held on their lands or regional inter-tribal seminars within the three-state region. Each tribal nation was afforded the opportunity to participate, some quickly took advantage while others took a 'wait and see' attitude, eventually reaching approximately two-thirds of the tribes by 2016. Peer engagement activities consisted of regional seminars where leaders and citizens of these tribal nations, representatives of other nations, irrespective of size, and researchers could discuss the results of ongoing research on

Indigenous governance and development and share their experiences with each other. The NNI was contracted to deliver nation-building content and, in the formative years, handled majority of the coordination of educational seminars; it continues to serve as primary faculty on the Native Nation-Building model.

A second component was *Technical Assistance and Support* via nation-specific workshops or other nation-building activities in tribal communities. This enabled tribal leaders, staff, community representatives and researchers to explore the practical challenges faced by the participating nation or community and consider how to put research results to work on the ground in support of nations' own goals. The Bush Foundation often hired consultants or contractors, such as NNI, with relevant expertise to assist their target audience. (NNI has completed more than thirty tribal 'house call' sessions from 2009 to 2019.)

The third component was shaped by the first two components and became known as the *Native Nation Rebuilders Program,* to be discussed in further detail.

The fourth component was *Grants for Nation-Building Activities* that involved a single tribe or intergovernmental work between different tribes or US Government entities at any level. This was managed by Foundation staff and no data is publicly available on their grant making, other than their own announcements of awards, for instance at monthly meetings.

THE NATIVE NATION REBUILDERS PROGRAM

One of the priorities emerging from the design lab and subsequent discussions was a need for programmes that could build the knowledge and skills of tribal citizens who, regardless of their occupation in formal leadership roles, could contribute over time to the strengthening of their own nation and the achievement of its objectives. This could be done individual-by-individual and nation-by-nation, but as the discussions proceeded and as we (the Bush Foundation and NNI) learned more about what might work elsewhere, the thinking converged on what we hoped would be a more effective strategy. We set up a programme that would engage a series of multi-national cohorts of individuals from across the twenty-three nations—one cohort each year—who could interact with, learn from and support each other.

Year by year, the cohort approach ideally would have two results: first, the gradual development of a critical mass of citizens in each nation who shared a substantial body of usable knowledge, who shared as well an understanding of the issues and decisions facing their nations and who could continue to work together to advance their nations' distinctive sets of goals; and second, a set of such cohorts who could communicate with each other not only vertically (across the years within a single nation) but horizontally (across multiple nations), vastly increasing the body of experience and support on which all could draw.

This was a major new step for the Foundation, but its leadership, recognising that the cohort effect would take time to develop, decided not only to support the initiative but to make a ten-year commitment, working with the tribes in the region and with NNI to bring the programme to fruition. With that commitment in hand, the programme was launched in 2009. The Native Nation Rebuilders Program is designed to 'inspire, equip, and connect citizens from the 23 Native nations who want to strengthen tribal governance' (See https://www.bushfoundation.org/fellowships/native-nation-rebuilders).

It is a competitive fellowship programme: citizens of the twenty-three nations in the three-state region can apply for fellowships, which last two years. Those who are accepted enter a structured programme of education and interaction that emphasises research results, reflections on personal and national histories, peer-to-peer learning and practical application.

Year 1 of the programme is about gaining knowledge and skills. In the course of the year, each fellow completes NNI's online course on 'Introduction to Native Nation Building' and attends four three-day 'executive education' sessions. These are designed to build knowledge of Indigenous self-determination, the governance issues facing Indigenous nations and the various strategies that Native nations are using—some that work and some that don't—as they pursue their own governmental and development goals. These sessions are spread out over the year and convened at various sites within the three-state region.

With content largely designed by NNI and the Harvard Project research, the sessions promote cross-national connections among fellows, encourage collaboration and group learning and equip fellows with facilitation and interactional skills. Fellows engage with questions such as, 'How did your nation come to be where it is today—politically, economically, culturally?'; 'What kind of people or nation or community do you want to be as you look forward across coming generations?'; 'What needs to change to get from here to there?' and 'How can you engage your community in a collaborative change effort?' They also consider how their own experiences, histories and personal styles of leadership or communication may reflect community dynamics and affect possibilities and strategies for change. The programme provides no stipends but covers fellows' costs of travel to and from the executive sessions and accommodations and meals during the sessions.

Over the course of the four sessions in Year 1, fellows also develop an action plan related to nation-building or a project for their community. The focus in Year 2 of the programme is on implementation of these plans.

Past projects have included, among other things, supporting the constitutional reform and governmental redesign efforts of some nations, initiating tribal-wide strategic planning, working with youth to introduce them to governance and leadership topics and tasks, and the enhancement of social services.

As the programme gained experience, these action plans increasingly shifted towards educating their nation on nation-building concepts. This shift was precipitated by difficulties rebuilders were experiencing in the implementation of their action plans. Here the consideration became one of how could Native Nation Rebuilders become catalysts, promoting broader education and discussion of self-determination and self-governance within their communities. Through 'open-to-the-community' discussions about nation-rebuilding, and related events and projects, most fellows apply Year 2 curriculum in Year 2 to stimulate new conversations and solicit new ideas about community development, self-determination and practical pathways of change.

No group gatherings are required during Year 2, but the programme facilitates continuing communication across cohorts and nations so that fellows can continue to learn from and support each other. There also have been several optional sessions organised over the ten-year history of the programme where rebuilders from multiple cohorts can come together if they wish, sustaining links not only within cohorts but also across them. These have turned out to be valuable learning opportunities as rebuilders draw on each other's insights and experiences.

The Rebuilders Programme was very different from the other activities of the Bush Foundation. In 2014 and half-way into the ten-year initiative, the foundation hired the Wilder Group—an independent company—to assess the growth and success of the programme. The report recognised the programme was young, uniquely operated by a philanthropic entity, identified what worked well and did not, and saw the impact the programme was having across nearly half of the tribes within the three-state target audience. It concluded, 'The Native Nation Rebuilders Initiative is a positive and significant force for change'. This assessment also convinced the foundation that it was time to find it an independent organisational home and planning was initiated to identify options and assist in its implementation, facilitated by independent contractor Clifton Larson Allen.

In 2016, the Foundation established the Native Governance Center (NGC), a non-profit outgrowth of the foundation, to take over responsibility for the programme and for future cohorts of fellows. The rebuilders programme is now operated by NGC, an Indigenous-run organisation and several persons involved are rebuilders themselves, where it has continued to thrive. NNI works closely with NGC and continues to deliver the programme's educational content on Native nation-building. The summary of the report can be accessed at the Bush Foundation website.[6]

WHO CAN BE A REBUILDER?

The Native Nations Rebuilders Program was designed to serve a wide range of individuals. Eligibility guidelines include any enrolled citizen of the twenty-three nations in Minnesota, South Dakota, and North 'who have a passion for learning about innovative tribal governance practices and ways to take these ideas and approaches to their own Native nations to make a positive difference'. They must be 25 years old by the date of the first session, and must be able to attend all four in-person sessions and complete assignments between these sessions. Many rebuilders are employees of their tribal nations or of nation-owned enterprises. Some work in education, some are tribal officials, others are community organisers. From my experience, most rebuilders are female, reflecting an occupational profile commonly found in higher education students and tribal workforces; many are college graduates.

Education aside, it is also generally recognised that females are often effecting change in their communities, essentially being a rebuilder. The age range has been large, but in the past three years, it appears to be in the late 20s to mid-40s range. While residency on their homelands is not required, all fellows must live within the three-state region. NNI and NGC have witnessed a greater impact in Year 2 from those rebuilders who live on their homelands or have strong contemporary ties to their homeland communities as their action plans require effecting change in their nation. Rebuilders commonly cited the challenge of trust and acceptance in their own homelands as a factor to their success. Those who lived off their homelands often had to reconnect or build new relationships to reach tribal audiences, and distance and time became factors in the implementation of their action plans.

From my insight into the process, the selection process is competitive. The application covers past experience and present activities, includes brief essays and requires reference letters. It also requires a written commitment from the applicant and, if relevant, from the applicant's employer for attendance at the four executive-education sessions. These are confidential processes and privileged information is kept accordingly. Cohort size has been limited by funding and logistics but has averaged between 18 and 25 individuals. Not all twenty-three nations are represented in every cohort, and most nations have placed more than one individual in a cohort. The eleventh cohort entered the programme in December 2019.

PROGRAMME RESULTS

By December 2019, the programme had graduated 188 individuals from all twenty-three nations in the three-state region. Graduates of the programme have been involved in a wide variety of activities, ranging from successfully running for leadership positions in tribal government or, in a few cases, state government, through to leading constitutional reform efforts in their nations. One is now president of a tribally owned and operated college; others are heading up social service programmes, natural resource departments and other initiatives. Several cohorts have organised their own networks, based on relationships built during the rebuilders programme, and continue to support each other professionally and personally.

Some examples of initiatives that rebuilders have undertaken, either individually or in concert with each other, to strengthen governance in their nations include:

- Developing an orientation programme designed to prepare newly elected members of a tribal legislature for their new jobs—the first such programme in that nation's modern history
- Establishing an independent newspaper committed to increased transparency and better education for citizens about tribal activities, opportunities and plans
- Starting a weekly talk show on one nation's radio station, covering current tribal governance issues
- Creating a grassroots non-profit organisation, Zaagibagaang, whose mission is to educate the citizens of the six-member tribes of the Minnesota Chippewa Tribe (MCT) about its constitution, government and history. Among other things, Zaagibagaang developed instructional videos and educational workshops and serves as an impartial resource as MCT explores revision of its constitution
- Documenting their native nation's governance history, either for a tribal civics class that is now being taught in the tribal college or a booklet for tribal citizens, and
- In several nations, supporting and helping to implement policy changes in various social programme areas to better address unmet needs or ensure fairness in programme services

Many rebuilders cite nation-building knowledge, personal development and confidence gained through the programme as key elements in their work to produce change in their communities or to seek positions where change can be effected. The impacts have been wide as reflected below and on the news page of the Native Governance Center's website at https://nativegov.org/news/:

Through the program, I developed lifelong bonds that not only benefit the work of Native nation building in our respective communities but also provide a supportive network that helps us heal. (Nikki Pieratos, Cohort 7 Native Nation Rebuilder)

I'm in my second term as an elected representative for the Leech Lake Band of Ojibwe. The Native Nation Rebuilders Program empowers leaders like me and prepares our future leaders to recover our sovereignty in both action and attitude. (LeRoy Staples-Fairbanks III, Cohort 1 Native Nation Rebuilder)

Being a Native Nation Rebuilder to me represents having hope. Hope for the future. Hope for the present. Hope for our leaders. And hope for our reservation. (Maggie Rousu, Cohort 7 Native Nation Rebuilder)

I immediately found new and exciting relevance for my work in both education and language revitalization. One of the most important ideas that I learned over the last year is that we can and we must create laws, rules, and systems that are based in our own ways of being. (Sunshine Carlow, Cohort 7 Native Nation Rebuilder)

SOME LESSONS LEARNED AND KEYS TO SUCCESS

The decade-long experience with the programme has given us insights into what has worked and not worked, its impacts and future pathways.

Up-Front Tribal Engagement

During the programme planning stage, the Foundation's Native Nations Initiative staff held long discussions with American Native nations in the region about the needs of their nations and their experiences with other programmes. Multiple visits by the foundation to individual nations were critical to the planning effort and major aspects of programme curriculum and operations can be traced directly to these early interactions. For example, several tribal leaders expressed frustration with their citizens' lack of knowledge about the powers, challenges and operations of tribal governments; others pointed to the need for opportunities to learn practical leadership techniques, including such things as presentational and facilitation skills that could improve communication and dialogue within their communities. Some wanted to know how other Native nations were bringing their values and traditional governance practices into contemporary, self-determined governing systems.

The NGC continues this strategy and regularly meets with tribal leadership of the twenty-three Native nations they serve to strengthen relationships with existing/new leaders and to identify tribal challenges or areas of mutual concern. The bi-annual NGC Newly Elected Leaders seminar, at which NNI presents Native Nation-Building, also includes a session to identify both challenges and successes for the three-state region. Both NNI and NGC programmes have come to be recognised as a governance resource to Native nations.

Learning from Others

While the Bush Foundation, the Harvard Project, NNI and NGC knew they were trying something new, they also knew they had much to learn and so looked to other programmes—some with Native nations, some not—for lessons. For example, the programme's emphasis on cohort effects (building up a critical mass of linked individuals who shared a usable body of knowledge) and on case accounts of Indigenously initiated change was inspired in part by the work of other organisations, such as the well-known Ambassadors programme of Americans for Indian Opportunity (AIO) (http://aio.org), the Honouring Nations programme that celebrates excellence in tribal government (https://hpaied.org/about) and Bush Foundation's own experience in leadership development (https://www.bushfoundation.org/learning/bush-papers).

A Long-Term Commitment

The foundation's commitment to a ten-year programme was essential and rare for the philanthropic sector. It removed the pressure for immediate results, allowed for a learning curve and adaptation, and sent a message to tribes that the Foundation was in it for the long haul and would not be cycling through new priorities every few years. This provided invaluable stability for the programme planners as well as participant cohorts. The Bush Foundation continues to financially support the Native Governance Center to achieve its strategic initiative of Native nation-building.

Periodic Assessment

Programme managers from Bush Foundation, NGC and NNI have continually sought feedback both from cohorts and from the nations that sent participants to the programme. They were asked about what is working, what is useful, what needs to change, what more could be done. Participant evaluations, recurrent staff debriefings, and a willingness to be flexible and adjust accordingly have led to improvements in both content and process over time. Two examples of changes having an impact on the rebuilder programme were: (a) to make the curriculum less academic/theoretical. Hence different teaching methods are now utilized including videos, decisional case studies, activities and discussions how topics impact their specific nation, etc.; and (b) establishing a minimum criterion of one educational session on Native nation-building for their Year 2 action plan. Some rebuilders had expressed that they were not fully supported, so group projects are now the norm, current rebuilders are expected to call upon past cohort members of their own nation, and the rebuilders themselves created a strong virtual support base through the use of social media and other networks.

The Cohort Model

The programme operates on the understanding that increased beneficial impact comes from growing the number of individuals in each nation who share a broad perspective and a body of knowledge about governance and nation-building, and can also support each other. When cohort members eat together, stay in the same hotel and attend rebuilder-only events, they not only create lasting professional connections but also personal friendships and bonds.

One location for some of the executive education sessions has proven particularly effective in this regard: it is in a canyon in an isolated rural region where both cell phone service and internet are unreliable and there are limited dining options. Consequently, rebuilders are able to spend intensive time with each other, away from the demands of work and social media. Additionally, at the first session of each new cohort, we take time to create agreed ground rules, shared commitments and expectations of each other. These provide reference points throughout the year, as individuals hold each other accountable to their own promises and to the group as a whole. Common examples are encouraging each other when faced with presentations/challenges, boasting about achievements of fellow rebuilders, being advocates for each other's programmes, joining forces on regional issues (e.g. the Dakota Access pipeline/No DAPL movement) and 'just being there' for each other.

Relevant Curricular Materials

A common complaint of Indigenous participants in many educational and leadership programmes has to do with curricular materials that are unrelated to, ignorant of, and often irrelevant to the realities of Indigenous communities and aspirations. The strength of the Rebuilders Programme has been its grounding in Indigenous knowledge, experience and concerns. This has been captured in case materials drawn from research on Indigenous self-determination and self-governance, by including numerous in-person presentations by

Indigenous leaders and practitioners and in peer-to-peer interactions among the fellows themselves.

Academic Partnership

Maintaining the flow of curricular materials that reflect evolving Indigenous experience takes significant investments in time and labour. The partnership with researchers at NNI and the Harvard Project has been a critically important component of the programme, providing, among other things, specific evidence-based case studies alongside broad comparative knowledge of what American Native nations in the United States and elsewhere are doing and learning as they assert self-governing powers.

Support for Year 2 Implementation

Implementation of the Year 2 projects has not always been as robust as we had hoped it would be. While some action plans have produced quick results, others have run into challenges, among them: overly ambitious projects, high costs of implementation combined with limited local resources; and for some rebuilders the difficulty of maintaining focus and energy outside the supportive framework of organised programme activities.

As mentioned previously, the shift, part way through the ten years, towards requiring a minimum of one educational presentation on native nation-building concepts to their tribal audience has helped, leading in some cases to new community conversations about self-determination, governance and long-term community goals. Many rebuilders have utilized that presentation as a foundation for longer term projects, such as creating youth programmes that educate them on their nation's governance and their role, to revising their constitution.

But we're still looking for additional ways to put Year 1 learnings into more effective practice in Year 2. The reality check here is that transitioning from a small cohort of committed rebuilders within a single nation, to enabling the nation as a whole to move more productively into nation-rebuilding, is a big ask. This may be where individual fellows will need to have stronger support, involvement in, and engagement from their own tribal governments in order to contribute to longer term action plans for nation-building.

Financial Support

The Rebuilders Programme is not cheap. Given the geographical breadth of the three-state region, transportation costs have been high, while lodging, meals, facility rental, curricular materials and educational staff for the twelve days of executive education (four three-day sessions) quickly mount up. A program of this kind or on this scale could not have been possible without the continued stable source of financial support provided by the Bush Foundation to NNI (now the Native Governance Center). One could imagine a stripped down, local programme serving one or two nations, thereby reducing transportation costs and further limiting the number of participants, but it has been apparent that one of the most beneficial aspects of the programme is the peer-to-peer learning, support and longer term relationships that come through the multi-nation cohort design. Nonetheless, cost is perhaps the largest obstacle to future replication.

Clarity of Purpose

This is not a programme in tribal management or tribal administration, as important as those may be. Its purpose is to support Native nations *as governments*: as substantive decision-makers exercising jurisdiction over their lands and their affairs in support of their own self-determined, long-term goals, whatever those goals might be—cultural, political, economic. It is a direct response to research findings that place the rebuilding of capable, culturally legitimate and resonant governance at the centre of the success of Native nations in achieving their objectives. At each point in programme design, execution and adaptation, a key question has been: how do we better prepare the fellows to serve their nations in that governance effort, regardless of where they live or the career decisions they make?

The Native Nation Rebuilders Program continues today under the auspices of the Native Governance Center. The centre continues to emphasise a nation-building vision for the programme and incorporate governance education into the curriculum. In 2018, the centre commenced an innovative pilot for a Youth Rebuilders component of the leadership development programme. Youth rebuilders evolved from the Nation Rebuilders Program as a way to equip youth with nation-building training and develop the next generation of Native leaders. In launching the youth programme, the NGC noted that:

> We ultimately want to change the conversation that we so often hear in Tribal communities from short-term, 'standard approach' thinking to long-term, strategic thinking. We believe that youth can play an important role in this shift. Youth Rebuilders will empower young people to consider their visions for the future and the contributions that they hope to make to their communities. Youth Rebuilders is a three-day summer experience that equips Native youth with nation building training, inspires civic responsibility, and encourages participants to dream big. (Native Governance Center n.d.(b))

This is an invaluable extension of the Native nation-rebuilding programme and its vision to a younger generation. It helps us ensure that intergenerational capacity and succession become an integral part of our nation-building objectives into the future.

NOTES

1. See https://hpaied.org/about.
2. http://nni.arizona.edu/about-us.
3. Note that NGC did not exist until Aug 2015, officially opened with staff in January 2016. See https://nativegov.org/our-story/ (Our History section).
4. 63 per National Conference of State Legislators, http://www.ncsl.org/research/state-tribal-institute/list-of-federal-and-state-recognized-tribes.aspx#State, accessed 12/17/19.
5. NNI researchers Cornell and Jorgensen hold research appointments at University Technology Sydney, Australia, and have been collaborating with Australian researchers on Australian Research Council funded research over the past decade.
6. https://www.bushfoundation.org/learning/bush-papers/lessons-learned-native-nations-initiative.

Chapter 10

Can a Self-Determination Strategy Improve Indigenous Health Care?

Evidence from the United States

Stephanie Russo Carroll, Stephen Cornell and Miriam Jorgensen[1]

Among the calamitous effects of colonisation in the CANZUS states (Canada, Australia, Aotearoa New Zealand and the United States (US)) has been drastic deterioration in the health of Indigenous peoples. In all four countries, Indigenous health status lags well behind mainstream populations (Anderson et al. 2016; Cooke et al. 2007). This has been a matter of deep concern to Indigenous nations. High indices of diabetes, heart disease, obesity and other ailments, poorly treated mental and behavioural health problems, short life expectancies and other health issues have profound effects on the ability of Indigenous nations to pursue their cultural, social and economic goals (see e.g. Durie 1999; Feir, Gillezeau & Jones 2018; Harvard Project on American Indian Economic Development 2008a; McMeeking 2019).

Indigenous peoples are not the only ones concerned. Numerous government reports and academic analyses have pointed to improvements in Indigenous health as one of the keys to improvements in other areas of Indigenous welfare, and considerable policy energy and money have been spent on the problem (Rainie et al. 2015). Over the years, settler-colonial governments have developed an array of centrally conceived and administered health programmes for Indigenous peoples. Yet Indigenous health disparities in the CANZUS states have proven stubbornly persistent.

This chapter asks whether an Indigenous self-determination and self-governance strategy could make a difference in improving health care in Indigenous communities. Research on this question is scarce but growing, and it suggests a positive response. Our purpose is to add details from the United States to assist in answering the question, with a focus on three things:

the logic of Indigenous—in this case, tribal—efforts to expand their control over health care, the forms that expansion is taking and the continuing challenges faced by the Indigenous nations involved. We begin by considering the existing literature and what it has to say on Indigenous self-determination in health-care delivery in the CANZUS states, and we present an historical overview of the shift towards the tribal control of health-care delivery in the United States. In the process, we draw on more than a decade of information from a series of research projects related to Indigenous health care in which the authors have been variously engaged, including:

- Interviews in 2007–2008 with health directors, health-related staff and tribal legislators at nine American Indian Nations. The interviews focused on decision-making in tribal health management, on the effect of an increased tribal role on citizens' access to health care and on the benefits and challenges of tribal control of health services.
- Interviews in the same period with nine individuals working on tribal health issues in supra-tribal health organisations, US Government agencies and academic institutions, with a comparable focus.
- Case studies of tribal health-care programmes in six American Indian Nations, carried out in 2009 and 2010. Our inquiries focused on the extent of tribal control of health-care delivery, reasons for moving to tribal control, management and delivery strategies, and changes, challenges and apparent benefits—if any—associated with increased tribal control.[2]
- Case accounts of health programmes operated by American Indian Nations or by consortia of nations that won awards between 1999 and 2016 from the Honoring Contributions in the Governance of American Indian Nations program ('Honoring Nations') administered at Harvard University, a programme that identifies and celebrates excellence and innovation in tribal governance.[3]
- A review of academic, professional and lay literatures, and electronic information sources on tribal health-care initiatives and access to health care in Native communities, published between 2006 and 2018.[4]

SELF-DETERMINATION: THE US CONCEPT AND PRACTICE

In the mid-1970s, through the *Indian Self-Determination and Education Assistance Act* (U.S. Congress 1976) and related actions, the US Government moved to a formal policy of tribal self-determination in American Indian affairs. There is some question as to whether the government had genuine self-determination in mind when it formulated its policy (see e.g. Barsh & Trosper 1975; Castile 1998: chapter 2), but in subsequent years, American Indian Nations, acting on their own interpretation of what self-determination meant, moved quickly to put it into action, displacing the Bureau of Indian Affairs (BIA) and other federal agencies as the primary decision-makers on Indian lands (Cornell 1988; Evans 2011; Johnson & Rhoades 2000; Nagel 1997; Noren, Kindig & Sprenger 1998; Steinman 2005, 2012).

This shift to practical tribal self-determination—whatever its original conception or intent—has served American Indian Nations well. Research shows positive results across a variety of issue areas, from economic development and natural resources management to justice systems. Tribal economies, for example, tend to grow more vigorously when tribal governments are the ones making organisational, development and resource-use decisions (Cornell & Kalt 2007). American Indian Nations that manage their own timber enterprises generally produce higher profits than BIA managers (Krepps & Caves 1994), and there is evidence that tribal forest managers can outperform federal forest managers on adjacent lands (Berry 2009). Several nations have shown that they do a better job than the BIA of managing Indian land title processes (Edwards, Morris & Red Thunder 2009; Harvard Project on American Indian Economic Development 2006). There also is evidence that justice system performance is enhanced under tribal control (Wakeling et al. 2001; Champagne & Goldberg 2012). This result may not be limited to the United States. There are accumulating indications of comparable results among First Nations in Canada, New Zealand and Australia.[5]

When using the term Indigenous self-determination in this chapter, we refer specifically to the vesting of substantial governmental authority, accountability and resources in Indigenous political entities (e.g. nations, tribes, iwi, hapu or communities) or in authoritative Indigenous organisational collaborations freely entered into by those entities to serve their purposes. Indigenous self-determination, in this view, is both collective and governmental; it is about Indigenous political collectives (not individual persons) taking control of their own affairs. While precise definitions may vary, in this chapter and in the context of health-care delivery, we use the terms Indigenous 'self-determination', 'control', and 'governance' interchangeably. In all of the cases we refer to below, this involves Indigenous nations having increased decision-making authority over and accountability for the purposes, design, organisation and implementation of health-care services.

To be sure, putting Indigenous nations or communities in charge of their own affairs is only the first step on the pathway to better results. Much of the research referred to above indicates that Native nations have to be able to back up decision-making power with capable and culturally resonant governance. Only then is the potential inherent in tribal control likely to be realised and sustained (e.g. Cornell & Kalt 2000; Jorgensen 2007). With that caution in mind, however, the evidence is clear across several policy domains: as a strategy for improving social welfare, Indigenous self-determination works. The question is, can it have comparable results in health care?

Emerging results suggest it does. For example, a US National Indian Health Board survey indicated that increased tribal control of health-care delivery led to expanded facilities, expanded services and increased user satisfaction (Dixon et al. 1998). The US Indian Health Service's Tribal Self-Governance Office reports that self-governance on the part of Native nations has led to innovations and improvements to care in rural locations, more wellness and prevention programmes, more chronic disease management, increased access to care through home health and transportation and reduced costs (US Department of Health and Human Services n.d.). In Canada, (Lavoie et al. 2010) found that Indigenous control of local health-care services improved hospitalisation rates, while other work has found that practical indications of collective self-determination are associated with improved health in Indigenous communities (e.g. Chandler & Lalonde 2009; Tiessen, Taylor & Kirmayer 2010). In a scoping analysis of sixty-two publications on Indigenous control of primary health-care services in the United States, Canada and Australia, (Harfield et al. 2018) found that Indigenous control led to more accessible health services, greater community engagement in health care, a commitment to continuous quality improvement, a more culturally appropriate and skilled workforce, increased flexibility in approaches to care, an holistic health-care model, and increased community and individual self-determination and empowerment.

THE SHIFT TO SELF-DETERMINED HEALTH-CARE DELIVERY IN THE UNITED STATES

Health conditions among American Indian populations located on reservations and in Alaskan Native communities are among the worst in the United States (Brenneman et al. 2000; Liao et al. 2003; US Department of Human Services 2018). For the period 1997 to 2014, following a persistent pattern since colonisation, life expectancy was lower and infant mortality rates were higher for American Indians and Alaskan Natives than for the total US population (Anderson et al. 2016). Poor health has adverse ripple effects within these communities, draining them of human and financial resources; complicating educational programmes, workforce development, and economic development; and undermining the cross-generational transfer of culture and kinship (Harvard Project on American Indian Economic Development 2008a).

The United States has a government-to-government relationship with American Indian and Alaska Native nations based on the U.S. Constitution, executive orders, statutory law and treaties concluded between the federal government and many of those nations. As part of that relationship, the US Government has committed itself to providing health services in those communities.[6] Since 1955, this has been the responsibility of the Indian Health Service in the US Department of Health and Human Services (IHS). While IHS efforts have improved a number of health indicators for these populations, such as rates of infant mortality and infectious disease, they have been less effective in addressing chronic diseases and behavioural health problems and inequalities in mortality and morbidity persist (Roubideaux 2002).

In 1975, responding to demands by American Indian Nations for greater control over their affairs, Congress passed the *Indian Self-Determination and Education Assistance Act* (Public Law 93-638). This legislation made it possible for tribes to contract with the US Government for tribal management of federally funded services, including health care. Contracts under this law, commonly known as '638 contracts', allow tribes to administer federally funded health-related services ranging from facilities construction and health education to direct care, as long as they provide at least the level of service that IHS previously provided.

While P.L. 93-638 led to a partial decentralisation of the Indian health-care system and a shift of some local administrative control into tribal hands, tribes believed that it did not go far enough (Kunitz 1996; Pfefferbaum et al. 1997). Congress amended the law in 1992, allowing tribes to engage in self-governance 'compacting'. Such 'compacts' fund tribes or tribal consortia through block grant-like mechanisms, which are often multi-year agreements (Dixon 2001; Pfefferbaum et al. 1997). Compared to 638 contracts, compacting gives tribes increased flexibility regarding service design, programme administration and use of funds. It also facilitates a further shift in authority from IHS to tribes and from IHS priorities to tribal ones (Roubideaux 2002). In effect, with compacting, tribes add a design and organisational role to the managerial or administrative role available through contracting.

Native nations took quick advantage of these new opportunities. By 1996, tribes were operating 12 of 49 hospitals on Indian lands and 379 of 492 ambulatory facilities, including 168 Alaska Village clinics (Johnson & Rhoades 2000), primarily through a shift from IHS to tribal control (Noren, Kindig & Sprenger 1998). This trend has continued. By July 2016, approximately 40 per cent of the IHS budget had been transferred to 350 tribes (of the then 567 federally recognised tribes in the United States) via 90 compacts (US Department of Health and Human Services 2016). In 2018, more than 60 per cent of the IHS budget was spent by tribes through contracts and compacts instead of by IHS directly and the majority of IHS facilities were operated by tribes (US Department of Health and Human Services 2018).

In addition, some tribes with significant discretionary revenues had begun to supplement federal funds with their own dollars, often in the form of third-party revenues from government or private insurance reimbursements, thereby further expanding the scope of tribal control (Government Accountability Office 2011).[7] Tribes today design and operate preventive care programmes, medical clinics, behavioural and mental health programmes, and hospitals. Some have taken almost complete control over the provision of health care to their own citizens.[8]

Indigenous control of health care can be organised in a number of ways. In the United States, it generally takes three forms. In some cases, it is organised nation by nation (i.e. tribe by tribe); an example is the Winnebago Comprehensive Healthcare System of the Winnebago Tribe of Nebraska. In others, it is organised through consortia of nations or associations of Indigenous organisations; an example is the Alaska Native Tribal Health Consortium. In some larger nations, control may be vested in sub-tribal or local governmental organisations; an example is Sage Memorial Hospital, managed by the Navajo Health Foundation and serving 8 of the 110 chapters within the Navajo Nation. In all of these cases, Indigenous control increases to the extent that Indigenous political collectives (nations, tribes) assume greater decision-making authority over the organisation and delivery of health-care services to their people.

What has been the effect of this transition to tribal control? There has been insufficient time for most long-term health outcomes—if any—to appear. However, it is not too early to consider how tribal control has affected the organisation and delivery of health care in Native communities or the challenges that the shift towards an increased Indigenous role in health-care organisation and decision-making pose for Native communities. And it is certainly not too early to consider the logic of the transition itself: Why are Native nations in the United States moving in this direction?

THE LOGIC OF INCREASED TRIBAL CONTROL

Our research identified a number of factors that were influential in tribal decisions to take greater control of health-care delivery. Some of those factors are national; others are local and context specific.

National Factors

The most obvious national factors—and those that probably affect the largest number of tribes—are perceived shortcomings in the IHS system. The one most often identified, both in our interviews and case studies and in the literature, is funding. IHS funding levels have been well below the demonstrated need for years, leading to inadequacies in personnel and programmes (Adams 2000; Harvard Project on American Indian Economic Development 2008a; Joe 2002; Noren et al. 1998; US Commission on Civil Rights 2004; Westmoreland & Watson 2006). Underfunding has persisted. In 2017, the federal government spent US$3,332 per IHS beneficiary for medical services compared to US$12,829 per Medicare beneficiary,[9] while the national health per capita spending was US$9,207 (National Tribal Budget Formulation Workgroup 2018). Complicating matters further with respect to tribal control, until at least 2012 tribes entering into contracts or compacts with the federal government for delivery of health services were insufficiently funded for administrative support costs (Government Accountability Office 2011; Roubideaux 2002).[10]

Another concern for tribes is a mismatch between community needs and the way IHS is organised for service delivery. In tribal communities where extreme and long-term poverty compounds health issues, it is difficult for IHS alone to provide the wrap-around services their clients need (Brown et al. 2002). Where tribes are small and/or remote, IHS tends to concentrate services in centralised locations, making access difficult and often generic (Pfefferbaum et al. 1997; U.S. Commission on Civil Rights 2004).

We also repeatedly encountered the view that the IHS system offers a top-down approach to health care in which policy is developed nationally and applied across diverse local situations. A number of our interviewees argued that this results in a disconnect between tribal priorities and IHS health concerns, between tribal preferences and IHS approaches to treatment, and between the cultural realities of local communities and centrally determined health policies. This view echoes earlier research (Dixon et al. 1998; Noren, Kindig & Sprenger 1998). Furthermore, with the exception of its diabetes programmes, IHS historically has tended to pay more attention to health services and sanitation issues than to the socially complex chronic disease and behavioural health issues that are of urgent concern across Native nations (Roubideaux 2002). On the other hand—and not surprisingly—IHS responsiveness makes a difference: Adams (2000) found that tribes were less likely to move towards tribal control of health-care delivery if they felt IHS took account of their concerns.

Tribal Factors

Most tribes are eager to take control of as much of what happens on their lands as possible. Health care is no exception. They would like to have control over their own health care if they can figure out how to do it well (Adams 2000; Dixon et al. 1998; Bylander 2017).

Experience and examples apparently matter. There is some evidence that tribes that have successfully assumed decision-making power in other federal programme areas may be more inclined to tackle health care (Adams 2000). Several of our interviewees also indicated that seeing another tribe successfully manage health care was a spur to action, especially if the other tribe's enhanced role led to increased community satisfaction with health-care delivery.

At the same time, some tribes that have treaties with the federal government (treaties in which that government promised to provide health care) understand the federal responsibility for Indian health care as a reason to limit their own involvement. They assert that tribal administration of health-care delivery lets the federal government off the hook on treaty promises (Dixon et al. 1998; Joe 2002). But this is not a universal view and has changed over time. Our interviews and case studies found more nuanced perspectives. While determined to hold the US Government to its promises, tribes increasingly recognise that federal treaty and trust obligations do not exempt tribal governments from their own responsibilities for citizen welfare. After years of largely ineffective lobbying for increased federal funding of health programmes, some tribal governments have concluded that if they want improvement in tribal-citizen health, they will have to assume a leading role in health-care delivery (Abourezk 2018; Bylander 2017; Ferguson 2016). This shifts some of the tribal focus away from urging federal action to organising Indigenous action and building self-governing capacity in specialist areas of expertise.

Our diverse but limited data[11] on effects are by no means conclusive, but they strongly suggest two points. First, the shift to tribal control of health-care delivery appears to offer significant potential advantages for Native nations. Second, realising those advantages appears to involve a recurrent set of challenges that those nations have to address.

POTENTIAL ADVANTAGES OF TRIBAL CONTROL OF HEALTH-CARE DELIVERY

The advantages of tribal self-determination in the health-care arena may not be realised equally across cases. Nevertheless, our interviews, cases and literature review all find evidence of the following effects.

Tribal Conceptions of Health and Tribal Health Priorities

This was succinctly captured by one senior official of a tribe that had taken significant control of health-care delivery, who said to us, 'We weren't happy with IHS's ability to address some of the problems we were most concerned with . . . Tribal management lets us focus resources on our own priorities'. Our evidence echoes this view. In our case studies and in the Honoring Nations examples, tribal control strengthened the link between community experience and health policy. As a result, both policy and programming were driven less by aggregate national data or Washington's policy priorities, and more by local needs, circumstances and visions.

A striking aspect of the tribally controlled programmes we looked at—and a contrast to IHS programmes—is the priority given to wellness and preventive care. For example, once in the driver's seat in health care, Tribe B shifted much of its attention from acute care to long-term wellness. Its wellness centre, adjacent to its health clinic, houses a gym with cardio and weight machines, a therapeutic swimming pool, an indoor track and exercise classrooms. The tribe moved its diabetes programme into the wellness centre where nutritionists work with exercise therapists. It also introduced educational components into many services, from one-on-one diabetes counselling to smoking cessation classes.

Tribe E, facing high rates of colon and lung cancers, launched an informational campaign that led to increased cancer screenings and increased reporting of family cancer histories to health providers. As one staff member put it, in contrast with the past, 'they're getting their colonoscopies'. Tribe F, which also has combined its clinic with a wellness centre, hosts wellness-themed community meals in conjunction with presentations on topics such as stroke, diet and healthy lifestyles, activities that were rare under IHS management.

Some tribes rethink the recipient unit of health-care delivery or focus increased attention on specific population segments. In Tribe A, we found a strongly held view that health originates in the home and then emanates outwards. In that tribe's culture, home is like a mother—the source and place of caring. This turns the home into a primary site of health care. Tribal care strategies therefore focus as much on families as on individuals. It also links health with collective identity. As Tribe A's health director said, 'Being unhealthy is not being [us]'. In several cases, increased tribal control led to increased attention to the elderly and youth populations' health-care needs. Tribe B helps elders purchase pharmaceuticals and other health-care items, Tribe C began a home visit program to monitor patients' health, and Tribe D established an on-reservation nursing care facility. The Fort Peck Assiniboine Sioux Tribes' tribally conceived and operated school-based health centres provide tribal children with access to bi-annual dental check-ups, mental health care, medication management and regular school-nurse visits.[12]

Across our six case studies, in the Honoring Nations cases, and in the literature, we also found new mechanisms for gathering information about local health-care priorities. One tribe used regular surveys of community experience with the health-care system to better understand preferences. Others relied on information gathering through community-level educational programmes and other forms of community outreach. Such activities gave tribes critical data for their own health policy-making and governance, data they would otherwise lack.

Expansion and Innovation in Locally Available Services

The shift in focus outlined above was accompanied by expanded services. It is not that tribes stopped doing the kinds of things that IHS does: rather they began doing things that IHS was not doing or not doing locally. For example, a senior health official at Tribe C said that before the tribe took over, the clinic operated on 'an urgent care model . . . where people would come in and get quick care, convenient care'. Anything more complex meant going 80 kilometres away, and many health problems would go unaddressed until they became acute. Now, when citizens ask if the clinic can help manage diabetes or heart issues or do breast or prostate exams, the answer is likely to be yes. The pharmacy offers an expanded range of medicines, the dental clinic offers a full array of services, and behavioural-health programmes are available on site. Efforts to produce more—and more accessible—services appeared in others of our cases as well.

Tribal control appeared to provide freedom to innovate that often is absent or heavily constrained in the federal bureaucracy, leading to experimentation in approaches to care delivery. Tribe E, for example, uses a sophisticated, centralised case-management system not available from IHS, through which case managers can work with citizens to track their individual medical conditions, medications and clinical visits. It requires effort to maintain but results in better-informed patients. It also frees the tribe from dependence on federal data sources for its own decision-making in health care.

Additional Funding Sources, Pooling Program Funds, Partnerships for In-kind Support

One result of chronic underfunding of Indian health care is that national and regional decisions often come down to, 'What can we pay for? There are only so many dollars; what will they cover?' Tribal health administrators in all of our case studies managed from a different starting point: 'What does this community need? Can we make it happen with available funds? If not, can we find additional resources?' Attention had shifted from what can be paid for to what needs to be done.

This shift was possible in part because case studies and interviewees reported that IHS managers operate within a narrower universe of spending guidelines.

As the degree of tribal control increases, tribes gain more discretion over uses of federal funds and the scope of specific programmes and can pool resources across programmes or even become self-sustaining. While the health directors in the tribally managed programmes we spoke to were severely constrained by budgets, they typically drew on multiple federal, state, tribal and philanthropic sources, gathering funds wherever they could find them. For example, as Tribe B moved into a compacting arrangement with the US Government, substantially increasing its freedom of action, it changed the allocation of federal dollars, found ways to bill for its services, and identified creative ways of financing new projects. It began work on improving efficiency, strengthening financial and operational management, and billing third parties for reimbursement. It also was effective in pursuing—and obtaining—additional federal funds and other outside funds to support clinic expansion and a wellness centre. In the mid-2000s, lacking the necessary dollars to better address elders' health needs, the tribe found a social and economic development-and-strategies grant programme from the Department of Health and Human Services that ultimately helped create a case-management system for elders.

Some tribes have found that more effective reimbursement policies are especially helpful in meeting funding needs. Tribes B and C have looked for previously missed opportunities for reimbursements through federal programmes (such as Medicaid and Medicare) and through third-party private insurers. Tribe B's third-party billing has generated millions of dollars that have been invested in clinic expansion, the wellness centre, an expanded set of medicines in the tribe's pharmacy and other improvements. Tribe C receives several million dollars annually from third-party billing and reinvests these funds back into its health-care system. While low-income or unemployed citizens in the United States are less likely than others to have either the privately purchased or employer-sponsored health insurance that fuels a good deal of third-party billing, federal insurance programmes still offer opportunities to generate reimbursement revenue.

In-kind support through partnerships beyond IHS is another strategy for self-governing tribes. Tribes B and C established relationships with nearby universities that had resources and ideas for expanding and improving tribal health care. Tribe F partnered with the surrounding county on aspects of health care. In 1990, the Coeur d'Alene Tribe pooled resources with the nearby city of Plummer, Idaho, to build and run a health and wellness centre that serves Native and non-Native local populations, increasing access to services for both. In subsequent years, they substantially expanded the facility, integrating preventive care and wellness into their array of services, and significantly increasing access to quality care in a rural region of Idaho (see Harvard Project on American Indian Economic Development 2000; Marimn Health n.d.).

An important element in the change in emphasis (from what can be paid for to what needs to be done) is heightened attention to the business aspects of health-care management. As a Tribe C interviewee noted: 'When we were under the IHS model, we weren't looking at it that way. When we started self-managing, we started looking at it as a business model'. At the same time, Tribe C's staff emphasise that the point of the business model isn't to make money but to increase resources for top-quality care and to be more effective by paying careful attention to financial processes and focusing on measurable outcomes.

Incorporation of Local Knowledge and Culture

Before Tribe C took over health-care delivery, education in maternal and child health depended on a practitioner who would visit periodically from the city, an hour away. But this person did not know the culture or the community and could not speak the language. Once the tribe assumed the major decision-making role, it found a respected community person, fluent in the tribe's own language and resident in the community, who could take over the teaching. This increased not only the availability of critical medical information but also the level of community comfort with the process. Tribe C also provides training to new health-care employees to ensure that they understand the tribe's culture, including why some things are difficult to talk about, which activities can be done only at certain times of year, and how ceremonies and other activities need to be accommodated in a holistic approach to health and wellness. Tribe A initiated a programme that pairs well-informed community representatives with IHS doctors and nurse practitioners to teach non-tribal providers about the tribe's culture and to build bridges between IHS and the community.

Recognising that many of the Ramah Navajo community's older women were not getting the preventative cancer care they needed—because they were intimidated by the health system and had trouble understanding what they were told (some speak little English)—staff at the tribally managed Pine Hill Health Centre tried something new. They turned breast cancer screenings into social events: they reminded women when screenings were due and organised monthly group outings to the screening site. The trips included transportation, lunch, breast health education and assistance in talking with doctors and nurses. This culturally informed approach significantly increased screening rates (Harvard Project on American Indian Economic Development 2008b).

Sometimes local knowledge is part of the healing process. Interviewees at Tribe C, for example, said that traditional medicine and Western medicine coexist within their tribe's culture. Providers are comfortable with the patient combining approaches to suit his or her needs. Said one official, 'Some people tend to go to the Western medicine here first, and later, kind of to finish out the whole process, go to the traditional way of healing. Sometimes the primary is traditional healing. So it really works together'. The health director at Tribe A also supported the integration of Western and traditional healing practices: 'We need to look at the strength present in the community and utilise people who have certain [traditional] roles. [Western] providers need to look to these systems and people. Hospitals are still needed and should still be present. But the real issues are in the family: fixing or strengthening families, helping them heal, and [identifying] how they help one another'.

Increased Attention on Access, Convenience and Compliance

Most of the tribes in our sample went to considerable lengths to make health care convenient for their citizens. Their efforts ranged from the bundling of services in comprehensive health centres to making sure citizens had adequate transportation to appointments, complied with doctors' instructions, had and took their medications and so forth.

One goal of Tribe F has been to create one-stop health-care opportunities, simplifying what previously had been a complicated process. As a result, a patient can see a practitioner, get a referral, obtain a prescription and get lab work done all in a single visit. The tribe established two clinic locations to serve Native people in their multi-county service area. At each location, virtually all the services that the tribe provides are available in a single building. Transportation to and from the clinics is available for all tribal citizens. Tribe D found that nearly one-third of its population lacked access to a vehicle, leading to missed appointments and under-utilised care. The tribe responded by obtaining a federal grant to initiate an on-demand transportation system. Tribe B, knowing how frustrated citizens were with long waits at IHS facilities, focused on eliminating wait times. With the exception of dental care, where the demand for services continued to exceed the tribe's ability to respond, it largely succeeded, making it more likely that citizens would use its services.

A Sense of Local Ownership

As the tribal role in the organisation and management of health care expanded, it appears that care was perceived less as a service provided by outsiders and more as a community enterprise. One interviewee said of Tribe C, 'They're calling the shots here. They own the health care of their own people'. Both in our case studies and among the Honoring Nations award winners there were conscious efforts to engage the tribal community in health care. We noted earlier that Tribes C and F sought feedback on their health programmes via community surveys. Tribe C publishes the results in its newsletter. Said one senior tribal official, 'One of the biggest things that has changed over the years is more community involvement and collaboration out of the simple fact that we cannot do it on our own'. Some of the sense of ownership comes when providers demonstrate a greater understanding of Indigenous cultures. Several tribes in our sample reported that citizens' sense of comfort and engagement with the health-care system rose as more knowledgeable providers became involved, typically as a result of greater tribal control.

Rethinking the Definition of 'Service Area'

For the IHS, service areas are geographical entities and service populations are limited to enrolled tribal citizens. Eligible residents within specified geographies and eligible tribal citizens can access IHS services. The tribes we talked to tended to think in terms of social boundaries instead. For example, Tribe B developed a programme to serve the health-care needs of non-Native spouses of its citizens as well as non-Native employees of the tribe. The previous exclusion of such individuals from the tribe's clinic undermined the provision of care to what the tribe considered its larger 'family'. The Fond du Lac Band of Lake Superior Chippewa set up a pharmacy in Minneapolis, 225 kilometres from the reservation, in part because the tribal government viewed urban tribal citizens as part of its responsibility (Harvard Project on American Indian Economic Development 2000). Tribe F, as a recently federally recognised tribe, created its own service area: a multi-county region where the majority of its citizens live. It also is investigating the possibility of providing services to non-tribal family members and to citizens outside the service area.

CHALLENGES IN TRIBAL CONTROL OF HEALTH-CARE DELIVERY

These changes were not easily achieved. Effective governance of health care is a daunting task anywhere. Health conditions in Indigenous communities and other legacies of colonial control make it particularly daunting for Native nations. Among the challenges most apparent in our research were these:

Complexity of Health-Care Systems

Not all tribes are increasing their role in the management of health-care delivery. Capacity issues doubtless play a role in this decision. Even those who have taken the plunge found it challenging.

A Tribe C official admitted that, while the tribe has created an innovative and effective health-care operation, it was tough to do and tough to maintain. At first, they underestimated the difficulty. Neither the tribe's organisational nor its physical infrastructure was robust enough. It took time to establish and learn the necessary processes. As a result, the tribe experienced not only impressive successes but also some rocky periods, with quality-control issues and turnover in directors. Said the official, 'We brought the gorilla home without thinking about how much it was going to eat'.

Capacity problems can be diverse. One tribe established a dialysis programme but then mismanaged it and lost the funding, so that patients again must make long-distance drives for care. Another tribe struggled with a lack of clear tribal health-department policies and procedures, leading to uncertainties and inconsistencies. Another treated its health-care programme as an employment service. Instead of finding a few people who could do high-quality work, it put multiple persons into low-paying jobs, only to discover that they lacked the skills to do their jobs well.

Data tracking is difficult and can be burdensome, particularly as tribes expand their universe of funding sources and have to respond to diverse data requirements. On the one hand, we found tribes were eager to track results and evaluate their own performance. Tribe B, for example, has an in-house peer-review programme and voluntarily submits data to a performance-rating programme run through IHS. Other tribes subject their programmes to outside evaluation by professional organisations. On the other hand, some tribes were required by funders or partners to gather data the tribes felt were of little use. Data collection also can prove fruitless if funding agencies don't report back to tribes on what they have learned from the data, allowing tribes to compare their work with that of other tribes and communities.

The tribes that appeared to be successful in operating their own health-care programmes tended to be entrepreneurial in a business sense and good managers in a public administration sense. They also were willing, if they could not find skills among their own citizens, to look outside. Tribes B and C had been proactive in seeking the best talent available, hiring a number of non-citizens—including non-Natives—to key positions. Their expectation was that at some point tribal citizens would fill those positions, but only when their training and expertise matched the best available elsewhere.

One priority of Tribe E's health department is to be responsive and accountable to both citizens and vendors: 'When we say we're gonna call you back, we really do call you back'. The department pays bills promptly, typically within two weeks. One result is strong relationships with partners and providers. 'They are very happy with us'.

Importance of Stability and Professionalism in Tribal Government

The health-care sector is often one of the biggest sources of jobs and outside funds on Indigenous lands. When tribes take over health-care operations, sector decision-making that was formerly in external hands moves into the hands of tribal health directors or health boards. Where elected tribal leadership is accustomed to controlling most tribal resources, and where resource allocations are highly politicised, this can produce problems.

Case-study tribes indicated that this issue was sometimes apparent in certification processes. To obtain health-care accreditation, boards of health programmes must become genuine governing boards. But this can diminish the decision-making power of tribal councils or executives, forcing tribal leadership to decide whether its commitment to health care is more important than its desire to retain such authority in its own hands. The challenge for tribal councils is to restrict their role to goal-setting and strategic direction and to cede authority over health system management to health programme boards, managers, and where appropriate, line employees.

Furthermore, many tribal communities are small, and relationships often are personal, including relationships among citizens, managers and elected officials. Turnover in tribal leadership can be frequent. This means that health programmes can be powerfully affected by the state of tribal government. Tribally managed health care can suffer if the tribal government's rules and procedures change from election to election, if policy and hiring decisions are seen as personal, political, or capricious, or if tribal leaders micromanage programmes. For example, the elected leadership of one tribe interfered in hiring and in priority-of-treatment decisions within the tribal health programme, favouring its own supporters. As a result, some highly qualified professionals left, unwilling to work under such conditions. The result was a reduction in quality of care for everyone. Staff in another tribe reported feeling political pressure in health-care decisions.

Some tribes in our case studies found ways to address these issues. Tribe E, for example, had a tribal council committee that was charged with health-care oversight. The tribe's health department worked to educate committee members about health care and encouraged them to join department staff in trainings. Committee members became familiar with programme requirements and better understood the complexity of programme decisions. The result, according to one interviewee, was that 'our council so far has been very supportive of our programmes and recognises that [staff] are the experts'. Interviewees at Tribe B indicated that success in their health programmes had been bolstered by stability in tribal government leading to the accumulation of knowledge about the practical requirements of health care, to a shared understanding within tribal government that tribal priorities include high-quality health care, and to decision-making rules that support those priorities.

Funding—a Major Challenge

Organising an effective health-care delivery system is one thing; paying for it is another. While some tribes have been creative and proactive in finding new sources of funding, and some have invested own-source tribal revenues in health-care programmes, the funding challenge remains.

Tribe B, for example, while aggressively pursuing management of health-care delivery, of necessity still received money from IHS. IHS funding requires tribes to serve any qualified American Indian, but in this case only a small portion of that funding was designated for services to non-Tribe B citizens. Meanwhile, thanks to the proximity of other tribes and the high quality of care Tribe B offered, a majority of its user population came from other tribes. This was expensive, requiring Tribe B to care for patients who were unaccounted for in its IHS funding, effectively penalising the tribe for quality improvements. This illustrates a broader problem. As tribes expand their funding sources, they can get caught in a mix of inclusion/exclusion criteria that vary from funder to funder and from service to service: a financial and administrative headache that all of our case-study tribes experienced.

There also are barriers to some tribal solutions. For example, IHS's electronic Resource and Patient Management System (RPMS) was designed as a medical record system, not a billing system. For years, case-study tribes interested in third-party billing had to purchase commercial software to operate alongside RPMS. IHS responded by modifying RPMS and offering third-party billing training. Unfortunately, problems persisted, driving tribes to commercial products.

Difficulties in Learning from Other Tribes

While some tribes taking control of health-care delivery have learned from others' experiences, there is no easy way to do so. Most interviewees knew there were health-care successes out there and wanted to know more about them: who's doing what, what's working where? But almost none of the tribal health directors we talked to in the interviews or case studies could give an example of an innovative tribal health programme outside their own area. Describing it as one of the 'biggest gaps' in their knowledge, one interviewee said, 'When you ask me . . . what other tribes are doing, I don't know!'

IMPLICATIONS

The data presented here suggest that the question that motivated our inquiry—can a self-determination strategy improve Indigenous health care?—deserves a qualified 'yes'. The qualification lies first in the limited scope of the data on which we've drawn in this chapter—diverse but small, non-random samples—and second, in the caution that the right to self-determination alone, absent capable tribal self-government, is insufficient for the realisation of health-care gains.

In regard to the first of these qualifications, one conclusion would be that the evidence presented here is sufficiently suggestive to justify a broader and more systematic study of the effects of increased tribal control. Our data suggest that these may include the following: It can better align health-care priorities with community needs and preferences; lead to expanded and innovative services; invite creative funding initiatives; bring local knowledge and culture into health-care decisions and policies; increase patient access, convenience and compliance; and create a sense of local ownership over health care. A broader and more systematic study also could look for innovative strategies that tribes are pursuing in the organisation and governance of health care that appear to amplify such effects. In other words, such a study could address not only the question of 'does a tribal self-determination strategy work?' but '*how* does it work?' and 'what can Native nations learn from each other's experience?'

In regard to the second qualification, we return to a point made in our introduction: self-determination has to be backed up by capability. As in other aspects of community life, increased decision-making power in the operation of a health-care system must be competently exercised. Tribes burdened with dysfunctional governing systems—systems that have difficulty establishing strategic priorities or sticking to them, difficulty in making decisions, difficulty in keeping politics in its place, difficulty in retaining good people or maintaining community trust—will find it difficult as well to maintain a functional health-care system. In short, the decision to move towards increased tribal control has to be careful, deliberate and informed. Operating a health-care system raises difficult questions for tribes about their institutional and management capacities, the role of politics in programme management and personnel retention, funding capabilities, and how they might learn from each other. System requirements are high, and the learning curve can be steep.

Some of the burden of addressing this issue should be borne by the federal government. Government policy can make sure the door remains open for tribes to consider transitioning to tribal control. It also can assist those who decide to transition by, among other options, providing grants for consultation or technical assistance (some of which are already available through

IHS and other federal sources), reassessing some IHS funding requirements, increasing funding levels, and supporting peer-to-peer learning across tribes. Investments along these lines, whether accomplished administratively or through legislative action, should pay attention both to tribal governments and to sub-tribal entities (grassroots organisations, Indigenous non-profits and local communities) where some innovations already are occurring.

In the meanwhile, the materials summarised in this chapter indicate that the payoffs to capable tribal control are potentially substantial, and they go well beyond health. Native nations have ambitious goals: addressing the legacies of colonialism; effectively exercising their rights and interests in contemporary contexts; replacing economies destroyed by colonial takings; becoming more independent and effective stewards of their remaining lands; assuring the intergenerational transmission of culture, language and spirituality; and more. All such goals are made more difficult when these nations' own citizens are crippled by chronic diseases; are struggling with behavioural and mental health issues; or cannot get the prenatal, neonatal and other care they need. In such situations, providing effective health care is a community priority.

The question is how to do it. The record of US Government policy in this regard is decidedly mixed: some successes, some failures, a lot of running in place, and a diminishing funding commitment. Perhaps a new strategy is needed. Fortunately, some American Indian Nations are showing that they can do a better job of providing health care to their people than anyone else can. Their record suggests that Indigenous self-determination, exercised through capable governing institutions, may be the health-care strategy and policy that works.

NOTES

1. The listed order of authorship is solely alphabetical; this chapter has been a joint effort. We gratefully acknowledge the W. K. Kellogg Foundation, the Morris K. Udall and Stewart L. Udall Foundation, the Nathan Cummings Foundation for their financial support of research on Indigenous health care at the University of Arizona's Native Nations Institute (NNI). Thanks also to the Harvard Project on American Indian Economic Development and its Honouring Contributions in the Governance of American Indian Nations (Honoring Nations) programme for assistance. We are especially grateful to the Native Nations, citizens and employees who participated in this research and shared their views and stories with us. Over an extended period, a large number of other individuals also have been involved in our research as interviewers, site visitors and research assistants. We thank Jaime Arsenault, Renee Goldtooth, Maura Grogan, Niina Haas, Denise Lum, Jackie Old Coyote, Tasce Simon, Rachel Rose Starks and Erin Suelmann. Our thanks as well to our sounding board members for their input: Alyce Adams, Chester Antone, Brenda Baptiste, Mim Dixon, Dorothy

Dupree, Jennie Joe and Phil Norgarrd. We especially thank Alyce Adams for her insights and advice and Diane Smith for helpful comments on an earlier draft.

2. Interview and case research protocols were reviewed and approved by the University of Arizona's Institutional Review Board and, wherever required, by the Native Nations involved. By arrangement with both tribal and other interviewees, we do not list individual names or affiliations. As per research agreements to keep case-study nations anonymous, those nations are identified only by the letters A–F. These nations varied in population size (from under 500 to 30,000 citizens), geographic location, and extent of managerial involvement and authority in health-care delivery. On the latter point, one nation had a self-governance compact with the federal government allowing it virtually complete control of health-care delivery; two were managing most health-care services under contracts with the federal government (so-called 638 contracts); two were managing more modest sets of services under similar contracts while the majority of services were provided directly by a federal agency; and one had a compact with the federal government allowing it to operate as a tribal managed-care organisation.

3. More detail on these programmes can be found on the publications page of the Honoring Nations website: https://hpaied.org/publications-and-research/search.

4. Those Native nations in the United States and elsewhere that are mentioned in this chapter, but were not in our case sample, are identified if already named in publicly available literature.

5. See, for example, Hemming, Rigney, and Berg 2011; McMeeking 2019; Murphy 2014; First Nations of Quebec and Labrador Health and Social Services Commission 2015.

6. This chapter concerns only federally recognised American Indian tribes or nations, as they are the only ones eligible to take over the federal duty to provide health care to their citizens. We also use the terms Native and Indigenous interchangeably to refer to the Indigenous Peoples of the CANZUS states. For a more thorough discussion of the history of health-care provision to federally recognised American Indian tribes, including a review of the literature on tribal control, see Rainie et al. 2015.

7. In the United States, health care is not organised through a single payer for services. In the US health-care system, the first and second parties that may be held accountable to pay for health care are the patient and the healthcare provider (doctor, nurse, clinic, etc.). If neither the patient nor the provider pays for services, costs may be covered by a 'third party'—for example, an individual's employer through an employer-sponsored insurance plan or, in the case of elderly and low-income Americans, the federal government through its Medicare or Medicaid programmes.

8. Many American Indian Nations specify criteria for tribal citizenship; therefore, we refer to those who meet those criteria as citizens.

9. Medicare is the U.S. federal health insurance programme serving individuals 65 and older.

10. In 2012, the U.S. Supreme Court ruled in *Salazar v. Ramah Navajo Chapter* that when the U. S. government enters into a contract with an American Indian or Alaska Native tribe or tribes for services, it must pay those contracts in full, including

the mutually determined contract support (administrative) costs. While the U.S. government settled with tribes that were party to the suit, it is unlikely the funds fully compensated tribes for the diversion of programme dollars into contract support or past decisions not to contract because it would have been too expensive.

11. The data sources for this chapter are diverse and largely consistent in their implications, but the samples are small and non-random, while large-scale, longitudinal, quantitative data on health policy effects in Indigenous communities are rare.

12. On Fort Peck, see https://hpaied.org/sites/default/files/publications/SchoolBasedHealthCenters-Final%20(2).pdf.

Theme Three

GOVERNING DEVELOPMENT AND RESOURCES

Thematic Introduction

Concepts, Issues and Trends

Diane Smith

In the twenty-first century, the power of development, entrepreneurship and related innovation to create social and economic progress is considered by many to be a universal phenomenon. International institutions such as the United Nations, the World Bank and global NGOs operate on the premise that 'good' governance is at the heart of sustainable human development and is a prerequisite for effectively responding to poverty, environmental and social concerns. There has been a concurrent international upsurge in concern among Indigenous peoples with matters of development. More and more Indigenous people are exploring ways in which they can most capably govern their hard-won rights and assets, to deliver tangible outcomes from development that make life better in ways they desire.

But amid this, there is heated debate about what constitutes 'development' and 'prosperity', and from whose perspective such definitions arise. Recently, a global Indigenous debate is questioning the colonial legacies of development pressures and the implicit acceptance of particular kinds of economic growth at the expense of Indigenous modes of development and cultural priorities. The United Nations Declaration on the Rights of Indigenous People has also identified informed consent and self-determination as keys to Indigenous development outcomes. There are equally diverse views as to what constitutes 'sustainable' development for Indigenous peoples. In addition, there are gaps in our knowledge about how to achieve it, in ways that maximise rather than undermine self-determination.

In the case studies under this theme, authors explore these fundamental issues and share their insights won through hard experience. They show the diversity of Indigenous aspirations for development, and the many pathways and assessments of success they use. At the same time, the authors' in-depth evidence and analyses suggest there are also some common strategic principles lying at the heart of such diverse solutions. One such principle is that Indigenous understandings, shared values and informed choice—rooted in their collective ways of being and doing things—must be given priority in shaping a nation's vision for their current and future development. A related principle for making a collective vision come alive is for self-determination and self-governance to be designed and implemented, within the nation, in ways that are inclusive, equitable and practically capable. These appear to be common denominators or principles for building the resilient internal bases needed within First Nations to achieve improved outcomes from development.

DEVELOPMENT—BY WHOM, FOR WHOM?

We take 'development' to mean the ability of people to support themselves over time in ways they desire: to sustain their self-governance and to provide citizens with the opportunity to live productive, satisfying lives. A common goal evident in the case studies emphasises beneficial change or transformation that makes life better in ways that Indigenous people want. That highlights the need for internal direction, choice and control by First Nations.

The concept of 'development' when applied to, and by, Indigenous societies is a complex one, and has been the subject of debate at national and international levels for some years (see, for example, Blaser et al. 2004; Bulloch 2018; Harvard Project 2008; O'Fairchellaigh 2018; Sen 2014). The concept's Western hegemonic assumptions about what constitutes 'progress' ignore the fact that 'development' is itself a cultural construct—and not culturally neutral. Therefore, the crucial questions become: Whose cultural values, norms, priorities and measures are adopted when considering 'development', 'progress', 'sustainability' and 'success'? Who gets to make the decisions about the forms they take? The authors in this theme resoundingly emphasise that Indigenous understandings and informed choice are the necessary preconditions to successful and flourishing societies.

In Indigenous contexts, desired development is shown to take a great variety of forms—ranging from resurgence and growth in traditional subsistence and cultural activities; community initiatives for the management of lands and waters, natural resource conservation and protection of collective intellectual property; through to increased participation in market economies, Indigenous-citizen entrepreneurship, and joint ventures by First Nations with each other and with non-Indigenous corporations. The authors provide rich accounts of the diversity of Indigenous cultures, further reinforcing that there no 'one size' model of development will suit all circumstances. Rather, local Indigenous conditions, aspirations, abilities and decisions give form to locally workable Indigenous pathways.

As they engage in a wide range of development endeavours, Indigenous nations and communities need to attract investment capital, to support citizens to move from welfare dependence to productive economic activity, to build relationships with other economic actors, deal with other jurisdictions and persuade their own citizens to remain in, or return to, their home communities and invest their skills, motivation and ideas there. All of these challenges are requiring nations to reconsider their governance arrangements and associated capabilities. Moreover, the additional challenge in this, as Sacha McMeeking and Jaimie Sterritt note, is not only to gain more control over their development agenda, but to find ways to make that control meaningful within their own communities. As the authors explore the strategies and outcomes being pursued to meet that ongoing challenge, an insight emerging from their accounts is that Indigenous people are pursuing 'development *with* culture and identity' (UNPFII 2016). Following Escobar (2008), this enables a modelling of Indigenous development as being a territory of difference that is as much cultural (and so relational and intercultural) as it is economic. This has profound implications for development practice.

WHAT IS PROSPERITY—THE GOOD LIFE?

The English word 'prosperity' is usually equated with a thriving condition linked to money, financial wealth and economic status. In the face of the intransigent socio-economic disadvantage and destructive legacies of settler-colonialism still apparent in many Indigenous communities across the CANZUS states and elsewhere, any sense of future prosperity seems overshadowed by urgent current needs for the most basic improvements in living conditions, health and well-being. However, it is clear from the chapters in this theme that First Nations have always had a more comprehensive understanding of what constitutes prosperity; of what the good life means to them. That understanding informs how people go about planning for the future together and using their resources in ways that have tangible, beneficial impacts in their communities.

That does not mean individual wealth creation is shunned or excluded. On the contrary, as Peter Yu and Jaimie Sterritt point out, it means that 'prosperity' takes on a wider sense of service and contribution to the well-being of the whole community, and that involves social, cultural and environmental aspects alongside economic ones. Prosperity is thus founded on interconnectedness. As a collective experience, it stresses the importance of relationships between people, country, natural resources and to traditional culture, which includes also seeking and integrating other critical elements of life such as financial security, decent housing and personal safety.

While a key Indigenous objective of development is to empower people through *individual and collective* wealth creation, the fundamental point emphasised by the chapters in this theme is that nations are pursuing culturally integrated strategies, where development initiatives contribute to this broader sense of prosperity, and don't simply respond to the pressures of a financial bottom line. The particular challenge that follows is to then build and sustain a sense of common purpose *and* personal investment in the commercial success of developing a First Nation's assets, in ways that align with its fundamental cultural and social values.

SUSTAINING INDIGENOUS DEVELOPMENT

In their case studies for this theme, the authors describe the internal 'tests' of sustainability and success applied by Indigenous people to their development initiatives, and to the effectiveness of how they govern development. This seems to involve coming up with answers to a common set of difficult questions, many of which call for 'future thinking'. They ask, for example:

- What kind of nation or community are we trying to build, not only for ourselves but also for future generations of our people?
- What kinds of development might be acceptable and consented to now, and be acceptable to our people in the future?
- What role should collective Indigenous culture play in development initiatives, and how might that change over time?
- Who should benefit from development, now and over time?
- What development strategies will best address current disadvantage along with future equity and inclusion issues?
- Moreover, who should make decisions about these matters? How should the nation be governed to maximise its development success and sustainability?

We see that answers to these probing questions engage nations and communities in considering new ways to build cultural resilience and 'future accountability' into current development initiatives and related governance arrangements.

Thirty years ago, the World Commission on Environment and Development's 'Brutland Report' was influential in proposing that development is 'sustainable' when it meets the needs of the present without compromising the ability of future generations to meet their own needs. However, as with self-determination, sustainable development as described by the Indigenous authors in this theme is a direction and a process (a sustainable journey) more than a final endpoint. As chapters by Jorgensen et al. and the

National Centre for First Nations Governance and Native Nations Institute make clear, this calls for value judgements about the preferred direction and speed of change. All the authors suggest that an Indigenous principle of sustainable development rests on four interdependent and mutually reinforcing pillars: social development; environmental and natural resource development; cultural development; and economic development. These four pillars operate across local, regional, national and global scales, and at individual and collective levels.

Under this Indigenous principle, development may be judged to be 'sustainable' when it delivers desired outcomes, reinforces cultural resilience, aligns with collectively identified directions and promotes the abilities of current and future generations to give effect to self-determination in their own terms. In which case, what constitutes sustainable development for one Indigenous group is unlikely to be the case for another.

INDIGENOUS INNOVATION

A growing number of First Nations in the CANZUS countries and beyond have been rejecting the limited and imposed models of development promoted by Western neoliberalism, and devising their own models as viable alternatives. They are also approaching the organisational task from very different starting points. Given that development priorities and goals can change dramatically over time, in this theme we are presented with examples of Indigenous innovation and experimentation by nations and communities to design governance solutions that are adaptive and 'fit' for particular development purposes. The authors consistently identify a direct link between exercising capable self-governance and securing desired development outcomes.

The purposeful Indigenous innovation in the ways development should be governed, described in this theme, offers an important reframing. It positions Indigenous people as 'innovation agents'—not as cultural problems or capacity deficits. Here the case studies describe how Indigenous people are strategically reshaping their governing institutions and practice in order to achieve desired development outcomes. The implication is that sustaining Indigenous development is best viewed as a socially instituted process of adaptive change in which culturally legitimate innovation is a necessary element—that is, a process of proposing, gaining support for and implementing novel ideas and solutions to address collective development priorities. Innovation of this kind is founded on everyday acts self-determination informed by inclusive Indigenous decision-making and consent.

GOVERNING INDIGENOUS DEVELOPMENT

Development involves change; by its nature it is unsettling. Sometimes treasured ways of life are put under the microscope, become vulnerable and reveal contending interests and aspirations. This means the decisions taken around development are often impressive, brave and risky. Many factors are influential in its success. The authors provide valuable insights into the practices, processes and strategies Indigenous nations and communities have designed to govern development in a self-determined way. All stress the central role of capable governance in managing development's unsettling attributes and sometimes unintended consequences. Conversely, poorly performed governance is quickly exposed in the context of development, raising the need for often urgent governance reassessment and renewal. The Harvard Project in the United States long ago identified the importance for Native American nations of rebuilding and monitoring their governance arrangements *before* leaping into major new development initiatives (Begay et al. 2008; Jorgensen 2007), an insight reinforced by later research and Indigenous practice in other countries.

In their case studies, authors describe some of the ways their nations have gone about rebuilding and strengthening governance in development contexts. One commonly practised strategy is to be vigilant about keeping cherished values and ways of doing things centred at the heart of development initiatives. For example, consensual decision-making is a common cultural tradition shared in common by many CANZUS Indigenous nations. In the chapters that follow, we read examples where leaders of change make sure that consensus processes are reinforced, by institutionalising them in the form of written rules and policies. In such ways, the tools of putting effective First Nation governance into practice become the tools of development.

The chapters highlight how nations are adopting a multifaceted approach to driving the profound shifts that are often called for at a local and regional level. Money alone cannot overcome decades of systemic exclusion from mainstream economic participation. And just as importantly, limited or vulnerable recognition of cultural rights to land cannot on their own grow and sustain a healthy, educated and cohesive community. Furthermore, in communities that are fragmented or in turmoil, trust is an issue. In situations where governance rebuilding and new development are occurring, members of a nation have to trust the reliability and fairness of their leaders and decision-making processes. The challenge described by authors in their chapters is for both leaders and members to work closely together at every stage of new initiatives. Mutual trust grows alongside a nation's capacity to protect and grow its cultural estate alongside its wealth and economic independence.

This speaks to a public-spirited quality needed for leadership and citizenship within a nation, which flows into the way development is undertaken, a point taken up in Theme Four that explores the role of transformative leadership in governance.

Several authors describe self-governance as residing in the whole community—not just in the capabilities and roles of leaders, but in citizens and members as well. While governance rebuilding at a national level is fundamentally important to generating self-determined development, there is also an equally, if distinctly, important entrepreneurial movement fomenting within Indigenous communities that has the potential to make significant contributions to social transformation and build the collective capability to be self-determining. Sacha McMeeking alerts us to a growing body of Indigenous entrepreneurship primarily being led by individuals and families, who can see opportunities to generate personal wealth as part of achieving tangible, meaningful social change that aligns with wider community priorities. In their hands, such entrepreneurship is both a tool for, and embodiment of, self-determination. Their practice is creating a groundswell of 'bottom-up' nation and governance building that empowers, inspires and activates a cycle of ever-growing self-determination.

Governing development puts leaders under pressure, especially if they get too far ahead of the community's vision and understanding of what is happening and why. Every chapter in this theme raises the issue of communication with nation members as being a critical one, no matter how small or large that membership is. This is what 'transparency' is about—keeping the beneficiaries of development (individuals, families, tribes, clans, organisations, the nation) informed about its progress, warts and all. This requirement entails internal and external communication responsibilities. There is also strong endorsement from authors that effectively (re)engaging with all Indigenous community members needs to be put back at the heart of development considerations, and therefore also at the centre of how to govern development.

Finally, development opportunities and goals are often ephemeral. In working to turn them into a reality, nations are routinely investing their precious financial, cultural and human capital. A distinctive feature in the success of such internal investment is being able to frankly assess the internal gaps in skills and knowledge available to govern and implement an agreed development agenda, and then to secure missing expertise, including from outside the nation if needed. Self-determination is exercised by making decisions not only to build a home-grown skill base but also to secure necessary missing expertise. This is because governance is about setting directions and making the decisions, and not expecting that all the hard work has to be done by the members and leaders of a nation.

REFRAMING DEVELOPMENT

Rather than being anti-development or an impediment to development, many Indigenous nations internationally are at the forefront of a paradigm shift in thinking around the substance and implementation of development. The message from authors in this theme is clear: rebuilding the social and cultural fabric of their societies is a core component of sustainable development. In that way, development initiatives can reinforce, not undermine, the ongoing cultural resilience of Indigenous First Nations and maximise their practical self-determination. By building these internal foundations for legitimate, capable governance of development, communities and nations are better positioned to renegotiate and renew their relationship with nation-state governments and other parties, from a position of equal authority (i.e. as a self-determining polity). From this vantage point, development can be viewed as a powerful governance and cultural resurgence tool that lies at the heart of nation building. Furthermore, the quadruple integrated pillars of Indigenous development could have substantial benefits globally.

Chapter 11

Rebuilding the Yawuru Nation

Activating Cultural Assets for Economic Growth and Stability

Peter Yu

The ferocity of Western domination of Indigenous peoples has been a global force. It is the story of empire, the story of modernity, resource exploitation and global trade. Indigenous societies and our traditional lands and waters have been ravaged and transformed by the expansion of Western commercial enterprises. Today humanity is desperately seeking a new paradigm which can enable a prosperity that accounts for our future generations and does not leave vast numbers of people mired in poverty and vulnerable to the vagaries of the market or to the impacts of climate change.

Indigenous peoples the world over are colonisation's greatest triumph. For we have survived. And we have survived to tell a different story to that of a destructive modernity. Our story is a beacon of hope for wider humanity, many of whom are confronting the legacy of the unbridled ravages of Western imperialism across the globe. The Indigenous view is at odds with the philosophy behind neoliberalism; we understand, have always understood, that human resilience is based on our relationship with each other and through connectedness to our lands and waters. We know that our culture, our languages, systems and practices that enable this connectivity are protective of our physical and mental health.

For Indigenous people, both prior to and after colonisation, our very survival as individuals and as distinct cultures has depended on our commitment to remaining connected to each other. Being narrowly self-interested runs contrary to how we are hardwired. Connectivity is part of our identity, of how we think about ourselves as forming part of a constellation of responsibilities to a wider network of kin and to country. It seems to me that this is something that Indigenous people globally are very good at: staying connected to each other, staying connected to cherished value systems that are under enormous pressure to change, and to the land and its natural environment. That is our holy trinity if you like. In our language, Yawuru, the term used to describe the interconnectedness between oneself, the wider community and the natural landscape is 'liyan'. Mabu liyan equates to a sense of well-being and living the 'good life'.

In the quest for mabu liyan, Yawuru stress the importance of family and community relationships and people's connection to country, to natural resources and to traditional culture, along with other critical elements of life such as financial security, decent housing and safety. Prior to British colonisation, mabu liyan was at the core of our cultural and social existence, informing our obligations to family, community and country. The impact of colonisation on our people has been traumatic, and we are now seeking to heal and work towards building 'mabu ngarrungu'—meaning strong community, and 'mabu buru'—meaning strong country.

Since our 2010 native title agreement with the Western Australian State Government, Yawuru have developed a range of programmes. These are aimed at achieving mabu liyan including language revitalisation and strengthening cultural practices and participation, best practice land and sea management, celebrating Yawuru cultural heritage, growing individual and family capacity, innovative home ownership approaches and developing pathways for Yawuru and other Aboriginal people to participate in the local economy.

We are fortunate that we have the resources at present to undertake this work. But for an Indigenous organisation like Nyamba Buru Yawuru—and the Yawuru people whose interests we work on behalf of—there has never been a moment yet since colonisation where we have arrived at a safe harbour, where we can rest from the constant need to defend our interests, to resist cultural and political assimilation and degradation. There has never been a time where we could simply consolidate the journey undertaken so far. But we are closer to this point—to the moment where we can say that we have arrived and that our nationhood is no longer under constant assault—than we ever have been since the colonisers invaded our country late in the nineteenth century. It has been a long and sustained battle, but the tides are turning in our favour. The journey towards self-governance and towards a healed community is itself an exercise in autonomous navigation; in sovereignty.

This chapter traces the Yawuru people's journey from systemic oppression by the Australian settler nation-state, through to the struggle for recognition of native title rights in the 1990s–2000s and to contemporary efforts to generate mabu liyan through strong leadership and self-governance. In doing this, it focuses on the renaissance of Yawuru language and culture, for these lie at the heart of our vision. Despite operating in a highly constrained legal and political environment, Yawuru are successfully building the physical and institutional infrastructure necessary to thrive in the modern economy, on our own terms. While a key objective is to empower our people through individual and collective wealth creation, the fundamental point is that this objective is being met through culturally integrated strategies, so that our investment outcomes also contribute to liyan, not just our financial bottom line. This chapter sets out some of the ways we are working to achieve this objective.

HISTORICAL CONTEXT

There are critical differences between the four countries of Canada, Australian, New Zealand and the United States in their processes of colonisation and Indigenous peoples' assertion of their sovereign rights. The striking difference for Indigenous people in Australia is that Britain and the subsequent Australian settler nation-state did not recognise the existence of Indigenous people at the time of colonisation, nor after it. Nor has there yet been a comprehensive, negotiated accommodation of our prior and continuing rights, responsibilities and interests. The British colonial instruction was 'To take possession of the great southern lands with the consent of the natives', but the second part of this instruction was never complied with.[1] Rather, the colonisers adapted the 'doctrine of discovery'[2] to reinforce a legal fiction of *terra nullius* in order to occupy and possess our lands. This was addressed in the Australian High Court's *Mabo* judgement in 1992, but the questions of settlement and domestic sovereignty are live issues.

The embryonic Australian settler state emerged from ruptures within the British Empire, especially with the United States and Canada. The lessons from South Africa and the Maori Wars also informed Britain's approaches to us. It is estimated that in 1788—when the British imperial flag was raised at Botany Bay in New South Wales—there were between 500,000 and 1 million Indigenous people inhabiting the Australian continent and surrounding islands (Taylor 2019). These people spoke several hundred languages and many more dialects and had developed deep knowledge of country, seasons and ecology, which among other things involved the adroit use of fire and enabled a reliable prosperity. It is only recently that scholars have researched and written about the skillful management of the natural environment by Indigenous Australians (Gammage 2012; Pascoe 2018). For the most part, however, our environmental intelligence—our knowledge and skills inherited over millennia—was historically represented as primitive, romantic and of no scientific value (Elkin 1938; Anderson & Perrin 2007). In truth, Aboriginal people through their stewardship had established the very landscape the British found so attractive in 1788.

In the mid-nineteenth century, global forces transformed colonial Australian settlement and economy. Industrialisation and associated social dislocation in Europe, the discovery of gold in Australia, the Irish famine and a massive expansion of agriculture and pastoralism across various frontiers, combined to cause an insatiable grab for land. A century-and-half later, we are confronted with the consequences of poor management of Australia's land, waters and seas. Countless species of terrestrial and marine animals have become extinct.[3] Introduced parasitic plant life and foreign animals have ravaged the nation's natural environment. On the critical measures of sustainability and reliable prosperity, the Australian settler state has been a monumental failure.

The seeds of this ongoing catastrophe are rooted in the rapid pastoral and agricultural expansion from the 1860s. The frontier settler, known positively in settler Australian myth as the 'squatter', rushed to occupy and gain legal title to vast tracks of land as leasehold allotments. As the frontier expanded, it did so on the back of the myth of *terra nullius*—the history of the Australian frontier is also a history of brutal dispossession, murder and trauma from which Indigenous people have yet to recover.

As Indigenous peoples, we have struggled long and hard for our land rights, which have never been given to us without us having to fight for them. When the court failed to overturn *terra nullius* in the Gove Land Rights Case (*Millirpum v Nabalco 1971*), the failure of the settler Australian legal system to deliver us land justice was fully exposed. The Australian Government subsequently enacted the *Aboriginal Lands Right Act (NT) 1976*, to return ownership of land to traditional owners in the Northern Territory. But it retreated from a commitment to extend that law into a national framework, in the face of fierce opposition from resource-rich states, their governments and the mining industry.

It took a further twenty years for the High Court of Australia to recognise our native title rights in the landmark *Mabo* Case. This was a turning point in Indigenous and non-Indigenous relations in Australia, as the High Court decision overturned the doctrine of *terra nullius* as the legal foundation of Australian colonial settlement. Significantly, the High Court found that the common law of Australia could recognise a continuing native title, where Indigenous people might still demonstrate that their cultural and customary rights and interests had not been 'extinguished' by non-exclusive settler title or by cultural disconnection. This legal decision was eventually enshrined in a legislated framework involving complex tribunal, mediation and court-determined processes under the *Native Title Act 1993*. But native title is effectively only for those who can meet its strict and often onerous requirements.

The Australian Government used its constitutional race powers to develop the *Native Title Act* as a national statutory regime that favoured the interests of state governments and development over those of Indigenous rights. Such was the politics generated by those hostile to Indigenous rights in the 1990s that the drafting of the original legislation in 1993 (and its subsequent amendments five years later in response to the *Wik* native title High Court decision)[4] involved the longest debates in Australian parliamentary history.

Australian courts have since adopted a conservative approach to native title jurisprudence in Australia. In the *Ward* case,[5] the High Court treated native title as a 'bundle of rights', which can be extinguished piece by piece. Under this approach, native title has tended to be confined to communal customary-use rights, such as a right to hunt, fish, or gather, or a right to be consulted rather than full beneficial ownership. More recently, there have been a small number of cases where 'exclusive possession' native title and certain commercial rights and interests have been recognised.[6] Importantly, native title does not deliver sovereignty, self-government status or a guarantee of financial resources, and it is not available to all Aboriginal people in Australia. So what has it delivered? And more to the point, what are Indigenous Australians themselves generating out of the opportunities created through the native title regime?

NATIVE TITLE RECOGNITION: SHIFTING FROM ADVERSARIAL TO COLLABORATIVE ENGAGEMENT

Native title is a legal concept, developed via the legal machinery and tactics of the settler-colonial state. In terms of Indigenous worldviews and value systems, it remains limited. It is not a political settlement.

Patrick Dodson, a senior Yawuru man, in speaking at the first formal native title mediation conference of the National Native Title Tribunal nearly twenty-five years ago, captured Yawuru's determination to negotiate as equals in the process, a determination that remains with us and underpins our contemporary operations in the town of Broome. His address is worth quoting at length:

> The Aboriginal people of the Broome region have been asked to lay our interests in land before you so that you can mediate between our interests and non-Aboriginal interests. We will in due course make known our interests, but we prefer at the outset not to talk to you of interests, but of rights.
>
> Our interests arise from our rights. We have ancestral rights to this land that are now, after many years of neglect, recognised in white Australian law as native title rights. Our interests flow from this. They are not a narrow list of wants. Our interests are as deep and complex as our culture, our history and our Law.
>
> We are very concerned about how these deep, complex and far-reaching interests can be presented within the confines of the Tribunal. It must be recognised

> from the start that there are strong impediments in the very process of structure of the Tribunal's compulsory mediation conference . . .
>
> . . . [W]e are not in fact equal. Our rights are prior, more fundamental, and bound up with our spirit. It is a matter of continuing hurt that we should be asked here to lay our rights down side by side with the so-called rights of those who have dispossessed and denied us. We meet here not as the recognised prior owners willing to concede rights to others in a spirit of co-operation and conciliation. We meet as supplicants pleading for our interests in the face of those who have in the past, and continue to, deny the existence of our rights . . . How can our deep complex and multi-faceted native title rights be reduced to a list of interests to be traded with others without making a mockery of our culture and our obligations both to our ancestors and to our descendants?[7]

Despite more than a century of brutal assault on Yawuru culture and society, we were able to prove—in more than a decade of bitter litigation against the State of Western Australia—that our cultural connection has remained intact. Under Australian law, Yawuru commenced our native title claim for recognition of our traditional connection to, and ownership of, the country in 1994. After an 'epic struggle'—as described by Justice Merkel (who determined the claim)[8]—the final determination of native title was made twelve years later in 2006.

It took the Western Australian State Government a further four years to conclude global agreements with us.[9] The agreements cover approximately 5,300 square kms of land in and around the town of Broome (which is approximately 2,250 kms north of Perth). As part of the agreements, future land development and heritage issues were resolved in order to free up land for residential and industrial development, tourism and an airport. In return, the Yawuru received monetary benefits for capacity-building, preservation of culture and heritage, economic development, social housing, and joint management of a conservation estate comprising conservation areas along the coast and a marine park covering much of Roebuck Bay. The agreements also provided land to the Yawuru for their own development and cultural heritage purposes.

Yawuru's objective in negotiating the agreement was to have a secure basis for income generation and to limit the influence of the state in the management of our affairs. We were also having to respond strategically to a rapidly changing economic environment in our region and identify the next steps to our future stability and self-reliance. When we were negotiating the original agreements with the Western Australian Government the oil, natural gas and mineral resources industries were booming—with all the opportunities and threats that present. Five years later, that industry activity has retracted and the Yawuru, like the broader regional economy, have needed to recalibrate our economic development strategies.

And herein lies our perpetual challenge as First Nations peoples. How do we achieve our ultimate goal of self-reliance and cultural integrity, when our future prosperity is dependent on our capacity to participate in the mainstream economy, an economy often at odds with the cultural values we hold in relation to land and natural resources?

For Yawuru people, the answer lies in transforming the modern settler-colonial discourse, which has historically locked us into a position of exclusion and deficit, into one anchored in inclusion and empowerment. That transformation of discourse must continue to take place, both internally and externally. Our native title determination has been a critical element of our progress in meeting these challenges but, in many regards, the signing of the two Indigenous Land Use Agreements (ILUAs) in 2010 simply marked the beginning of a new phase in our journey towards autonomy. That turning point also signified the handover of significant assets to a nascent entity—Yawuru—whose members had been single-mindedly focused on litigating the native title process for over ten years.

The shift from a political consciousness that arose from more than a decade of native-title claim advocacy and litigation to one that seeks to build community assets and well-being was a massive one. It began with a careful consideration of our governance structures. The several Yawuru corporate governance structures set up to hold and manage our various native title and agreement assets were designed to protect them for future generations, and the relevant Yawuru Boards have committed to ongoing governance training and development to ensure that continues to be the case. For example, the Yawuru Prescribed Body Corporate (PBC) represents the community and holds their native title in trust. It makes decisions about sustaining the integrity and substance of native title in the face of current and future development interests on Yawuru country. To do so, it obtains the free, prior and informed consent of the Yawuru community about important decisions impacting upon culture, country and people.

Nyamba Yawuru Buru (NBY) is a private subsidiary development company, established and fully owned by the PBC to generate income from the activation of Yawuru capital assets that are assigned to it by the PBC. Critically, it incorporates commercial success with the philosophy of mabu liyan. It is not an easy task building and enhancing mabu liyan while at the same time running a commercial business. In the first instance, NBY is tasked with delivering benefits for the well-being of the whole Yawuru community, and second, it must ensure benefits also flow to the broader settler community for the economic sustainability of the town. The considerable challenge for NBY has been to align itself with wider markets and investment partners in a way that will sustain Yawuru's cultural, social and environmental assets, without compromising our native title rights and ability to practice traditional law and culture. We have been actively building strategic partnerships with government agencies and other third parties who are willing to invest in such a culturally integrated approach, and to achieve our goals. Slowly but decisively we have been building a strategic approach to such engagements that emphasises negotiation and collaborative futures.

REDEFINING RELATIONSHIPS WITH THE SETTLER COMMUNITY

We recognise that sustainable economic development cannot be achieved without a fundamental shift in the relationship Yawuru have with the broader settler community. In 1991, following the devastating findings in Australia of the Royal Commission into Aboriginal and Torres Strait Islander Deaths in Custody (Australian Government 1991),[10] Prime Minister Paul Keating instituted through legislation a national process of 'reconciliation'. The intent was to heal the wounds of our nation's historical injustices and include Aboriginal and Torres Strait Islanders in a modern Australia under the terms of an agreed political settlement. While this widely supported movement has done much to raise awareness about institutionalised racism and historical injustice, almost three decades later, it has lost much of its moral and political gravitas. Australians have issued an apology for past injustices, but keep stalling at the confessional, refusing to accept the real price of legitimately founded statehood. Respected historian Mark McKenna (2018: 16) succinctly captures their dilemma, noting that, 'It's precisely this recognition—that the material success of Australian society was built upon the dispossession of Indigenous Australia, a history that clearly demands treaty and settlement—that causes so many to avert their eyes'.

Despite the odds, Australian First Nations communities are gathering momentum and public debate is once again intensifying over the need for constitutional change. Demands include recognition of Aboriginal and Torres Strait Islander people's unique status as First Peoples of Australia and the need to reform that founding document to remove indefensible racist clauses and guarantee there are no legal bases for future generations to be subjected to the injustices of the past. There are also proposals[11] to enshrine a 'Voice to Parliament' within the Australian Constitution, whereby Indigenous people would be guaranteed a say on legislation directly impacting upon their rights and interests.

Amid these sometimes competing agendas, one clear message is emerging; namely, that Australian First Nations must have their cultural jurisdiction recognised over their local territories, particularly those recognised under common law. The time has come for a new paradigm that provides the legal, political and economic mechanisms necessary for our people to 'own our own risk'. In other words, any dramatic shift and change in our circumstances for the betterment of our children and families can only come from our own determination, our own discipline, commitment and leadership at an individual and collective level to drive the change required.

The idea of a national framework agreement or treaty which supports localised agreements incorporating traditional owners or native title holders, the Australian and State Governments, local governments, and industry and community stakeholders should supersede the current dysfunctional federalism arrangements which we all know are failing. Like many native title holders across Australia, we are already heavily engaged in this larger national project by recalibrating our approach to negotiations with government and regional development agencies, such as the Shire of Broome and the Broome Chamber of Commerce and Industry. Yawuru are working hard to create a political, cultural and economic environment whereby we can effectively leverage our rights as equity shareholders in the local and regional economy. Yawuru also are reassessing our global agreements with the nation-state, with a view to better defining the relationship in perpetuity, and have proposed a comprehensive settlement agreement which seeks to support the economic development of the Yawuru Nation through the negotiation of a growth and investment enhancement package for our members. Consistent with the idea of such a national framework agreement, Yawuru are involving the Australian government in these negotiations and are seeking to channel its programme funding, infrastructure and capacity-building investments through Yawuru in order to promote economic growth in the broader region.

The approach adopted by Yawuru is to negotiate future development in the region from a position of strength and in alignment with core Yawuru social and cultural values. This is a change in the discourse and a change of relationships. Rather than waiting for the next ill-conceived 'northern development' scheme or bureaucratic 'project of the day' to be foisted upon us by government or industry with the promise of trickle-down benefits, Yawuru are seeking to leverage our economic and cultural assets and trading links to Asia, to drive economic development in the Kimberley—and to place Yawuru's interests front and centre of that.

In the post-native title local environment, there is a growing realisation within government and the broader community that it will not be possible for development to occur in Broome and its surrounds without the informed involvement and consent of Yawuru. Within Yawuru, there is also increasingly an understanding that for social advancement to occur on our own terms, there needs to be a well-considered engagement in the mainstream economy. This is the only way to protect our cultural estate in the modern economy. We must move beyond a contested, adversarial approach to development towards a more collaborative, interest-based, culturally integrated approach focused on building partnerships and the capacity for enhanced Indigenous participation to support the growth and well-being of the Yawuru *and* the broader regional economy.

REBUILDING THE SOCIAL FABRIC OF YAWURU

Intergenerational Transfer of Cultural Knowledge

Throughout the twentieth century, Yawuru people were subject to laws of the Australian nation-state that allowed government officials to forcibly remove children from their families, fracturing intricate kinship systems and generating transgenerational trauma. The impacts of this experience manifests today in social disharmony, substance abuse and high rates of incarceration for our people. These policies also placed in jeopardy the survival of the Yawuru language and cultural knowledge handed down by our ancestors.

A key initiative in turning this around is the Liyan-ngan Nyirrwa Cultural Healing Centre, officially opened in June 2019. By integrating and extending the Language Resource Hub and the Mangara Knowledge Archive with new training facilities, this institution will become a pillar of Yawuru learning in the community, offering a space to record, document, and perform traditional songs, stories and dances. The Centre will enable Yawuru to deliver cultural and community development programmes grounded in the philosophy of mabu liyan and serve as a contemporary and physical manifestation of reasserting Yawuru values. It will also provide an opportunity for senior and young Yawuru people to work together to develop an understanding of the value of mabu liyan and to ensure the transmission of knowledge and understanding of such Yawuru language terms. A major focus will be on young children in their formative years up to the age of six years, creating a Yawuru cultural environment for them to grow. Nini Mills, Yawuru Manager of Community Development, said at the Centre's opening that

> Seeing it finally open is very heartening for us all and delivers on a promise to increase our services and programs within a welcoming space. This Centre nurtures our culture and cultivates a strong sense of purpose and connection for our community and what it means to be Yawuru. (Nyamba Buru Yawuru 2019a)

The already established Mabu Yawuru Ngan-ga Language Resource Centre has been central to the revitalisation and preservation of Yawuru language and culture. Today, Yawuru and non-Yawuru people are learning language in schools, and the language centre offers a two-year study programme for Yawuru adults. This programme is bringing Yawuru language back into daily use as a family activity, through comprehensive and immersive training. Its aim is to have twenty Yawuru language speakers by 2021. Graduates of the programme will be supported with opportunities to work in tourism, land management and other industries. Some may continue to study through the Department of Education and gain accreditation to become school language teachers. As Maya Shioji, the new coordinator at Mabu Yawuru Ngan-Ga put it, 'I now feel like I am contributing to my grandmother's vision to keeping the Yawuru language alive' (Nyamba Buru Yawuru 2016: 8). With these language and other initiatives, we aim to keep our Yawuru culture strong and at the very heart of our future development.

Investing in Our Young People

We recognise that investing in our young people is absolutely critical to transforming the old deficit discourse and achieving intergenerational change. We are seeing a number of young cultural leaders emerging through initiatives such as the Yawuru Youth Forums. These forums provide a platform for young people aged between twelve and thirty years to come together, share ideas, make collective decisions and set their own agenda for change. The forums have seen substantial contributions from young people to tackling the tragically high levels of youth suicide in our region, with a number participating in the Australian Government's Suicide Prevention Roundtable in 2017.

We know that nurturing a strong cultural identity in young people is essential to their emotional well-being, but it also increases their capacity and resilience to engage in education and employment later in life. This is why Nyamba Yawuru Buru (NBY), the Yawuru-owned and controlled not-for-profit organisation, also directly delivers services to young people such as the Australian Government's Transition to Work Program, an intensive pre-employment support for fifteen- to twenty-one-year-olds. As well as developing practical skills to enhance employability, NBY is collaborating with partner organisations to provide cultural leadership training, and utilising digital media to share stories that reflect our local history and Yawuru culture. The Yawuru Youth Excellence Fund provides a scholarship programme to improve the delivery of support to young people who are either high achievers in their field or those seeking assistance to further their education or training. In such ways, we are working to mentor and support the next generation of Yawuru leaders to have a strong commitment to collective well-being and shared prosperity for all Yawuru.

Individual and Collective Wealth Generation

Yawuru people are effectively engaging in an adaptive cultural process, one where we have reorientated ourselves towards our cultural knowledge and practices, but also embrace the reality of Western economic success. This is a hard balance for any First Nation to achieve in the real world. But we are finding that by making sure mabu liyan is repositioned at the heart of what we do, we are building cultural resilience and integration into our economic development decisions and priorities. Cultural knowledge and practices such as mabu liyan have always been there, underlying Yawuru life, but due to historical circumstances, they have not always been publicly acknowledged and promoted. The native title determination has empowered us to make the decisions about these matters—to give greater focus and definition to our knowledge and practices in a contemporary context. For example, some Yawuru people now have the ability to obtain capital assets (e.g. freehold property) and this in turn has enabled us to give greater definition to the social value of our country, language, ceremonies and customs.

Housing is a good example of where we are imbuing our economic development strategy with the philosophy of mabu liyan. A house is a tangible financial asset for an individual, but is integral to building capacity of the whole community, offering stability and health benefits and creating well-being for families. This stability in turn underpins our young people's capacity to participate in education and employment, and succeed. NBY's strategic investment over the past six years has demonstrated that we can operate a successful housing development model, providing a housing pathway that incorporates all stages of the housing continuum—from rental relief and social housing through to private home ownership. NBY has signed a Memorandum of Understanding with the relevant WA State Government agency, which allows us to work collaboratively to improve housing opportunities for a broad cross-section of our community.

Another initiative that aligns mabu liyan with economic development is the Yawuru Ranger Program. This was established with the WA Department of Parks and Wildlife for the training and employment of Yawuru to actively manage our own country. The work of Yawuru Rangers includes managing introduced challenges such as weeds, feral animals and uncontrolled fires. A combination of pristine marine and conservation parks fall within our native title determination area. Yawuru are working with external scientific experts at the forefront of geospatial mapping technology[12] and bringing them together with the expertise of our own Elders to develop a land-use decision-making tool to help protect culturally and ecologically significant wetlands and pastoral land. Yawuru country managers who are trained in this gain formal qualifications in conservation and land management and are engaged in projects such as comprehensive fauna surveys, fencing, weed-management and bio-security training. Yawuru country managers are also collaborating with other First Nations' ranger groups across Australia to research endangered species across our region.

Looking after country in this way is not only important for protecting and exercising our cultural and native title rights but it also an opportunity to open up other economic development opportunities for Yawuru people. For example, much of our cultural mapping work is being undertaken on Roebuck Plains Station, a successful cattle station on Yawuru country. Increasing our involvement in the commercial operation of Roebuck Plains Station is a priority for NBY and there is potential to lead an integrated regional beef strategy and leverage the Roebuck Export Depot Cattle Yards in the future. Other promising commercial opportunities for the station include cultural tourism, fodder production, tropical horticulture, aquiculture, and bush foods and medicines.

Yawuru are also continuing to explore options for low-impact development on waterfront land suitable for tourism. This land is currently unregulated and heavily used by non-Indigenous people and was included in the original settlement agreements with the WA Government, following our native title determination. This project will require careful cultural consideration and natural resource management in order to imbue and sustain it with mabu liyan for our people. Having an equity interest in such a facility is potentially the most strategic way for Yawuru people to regain control over access to these areas and ensure long-term cultural and environmental sustainability, as well as financial benefit for Yawuru people. NBY takes considerable care in navigating and negotiating such proposals with the community, beginning with discussions that occur at a Board level.

Demonstrating Leadership for Intergenerational Growth and Stability

Yawuru people are engaged in the reconstruction of the social and cultural fabric of our society, following more than a century of marginalisation and disenfranchisement. To achieve this formidable goal, we need to build a cycle of success in which a key element is unity of purpose and confidence within the community. Leadership is key to our social and economic transformation. We must rebuild the foundations of cultural knowledge and respect and integrate that into Yawuru contemporary governance, while at the same time develop the agility and resilience necessary to leverage opportunities to secure the economic future of our people in the emerging economy. This calls for a particular kind of public-spirited leadership, one that puts mabu liyan and the well-being of our people ahead of self-interest.

In this context, Yawuru must have at our disposal a 'modern weaponry' of capabilities, such as fit-for-purpose corporate structures, adaptive governance and trustworthy expert advice. But, just as importantly, our community members must accept responsibility and own the risk of change—individually and collectively. To be able to do that, we must have the confidence to make and implement decisions about our future, plus have workable accountability mechanisms so there is transparency as well as a safe environment in which to conduct respectful discussions when there is dissent or alternative points of view.

The risks for Yawuru are both internal and external. While our corporate entities are busily engaged in relationship-building with government and commercial investment partners, we also have to manage the risk posed by disputation between various sections of the Yawuru community or other Aboriginal groups. The challenge for our leadership is to work with community members to overcome decades of learnt behaviour, where development and change has historically been imposed upon us and so compounded the trauma of colonisation rather than relieved it. The challenge now is to build a sense of common purpose and personal investment in the commercial success of community assets, while remaining true to fundamental Yawuru cultural and social values.

Of course, the other leadership challenge is to manage this work of social repair and resurgence, alongside the pressure to grow the business side. The key for Yawuru is to build on our success. We must capture and channel the optimism and confidence that we can see being generated when our social and cultural programmes are able to break cycles of long-term unemployment, when a Yawuru student becomes the first member of their family to graduate from university, when a business proposal attracts capital investment from a new commercial partner, when a Yawuru person makes a decision to establish a cultural tourism enterprise or other business. Each one of these victories builds the strength and capacity of the whole community and helps to create a shared vision as to how culturally integrated development strategies can deliver stability and prosperity for future generations of Yawuru. This helps reproduce an environment where our own members are confident about investing their time and energies into our collective future.

Yawuru people have a proud history of strong leadership, not just at the community level but also at a state and national level. From the beginnings of the land rights movement through to the negotiation of the *Native Title Act* and reconciliation agenda, Yawuru leaders have demonstrated the importance of strategic public engagement in policy issues that impact upon our people. I see the next generation of Yawuru leaders as not only leading the debate on how to best meet the diverse and unique needs of First Nations peoples in our region and across Australia but also as commercial pioneers and leaders in the industries in which Yawuru chose to target economic opportunity.

Yawuru are already at the forefront of a paradigm shift in thinking around the Australian Government's 'Northern Australia Development Agenda'.[13] A good example of this leadership is our participation in the Indigenous Reference Group (IRG) advising the Australian Ministerial Council on Northern Australian Development. NBY's chief executive officer chairs the IRG and, together with other First Nations' colleagues, is working with all levels of government to open up access to rapidly growing Asian markets and ensure that employment, training and enterprise development are incorporated as a matter of course into our broader nation-building strategy.

It is vital that we demonstrate to our young people that they have the power and capacity to lead their generation into a stable and positive future; to honour, protect and leverage the cultural assets of language, law and country handed down to them by their ancestors. But it is also vital that they use this strength and mabu liyan to flourish and succeed in the contemporary Australian society and economy.

CONCLUSION

As Yawuru people, we find ourselves at a pivotal moment in our history. We are transitioning from more than a century of adversarial struggle against an aggressive colonial-settler regime towards recognition of our status as First Nations people, with all the risks and opportunities that journey produces. Following our native title determination, the message from our community was clear: rebuilding the social and cultural fabric of our society had to be a priority focus. We need to recover and strengthen mabu liyan and incorporate this philosophy, handed down by our ancestors, into all our development strategies for the future. In that way, we know that our development initiatives will reinforce, not undermine, our ongoing cultural resilience and maximise our self-determination.

This is a 'nation project' layered in complexity due to a highly dynamic mainstream political milieu that is alert, but not always responsive to the competing demands of a contemporary Indigenous society. As a post-colonial settler state, Australia is still working through its own extended, troubled adolescence, anticipating a move towards an independent republic when it has not yet fully come to terms with the illegitimacy of its founding moment. As a consequence, efforts to reconcile the relationship between Indigenous and non-Indigenous peoples have remained fragmented and service-delivery focused, failing to produce the comprehensive transformation of colonial power dynamics that is required. While native title rights and interests have been recognised at law, there remains an ongoing challenge at the local level to translate these technical rights into practical outcomes that will sustain future generations of cultural leaders.

Nonetheless, there are signs that the mood of the nation is shifting. There is enormous goodwill in the wider community and business sectors to support the recognition of Indigenous people's place at the heart of the nation. There is hope for future generations of Indigenous people that, for the first time since colonisation, they will not be forced to fight to have their rights and culture recognised but will be able to dream of, aspire to and achieve in whatever endeavour they pursue, proud of their Indigenous heritage and confident in their sense of self.

The challenge for governments and for Indigenous Nations will be to channel this hope and aspiration to support the collaborative future development of Northern Australia. The focus should not just be to develop industry and the economy in the northern half of our continent to support a neoliberal vision of growth but to fundamentally transform the livelihoods of Indigenous people through prioritising Indigenous-identified opportunities and via investment in the capacity for Indigenous groups to work towards the practical realisation of self-determination. This will require explicit attention to and support for our political bases and our political processes from the wider Australian state and community.

We are adopting a multifaceted approach to drive this more profound shift at a local and regional level. Money alone cannot overcome decades of systemic exclusion from mainstream economic participation. Just as importantly, limited recognition of cultural rights to land cannot on their own grow and sustain a healthy, educated and cohesive community. The challenge for Yawuru leaders is to work closely with community to pursue their goal of mabu liyan, by leveraging the capital value of cultural assets—to forge new partnerships that support sustainable development on our country in a way that promotes and protects country, language and our people. Trust will grow alongside our capacity to protect and grow our cultural estate.

This process will take time. While our ancestors have provided the values and deeper reference points that are necessary to reconstruct our social fabric and collective well-being, they could never have envisaged how Yawuru culture might manifest and survive in a technology-driven, emergent northern economy that is increasingly driven by Asian markets and capital. We must learn how to sit comfortably with the risk and responsibility this environment brings. If we are strong in our understanding of who we are and understand the value of our cultural assets, we can assert our position as genuine equity shareholders in the northern Australian economy and, through the fulfilment of our potential, contribute significantly to the future prosperity of our nation, and the nation as a whole.

NOTES

1. In the process of colonising Australia, Captain James Cook was instructed by King George III to take possession of the 'Convenient Situations in the Country . . . with the Consent of the Natives' (Museum of Australian Democracy n.d.).

2. The doctrine of discovery is a concept of western international law expounded by the United States Supreme Court in a series of decisions, which purported to explain and apply the way that western colonial powers laid claim to lands belonging to Indigenous sovereign nations during the 'age of discovery'. The doctrine has been primarily used to support decisions invalidating or ignoring Indigenous possession of land in favour of settler colonial governments. See also Newcombe S. http://ili.nativeweb.org/sdrm_art.html.

3. For example, a 2019 Interim Report from the Australian Government inquiry into Australia's Faunal Extinction Crisis, notes that Australia is in the midst of an animal extinction crisis and the loss of almost 20 unique species in coming years is inevitable without drastic change (Commonwealth of Australia 2019).

4. *The Wik Peoples v The State of Queensland & Ors*; *The Thayorre People v The State of Queensland & Ors* (1996) HCA 40.

5. *State of Western Australia v Ward* (2002) HCA 28 at [76].

6. In 2013, the first litigated native title decision in relation to commercial rights and interests was handed down by the High Court in Akiba on behalf of the *Torres Strait Regional Seas Claim Group v Commonwealth of Australia*, which found that a native title right to commercially exploit fish did exist in a determination relating to 13 Torres Strait Island communities. The following year, the Federal Court found, in two native title determinations in the Western Desert in Western Australia, *Willis on behalf of the Pilki People v State of Western Australia* and *BP (Deceased) on behalf of the Birriliburu People v State of Western Australia*, held that the native title holders had always held the right to access and take the resources within their territory for any purposes, including commercial purposes, provided the right was consistent with the group's traditional system of law and custom. *Griffiths v Northern Territory* [2007] 165 FCR 391]; *Akiba on behalf of the Torres Strait Regional Seas Claim Group v Commonwealth of Australia* (2013) HCA 33. See National Native Title Tribunal (2017).

7. Patrick Dodson, Introductory speech to His Honor, Mr Justice French (NNTT President) at the first compulsory mediation conference convened by the National Native Title Tribunal in Broome, 19 September 1994.

8. *Rubibi Community v State of Western Australia (No 7)* [2006] FCA 459, 28 April 2006, per Merkel J.

9. The Yawuru Agreement includes two Indigenous Land Use Agreements (ILUAs)—the Yawuru Area Agreement and the Yawuru Prescribed Body Corporate Agreement, registered by the National Native Title Tribunal on 6 August 2010. The signatories to the Agreements are the State of Western Australia, the Shire of Broome and the Yawuru Native Title Holders Aboriginal Corporation.

10. The recommendations from the report are available at http://www.austlii.edu.au/au/other/IndigLRes/rciadic/national/vol5/5.html.

11. A constitutional convention bringing together over 250 Aboriginal and Torres Strait Islander leaders met in 2017 at the foot of Uluru in Central Australia on the lands of the Aṉangu people. The majority resolved, in the Uluru Statement from the Heart, to call for the establishment of a First Nations Voice in the Australian Constitution and a Makarrata Commission to supervise a process of 'agreement-making' and 'truth-telling' between governments and Australia's Indigenous peoples. With subsequent changes of national government in Australia, support for the recommendations have swung from bipartisan to highly divergent, sometimes oppositional posturing by political parties. See '1 Voice Uluru' (n.d.) at https://dosomethingnearyou.com.au/cause/1-voice-uluru/.

12. NBY has a geospatial mapping partnership with the Fenner School of Environmental Studies at Australian National University that helps Yawuru better understand country and improve land-use decision-making. The MOLA (Multi Objective Land Allocation) project utilises sophisticated technology and other tools along with cultural knowledge to increase the information about Yawuru country and to evaluate its values and potential uses. MOLA is also used to produce information in collaboration with other partners such as the Shire of Broome, which regularly undertakes coastal mapping with us (Nyamba Buru Yawuru 2019b).

13. The Australian Government's 'Our North, Our Future: White Paper on Developing Northern Australia' was released in 2015, and sets out the priorities to drive growth in Australia's north. It is a twenty-year plan for investment and support to grow the north through six key pillars: a trade and investment gateway, diversified northern economy, Indigenous entrepreneurship and businesses, world-class infrastructure, water infrastructure investment, and research and innovation (see Australian Government 2019).

Chapter 12

The Red Lake Walleye Recovery Project

Tribal Governance for Sustainable Success

Miriam Jorgensen, Allen Pemberton, Pat Brown and David Conner

In 1997, the members of the Red Lake Fisheries Association (RLFA), a business cooperative established by commercial fishermen from the Red Lake Nation,[1] voted to discontinue all commercial gillnet fishing on Red Lake, Minnesota, the United States (US). Less than a year later, the Red Lake Tribal Council passed a resolution banning hook-and-line subsistence fishing for walleye,[2] effectively ending all fishing on tribal waters. Several hundred tribal families lost income from the demise of commercial walleye fishing and, with the overall fishing ban, every tribal citizen lost access to a significant food source. But witnessing first-hand the stark decline of the walleye and recognising that a vital cultural and economic resource was slipping away, the Red Lake Nation had taken a stand: it needed to do everything it could to save the walleye and make its lake healthy again.

The decisions taken by the RLFA and the tribal council were impressive, brave and risky. They did not know if Red Lake Nation citizens would abide by the fishing ban. They did not know if a recovery effort on such a large lake, overfished for decades, would be possible. And because the Red Lake Nation shares jurisdiction over Red Lake with the state of Minnesota, they did not know if fishing from the Minnesota side would compromise the tribal efforts to revive the walleye population.

Yet, by 2006, walleye recovery was essentially complete. Red Lake Nation citizens were fishing again and utilising practices that reduced pressure on the fish population. The tribe had developed strong and respectful relationships with partner government agencies engaged in fish recovery. And new economic opportunities were open to both tribal citizens and non-Native residents of the surrounding region. In 2019, more than a decade after Red Lake's waters reopened for fishing, the lake ecosystem remains in robust health. The Red Lake Nation-owned fish processing facility provides employment for tribal citizens and revenue for the tribal government; a thriving sport fishing sector is an economic boon to off-reservation non-Native communities; the tribal government and state government continue to work collaboratively on fish population management; science and public policy advanced by the Red Lake walleye recovery effort is benefiting lake ecosystems throughout the Great Lakes region and into Canada; and once-frayed cultural and spiritual connections between the Red Lake Ojibwe and Red Lake itself have been restored.

How did all of this occur? How did the walleye population reach its low point? What did the Red Lake Nation do to turn things around? What explains the Red Lake Nation's trajectory from near-loss of its fish resources to recovery and sustainability? As this case story explains, success was the result not only of sound environmental science but also of effective tribal governance.

FROM PLENTY TO FEW

The Red Lake Nation is an Ojibwe Nation, having kinship and cultural ties with the Ojibwe peoples that span the Great Lakes region of North America. The Red Lake Reservation, which is home to 7,000 of the Red Lake Nation's 12,000 citizens (Smith 2017),[3] shares a geography with the north-western part of the US State of Minnesota. Red Lake, the reservation's namesake, is a pre-eminent feature of the landscape. At 116,870 hectares, it is the largest lake in Minnesota and the sixth largest natural lake in the United States.[4]

In the late 1800s, the Red Lake Nation's leadership experienced unusual success in preventing allotment (the division of reservation land into individually assigned parcels)—success that in turn prevented the sale of 'surplus' reservation land to non-Ojibwe immigrants. But Red Lake's leaders were unable to fully thwart resource-hungry settlers. While they believed their 1889 negotiations concerning allotment and the reservation's boundaries had secured not only the reservation land base but also the entirety of the lake for the tribe, final treaty documents assigned the eastern portion of upper Red Lake to the State of Minnesota. As a result, the Red Lake Reservation is a contiguous land base under the jurisdiction of the Red Lake Nation Government and subject to trust oversight by the United States Bureau of Indian Affairs (BIA)—as is 83 per cent of the lake. The remaining 17 per cent of the lake is under Minnesota's jurisdiction.[5]

The Red Lake Ojibwe view their lake as a gift from the Creator and have long relied on its fish, especially the prized walleye, as a primary source of nourishment. They even have referred to the lake as their 'food store' (Haga 2006; Kolpack 2006). Historically, subsistence fishing on Red Lake was a way of life. For several months each year, families would move to lakeside fish camps and work together to bring in the harvest. Men and older children would set and pull the nets; women and younger children would remove the fish and dry the nets. It was hard work, but the walleye were plentiful and the people were grateful, offering their thanks each fishing season with a gift of sacred tobacco to the lake.[6]

Despite the loss of a portion of the lake in 1889, the Red Lake people's relationship with the lake remained largely unchanged until 1917, when the United States entered World War I. The war effort caused regional food shortages, and Minnesota was hard hit. Widespread hunger and the threat of substantial illicit and unregulated fishing turned the state's attention towards fish as a food source (Avery 1918; van Oosten & Deason 1957). While the State of Minnesota also opened several other lakes for commercial fishing, it first developed a plan for commercial fishing on Red Lake, which the BIA permitted on the condition that the plan provide 'certain benefits' to the tribe (Avery 1918).[7] The state responded by offering to help the Red Lake Nation establish and operate its own commercial fishery. From 1920 to 1928, Red Lake citizens sold their catches to the state, which then sold the fish wholesale to mid-western and eastern markets (Meyers 1992; van Oosten & Deason 1957).

Red Lake fishermen soon became dissatisfied with this arrangement. In 1922, tribal leaders objected to state involvement, arguing that the presence of state fishing crews disadvantaged tribal fishermen. They contended that the state's control of marketing did not bring the best price for the tribal catch and that the state underpaid Indian fishermen by weighing their fish inaccurately (Meyers 1992; Walter Butler Company 1978). Nevertheless, crews of both tribal and state commercial fishermen continued to fish on Red Lake and were able to provide food to Minnesotans and others at affordable prices for the remainder of the decade. Because it was standard practice at the time, all fishing occurred with an eye towards market demand—not fish population sustainability (van Oosten & Deason 1957).[8]

In 1929, a non-Indian fish wholesaler from southern Minnesota sued the state for unfair competition. It was this challenge, not the tribe's concerns, that led to the state's exit from the fishing business at Red Lake. The suit resulted in a Minnesota Supreme Court order that restricted the state to a regulatory role in commercial fishing operations on state waters. Complying, the state legislature transferred the fishing operations on Red Lake to the BIA (van Oosten & Deason 1957).

To fulfil its new responsibilities, the BIA developed fishery regulations that mandated harvest monitoring and scientific resource management

(USA Code of Federal Regulations No. 242). If followed, these federal regulations might have worked. But as contemporary tribal managers have observed, it was as if the BIA put a regulatory framework in place in 1930 and then forgot about it—at the cost of fish and lake health (Anderson 2006).

Regulatory monitoring and enforcement were sorely needed. On the Indian-owned portion of the lake, there essentially was no limit on the number of Red Lake citizens setting gillnets or on the number of nets each set. The tribal fishermen's cooperative, the RLFA, routinely asked the BIA to expand the quota, requests that routinely were granted (Dokken 2000; Haga 2006). On the lake's state-controlled waters, scores of non-Indian anglers regularly exceeded their walleye catch limits, a flouting of the law fuelled both by competition and a sense of entitlement. As one fishing insider put it, the mindset developed among sport-fish anglers that, '"If the Indians are going to net them anyway, I'm going to take more than my limit." It was a race to catch the last walleye' (Kelly Petrowske, quoted in Dokken 2009, para. 29).

The lack of quota enforcement also fuelled a black market. Fish were provided to family and friends as gifts or in trade; they were sold for quick cash to people passing through the reservation, and they were sold out of the backs of cars at schools, churches and sporting events as far away as the state's largest metropolis, the 'Twin Cities' of Minneapolis and St. Paul (Anderson 2006; Dokken 2009; Niskanen 2006). Illicit sales reportedly doubled the annual legal take of walleye, which already was well above a sustainable harvest level (Gunderson 1998).

In the 1970s, after five decades of overfishing, Red Lake's walleye population began to experience boom-and-bust cycles, an omen of the species' collapse. But soaring walleye prices, which continued through the 1980s and 1990s, lured more and more Red Lake citizens in search of a good living into commercial fishing. The RLFA membership surged to 700 in the late 1980s and early 1990s and produced its largest documented annual harvest in 1989—430,435 kilograms (Dokken 2000). This level far eclipsed both the BIA's static quota and the lakes' capacity. By 1996, the harvest fell to 6,804 kilograms (Red Lake DNR 2016).

How many population booms and busts could the Red Lake walleye survive? Might things reach a point where the walleye simply died out? If so, what might this imply for Red Lake community members as a tribe and as a people? As some community members observed, 'The tradition of fishing has been passed down from generation to generation. It is part of who we are as a nation, so when the fish left, so did part of our identity' (Red Lake DNR and Project Preserve 2008, at 00:01).

WORKING TOWARDS RECOVERY

In 1997, in an eleventh-hour effort to save the walleye, the RFLA voted to end all gillnet fishing on Red Lake. Fishermen left the work that had supported their families for generations, sold their boats and gear, and began looking for new ways to make a living. Less than a year later, the Red Lake Tribal Council backed up the fishermen's actions by banning hook-and-line fishing on the tribe's portion of the lake. The State of Minnesota was slower to respond, but by 1999, the state legislature also had placed a moratorium on fishing in the Red Lake waters it controlled.[9] What made these decisions possible and what made them sustainable?

Regaining Tribal Decision-Making Authority

In part, the Red Lake Nation's success was born of its ability and desire to take advantage of changes in US law. In 1988, the US Government began testing (through a demonstration programme) a policy it called 'self governance'. Under the United States' standard model for channelling monies to tribes, the BIA would hire its own personnel to manage federally funded programmes in tribal communities. Under the new policy, tribes could sign a Self-Governance Agreement, take over a programme that the federal government had managed on the tribe's behalf and manage the programme and programme monies as it saw fit. When Congress expanded the programme beyond its demonstration status in 1994 and allowed all tribes to pursue Self-Governance Agreements, the Red Lake Nation seized the opportunity. By 1997, it was operating its own natural-resource programmes, free of the BIA's bureaucracy. Streamlined decision-making facilitated by tribal control made it possible for the Red Lake Nation Department of Natural Resources to act quickly and authoritatively, particularly in regard to the fishery, which was one of its first major projects as a self-governance tribe (Simcosky & Holmes 2005).

Building a Relationship with the State

Given its partial jurisdiction over Red Lake's waters, the tribe knew that involvement by the State of Minnesota was critical to walleye recovery. In 1997, even before the tribal council took decisive action, then-chairman Bobby Whitefeather initiated a dialogue with the state's Department of Natural Resources.[10] These early meetings took place in cafes and restaurants—neutral ground that supported an honest exchange of views. Despite initial tensions, the participants openly discussed their shared goals and, remarkably, made an explicit decision to leave behind any blame.[11]

The discussions culminated in an historic memorandum of understanding (MOU) signed by the Red Lake Nation, State of Minnesota and US Bureau of Indian Affairs. A first in the history of tribal–state relations in Minnesota, the 1999 agreement reaffirmed the Red Lake Nation's walleye ban, prohibited walleye fishing on Red Lake's state waters and mandated strict regulation of the moratorium on both parts of the lake. It also established a multi-partner technical committee composed of scientists and other representatives from the Red Lake Department of Natural Resources (Red Lake DNR), RLFA, Minnesota Department of Natural Resources (Minnesota DNR), University of Minnesota, BIA and the US Fish and Wildlife Service—and charged it with planning, managing and sustaining walleye recovery.[12] At the signatories' option, the MOU could be renewed in ten years.

Following the operating principles of mutual respect and shared science, the technical committee launched an unprecedented recovery plan designed to bring the walleye back to Red Lake. This aggressive plan incorporated staggered fry stocking,[13] stringent enforcement of the fishing ban, public education, and comprehensive data collection and sharing to assess the quantity, maturity, diversity and natural reproduction capability of the walleye population as it recovered. The two parties also agreed to share the cost of the restoration.

Recovery efforts had little chance of success without tribal–state collaboration, and yet a variety of circumstances suggested that cooperation would be difficult. As noted, resource competition had developed between Native commercial fishermen and non-Native sport fishermen. For some, the perception of competing interests also was fuelled by racism (Dokken 2000). Furthermore, the state and tribe had no history of collaboration on fishery management or, realistically, on any issues at all. As journalist Dennis Anderson describes it, the Red Lake Nation and State of Minnesota, as peoples and as governments, were 'separated by vastly different histories and traditions, shady land deals, and centuries of mistrust that hang over northwest Minnesota like ghosts' (Anderson 2006, para. 1).

The technical committee was a key vehicle for addressing these concerns and ensuring ongoing cooperation. Three aspects of technical committee design and operations were particularly helpful to maintaining the tribal–state partnership:

1. Strategic representation: Appointees to the technical committee included practising fisheries biologists, fishermen, politicians and a university professor. The tribal, federal and state representatives were able to keep key stakeholders within their respective governments informed. Those with environmental expertise kept the focus on sustainability, and those with programme management skills kept the focus on practical

implementation. The university professor brought scientific know-how, historical perspective (in the 1980s, he had helped start the Red Lake Nation's fishery programme), and a degree of neutrality as he had not been directly involved in any of the activities that led to fish-stock depletion. RLFA members brought the knowledge of multiple generations of Red Lake fishermen and a grounded perspective that reminded experts of the real-life needs of the tribe's fishing families.

2. Consensus decision-making: Early on, the technical committee agreed to make all decisions by consensus. The committee's protocol was to discuss disagreements until everyone could agree on a course of action. These discussions helped committee members understand and respect each other's commitments and develop trust in the process.

   Stocking was an early contentious issue for the technical committee: given the unique genetics of Red Lake walleye, should it recommend rebuilding the walleye population with juvenile fish reared outside Red Lake? Committee members discussed the arguments for and against stocking for weeks, ultimately forming a subcommittee to explore the options in greater depth. These conversations made it clear that the controversy involved scientific unknowns rather than a one-dimensional 'tribe versus state' fracture: would it be possible to find a close enough genetic match to limit ecological damage to the lake? Would enough such fry be available to make a real commitment to restoration of Red Lake's walleye population? If so, would stocking mean the end of the unique Red Lake walleye genome? As one fisheries specialist put it, the decision to stock Red Lake was 'agonizing' (Smith 2015). Eventually, the technical committee found a compromise that all members could accept: stock Red Lake no more than five times with fry that were a close genetic match to the naturally occurring walleye population and actively monitor the population over time in order to supply just enough non-Native walleye to support recovery (Logsdon, Anderson & Miller 2016).
3. Freedom from political interference: Without question, numerous state and tribal government constituents were dissatisfied with the fishing ban. Commercial fishermen lost income, sport fishermen lost recreational opportunities and tourism-oriented entrepreneurs lost business. Yet successive tribal chairmen and councillors, governors and state legislators did not play politics with these constituent concerns. They respected and supported their experts, freeing the technical committee to make decisions based on biology, not politics.

This attention to technical committee design and processes paid off. Comments such as those from Bill May, an RFLA representative to the committee, show how the protocols resulted in mutual respect among members and a commitment to forward progress:

> I really listened to what the guys had to say, and everything they said made a lot of sense to me . . . The biologists were using all their techniques to develop a plan. And what I liked about it is nobody in the group was there to say, 'It's because of you guys'. Never did that attitude come out. It was just this group of people saying, 'What can we do together?' (quoted in Dokken 2000: 16)

Communicating with the Public

In addition to building a relationship with the state, Red Lake Nation leaders knew they needed to keep the tribal community informed about walleye recovery efforts. As Pat Brown, Red Lake DNR Fisheries Director, put it, 'We had a very simple plan to bring back the walleye . . . that was the easy part. The hard part was when we had to start managing people, or the social aspect' (quoted in Record 2010, at 14:39). Because there would have been no chance of success if tribal citizens failed to cooperate with the fishing regulations, the tribe complemented its scientific efforts with a systematic and conscientious citizen-information campaign.

Elected leaders and tribal DNR staff organised forums and town hall meetings to share the technical committee's recommendations and gather grassroots feedback. These were held across the reservation and in several off-reservation metropolitan areas in an effort to reach both resident and non-resident Red Lake citizens. Tribal council representatives and the Red Lake Nation's seven hereditary chiefs served as points of contact for tribal members. Up-to-date information about the recovery also was available in tribal council minutes and in the tribal newsletter, which were distributed widely.[14]

This transparency generated critical support from tribal citizens for the fishing moratorium. While anecdotal evidence points to some smaller-scale poaching by tribal citizens,[15] the Red Lake DNR formally recorded very few violations by tribal citizens between 1997 and 2006 (Record 2010). Tribal leaders also testified to Red Lake tribal citizens' support and cooperation. Press coverage of the tribe's May 2006 ceremony and feast in celebration of the walleye recovery notes that Red Lake Tribal Secretary Judy Roy 'expressed thanks to all the people who observed the fishing moratorium' (Miron 2006, para. 13). In a contemporaneous interview, former Tribal Chairman Bobby Whitefeather remarked, 'I commend the membership in their refrain from exploiting that body of water we all hold so sacred' (quoted in Kolpack 2006: 1).

Of course, successful walleye recovery required buy-in from both sides of the lake—from tribal citizens *and* non-Indian fishermen. Dave Conner, a biologist and administrator with the Red Lake DNR, bluntly framed the problem: 'People everywhere are going to see walleyes, and they're going to want them' (quoted in Dokken 2000: 17).

Marketing the initiative off the reservation included information about the recovery project and how state–tribal collaboration made the Red Lake recovery project possible. From the start, Minnesota DNR officials assembled and consulted with a Minnesota citizens' advisory committee for input on public relations' issues and proposed regulations.[16] Among others, its members included representatives of the Minnesota Fishing Roundtable, Minnesota Sportfishing Congress, Sportmen's Club of Lake Vermilion and a variety of area tourism interests (Dokken 2005; Vermilion Lake Association 1999), who were able to represent and provide outreach to a diverse group of stakeholders with interests in Upper Red Lake. It was through the Minnesota Fish Roundtable, for example, that the DNR was able to make an early announcement about plans to reopen Red Lake and to have preliminary discussions about the number and size of walleye that sport anglers might take (*Brainerd Dispatch* staff 2004). The technical committee also jointly hosted several meetings with the Bemidji Area Race Relations Council. These engagements taught people about the joint recovery effort and presented the state–tribal collaboration as a lesson in interagency cooperation.[17] The meetings also provided the broader public with opportunities to interact with officials from the tribe and state.

Combined with stepped-up enforcement, education efforts by the state and technical committee appear to have resulted in substantial compliance by non-Native fishermen. The press reported only a few verified poaching incidents during the moratorium,[18] which suggests that the results of joint state–tribal conservation enforcement efforts in 2002, described in the minutes of the 28 December technical committee meeting, were typical:

> [The officer] reported that work efforts entailed 634 lake patrol/man hours, 973 fishermen checked, and one violation . . . He also reported that officers would be patrolling the lake on a daily basis. They have also set up check points at the shoreline and lake and have an underwater camera this year. He concluded that overall, things went well during the year, fishermen were cooperative and concerned about walleye recovery.[19]

THE RECOVERY

Neither fishermen nor fisheries biologists were certain that the Red Lake walleye recovery effort would succeed (Dokken 1999; Gunderson 1998)—especially given Red Lake's immense size and complexity as a fish incubator

(Anderson 2006). Experts estimated that, at best, it would take a decade for the fish population to return to a self-sustaining level (Niskanen 2006)—if recovery was feasible at all. But as Henry Drewes of the Minnesota DNR observed, through the combined efforts of the tribe and state, the recovery 'ended up being quicker and more successful than we possibly could have imagined' (quoted in Dokken 2014, para. 20).

Ecological Restoration

In 1997, the Red Lake Nation DNR counted only twelve walleye in its test nets, leading to a population estimate of 100,000 to 200,000 walleye throughout the lakes' nearly 121,406 hectares (Bowden 2010; Boyd 2011; Haga 2006; Kolpack 2006). In other words, assessment data suggested that there were no more than two walleye for every 1.2 hectares acres of lake waters. Worse, test nets captured no female walleye, making population replacement, let alone growth, doubtful (Dokken 2016).

By the mid-2000s, the data told a very different story. In 2005, the Red Lake DNR counted 1,230 walleye in its test nets (Haga 2006) and estimates placed the 2006 population in the range of 7.5 to 8 million fish (Bowden 2010; Boyd 2011). Moreover, the population consisted of several strong year-classes of spawning age walleye and a significant percentage of naturally reproduced fish, clear signs of the renewed health and sustainability of the species. A sustainable fish population is characterised by multiple year-classes of mature fish that are able to naturally reproduce. By 2016, population models showed a combined Upper and Lower Red Lakes walleye population of 13 million fish across ten spawning classes (Dokken 2016). It indicated that the technical committee's recovery plan had worked.

Of note, the collaborating tribal and state DNRs gained this detailed understanding of the walleye population through scientific innovation. By using and refining a new technique for marking fry,[20] biologists could later determine whether a fish had been stocked. Thus, test net data not only supported estimates of the total population size and age structure but also of the proportions of stocked, native and naturally reproduced fish (Haga 2006; Logsdon 2006; Logsdon, Anderson & Miller 2016; Rivers 2006).

Economic Revival

The walleye's resurgence prompted the Red Lake Nation and the state of Minnesota—with the technical committee's endorsement—to reopen Red Lake to subsistence and sport fishing in the spring of 2006. In late 2007, the tribe re-established the commercial fishery on Red Lake.

Initial post-recovery regulations were conservative. Only hook-and-line fishing was allowed. On state-controlled waters, the sport fishing catch limit was set at two walleye (of regulated size) per day. On tribally controlled waters, subsistence fishermen were limited to ten walleye per day, and commercial fishermen were allowed fifty, provided they first registered with the tribe (Robertson 2008).[21] The technical committee also set harvestable limit of 446,788 kilograms as a further constraint on the maximum catch that could be taken from the lake and allocated the quota to the Red Lake Nation and State of Minnesota based on their proportional ownership of the lake. If ongoing monitoring proved these limits were either too restrictive or too liberal, Red Lake fisheries regulators could adjust within the suite of the rules concerning fishing gear, daily takes, fish size and season opening and closure dates to ensure a catch of the appropriate size.

In fact, in the years since the lake reopened, rising quotas have been the norm. The combined tribe and state harvestable volume rose to 452,458 kilograms by 2010 and to 562,455 kilograms by 2016. Catch limits for sport fishermen rose from two to four fish in the early 2010s, were pulled back to two in 2014–2015 and returned to four in 2016. While the Red Lake Nation maintained a subsistence limit of ten walleye per day, it raised the catch limit for tribal commercial fishermen to 75 in 2009, 100 by 2013 and 150 in 2018. The tribe also began a controlled netting programme in 2009. Conducted exclusively by crews working for the Red Lake fisheries, netting serves both as a mechanism for aligning the tribe's total catch with its harvest quota and as a way to supplement processing plant supply during the hook-and-line low season.[22]

With the recovery's success, fishing is again a source of employment and income at Red Lake. A year after the fishery reopened, more than 400 tribal citizens had registered to fish commercially (Robertson 2008). The practical benefits are clear: a tribal commercial fisherman who regularly catches his limit can earn US$1,000 a week during the fishing season.[23] Tribal members with other jobs can fish a few evenings a week to supplement their incomes; one father reported that his supplemental fishing earnings paid for his daughter's orthodontics (Record 2010). Families can fish as a form of recreation that also brings in cash. Teenagers can fish with friends for recreation and for spending money.

The tribally owned and operated fish processing plant in Redby, Minnesota, is an important link in this chain of economic opportunity. With US$2 million in grants from the Shakopee Mdewakanton Sioux Community, the Red Lake Nation was able to restore, update and reopen its fish processing facility (Robertson 2008). Prior to the fishery's collapse, processed fish were sold to off-reservation wholesalers. Post-recovery, the processing plant allows the Red Lake Nation to cut out the middleman. The plant sets a price and buys walleye from tribal-citizen fishermen, processes the fish and sells them locally and nationally through its marketing arm.[24] This vertical integration helps the Red Lake Nation and its citizens reap more of the economic rewards from fish sales and provides another means for monitoring the total catch. In 2011, the plant employed 90 people, processed 294,835 kilograms of fish and generated US$2.5 million in revenues (Allen 2012). By 2017, the processed volume rose to nearly 453,592 kilograms (Enger 2017). Also in 2017, the joint Safina Center and Monterey Bay Aquarium Seafood Watch programme designated walleye sold by Red Lake fisheries as a 'Best Choice/Green' product (meaning that the fishery is well-managed and that fishing causes little harm to habitats and wildlife), the highest sustainability rating it awards (Safina Center 2017): a classification that further increases demand for the Red Lake Nation walleye.

Not only the tribal community but also local non-tribal communities experienced economic hardship during the walleye fishing moratorium. In 1999, the paying membership of the Upper Red Lake Area Association, an off-reservation tourism organisation, had dropped to eight. As Joe Corcoran, the association's president at the time, put it, 'It was devastating to watch how [the moratorium] impacted upon the community and especially the business people who had, you know, relied on the tourism industry to help them and to stay afloat. It was not good up here' (quoted in Robertson 2006, para 2). Businesses closed, lakeshore property values plummeted and young people moved away.

When the walleye fishery reopened, however, property prices tripled, anglers returned in droves[25] and the resort industry rebounded (Robertson 2006). In 2019, the Upper Red Lake Association listed thirty-four business members on its website, half of which cater to tourists (Upper Red Lake Association 2019). In fact, tourism-focused investments made during the moratorium, including creation of a boardwalk 'bog walk' through Minnesota DNR-managed Big Bog State Recreation Area, now combine with walleye fishing to make Upper Red Lake a premier destination for outdoorsmen and outdoor-oriented vacationers. If anything, the problems residents on the shore of Upper Red Lake face are those of economic success: increased fishing and hunting activity has generated more litter and trash, wetland protection laws limit the development of new resort properties, and the seasonality of current tourism employment puts pressure on community leaders to develop year-round employment opportunities (Dokken 2014, 2016).

Community and Cultural Renewal

Red Lake tribal citizens often describe themselves as having a spiritual connection to the lake (Gunderson 1998; Kolpack 2006). As an elder from the

Red Lake community of Ponemah explained, 'There are spiritual beings in that lake, that's why we worship this lake. There are spiritual beings there, and we think a whole lot of them' (Eugene Stillday, quoted in Robertson 2004, para. 18). But the opportunities and obligations this relationship creates have not always been clear. Does the Red Lake Ojibwe's identity as a fishing people and their cultural connection to the lake mean that tribal citizens should be able to fish as much as they want, however they want? Or does their relationship create other responsibilities?

Answers to these questions were important to the Red Lake Nation as it moved towards reopening the lake for fishing. They helped define the types of renewed access to Red Lake that would best restore the bonds of culture and community—bonds that had weakened during the moratorium and may have begun to fray long before. Then tribal secretary, Judy Roy, provided her views at a 2006 tribal public meeting:

> [the lake] is neither a reservoir nor a fishery, it's a sacred, living body to us who are Red Lakers. It's something that our Chiefs kept for us. They had a specific reason for keeping it for us, and that was for subsistence, for sustaining our families into the future. Now I think we kind of started in the middle when we started with the question, 'do we want sport fishing or commercial fishing on Red Lake when we can open it again?' . . . We need to go back, we need to ask ourselves, what is that lake, what does it mean to us, and what would be the proper and appropriate use for it? Do we want it to provide jobs? Do we want it to provide economic development? Do we want it to be subsistence for every member of the Band to have access to fish to feed their family? However we answer that question, that will determine how we're going to use that lake . . . We have to take the time, like our Chiefs did, to ensure that we know what that lake means to us, and what it means to future generations, and so if we need that time, let's take it. Who's pushing us? Who's pushing us to make a choice one way or another? It's our decision to make. Let's do it right, because it will determine the future, it will determine if the dads or the mothers can take their kids out and teach them to fish one way or another. It'll determine what we're going to do with our great-grandchildren . . . So I hope that we're not driven by this ticking clock that doesn't exist, by our need to rush out there and make sure we get our share before the white people get it. We'll get our share. It's our lake. But one thing that I'm going to still insist on . . . we have to learn by our mistakes in the past. We have to learn why the lake collapsed, whether we think it was totally [dead] or there were still walleye in there, it was not enough to sustain us, and it would have not been back up if we wouldn't have intervened . . . So I urge us, not to feel like we have to just do something for the sake of doing something. That's one of our most precious holdings, one of our most precious resources. People go out to the lakeshore when they're feeling down

> . . . The lake heals us, it reminds us of who we are, it reminds us of the best we can be and where we came from, as well as what our ancestors gave up for us. One should not see dollar signs, nets, and quotas when looking at the lake, but see what we have determined from that lake [to be]. (quoted in Iceman 2006)

Arguments like Roy's eventually won the day. The Red Lake Tribal Council enacted a set of regulations that provided fishing access for all tribal citizens. It also offered those who were interested in the opportunity to fish commercially and ensured that the tribe's DNR had multiple tools to monitor and manage the walleye harvest. Commercial fishermen who had advocated for a return to netting were persuaded to give the new rules a chance, and whenever questions arose about the possibility of individual fishermen returning to netting, Red Lake DNR officials were empowered to reply, 'No, we have to keep track of what comes out of the lake'. More broadly, through its website, seasonal newsletters, reports to the tribal council and presentations to school children, college students and community members, the Red Lake DNR actively educates all Red Lake Nation citizens about the part they must play in sustaining the lake and its iconic walleye for future generations.

Red Lake Tribal Council member and Red Lake DNR director, Al Pemberton, has described the process of 'cultural change' concerning fishing as follows:

> The way I felt was if we could just get through eight to ten years of a new management system, and show that it worked, it could become the new norm and become 'how it was' . . . That's pretty much what happened. When [tribal members] did start fishing and found out that they could make some money at it, it changed the culture of fishing . . . We got a lot of people who liked it, and many didn't want to go back [to the way fishing was]. (pers comm., 9 August 2018)

Ultimately, tribal members have come to a new understanding—reflected in their behaviour—of what it means to say the lake is 'sacred and alive and must be paid the utmost respect by the people whom the lake has fed for centuries' (Meuers 2018, para. 2).

Unquestionably, motivating change has been difficult, but the payoff has been community and cultural renewal. Red Lake Nation citizens take pride in having accomplished something rare and remarkable—they restored a resource given to them by the Creator. Although the moratorium created a gap in tribal citizens' engagement with fishing and in the generation-to-generation sharing of knowledge about fishing, interest in fishing did not decline. When Red Lake was once again open for subsistence and commercial fishing, tribal citizens seized the opportunity. Now, while fishing, parents spend quality time with their children and can re-invest in passing on their knowledge;

youth learn work values; and family and community members strengthen their bonds with one another, the lake, Ojibwe culture and the tribe.

GOVERNANCE SUCCESS

While many factors contributed to the success of the Red Lake walleye recovery effort, much credit is due to the Red Lake Nation's effective exercise of tribal governance. For example, the Red Lake Nation acted proactively in taking a leadership position on the fishing ban. It greatly desired the State of Minnesota's cooperation, but decided it needed to take steps on its own to encourage the walleye's return. The tribe's decision to become a 'Self-Governance' tribe under US law was helpful in this regard. Self-governance status allowed the Red Lake Nation to assume administration of the Red Lake DNR, swiftly enact the fishing moratorium and implement recovery efforts free of BIA bureaucracy.

Further, the Red Lake Nation invested financial and human capital in the process of walleye recovery. It hired knowledgeable biologists and enforcement personnel, invested in cutting-edge scientific data collection and data assessment capacities, and covered a substantial portion of the recovery effort costs. Significantly, the tribe's investments in skilled personnel and data capacities not only positioned tribal DNR staff as authorities on the health and management of Red Lake but also as experts on walleye fisheries management more generally. The tribe's research on the Red Lake recovery effort contributed to the Minnesota DNR's statewide 2010–2015 walleye stocking plan (Niskanen 2011), and three First Nations in Canada and the government of Ontario have sought advice from Red Lake about addressing their own walleye population decline.

Red Lake Nation leaders did not politicise recovery management. Four different tribal chairmen served during the walleye fishing moratorium,[26] and tribal council membership turned over, but these political changes did not alter the tribe's support for the technical committee. Nor did new elected leadership recall appointees and replace them with political allies. Throughout these critical years, Red Lake leaders were committed to the strategic composition of the technical committee and to allowing the tribe's natural resource managers to do their jobs. The pattern has continued post-recovery as well. The Red Lake Nation elected yet another tribal chairman in 2014 and re-elected him in 2018; he too has respected the independence of the technical committee and upheld its efforts to sustain the Red Lake walleye.

Tribal government operations and decisions relating to the recovery were made transparent to Red Lake Nation citizens. Citizens were kept informed through public meetings, print media, and identified points of contact. This engagement was essential to gaining tribal citizens' trust, generating community-wide commitment to the recovery effort, and motivating adherence to the walleye fishing ban. It has been equally essential to motivating community members' adherence to post-moratorium fishing regulations.

The Red Lake Nation engaged with the State of Minnesota on a government-to-government basis, which positioned the tribe and state as equals in all the work that followed. The MOU enshrined and institutionalised this understanding, which has helped it last. The government-to-government approach educated Minnesota government officials about tribes, generated respect for treaty rights, and gave legitimacy to Indigenous knowledge and tribal ways of doing business (consensus decision-making, for example). Ultimately, it also created a group of allies within state government who continue to support the tribe in the post-recovery era. As Mike Carroll, Bemidji regional director of the state DNR, put it, 'They're sovereign, and we need to be respectful of that' (quoted in Dokken 2009, para. 38).[27]

Looking to the future, effective tribal governance also will be critical for addressing the challenges that remain. For example, in 2013 ten people were caught illegally selling walleye from Red Lake and Leech Lake, four of whom were Red Lake Nation citizens. In attempting to prosecute the violators, the US Government, the tribe's jurisdictional partner under US law, discovered that the relevant US statute (25 US Code of Federal Regulations No. 242.1) had not been updated and could not support the charges. Because of the tribe's separate sovereignty, prosecution in tribal court was still possible,[28] although the penalties are lower (again, as dictated by US law). To change this situation, the nation must again exercise its self-determination and sovereignty.

Maintaining the composition and character of the technical committee, which continues to meet twice a year, is another challenge. Many members have served for much of the committee's twenty-year existence. Ideally, as these individuals retire, they will be replaced with equally talented committee members, who can absorb institutional knowledge and sustain the commitment to tribal–state collaboration. For both governments, preserving the independence of the technical committee throughout this rejuvenation process is an act of effective governance.

FOR ALL THE GENERATIONS TO COME

In 2019, business as usual is very different than it was in 1999, when both the Red Lake Nation and the State of Minnesota finally suspended all walleye fishing on Red Lake. Today, Red Lake produces so many walleye that some have dubbed it a 'walleye factory' (Smith 2012). Where a lack of regulation was once the norm, the walleye harvest now is managed methodically, cautiously and sustainably. A lake-wide harvest quota, based on the health of the spawning walleye stock, is allocated to the tribe and the state based on their proportional ownership of Red Lake. First signed in 1999, renewed in 2010 and in 2015, and on track to be renewed again in 2020, the Red Lake Nation and State of Minnesota MOU continues to guide the two governments' mutually beneficial management activities on Red Lake.

The tribe and the state regularly collaborate to educate the public about fish population management, enforce walleye fishing regulations, collect and share data, and plan new projects. The Red Lake Nation has proven that a hook-and-line commercial fishery is feasible, even for one of the largest freshwater fisheries in the United States. Ecologically viable economic ventures—walleye processing and sales, sport fishing, camping and other lakeside recreation, wild rice cultivation, pleasure boating, the bog walk and so on—are thriving. In the midst of all of this activity, the technical committee continues to serve as an effective, dynamic mechanism through which the Red Lake Nation can advance its fishery goals. Because of the Red Lake Nation's governance success, walleye can bring untold future generations of Red Lake people the same physical and cultural sustenance that the fish brought their ancestors.

NOTES

1. The authors wish to thank Megan Hill (Program director, Harvard Project on American Indian Economic Development, and director, Honoring Nations), who initiated this update of the case study and helped coordinate the author team. The version of the case extends and updates the Honoring Nations case study 'The Red Lake Walleye Recovery Project', by Jamie Dolan, Ian Record, Miriam Jorgensen and Eileen Briggs (2015) and relies substantially on Dolan (2009) and Record (2010).

   This American Indian tribe is also known as the Red Lake Band of Chippewa Indians. The nation's website uses this terminology: 'Red Lake Nation: Home of the Red Lake Band of Chippewa Indians'. See their website at http://www.redlakenation.org/

2. Walleye, or yellow pike, is a freshwater perciform fish native to Canada and the northern United States. It is both a commercially valuable food fish and a popular sporting fish.

3. At the beginning of the walleye recovery project in the late 1990s, there were approximately 10,000 Red Lake Nation citizens, 5,000 of whom lived on the Red Lake Reservation (Tiller 2005).

4. This count considers lakes by surface area, not volume, and excludes lakes under the joint jurisdiction of Canada and the USA, man-made lakes, and Lake Pontchartrain in the state of Louisiana, which many consider to be an estuary rather than a lake (US Census Bureau 2012).

5. For a complete history of the Red Lake Nation, see Treuer (2015).

6. As one Ojibwe elder put it, 'a long time ago, the fish, animals and humans could all communicate with each other. The Manidoog [deities] put us all here to live a good life, and humans needed subsistence. The fish felt it was important to protect and provide for the humans, and so they told the humans that they were willing to sacrifice and give their lives so the humans could live. The only thing they asked in return, was that we only take what we need, that we always be respectful and put our tobacco down, and make sure the Manidoog always know that we respect the walleye and will make our own sacrifices to help the fish if we need to do so' (recounted by Benjamin in Erickson 2015: 1).

7. In other words, the Red Lake is both the largest and oldest commercial walleye fishery in the USA (Safina Center Seafood Analysts 2017).

8. In an article written in part to justify opening the fishery, Carlos Avery wrote, 'It is apparent that Red Lake can give up a large volume of fish for a long time before any diminution will be noted' (Avery 1918: 63).

9. According to the Minnesota Department of Natural Resources (DNR), the state's slower response was due in part to the need to gain public support. As Henry Drewes, a Minnesota DNR regional fisheries supervisor in Bemidji explains, after a period of citizen education and engagement, 'There was an amazing transformation from some of the earlier informational meetings where even the suggestion of reduced walleye limits and cooperation with tribal DNR generated anger and distrust' (quoted in Dokken 2000: 16).

10. The Chairman of the Red Lake Nation is the tribe's chief political officer under its constitution; it is an elected position. The nation's other elected officers are a secretary, a treasurer and eight representatives from geographic districts across the nation's territory. The Red Lake Nation also has hereditary chiefs, who serve for life as advisors to the elected officers and district representatives. See "'Miskwaagamiiwi-zaaga'igan: Tribal Council Members,' http://www.redlakenation.org/tribal-government/tribal-council-members

11. Henry Drewes asserted, 'If we'd wanted to assess blame, there was plenty of it to go around. Instead, we committed to sharing information, working together on all aspects of the recovery, and coming up with a plan that we thought would turn things around' (quoted in Rivers 2006: 14).

12. The specific allocation of seats at the table was as follows: two representatives from the RLFA, four to five representatives from the Red Lake DNR, four to five representatives from the Minnesota DNR, one representative from the University of Minnesota, one representative from the US Fish and Wildlife Service, and one representative from the BIA.

13. Fry are recently hatched juvenile fish. 'Stocking' refers to the process of rebuilding a fish population by introducing fish reared elsewhere.

14. As of 2019, evidence of this information campaign remains visible on the Internet. The article 'Red Lake Fisheries Technical Committee Reports on Walleye Recovery Progress' appeared on 22 November 2000 in *Anishinaabeg Today* V(22), 5. See https://d-commons.d.umn.edu/bitstream/10792/598/1/Anishinaabeg%20Today%20%282000-11-22%29.pdf. *Anishinaabeg Today* is a publication of the White Earth Nation but is read across the Ojibwe communities that share a geography

with the State of Minnesota. On 8 March 2007, Brad Hawthorne, a member of the online forum 'lakestatefishing', posted what appear to be partial minutes from the 9 September 2003 Red Lake Tribal Council meeting, at which technical committee members reported on progress (Hawthorne 2007). The discussion shows tribal council members urging the committee to conduct even more outreach, which they promise to do through additional public presentations at council meetings. They also remind tribal council members that they publish the committee's minutes and distribute a newsletter. Dokken (2005) recounts a conversation with the administrative officer for the Red Lake DNR, who reported that tribal officials had started a series of public meetings the week of 20 March 2005; meetings were to be held at various sites across the Red Lake Reservation and in Minneapolis/St. Paul and Duluth, MN. Harvest options for individual tribal members, tribal commercial operations, and non-tribal members were discussed at the tribal public meeting: How Should We Harvest and Protect the Red Lake Walleye into the Future?, held at the Red Lake Humanities Center on 17 January 2006 (Iceman 2006).

15. For example, the minutes of the 17 January 2006 tribal public meeting (Iceman 2006) recount one Red Lake citizen's comments as follows: '[She said] that they were going to need more game wardens than what they currently had because there were people already selling fish. She said she was asked the other day if she wanted to buy some walleyes and she refused the offer. And there were quite a few of them out bootlegging fish' (para. 44).

16. The historical record shows that the Minnesota DNR consulted with its Red Lake recovery project citizen advisory group on issues as diverse as fry harvests from the supply in Lake Vermilion (Vermilion Lake Association 1999); regulation development, including the effectiveness of various size-based regulations (*Brainerd Dispatch* staff 2004); and the overall recovery and management plans ('For the First Time Since 1999' 2006, Northland Fishing Tackle 2016).

17. For example, the Bemidji Area Race Relations Council hosted One Lake, Two Traditions: A Forum on Red Lake Walleye Management, at the Bemidji High School on 27 March 2006, six weeks before the lake reopened in May 2006.

18. 'In winter of 2002 a man landed his floatplane on Lower Red Lake, within the reservation boundary, and began fishing. The tribe confiscated the plane, and the pilot had to pay more than US$4,000 in fines and fees to get it back' (Treuer 2012: 44); this event became well known across the reservation and in the region (Robertson 2006). In April 2005, a state conservation officer received a report of poaching and found three adults and a juvenile on Upper Red Lake with six walleye in their possession and making an attempt to dispose of another, an incident that received significant coverage in the Minnesota fishing community. See Vermillion Lake Association newsletter, *The Vermilion* 2005, and *Star Tribune* article quoted in Jordan 2005.

19. See Hawthorne 2007, which includes minutes from the 28 December 2002 technical committee meeting.

20. Tribal and state biologists overseeing the stocking process were able to create a long-lasting stain on the ear bones of each stocked walleye by immersing fry at an appropriate stage of development in a specific chemical solution for a specific amount of time. See Logsdon (2006) and Logsdon, Anderson and Miller (2016) for detailed

discussions of the technical committee's use of oxytetracycline hydrochloride as a chemical marker and of the ways it progressed the science of fish stocking overall.

21. In Red Lake Nation law, fishing on tribally controlled Red Lake waters is restricted to tribal citizens.

22. Of note, these adjustments to harvest volume also are evidence of the health of the Red Lake walleye fishery, and part of the sustainability plan. As the Minnesota DNR explains, 'Surplus spawning stock means that there are more adult spawners than needed for good reproduction. Removing some of the excess is good for the population since it will improve growth and survival of young fish' (Minnesota DNR 2018, para. 6).

23. Calculated using 2008 USA prices.

24. See www.redlakewalleye.com/about-us/red-lake-fishery.

25. In the early post-moratorium days, weekend fishing traffic was so heavy that the Minnesota Highway Patrol had to deploy additional officers to the area (Dokken 2014).

26. Bobby Whitefeather served as tribal chairman from 1994 to 2002; Gerald 'Butch' Bruns served from 2002 to 2003, when he died in office; George 'Billy' King was appointed as an interim chairman and served from 2003 to 2004, when a special election was held; Floyd 'Buck' Jourdain served from 2004 to 2014; and Darrell Seki was elected in 2014 and again in 2018 (Barrett 2014).

27. Another example of state allies' willingness to defend and support the tribe is the email response from Minnesota DNR Bemidji Area Fisheries specialist, Gary Barnard, to a member of an online sport fishing forum. When simplistically asked who paid for the recovery, Barnard replied: 'Estimated costs for egg collection, hatchery, and administrative costs were approximately US$68,000 per stocking event. The Red Lake Band and the Bureau of Indian Affairs reimbursed the MNDNR $40,000 per stocking event. All three of these stocking events were exceptionally successful. I am certain that the restoration cost to MN anglers will be very quickly recovered in angling opportunity and economic return from the incredible fishery that has developed . . . Since the Band did the egg collection and the State did the incubation, no reimbursement was exchanged for these collaborative efforts. It should be noted that besides the actual costs and monetary reimbursements there has been considerable collaboration on all aspects of this recovery effort, of which egg collection and fry stocking has been just one part of a much larger process' (quoted in Farmboy1 2006).

28. The fishing regulations approved by the Red Lake Nation Tribal Council on 11 April 2006 not only describe allowable forms of fishing on the tribe's portion of the lake (hook-and-line fishing), but also what is not allowed (tribal-citizen netting, overfishing, illegal sales) and what the penalties are for breaking the law. For example, Red Lake Nation law specifies that tribal citizens themselves may only sell walleye to other tribal citizens on the reservation. If they transport their personal catch off the reservation, the fish must be packaged and sealed with a special permit from a tribal warden. It creates penalties for tribal citizens who violate daily possession or size limits; the initial fine level was US$100 per walleye, and Red Lake Nation citizens with 20 fish or more over the limit are subject to loss of their fishing rights for six months (Niskanen 2006).

Chapter 13

Making First Nation Law

The Listuguj Mi'gmaq Fishery

National Centre for First Nations Governance (NCFNG) and Native Nations Institute (NNI)[1]

On 19 May 1993, the Listuguj Mi'gmaq First Nation took over the management of the salmon fishery in the Restigouche River where it flows between the provinces of New Brunswick and Quebec, waters the Listuguj Mi'gmaq people had fished for many generations. They did so not under a contract with provincial or federal authorities; the province of Quebec, Canada, in fact opposed them. Nor did they do it by asking permission or receiving a request from some other government—they asked no permission and received no such requests. Nor did they do it by force, although their actions were shaped in part by violence. Ultimately, the Listuguj Mi'gmaq fought back with the tools of governance: by passing, implementing and enforcing a law.

But this law was not simply a by-law of the *Indian Act*. It was a Listuguj Mi'gmaq law, an assertion and manifestation of the nation's right to fish and to govern its people, lands and waters in its own ways. The law begins by pointing out that 'we the indigenous peoples of Gespe'gewa'gi[2] are vested by Gisiteget with sacred responsibilities for stewardship of the land, waters and all living things'. It goes on to state that the law 'is enacted pursuant to Mi'gmaq custom and in the exercise of the inherent jurisdiction of Listuguj First Nation'. The law specifies—among other things—where it applies, how it will be enforced, how the fishery will be managed each year and how the resource will be used.[3]

Since its adoption, the Listuguj Mi'gmaq First Nation Law on Fisheries and Fishing has been the effective law governing salmon fishing on the Restigouche River, displacing provincial and federal authority. This is the story of that law: its genesis, application and effects. It is the story of a

First Nation not only reclaiming inherent jurisdiction over the resource but reclaiming governance—including law-making and enforcement—as an inherent Indigenous right, tradition and practice. The Restigouche River rises in the Appalachian Mountains of eastern Canada and flows approximately 200 kilometres into the Gulf of St. Lawrence and the Atlantic Ocean. In its lower reaches, before it empties into the Bay of Chaleur, the river marks the boundary between the provinces of New Brunswick and Quebec. The ancestors of the Listuguj Mi'gmaq depended on the resources of the Restigouche River, its watershed, and neighbouring lands and waters. One species of fish that they particularly cherished was the salmon. Fishing for salmon had been a way of Mi'gmaq life long before Europeans came to North America. The lives of the salmon and the lives of the Mi'gmaq were intertwined; they took care of each other.

CRISIS BRINGS US TOGETHER

John Martin, a former Mi'gmaq chief of Gesgapegiag, another Mi'gmaq community, notes that 'For countless generations the Mi'gmaq have had a special relationship with the salmon' (quoted in Metallic & Chamberlin 2006: 8). According to the Gespe'gewaq Mi'gmaq Resource Council, 'Salmon has provided the people of Gespe'gewa'gi with strength and nourishment for thousands of years'.[4] The salmon played multiple roles in Mi'gmaq life as food, in ceremony and in trade. Fred Metallic explains how:

> In Mi'gmaq I say 'the salmon is my brother.' If the salmon is my brother, then he's no different than my uncle, my cousin, my aunt's husband who has passed away. And all these people are buried here, all these people who shared their experience and understanding of salmon fishing; they shared their experiences and knowledge of this territory. They taught my father everything that he knows about salmon fishing . . . and he taught me . . . we continue to give back to people through the salmon so that we can continue to acknowledge and strengthen that we are connected. But by the mid-1800s, the combined effects of Canadian Government policy, the spread of non-Indigenous settlements, and the imposition of provincial law had severely restricted Mi'gmaq hunting and fishing activities and reduced Listuguj Mi'gmaq land holdings to just over 4,000 hectares on the north shore—the Quebec side—of the Restigouche River.[5]

Under the Canadian Constitution, the provinces have authority over natural resources, including most fish. But salmon are anadromous: that is, they migrate, spawning in fresh-water streams but spending most of their lives in the ocean. They therefore fall under federal jurisdiction, even when in provincial waters. But in 1922 the Canadian Government gave Quebec jurisdiction over Atlantic salmon in its waters, and Quebec took over management of the fishery on which the Listuguj people depended. Soon the province was limiting who could fish, where, when and how much.[6]

MAKE FISH SACRED AGAIN

The Mi'gmaq of Listuguj paid little attention to the provincial laws governing the salmon fishery. These weren't their laws, they had never given up their right to fish and much of their life revolved around the salmon. So they kept fishing according to their traditional values and harvesting practices. Meanwhile, salmon were declining throughout much of the North Atlantic. From the mid-1800s onwards, agricultural and industrial development in the Maritime Provinces and New England affected salmon spawning habitat, while commercial and recreational fishing put growing pressure on mature fish. As numbers dropped, competition rose, including competition on the Restigouche River; a premier stream for Atlantic salmon. But the Mi'gmaq continued to fish and support their families as they always had.

By the middle of the twentieth century, commercial fishermen and upstream sport fishermen were claiming that Mi'gmaq fishermen were affecting their catch, while the province claimed the Mi'gmaq were violating provincial fishing laws. During the 1970s, provincial authorities began charging Listuguj citizens with illegal fishing, illegal sale of fish, and other violations, criminalising non-compliant fishing and enforcing regulations against gill netting, food fishing and small-scale catch-and-sell efforts by Mi'gmaq citizens. As the decade progressed, tensions between the province and non-Native fishermen, on one side, and the Mi'gmaq, on the other, continued to rise. There were threats of violence against the Mi'gmaq but, as one Listuguj citizen put it, 'They told us to stop fishing. We never stopped'.[7]

In 1985, after on-again, off-again efforts and in the face of declining fish populations, the provinces of New Brunswick and Quebec banned commercial fishing throughout the Bay of Chaleur (see Parsons & Lear 1993). This was a devastating blow to the regional economy. It was a blow especially to the Listuguj Mi'gmaq, who fished for both consumption and sale. A resource that once had been more than sufficient to feed and support the people was now in trouble. But the Mi'gmaq attitude was, 'we've always fished these waters. We are not the ones overtaxing the resource. We did not create the crisis. We will continue to fish'.

In 2014, Listuguj comprised 4,058 members: 2,108 Mi'gmaq members living on reserve and occupying some 650 homes, and 1,950 members living off reserve.[8] However, in the early summer of 1981, the community was about a third of that size, with just over 200 dwellings. It was about to be overrun. On 9 June 1981, just as the fishing season got underway, Quebec's Minister of Recreation, Fish and Game, sent word to Alphonse Metallic, Chief of the Listuguj Mi'gmaq First Nation, that the community had thirty-six hours to remove all Listuguj Mi'gmaq fishing nets from the Restigouche River. The Chief and Council refused. On 11 June, without warning, an armed force of some 500 Quebec Provincial Police, fisheries officers and game wardens, some in helicopters and boats, launched a violent raid on the Listuguj community. Scenes of police marching down the streets, beating Listuguj citizens, arresting people, seizing boats and other property, and ripping fishing nets to pieces made the national and international news. Outraged Native people from across Canada and even the United States rushed to Listuguj to support their relatives. On 20 June, the police launched a second raid, but Listuguj Mi'gmaq citizens, this time prepared and organised, stopped them from entering the community.[9]

Almost thirty years later, the events of that June remained vividly alive in the minds of those who were there, and the costs are still apparent. One person who had been a teacher at the time remembered that Listuguj children 'were traumatised. Those kids are now in their thirties. The government, the church, the schools never did anything to counsel them. My daughter was eight. She had nightmares for years'. Said another, 'My children were so young then. For so long afterwards, they couldn't understand why, whenever they heard a helicopter, they felt scared'. Others described the helplessness they felt as they watched relatives being beaten or handcuffed and provincial officers mocking their Chief. The raids transformed the community. 'We fight all the time', said one resident, 'but if trouble starts, we're like glue. We have one voice'. While another resident noted that, 'The salmon raid brought people together. We were invaded. The raid cut across family divisions'. One older woman, remembering those days, said: 'I've never been so proud of my people as I was then. It awakened something in us'.

Part of that awakening was a reinvigorated sense of identity and an effort to figure out how to respond not only to the raids themselves, but to the violation of community, the attack on Listuguj livelihood, and the affront to Mi'gmaq values and culture. Reflecting on her experience at the time, one woman said, 'Prior to '81, my generation didn't really put a lot of thought into being First Nation. You got up and went about your day. We exercised our rights, we fished for salmon . . . But when you have to band together to protect yourselves, you begin to see things a little differently'. The raids also encouraged people to think differently about the fishery. After the raids people were saying, 'Let's stop this nonsense. Let's try to make an agreement. Take control of the fishery. Make our own rules'.

On 23 June, three days after the second raid, the Listuguj Mi'gmaq Chief and Council met with the Quebec Minister of Fisheries. At that meeting, Councillor Mike Isaac stated clearly that the Listuguj Mi'gmaq people would continue to exercise their right to fish, a right that pre-existed the government of Quebec and even the government of Canada. He stated that the province of Quebec had no right to regulate Mi'gmaq Nation fishing and would not be allowed to do so, that it had no jurisdiction within the territory of the Mi'gmaq Nation and that it had exceeded its authority in its effort to exert its power on Listuguj Mi'gmaq lands. He said it would be up to the Listuguj Mi'gmaq Government and the Federal Government of Canada to decide jurisdictional issues together.[10] With that meeting, the Listuguj Mi'gmaq people began a nation-rebuilding journey that would last more than a decade, culminating in 1993 when they established a framework—in the form of a Mi'gmaq law—for the effective exercise of their right not only to fish but to regulate the resource on which they depend.

In their discussion of Listuguj Mi'gmaq governance, Alfred Metallic and Amy Chamberlin write that, 'In the fisheries, the pathway followed by the Mi'gmaq over the years has been one of resistance; the path is also one of affirmation: to use, manage, and occupy the land and the water in accordance with Mi'gmaq values, philosophies, and ways-of-being' (Metallic & Chamberlin 2006: 24–5). Ultimately, Mi'gmaq resistance did open the door for Mi'gmaq affirmation, but it was not a simple process and it took a long time. When the second raid occurred on 20 June, the Listuguj community knew what was coming. They turned out in force, blockaded the roads into the community with trucks and cars, stood their ground, turned back the provincial police and compelled Quebec to abandon force as its primary strategy. In effect, the Listuguj Mi'gmaq forced Quebec to come to the table and talk. At the 23 June meeting, they made it clear to Quebec what their own starting point would be.

The result, over the course of the 1980s and early 1990s, was a series of conservation agreements between Quebec and Listuguj called Atlantic Salmon Conservation Agreements. Both parties wanted to avoid further conflict, and the Listuguj Mi'gmaq Government (LMG), concerned about the long-term health of the resource, was willing to compromise: they would work with Quebec to establish rules that would govern the fishery.[11] These agreements allowed Listuguj to continue fishing and provided for hiring and training Listuguj citizens as conservation officers. But, in return, the community had to agree to quotas on its annual catch. The quotas started in 1982 at just over 36,000 pounds, of which 15,390 pounds were set aside for domestic consumption.

Over time, pressure from the province, sport fishermen and others to reduce the Listuguj quota drove the numbers down. By 1985, Listuguj's allowable annual catch had dropped to 15,390 pounds, interestingly the same amount set aside in 1982 for domestic consumption. Eventually the reductions threatened people's ability to get enough to eat. While the provincial and federal argument for these reductions was conservation, it appeared to the Listuguj Mi'gmaq that they were being forced to forego fishing, not so much to protect the fish as to leave more to be caught by others, often sportsmen from corporate and other fishing camps upstream.

By the late 1980s, it was clear that these agreements were not working. There was little transparency in the negotiation of the agreements. The province took the lead in setting the rules, changing them more or less at will, while Listuguj quotas continued to fall. To top it off, Listuguj citizens were again being charged for violations of provincial or federal fishing regulations. By 1990, Quebec was cracking down on violations of provincial fishing laws. In June and July of that year, Quebec launched undercover operations involving telescope surveillance of Mi'gmaq fishermen, undercover sting operations, river raids and other techniques, yielding a flurry of charges. Over the four seasons from 1989 to 1992, Listuguj citizens accumulated seventy-four charges for either fishing illegally or illegally selling Atlantic salmon.[12]

Furthermore, there was continuing concern about the state of the resource. Listuguj fishermen had noticed the declining salmon runs; traditional knowledge passed on through the generations made them acutely aware that the runs were nowhere near what they used to be. Canada's determination that the salmon were endangered had only confirmed what Listuguj fishermen already knew: something had to be done to save the fishery. While conservation arguments made by other governments rang hollow in view of continued high takings by non-Native fishers, the Mi'gmaq knew that the conservation challenge was urgent. It was more than their livelihood at stake. Salmon was more than food. It infused Mi'gmaq culture. They felt a responsibility to preserve the fish for their grandchildren, to protect a resource essential to their way of life. They were looking for something that not only would address overfishing but would 'make the fish sacred' again.

But if the issue was conservation, it would have to be conservation on Mi'gmaq terms. According to Wendell Metallic, a Councillor in the LMG, the attitude was that the Mi'gmaq have to preserve the salmon, but 'we will be the last to stop fishing. This is an Aboriginal right. These other groups have to stop first'. Traditional Mi'gmaq governance also played a role in the community's thinking about the fishery. The Listuguj Mi'gmaq First Nation is one of three Mi'gmaq communities located in Quebec and one of eight communities making up the seventh district of Gespe'gewa'gi, Mi'gma'gi. The traditional governing structure of the Mi'gmaq people is the Mi'gmaq Grand Council, created long before European contact, representing the seven districts into which Mi'gmaq people and territory are divided.[13] Each district has its own District Keptin, whose task is to help the community achieve its objectives. Among other things, the Keptins have to think about the appropriate use of resources in the whole of Mi'gmaq territory, including traditional lands beyond the boundaries of the reserves. The Keptins help to ensure strategic thinking and resource stewardship, taking a long-term view of the health of the resource and the community.

The chief at the time of the salmon raids, Alphonse Metallic, was also District Keptin for the seventh district. He eventually passed the role of Keptin on to Gary Metallic, Sr. Seeing the need of the people to have control over the salmon resource, Gary began to ask how to make a law for the river, assuming as a starting point that this was—as it always had been—within Listuguj Mi'gmaq power, regardless of what Canada would say. His vision and support were critical in organising the community, in developing the political will among Listuguj citizens to take control of the fishery and in grounding the assertion of governing power in Mi'gmaq traditions.

Meanwhile, legal developments also were having an impact at Listuguj. The first was the 1990 Supreme Court of Canada decision in *Regina v. Sparrow* (1990, 1 S.C.R. 1075). Section 35(1) of Canada's *Constitution Act, 1982* provides constitutional protection to the Aboriginal and treaty rights of the Aboriginal peoples of Canada.[14] However, it does not define those rights—a task effectively left to the courts. Ron Sparrow, a citizen of the Musqueam Band, was arrested in 1984 for fishing on the lower Fraser River—a traditional Musqueam fishing ground—using a net that violated the terms of his band's fishing licence, granted by the Crown.[15] At trial, Sparrow's defence argued that the licence restrictions were inconsistent with s 35(1) of the *Constitution Act, 1982* protecting Aboriginal and treaty rights and that fishing rights were among those protected. This defence failed in the lower courts, but, on appeal the Supreme Court—in a unanimous decision—found that Ron Sparrow was indeed exercising an Aboriginal right that existed at the time of the passage of the Act and for which the Act provided protection. It decided further that once conservation goals are met, Aboriginal fishing for food, social and ceremonial needs must take priority over other uses of the fishery. 'Sparrow was a turning point. It affirmed our right to fish', says Brenda Gedeon Miller, Chief of the Listuguj Mi'gmaq, in the mid-1990s. The Mi'gmaq had long known they had that right. With Sparrow, Canadian law caught up with them.

In the early 1990s, these factors came together with new Listuguj Mi'gmaq leadership. When Brenda Gedeon Miller became Chief in 1992, the Listuguj Mi'gmaq Council met to discuss its priorities. Fisheries was high on the list. Action was needed. But what action? The nation's internal discussions had two sides. On one hand, in the aftermath of Sparrow, many fishermen wanted simply to exercise the right that the court had recognised: go out there and fish. On the other hand, the affirmation of the right raised a new question:

how do you exercise that right responsibly and effectively, particularly in view of the threat to the survival of the salmon? This was a governance question. What if Listuguj were to manage the fishery itself? This would be a major step in a return to Mi'gmaq self-government, but it would have to be done well. Not only was survival of the resource at stake, but mismanagement could be used by opponents of the Mi'gmaq to undermine the rights argument. Brenda Gedeon Miller identified the challenge, 'You have to balance the exercise of the right with the responsibility to manage and protect the resource'.[16]

This meant compromise. Unlimited fishing was not an option, for the resource couldn't bear it. Any realistic management plan would have to limit fishing to certain times and places, and these limitations would have to be enforceable by the LMG. But any such compromise would have to have community support. Engaging with the community, therefore, was critical. Listuguj people were accustomed to just going out on the river and catching fish. But if their own government took over responsibility for the resource, it was going to have to impose its own rules. It would have to take governance seriously. 'We had to get past the "you can't tell me I can't fish on Saturday. This is my right."' The community was going to have to decide: 'Do we like the idea of being self-governing?'

As Peter Hutchins, an attorney who worked closely with the LMG, remarks, the Listuguj Mi'gmaq strategy that emerged was:

> . . . to seek an appropriate alternative to the application of federal and provincial fisheries laws and regulations . . . and to devise, in their stead, rules for the fishing of salmon and conservation . . . that made sense to Mi'gmaq fishermen . . . The technique was to formulate Mi'gmaq fishing rules and a conservation program . . . with the Mi'gmaq fishermen and to enact them in virtue of the inherent Mi'gmaq jurisdiction.[17]

The response, in other words, was to assert and exercise Mi'gmaq self-governance over fishing activities and fishing resources.

In 1992–1993, the traditional and the elected leadership of the community began to plan for taking over management of the river and the fish, talking with various stakeholders within the community about what community management of the fishery might look like. Fishing affected everyone. 'The fisherman's circle of family and friends had to understand and support the new fishing system . . . Otherwise, the whole family was in chaos'. These were sometimes difficult discussions, but over a period of about eighteen months an understanding of the need for active management grew. The LMG also reached outside the community, talking to non-Native groups, the Canadian Department of Fisheries and Oceans, and others. Knowing that effective management would require information and training, it began to look for partners who could provide both. It sent its Mi'gmaq rangers to the First Nations Tribal Justice Institute for training, and it engaged a biologist and a technical team to advise it on conservation and management issues

By 1993, Listuguj had developed a draft of a fishing law and a fisheries management plan. The Listuguj Mi'gmaq 'First Nation Law on Fisheries and Fishing' specifies, among other things, the goals of the law and of fisheries management, the territory within which the law would apply, a schedule for development of an annual fishery management plan, and how the community would be consulted. It provides for co-management agreements with adjacent governments in the interests of conservation and effective management of the resource. It also establishes means of monitoring the condition of the resource, setting harvest limits and carrying out other management activities. It places responsibility for enforcement and compliance with the new Mi'gmaq Rangers Division of the LMG, sets out rules to be applied by that Division, and states that 'no person or agency other than a duly appointed Mi'gmaq Ranger shall interfere with or molest the Mi'gmaq in fishing and conducting fishing related activities, including landing, storage, transport, use, and disposal of fish by sale or otherwise'.[18] It rules out quotas or other allocations for Mi'gmaq fishing unless it can be demonstrated that the Listuguj Mi'gmaq are 'exclusively responsible for endangering fish stocks'.[19] It empowers the nation to regulate the days and areas where fishing will be allowed.

Listuguj showed these documents to the Quebec authorities. 'It was not a submission. It was a statement. Here's what we're going to do. We informed the non-Natives that we're retaking control of our river'. Quebec's response, delivered in a letter to the Listuguj leadership on 4 June 1993, was to the point. It said, in essence, 'You can't do that'. When it became clear that Listuguj was going to pass its law and implement its plan regardless of Quebec's reaction, the province threatened to withdraw more than CA$419,000 that the LMG badly needed for fishery management and conservation. Listuguj decided to go ahead anyway. It swore in its own conservation officers, the Mi'gmaq rangers, to enforce the new management plan, telling them, 'Here's the plan. Go enforce it'. It scavenged funds wherever it could to pay the rangers and equipped them. The attitude, in short, was: never mind what Quebec says: 'Just do it.'

Quebec now faced a dilemma. It had a resource management and conservation responsibility, and it was under pressure from non-Native users to meet that responsibility. But the LMG was actively taking over both management and conservation. Eventually the two sides sat down together to talk, in an effort to avoid a repeat of the 1981 conflict, but subsequent discussions were difficult. It was not until 1995, some fourteen years later, that Quebec agreed to the Mi'gmaq plan and restored the lost funds. But one of the provincial demands was that the Mi'gmaq rangers be sworn in by Quebec. Their authority, in other words, would come from the provincial government. Listuguj refused. 'They'll only be sworn in by our own government'.

IT'S MI'GMAQ LAW

In 1995, traditional Listuguj leaders[20] acting pursuant to Mi'gmaq custom and First Nation Law adopted the *Listuguj Mi'gmaq Fishing Law 1993* that had been developed by Chief and Council.[21] Attached to the law is the fishing management plan, subject to annual amendment in response to the condition of the fish and the watershed. The plan establishes conservation targets and sets out rules governing harvest techniques and areas subject to special protections. It is a comprehensive guide to responsible management of the fishery. Critically, the fishing law is not a by-law of the *Indian Act* nor is it a product of delegated authority originating in some other government. Instead, it is a Mi'gmaq law created by Listuguj Mi'gmaq governing institutions in a deliberate exercise of self-governing power. This was a ground-breaking step in reclaiming governance as a Mi'gmaq right and practice. The law is about the fishery. But it has significance far beyond the management of the river and the salmon, as important as those are. It restores to the government of the Listuguj First Nation its status as a law-making body.[22] That body is not simply an administrative entity, managing social programmes and tracking funds. It makes law. It enforces law. It governs.

The Listuguj Mi'gmaq Fishery Law has force both on and off the reserve. The boundary of the reserve along the Restigouche River is the high-water mark; the area beyond that point falls under federal or provincial jurisdiction. But the fishing activities that the fishery law addressed occur both on reserve and in traditional Mi'gmaq territory off reserve. In this off-reserve area, the elected Chief and Council of the Listuguj Mi'gmaq First Nation—political entities established under the federal Indian Act—have no legislative jurisdiction granted by the Canadian Parliament. To make the law effective in this area, the nation had to turn to a source of authority arising from Aboriginal title. This was why the community asked the traditional leaders, represented by the Listuguj Overseers' Tribal Council, to sanction the fishery law. Thus, the law was made to apply not only on reserve but in designated, off-reserve, traditional Mi'gmaq territory, an area of approximately 518 square kilometres of land and 130 square kilometres of water. Within this area, the law is enforced by the Mi'gmaq rangers, whose authority is now duly recognised by the Crown.

But the LMG did not simply create and pass a law. It backed up its new law and management plan by investing in training staff, building relationships with other governments and entities with knowledge or interests in the fishery, and combining Mi'gmaq knowledge with top-of-the-line science. The Listuguj fish management plan is amended each year in response to new data and changing conditions, and each amendment involves consultation with the community. In a very real sense, the fish management plan is a community plan.

As Alfred Metallic and Amy Chamberlin suggest (Metallic & Chamberlin 2006: 24–25), in the fishing law and the management plan, Mi'gmaq resistance becomes Mi'gmaq affirmation—of their right to fish, their right to govern and their centuries-old relationship with the salmon. Federal and provincial regulation was about days of fishing and numbers of fish, and the Listuguj Mi'gmaq have adjusted to that, to some degree, in their management plan and their awareness of the conservation challenge that they—through no fault of their own—have to address. But when it comes to implementation, they also bring to the plan generations of intimate knowledge:

> We know that you have to pay attention to the moon, the birds and the moon tides. All of this has an effect on when the salmon decide to move up river. You need to pay attention to the moon, to the birds, to the bugs and the wind. When the bugs are out in June and the birds—when they're around in the afternoon and the winds start picking up; there's certain times when you know it's good fishing, you just know. You know that's a sign: the salmon are on their way in, the salmon are coming.[23]

Is the plan working? From 1992 to the first 2010 publication of this study, no Listuguj Mi'gmaq citizen had been charged with violating federal or provincial fishing law on Listuguj-regulated waters. Meanwhile, Mi'gmaq rangers enforced the plan, confiscating equipment from an occasional Mi'gmaq violator of the community's own regulations and enforcing the law with non-Native fishermen as well. The LMG reached out to other governments, concluding agreements for scientific and management services with the Federal Department of Fisheries and Oceans and the Quebec Department of Environment and Wildlife. One of the most satisfying indicators of success came in 1995 when the Atlantic Salmon Federation of Quebec (ASF)[24] awarded the Listuguj Mi'gmaq First Nation recognition as the best-managed river in the province.

By 2010, Listuguj management of the river and the fishery was well-established. Mi'gmaq rangers enforced the law, and Listuguj Mi'gmaq citizens continued to fish and to honour the salmon. As a result, said one citizen, 'you wouldn't see what I call a foreign government patrolling our waters and telling our fishers when and how they could fish. It's nice to know that we can employ our own people to patrol our waters and protect our fishers'. There have been economic benefits as well: fisheries management jobs in the community and yearly funds from the federal Department of Fisheries and Oceans and the Quebec government support the Rangers programme and related activities.[25]

Not everyone is satisfied with the results. Some citizens feel the community role in the annual development of the fishing plan has been diminished over the years; it has become less community consultation and more community notification. Others see politics and family connections creeping into fishery decisions, enforcement and the distribution of jobs. 'It's all family politics,' said one LMG employee, while another saw elected leaders using the fishery for their own ends, cheapening the community's accomplishment. Some worried about how to make the fishery more of a community enterprise, arguing that their own citizens should be treated like shareholders in the fishery, sharing profits and losses. One person involved in the fishery argued that 'we need to revisit the law, look at what's working and what's not. I hardly call that a failure. It still works. It's unique. But it's been close to twenty years'. A few citizens resist the law. 'Who made these laws?' they ask. The answer is, 'We made these laws'. But some individuals still claim that they have the right to do what they want in the fishery'. Some people try to take advantage of the close relationships that are typical of First Nations communities.

The law has had positive ripple effects that reach well beyond the fishery. The LMG has expanded the scope of its own governance. It has developed agreements with municipalities, the provinces of Quebec and New Brunswick, and Canada in other areas, such as municipal infrastructure, social services, education, police services, justice systems and forestry. These have not involved law-making, but they have involved Listuguj Mi'gmaq assertions of the right to decide what happens in their community and on their lands. As one community leader, long involved in these activities, put it, 'The effort to expand self-governance is a product of the fishing law'. There have been intangible benefits as well. One citizen saw the entire process, from salmon raids to fishing law, as an education: 'I learned about my rights. I knew I had them, but through this process, I learned more about my treaty rights'. New community activities that express Mi'gmaq values and traditions began to emerge. For many Listuguj Mi'gmaq citizens, the community began to feel more and more as if it was truly theirs.

The fishing law was a Listuguj Mi'gmaq creation, an act of will by a people determined to retain not only their rights but their own ways of living in the world. As one leader stated: 'When the law comes from your own people, their words, you can justify it. This is your own law. You created it. It revitalized pride in who we are'.

Plenty of work remains to be done. Governance is a challenge. Continuity of effort can be a problem in a community where elected officials serve only two-year terms, and the march of elections is relentless. The council is the ultimate authority on nearly everything, which means that keeping politics at arm's length from the fishery, from other economic enterprise and from other programmes is a daily battle. The community also needs a way of resolving its own internal disputes—about the fishing law and other things—that keeps the politics out of it and is perceived by the citizens as fair. Plus, there's a revenue issue. As long as the Listuguj Mi'gmaq First Nation depends on federal funds to carry out its programmes and manage the fishery, it will be hostage, to some degree, at least to federal priorities and decisions. 'The way out,' as one senior LMG employee said, 'is economic development' that can produce own-source revenues. But that will take a while.

Perhaps most important for many Listuguj citizens is the generational challenge. As one councillor said, 'Everyone knows about the '81 raids. But, a lot of young people don't know why. Why did it happen? Why was the Ranger Program started? Some of them only see the uniform on the Ranger, not the reason for it. It's just another authority figure. We aren't doing a good job of educating our youth on what it's all about: the conservation of fish, the culture'. Others agreed: 'Everything I was taught, I taught my kids. But many parents don't teach their kids about fishing. In a couple of generations, no one knows anything'. Some citizens wonder if the fierce attachment to Listuguj Mi'gmaq rights and self-governance will last as the generation that faced the salmon raids ages and young people grow up with no memory of what the community went through. It may be that crisis brings people together, but what will sustain that togetherness when the memories of crisis fade?

For many generations, the Listuguj Mi'gmaq were a fishing people with a complex, intimate relationship with the salmon. But from the early 1800s on, as European settlements and provincial and Canadian governments asserted ever greater control over Mi'gmaq lands and waters and the animals within them, that relationship became more and more difficult to maintain. The Mi'gmaq defended their rights as best they could, continuing to fish as their ancestors had and defying efforts to make them stop.

The resulting conflict came to a head in the salmon raids of 1981. The raids brought the community together and produced a determination to reverse the downward spiral of Mi'gmaq history. Out of the trauma of 1981, a vision began to emerge of a revitalised people, exercising their right to fish and their right to govern themselves and their resources in their own ways. But the vision raised questions. How do you make it a reality? How do you fight back? The answer, it turned out, was not guns or litigation or marching in the streets. Ultimately, the Listuguj Mi'gmaq fought back with the tools of governance: by making credible law—Mi'gmaq law—and then backing it up with competent management and enforcement.[26]

This is a key lesson emerging from this story. The vision was essential. Its power came from the fact that it was an Indigenous conception, rooted in the community and in the centuries-old, Indigenous traditions of governance. But the challenge was to make the vision come alive. To do that, the LMG turned to law-making; one of the core functions of any government. Drawing on customary practice and building on generations of accumulated knowledge of the fishery, they put in place a law and a management plan that could support their own subsistence and commercial needs and conserve the salmon.

But there was a further step as well that was required. Asserting rights, control, passing a law and developing a plan were not enough. The LMG had to exercise that control effectively and responsibly. They had to back up that law and that plan with competent management and enforcement. As one of those involved in the process said, 'Be prepared. You need very high performance in law-making and policing'. The lesson of 'Just do it' is not enough. As one Listuguj Mi'gmaq leader said, 'We needed to do it right'.[27]

Other factors also played a part in the Listuguj Mi'gmaq success. The effort to reassert self-governing power had broad community support and participation. 'We were all involved in making it', said one citizen about the fishing law. The community also was fortunate in its own people. They had a District Keptin who was determined to find a way to meet the people's needs and conserve a precious resource. They had elected leadership willing and able to engage other governments in dialogue without abandoning the community's principles and priorities, to engage the community in developing an Indigenous solution to the challenge they faced, and to seek out the legal and technical advice they needed. They had individuals who understood and could work with Mi'gmaq traditions and protocols, and they had individuals who could navigate the legal/bureaucratic/administrative maze of provincial and federal governments. These were critical assets during a drawn-out process of assertion and negotiation. They also could draw on the experience of other First Nations. In a fundamental sense, they were not alone.

REBIRTH OF OUR NATION

This is much more than the story of a fishery. It is a nation-rebuilding story. In 1993, as the LMG was putting its fishing law and management plan in place, Chief Brenda Gedeon Miller testified before the Canadian Royal Commission on Aboriginal Peoples. She said, 'We believe we have embarked on a critical path. This critical path leads to what you refer to as self-government in modern-day contemporary terms, but what we refer to as the rebirth of our Nation' (Miller 1993: 54–5).

BRIEF UPDATE: 2019

The work of nation-building through fisheries governance has continued. On 12 November 2018, LMG Chief, Darcy Gray and Marc Miller, parliamentary secretary to the minister of Crown-Indigenous Relations, met with Rémi Massé, Member of Quebec Parliament, in Listuguj and signed the Listuguj First Nation–Canada Fish Framework Agreement.[28] The agreement outlines Listuguj's fish interests, positions parties to explore innovative fish arrangements and reaffirms the parties' commitment to advance Listuguj's fishing rights. The agreement will also help establish a process to strengthen a nation-to-nation relationship between the Canadian government and the LMG. More directly, there will be negotiations between the LMG and Canada, and further talks will focus on managing the lobster fishery. In 2019, LMG circulated its most recent Fishing Plan[29] for consultation and discussion with citizens at a series of public meetings. These recent events led Chief Gray to reiterate that:

> The Listuguj Mi'gmaq Government recognises that fishing is our inherent right that stems from our traditional way of life . . . As an elected government, we will continue to exercise our jurisdiction over and responsibility for our fisheries as a community. Usgaqa'nminew aq ango'tesnug—our fisheries belong to us and we will take care of it.[30]

NOTES

1. This chapter is an abridged and edited version of a case study published in 2010 by the NCFNG and the NNI, with permission. The editors of this book extend their thanks to the Listuguj Mi'gmaq Government for permission to use it here. We also extend our gratitude to the numerous Listuguj Mi'gmaq citizens and others who agreed to be interviewed, shared their thoughts and experiences, and commented on drafts of the original publication. The original case-study research team was made up of: from NNI: Stephen Cornell, Renee Goldtooth, Miriam Jorgensen and Rachel Starks; from NCFNG: Michele Guerin, Beaver Paul, Sheldon Tetreault and Anisa White.

2. Gespe'gewa'gi is the seventh district of Mi'gma'gi, the Mi'gmaq homeland. It includes what is known today as northern and north-central New Brunswick, the Gaspé Peninsula, parts of the mainland of Québec, as well as the islands and surrounding waters. See http://nutewistoq.migmawei.ca/gespegewagi, accessed 25 July 2010. Gisiteget is a Mi'gmaq word for Creator.

3. 'Listuguj Mi'gmaq First Nation Law on Fisheries and Fishing' (n.d.), see https://listuguj.ca/wp-content/uploads/2019/04/Migmaq-Fishing-Law.pdf.

4. The Resource Council quote is from Gespe'gewaq Mi'gmaq Resource Council's Notes, see http://www.facebook.com/note.php?note_id=129532063006, accessed 14 May 2010.

5. From F. (Gopit) Metallic, 2008, 'Strengthening our Relations in Gespe'gewa'gi, the Seventh District of Mi'gma'gi'. Unpublished paper, courtesy of Fred Metallic.

6. First Nations have argued that the Canadian government is obligated to rescind this delegation of authority to the Quebec province.

7. At a number of places in this chapter, we quote from interviews with Listuguj citizens carried out in the winter and spring of 2010. Most of these interviews included assurances of anonymity and unattributed quotations in this chapter are from those interviews.

8. See the Listuguj Mi'gmaq First Nation Government website at: http://listuguj live.wpengine.com/about-listuguj/.

9. These raids are the subject of Alanis Obomsawin's powerful 1984 documentary film, *Incident at Restigouche,* which includes some of the news footage shot at the time. The film can be viewed at the National Film Board of Canada website: http://www.nfb.ca/film/incident_at_restigouche/. The film features a remarkable on-camera exchange between Obomsawin herself and provincial Minister of Fisheries Lucien Lessard, the man who ordered the raid.

10. Listuguj Mi'gmaq First Nation, 1981, Minutes of Meeting with the Minister Lucien Lessard, Chief and Council of the Restigouche Band Council, 23 June 1981, pp. 6, 8, 9. Unpublished document, courtesy of Donald Germain.

11. This is apparent in the minutes of the 23 June meeting; see Listuguj Mi'gmaq First Nation, 1981.

12. Hutchins, P.W. 2006. We are all here to stay: Managing lands and resources for cultural integrity and mutual advantage. Paper prepared for the Aboriginal Jurisprudence Conference, Winnipeg, 26–28 June.

13. On the seven districts, see the testimony given on 2 December 1999 by Chief Augustine at www.johncummins.ca/docs/Dec2.doc (accessed 25 August 2010).

14. 'Aboriginal peoples' is defined in the *Constitution Act* as the Indian, Inuit, and Métis peoples of Canada.

15. The Musqueam are Coast Salish people whose traditional territory encompasses much of Vancouver, British Columbia, at the mouth of the Fraser River.

16. Interview with Brenda Gedeon Miller, 9 February 2010.

17. Hutchins, 2006, pp. 34–35.

18. 'Listuguj Mi'gmaq First Nation Law on Fisheries and Fishing' (n.d.).

19. 'Listuguj Mi'gmaq First Nation Law on Fisheries and Fishing' (n.d.).

20. The Listuguj Overseers' Tribal Council is an advisory body to the Keptin.

21. See 'Listuguj Mi'gmaq First Nation Law on Fisheries and Fishing' (n.d.).

22. On traditional governance among the Listuguj and other Mi'gmaq of the region, see Metallic and Chamberlin, 2006 and Miller, 1993.

23. Metallic 2005: 8.

24. ASF's mission is to conserve and restore wild Atlantic salmon and their ecosystems. See: https://www.asf.ca.

25. Information supplied by Robert Smith, Director of Finance, Listuguj Mi'gmaq First Nation, 10 February 2010.

26. Peter Hutchins, an attorney who worked with the LMG, argues that it was important that LMG chose to make law instead of entering into negotiations with other governments. If they had chosen negotiation, he argued, 'they'd still be at it now'. Interview with Peter Hutchins, 8 April 2010.

27. The Listuguj Mi'gmaq experience lends support to the core findings of the Harvard Project on American Indian Economic Development, which found that success in achieving collective goals came to those Native nations who asserted self-governing power and backed up that power with competent, responsible governance that reflected their own values and therefore had legitimacy with their own peoples. See, for example, Jorgensen, 2007.

28. The LMG Natural Resource Directorate, November 2018 'Fisheries Newsletter', available at https://listuguj.ca/wp-content/uploads/2018/11/Fisheries-Newsletter-Nov-2018.pdf.

29. See Listuguj Mi'gmaq Government Natural Resource Directorate, 2019 Draft for Discussion at http://listuguj.ca/wp-content/uploads/2019/05/Listuguj-Migmaq-Fishing-Plan-2019_DRAFT1.pdf.

30. Quoted in LMG Natural Resource Directorate, November 2018 'Fisheries Newsletter', available at https://listuguj.ca/wp-content/uploads/2018/11/Fisheries-Newsletter-Nov-2018.pdf.

Chapter 14

Instilling Good Governance for Community Prosperity

A Canadian Perspective

Williams James (Jamie) Sterritt

> We cannot seek achievement for ourselves and forget about progress and prosperity for our community . . . Our ambitions must be broad enough to include the aspirations and needs of others, for their sakes and for our own.
>
> —Cesar Chavez[1]

This chapter focuses on the issue of prosperity for First Nations communities in Canada and the roles that all involved play in its achievement. In the spirit of the community referred to by Cesar Chavez above, there must be a balance that enables the advancement of social, cultural, economic and environmental aspects of community life for Indigenous peoples. However, achieving that balance is challenging. There are roles that every individual in the community must play, including the citizens, staff and the governing body, as well as external factors such as the roles of municipal, provincial and federal governments. Furthermore, while Indigenous communities across Canada at the time functioned effectively within their traditional social systems and traditional territories, the introduction of Western civilisation and the colonial imposition of the *Indian Act 1876* have all disrupted the balance. Accordingly, our understanding of what constitutes 'community' and 'prosperity' as First Nations have been compromised.

In this chapter, I consider how we might reconceptualise our understanding of these critical terms and the implications for our current governance. In particular, this chapter focuses on the roles and responsibilities of First Nation citizens, chief and council, and their governing organisations. All too often, it seems we focus on the governance importance of the latter; that is, the organisation and the role of chief and council. However, I argue there is a broader, more fundamental two-way relationship that is critical for the effectiveness of First Nations governance; namely, the *mutual* responsibilities and investment of citizens back into their organisations and the way their leaders operate. Finally, the chapter looks at the kinds of governance arrangements that we need to build as First Nations based around this 'whole of community' approach to roles, responsibilities and capacities, to achieve our vision of prosperous communities.

CANADIAN FIRST NATIONS: AN OVERVIEW

The First Nations are the predominant Indigenous peoples in Canada south of the Arctic Circle. Those in the Arctic area are distinct and known as Inuit. The Métis are comprised of descendants of First Nations and European settlers in the early decades of colonisation. Today there are 634 recognised Canadian First Nation Governments or 'bands', roughly half of which are in the provinces of Ontario and British Columbia. Approximately 40 per cent of First Nation peoples live on reserve lands[2] and, across these First Nations' communities, roughly seventy distinct languages are spoken.[3]

Historically, each First Nation was a self-governing community and had its own culture and customs, all of which had traditional governance structures, hierarchy, laws and policies—but not as we define them now. Today, many First Nations in Canada have some measure of control over their reserve lands, but in nearly all such cases, the areas are minuscule in extent.[4] Traditional lands to which we have some rights may be more extensive. Still, our level of control is significantly reduced as a result of settler governments imposing their own statutory definitions of individual identity and establishing related processes requiring people to prove their Indigeneity. The typical impact has been to exacerbate conflict and dispute within many First Nations about their own citizenship. Neil J. Sterritt has noted the culminating problems that have arisen in communities as a result, including,

> insufficient power and jurisdiction, excessive government controls, unclear lines of authority and accountability, inadequate funding and training, lack of enforcement mechanisms, confusion about the impact of provincial [government] laws, confusion about leaders' roles and responsibilities, and confusion about governance matters. (Sterritt, 2001: 9)

While the Canadian Government retains a primary role in relations with our nations, the part of the provincial governments has been substantial, especially in recent years, with both provincial and federal governments imposing their own ideas of 'government' on Indigenous peoples. Since 1975, Canada has signed twenty-five additional treaties (the so-called 'modern treaties' or 'comprehensive land claim agreements') with First Nations in Canada. Some of these treaties include the rights of self-government. While such treaty-making constituted a form of political recognition for some First Nations, the administration of Indian Affairs has fragmented many of them, turning localised or temporary separations into inflexible political, administrative and geographical divides. Meanwhile, small land bases and populations, together with the historical underfunding of essential services and infrastructure by the state, mean many of our First Nations have only limited human capital pools and assets to use in productive economic activity.

The majority of our nations had limited self-government under the terms of the *Indian Act 1876* ('the Act', along with its assorted amendments in later years) and are substantially dependent on federal and provincial funds. In the last three decades, a number of crucial Canadian court decisions have recognised expanded rights of First Nations and strengthened our hand in negotiations with federal and provincial governments. Self-government has given chiefs and their 'councils' significant powers that combine those of a province, school board, health board and municipality. Councils are also largely self-regulating regarding utilities, environmental protection, natural resources, building codes and so on. Not surprisingly, the governance and development challenges facing First Nations are substantial, not the least because our population is growing—in the next two decades, the Indigenous people in Canada are likely to exceed 2.5 million persons.

Looking to the future, a growing number of First Nations are adapting where they can, or are breaking away from the *Act*, to establish their own governance structures and expand both their governing powers and development bases. Given that dependency on government funding to achieve these goals is not ideal, communities need to expand their economic bases and find creative ways to build their own-source revenue. At the forefront of their strategic deliberations are the questions of what 'community' and 'prosperity' mean to First Nations and, in turn, how First Nations can best govern to achieve prosperity for their community.

UNDERSTANDING AND CREATING COMMUNITY PROSPERITY

My experience in delivering governance training workshops[5] with First Nations in Canada leads me to conclude that 'community' and 'prosperity' are integrally entwined with each other and that the condition of both is directly influenced by our governance arrangements. For the purposes of the discussion in this chapter, community is defined as 'a social group of any size whose members reside in a specific locality, share government and often have a common cultural and historical heritage'.[6] Overall, this definition fits for Indigenous peoples in Canada; however, more and more nation citizens now live outside of the geographic boundaries of their traditional lands or reserves. This has created what could be called 'dispersed communities of identity' and has led to many associated challenges for our internal governance systems. For example, if we are being effective in our governance and looking at prosperity for all, how do we include and interact with all citizens, no matter where they live in the world? No matter where you reside, as an Indigenous person you are part of your community and should be recognised as such.

When we hear the word 'prosperity', we usually equate this to money and financial status, as prosperity is traditionally defined as 'a successful, flourishing, or thriving condition, especially in financial respects; good fortune'.[7] However, it is clear from our own histories that First Nations in Canada have always had a much more comprehensive understanding of what constitutes prosperity, what the good life means to us. While financial gain and a lucrative bank account are still welcome, our understanding is more about how we plan for the future and use our resources in ways that make a real impact in our communities. So the word takes on a sense of service and contribution to the well-being of the whole of 'our community'. There are social and environmental aspects as well to include when considering the broader dynamics of building a prosperous community. Furthermore, there is significant diversity amongst our nations and, given the varied locations of our communities, the opportunities may not be as financially plentiful or equally available for all nations. Communities closer to urban centres or those that are ideally geographically situated definitely have an advantage over those that are remote. Many First Nation communities still struggle to obtain a decent quality of life, with only one in five having median incomes over the poverty line (Statistics Canada 2016).

As our communities move forward, then, it is clear that the old paradigm of government aid will not fulfil our needs long term. In fact, it may hold us back. Fortunately, many now embrace the idea of self-governance and autonomy. The caution here is that focusing solely on finances and building wealth as the way to achieve those goals can negate the cultural, social and ethical values and relationships of our lives. No community is truly prosperous unless its citizens are healthy, happy, engaged and living in a community that reflects their shared values and can function with integrity. Relying on the status quo neither makes sense nor provides hope for the future. Instead, we need to foster innovative solutions to encourage self-determined economic growth and care for our people and our lands, no matter where we are located.

When looking at our communities, we must ensure that citizens have the necessary resources to be able to participate in modern life on par with the broader 'general population'. This means that merely providing our communities with an equal level of services to those of the broader population may, in fact, not be 'fair'. This is because they already are at a disadvantage for a host of reasons (including location, social upheaval and other systematic constraints forced upon them since colonial contact). Instead, equitable efforts are needed to address the historically low levels of infrastructure, the absence of essential services and the entrenched socio-economic disadvantage of our citizens' experience. That benchmark for 'equity' is, therefore, the standard that needs to be instilled because it provides the necessary resources to bring First Nation communities up to a level playing field. In other words, creating a prosperous community must include proper healthcare services for its citizens; it must consist of care for its children and offer educational and job opportunities to carry us into the future; it must care for its elders and aid the disadvantaged.

A strong, prosperous community also is one that strengthens and unites. It works to unify its citizens, healing old wounds and trauma, and building individual and collective capacities. It helps the leadership make wise decisions regarding resource use and allocation of benefits, and fiercely protects its interests based on community morals and values instead of individual self-interest. It seeks constructive partnerships and increases its competitive abilities. This is a viewpoint that suggests leaders are not the only critical driver for community governance; instead, it is the community as a whole. It also suggests that, without addressing our fundamental collective social needs, no community is truly prosperous. Combined or integrated social and economic prosperity is arguably the path to self-sufficiency and self-determination. But perhaps most importantly, producing prosperity of this inclusive kind will only come about by having effective governance in which both leaders and citizens are prepared to invest and take responsibility for.

FOCUSING ON WHAT MATTERS TO US

All communities have specific issues of high importance to them, and no two communities are alike. At the same time, we are also interconnected and often share many of the same concerns and challenges. We all want safe communities, peace and happiness, non-dependant citizens, and economic and social well-being. Fostering sustainable growth of the kind we choose requires innovative solutions, and leaders have an essential role to play in either enabling or disabling such innovation. Leaders need to be able to think outside the box, change mindsets and employ good governance practices to achieve this. By creating positive, responsible and respectful relationships, we help to eliminate confrontation and create prosperity instead.

At the same time, change must also begin within our own communities at the grassroots level of our citizens. It must foster all citizens' access to learning, social inclusion and security. It must improve the quality and range of educational opportunities for citizens from childhood through trade, college or university education, regardless of whether they live within or outside of the boundaries of the community. Otherwise, the same detrimental issues are bound to continue or even grow. Money alone cannot satisfy our needs. The view of prosperity that I propose demands new forms of organisation, fiscal and fiduciary responsibility, the rebuilding of our community infrastructure and the workforce, and culturally respectful resource practices. In other words, prosperity is a governance issue. Our communities need to forge internal and external partnerships and connect on the regional and national levels, as well as internationally. To do that, we need to rebuild robust governing arrangements. And every citizen has a role to play in that.

In working with one community on their strategic planning, I raised the question, 'What is your community looking for?' One councillor put up his hand and said 'houses', and the chief questioned him on that. 'You say houses, but what are they really asking for?' After much discussion, it came around to, 'They are asking for "homes". House is an infrastructure issue, a building, a place to hold your belongings. A home is much more. It includes the physical structure, but also healthy, educated, and working family members—yes, our communities need homes'. This brief discussion goes to show how the governing body needs to take that step back, let the programmes and services worry about the means (houses) and look at the bigger picture vision of where the nation wants to head—which, in this case, is to create homes. That particular chief and council can now set this as a goal: 'We want homes for our members'. Their staff can start to work collaboratively through all programmes to see how they can reach that goal. This is where a community begins to prosper—by collectively forging a clear vision for their future and ensuring that vision continues to inform their leaders' decisions. It points to a way of thinking that chiefs and councils need to employ throughout their organisations.

Only when social and economic interests align can we build a lasting social fabric that sustains self-reliance and sustainable prosperity, focusing on the health, well-being and respect for our lands instead of solely on money. Nowhere has the latter been more damaging than in Maskwacis (formerly Hobbema), Alberta. Made up of the four First Nations of Samson, Ermineskin, Louis Bull and Montana bands, Hobbema's Pigeon Lake was the centre of significant oil discoveries in the 1950s. Although not of immediate benefit to the members, by the 1970s royalties were being handed out monthly to each member, in the neighbourhood of $3,000 cash per person. As well, when a citizen turned 18 years, they were given $30,000 (York 1990: Ch. 4). With little to no education about fiscal management or any long-term planning regarding the benefits and funds derived from oil royalties, drug and alcohol abuse became common in the communities, which have suffered since with substance abuse, suicide and gang violence. Today the population is no longer rich with royalties. And they still struggle with the same barriers most First Nation communities face right across Canada, even though at one time they had this massive influx of dollars. However, it must be noted that, collectively, they are still rich with culture, and the Ermineskin Cree Nation Pow Wow[8] is one of the biggest in Canada, with dancers from across North America attending yearly. Never having totally lost their culture, the communities are slowly building their capacity in all areas, including the emergence of better governance practices, leadership taking a more proactive role and community members banding together.

This is a familiar story for many First Nation communities when they encounter significant development opportunities. Sometimes quick opportunities for poor communities are hard to resist. In hindsight, how could leadership have helped its citizens to prosper over the decades? How could citizens have supported their leaders to stay on track? How could more effective governance have played a role in ensuring that the community's vision stayed clear and strong, that well-considered goals and priorities were set, policies implemented and local capacity supported? Were there multiple parties at blame here, from the community leadership to the provincial and federal governments? We will never know the full breadth of what could have been, but it is to be hoped that lessons can be learned, and possible solutions can be taken from this experience. The following section of the chapter presents some insights into how these questions might be addressed in other First Nation contexts.

GOVERNANCE: WHAT IT IS AND WHY IT MATTERS

In particular, true self-determination means that we can now decide how we want to move forward—it is up to us, not others. It may equally mean that the correct path to prosperity blends social, cultural and financial needs and solutions. Social and economic prosperity is at the heart of any healthy community. If we want to build an enduring community that serves us well, we need to create a careful balance between the two. Our First Nations in Canada can create harmony, grow the community, care for our lands and prosper financially when we include our social and cultural needs in our planning. It isn't a matter of either building our own-source revenue or caring for our people. We can and must do both, with whatever means we have been given. The strong lesson from our collective experience to date is that the best path to inclusive prosperity is through our own governance, specifically, how well we all participate in building the kind of governance that delivers the type of success and community we want.

Canadian First Nations have always had our own ways of governing. Broadly, governance is about how a nation, group or community organises itself collectively to make decisions and get things done. When a group of people come together to accomplish their collective goals, they need to decide who has the authority to make decisions on their behalf, how those decision-makers will be s/elected and kept accountable, and how the citizens will be given a voice and heeded. Once answers to these fundamental issues are determined, the governing leaders can operate with a mandate from their people to establish rules and policies, properly implement and enforce those, and monitor progress with an overreaching goal of increased group viability and prosperity.

'Good' governance includes strong leadership, decision-making and implementation. It is also about communication with the nation's citizens and having an effective, open process by which to reach decisions and give direction. Furthermore, everyone must understand how and why decisions are made and the role and responsibilities of each individual involved in the process. Additionally, while we often give a lot of attention to the functions, capacities and responsibilities of leaders and governing bodies (especially chief and council), it's just as vital that the citizens of the nation are able to fully and inclusively participate in s/electing their leaders, and that the citizens are able to hold leaders to account.

It is clear that governance can have a direct and substantial impact on the prosperity of a community. Poor governance can hinder prosperity; effective governance can build it. It also seems to be the case in Canada that some forms of governance work better than others in building strong, prosperous communities of the kind described above. Next, I consider some of the factors that appear to be critical in determining whether governance either supports or undermines this broader understanding of community prosperity. I emphasise the vital reciprocal roles and responsibilities that need to be undertaken to achieve the kind of governance needed to rebuild community and prosperity. The first steps start with the citizens themselves.

THE ROLES AND RESPONSIBILITIES OF CITIZENS

There are several core areas where citizens play a vital role in the design and exercise of their own governing structures. This is an opportunity for them to exercise real-life self-determination. How well they play their part has direct consequences for the viability and effectiveness of their collective governance arrangements.

In the Governance Structure

A core area in which a community can take action and adapt is its current governance structure. It is clear that the default governance processes established under the *Indian Act* have caused considerable troubles. As First Nations, we have been handed a system built by and for non-Indigenous culture, which aims to instil Western ways of governing. These imposed processes enable individuals to run for leadership positions in First Nation Governments in ways that are typically based on a popularity contest, with the hope that individually they can create change for their constituents.

Consequently, we often hear the old question: 'What are you going to do for me if I vote for you?' This is a question which is still prevalent in many communities today. This self-interested focus has created significant problems for the growth and prosperity of our communities and, more importantly, for our progress towards self-governance. Typically, in most communities, chief and council revert to serving their 'constituents' (i.e. their supporters) and not the community as a whole. An example of this thinking is evident in a few communities I work with in Manitoba, where Video Lottery Terminals are one of the consistent sources of own-source revenue. However, given the distance of the communities from more urban centres, typically only community citizens use these terminals. The profits are then sometimes used as discretionary funds by chief and council for council citizens to hand out monies for items such as gas or food to community citizens of their choice, typically their supporters. This largesse could be seen as 'buying votes', as a council member will only be providing the dollars to someone they like or have a particular relationship with. Furthermore, it generally means the revenue is a revolving pot of money that comes in from the lottery terminals, instead of there being future planning for how to use the revenues to improve life in the community for all citizens long-term.

The typical contemporary governing structure found in many Canadian First Nation communities that are still subject to the Act is that of the 'council' with its senior governing official being the 'chief'. A council is made up of elected citizens voted in to make decisions collectively for the future of the community, over a defined term of office. The term 'chief' refers to the elected member who generally becomes the face of the council and community. Her or his general role is to keep the council focused on community goals and priorities and ensure that good governance is upheld while making group decisions. Some communities within Canada do select or appoint their chief and council (sometimes for life) based on their historic hereditary structures and processes. As with the contemporary elected councils, hereditary councils have also met with mixed success.

One example of the barriers created by the typical form of governance model created under the Act is the fact that, by default, under the Act, chief and council hold office for only two years—a short timeframe for any positive change or strategic planning to happen. Therefore, there is no guarantee that successful candidates will be in office after the next election, allowing for a wholesale shift in the governing body and, in turn, potentially an entirely new direction each time. Additionally, under the Act, First Nations may have one councillor per 100 members, with the result that some governing councils reach sizes of twelve or more. That is a sizeable body to be effective and efficient in making informed decisions. All these factors play a part in the extent to which communities can effectively govern themselves and create sustained positive change.

While the long-term goal of many nations is self-governance and total autonomy, we strive to get there incrementally, given the above constraints. There has been progress, and there are means for tweaking the election process under the Act to enable communities to modify certain areas of their governance responsibilities. Historically, factors like the size of council, the term of council chief and members, etc. were all embedded in the Act. However, through the relatively new 'band custom' process or the *First Nations Elections Act* of April 2015, two other ways have been created, providing communities with mechanisms by which to actively modify and build a more suitable governance structure in their steps towards self-governance. For example, the new opportunities provide for customised electoral systems, the chance to increase terms of office to three or four years, and more robust processes for nomination of candidates, size of councils, and other initiatives such as ensuring council candidates have a clean criminal record or have completed specific education requirements such as graduation from high school. All of these measures could help First Nations to create the political stability necessary to undertake long-term planning and build relationships with potential investors, which could lead to increased economic development and, in turn, community prosperity.

An excellent example of such adaptation of a governance structure to better reflect traditional governance was undertaken by Blueberry River First Nations in northern British Columbia. They wanted longer leadership terms and equal family representation. The community as a whole was comprised of five family groups, each of varying sizes. Yet demographically, one particular family held just over half the community's population base. Under the earlier Indian Act system, because of the larger size of one family, they held the majority of council seats for many years. In recent years, they started to work on designing a community or Custom Election Code, which would enable a better representation of the whole community at the council table. The customised code they developed would allow each family group to vote one person from their group to sit on the council, and then the position of chief would be chosen from the whole community. This system, while it still has its challenges, is an example of how communities can work together to establish greater internal governing credibility and collective autonomy within their nation.

In the Voting Process

In light of the legal ability to adapt their election codes, many communities I work with are, in fact, nervous about making changes such as moving beyond two-year terms, for fear of a council coming into office that lacks internal cultural integrity and values. The concern is that, if such a council was in place, it could do far more damage in three or four years than in two. So how can this 'culture' of fear and distrust in communities be changed?

First and foremost, citizens must be cautious, strategic and well-informed throughout the voting process. The decisive question is: What role do First Nation citizens play in elections? Further, what are their responsibilities to the collective and for the way their own tribal governance is exercised? For example, do we act out of self-interest or unselfishly? Do we vote for our friends and family because we personally want to gain? Or do we take a step back and consider the collective good? How do we start to ensure we have a variety of complementary skills at the governing-body table so that the right decisions are made for our community as a whole? Only by giving these hard questions deep consideration, and working together to build fair and inclusive participation by *all* citizens in our governance processes, will our governance improve and community prosper.

From this perspective, it is the member—individually and collectively—who takes on one of the most essential roles and responsibilities in the governance process: that of exercising their participation and voice. Primarily, citizens must vote based on potential candidates' skills, experience and the leadership they will bring to bear if they are successful in gaining a seat at the governing table. The citizen must take the time to understand each candidate running for a position and ensure that they are bringing something worthwhile to the collective group. That might mean their support will not be given to a direct family relation. It might even suggest that the citizen will not personally benefit, but it will help ensure that the community will flourish and be prosperous over the long term. This is exercising your vote in the spirit of community service.

Furthermore, once the election process is complete and a council is sworn in, citizens then have to respect the organisation and follow the chain of governing command. The citizen must understand the limits and extent of matters on which chief and council can and cannot make decisions and respect and actively support those boundaries. This is the crucial point at which citizens turn from being the source of mandated power to the council (by electing them) to then being the receivers of the decisions, programmes and services from council. If citizens do not understand and honour that transition in their own role, they can end up sabotaging the effectiveness of the council and chief.

Running for Council

As a citizen interested in joining the council, each person must first ask themselves, 'Why am I running for Council'? Is it because they personally want their family or self to benefit? Or is it because they want to start building the long-term prosperity of their community and ensure that all citizens have the right programmes, services and opportunities to start building independence? There's a big difference between self-interest and public-spiritedness. Most times, when asked, councillors say they run for office because they want to see change, and they aren't happy with the previous leadership and the direction (or lack of) being taken. However, once in office, they can display similar tendencies towards self-interest that former councillors were guilty of. The result is that new faces are now typically going through the motions of being in a leadership position. However, their actions usually lead to such things as micromanaging staff or reactively making daily decisions. There are various reasons this may happen, from no orientation process or training on their roles and responsibilities to the remaining previous councillors instilling their dominance when decisions are being made or action has to take place, eventually leaving new eager citizens feeling helpless or powerless and not part of the team.

Citizens hoping to run as councillors must also ensure they have a reasonable understanding of their future role and duties if they are successful in their campaign. For example, they must understand that individually, as a single councillor, they cannot act unilaterally, but are taking up a governing role, collectively, as a unified body. It is through the collective mechanism of the governing body that councillors can then give the 'council' direction to their one employee—the top manager or CEO. It is the top manager, not the councillor, who then directs the staff on the next steps. This is the chain of governing command necessary for our organisations to move forward as one. While this command chain sometimes is activated on a daily or weekly basis, it is one of the first areas of governmental authority that a council collectively exercises after being voted in and starting their planning process.

To further complicate the practical exercise of governance, in some communities, the chief and council are financially compensated for full-time positions. This can cause several issues to arise, first and foremost of which is the question of what is their 'job description'? Daily, what are the roles and responsibilities that chief and council must and can undertake that don't adversely impact on the administration of the organisation or its ultimate governing hierarchy (including lines of communication with and authority over staff)? It is common to see poor governance practice here, where both chief and council use various avenues to micromanage staff and, in turn, staff seek to bypass their top manager to have direct daily contact with their governing body. This bypasses the essence of good governance, in that the top manager is the single employee of the council. Neither the staff nor the organisation will operate efficiently if there are 'multiple' bosses giving different directions. Nor will the top manager be able to keep across the work being done or the resources, both human and financial, that are being used to carry out the daily workloads.

As well, many challenging issues flow from having council positions paid full-time. For example, we may find that a successful candidate has to take a leave of absence from their career, leaving them at a potential disadvantage if they are not successful in obtaining a multi-term council position. On the other hand, if a citizen is unemployed and runs for council, is successful in their election and begins making a comparatively substantial amount of money, will that cause them to use their power in office to maintain their position as long as they can? In working with one community where councillors were paid a full-time wage, a first-time councillor made this exact point: 'John down there was on income assistance before being successful on the council, bringing in around $250 a month. Now he is making $60,000 tax-free a year. Can he go back to $250 a month if he's not successful next election? What will he do to secure his seat in the next election? Make good decisions for "all members" or ensure that the persons who voted for him will vote again by making sure they are kept happy, which could be perceived as buying votes?'

As you can see, when a council member or chief is paid full time, the roles and responsibilities can get very confusing both for the leaders themselves and for staff looking for direction. It is very easy for the council or staff to bypass the top manager if individual councillors or chief are readily available to influence directly. Early in-house inductions for chief and council, and ongoing shared council conversations about the challenges and responsibilities associated with receiving remuneration, will go some way to supporting them in their roles. Typically, when monies are involved, the organisation should have a policy that outlines the limitations that council members can work within to ensure they stick to the roles and responsibilities of leaders and not wade into the job of the administration.

Holding the Elected Body Accountable

How can the citizens or members of a First Nation hold their elected body accountable? This is one of the most fundamental roles that citizens can play and one of the hardest to do consistently and well. If done poorly by citizens, a council may get out of control and be unaccountable to citizens for their decisions. Corruption and greed may take over with the result that a community is put into financial despair or tied up in exhaustive legal action. Westbank First Nation (WFN), one of the few self-governing nations in Canada, has utilised means within their tribal constitution to aid citizens in holding their leaders accountable. This includes provisions for the membership to remove council members if they violate the Westbank First Nation Constitution or their oath of office (Westbank First Nation 2019).

It is not sufficient just to vote people into office. Citizens must also give overall direction to the council. One of the best ways to do that is by having a say in community strategic planning processes. For example, in many communities, citizens are undergoing a Canadian government-initiated process called 'comprehensive community planning' (CCP) which is, in effect, a long-term strategy for setting out the priorities and vision of how a community agrees it wants to develop into the future (Government of Canada 2010). The process includes planning about land, culture, and language, programmes, services and sometimes even governance. Westbank First Nation (2015) has been very progressive in the CCP process and has developed a plan that includes various strategies around governance, economy, land, culture and language, health and wellness, community safety, education and so forth. While all are important to a thriving community, the governance component especially helps the community give direction to their leadership regarding the WFN Government and its initiatives and policies on intergovernmental relationships, Indigenous rights, taxation, employment and economic development, and non-member residents.

This plan is the community's voice and provides the council with the opportunity to use it as a guiding document in developing its own organisational 'strategic plan'. However, making the plan is only the start. Communities do need to understand that CCP is very thorough and can cover a lot of big issues, most of which cannot be achieved in a two-, three- or even four-year term. So councils—in collaboration with their citizens—need to identify three or four priority goals which they can work towards and execute the necessary steps to achieve, including allocating human and financial resources through their budget process. Council then needs to report to the community on progress at regular intervals.

In my work with a Nation's leadership in the Fraser Valley region of British Columbia, I have seen how the CCP can be treated as a living document, where chief and council continuously use the plan to revise their yearly strategic plan. While their CCP has a community vision, the council has nevertheless moved to create and continually affirm its leadership vision, which is a more succinct variation on that of the community. They also ensure that the goals and priorities within their strategic plan are achievable for their term in leadership. This integrated process ensures the community feels they are part of the overall effort and are able to strive to hold their chief and council accountable while also giving them a long-term vision for their community. While this doesn't always work perfectly, it's a step in the right direction and offers a holistic approach to the governing of the nation.

THE ROLES AND RESPONSIBILITIES OF CHIEF AND COUNCIL

Once citizens are s/elected into office and performing the task of collectively governing, the chief and councillors face several immediate challenges.

Demarcating Power and Authority

An area that is often fraught with tension is the often-blurred lines between what chief and council should be doing and what the management and staff should be doing. Sometimes this is a simple consequence of the fact that First Nations are often small and closely related to each other so that people are called upon to contribute their expertise and skills in many different contexts and work with people who are friends or family. People usually wear many 'hats'. That is a positive strength in our communities. However, when it comes to governance, there is a line which, when crossed, can cause significant headaches for everyone. This is especially the case when our interconnections are used for *selfish* determination.

Once coming onto council, individual councillors get bombarded by the reactive nature of the position. Some community members often resort to the old assertion that 'I voted you in, so what are you going to do for me now?' Councillors, in turn, feel they need to act in such ways to be seen as responsive to, and engaged with, citizens. That is a fundamental misunderstanding of their roles. These blurred lines of who has power and what for, cause confusion and can instil further dependence by citizens on others to do things for them, and exacerbate internal conflicts within the community. As Chief Clarence Louie of the Osoyoos Indian Band stated in November 1993:[9]

> The band does not owe its membership dependency. It owes them opportunity and a chance to become independent.

If we as First Nations hold this view, then the role of chief and council needs to move away from doing things for self-interest or for particular individual citizens, and away from nepotism, and move to do things for the community as a whole. That means operating in a public-spirited way, for the collective good, to find ways to rebuild the pride in who we are and work to instil that former independent way of life. An example of this is Chief Louie's community mentioned above, today, possibly one of the most prosperous First Nation communities in all of Canada. While the community is ideally situated in the southern Okanagan, at one time it was not so prosperous. It struggled with the same issues the majority of First Nation communities face today. Since Louie's election as chief in 1991, he realised that things couldn't be done the same way they had in the past if his nation wanted to break the culture of dependency that had become established and return to being self-sufficient as they were prior to European contact and the application of the Act. Through various mechanisms including a community-initiated long-term development plan, clear accountability and transparency measures throughout the organisation, and supporting local entrepreneurs and economic opportunities, the community today is thriving—both fiscally and culturally, with nearly no unemployment.

A Shared Vision

The primary job of the council is to set a vision for its nation or community. This is about 'the act or power of anticipating that which will or may come to be'.[10] Through this process of 'future thinking', the council steers a direction and develops further clarity about how to achieve that, enabling it to better focus on the overall state of the community over the long term. As well, a community vision should clearly define what the roles of chief and council are in respect to ensuring the vision remains at the heart of their work and is carried out. That means also setting out clearly the roles of the top manager, staff and even the citizens in working to secure the shared vision. These roles are likely not to be all of the same kind and will involve different layers of decision-making about different things.

A strong collective vision of where you want to be in the future helps everyone within the organisation and nation understand and carry out their particular responsibilities. Together, that *joint* effort is what will make it happen. Furthermore, unless the council and community share a common core vision, when crises happen or significant opportunities arise that have potential to destabilise the nation, it is easy for leaders to simply react, make poor decisions, or for community members to feel that they are being taken in a direction they don't want to head. A council is remiss if they do not establish and regularly review a strong vision for their nation and then base their work at the governing table on achieving that vision.

For example, in talking with one Canadian First Nation, the council has a transparent process they follow annually to ensure they are all-inclusive through the planning process. The early stage involves engaging with their citizens. Through a series of predetermined questions, community citizens are invited to provide their input to the council, which facilitates the public session. The second phase is to compile all information, and then the council sits with the staff to work through a similar process. Finally, once all this information is collected, the council will attend a multi-day facilitated retreat, with the end result being a collective strategic plan.

Implementing a Shared Plan

Once a vision is set, then the council must sit down and plan how it can be applied. What are the goals for their time in office, whether it be a two-, three- or four-year term? How are those goals going to be achieved? This process helps the new governing body come together as a team and discuss the most important items they wish to accomplish.

As mentioned above, if a community has undergone a CCP process, this can serve as a document that chief and council can refer to as their starting point. Importantly, once the plan is in place, the organisation as a whole has some guidelines to follow in setting out the operational plan and the annual work plans for staff, and so are better able to measure whether they are achieving the desired outcomes, as well as the effectiveness of the organisation. In effect, the council should be concerned with the ends, the outcomes; management and staff should be concerned with the means to get there.

Communication

Open and regular communication based on accurate information is one of the essential criteria of effective governance. The citizens of a nation or community have a responsibility to insist that their leaders communicate with them, no matter where they reside. For example, First Nations can do this regularly through various mediums such as community meetings, newsletters, radio, web pages and other forms of social media. In turn, the council should ensure frequent formal reporting (e.g. quarterly) to its citizens on the financial status of the organisation and do that in a way that citizens can fully understand.

One effective way of reporting used by governing organisations to their citizens is as a sequence of approved information processes. For example, whereby staff report to the top manager on the progress of the work plans, the top manager reports up to the council on the progress of the operational plans, and the council publicly reports to the community at large on the progress of the strategic plan. This reporting and information cycle can become a very effective communication routine.

ROLE AND RESPONSIBILITIES OF THE GOVERNING ORGANISATION

The administrative body that is established to put governance into action for getting things done for the nation has a pivotal role to play in delivering on the promise of prosperity. Here we have to remember that an organisation is not just a structure; it means people. The calibre and commitment of the people in an organisation can make or break it.

The Top Manager

Given the tight webs of the relationship of most First Nation communities and the need for clear lines of authority and direction for all staff in a governing organisation, it is imperative that the top manager of the organisation is in effect the single employee of chief and council. In other words, the top manager takes his or her work instructions from the chief and collective council, not from individual councillors. The top manager is the 'gateway' between the council and the rest of the staff, and vice versa. The top manager, no matter their title, must be able to build the organisation to run effectively and efficiently, ensure staff understand the council's goals and priorities, and coordinate the development and implementation of the operating plan to reflect them.

Given these responsibilities, the person in this top role must have the necessary skills and experience to carry out the range of work duties, including the ability and desire to delegate down through the organisational structure appropriately. Further, they must have the full support and trust of the council collectively, with no interference in decisions or micromanagement of staff under their supervision. They must also be open and willing to develop their skills and, in turn, the council must ensure there are resources available to them to keep building their professional skillset. One of the top priorities of the council is to ensure they have the right person in this role, and if this role is vacant, then they work proactively to fill it. When they get the right person, their next job is to ensure they regularly review the top manager's performance.

Staff and Programmes

The requirement for staff is to understand that they are an employee of the organisation and, in their work, act like one. This means that they do not work for single councillors or for only one section of the community. They must remain apolitical and not get caught up by community factions. It also means being accountable, showing up to work on time and ensuring while at work that they are representing the organisation to the utmost level. Staff must also respect, implement and uphold the organisation's policies and hopefully look beyond the job as a mere source of money. First and foremost, they are responsible for carrying out the implementation of council policy frameworks, through programmes and services.

Policies

Policies are the guidelines and rules not only for the organisation as a whole but also for the governing body itself. They also tell the wider community the standards and strategies that their leaders and organisation are adhering to. The leadership must focus on policy development and implementation so that politics are taken out of the decision-making at the management level. This enables community members to see that decisions are not being made in an ad hoc way or because of who is at the governing table but rather because of the policy that has been developed and followed in making decisions fair for all citizens. In this way, agreed polices act as buffers at all levels against misconduct and encourage cooperative behaviour.

In other words, the collective effort and implementation of all the above areas of practice, not only by councils, chiefs and their staff, but also by citizens, will help enable the functional achievement of the organisation's governance and ensure the effective means of delivering programmes and services to the nation while moving forward proactively.

CONCLUSION

There is a more profound idea of prosperity in our communities that is about more than just financial wealth. Many First Nations in Canada are keenly concerned with cultural and language resurgence and vitality, improving the health and well-being of all their citizens and rebuilding the social harmony within their communities that has been shattered by the experience of settler colonisation. That is our fuller sense of prosperity.

I maintain that there is a critical role for good governance practices in building and sustaining this broader view of prosperity. In this chapter, I have explored only the tip of the iceberg, so to speak, of issues and practices that First Nations need to consider for building the kind of self-governance that is required to achieve such prosperity. In particular, and perhaps contrary to the more common approach, I have emphasised that *everyone* in a nation and community has a role and responsibility to play in achieving that kind of governance—it does not only lie with the chief and council, or even the organisation. The role played by individual citizens in ensuring they are part of the governance process is crucial and is the very first step in achieving and then sustaining effective governance. In other words, 'participation' and 'voice' not only have to be demanded as a citizen right; the responsibilities attached to those rights have to be carried out. In a real and practical way, good governance has to run through the whole community, and it effectively starts with the citizens of the community or nation choosing their leadership. It means citizens have to ensure they choose leaders wisely and this may not always mean a family member or someone they really like.

This suggests a new agenda for governance reform amongst First Nations: one that focuses on the collective good, not individual self-interest; on all citizens having a responsibility to consider the public good when they exercise their 'vote'. This has implications for the kind of leaders we should be looking for to run our governance. Our leaders must be accountable and transparent, willing to work together for the collective good and make the tough decisions that often may not be the popular decisions. This type of leadership will help us collectively to move away from the dependency instilled by the 'Act', into a self-sufficient pathway towards prosperous communities. This means that further sustained work is needed to build better awareness of these issues among our citizens. Indeed, communication with and between citizens needs to become a priority at every step of our governance processes. The culture of dependency and apathy must be turned around, so we can rebuild our independence and develop the necessary skills and capacity to be able to support our communities under self-determination for years to come; all the while keeping culture as the essence of our being.

NOTES

1. American farm worker, labour leader and civil rights activist, Cesar Chavez launched the National Farm Workers Association on 31 March 1962. He had a bold vision for a strong farm workers' union as well as services that would support that union by building communities up beyond the workplace. Cesar Chavez knew it would take an entire movement to empower his community to overcome the burdens of poverty, discrimination and powerlessness (see Cesar Chavez Foundation 2016).

2. A 'reserve' is a 'tract of land, the legal title to which is vested in Her Majesty, which has been set apart by Her Majesty for the use and benefit of a band' (Indian Act, 1867, Section 2(1)).

3. See Norris, M.J. 2003, 2006. See also: https://www.thecanadianencyclopedia.ca/en/article/aboriginal-people-languages.

4. See https://indigenousfoundations.arts.ubc.ca/reserves/ See also Canadian Government website of the Department of Indigenous and Northern Affairs Canada, sections on land and development, available at: https://www.aadnc-aandc.gc.ca/eng/1100100034731/1100100034735 And also Canadian Government report on inventory of lands secured by First Nations, available at: https://www.aadnc-aandc.gc.ca/eng/1100100034846/1100100034847.

5. Under the business name Sa'hetx̣w Consulting, I work with First Nations communities and Boards of Directors throughout British Columbia, Manitoba, and the Yukon delivering governance workshops on such matters as 'Roles and Responsibilities of Leadership' and 'Establishing Good Governance Practices'. This work also includes developing policy, strategic planning and advising First Nations on a variety of issues that arise about their governance at community and organisational levels.

6. See: www.dictionary.com.

7. See www.dictionary.com.

8. Pow wow is 'a large gathering organised by North American Indians for socialising, dancing, singing, and celebrating their culture' (www.dictionary.com).

9. This statement appears on the wall of one of the Osoyoos Indian Band's enterprise offices.

10. See www.dictionary.com.

Chapter 15

Nation-Building through Social Enterprise in Māori Communities

Sacha McMeeking

Regenerating self-determination in Aotearoa-New Zealand is predominantly perceived as led by Māori tribal organisations that have received cash injections through settlement agreements with the government, thereby regaining the financial independence to self-determine their future development. While nation-building at a tribal level is fundamentally important to a new era of self-determination, there is also an equally, if distinctly, important entrepreneurial movement fomenting within Māori communities that has the potential to make significant contributions to social transformation and build collective capability to be self-determining. This growing body of Māori entrepreneurship is primarily led by individuals and families, who can see opportunities to achieve tangible, meaningful social change that aligns to community priorities. In their hands, entrepreneurship is both a tool for and embodiment of self-determination because it involves identifying desired social, cultural and economic futures and making progress towards them with independent ingenuity. Their practice is creating a groundswell of 'bottom-up' nation-building that empowers, inspires and activates communities in a virtuous cycle of ever-growing self-determination.

This chapter describes the characteristics of Māori entrepreneurship that are contributing to self-determination in our communities, drawing on case studies to exemplify the potential value and challenges facing these approaches to nation-building. The role of entrepreneurship in creating social change is first located in the global body of work pertaining to social entrepreneurship, and then its distinctive practice within Māori communities is exemplified by three case studies that illustrate diversity and impact. The chapter then extrapolates transferable insights into the value of social enterprise for Indigenous nation-building.

SOCIAL ENTERPRISE

Entrepreneurship has always contributed to social change, for better and worse, through economic value creation and disseminating disruption in many forms (Boettke & Coyne 2004). The term 'social enterprise' emerged in the 1970s to refer to intentional social value creation, or social change, through entrepreneurship (Trivedi 2010). Since then, social enterprise has become a global phenomenon attributed with solving embedded social challenges with greater agility, durability and impact than government (Martin & Osberg 2007; Santos 2012; Dacin et al. 2011; Mongtogmery et al. 2012). In an age of government retraction from social welfarism, social enterprise is also positioned, perhaps unreasonably, as a societal saviour capable of generating desirable social change through an ethic of empowerment and disruptive approaches (Martin & Osberg 2007; Santos 2012; Dacin et al. 2011; Montgomery et al. 2012). Iconic examples of social entrepreneurship are the Grameen Bank[1], Barefoot College[2] and Aravind Eye Clinic[3], among many others, which aim to generate a societal impact of alleviating poverty through micro-enterprise loans, capability development and overcoming health barriers.

Social entrepreneurship operates at many scales and across social, cultural, environmental, economic and political spheres, ranging from localised employment programmes for disenfranchised groups such as prison inmates, through environmental protection initiatives that increase youth employment as well as community regeneration[4] and beyond (PEP 2018; The Howard League 2008). Successful social enterprises are generating meaningful, tangible, life-changing outcomes for and with communities experiencing some of the most pressing and distressing issues of our time.

Social enterprise has been variously defined, but the two consistent elements are, first, an overriding social mission, and second, an element of trade that supports the achievement of the social mission (Martin & Osberg 2007). The character of a 'social mission' can be diverse, spanning social, cultural, environmental and political objectives. The core character of the 'social mission' is that a 'problem' or 'need' is being addressed (Lyon & Sepulveda 2009). The trade element is flexible, encompassing selling products or services to the open market, through generating revenue through service agreements with government. The key determinant is that social enterprises are not solely reliant on grants (Lyon & Sepulveda 2009). Importantly, it is not necessary to be fully self-sustaining through trade for an activity to be recognised as a social enterprise; many receive significant amounts of their income from government and philanthropic grants. Some definitions also emphasise that the use of profit or surplus is primarily directed to the social mission (Martin & Osberg 2007). For Indigenous communities, as for many others, one of the values of social enterprise is that the economic mission creates financial autonomy to pursue the social mission considered to best serve their community, freeing them from being beholden to an external grant maker's priorities and funding cycles.

SOCIAL ENTERPRISE WITHIN MĀORI COMMUNITIES

Māori have a rich body of social innovation spanning from well before the colonial period to the present day. It encompasses diverse forms of social value creation from early models of collective capitalism that sought to sustain tribal communities in the face of colonisation, to world-leading cultural revitalisation initiatives and solutions to the disproportionate socioeconomic disadvantage that Māori, in common with Indigenous peoples globally, experience across every measurable quality-of-life indicator. While social enterprise is a new term within the Māori community, the practice of social enterprise has a long genealogy in Māori approaches to the role of wealth creation within communities and is pervasive across the contemporary Māori economy.

Pre-contact and early contact economic activity within the Māori community arguably falls within the definition of social enterprise. Pre-contact intertribal trade in food, pounamu and other goods was conducted for the purposes of hapū[5] sustainability and prosperity (social mission) through barter (trade). The early contact economy comprised a diverse range of collectively driven cropping, producing and trading relationships that similarly served hapū sustainability objectives. Until the 1860s, these collective models of economic activity became progressively larger in scale and more nuanced in their operations. They included, for example, the 'roving working bees' that were used to harvest cropped blocks of Māori land and the pooling of capital used to pay for the construction and operation of Māori owned flour and wheat mills (Petrie 2013). As is widely documented, the Māori economy went from being the powerhouse of the early New Zealand economy, through various phases of decline, principally as a result of Crown actions in the forcible dispossession of Māori from their collective ownership of lands and resources (Petrie 2013).

Significantly, the contemporary Māori economy, which now has a compelling NZ$50 billion asset base (Chapman Tripp 2017), is arguably comprised predominantly of social enterprises. Using a broad definition of social enterprise that requires solely the presence of a social mission and some element of trade (including contracts with government), it could even be argued that non-social enterprises are the minority within the Māori economy. In this chapter and elsewhere, I argue that the reason for this distinctive character is the prevalence of a strong social mission across the Māori economy at all scales and sectors, ranging from tribal organisations charged with major social, environmental and cultural transformation, through small family businesses that have a social mission of employing family members (McMeeking, Grant & Melrose 2017). The diversity of social impact and economic models evident within the contemporary Māori economy is illustrated in the three case studies below, which describe a tribal organisation, a disruptive health venture and a traditional village business selling traditional food. The important correlation between the different approaches to Māori social enterprise and nation-building is discussed in the following section.

Case Study: Te Rūnanga o Ngāi Tahu

Te Rūnanga o Ngāi Tahu is a tribal organisation representing the Ngāi Tahu tribe, who now number over 55,000 members and have a traditional territory spanning most of the South Island of New Zealand (Te Rūnanga o Ngāi Tahu 2018). In 1998, Ngāi Tahu received a settlement from government, as redress for the historical appropriation of lands and resources, to a value of NZ$170 million as well as their entitlement under the pan-Māori fisheries settlement in 1992. This resulted in the tribe gaining settlement-derived assets of fisheries quota (the regulatory tool that enables commercial fisheries harvesting), extensive rural land holdings predominantly used for forestry at the time of settlement, some urban land holdings and cash.

In the twenty years since settlement, Ngāi Tahu has grown its asset base to a value of NZ$1.3 billion (Te Rūnanga o Ngāi Tahu 2017) with active subsidiary businesses in tourism, seafood, agriculture, property development and an investment portfolio. Ngāi Tahu generates social impact from these significant funds and resources through a dividend model. Under this model, the commercial entities are charged with generating wealth with minimal directives for social or cultural performance. Rather, an annual dividend is transferred to the parent tribal development arm which delivers a broad suite of programmes across social, cultural, environmental, economic and political spheres. The annual tribal development dividend is now close to NZ$50 million (2017) which can be expected to grow over time.

The social impact created by the tribal entity is diverse both in objectives and mechanisms. The social impact objectives are anchored in a tribal vision document that was developed by tribal members shortly after receipt of the settlement assets (Te Rūnanga o Ngāi Tahu 2013). The document gives expression to intergenerational aspirations for cultural revitalisation; social well-being in educational, health and wealth outcomes; regional development supporting traditional villages; commercial growth; political influence; and reactivating the tribal footprint in an environmentally rejuvenated tribal territory. The mechanisms for achieving these objectives range from direct distribution of funds to individuals and subtribal collectives, as well as programmatic delivery akin to governmental service-delivery approaches.

The highest profile social change initiatives use direct distribution to support individual and family savings through the Whai Rawa Scheme and the Ngāi Tahu Fund, which supports cultural revitalisation initiatives driven by tribal members. Whai Rawa is a matched savings scheme, with individual contributions matched by the tribal organisation to an annually capped figure that can be accessed for prescribed purposes including tertiary education, first-home purchase and retirement (Te Rūnanga o Ngāi Tahu 2006b). The fund is significant because its direct impact of increasing the financial security of tribal members has powerful ancillary benefits that come from peoples' improved access to education and better-quality housing. The Ngāi Tahu Fund has invested close to NZ$10 million in cultural revitalisation initiatives spanning language, cultural practices, knowledge of genealogy, and tribal histories, as well as the redevelopment of marae, the paramount cultural facility and heart in Māori communities (Te Rūnanga o Ngāi Tahu 2006a). These initiatives similarly have the direct benefit of the cultural regeneration project, as well as wider contemporary vitalisation within the tribe that is enabled by strengthened connectivity among tribal members.

But these various forms of social impact generated by Ngāi Tahu are about more than simply social enterprise development. They reflect the contemporary realities and potential of tribally driven nation-building. Their broad terrain of priorities carries a mandate from the tribal membership, through the vision document, with annual consideration of relative priorities, and determination of the way to achieve desired outcome being set by the tribal governing body. The right and ability to make decisions on how to invest tribally generated funds, for tribal benefit that aligns with tribal priorities, is decided solely by tribal machinery. This is collective self-determination in action. While it may not be self-determination's apex of political authority and jurisdiction across a territory, it is a manifestation of the tribe, through its exercise of governance, shaping the social, cultural, economic and environmental inheritance of future generations.

Case Study*:* iMoko

iMoko is a disruptive virtual healthcare provider for children that aims to democratise healthcare and overcome access barriers that are known to contribute to negative health outcomes within rural and marginalised communities. iMoko uses technology to enable remote diagnosis of a suite of common childhood illnesses. A lay community member, often a volunteer or teacher aid, is trained to submit relevant diagnostic information (such as weight, temperature, a short narrative of the issue and pictures) based on a child's presenting complaint. All diagnostic information is uploaded to a cloud-based web platform for assessment by a team of telehealth clinicians. A treatment plan is developed, reviewed by a doctor and, if relevant, a prescription for pharmaceuticals is sent directly to a pharmacy near the patient, with the parents notified of their child's diagnosis and that a script is available to be picked up (McMeeking et al. 2017).

iMoko currently offers free health checks to 10,000 children across 260 sites throughout New Zealand. These health checks occur at Kōhanga Reo (Māori language early childhood centres), early childhood centres and schools within lower socioeconomic areas, many of which are rural. Currently, iMoko provides remote diagnosis and treatment for skin, dental and throat infections, with the latter being particularly important to arresting the growth in rheumatic fever.

iMoko was founded by a high-profile Māori doctor and public health advocate, Dr Lance O'Sullivan, who was celebrated as 'New Zealander of the Year' in 2014.[6] While the service is not confined to Māori children, the areas in which the service operates have a high Māori population, and the organisation places a high priority on improving Māori health outcomes. The service also has a strong integration of Māori language and cultural protocols (McMeeking et al. 2017). Such has been its success that iMoko has been approached by Indigenous communities in the Pacific and North America to expand the service into their countries.

iMoko reflects a different type of nation-building: as 'ground up' solution building from within Indigenous communities that may or may not be directly connected to tribal economic development. There are now a large number of Māori social enterprises with this characteristic: passionate individuals who bring their insights and entrepreneurial talent to create social transformation for and with their community (McMeeking et al. 2017). Māori, and more broadly Indigenous, social enterprise has not formally been connected with nation-building, perhaps because of the perception of weak institutional linkages with the attainment of political authority or tribal development. However, social enterprise of this kind directly addresses social ills while building empowerment, aspiration and capability within Indigenous communities. That is arguably a critically important companion to institutional nation-building and tribal development programmes that can, at times, mimic the 'top-down' nature of government services. The role of this type of Māori social enterprise in nation-building is developed more fully below, with a particular exploration of the import of an organic social movement born out of Indigenous communities and aiming to address some of our communities' most pressing issues.

Case Study: Koukourārata Development Hāpai Produce

Koukourārata is a traditional Ngāi Tahu village in a particularly picturesque part of the South Island that shares a colonial legacy and contemporary aspirations in common with many Māori communities. Land loss during the colonial period resulted in the Māori villages being stripped of their economic assets, materially contributing to twentieth-century diaspora as members of communities sought employment opportunities no longer available in their traditional territories. Koukourārata are now actively seeking to repatriate their dispersed people to the village by creating contemporary employment opportunities; an aspiration and strategy shared with a number of rural Māori communities across Aotearoa-New Zealand.

One of their suites of village regeneration initiatives is a boutique produce business that grows and retails a traditional variety of Māori potato, known as taewa. The business uses land owned by the community, but that has been leased to non-community members due to a lack of capability in the community to put it into productive use (McMeeking et al. 2017).[7] The cropping practice is informed by mātauranga Māori (traditional knowledge) and a research partnership with a local university. In addition to job creation, the initiative is supporting an education programme for community members to learn about the horticulture industry. These aspects of the business align to the community aspiration to grow and diversify crops over time, creating a growing circle of community members to step into a business, which—as it becomes stronger—creates more employment opportunities thereby enabling more families to return home.

This type of Māori social enterprise is also a form of ground-up nation-building that has as its principal aim rebuilding sustainable communities in traditional homelands, through community-led business growth. Regenerating the economic vitality of traditional villages is a necessary, but not particularly visible, precursor to many of the aspirations that drive nation-building, because it anchors and actively regenerates the presence of a community. The more people who can reside close to our marae (cultural centres), the stronger the community presence becomes to anchor cultural practices. This is especially the case for practices which can only be maintained as a group or collective, such as language, knowledge of genealogical relationships, governance and many other dimensions of nationhood that require the presence of people in, and acting as, a community. In the contemporary era, meaningful employment opportunities enable families to reside close to the marae, with consequential positive impacts of increasing the resilience, vitality and momentum within the community.

These three case studies reflect the diversity of Māori social enterprises and the type of contributions that are being made to contemporary nation-building, that to date have been largely confined to the periphery of discourses about nationhood, perhaps due to the pre-eminence given to institution-building within Indigenous communities (see e.g.[8] Cornell 2007a, 2007b, 2013, 2015; Smith 2004, 2008; Joseph 2005; Jorgenson 2007). As important as institution-building is to reclaiming political authority, the social, cultural, environmental and economic dimensions of nation-building arguably require more tangible practical processes of change, to which this chapter now turns.

TANGIBLE CHANGE: MĀORI SOCIAL ENTERPRISE AND NATION-BUILDING

Pursuing the right to self-determination has, fairly, captured much of the discourse on Indigenous nation-building. Legalistic commentary and advocacy on domestic and international doctrines have been instrumental in enabling Indigenous peoples in the CANZUS[9] nation-states to engage more fully, if not completely, in the activity of nation-building. The United Nations Declaration on the Rights of Indigenous Peoples (UNDRIP) and various, if still wanting, domestic advances have enabled Indigenous peoples to define their own futures beyond the constraints our ancestors experienced in the colonial era. The body of knowledge on how to activate hard-won Indigenous rights and translate those into the kinds of practical outcomes Indigenous peoples are seeking is, however, slender and perhaps lagging behind the pioneering leadership and innovation of Indigenous leaders and social entrepreneurs. There are three emergent theories guiding the practice of self-determination that Māori social enterprise appears to contribute to, offering further insights to each and encouraging deeper consideration of the relationship between self-determination and social change within Indigenous communities.

The theories of self-determination are: first, ensuring the 'cultural fit' or 'cultural legitimacy' of contemporary Indigenous institutions (see, e.g.[10] Cornell & Kalt 2000; Cornell 2007a, 2007b, 2013, 2015; Smith 2004, 2008; Joseph 2005; Jorgenson 2007); second, encouraging practices of 'everyday resurgence' that incorporate Indigenous language and varied cultural practices into daily life (Alfred & Corntassel 2005); and third, promoting collective capability development. The latter additionally builds on Amartya Sen's thesis that achieving the fundamental freedoms embodied by human rights is best done by building capabilities that the community values (Sen 2009; Murphy 2008). These theories each have different foci, which create a high degree of complementarity and synergy, resembling a layer cake.

The 'cultural fit' thesis is principally concerned with the architecture of tribal organisations and their forms of governance and, as such, provides a primarily top-down approach to nation-building. The premise is that, if the central tribal institutions are developed through a culturally sound process and perform according to cultural values and expectations, they are both constitutive of and maintain ongoing self-determination (Anaya 2011). The 'acts of everyday resurgence' theory focuses on individuals, in effect representing the bottom layer of the cake. For example, by choosing to incorporate language and cultural practice into daily life, individuals are furthering the Indigenous cause and being self-determining (Alfred & Corntassel 2005; Corntassel 2012). The middle layer, promoting collective capability development, is the least developed of the three theories. This places the priority on building community capability to identify and enact their own priorities, with capability development being both the means and the end. Under this framework, building the capability to be self-determining has both a constitutive role in regaining self-determination and is an intrinsic good in its own right (Murphy 2008, 2014). Critically, it also provides the glue that holds the overall endeavour of self-determination together, creating the practical connections between higher level institution building and individual acts of resurgence.

The practice of Māori social entrepreneurship correlates to some but not all of these propositions, while inviting a deeper questioning of the importance of social transformation in Indigenous self-determination. The cultural fit thesis is most obviously invoked in the Ngāi Tahu and Koukourārata case studies, both of which involve contemporary tribal organisations with cultural roots and community mandate to act. In contrast, the iMoko example is not attached to any tribal organisation. Rather, institutionally it uses a mainstream legal entity to facilitate its community services, and the priority placed on incorporating language and cultural facets are solely at the discretion of the Board of Directors.

There are many Māori social enterprises, like iMoko, that do not have an *a priori* community mandate for their work, rather as entrepreneurs they are inspired mavericks who act on their own volition. The incorporation of cultural elements reflects the ad hoc preferences of the founders, which appears not to meet the formality implied in the cultural fit thesis. These entities are, however, celebrated and championed within the Māori community (Hemi 2018; Treacher 2016; Trup 2017). This suggests that the cultural fit thesis may have an exemption clause for initiatives of this ilk, the common feature of which intuitively appears to be demonstrable service to, and social gains for, the Māori community. It also suggests that the role of individuals in producing innovative cultural elements in their social entrepreneurship, which in turn gain wider cultural credibility or cultural fit, is important and needs to be considered more closely.

Acts of everyday resurgence as a mechanism for practising self-determination appear to be an ancillary feature of many Māori social enterprises, if not their principal cause. Koukourārata, for example, has the primary objective of creating employment opportunities that enable people to return to their village, in turn sustaining the vitality of the village community. The mechanism for doing so is an act of 'everyday resurgence', in that they are reinvigorating a traditional food source, re-engaging in trade practices with an historical precedent, and branding their product with Māori language and narrative. iMoko integrates language and cultural protocol into how they perform their service (the means), but, as with Koukourārata, the end is a social transformation objective. Both examples demonstrate the value of social enterprise as a vehicle for acts of everyday resurgence, which enable Indigenous communities to achieve greater autonomy and visibility for language, cultural practices and other resurgence priorities they choose to integrate into social change initiatives.

The social change purpose of Māori social enterprises is most directly aligned with the collective capability thesis but clearly infiltrates and contributes to the others. As exemplified by Koukourārata which incorporates an educational component to grow their people into the horticultural industry, Māori social enterprises commonly contribute to community capability development as an explicit goal or indirectly through their means of delivery, such as iMoko's training of lay community members to collect information from patients. A recent study of twenty Māori social enterprises found that all the ventures intended to build community capability in a way they believed would contribute to positive social gain, indicating that capability development is likely to be pervasive—indeed, arguably to the extent of near universality in Māori social enterprises (McMeeking et al. 2017).

The deeper question posed by social enterprise is the relationship between self-determination and social transformation within Māori communities. Self-determination has in part been pursued as an end in itself, rightly, to repatriate the authorities that were eroded through colonisation. However, there has also been recognition that the true test of self-determination is 'whether Indigenous Peoples themselves actually feel they have choices about their way of life . . . [and therefore] to live well and humanly in their own ways' (Ferrell 2001, 263–4). The test of choices and 'living well' is a considerable one in the context of the disproportionate social and economic disadvantage experienced by Māori, in common with our Indigenous relations globally. It also speaks to an implicit if somewhat opaque relationship between self-determination and social change, as the ability of Indigenous peoples to have real choices and live well necessitates significant changes to the socio-economic and cultural legacy that colonisation has left our communities. Contemporary government by nation-states has failed to remedy, and many would argue has worsened, this colonial legacy. It is perhaps unreasonable then to expect that tribal organisations by themselves can correct the levels of embedded disadvantage or within a timeframe that is worthy of our communities' faith.

Nevertheless, in spite of the enormity of the work involved in overcoming that colonial legacy, social enterprise has potentially three important contributions to enabling our communities to attain the goal of freedom of real choices and living well. First, social enterprise is free from some of the institutional constraints that accompany tribal development initiatives. Māori social entrepreneurs typically do not access tribal funds to pursue their venture (McMeeking et al. 2017), and so are not subject to the accountability politics experienced by tribal institutions. They typically reside within the community they are aiming to serve, have a track record of service producing social gains, and are bringing new external funding and resources to the community. In combination, these factors grant them a licence to operate and an implied encouragement to be innovative, disruptive and experimental: a set of permissions arguably more difficult for tribal institutions to obtain and sustain.

One of the certainties about the experiences of Indigenous peoples today is that replicating the status quo will not only perpetuate the social disadvantage faced by our people, but is also likely to limit the regeneration of our self-determination. Pioneering the new is, however, inherently risky; being new means, it is unproven. Social entrepreneurs have appetite, implied community permission and, most commonly, an aptitude to experiment with the new, to prove a novel approach to social change and improve it iteratively. Their implied mandate is sustainable as long as they do so with integrity and an ethic of service to their community. Social entrepreneurs are therefore an important companion for tribal organisations, able to innovate at the margins to create the new, with wider latitude than a tribal organisation may have.

Second, social entrepreneurship appears to be gaining prominence within Māori communities as a quasi-social movement that promulgates self-belief and aspiration not only within the individuals involved but also within the community, as well as building community capability. Social movements involve a common cause, visible constituency with some degree of collectivisation, engagement in collective actions with some continuity and clarity of purpose over time (Batiwala 2012). Māori social entrepreneurship has a common cause of Māori transforming our own communities through novel solutions that embody our values, priorities and ideals, which is the essence of self-determination (McMeeking et al. 2017). Existing practitioners have a strong desire to increase their collective impact and coordination, which may foment into a sufficient degree of collective action and continuity over time to constitute a social movement. If this occurs, it will become a community-generated social movement that aims to grow the tangible realisation of self-determination's promise for social transformation, continuing the work of previous generations of Indigenous advocates who championed the rights recognition movement.

Finally, achieving sustainable social change requires the creation of new social habits: new expectations, practices and processes that wear away at the structural anchors of the status quo (da Silveira 2014; de la Sablonniere 2017; Cooper 2001). For self-determination, there are arguably two types of new social habits required: first, re-imprinting the institutions of nation-states to recognise and provide equitable space for Indigenous self-determination and second, re-embedding aspirations, expectations and practices within Indigenous communities to chart our own destinies on our terms, in contrast to the progressive colonial erosion of our autonomy. Māori social enterprise, by pioneering novel approaches to self-determination, is an important part of creating new social habits within our communities as progressive waves of agents of change deliver a body of proof to their peers and relations that we can design and enact the social change our communities aspire to. When the density of this kind of social entrepreneurship reaches a tipping point of sustainable success, it becomes the foundation for a social movement that directly contributes to maximising collective Indigenous self-determination.

CHALLENGES FOR MĀORI SOCIAL ENTERPRISE

The potency of Māori social enterprise to contribute meaningfully to self-determination is jeopardised by a number of factors, paramount among them is navigating their dual social and economic objectives. Organisations which have social and economic aims are known by management theorists as 'hybrid organisations' (Battiliana, Lee, Walker & Dorsey 2012). The literature identifies a common set of complex challenges recognised as affecting these types of organisations, which Māori social enterprises are likely to experience to varying degrees.

It is common for hybrid organisations to experience tension in reconciling social and economic objectives. Two predominant approaches to reconciling these twin objectives have emerged: coupled and decoupled (Doherty, Haugh & Lyon 2014). Coupling the dual objectives results in achieving social aims through the commercial model (Haigh, Walker, Bacq & Kickul 2015). An example of this 'coupled strategy' is a business that seeks to create employment opportunities for a marginalised segment of society, for example, Koukourārata seeking to create employment opportunities for members of the community to encourage them to return home. The more successful the business is, the more employment opportunities are created, thereby unifying the economic and social objectives. A 'decoupled strategy' is an approach that separates the dual missions; for example, Te Rūnanga o Ngāi Tahu, which has a structurally separated commercial arm charged with generating high profit and then using that profit through a dividend funding model as the sole way to achieve the social objectives of the community. The different strategies have a cascading suite of impacts.

Coupled approaches to the dual objectives, while offering a greater unity of purpose across the organisation, may be more difficult to initiate and scale. Many Māori social enterprises of this ilk are experiencing difficulties attracting funding due to their dual objectives: they don't look like a typical charity because they generate some portion of their revenue, and they don't look like a typical enterprise that is familiar to venture and capital investors because of their overriding social change objectives. As such, social enterprises with coupled objectives can land betwixt and between philanthropic, government and venture capital sources, adversely affecting their ability to both deliver proof of concept and survive the awkward transition phase to generating sufficient revenue to sustain their social impact (McMeeking et al. 2017). Decoupled approaches can result in a simpler commercial model, but make it difficult for staff and stakeholders to understand the relationship between the dual objectives, resulting in loyalty conflicts and perception challenges (Haigh et al. 2015). For Māori social enterprises, the question of whether to couple or decouple the achievement of social and commercial objectives will also impact on the nature, timeframe, scale and impact of the desired social change and, at a deeper level, the advancement of self-determination within communities.

Māori social enterprises are engaging with these challenges without a supporting body of evidence on the correlation between self-determination, social impact and different approaches to reconciling social and commercial objectives. There are emerging bodies of work on the importance of values alignment within Māori enterprise (Awatere et al. 2017), the distinctive characteristics of Māori entrepreneurship (Kawharu, Tapsell & Woods 2012), and regenerating tribal economies through internal trade relationships (Barr & Reid 2014). However, there is not yet sufficient evaluative work that can inform those engaged in rebuilding self-determination as to the likely impact of their strategic choices, both for the social realities within their communities and the pursuit of nation-building. Māori practitioners and entrepreneurs will continue to innovate at the apex of social transformation; it is contingent on the academy to keep pace, validating, questioning and accelerating their contributions to self-determination and the realisation of intergenerational aspirations.

CONCLUSION

The legal affirmation of Indigenous peoples' right to self-determination is barely a decade old, but the practice of self-determination extends across generations overcoming a plethora of challenges, not least of which continues to be settler-colonial incursion and dispossession. At this time in our collective history, one of the most important endeavours of Indigenous peoples is that of re-creating our practices of self-determination according to our own values and priorities. If self-determination is to mean more than political autonomy, if it is expected to regenerate agency within Indigenous communities and transform the lived sociocultural and economic realities within our communities, then the important work of tribal institution building will never be sufficient in isolation. Embedding social habits and expectations to define our own trajectories, within our communities and the wider nation-state, necessitates a movement comprised of many people creating the change our communities aspire to. One thread of that movement will need to be advocacy reminiscent of the fearless leadership within the rights recognition movement. But equally important are the threads of tribally led nation-building and community innovation that collectively contribute to culturally founded Indigenous institutions, practices of everyday resurgence of indigeneity and community-wide collective capability to be self-determining.

The role of community innovation in contemporary self-determination has not, to date, been adequately recognised as a source of ground-up momentum and transformation that is quietly building aspiration and capabilities within our communities to chart our own destinies. Māori, and more broadly Indigenous, social enterprise is a distinctive frame through which to understand the contribution of community innovation to the regeneration of self-determination. Furthermore, to fully understand this collective impact, we need to move beyond viewing Indigenous social entrepreneurs as stand-alone, isolated individuals and look to the larger scale social and cultural momentum they are generating. Today, Māori are recognising that the language and knowledge pertaining to social enterprise are simply tools that Indigenous peoples can use for our own purposes. We are creating and sustaining initiatives that do not neatly subscribe to global social enterprise discourse but rather demonstrate that we can learn and adapt what is useful to our journey of self-determination.

NOTES

1. The Grameen Bank (GB) has reversed conventional banking practice by removing the need for collateral and created a banking system based on mutual trust, accountability, participation and creativity. GB provides credit to the poorest of the poor in rural Bangladesh, without any collateral. At GB, credit is a cost-effective weapon to fight poverty and serves as a catalyst in the overall development of socio-economic conditions of the poor who have been kept outside the banking orbit on the grounds that they are poor and hence not bankable. Professor Muhammad Yunus,

the founder of the Grameen Bank, reasoned that financial resources can be made available to the poor on terms and conditions that are appropriate and reasonable, 'enabling them to start or expand tiny businesses and ultimately lift themselves out of poverty . . . Grameen Bank is owned by the poor: Ninety-four percent of the ownership shares of the institution are held by the borrowers themselves' (Yunus 2009, 34).

2. The Barefoot College started in India in 1972. Its website states:

> For more than 40 years, the Barefoot College has designed new ways to nurture and support a journey to empowerment, one village at a time, one woman at a time. We demystify and decentralise technology and put new tools in the hands of the rural poor with a singular objective of spreading self-sufficiency and sustainability. With a geographic focus on the Least Developed Countries, we train women worldwide as solar engineers, innovators and educators, who then return to their villages to bring light and learning to their community. (Barefoot College n.d.)

3. Aravind is innovative in its mission of eliminating blindness by providing high-quality eye care for all. The hospital started in 1976 with 11 beds in Madurai, India. Today, Aravind provides 3,500 beds at its facilities in 12 Indian cities. Each hospital also houses specialty clinics that treat cataracts, low vision, cornea injuries, glaucoma and other common eye ailments. Seventy-five per cent of its surgeries are free, but it still manages to run at profit (Aravind eye hospitals 2019).

4. See for example the Hunts Point Riverside Park and the South Bronx Greenway, led by Majora Carter in the Bronx, NY (Carter 2006).

5. Hapū is interpreted as 'subtribe' and were the principal collective unit of political authority prior to contact.

6. For further information, see iMoko homepage. Available at http://public.imoko.com/.

7. See also S. McMeeking. 2017. *Preliminary insights into Māori social enterprise.* A commissioned research report for Te Puni Kōkiri (Ministry of Māori Development), unpublished. Available at http://hdl.handle.net/10092/15663.

8. Cornell, S. 2014. From rights to governance—and back: Transformations in contemporary Indigenous politics. Revised version of a lecture presented at the Joseph A. Myers Center for Research on Native American Issues at the University of California, Berkeley, 19 April 2012. Available from author.

9. CANZUS represents the Indigenous interests of nation-states: Canada, Australia, New Zealand and the United States of America.

10. Cornell, S. 2014. From rights to governance—and back: Transformations in contemporary Indigenous politics. Revised version of a lecture presented at the Joseph A. Myers Center for Research on Native American Issues at the University of California, Berkeley, 19 April 2012. Available from author.

Theme Four

GOVERNING AS TRANSFORMATIVE LEADERSHIP

Thematic Introduction

Concepts, Issues and Trends

Diane Smith

Whether it be for a nation, community or organisation, the conduct of governance has a remarkable capacity to unite diverse people under a common purpose, or to produce fragmentation and discord. The extent to which Indigenous leaders can exercise culturally credible leadership and bring people together to govern collectively—as a nation or a community—is a critical factor in which of these outcomes eventuates. Governance is about more than just leadership, but without visionary, capable and accountable leaders it can quickly deteriorate into dysfunction and lack of direction. When leaders and governance arrangements have poor credibility, it diminishes people's trust and preparedness to invest their time and support. This can become a debilitating downward spiral that exacerbates existing problems within a community or nation.

Through decades of settler-colonialism across the CANZUS states and beyond, discriminatory policies and Western governance practices have been imposed upon and undermined Indigenous forms of authority and social order, creating conflict, despair and apathy within Indigenous societies. As Bhiamie Williamson points out in his chapter for this theme, some Indigenous communities have been driven apart by the trauma-based disputes that result. When a community has trauma-informed leadership and decision-making (see Atkinson 2013; Clements et al. 2010; Oscar 2018), internal division and disunity will remain unmediated and persevere, sometimes in perpetuity. Community members with unresolved grievances can thwart attempts to get new things done, even when innovative action may be for the common good. Under these conditions, people's ability to come together, discuss ideas and place the interest of the collective above the self may be severely diminished. This can be a major obstacle for governance resurgence and achieving a shared development agenda.

Leadership makes a difference, not just for securing rights, but perhaps even more importantly, for subsequently exercising those rights and rebuilding nations. As James S Anaya suggests in his chapter, a transition occurred with the passage of the UNDRIP from a 'rights recognition' era to a 'rights implementation' era. In the latter era, the challenge has become how to translate rights into effective governance practice (see also Cornell 2019; and Neil Sterritt this volume). This means leaders must be able to grow and mature in their skills and insights, adapt to changing demands on them, and yet continue to keep the whole nation in their hearts. It often also calls upon leaders to undertake a wider set of contemporary requirements for representation and accountability.

In this theme, we read accounts of Indigenous people tackling fundamental questions as they go about revitalising their leadership for exercising governance and development purposes. They are asking:

- What is Indigenous leadership in today's world and why is it important?
- What kind of leadership contributes to effective, legitimate governance in nations and communities?
- Who should take up leadership roles today?
- How can leadership for self-governance be evaluated and rebuilt?
- How can gender equality be embedded in new leadership frameworks?
- How can the next generation of strong leaders be mentored?

INDIGENOUS LEADERSHIP

A leader is someone who is recognised by their own group members as having the personal style, values, skills, experience and knowledge that enables them to provide direction, mould consensus and mobilise members to act towards achieving a common goal together. Leadership and management are not the same thing. These days, nations, communities and organisations need to have both—but not all good leaders are good managers and equally, not all managers are good leaders. The chapters in this theme testify that the form, function and qualities of leadership are as varied as the Indigenous cultures across the CANZUS countries.

In general, leadership style of Indigenous nations is socially and politically complex. This is because it is distributed amongst particular community members who take on differing leadership responsibilities, at different social layers, for diverse matters such as ceremony, gendered and site-specific knowledge, economic exchange, dispute mediation and so on. It is hierarchical in that it is based on a personal accumulation of valued knowledge and experience, which in turn has important age and gender dimensions creating recognised areas of women and men's leadership. As we see in this theme, not all leaders are equally powerful; some are more influential than others. The individual authority of leaders is influenced by their cultural knowledge, reputation and their ability to 'look after' others—not only their community but also the land, its resources and related systems of knowledge and law. This means that leadership in Indigenous nations is not just about people at the top. Building the collective capacity of citizens for leadership is therefore an important aspect of nation-building and governance resurgence.

Several of the authors emphasise that the legitimacy of governance is stronger and more sustainable when leaders gain the respect and trust of their members and when there is regular open communication between them. In the case studies presented in this theme, we see leaders doing that by:

- Acting in a public-spirited way that accords with shared cultural values and standards of behaviour.
- Being accountable, fair and inclusive in representing all the members of their community or nation.
- Understanding and carrying out the responsibilities assigned to their governing roles.
- Inspiring people to work together to achieve collective goals.
- Knowing when to seek further knowledge or expertise, from themselves or others.

A leader's style—the way they put their values, expertise, vision and sense of purpose into action—is described by authors as making an important difference to their own and other people's performance and accomplishments. How leaders marshal resources, engage members and other parties, mobilise assets and generate support to enact a nation's vision are crucial elements of effective governance and collectively achieving the things that matter to a nation.

DECOLONISING LEADERSHIP

Settler-colonisation has been deeply shaped Indigenous modes of leadership and governance (Begay et al. 2007; Champagne et al. 2005; Evans & Sinclair 2015). Several authors testify to the deep reflection that is occurring within First Nations about how to actively rebuild culturally informed leadership for self-governance and self-determined development. Given settler-colonialism is a dynamic, ongoing process across the CANZUS states, then Indigenous approaches to leadership will also need to be dynamic, willing to adapt and take into account diverse modern experiences of dispossession and marginalisation. Examples described by the authors of the contributions in this section of the book show this has required a supported process of individual rediscovery and recovery that can have transformative impacts in Indigenous communities. Here we see the potential of revitalised leadership to heal a nation's internal trauma, intergenerational antipathies and internal disputes.

Authors such as Bhiamie Williamson therefore pose healing as a process of therapeutic change through social, cultural and spiritual renewal in which leaders can play a valuable part. At the individual level, it requires a willingness to reflect on personal relationships and behaviour in often stressful circumstances, while at the community level it requires the ability to come together to support one another and work collectively and collegially towards an end. Neil Sterritt's chapter shows us that the act of coming together and working as a group over time is the foundation stone of governance, one that marks out a particularly influential intersection between leadership, governance-rebuilding and the incremental assertion of sovereignty over development.

INSTITUTIONAL LEADERSHIP SOLUTIONS, TOOLS AND BEHAVIOUR

In this theme, authors provide compelling insights into the strategies and tools that work to support the complex and challenging set of contemporary leadership tasks involved in governance and nation-rebuilding. Several communities and nations set out their agreed understandings about *who* they want to be and *how* they want to treat each other (including as leaders) in written laws, policies and charters. Such new institutional frameworks embrace Indigenous ways of knowing, doing and being, attempting to reinforce societal norms and responsibilities that served to guide a nation through generations. But that does not exclude adopting innovative practice and new technologies. Both Mera Penhera and Karen Diver showcase how new generations of Indigenous leaders are productively engaging with gender equity and digital activism to create new opportunities and spaces for leadership. They also describe initiatives to ensure that the governance capacity and confidence of the nation's members are being actively developed and continuously promoted. Karen Diver points out that this is a long-term process requiring careful leadership planning, sustained organisation and direction over a prolonged period.

A critical leadership service provided by many of the Indigenous leaders described in authors' accounts is to create a culturally safe space for community members to gather, share their experiences, renew relationships, and rebuild trust and mutual reciprocity. We see leaders designing ways to include community members in planning and implementation. Increased engagement by citizens enables more inclusive planning for the future that sustains community credibility and personal commitment. It elevates the legitimacy of representative organisations and their leadership (including the decisions they make), through greater participation. The case studies describe how this increases the likelihood of more active engagement by members in the wider projects of governance and nation-rebuilding.

First Nation leaders are flooded by the demands of government, industry and their own citizens. Leaders need to be strategic and realistic about their resources and capacity. Neil Sterritt notes the often small size, remoteness and low levels of capital resources of many communities, leading some leaders to make strategic decisions about how to concentrate on a few agreed priorities, achieve success there and then build on that success. In other words, they are undertaking a strategic, incremental approach to governance and nation-rebuilding. With continued success, leaders are then tackling a broader range of issues in a comprehensive approach to change.

Another common strategy evident amongst the nations discussed in the chapters is to renegotiate relationships and networks of support with external parties, from a position of governance strength. Many are also putting priority on creating strategic alliances with other Indigenous nations. Non-Indigenous supporters can help compel governments to make systemic changes and implement Indigenous laws on the ground. When rights as a nation are reaffirmed in these ways, Indigenous people effectively regain greater control of their lives.

Governance resurgence calls for experimentation and new solutions to be designed within the nation. It is risky business. Several authors describe the ways nations are monitoring and periodically reviewing their institutional checks and balances, including scrutinising their leaders. Indigenous peoples have survived because of their cultural institutions and values. But Indigenous leaders today are looking hard and afresh at what constitutes workable cultural solutions. Therefore, leaders who successfully promote cultural innovation are the ones who work hard to unite all their citizens to secure their mandate for proposed changes, not just those who support their ideas and goals. The case studies all conclude that rebuilding self-governance calls upon the participation of all generations. Here the chapters emphasise the critical need to make sure succession plans are in place and that young leaders can contribute their new ideas now, not later. Too often, charismatic leaders have been amazingly successful, but when they retire or fail in their leadership acumen, communities can fall apart. Leaders build for the future by mentoring youth who will carry on their good work long into the future.

TRANSFORMATIVE LEADERSHIP

The diverse aspects of governance resurgence described by the authors in this theme indicate that a new agenda for leadership transformation is occurring in parallel amongst many First Nations. This focuses on recognising the role of women as leaders; on the collective good rather than individual self-interest; and on all citizens having a responsibility to consider the public good when they exercise their 'vote'.

Leadership is perhaps even more demanding than it used to be. Not only is it informed by traditional values, laws, knowledge and extended family relations but leaders also have to operate within contemporary intercultural environments of governance, where often competing standards and expectations intersect. Karen Diver and Neil Sterritt describe how leaders today are required to undertake a raft of new forms of accountability and transparency, wear many different hats and be willing to make tough decisions that often may not be the popular decisions. Bhiamie Williamson alerts us to the fact that a significant area of contemporary leadership is also to meet the challenge of transforming communities through social repair and healing. This type of 'transformative leadership' is helping nations collectively to move away from dependency.

To undertake these twenty-first-century roles and responsibilities, we see many leaders further developing their own expertise and ability for 'connected up' leadership, as digital leaders. Mera Penhera describes how they are harnessing the power of new media and information technologies to expand conversations and shape political change with their community members, many of whom are residentially dispersed. Several authors examine the fresh contributions Indigenous women are having as leaders, as they reassert their collective voice as gender and cultural advocates by harnessing social media and Indigenous networking websites. They are seeking not only to practice what Penhera calls a politics of visibility that unsettles colonial power relations but also to cultivate internal solidarity and leadership for shaping positive transformation within their nations. This expands the substance and practice of self-determination in nations.

A nation-rebuilding approach requires a new conversation about the role and the strategic vision of self-governance, and how to go about achieving it. A critical component in that is rebuilding leadership. Initially it may be about a small area of leadership, decision-making control and responsibility, or cultural values. Whatever the focus, under a nation-rebuilding approach, the leadership arrangements must, first and foremost, be the result of informed decisions made by the Indigenous members of the nation or community involved. Action of this kind to transform leadership arrangements is, in effect, a sovereign decision—it is what 'self-determination in action' is about.

Chapter 16

Healing, Decolonisation and Governance

Bhiamie Williamson

Indigenous governance is a philosophy, theory and practice performed in the context of contemporary settler-colonialism. Whether they be organisations, corporations, First Nations governments or others, Indigenous-governing entities are often the point of entry for non-Indigenous parties to engage Indigenous peoples, communities and nations.

'Good' or 'effective' governance is recognised as the foundation stone upon which Indigenous communities can build prosperous futures for their peoples (Dodson & Smith 2003: 1–2). The importance of governing effectively is reflected in the large body of literature on Indigenous governance that is being produced throughout the world (Australian Indigenous Governance Institute 2018; Dodson & Smith 2003; Harvard Project on American Indian Economic Development 2008; Hunt et al. 2008; Sullivan & Oliver 2007; Von Der Porten 2012). Much of this literature focuses on the organisational, political, legal and economic elements of Indigenous governance. Literature that focuses on the sociocultural elements of Indigenous governing tends to speak to the idea of 'cultural match' or 'cultural legitimacy'—that is, governing structures and institutions that are adaptable and fit particular cultural groups (Australian Indigenous Governance Institute 2019; Harvard Project on American Indian Economic Development 2008; Hunt et al. 2008). While valuable contributions in their own right, this chapter considers these attempts to engage with the sociocultural foundations of Indigenous governance as insufficient.

What is largely missing is a deeper reflection on the integrated and inherently social aspects of Indigenous governance in communities. The rare engagements of scholars in this area tend to be through localised case studies of particular Indigenous communities or nations at particular points in time (Hunt et al. 2008; Jorgensen 2007; Rigney et al. 2015). Yet there remains a scarcity of literature that questions why some Indigenous communities just cannot seem to emerge as functional, well-organised groups in the modern world. Even rarer is literature that identifies how Indigenous leaders can exercise culturally informed notions of leadership and bring communities together to govern effectively. This chapter explores these deeper issues underlying the exercise and goals of Indigenous governance.

The chapter begins with a discussion of settler-colonialism, which it identifies as an ongoing process. In particular, moving away from colonial mentalities requires the decolonisation of Indigenous peoples and how they govern their communities. The chapter then discusses the notion of healing: exploring the roots of healing as a concept, its emergence in recent discourses, and how the term has been adapted in settler-colonial states today. Then follows a consideration of the field of Indigenous governance, where the common foundations of governance are identified before turning to the issue of what makes Indigenous governance unique in settler-colonial states. Understanding the overlap between decolonisation, healing and governance reveals that they are connected and interdependent processes. The chapter finishes by suggesting that Indigenous leaders can apply the distinct Indigenous craft practice of weaving in order to bring together decolonisation, healing and governance into an organised vision for the future.

DECOLONISATION

Settler-colonialism,[1] while emerging from and related to colonialism, is fundamentally different from it (Veracini 2011). Unlike colonialism, whose main purpose is to enrich a ruling nation-state (usually from European or Asian centres of empire) by conquering and subjugating external colonies, the purpose of settler-colonialism is to sever the historical ties to the ruling state from which the new nation has emerged (Veracini 2011). In this way, new states, such as Aotearoa-New Zealand, Australia, Canada or the United States, in turn become the colonising force, not England, which is the common coloniser in these states. Veracini, explored this distinction in great depth, noting that '[w]hereas colonialism reinforces the distinction between colony and metropole, settler colonialism erases it' (2011: 3).

Settler-colonial forces arrived throughout the 'new world' in various historical periods. They continue to occur in different places and in different ways. However, no matter at what period in history nor the narrative employed to establish and justify the existence of a new nation, the primary agenda of settler-colonialism remains to acquire and rule land (Tuck & Yang 2012: 5; Wolfe 2006). This agenda is mobilised through many state institutions such as courts, parliaments, and governmental and private interests, as well as carefully cultivated social engineering projects such as the 'White Australia policy' in Australia[2] or the *Indian Act* in Canada[3]. Settler-colonialism is a social process,[4] not simply an economic one, and is accepted, normalised and perpetuated by mainstream populations (Tuck & Yang 2012: 5; Veracini 2011). This settler-colonial mentality can be observed through the telling and re-telling of stories of 'explorers' and 'pioneers' (Veracini 2011: 3). Taming the wilderness, building industry and venerating historical figures as founding fathers (usually always fathers and not mothers) are common narratives embedded in this mentality (Veracini 2011: 3). This ongoing quest to dominate lands and waters places settler-colonial forces in diametric opposition to Indigenous peoples.

Indigenous peoples are just that, indigenous to the lands and waters they occupy (Alfred & Corntassel 2005: 597; United Nations Department of Economic and Social Affairs 2019: 5). They share a deep connection born out of millennia of being in and living on their lands and waters (United Nations Department of Economic and Social Affairs 2019: 5). Indigenous peoples possess an ancient jurisdiction evidenced by their linguistic diversity, their unique diets, cultural customs and stories of creation. It is this existence, as people of a particular place, that settler-colonialism strives to eradicate (Alfred & Corntassel 2005).

The eradication of Indigenous peoples has taken many forms, beginning with their physical extermination through introduced diseases and violent frontier conflict. Later, settler-colonial forces moved Indigenous peoples to various reserves, camps and missions in the hope that they would simply die out (Archibald 2006). Following this were assimilatory processes to remove the cultural, spiritual and linguistic institutions so central to Indigenous peoples' lives. More recently, 'recognition' has been identified as a political strategy to continue this process of removing Indigenous peoples, by absorbing them into a settler-colonial edifice (Coulthard 2014).

Reflecting on the violent histories manifest throughout almost every part of the settler-colonial world reveals that settler-colonialism, no matter how well disguised, has never—and nor could it be—beneficial to Indigenous peoples. This is the necessary lesson to inform understanding: that a settler-colonial system, no matter how well-meaning or asserting the rhetoric of equality, will always be committed to removing Indigenous peoples from their own lands. As Alfred and Corntassel explain:

> Contemporary Settlers follow the mandate provided for them by their imperial forefathers' colonial legacy, not by attempting to eradicate the physical signs of Indigenous peoples as human bodies, but by trying to eradicate their existence as peoples through the erasure of the histories and geographies that provide the foundation for Indigenous cultural identities and sense of self. (2005: 598)

In response to the unyielding and frequently overwhelming forces of settler-colonialism, Indigenous peoples throughout the settler-colonial world have responded by moving away from the ideas, practices and philosophies that enable the existence and acceptance of settler-colonialism.

'Decolonisation' is born out of a deep commitment to the future of Indigenous peoples and Indigenous ways of life (Archibald 2006: 25; Leanui 2000). The act of decolonisation is rooted in local Indigenous histories, laws, customs, traditions, stories, languages, and ways of knowing and being (Leanui 2000). It protects that which makes a group of people distinct as Indigenous people: that is, people of the land. Unlike the decolonisation of Africa and parts of Asia where many colonising forces have progressively relinquished control over local jurisdictions, decolonisation in countries, such as Aotearoa-New Zealand, Australia, Canada, and the United States, must occur in the lived context of contemporary settler-colonialism. Decolonisation, like settler-colonialism, can also be thought of as a social process (Archibald 2006: 25; Leanui 2000: 79). As settler-colonialism occurred in different places, in different ways and at different times, it is completely reasonable that decolonisation occurs in much the same diverse ways (Archibald 2006: 25).

A common misconception of decolonisation is that it is a process of 'going back'; it is not. Rather, it is a social, cultural and political process that centres Indigenous ways of knowing and being in the future. While deeply embedded in Indigenous life projects, decolonisation provides agency for Indigenous peoples, including their communities and nations, to negotiate a relationship with larger settler-colonial forces that is rooted in their own notions of justice and sustainability. Decolonisation requires Indigenous peoples and communities to see beyond their own circumstances, to identify what a desirable future looks like *for them*, decide how they might realise that together and take actions they need to take to achieve it. Tuck and Yang consider that decolonisation is a targeted, purposeful and active process:

> Decolonization is not a metaphor, it cannot be grafted onto other discourses or frameworks, even if they are critical and even if they are anti-racist, and even if they are justice frameworks . . . Decolonization is not a swappable term for other things we want to do to improve our societies and schools. Decolonization doesn't have a synonym. (2012: 3)

Decolonisation occurs at many levels, internationally through alliance-building and trade, regionally through nation-to-nation treaties and landscape-scale environmental management, and at the community level through local organising and self-governing. However, first and foremost, decolonisation begins with oneself. As Alfred and Corntassel suggest:

> Decolonization and regeneration are not at root collective and institutional processes. They are shifts in thinking and action that emanate from recommitments and reorientations at the level of the self that, over time and through proper organization, manifest as broad social and political movements to challenge state agendas and authorities. (2005: 611)

Although a complex philosophy, decolonisation can be boiled down to a simple principle. If settler-colonialism is about erasing Indigenous peoples as political, cultural, spiritual and physical beings, then decolonisation is about restoring that which the coloniser seeks to erase. It is a process of recovery, reclamation, reproduction and resurgence. Although decolonisation as an action is inextricably linked to larger sociocultural groups (such as Indigenous communities or nations), decolonisation is a process that must have its beginnings at the level of the self. Only by a person's willingness to deeply reflect on how colonisation has shaped their worldviews and then actively move away from settler-colonial ways of being and knowing and towards their own culturally informed notions of a good life can the process of decolonisation begin. Clearly, though, a coordinated process of individual rediscovery and recovery can have transformative impacts in Indigenous communities. One of the most significant ways that decolonisation can transform communities is in its ability to heal.

HEALING

Healing is not a new concept within Indigenous worlds.[5] Indigenous peoples throughout the world have many and varied traditions of healing (Struthers & Eschiti 2004: 13; Yeh et al. 2004). These are centred in their own social groups and appropriate to the lands and waters from which they come (Struthers et al. 2004; Yeh et al. 2004). A shared philosophy among Indigenous peoples throughout many parts of the world is interrelatedness or interconnectedness (Struthers & Eschiti 2004: 22; Yeh et al. 2004). Everything is connected and a healthy system requires the balancing of these various components (Hemming et al. 2019; Robbins & Dewar 2011: 3). Imbalance is often attributed as the cause of illness or conflict. In response to this worldview, Indigenous healing practices are holistic and aim to connect the physical, cultural and spiritual elements in one's life (Robbins & Dewar 2011; Struthers et al. 2004; Yeh et al. 2004). It also often has a social context whereby individual healing has positive repercussions within the person's own social group. Healing is seen as a journey to uncover an imbalance and take steps to rectify it.

Traditional healers (also known as medicine men/women, tohungas, shamans or clever men/women) are repositories of knowledge and revered members of communities. They are immersed in culture and are often viewed as extensions and powerful agents of the spiritual world. They also have an acute awareness and intimate knowledge of the various plants, animals, lands and seasons which can be called upon to assist in the healing of another person (Robbins & Dewar 2011: 3). Perhaps not surprisingly, in many settler-colonial nations, traditional healing was often outlawed (Robbins & Dewar 2011: 4; Struthers et al. 2004). As Struthers et al. explains, '[t]he medicine man was long recognized by the settlers or whites as a principle barrier to the eradication of Indian culture' (2004: 143).

Aotearoa-New Zealand offers a case study in how traditional healers were institutionally suppressed in settler-colonial states. The *Tohunga Suppression Act 1907* states that

> Every person who gathers Maoris around him by practising on their superstition or credulity, or who misleads or attempts to mislead any Maori by professing or pretending to possess super-natural powers in the treatment or cure of any disease, or in the foretelling of future events, or otherwise, is liable on summary to a fine not exceeding twenty-five pounds or to imprisonment. (*Tohunga Suppression Act 1907*)

Despite the best efforts of settler-colonial societies and governments to suppress Indigenous healing and healers, Indigenous healing remains deeply embedded in cultural practices (Robbins & Dewar 2011: 4; Yeh et al. 2004: 411). Even today, individuals continue to be recognised as holders of valued healing knowledge and practices (Robbins & Dewar 2011: 4–5). It is ever-present in the lives of many Indigenous peoples and often holds more sway in their lives than Western medicine[6] (Struthers & Eschiti 2004: 17–19; Yeh et al. 2004: 411). However, in recent times, the term 'healing' has evolved to take on new meaning.

Healing has emerged in public discourse through the many reports, commissions and enquiries investigating the experiences of Indigenous peoples throughout various parts of the settler-colonial world (Archibald 2006). For example, in Australia and Canada a concept and practice of healing has been developed largely through national investigations and recommendations arising in response to the long-term effects of the forced removal of Indigenous children from their families and communities. In Australia, this policy of forced removal has become widely known as the 'Stolen Generations' and, in Canada, the 'Residential Schools' (Archibald 2006; DeGagne 2007). Healing has also emerged in other settler-colonial states including Aotearoa/New Zealand and the United States as well as other post-colonial[7] states such as Greenland and South Africa (Archibald 2006;

South Africa TRC 1999). Through these national enquiries, the term 'healing' first appeared and became normalised in national discourses (Archibald 2006).

Generally speaking, healing is defined and applied as a process of recovery, both collective and individual, from trauma (Archibald 2006; DeGagne 2007). Although healing as a concept emerged in response to the specific circumstances of the forced removal of Indigenous children from their families and communities, it has evolved to include the general experiences of Indigenous peoples in settler-colonial states. The term is used to describe the journey of recovery for Indigenous individuals and communities that have suffered and continue to suffer the effects of settler-colonialism (Archibald 2006).

To engage deeply with how the lived reality of Indigenous peoples continues to be impacted upon by settler-colonialism, it is vital to understand it as a process without end. Alfred and Corntassel identify the shape-shifting nature of settler-colonialism. They note that Indigenous peoples,

> live in an era of postmodern imperialism and manipulations by shape-shifting colonial powers; the instruments of domination are evolving and inventing new methods to erase Indigenous histories and senses of place. (2005: 601)

Australia offers a case study of such shape-shifting settler-colonialism. In 2008, former Australian Prime Minister Kevin Rudd apologised for the forced removal of Aboriginal and Torres Strait Islander children from their families and communities. In this now famous address, he stated:

> We apologise especially for the removal of Aboriginal and Torres Strait Islander children from their families, their communities and their country. For the pain, suffering and hurt of these Stolen Generations, their descendants and for their families left behind, we say sorry . . . We the Parliament of Australia respectfully request that this apology be received in the spirit in which it is offered as part of the healing of the nation. (Rudd 2008)

Prime Minister Rudd went on to lay claim to a particular rendition of the future: 'where this Parliament resolves that the injustices of the past must never, never happen again' (Rudd 2008).

This apology was a watershed moment in Australian history and represented the culmination of decades of advocacy by survivors and those who sought justice on their behalf. There is no questioning of the positive impact of the national apology for Indigenous Australians, nor the potential impact of commitments by governments to act differently. However, one can challenge the assertion that a modern settler-colonial state, such as Australia can lay claim to a future where injustices against Indigenous peoples, including the removal of Indigenous children from their families, should not or would not continue to occur. For promises of future good behaviour can serve to gloss over the deep continuity of settler-colonialism at systemic and normative levels.

For example, in January 2018, the Australian Federal Productivity Commission released its annual Report on Government Services (Productivity Commission 2018).[8] The report details the statistics of child protection services throughout every state and territory as well as nationally. It revealed that the number of Aboriginal and Torres Strait Islander children in out-of-home care at 30 June 2017 was a shocking 17,664 children (p. 58, Table 16A.20). At the time of the National Apology to the Stolen Generations in 2008, the number of Aboriginal and Torres Strait Islander children in out-of-home care was 9,070 (p. 64 of Table 16A.20). This represents a staggering 94.65 per cent increase in the number of Aboriginal and Torres Strait Islander children in out-of-home care in the generation *after* the National Apology for the forced removal of Aboriginal and Torres Strait Islander children from their families. Furthermore, the percentage of Aboriginal and Torres Strait Islander children in out-of-home care who were placed with relatives or kin or in Aboriginal and Torres Strait Islander residential care over this same period decreased from 74 per cent to 67.6 per cent (p. 20: 16.20). Not only are more and more Aboriginal and Torres Strait Islander children interned in out-of-home care, less of them are being placed with family or in culturally appropriate care. Former Victorian Aboriginal Children's Commissioner, Andrew Jackomos, described the continued removal of children from their families and communities as a 'national disaster' (quoted in Brennan 2018).

The persistence (indeed increase) in ongoing removal of Aboriginal and Torres Strait Islander children from their families in the decade after the national apology for the same act demonstrates in devastating clarity that the settler-colonial agenda in Australia is, as it is among other comparable nations, as active as ever. It supports Alfred and Corntassel's observations that settler-colonialism is a shape-shifting force, one that adapts and finds new methods to reproduce the colonial project. This characteristic has been identified by Jacynta Krakouer who, in writing for the Indigenous media platform *IndigenousX*, states, 'The stolen generations never ended—they just morphed into child protection' (Krakouer 2019).

It is critical to understand the persistent ongoing process of settler-colonialism as it directly informs our ability to promote the meaningful healing of Indigenous peoples, communities and nations. If settler-colonialism is a dynamic, changing and modern process, the response must also be dynamic, be willing to change and adapt, and account for modern experiences of dispossession and new guises of displacement.

Healing cannot be thought of as a singular fixed concept that can apply to all Indigenous peoples in the same way (Archibald 2006; Krawll 1994). Nor is it realistic to approach healing as a one-off activity, as something that can be facilitated at a single time and place, with a defined objective and outcome (Krawll 1994). Rather, healing is best understood as a long-term process. As highlighted by Krawll (1994: 23), there is '[n]ot a single definition for healing but rather, a growing consensus of a vision and process for healing'.

This process is something that an individual or group of people embark on willingly and purposefully (Yeh et al. 2004: 412). It is a process committed to identifying the root causes and addressing these through appropriate strategies and practices (Archibald 2006: 26; DeGagne 2007; Krawll 1994). This philosophy of identifying and addressing the root causes has been identified by the Aboriginal and Torres Strait Islander Healing Foundation in Australia, which notes that '[a]ddressing the underlying trauma of these issues through healing is the only way to create meaningful and lasting change' (2017: 4).

It is important to think about healing as a journey with multiple and intersecting methods that occur in different stages. Marcia B. Krawll, in her seminal report to the Solicitor General of Canada, describes this lack of a common definition of healing and introduces the idea that it is tied to cultural reclamation:

> The word 'healing' has been widely used to describe the changes that must take place within our society, and in particular, within Aboriginal communities. 'Healing' for each of us seems to be culturally based and carries many definitions within the context of different languages. It is a word used frequently, but in many ways it lacks a common definition which enhances our ability to work more collaboratively towards its end. (1994: 23)

The centrality of culture in the healing process for Indigenous peoples is increasingly well understood. Gregory Phillips, a highly respected Australian medical anthropologist, describes healing as '[f]undamentally about therapeutic change and cultural renewal' (quoted in Feeney 2009: 3). If we accept that healing cannot be achieved meaningfully without addressing root causes, and if we accept that for Indigenous peoples the root cause is settler-colonialism (both past and ongoing), then reclaiming and re-centering that which makes Indigenous peoples distinct and unique must form the heart of the journey.

For Indigenous peoples then, healing is a process of therapeutic change through social, cultural and spiritual renewal. At the individual level, it requires a willingness to heal, while at the community level, it requires the ability to come together to support one another and work collectively and collegially towards an end. This act of coming together and working as a group is the foundation of governance, one that marks out a particularly significant intersection between governance and healing. In the second part of this chapter, I turn to examining that intersection and its potential.

GOVERNANCE

Pre-colonisation, Indigenous Australians possessed highly complex and deeply rooted governing arrangements that varied greatly between different cultural, linguistic and familial groups. Indigenous governing institutions were fit for purpose in the lands and waters that Indigenous groups occupied. Highly effective and organised governance was required in order for groups of people, whether communities, iwi, tribes or nations, to persist through millennia. Yet, in all the complexity and diversity of these governing arrangements, there existed common values that were shared between Indigenous groups—values such as justice, respect, reciprocity and accountability (who answers to who) (Simpson 2008: 8). However, since the onset of settler-colonialism, Indigenous governance practised through Indigenous organisations has evolved to take on new meaning.

For the purposes of this chapter, Indigenous organisations such as national representative bodies the Assembly of First Nations (AFM) in Canada, the National Congress of American Indians (NCAI) in the United States, the National Aboriginal Community Controlled Health Organisation (NACCHO) in Australia, to name a few, fall outside the ambit of discussion. The reason is that they are peak bodies and/or sector-specific advocacy groups. The grounds for this distinction is that the functions and purposes of these national bodies are significantly different to those of community-based groups. An example of this can be seen in the United States with the NCAI. It is a peak group that represents the interests of Indian tribal governments, whereas tribal governments are embedded in and directly answerable to the specific communities from which they arise. This is not to say that a body such as the NCAI does not have community at its heart. It simply acknowledges that in the specific circumstances of individual communities, tribal governments are more directly accountable to, and can reach, community members at an individual level, whereas a body such as the NCAI cannot. As such, the Indigenous organisations referred to in this chapter include those with a direct local base and mandate, such as Indigenous community-based corporations, tribal governments, First Nations band councils, prescribed bodies corporate (PBCs)[9], Aboriginal Medical Services (AMS), Aboriginal ranger groups and land management or First Nations guardianship programmes. In other words, organisations that aim to represent directly the interests of distinct nations or communities of people.

The scope and services provided by Indigenous organisations is vast (Australian Indigenous Governance Institute (2018); Hunt et al. 2008;

Sullivan & Oliver 2007). They vary significantly in their purposes and operate in diverse localised contexts. Indigenous organisations provide a range of services for communities and hold different responsibilities, including, to local Indigenous communities, as well as to governments and other (predominantly) non-Indigenous interests. However, because these organisations are accountable to non-Indigenous interests, especially when reliant on funding from governments, there are persistent questions regarding their validity as 'Indigenous' organisations.

In Australia, a comprehensive project looking at Indigenous governance garnered views from many communities and governance practitioners (Bauman et al. 2015). The final report, 'Building Aboriginal and Torres Strait Islander Governance', details important findings that speak directly to this perceived imbalance. One participant noted that Indigenous organisations are spending most of their time 'complying to imposed rules and regulations, rather than their own (Indigenous) rules' (Bauman et al. 2015: 11).

These findings supported previous research done on Indigenous governance in Canada (Von Der Porten 2012) and through the Indigenous Community Governance Project (ICGP) in Australia (Hunt et al. 2008). In the final publication of the ICGP, the clash between organisation and community was identified as a significant and shared challenge (Hunt et al. 2008). The authors explored this contestation in relation to the 'mainstreaming' of Indigenous organisations and service providers over time, identifying that, '[Indigenous] organisations are finding themselves caught at an uncomfortable intersection between communities operating with one set of assumptions, and government another' (Hunt et al. 2008: 27).

On the one hand, Indigenous organisations carry the legal and financial obligations of Western corporations, while on the other hand, they are accountable to the unique values of Indigenous peoples, communities and nations (Australian Indigenous Governance Institute 2019; Hunt et al. 2008; Sullivan & Oliver 2007: 184; Von Der Porten 2012). It is these differing values that have led academics to refer to Indigenous governance as 'contested governance' (Hunt et al. 2008). This highlights Indigenous governance as a site of power struggle between settler-colonial states and Indigenous peoples (Hunt et al. 2008). Indigenous organisations are constantly engaging with, and attempting to balance, governance stemming from Indigenous peoples' ancient laws and customs and governance stemming from Western expectations and requirements (Hunt et al. 2008; Von Der Porten 2012). As such, Indigenous governance is often described as being 'intercultural'. As Smith and Hunt explained: '[Indigenous] governance is not culture-neutral. Assessments of what is "good" about governance cannot be separated from culturally-based values and normative codes about what is the "right way" to get things done. In an intercultural milieu, determining whose way is the "right way" is frequently a contested issue' (2008: 10).

Indigenous governance is thus an intercultural exchange where power is negotiated and renegotiated with larger settler-colonial forces (Hunt et al. 2008; Von Der Porten 2012). Due to its significance as a site where power is negotiated, as well as being the primary vehicle through which Indigenous peoples can promote economic and community development, the practice of governing through Indigenous organisations has become a site of increased academic enquiry (Dodson & Smith 2004; Harvard Project on American Indian Economic Development 2008; Hunt et al. 2008; Sullivan & Oliver 2007; Von Der Porten 2012).

Two of the most well-developed research programmes investigating Indigenous governance have been the Harvard Project on American Indian Economic Development in the United States and the aforementioned ICGP in Australia. Both of these studies demonstrated that Indigenous governance is both a contested space and that effective Indigenous governance is a powerful predictor of community and economic development (Harvard Project on American Indian Economic Development 2008; Hunt et al. 2008). But these research programmes also highlight the unique culturally based values that inform what makes organisations successful.

These research programmes, as well as others, have led to the establishment of various organisations and institutions whose shared goal is to better understand and support Indigenous communities and their governing groups. These include the Centre for Maori and Indigenous Governance in Aotearoa-New Zealand, the Australian Indigenous Governance Institute in Australia, the National Centre for First Nations Governance in Canada, and the NCAI and the Native Nations Institute in the United States. These institutions share the common goal of supporting the development of effective Indigenous organisations. The support varies and includes the provision of training and education, resources, services, research and advocacy.

Another way that these significant research programmes have advanced the Indigenous governance agenda has been through the creation of awards such as the 'Indigenous Governance Awards' in Australia and the 'Honouring Nations Awards' in the United States. The Honouring Nations Awards celebrate examples of tribal governance excellence (see chapter 9, this volume). The Indigenous award winners often recognise that high-functioning tribal governments and community governing groups embed their own notions of success in order to better articulate why their programmes are so effective. What makes award-winning groups 'successful', in their own terms, is their ability to operationalise culturally informed values and locally appropriate governing arrangements (Australian Indigenous Governance Institute 2016, 2018; Harvard Project on American Indian Economic Development 2018).

These unique values and arrangements are then integrated into Western governing and reporting structures.

The Native Village of Kotzebue offers an insight into how Indigenous peoples and their governing groups embedding cultural values in their ways of operating. Kotzebue is a federally recognised tribe in Alaska. The tribe administers a number of programmes including tribal and family services, realty programmes, transport/roads services, and a well-established environmental programme (Native Village of Kotzebue 2019). The environmental programme is of particular relevance when examining the role of culture. It was first established in 1997 and responded to key issues in environmental management that were of concern to the tribe, including water quality and the health of subsistence species that the group relies on for food, medicine and cultural practices (Native Village of Kotzebue 2019: 9).

The programme integrates Western scientific knowledge with local cultural knowledge to produce in-depth cultural and/or scientific analyses. A significant component of the programme is the monitoring and safeguarding of key fish and wildlife resources that the community relies on for their cultural ways of life (Native Village of Kotzebue 2019: 10). But what makes this programme successful, according to the Native Village of Kotzebue, is their ability to both administer and report on the programme to federal funding agencies as well as to consult and communicate with their community and prioritise community values in the environmental programme. It is because of their ability to embed cultural ways of organising and governing with Western reporting requirements that the Native Village of Kotzebue was recognised as a finalist in the 2018 USA Honouring Nations Awards (Harvard Project on American Indian Economic Development 2018).

The ability of Indigenous organisations to function in the Western world, while embedding and supporting locally appropriate and culturally informed governing structures is paramount as a marker of their success (Australian Indigenous Governance Institute 2018; Sullivan & Oliver 2007: 189; Harvard Project on American Indian Economic Development 2018; Rigney et al. 2015: 343). These Indigenous organisations are functioning against the backdrop of dynamic settler-colonial forces, with many experts adapting and refining their governance in order to respond to changing internal and external circumstances and opportunities.

Clearly, Indigenous governance is a complex and evolving practice. Functioning successfully requires bringing together the right people to make and enact important decisions. Yet what makes 'effective' Indigenous governance practice is the ability of leaders to articulate the cultural values of a group and embed them into the fabric of an organisation. These values centre community, culture, language and Indigenous peoples' lands and waters. Indigenous governance promotes political and economic independence and is rooted in culturally informed notions of a good life. This process of recovery and rediscovery, and embedding Indigenous values and normative institutions into ways of contemporary self-governing, can also be thought of as a process of decolonisation.

THE METAPHOR OF WEAVING

Examining decolonisation, healing and governance reveals that these concepts share striking similarities. The three concepts complement, reinforce and enable each other. The challenge Indigenous leaders face is bringing together each of these components and giving them a practical direction. The Indigenous practice of weaving offers, I suggest, a framework for this vision.

For many Indigenous communities throughout the world, weaving is a distinct cultural practice and a powerful cultural identifier. It involves drawing on Indigenous ecological knowledge to harvest plants, bark, leaves, sticks or grasses and applying techniques to soften, lengthen and make the textile more durable. Many weaving techniques involve using three strands of fabric, flax, pandanus, grass, bark or soft wood. After the textile or strands have been prepared, weavers, usually women, carefully and methodically bring the strands together. Master weavers are some of the most highly skilled and respected people in Indigenous communities, even today. To gain knowledge of how to harmoniously bring together different elements to create strong, resilient, useful and peaceful objects is a practice that takes time, perseverance and commitment. Isabel Rorick, a master spruce-root weaver from the Haida First Nation in Canada[10] was interviewed as part of an online exhibition through Simon Fraser University in British Columbia. She spoke about what is involved in becoming a master weaver:

> It takes a lot of discipline to get to a point where it looks really beautiful. From gathering the roots properly, to cooking them in the fire properly, to learning how to split, to weaving. The whole process is time consuming and takes a lot of work to become a good weaver. You can't fake it. You can't go out and just purchase the materials. You have to go right to the source and create the whole thing yourself. (Rorick n.d.)

This ancient and ongoing practice is also a deep metaphor for preferred ways of being, knowing and doing that emphasise people and place within a deep web of reciprocal rationality.[11] As such, weaving offers a highly effective framework by which we can bring together the strands of decolonisation, healing and governance.

Weaving begins with a single thread, decolonisation. Decolonisation as an act starts with oneself and emanates out. It is not an act of going back but rather a purposeful action with specific future goals. It is fundamentally about training oneself to identify the lie inherent in the colonial logic and its influence on one's own thinking and behaviour. This lie is devastating in its simplicity: namely, that Indigenous peoples including their customary governance and laws, languages, cultures, kinship and lands held in common, are the problem. Understanding decolonisation as a distinct thread with its own purposes and objectives reveals that healing naturally folds through and around it.

Healing has ancient traditions among Indigenous peoples throughout the world. But healing has evolved since settler-colonialism and is best understood now as a process of therapeutic change through social, cultural and spiritual renewal. It is not a singular concept, but a journey with multiple and intersecting points. It occurs differently between Indigenous peoples and groups, and over time.

Decolonisation and healing require a willingness to be confronted, to be mindful and to overcome. Both decolonisation and healing require active, prolonged and meaningful engagement with the cultural and spiritual aspects of Indigenous peoples' lives (Archibald 2006: 30). Only by a person's willingness to deeply reflect on how settler-colonialism has shaped their worldviews, and to actively move away from the imposed settler-colonial ways of being and knowing towards one's own culturally informed notion of a good life, can the concurrent interlinked processes of decolonisation and healing take place (Archibald 2006: 29–30). Corntassel has identified this link, noting that, '[w]hen considering how colonization systematically deprives us of our experiences and confidence as Indigenous peoples, the linkages between colonialism, cultural harm, and the disintegration of community health and well-being become clearer' (2012: 88). Folding healing with decolonisation into a foundational plait creates a strong anchor. It is then possible to braid governance with healing.

The foundational building block of governance is the ability of a people to come together, discuss important matters, and make and affect decisions (Dodson & Smith 2003: 1). But the reality in many Indigenous communities is that the legacies and ongoing practices of settler-colonialism have caused immense ongoing trauma. How can a community of people who have unresolved trauma be expected to come together in an organised, efficient and respectful way? It may be unrealistic to expect that communities can do so in such circumstances.

A community that does not function socially cannot be expected to govern effectively. Indigenous communities that might identify with such circumstances are often required to embark on a communal journey of healing *before* they can come together and work out the ways they want to govern together. In the absence of effective healing, the capacity for communities to come together, discuss ideas and place the interest of the collective above the self is diminutive. Moreover, as the membership of many Indigenous organisations are predetermined (according to set cultural, familial and linguistic lineages), conflicts left unresolved can persevere, sometimes in perpetuity.

Communities with unresolved tension often thwart attempts to get things done, even when it may be for the common good. This is not to say that Indigenous peoples are petty and cannot overcome their differences. It is simply an acknowledgement that, through generations of settler-colonialism, prejudicial policies and imposed Western practices have placed immense and unfair pressures on Indigenous peoples, creating conflict, despair and apathy which has over time been internalised by communities. As a result, some Indigenous communities can be said to have been driven apart by trauma-based disputes and poor leadership and decision-making. The critical question within a decolonisation framework then becomes: Who is equipped to respond to these issues?

This chapter suggests that Indigenous organisations are, in fact, eminently well-placed to promote healing. Many Indigenous organisations such as Prescribed ody Corporates, local land councils, iwi or clan corporations, tribal governments, community-controlled health organisations and Indigenous ranger or guardianship groups carry specific rights and responsibilities for the social, cultural and environmental assets of communities and nations. These assets (through connection to traditional lands) are also identified as being critical to Indigenous health and well-being and to healing processes (Archibald 2006; Sullivan & Oliver 2007).

As healing is a long-term process, it requires careful planning, sustained organisation and economic resources over a prolonged period. Indigenous communities looking to rebuild from the effects of settler-colonialism would benefit greatly from embedding healing as a standard operation within the governing structures, processes and visions of their organisations. Doing so increases the likelihood of constructive engagement with families and community members and insulates communities against new trauma. In this way, Indigenous governing institutions become bodies that *require* as well as *promote* the ongoing healing of Indigenous communities. Creating a culturally safe space for community to gather and renew connections builds trust and mutual reciprocity and increases the likelihood of engagement by members. Increased engagement enables more inclusive planning for the future that sustains community credibility and personal commitment. It elevates the legitimacy of organisations and their leadership including the decisions they make, through greater participation. Braiding healing and governance arguably grows the very fabric of community. It nurtures the work of reconnection that began by folding decolonisation with healing and presents an opportunity to close the loop by threading governance and decolonisation together in ways that are self-determined by Indigenous peoples.

Indigenous organisations are often answerable to the Western mainstream legal mechanisms that give them status as incorporated bodies. But even more so, they are accountable to the expectations of their own communities, the people whom they service and represent. From this perspective, what makes an Indigenous organisation 'successful' or 'effective' differs greatly, making Indigenous governance a highly dynamic and influential field of practice (Rigney et al. 2015). While all Indigenous organisations require financial stability, their markers of success must accord with the values and priorities of their community. These values are often grounded in the cultural needs of communities and respond to local circumstances. Identifying and articulating those values can also be thought of as a fundamental part of the process of decolonisation (Rigney et al. 2015).

Decolonising the values and institutions (rules) that underpin Indigenous groups allows communities to establish unique goal posts for their organisations. These often incorporate the universal Indigenous values of justice, respect, reciprocity and accountability, as well as local cultural customs. In this way, in order for Indigenous organisations, corporations or tribal governments to meaningfully enact Indigenous governance, they must be committed to decolonising their governance structures, processes and philosophies and bring those closer to their own philosophical and cultural worldviews. Where could this decolonising process start? For many communities, the process has already started.

Some Indigenous groups have successfully weathered settler-colonialism, maintaining important ceremonial and linguistic connections that hold the people together as distinct groups. This can be attributed first to the strength of these groups in ensuring that the bonds of culture and tradition are not severed by settler-colonialism and second, due in part to their remoteness and isolation from major Western developments and urbanisation. For Indigenous groups who have not enjoyed the isolation from settler-colonial forces and, as a result, have been more heavily impacted upon by settler-colonialism, there remain important and deeply rooted cultural bonds of family, respect for elders, and connection to traditional lands and waters. However, regardless of the circumstances of Indigenous groups, the act of governing requires the common foundation of bringing together a specific group of people. It is these groups of people that settler-colonialism continues to attempt to erode and eradicate. The act of coming together as a distinct group, then, is itself the first act of decolonising. It is a purposeful action to remember who people are, what binds them together, and the acceptance that they do in fact belong together and to their lands and waters.

For Indigenous peoples, remembering who they are as a sociocultural group, attached to their lands and waters, is the starting point on the road to decolonisation. By starting with and caring for the group, Indigenous governance reinforces cultural bonds and traditions and allows communities and nations to get things done that are important to them. Highly effective Indigenous governance, as observed through the Indigenous Governance Awards in Australia, builds on these foundations and incorporates distinct Indigenous principles into the fabric of an organisation. Effective Indigenous governance then, *requires* the decolonisation of organisations, including their ways of gathering, their values, visions and objectives.

All three processes—decolonisation, healing and governance—are long-term processes to which a person or people must consistently apply their efforts in order to fully achieve. Like weaving, this takes time, perseverance, practice and commitment. And like weaving, the strength and resilience of the thread are increased as more is produced. It requires highly skilled leaders with vision, intent and purpose. This philosophy of leadership as a conduit for governance-as-healing is deeply rooted in Indigenous ways of being, knowing and governing.

Maori scholar Dr Annie Te One, when discussing Maori philosophies of leadership and governance, states:

> The [Maori] word for leader is Rangatira. The root of this word however comes from two separate words. The first is Ranga or Raranga, which means to weave. The second part of that is Tira, which means group. So taken together our word for leader literally means to weave a group together. That is a person's role in holding a leadership position, like that of a governance board for example, is to ensure the cohesiveness of the Iwi . . . This is what the language system of Rangatira, the governing language of Maori, teaches us about leadership. (Te One 2018).

Decolonisation, healing and governance are unique strands in the fabric of community that must be folded, braided and threaded together at different points and in different ways. Carefully and methodically combining the three strands together, one over the other, on and on, over time, has the potential to create a rich sociocultural tapestry. Just as master weavers are some of the most highly valued and skilled members of Indigenous communities, so too may Indigenous leaders can recover their place as people who weave their communities together.

CONCLUSION

Decolonisation, healing and governance are three strands that can be woven together to create strong, resilient and vibrant Indigenous communities. This goal is a fundamental component of development. From such a basis, communities can engage in determining their own futures and visions for further development. It is already within the capacity of Indigenous peoples through their organisations to promote meaningful and sustainable healing. As organisations (whether they be incorporated for community or self-governing purposes, or indeed a non-incorporated community group), the basic functions remain the same—to bring people together. In so doing, these organisations and their leaders occupy a delicate space reliant on respectful relationships and functioning communities.

Where divisions occur, the root is frequently traceable to settler-colonialism, both past and ongoing. Addressing this root cause is a process of decolonisation. It is a process of remembering what makes a group of people Indigenous, with a shared collective identity, and actively moving towards those ideals. This can be undertaken both at the individual and collective level. In so doing, Indigenous communities and community members embark on their own process of healing. These concurrent and interdependent activities support and reinforce one another, creating their own locally appropriate structures derived out of weaving together decolonisation, healing and governance. Embarking on a long-term journey of recovery and regeneration equips communities with the tools to recreate their own expressions of who they are in the world today. Only then will Indigenous peoples and communities realise the true potential and power of their governance.

NOTES

1. 'Internal colonialism' is another term used by academics to describe the act of a colonising force that has established permanent settlements on lands and waters occupied and owned by Indigenous peoples (Tuck & Yang 2012: 4).

2. The 'White Australia policy' was a federally legislated policy, enabled through the *Immigration Restriction Act 1901 (Cth)*) that prohibited non-European immigration to Australia. Although the policy was enforced less stringently from the 1950s, it was not until the mid-1970s that the then Labor Government ended the policy (Encyclopaedia Britannica 2019).

3. *The Indian Act* is a federal law, first passed in Canada in 1876. The Act is 'the principle statue through which the federal government administers Indian status, local First Nations governments and the management of reserve land and communal monies' (Henderson & Parrott 2019). The Act was designed to structurally institutionalise the assimilation of Native peoples into Canadian law and has been attributed with allowing multiple human rights violations and creating intergenerational trauma for Native peoples in Canada. The Indian Act remains federal law in Canada today.

4. A 'social process' is a pattern of observable, repetitive behaviour between people that has a consistent direction, quality or inherent values (Bardis 1979: 148).

5. There exists a vast literature base on 'healing', including associated terms such as 'health', 'wellbeing', 'social and emotional wellbeing', and so on. While this discussion uses the specific term 'healing' to describe a process of recovery and regeneration, associated terms may also be applied that describe this process.

6. In Australia, there have been recent investments by mainstream health services in Aboriginal healing. One example is at Lyell McEwin Hospital in South Australia where Aboriginal healers treat patients alongside Western medical practitioners. Under this programme, Aboriginal patients have the option of being treated by Aboriginal healers, known as Ngangkari, while at the hospital. This initiative is widely viewed as both enhancing the care of patients as well as creating a culturally safe space within the hospital. By creating a culturally safe space, it is expected that higher rates of Aboriginal people will seek medical care as they know they can access Aboriginal healing services (Burnie 2019). Additionally, in Aotearoa/New Zealand, an urban Maori health clinic in Auckland employed Tohunga (Maori healers) to treat Maori patients (Jones 2000).

7. 'Post-colonial' or 'postcolonialism' is generally understood as a period of time or state of affairs that occurs after a colonial power has relinquished control or been removed from power (Ivison 2018). However, even (or especially) in the cases of states such as South Africa and Greenland, postcolonialism should not be confused with the idea that these states are devoid of colonialism or are somehow not subjected to ongoing colonial power (Ivison 2018). Indeed, in an ever-globalising world, states including South Africa and Greenland remain embedded in and subject to economic factors through trade and international legal frameworks (e.g. the United Nations), and geopolitical powers (e.g. military influences of the United States or its allies in Europe), which continue to influence the internal law making of these nations.

8. Figures quoted in this publication were retrieved in November 2019. From time to time, The Department of Human Services updates these figures. As such, if this report is accessed at a later date, the exact figures may be different than those outlined in this paper. Nevertheless, the general trends of Aboriginal and Torres Strait Islander children being removed from their families highlighted in this chapter remain.

9. In Australia, the *Native Title Act 1993 (Cth)* states that, when a determination of native title is made (that is, a determination whereby the rights and interests Indigenous peoples have in land and waters is recognised by the government of Australia), native title holders must establish a corporation called a prescribed body corporate (PBC) to manage and protect their native title rights and interests (Cawthorn 2019).

10. Haida territory also extends to the United States where small communities of Haida people live, such as Hydaberg, Alaska. Nevertheless, the greater Haida territory and population live on the Island of Haida Gwaii, which was formerly part of the province of British Columbia in Canada. Available at https://www.sfu.ca/brc/online_exhibits/spruce-root-weaving/spruce-root-weaving.html.

11. See Johnson et al. (2016) for a similar use of the 'weaving' metaphor in relation to Indigenous and Western (scientific) knowledges.

Chapter 17

'You're Not Just a Leader, You Are an Indigenous Leader'

Empowering Native American Women for Governing

Karen Diver

Growing up as a citizen of the Fond du Lac Band of Lake Superior Chippewa in the State of Minnesota in the United States (US), I was well aware that most of the current governance structures of Native American Tribal Nations are the result of paternalistic federal policy. In the early 1900s, the US Government required that Native American tribes adopt written constitutions in order to access grants and other opportunities. These constitutions, originating in Washington, DC, typically left tribes subject to federal government oversight. They also called for popularly elected positions: a chairperson and a secretary/treasurer usually elected at-large[1] and a council composed of elected representatives of districts established on American Indian reservations—lands reserved to tribes under treaty or other federal action. In many cases, including ours, this representative body was called the Reservation Business Committee.

This form of governance was completely foreign to many tribes. The traditional forms of governance of the more than 500 tribes in the United States came from their unique historical and cultural backgrounds, and most were very different from the models imposed by the U. S.government. For instance, my people, the Fond du Lac Band of Lake Superior Chippewa, were traditionally governed by a hereditary male chief and a clan system identified roles and responsibilities within the community. While not in the chieftainship, women had leadership roles in numerous aspects of Chippewa life. Western notions based on patriarchy misunderstood much of this, distorting the role of the chief and discounting our complex clan systems.

My tribe had never had a woman elected as chairperson. In fact, only two women had served as elected officials previously, both as district representatives: one in the 1950s and another in the 1970s. In all of Indian Country across the United States, there were only two female tribal leaders who I can recall knowing about, as role models, when I was growing up. The most famous was Wilma Pearl Mankiller (A-ji-luhsgi Asgaya-dihi) of the Cherokee Nation, who was chief of that nation in the late 1980s and 1990s, and the first woman to hold that position. Wilma (1945–2010) was born in Oklahoma, was known for being an astute leader and, over time, we came to learn more about the added burden of her efforts to break gender barriers within her community. The other was Marge Anderson, long-time leader of one of our neighbouring tribes, the Mille Lacs Band of Ojibwe. Marge was also the first woman leader of her tribe and served with distinction at a critical time for American Indian Nations as they began to grow governmentally and economically in the 1980s.

Over a couple of our election cycles in the early 2000s, the Fond du Lac Band Tribal Government[2] experienced profound changes. In our system, elections happen every two years, with staggered terms. The five-seat council is made up of two at-large positions and three district representatives, including the chair. After fifteen years of stable leadership, an election in the early 2000s produced five new members of the council, only one of whom had any previous council experience. Pretty quickly, this lack of experience began to show. While feeling immense pride in the contemporary growth of my tribe, I was critical of how the new members of the tribal government managed and planned. They were becoming less transparent and more isolated from their constituents. The bureaucracy was inefficient. Decision-making had become cumbersome. It often took place in reaction mode, lacking any form of long-range planning. Our workforce was becoming increasingly demoralised by a sense of instability and drift.

As the tribal population saw what was happening, they again voted for change, but this time they focused on reform candidates who brought with them professional or previous governmental experience. We ended up with a mix of old guard and new, leading to conflicts that in turn led to the resignation of the tribal chairperson.

Meanwhile, I had returned to Fond du Lac after some time away and had been working in the tribe's government. I returned having spent over a decade in the non-profit sector building skills in advocacy and in programme and community development. During that time, I had also done a public administration degree at Harvard University's Kennedy School of Government. My work at the tribe was heavily focused on new programme development, especially in housing. Because I had a strong management background, the tribe made use of me in various interim management roles in departments that needed assistance, including our community centres, early learning centre, the hotel and others. I drafted new policies for the Fond du Lac Tribal Council to consider in areas such as land use and zoning, tribal citizen assistance programmes and our tribal court.

While my initial motivation for returning to Fond du Lac was to contribute on the administrative side of tribal government, I soon realised it was the elected leadership that sets the direction and tone of tribal activity and oversees the practical processes that are necessary for getting the essential work of the tribe done. When the government is in disarray or the leadership is confused about its purpose, things soon go wrong. I also had encountered, during my graduate work at Harvard, the research carried out by the Harvard Project on American Indian Economic Development, which emphasised the importance for Native nations of rebuilding their own governance capacities and designing governing institutions that are not only effective but compatible with the culture and traditions of the tribe.

With another round of elections looming, I decided to run for the chair position in the Fond du Lac Band Tribal Government. And I decided that my focus would be on nation-building—on strengthening Fond du Lac governance. I survived a field of twelve candidates in the primary in 2007, and in the 2008 general election, I was elected chair: the first woman to lead my tribe. This chapter presents a personal account of my leadership journey that then followed. Over several decades, I have been honoured to share many exceptional opportunities and experiences, which have enabled me to now reflect on Native American women's leadership, our strengths and contributions, the challenges we face in developing our leadership abilities and effectiveness, and how such challenges might be addressed and women's leadership empowered.

WORKING IN TRIBAL GOVERNMENT: THE EARLY CHALLENGES

The subsequent learning curve was steep. Despite coming from a tribal government staff position into elected office, there was a lot I didn't know. Hitting the ground running entailed being briefed by our legal counsel on current legal issues; talking to the planning department to see what plans were in the works and what they perceived as gaps; reviewing the past several years of financial audits, current year financial statements and budgets; consulting with tribal department managers on current issues; and much more. I convened most of these information sessions as meetings of our entire government to make sure that I was up to speed and that we were all on the same page in understanding the current state of affairs.

I also realised that Fond du Lac was part of something bigger happening across Indian Country in the 2000s—tribes were working hard to 'up their game' in the governance arena, that is, to become more capable of defending their rights and pursuing their own goals for their people. Several of the issues we were dealing with illustrate some of the development challenges we were facing and the governance arrangements we tested and put in place. For they all spoke to the same shared concern: getting our governance up to speed, in ways we wanted.

Governing Our Environment

One particularly big concern for Fond du Lac that demonstrated this issue was environmental threats. The Fond du Lac Reservation is located in the northern part of the State of Minnesota, west of the western end of Lake Superior, which is the largest body of fresh water in the world. It is a land of forests, lakes, rivers—and mining. Mining activity in northern Minnesota was threatening the tribe's lands and health.

The Fond du Lac Band's interests in the land go well beyond the reservation. In treaties historically negotiated between the US Government and American Indian nations, some nations reserved their rights to hunt, fish and gather not only on reservation lands but also on much broader swathes of their traditional homelands. Under several treaties,[3] Fond du Lac had retained such rights in ceded territory through northern Minnesota, Wisconsin and Michigan. We managed the implementation and protection of these treaty rights, through a consortia, with other tribes in Wisconsin and Michigan, and over the years we had made significant investments in our ability to manage natural resources responsibly. Our tribal government's natural resources division was active throughout the region—on everything from habitat protection and renewal to fish and game management, from water and air quality to historic preservation. Among other things, we had invested in individual staff in order to develop a collective scientific capacity to expertly monitor, participate in and, if necessary, challenge state and federal permitting processes.

Northern Minnesota has long been home to iron mining, and now there was interest in copper-nickel mining. Mining tends to increase sulphide levels in water. Sulphides have destructive impacts on wild rice, which grows in water and is one of our most sacred and traditional foods. Wild rice is a resource that our people have depended on for many generations. Sulphides also contribute to the bio-accumulation of mercury in fish, another staple in a traditional and healthy diet. Within the region, mercury from fish was resulting in two out of ten Indigenous babies having elevated mercury levels (Borkholder et al. 2002). Copper-nickel mining has never been accomplished world-wide without severe impacts on water resources.

As the threats to our lands, waters and foods increased, we held firm in our belief that the exercise of our treaty rights are being impacted upon whenever these resources are diminished in quality or quantity. We never opposed mining itself. We opposed the environmental degradation that resulted from mining. The State of Minnesota had official water quality standards that could have been used to protect wild rice, for example, but these standards were never enforced. For this reason, it looked like the State of Minnesota was trading off the protection of water resources and public health against perceived economic development gains, but bypassing Fond du Lac's tribal rights and interests. This was not only an environmental and development issue for the tribe, it was a governance issue as well.

We decided that we would have to be proactive on these issues and reached out for allies. We undertook a multifaceted campaign to protect our resources and our people. In 2010, as the iron mining interests were lobbying to get sulphide regulations loosened, we joined with other tribes and the State of Minnesota to enact a public health campaign to educate pregnant women about the dangers of eating potentially contaminated fish. We contracted with a local university to undertake a longitudinal study of the effects of sulphides on wild rice.[4] We launched a summer environmental internship programme, sending a team of students out to gather core samples from lakes to show that previous stands of wild rice were being eradicated by industrial discharges. We partnered with other tribes to share the costs of technical training so that we could do more independent assessments of the hydrological impacts of discharges from mine tailings.[5] We did the same in hiring legal counsel with environmental expertise who could take full advantage of our treaty-based standing in state and federal licence permitting processes and found allies to partner with when proceeding into litigation. We also commissioned a report that showed the monetised value to the public of having a clean Saint Louis River to northern Minnesota (Fletcher & Christin 2015).[6] Findings from this report challenged the argument made by both the mining private sector and government that mining was economically necessary, seemingly at all costs.

This environmental battle is continuing today, and while we have made progress, we cannot yet claim success. But we learned some important lessons: one of which was that the effective defence of our rights and stewardship of our resources would require us to become a more capable government. We also learned the value of being able to develop our own expertise (e.g. in diverse areas such as our cultural knowledge, environmental science, conservation and negotiation), to find allies and build partnerships with them, to engage intelligently and strategically with state and federal governments, and to maintain and mobilise the support of our community.

Governing Economic Development

During this early period, we also faced a major economic development challenge. When I assumed office as tribal chair in 2007, one of my most urgent and daunting tasks was to manage the tribe's largest ever development project, a US$120 million upgrade to our casino/resort complex. While the Fond du Lac Band is not a wealthy tribe by many US standards, we had two gaming casinos: one in a city of 80,000 people about 32 kilometres from the reservation and another on our reservation lands in rural Minnesota.[7] Revenue from these operations gave us flexibility through having an income source we could use on tribal priorities that were either otherwise unfunded or reliant on external grant funding.

Our future stability and freedom of action were at risk if we didn't manage this development project correctly, as the tribe's entire portfolio of assets was tied to it. But there were indications that the project had some problems. My immediate task was to figure out the current state of the budget, expenses, timelines and implementation. We soon realised that at the current pace and spending, we would be US$20 million short of what was needed to finish the project, and the US$20 million was nowhere in sight.

We decided to meet every two weeks with project staff to maintain a tight watch on expenses and timelines. Some might call this micro-management, but we called it 'getting a handle on the details'. Most critically, we decided to scale back the renovation to something more like 'updating' than a complete 'rebuilding'. We built a mock hotel room so we could see how the renovations would come together and hopefully avoid the costs of making additional changes. We subjected every single purchase to careful approval, down to lamps and bedding for the hotel rooms. We told vendors to bring in their products so we could gauge quality and price before purchasing. This informed our eventual decision to lease some items for the casino instead of purchasing them. And then we all heaved a sigh of relief when the project came in on time and US$3 million under budget.

The lesson we learned from this was not, as the story might suggest, to micro-manage development. Rather, it was to put effective processes in place that could reliably review and track spending against budgets, and also identify and address issues before they turned into crises. Once such processes were agreed upon and created, the tribal leadership could be more hands-off from the project implementation. These considerations and processes were all part of maturing as a government.

Governing Our Relationship with Duluth City

Another issue during my time as chairperson (2007–2012) had to do with our relationship with the port city of Duluth in Minnesota, the nearby city of

80,000 people about 32 kilometres from the reservation. One of the Fond du Lac Band's gaming casinos is located in that city. The casino was the result of a complicated set of agreements, reached some years before, between the tribe and the city. These agreements were guided by the *Indian Gaming Regulatory Act 1988*, which provided a legislative basis for tribes to generate revenue through gaming on tribal land. Under the Act, tribal land is under tribal sovereignty and, because of this, states are limited in their ability to forbid gambling there. The Act established a regulatory framework and a new federal agency (the National Indian Gaming Commission—NIGC) to monitor and define the scope of tribal economic decisions related to gaming. The Act also established guidelines for the relationship of gaming enterprises to other jurisdictions, including cities, counties and states.

The agreements between the tribe and the city of Duluth included the city receiving a financial benefit from the casino by taking a share of the revenue from gross profits. That contribution was intended to offset access to city services enjoyed by the casino. Over the years, the city became reliant on these funds and used it to meet obligations that most jurisdictions funded through ordinary taxes—in this case, for roads and street repairs—a big deal in northern Minnesota's harsh winters.

However, as we monitored our financial situation, we couldn't help but notice that as the casino grew, the city took a larger share of the profits each year, approaching a third of the profits. Because the agreement for the city's share was based on gross profit (revenue), as the casino's operational expenses went up, the tribe's net profits declined. This seemed inherently unfair to us; it felt like a growing tax that the tribe could not control. Most businesses pay some level of taxes, and the tribe certainly benefitted from city road maintenance and other services, but in this case, the cost to the tribe seemed disproportionate to the benefits it received.

We began to look more closely at these legal agreements and how they fit with regulatory decisions that were made by the NIGC, which is the federal agency responsible for the management of tribal gaming. We found that the profit-sharing agreements did not comply with relevant federal law. Simply put, the relevant federal law stated that tribes need to have a sole proprietary interest in their gaming enterprises—because the city's share of profits (19% of gross revenue from 1994 to 2011; see Leagle 2017) was disproportionate to the services provided, the agreement was not compliant.

The tribe tried several times, informally, to engage the city to discuss upcoming renewals of the agreements, but we were rebuffed. Eventually, as the tribal government, we decided to stop paying the city a share of the gross profit. We made this decision for a number of reasons. Mainly, however, we thought it was the best way to get the city's attention and bring it to the table to discuss the matter and negotiate a new contract, which was also encouraged by the NIGC.

It brought litigation instead. The city of Duluth didn't even try to engage with us, but instead the authorities went directly to the US District Court. In addition to litigation, the city took the issue into the 'court of public opinion'—the news media. The city's Mayor used his office as a bully pulpit to vilify the tribal government and our people in the media. It has always been our view that this issue was a contract dispute over a revenue-sharing agreement. However, it was not framed as such in the media by the city authorities. Instead of keeping the door open to future good relations between the city and the tribe, the mayor used rhetoric that was inflammatory, and some of the fallout was decidedly racist.

Native Americans are one of the largest communities in northern Minnesota. Through the media, the citizens of the city were being told that Native Americans, and in particular citizens of the Fond du Lac Tribe, were taking advantage of them. The rhetoric exploited the general population's ignorance of the unique, political status of American Indian Nations. For its part, the tribe kept its citizens informed through its own newspaper and radio station and in public meetings. We felt the tribal government had a duty to protect its citizens and to be a responsible steward of the tribe's financial resources. While we had hoped for, and tried to maintain, good relationships with the city, it was not our duty to keep the city happy.

The agreements at issue in this case were exceedingly technical, and the regulatory environment was evolving. Once our efforts at constructive engagement and negotiation with the city had been rebuffed, we spent months learning the law, seeking advice and discussing our strategy for the court hearings. Eventually, the courts and the regulatory agencies supported our view, concluding that the city was only entitled to a share of profits commensurate with the cost of providing services. In other words, the city was only entitled to a payment in lieu of taxes, such as those that other businesses would pay. This meant that the city was entitled to about US$150,000, rather than the approximately US$6 million per annum it had been receiving previously. It was a major win for the Fond du Lac Tribal Government and the nation.

Again, we learned important lessons from this experience. One was the strategic value of pursuing open and cordial engagement with the other government and political entities in our region. But at the same time, we also learned the importance of knowing the law and being prepared to fight on legal terrain. Our diligent efforts to learn the law, seek advice and discuss our strategies paid off.

Governing Relations with Outside Government Agencies

Relations with external governmental agencies were another area where we found that strategically using our own human capital and expertise produced results. We had realised that a more effective approach to dealing with federal agencies was to be part of the solution that tribes were seeking to achieve. This turned the tables around. Too often, tribes rely on the historical political relationship between the federal government and the tribes that was created by the original treaties. Treaties committed the US Government to provide for certain tribal needs in perpetuity. This is referred to as the 'trust responsibility'. It was my view at the time that there was ample evidence to suggest that the federal government is incapable of figuring out how to effectively serve tribal needs. Tribes can be part of the solution to this frustrating historical relationship, by identifying their own priorities, building institutions that are capable of serving their own people and negotiating effectively with external agencies.

Adopting this partnership attitude, as opposed to just complaining, helped me be an effective advocate for tribal interests with other governments. For example, during my tenure as chair, the Fond du Lac Tribe experienced a significant flood in 2008 that caused widespread damage to roads, buildings and homes. We were unprepared for the flood, as this type of disaster had no precedent in our area. While we made it through the initial event with common sense, collective effort and available resources, it was clear that existing state and federal emergency management processes failed to include tribal communities.

The tribe had to start navigating complex state and federal government processes in order to repair and rebuild our community, and we had to help tribal citizens navigate the various assistance programmes as well. While we had been unprepared for that particular disaster, over the years Fond du Lac had built up capable government departments staffed with professional expertise.[8] This enabled us to be effective partners with federal and state agencies, greatly facilitating the rebuilding process.

Governing Relations with Tribal Citizens

Of course, relations with our own citizens also posed some challenges. When I became chair, the Fond du Lac Band had about 4,000 citizens. Between its governmental services and its businesses, it employed over 2,200 people, a very large workforce for northern Minnesota.[9] But everything was not perfect. There was still a critical lack of housing. Graduation rates from high school were still below average. Not all citizens were participating in the workforce. Drug and alcohol abuse rates were higher than the general population. In other words, the effects of colonialism were still apparent in various social indicators. Years of depending on the federal and tribal governments to solve these problems had led to a sense of entitlement among many of our citizens.

Early in my tenure as chair, we undertook a year-long effort to develop the first strategic plan for the tribe, consulting at length with our citizens. I was surprised by the results. Overwhelmingly, citizens wanted tribal government to put a large focus on promoting personal responsibility and self-sufficiency among tribal individuals. The strategic plan we developed set out a strong positive response to that feedback and has been included in our ongoing plans since then:

> The Fond du Lac Reservation Business Committee, through a continuing dialogue with the people, shall develop ways to improve the health and well-being of the people of Fond du Lac Reservation by insuring the quality delivery of services, maintaining a continuing commitment to quality education, striving for economic development that will be both financially sound and provide long term employment, ensuring safe and affordable housing, and providing an environment for the people that reflects professionalism and encourages and supports training and career development opportunities.
>
> We shall protect and defend our sovereign rights as a tribe, protect and promote Tribal self-determination, enhancement of individual opportunities of its members and participate with its members in promoting and preserving Ojibwe tradition while being fiscally responsible and accountable. (Fond du Lac 2019: 5)

This call to take on personal and collective responsibility was consistent with what I was learning about nation-building at the Native Nations Institute, University of Arizona (Native Nations Institute 2019), namely, that a tribal government's role is to build the systems and institutions that can effectively serve our citizens, not to solve everyone's problems. So we started to try changing the conversation and our behaviour. It was not always easy to get people on board.

One day a young woman came to see me. She was in a housing crisis. She bluntly said, 'I need you to get me a house. I'm a single mother'. I asked her questions about her circumstances, such as, was she working or going to school? She wanted to know why I was asking her questions, saying that it was my job to help her. I explained that there were several available housing programmes, but because she was not working, she only qualified for one programme and that programme already had an extensive waiting list. I explained that she was more likely to qualify for a housing programme if she was working, and I asked if I could help her get a job. I showed her the human resources web page and printed out the job listings. We discussed which ones she might qualify for. She was reluctant to apply, believing she wasn't qualified for 'good jobs'. We then discussed entry-level employment and how to get promoted. We talked about the tribal college and the tribe's scholarship programmes. She left my office with contact information, tasks to carry out and decisions to make, but clearly unhappy that I didn't simply solve her problems.

Near the end of my time as chair, I was taking a break outside my office when the same young woman sat down beside me. Still prone to bluntness, she said, 'I didn't much like you when you first got elected'. She said she remembered the time she came to my office looking for housing, and had left my office thinking I wasn't very helpful at all. But then she told me she had been working continuously since shortly after that meeting. She eventually qualified for a home-ownership loan, and she had nearly finished paying it off. She had nearly completed college and had been promoted in her job. She said she was proud of herself and felt she was a good role model for her daughter. She said simply, and with a smile, 'You did that for me'. I could reply honestly, 'No, young woman, you did it'.

That encounter, among other things, emphasised for me that the stories told by our constituents can tell us where our institutions are working and where they aren't. From having an array of housing options, to being thoughtful about workforce development and career-laddering, tribal government is informed by its citizens, but it should not simply be reactive. We need to be less problem-solvers for every individual rather than institution and system builders.

MOVING INTO THE NATIONAL ARENA

The Tribal Nations Conference

The chair of the Fond du Lac Band was responsible for representing the Band publicly. For me, this often meant trips to Washington, DC, to meet with legislators and federal government agencies, and it was in this capacity that I first met President Barack Obama. In late 2009, Obama's first year in office, the president held a gathering called the White House Tribal Nations Conference, convening leaders from all of the tribes in the United States. Prior to this gathering, he held a smaller meeting, with twelve tribal leaders, that I was fortunate to be part of.[10]

This meeting gave tribal leaders an opportunity to discuss a number of concerns with the president at the very highest level. At the time, the country was in a severe economic recession, and the tribes were worried that the burden of balancing the budget would fall disproportionately on tribal communities by leading to cuts in services upon which many of them depended. We also wanted the US Government to endorse the United Nations Declaration on the Rights of Indigenous Peoples (UNDRIP), which it had opposed in the General Assembly of the United Nations on 13 September 2013.[11] Following our meeting with President Obama—in fact, the next day—we learned that the US Government planned to increase the budget for tribal communities and announced plans to endorse the UNDRIP and increased the following year's budget for tribes. Clearly, President Obama's support for tribal nations was sincere and not just rhetorical.

The Task Force on Climate Preparedness and Resilience

After my meeting with President Obama, I began to get more involved in tribal issues at the national level. Here, the 2008 flood our community had experienced turned out to have an unexpected indirect effect. Many tribes and members of the general public in the United States felt that these types of disasters were the result of climate change. On 1 November 2013, President Obama established a task force focused on climate resiliency at the state, local and tribal level, known as the Task Force on Climate Preparedness and Resilience. I was invited to join the task force, to represent tribal interests. This was a fundamental change in the federal process. Up until then, tribes were often not included with other jurisdictions on federal mechanisms for decision- making and advice. Tribal consultations were usually held separately. But it made sense to include tribes in discussions of climate resiliency, as the impacts of climate change are at the scale of whole landscapes, not simply particular groups of people.

Reggie Joule, Mayor, Northwest Arctic Borough (Native village in Alaska) and I were chosen to represent American Indian and Alaska Native communities on the task force on climate resiliency. At the time, about half the total U.S. 567 tribes were located in Alaska, and half were located in the lower 48 states of America. We sat on the task force with city mayors, county commissioners and state governors: government jurisdictions that more often than not failed to coordinate planning with their neighbouring tribal jurisdictions (see US Government 2009). The task force was given a year to deliver to the president a set of recommendations for the federal government on how to prepare for the effects of climate change. With strong tribal engagement and support, we not only built tribal recommendations into the full task force report[12] but also issued a separate set of tribal recommendations designed to meet local needs.

Special Assistant to the President for Native American Affairs

Obama was the first US president to have a senior-level adviser focused on tribal policy interests. His administration also had a dedicated tribal person in inter-governmental affairs to liaise with all tribes on Indian Country. In 2015, two years before the end of Obama's presidency, his Native American adviser left the White House for another position. Because of my previous work with the White House and other federal agencies, I was invited to take the post of, and subsequently appointed as, special assistant to the president for Native

American Affairs, which was then part of the White House Domestic Policy Council.

In 2015, I resigned as chair of the Fond du Lac Band, left home and moved to Washington, DC. I took up my position in November that year and served for the remainder of the Obama administration. My job entailed working with federal government agencies on programmes and deliverables for Native American Tribal Nations. It was mentally and physically exhausting. The volume of email, meetings and reading was enormous, and the pace was relentless; requiring ten- to fourteen-hour days just to keep up. All policy initiatives coming out of twenty-seven federal agencies with funding equities for tribes needed final review and sign-off by my office before proceeding to the next level in government. I found that being a former elected leader of a tribe was an immense benefit in the work. Because I had spent nearly nine years leading a government that was on the other end of federal policy-making, it gave me a unique perspective to the federal government. I was able to be an effective advocate from within the system.

One such area of effective advocacy was in respect to the accuracy and governance of data. The Obama administration prided itself on being data-driven. In most instances, that would be a laudable feature of policy-making. However, for Native American tribes, it is more often problematic. For example, while the US Population Census has made progress over the years on tribal data, there is still a lack of consistent information on land ownership within tribal boundaries, which often skews data collection, including problems from mixing tribal data with data on non-tribal property owners. Even defining who is or is not 'Native American' is tricky; many Native Americans identify as being biracial.

I remember a meeting where White House staff were discussing a policy issue affecting tribes, in this case, the issue on how some provisions of the health-care-focused *Affordable Care Act 2010* applied to large employers. The health-care advisers made a lot of assumptions, based on a Western point of view, lumping tribal enterprises with other businesses in the United States and assigning them the same attributes. For example, they assumed that tribal businesses would be driven by profit at the expense of their workers. As a former tribal leader, I explained that tribes are employers of their own citizens and their families and that most of them show substantial care for their workforces. These advisers told me that there was no data to back up my assertions. This was true. But I was able to point out that there was no data to back up their assertions either, so my anecdotal evidence was superior to their ignorance of tribes as employers. The issue was put on hold to get more information. By being present at that moment, I felt I was able to subvert institutional ignorance and racism.

In the autumn before the end of the Obama administration, the White House scheduled its final White House Tribal Nations Conference. Tribes knew that President Obama's agenda to benefit tribes was unprecedented, and that some of his initiatives had made tribal communities better. American Indians are not a significant political constituency in most of the United States, but Obama had fought for us; not because he needed our votes, but because he thought it was important and the right thing to do.

As I was on the sidelines waiting for the president's final speech to tribes, a US Secret Service agent told me that I was wanted backstage. When I got there, I saw the president pacing back and forwards before going on stage. When he saw me, he came over and gave me a hug, thanking me for my work. He said that his administration's work, on behalf of tribes, was something he was proud of, and that even though he was leaving the office of the presidency, he would never stop being an advocate. I watched through tears as tribal drummers sang an honour song for him, and tribal representatives wrapped him in a blanket to signify the gratitude and respect of tribes for his efforts on our behalf. My time at the national level gave me another set of insights into leadership. It became even clearer to me that as leaders of Native American Tribal governments, we have a valuable role to play in rebuilding governance for our nations.

INSIGHTS FOR NATIVE AMERICAN WOMEN AS LEADERS IN GOVERNANCE-BUILDING

I'm sometimes asked how being a woman has affected my experience of leadership for building tribal governance. My gender has caused me difficulties—some people take you less seriously as a leader if you're a woman—but it also has helped. I have often mused that being the chair of my tribal government felt like I had 4,200 children. These maternal instincts were about righting wrongs, about protecting and safeguarding from harm, about not having a favourite child, and therefore working equitably. At the same time, they also involved facing head-on the display of patriarchy that manifested itself in power plays and bullying behaviour. I often felt my gender was an asset in leadership.

Being the first female chair of the Fond du Lac Band was made easier by the fact that, after my election into office, three of the five seats on our council were filled by women. The women brought a practical manner to tribal government. They were not swayed by constituents who tried to use emotional appeals to get their way. We talked to one another about decision-making and supported each other with a shared cohesive message—we were not in competition with each other, so knowledge was shared freely with each other. When we questioned or disagreed with each other, we did not take it personally, and no disagreements were had in front of constituents or employees. We did our homework and came to meetings prepared, ready to make decisions or otherwise move things along. We held each other to a high standard of professionalism and personal and professional maturity. And we got support from our two male colleagues, who were comfortable in their own leadership roles, were open to frank discussions and listened to their co-workers. And importantly, we got things done. It was not enough to be elected into office. We wanted to deliver real results for our citizens.

I met other Native American women leaders through some of the inter-tribal groups that convened in Indian Country, and they impressed me. They were remarkable women. They were educated—many with advanced degrees—and they came to their leadership positions with professional experience. Each woman carried a story of personal resilience. Each was balancing careers with family. And they never, ever forgot that they were Indigenous women and that their Indian cultures informed their leadership.

These women were also developing ways to encourage Native American women's leadership, whether in tribal government or at the community level. For example, one group founded Women Empowering Women for Indian Nations (WEWIN), a support network for Native women who wanted to grow their leadership and governance abilities. WEWIN's mission statement set out an agenda that included a strong governance role for Native women in protecting the inherent rights we exercise for the good of our people:

> We, the Indian women founders, who have common values and goals, do hereby establish 'Women Empowering Women for Indigenous Nations' because we are committed and dedicated to the following purposes:
>
> - To strengthen and sustain tribal cultures for the benefit and destiny of the children;
> - To educate about tribal cultures, the history of Native people, the inherent rights we exercise for the good of our people and others, and of current issues that affect our well-being;
> - To promote honest dignified tribal leadership who reflect pride for those we represent; and
> - To support and encourage tribal leadership. (Women Empowering Women for Indian Nations n.d.)

At every level, there seemed no need to explain that we needed to support one another, amplify each other's voices, and encourage and mentor younger women who might be in our positions in the future. Native American women were working together to do all that and more. And more and more are taking up top positions in the governance of their tribes.

My career is now focused on building the next generation of Indigenous leaders, female and male. Their challenges may differ from the challenges I have faced or the challenges faced by the Fond du Lac Band. But developing your own personal leadership abilities will be one of the best investments you can make—not just for yourself but for your own community. When I reflect on the opportunities that have given me a chance to make a positive impact on the governance and lives of Native American communities, there are some specific practical things that Indigenous women can do to prepare themselves for increased leadership.

Prepare yourself. Indigenous communities, like most, are full of charismatic leaders who have plenty of rhetoric, but little substance. We need better leaders than that. Whether it be through formal academic programmes, volunteering or work experience, develop your understanding of how systems work, about how all the pieces of the environment in which you are operating fit together. For example, the education system is tied to workforce development, which in turn is tied to economic development outcomes. Child care and transportation are key to educational attainment and workforce development, so they need to be taken into account in your strategic planning. Build your knowledge of these and the wider systems they fit into. Be a lifelong learner and do your homework.

Build networks. The broader your network, the broader your opportunities for impact. Sociologists know that networks are how the majority population sustain their grip on decision- making and governance institutions. Your networking increases your chances of being present in places and discussions that matter for your own people. Your network is a source of support, potential partnerships and joint advocacy.

Take risks. Change is difficult. It is human nature to avoid those things that make us uncomfortable. Part of taking risks is to determine your tolerance for risk and make plans to mitigate it. For example, if you're a primary wage earner, you may feel stuck in your current employment. If you build your savings, it may relieve some of the stress of trying something new. Leadership is always risky, especially when you are the one making important decisions or setting a new direction. If you have prepared yourself, then the risks are more manageable.

Take care of yourself. Understand what your physical and emotional needs are and make sure you have balance and set boundaries. Don't be afraid to articulate what you are willing to do and not do.

Have a support system. Leadership can be exhausting. Find mentors who can guide you and share what they have learned. The people who believe in your abilities can lift you when you are doubting yourself. Work and share your ideas with other women who are also rebuilding tribal governance.

Be confident. As women, we are conditioned to think that having confidence means having an ego or being arrogant. Let's change that narrative to mean that we understand our abilities and are self-assured.

Handle criticism. No one is perfect. You don't have to be either. Forgive yourself, learn and move on. Don't dwell on past mistakes or disagreements. Sometimes the criticism is misplaced. If—after you given it some thought—you disagree with the criticism, let it go. It's not your job to make everyone happy.

Be Indigenous. Someone once said that we are the dreams of our ancestors. Never forget who you are and where you came from. The trauma of our past is countered by the steadfast resiliency of our communities. You're not just a leader, you are an Indigenous leader.

NOTES

1. The term 'at-large' refers to when members of a governing body are elected or appointed to represent the whole membership of a community, nation, city, etc. rather than to represent a subset of that membership according to a voting ward, district or type of member.

2. The history, culture, governance arrangements, programmes and services of the Fond du Lac Band Tribal Government can be viewed at the Tribe's website (Fond du Lac Band of Lake Superior Chippewa 2019).

3. The Ojibwe people of the Fond du Lac and Lake Superior region had dealings with European governments for hundreds of years before the arrival of representatives of the US Government after the War of 1812. In the years following, a number of treaties were negotiated between the Ojibwe and the United States, first to establish a peaceful relationship and then to transfer or 'cede' title of lands to the control of the United States (Fond du Lac Tribal Government 2018).

4. The Fond du Lac Tribal Government's Natural Resources Program is responsible for the wild rice management and restoration activities. There are five primary wild-rice lakes on the Fond du Lac Reservation, where the total area on which wild rice is currently present on these lakes is 367 hectares. The primary method of wild-rice lake management is by controlling water levels on the lakes by operating water-control structures (dams), ditch maintenance and beaver-dam management. The programme works full time on water-level management and data collection, restoration planning and implementation (Fond du Lac Tribal Government 2019b).

5. See various resource management programmes and reports produced by the FDL Government on these critical concerns, see Fond du Lac Tribal Government (2019b).

6. The Saint Louis River is the largest tributary to Lake Superior, which is itself the largest body of fresh water in the world.

7. For further information on the operation of these casinos, see Black Bear Casino Resort (n.d.) and Fond du Lac (2018).

8. These include, for example, a tribal government council and community services division, emergency services, police department, human resources and services,

a planning division, a resource management division, housing division and several others. See Fond du Lac Band of Lake Superior Chippewa (2019b).

9. The Fond du Lac Band itself employed about 2,200 in 2013, making it the second largest employer in northeast Minnesota, according to a study commissioned by the Fond du Lac by the Bureau of Business and Economic research. The study estimated the band's economic activity creates an additional 1,400 jobs (Kraker 2013).

10. See overview of the 2009 conference and President Obama's speech at US Government 2009.

11. See James Anaya, chapter 1, this volume, regarding this US position on voting against UNDRIP.

12. The report presented the Task Force recommendations across seven cross-cutting themes: resilient communities; infrastructure resilience; natural resources resilience; human health and population resilience; climate-smart hazard mitigation, disaster preparedness and recovery; the economics of resilience and building capacity for resilience. A summary of the report is available at Environmental and Energy Study Institute (2015).

Chapter 18

Mana Wāhine

We Care So Much It Exhausts Us!

Mera Penehira

Māori women in Aotearoa-New Zealand have an identity that is unique to them and their ancestry. Yet the voice of Māori women has been silenced in many ways through the process of colonisation (Mikaere 2003; Pihama 2005). This chapter speaks to that silence, describing three short case studies of how Māori and Indigenous women are reasserting their collective voice by engaging as gender and cultural advocates with social media and networking sites. I consider the social media tactics and strategies used by a group of Māori women, in seeking not only to practice a politics of visibility that unsettles colonial power relations but also to cultivate internal solidarity and leadership for shaping positive transformation within Māori society.

The chapter title is borrowed from one of our most prominent Māori academics, Professor Linda Tuhiwai Smith (2018), who vehemently resists the notion that Māori, Native and Indigenous peoples do not care about education:

> Hundreds of Māori education hui have been held; super big ones, small ones, and ones that lasted until dawn. I have attended many of these hui. So many in fact, that it gives a lie to any claim that Māori don't care about education. We do care. We care so much it exhausts us. Our hui are never meaningless as they enable us to voice our concerns, share knowledge, identify capacity and strategise. Our hui processes are intense and at their finest are the best educational gatherings I have ever participated in. Mostly they reaffirm that we are not alone and our experiences are not isolated. But, we rarely have the system power to make the changes we need and when we do, for example Kura Kaupapa Māori, they never have the investment to make the changes sustainable.

Not only do Māori women care about and invest their leadership energies in Māori identity and knowledge, many are working together for the purposes of what Duarte (2017) calls 'connected activism', where they are harnessing the power of new media and information technologies to enable bigger conversations and shape political change. In this chapter, I argue that this kind of strategic engagement with digital platforms by Māori women has the potential to be a powerful transformative mechanism for accessing and activating what Linda Tuhiwai Smith refers to in the quote above as 'system power'. Specifically, it may contribute to a decolonising process and systemic change. The voices of three Māori women (including the author), and their social media writings, are presented here. Each of them has been part of the Hina Matarau collective and worked together for shared political, protective and leadership purposes. They are active in politics and, in particular, the politics of resistance and decolonisation. As such, they are each leaders in their own right within family, tribal groupings, community, politics and/or academia.

Hina Matarau is a national collective of Māori and Indigenous women political activists and leaders in Aotearoa. With the well-being of Māori women, children, families and community at its heart, this collective provides a wāhine (women's) voice on relevant issues through any channels available to them. In particular, its members have proactively engaged in using multiple forms of media over the past three years, as a platform for new Māori women's activism and leadership. Women of the Hina Matarau collective assert that theirs is a reflective space where women can actively affirm their responsibility to protect Papatūānuku (our ancestress mother earth) and to sustain all living and loving systems in the environment. Not limited to concern for the rights of Māori in Aotearoa, they work broadly to support Native and Indigenous solidarity worldwide.

Each of the three women profiled in this chapter are Māori wearers of moko kauwae, or traditional facial skin carving. And indeed, this will be the focus of some of the writings examined here. Moko has been shown to be an effective expression of identity and one that adds to their well-being as Māori women (Nikora, Rua & Awewkotuku, 2007; Penehira 2011). Moko provides another narrative through which the ongoing colonial silencing of women in particular is directly challenged. Ironically, one of the most blatant forms of colonial silencing of our women was grounded in the Women's Christian Temperance Union (WCTU) which underpinned the Women's Suffrage Movement. In order to participate in the suffrage movement, our women were required by the WCTU to sign away their right to wear moko.[1] The women in this chapter have actively spoken back to the silence, as did their ancestors. A sample of both their individual and collective women's voices are shared in the following sections. By examining both the challenges and successes the women of Hina Matarau have experienced in this arena, the chapter also draws a link to the broader roles and leadership of Māori women in the socio-political context of Aotearoa.

DIGITAL ACTIVISM

The political usage of social media and digital technologies has grown rapidly in Aotearoa-New Zealand and around the world, including among Indigenous women who face the gender discrimination and social disadvantage that arises out of ongoing settler colonialism (Duarte 2017; John 2015; McMillan, Young & Peters 2013; O'Carroll 2013). Given the power of using social media for communicating messages about Indigeneity and identity, and as part of creating and responding to social change, this chapter presents three short case studies to demonstrate how Māori women are mobilising digital technologies and social media.

Mera Penehira

As a mother and academic active(ist) in my community, I descend from the Māori nations of Ngāti Raukawa, Rangitāne and Ngaiterangi. With a master's degree in educational psychology completed at the University of Auckland, my research and political advocacy has long centred on Māori women's health, well-being and traditional healing practices, in particular moko—the traditional Māori skin carving. As noted in the introduction to this chapter, the resurgence of traditional facial tattoo is a significant part of Māori women's language reclamation, for the moko or skin carving is its own narrative. We know this is not the domain of Māori women alone—Indigenous peoples of many other nations, including the Ainu of Japan, Inuit of Alaska, Samoa and Kanaka Maoli of Hawai'i, to name a few, share this tradition of skin carving (Nikora, Rua & Awewkotuku, 2007; DeMello 2012; Penehira 2011). For Māori, moko is a multi-layered journey, carrying with it a multiplicity of meaning for both the 'creator' and the recipient (Penehira 2011). Te Awekotuku and Nikora (2007: 208–09) have summarised its great value as follows:

> Moko has many meanings to those who carry it. Moko is about identity; about being Māori in a Māori place, being Māori in a foreign place, being Māori in one's own land and times, being Māori on Māori terms. It is about survival and resilience. It reflects Māori relationships with others; how they see Māori, and more importantly, how Māori want to be seen.

Recently in Aotearoa, the issue of non-Māori, non-Native women receiving moko kauwae (traditional women's facial skin carving) has come to the fore.

Alongside a number of my colleagues and friends, I took the opportunity to make a stand when this happened. Across social and news media, we probably hit in excess of 500 online engagements. We argued simply that the right of moko kauwae was a right determined by whakapapa (genealogy) and was not the right of any Māori to give to a non-Native, non-Māori woman (Pākehā). We saw this as an opportunity to engage in educated conversations and, importantly, to claim our role as kaitiaki or caretakers of this domain of knowledge and expertise.

Following a flurry of discussion on social media sites, in particular Facebook, the following media statement was released on 22 September 2018. It is presented in full below as it reveals the range of issues and depth of concerns raised by Māori:

> Recent social media spaces have seen the emergence of a heated yet very articulate and informed discussion as to the right of non-Māori to wear moko kauwae, or traditional Māori women's skin carving. Although instigated by what some would describe as the heinous mistake to apply a 'chin tattoo' on a woman lacking any genealogy to Māori, the national Indigenous Women's collective, Hina Matarau, say the discussion is much broader than that.
>
> In response to Pākehā or other Europeans wearing Māori women's facial tattoo, Te Whare Wānanga o Awanuiārangi Associate Professor Mera Penehira, states 'Moko kauwae is the sole right of Māori women. Not only is it "okay" to make a race-based decision in applying moko kauwae, but it is a "requirement". In my view the gifting of moko kauwae to Pākehā is not the right of any Māori, be they wāhine or tāne, irrespective of what has gone before'. (Quoted: http://www.scoop.co.nz/stories/CU1805/S00248/its-about-whakapapa-moko-kauwae-is-not-for-pakeha.htm, 23 May 201)

Yet, in this day and age where traditional skin carving and other forms of tattoo are more commonly practised and indeed increasing in popularity, moko artists are often asked to perform specific tribal work on non-Māori. Renowned moko artist (skin carver) Anikaaro Harawira-Havili says it is different though when it comes to moko kauwae:

> Putting it on Pākehā unravels and aggravates a long history of whakapapa (genealogy). It's hard enough to receive it as Māori because of the stigma and fear from colonisation, without seeing Pākehā parading it and using it as a business brand! For us it gives us a sense of rangatiratanga that is purely ours through whakapapa. One taonga I won't allow to be stolen by Pākehā. (Quoted: http://www.scoop.co.nz/stories/CU1805/S00248/its-about-whakapapa-moko-kauwae-is-not-for-pakeha.htm)

Associate Professor Leonie Pihama agrees, stating:

> Pākehā women wanting to take on our taonga of moko kauwae and be justified in doing so smacks of white privilege! Māori women have been struggling to reclaim this taonga for generations and Pākehā women need to stop their co-option of our taonga! (Quoted: https://www.rnz.co.nz/news/te-manu-korihi/358026/pakeha-woman-with-facial-moko-draws-backlash)

The Hina Matarau collective are adamant that Māori—and in particular Māori women—have a responsibility to maintain the sacred space of moko kauwae. 'But this does not mean you have to jump through extra hoops or reach anyone else's standards except your own and those of your whānau and hapū, in order to wear moko kauwae. As long as you are wahine Māori, this is yours as of right! It speaks to whakapapa Māori, to being Māori!', says Penehira:

> There is some concern that media discourse generally presupposes Māori women need to reach certain milestones before being 'worthy' of receiving their moko kauwae. However, as long-time language advocate, Tere Harrison, states, 'kauwae are taonga wāhine Māori, and whakapapa is the guideline for the practice of applying or receiving. There is no other measure necessary.
>
> (Quoted: http://www.scoop.co.nz/stories/CU1805/S00248/it-s-about-whakapapa-moko-kauwae-is-not-for-pakeha.htm?from-mobile=bottom-link-01)
>
> Whilst it has been suggested in social media that the group would not encourage fair-skinned Māori to take on moko kauwae, as academic and collective member, Ngahuia Murphy, clarifies: 'Skin colour is irrelevant. It is about whakapapa back to the tupuna, atua and our own spiritualties. We have had the taonga of moko kauwae stolen from us as well as our language and lands. The reclamation of this is for us'!
>
> The centrality of genealogy is further iterated by Taranaki artist, Ngaahina Hohaia: 'Moko kauwae is the DNA blue print of Māori women. It speaks to our whakapapa and stands as a bastion of our survival. Cultural appropriation has pillaged almost every other taonga sacred to our people. The line is drawn here'.

What ensued was a continued dialogue on social media that ranged from well-articulated and informed discussion to general harassment and online trolling towards those of us who took up the space to show both leadership and inform opportunities for conversation and education. Other media picked up on this, including both English and Māori news and current affairs (see e.g. Matata-Sipu 2018). This was a time that tested our stamina and integrity.

Did we succeed? Since this publicity, we are seeing both the quality and quantity of the resurgence of our facial skin carving increase. Along with a growing demand for moko kauwae, there is a growing number of moko artists coming forward with increased expertise to match. There are more Māori women than ever putting their hands (or rather chins) up to participate in this part of the resurgence of Māori women's voice and spaces for our leadership. While just a couple of short decades ago we could count on one hand the number of people attaining moko kauwae in a 12-month period, it is not unusual now to see twenty new moko kauwae in just one month. We count this as success, as evidenced in one of the most eloquent responses to this dialogue from a Māori woman:

> I've been thinking about taking on moko kauwae for a long time now, but felt I wasn't worthy enough. I know now, I am okay. I am a wahine Māori and it is my right! My birth right! (Anonymous pers comm., 2019)

In this instance then, the mobilisation of a social media debate did more than simply focus attention on what was, in effect, a further colonisation by Pākehā of Māori cultural symbolism and knowledges. Perhaps, even more importantly, it supported an internal resurgence among Māori women of individual cultural confidence and collective voice.

Leonie Pihama

A descendant of the Māori nations of Te Atiwa, Ngā Māhanga a Tairi and Ngāti Māhanga, Leonie is a mother of six and a grandmother of five, and a leading Kaupapa Māori educator and researcher. She has extensive expertise connecting her to a wide range of communities and iwi (tribal groups), which enables her to relate to people throughout Aotearoa-New Zealand. Leonie is an active blogger and comments broadly across multiple media platforms on issues of relevance to Hina Matarau and to shed light on critical issues of continued colonial oppression in her lands.

One such instance occurred in 2016, when the hotel chain Novotel announced its decision to rename the hotel that stands in Leonie's region of Taranaki[2] 'Novotel New Plymouth Hobson', with the restaurant being named 'The Governor'. This sparked an immediate and staunch response from Leonie: 'I was immediately sickened by the lack of any sensitivity or thought for the impact of such naming on our people' (Pihama 2016).

The blog from which this quote is extracted (Pihama 2016) is used as the basis for this case study, to examine Leonie's engagement with social media initially around this issue and, secondarily, her broader media engagement, aimed ultimately at resisting ongoing coloniser domination in her lands. Specifically, in this instance, Leonie drew on both her lived experience and her academic knowledge of historical trauma (Walters 2006; Pihama 2016) to lead a critical public discussion about, and encourage greater depth of understanding of, the impact of naming. Leonie has been at the forefront of historical trauma research in Aotearoa and how it continues to impact upon us and potentially our future generations (Pihama et al. 2014). For, as Leonie states in her blog: 'Naming is important. Names carry memories, names carry meaning, names carry history' (Quoted: https://tewhareporahou.wordpress.com/2016/02/19/colonial-naming-reproduces-historical-trauma/).

There is an emerging body of work which further affirms the significance of naming more widely to Native and Indigenous cultures (See Pihama 2017). The global impacts of patriarchal and locational naming practices by settler–colonial and then nation-states are also well-documented. In Aotearoa, part of the resurgence of Māori language and identity has to do with naming. For example, we are much more likely now to have children with at least one of their first names being Māori, and a growing number of young parents choose to completely name their children with ancestral names or names in our own language. It is significant to note also that many Māori of my generation have sought to return to ancestral names—by choosing one themselves, by virtue of seeking the affirmation from an elder, or by simply translating their given English name to Māori. All of these are signals that naming is important to our identity and, indeed, to reasserting leadership of ourselves and our lands as forms of individual and collective self-determination (Lee 2012; Penehira 2011).

All too often, however, the experience of Māori in Aotearoa is one where this fundamental aspect of our self-determination has been denied, as Leonie stated in her blog:

> Being raised in Waitara, every day we were surrounded by streets named after the colonial militia and colonial governors who instigated and led the invasion of our lands. We were raised on the Pekapeka block. Everyday street signs remind us of those who forcibly removed our ancestors from our lands, those who invaded and occupied our lands, those who killed and imprisoned our people, who placed our men in chains and imprisoned them in Otago, who led the militia that raped our tupuna wahine. (https://tewhareporahou.wordpress.com/2016/02/19/colonial-naming-reproduces-historical-trauma/)

There is a direct and undeniable link between naming and historical trauma in the ongoing colonial experience of our people. Being prepared to speak out against this is both brave and necessary if we are to interrupt this pattern of trauma and take back active authority over our own names and naming processes. It will not otherwise be recognised, either by the Crown, the colonial 'namers', nor even our own people, whom for so long have lived this. As Leonie goes on to say:

> What the owners of the Novotel New Plymouth Hobson, and the New Plymouth District Council fail to understand is the depth of the insult and offense being perpetrated through the continued privileging of colonial names over and above those of hapū. For many of our people, the history of Waitara can still be felt in the land and air. The historical trauma of that history has been carried by generations of whānau, hapū and iwi of Taranaki. The pain and struggle of a colonial past, of war and raupatu can be felt. (Quoted: https://tewhareporahou.wordpress.com/2016/02/19/colonial-naming-reproduces-historical-trauma/)

For Māori, as is true with most if not all Native and Indigenous peoples, we are not just raised on our lands, we do not just feel connected to our lands. It is more than that. Our land, our rivers, our mountains and our oceans are indeed our ancestors and are named as such. So too are our traditional buildings. They are named for ancestors who are considered to be true leaders, chiefs of our nations, to whom we pay tribute and remember for their leadership, which has contributed to our current standing. So to continue to have the names of colonial settlers who were responsible for the savage murder of our people and desecration of lands and waterways forced upon us in our everyday communities is considered by many Māori to be an atrocity.

Speaking out and taking leadership in this area of our cultural resurgence is critical to our survival and to our rightful ownership and control within our territories. Though there was no name change as a result of Leonie's blog, it no doubt opened the space for courageous conversations among Māori and non-Māori alike. Of note, since drafting this chapter, the hotel was sold in November 2018 to a local iwi (tribal) business consortium. At the time of writing, the hotel and restaurant names remain unchanged. However, with the power for change now clearly in the hands of Māori, there is a clear expectation from many that this should eventuate. This section concludes with the final words of Leonie's blog, which capture in essence both the birth-right and birth-responsibility we have as Native and Indigenous women to speak back to colonial oppression:

> I was born and raised in Taranaki.
>
> I have lived under the korowai of the Maunga and have experienced the awe of seeing Taranaki stand firmly on the landscape, defining the geography in a way that we who live under his shadow may never achieve.

I have lived alongside the awa and the Moana. Known them in their strength and beauty. Known them in their provision of kai, before they were poisoned.

I have lived on land that was taken from my people and watched as my parents struggled to 'pay the rent' on land that was rightfully ours.

I was schooled alongside Owae Whaitara, the marae that stands above the township. We walked through and around that space every day and were never schooled within its bounds. It was an 'out of bounds' area.

I learnt of a history of this land that told us of Cook and Tasman and Browne. And I knew these names because they named the streets upon which I walked. They named my world. Waitara.

I was told we were all the same. New Zealanders/National identity/Kiwi/ Egalitarian/National identity/One New Zealand/One identity.

But I knew that to be Māori wasn't the same. And I see now why we were never to know who we were. Identity had to be controlled. So the system could be maintained. As without the system the 'Nation' would be fragmented.

And we would be left with a Nervous System. (Pihama 2018)

Tina Ngata

Tina Ngata descends from the Māori nation of Ngāti Porou. A mother of two, her work involves advocacy for environmental, Indigenous and human rights. This includes local, national and international initiatives that highlight the role of settler colonialism in issues, such as climate change and waste pollution, and promote Indigenous conservation as best practice for a globally sustainable future. Tina is well-known across Aotearoa for her fearless approach in utilising public forums to speak out on important matters of social justice for all. Recently, she spoke out against a local initiative that served to denigrate Indigenous peoples in an inexcusable fashion.

In 2019, the Waimamaku Wild Festival, which is held annually in the northern region of Aotearoa, engaged in perpetuating what were seen to be racist portrayals of Native American people and culture. The festival was promoted, primarily on Facebook, in the weeks leading up to its opening. Organisers chose to post images of people in cheap, fake Native American regalia, with others dressed as cowboys, some of whom were enacting the shooting of Native Americans. Furthermore, there were images of fake Tipi and potential festival-goers were encouraged to 'visit our reservation'. This disregard for the sanctity and sovereignty of Native American peoples is neither new nor isolated (Walters 2006). Tina chose to speak out:

> The American West was not 'Wild' to anyone but the colonial invaders—who then attempted to settle it by means of genocide, including bounties for Native American scalps, mass displacement, forced marches, massacres, the theft of Native American children, and purposeful infection. This is not a period to be festive about at all, and there is literally no way to hold a 'Wild West Festival' without being racist and colonial. From the concept to the costumes, this is a thoroughly offensive, redneck event. (Ngata 2019)

Showing a forthright approach to the issue, Tina took this as an opportunity to expose the racism and the inherent and ongoing historical trauma issues associated with it. She and colleagues related the history of the Choctaw and other Native American Nations, who were forcefully removed from their homelands, along what is now known as the Trail of Tears (Walters et al. 2011). However, as Tina made her online stand, both in calling for the removal of offensive imagery and a shift away from the overall theme of the festival, she also took up the opportunity to educate and transform. Part of the open letter to the festival organisers Tina wrote is as follows:

> Hey Waimamaku Wild West Festival
>
> I see you have a super colonial shindig planned and you're censoring the comments on your own page. That's ok we will just share the heck outta your page.
>
> So first of all—the period of time you are commemorating here for your festival is one of genocide. The west coast of Great Turtle Island was not 'wild' to the nations who already lived there. It was already occupied and well known. And there were no reservations.
>
> It is called 'wild' because the invasions began in the east and the racist, bigoted invaders considered Indigenous people as little more than animals with no rights, which meant the land was, in their eyes unoccupied, awaiting 'discovery' and settlement and therefore 'wild'.
>
> The period of time you are referring to as the 'Wild West' was one of rampant invasion, land theft, rape and massacre. It is the period of the 'Trail of Tears' where tens of thousands of Choctaw Cherokee and Seminole people, after having their lands stolen under the Indian Removal Act, were force-marched by militia to lands thousands of kms away. Thousands and thousands died; just

> in this instance—and there were plenty of these instances all over Great Turtle Island.
>
> That's how reservations started. By true landowners being pushed off their territories and forced to live in small plots of land so that settlers could farm their land. 'Come see our Indian reservation'. Good lord.
>
> Other ways settlers 'conquered the Wild West' was 'Indian scalp bounties'—yep the national and state colonial governments paid the white settlers you are celebrating for the skinned top of a Native American head. Oh and of course there was also the time honoured colonial practices of purposeful infection and rampant child theft. Even *if* you survived the massacres and forced marches thousands of miles from your home, you were often subjected to horrid, infectious conditions, and men would show up to literally take your children from you to places where unspeakable horrors were done to them under the pretence of making them 'less wild'.
>
> That is the 'Wild West' you are having your 'fest' about. That is the 'Indian Reservation' you are promoting here. So anyway—go learn some history and quit perpetuating racist stereotypes, Waimamaku. (Ngata 2019)

As a result of Tina's public blog and open letter, there ensued a major public debate on the issue. Her online activism mobilised and connected up a large reservoir of support and back-up from colleagues, peers and some members of the general public via Facebook, news and television media. In this instance, the leadership stand of this one Māori woman achieved the ultimate goal—festival organisers issued a public apology. Furthermore, they removed all offensive imagery and reshaped the festival theme removing all negative reference to Native Americans. This was leadership that transformed the conversation and led to a successful practical outcome, as outlined below in the apology that appeared on the Facebook page:

> Waimamaku has a long history of organising a community event called the Waimamaku Wild West Fest. However, it has recently come to our attention that in doing so we have been culturally appropriating indigenous cultures and have caused offence.
>
> The Waimamaku Wild West Festival Committee would like to publicly and unreservedly apologise for any hurt we might have caused through our ignorance.
>
> Cultural appropriation is a significant issue that we are on a journey to understand. The long history of colonisation within the Americas has had an

> enormous detrimental impact that cannot be understated. This has been a steep learning curve for us and one we are undertaking with great care.
>
> The event originated as a way to incorporate and celebrate the wild West coast of New Zealand where we live, horse riding, our history of cheese production, and promotion of our community, arts, crafts and environmental issues. Historically, the Wild West Fest has been a significant fundraising event for Hokianga Health and our community. Our intent was never to offend.
>
> We as a community are trying to redress any harm done, by eliminating any aspects of cultural appropriation and to take it back to our roots celebrating our place on the West Coast of Northland, New Zealand.
>
> We would like to extend an invitation to anyone who would like to have a stall at our event providing education to the wider community about these issues. We hope that with this event and with all future events Waimamaku will be inclusive and welcoming to all peoples. (Wild West Festival 2019)

The Hina Matarau collective acknowledged the integrity and sincerity that conference organisers applied to their response. It is rare—so it is to be celebrated! It encouraged us to look forward to further opportunities for education and positive transformation as, building on that of our forebears, Māori women's leadership continues to revitalise and strengthen our collective identities.

THE TRANSFORMATIVE POWER OF DIGITAL LEADERSHIP

In discussing this chapter with the women who are mentioned in the case studies, there is common agreement that preparedness to speak out and take a lead approach against the current impacts of historical trauma and work for political and educational transformation comes with both costs and benefits. There is also a shared understanding that not only is this work important to do at this time; indeed, it is also our responsibility. In the words of Angelou Maya: 'History, despite its wrenching pain cannot be unlived, but if faced with courage, need not be lived again' (quoted in Peters 2014). There are three key themes that have emerged in this chapter, which highlight how we can create change so that our history 'need not be lived again', themes which point to the potential of social media for rebuilding and asserting women's leadership for political advocacy and cultural resurgence.

Transformation through Education

The first of these themes is that of leading the positive transformation of people and society through education, and in this case through harnessing the educational influence of digital platforms. Each of the three stories has components of education that have resulted in positive change.

The first section of this chapter described how the debate regarding moko kauwae resulted in a shift for Māori women in the public and their own understandings of the cultural value of moko. Previously believing they were 'not worthy' of attaining the sacred chin skin carving, following the media discussions more Māori women came to know that it is a valued part of their birth-right. The second section of the chapter examined how Leonie Pihama took the opportunity to engage social media to lead a conversation about naming and the impact of colonial naming on people in the region of Taranaki. She further used the forum to discuss the historical nature of trauma that was associated with the colonial practices of naming, which enabled people to reflect on and potentially analyse their own experience in this context.

In the final section, Tina Ngata's stance gave festival organisers the opportunity to reflect on and analyse their marketing in respect to its racist and offensive impacts. Ultimately this resulted in an apology and the changing of the festival theme by the organisers. While not all were in agreement with the decision, important new understandings of both an historical and contemporary nature came to fruition. In all three cases, online formats offered a compelling set of communicative tools that the women were able to use to present further information, correct inaccuracies and promote a more informed debate about specific issues of concern to them.

Speaking with Purpose

The second key theme to emerge in this chapter is the direct relationship between leadership, speaking with purpose and creating change. In each short case study, the women's information and arguments are clear and simple, unencumbered by overly academic or subject-specific technical language. They also spoke from personal experience which they integrated into their overall argument, helping to share the human qualities of their concerns. Where sometimes less familiar terms were necessarily used (such as Māori language words) these were explained, thus ensuring the content was accessible to all and broadening the educative opportunities. Given the transformative results outlined above, it could be argued that systemic change is far more likely when the messages are focussed, clearly articulated and raise awareness by resonating shared human concerns and standards.

A related insight is the substantial value that digital platforms provide as participatory spaces for Māori women to practice a politics of visibility and cultivate solidarity. Important kinds of cultural knowledge work have to happen prior to and around activating digital tactics. In each of the three studies, the women discussed and made choices about their messaging and the discourses of Indigeneity that they wanted to positively promote. There is considerable potential for Māori women to use digital communication platforms as mobilising grounds to build and assert connected activism.

Solidarity with Other Indigenous Nations

Although not an immediately visible feature of each of the studies, there is an undeniable opportunity for the digital activism described in this chapter to contribute to the work of other Native and Indigenous nations. Clearly, this is most apparent in Tina Pihama's story in relation to the Wild West Festival. When exploring more broadly the work of each of the women, it is apparent that they make use of opportunities to work with other Indigenous people on a regular basis.[3] It is widely understood that change for Indigenous nations will be more effective when global solidarity is enacted and we can leverage off our shared insights and expertise. In this context, the notion of reciprocity and shared responsibility (e.g., in terms of guardianship of sacred lands and waterways) is understood and practised among Indigenous women's leadership and has an important role to play in building this wider global network. Our engagement with social media as connected activists is likely to play a major part in enabling Indigenous women's voices to be heard more widely beyond our own countries and have a transformative impact.

This chapter has presented three examples of women engaging in multimedia in order to inform, educate and effect change. The Hina Matarau collective takes seriously the digital space they have created where women can actively affirm their roles and responsibility to protect Papatūānuku and to sustain all living and loving systems in the environment. As such, the importance of being active in politics and in particular the politics of resistance and decolonisation has been highlighted and the influential part that digital platforms will play in that. Christensen found that the Inuit 'are generally embedding offline life into cyberspace' and that '[t]he Internet is not necessarily a space to hide in, nor is it a space that mysteriously filters away the cultural identity of people' (2003: 23). This chapter indicates that in fact the internet and social media platforms can be harnessed as spaces that make visible and promote the cultural identity of Indigenous people.

I close with a well-known proverb from Parihaka (village in the Taranaki region of Aotearoa/New Zealand), which speaks to the strength of women to stand, in the absence of others, to maintain the well-being of all: 'E tū tama wāhine i te wā o te kore'! (quoted in Penehira 2011).

NOTES

1. See, for example, an outline of this history at Pihama (2018).
2. Taranaki is a region in the west of Aotearoa North Island. It is named after its main geographical feature, the volcano of Mount Taranaki, which is sacred to Māori.
3. For instance, Mera Penehira works regularly with First Nations located in the Pacific Northwest of the United States of America, and kanaka Māoli of Hawai'i supervising and teaching doctoral candidates, and presents regularly at Indigenous conferences. Leonie Pihama is often invited to present to Indigenous academic audiences across many Native and Indigenous nations and has been involved in collaborative Indigenous research projects for many years. Tina Ngata is a regular representative at United Nations gatherings and also a frequent presenter to Indigenous academic audiences.

Chapter 19

The Trials and Legacy of Delgamuukw

Transforming Rights into Outcomes for Canadian First Nations Peoples

Neil J. Sterritt

The Indigenous peoples of Canada exercised their self-determination for millennia before the British arrived at the shores of our continent. Moreover, we continued to be self-governing for far longer than some might realise after the British planted their flags. Our independence, however, would eventually wane as settlers spread across the continent, as the British sought to assimilate our peoples to their values and way of life and imposed legislation and policies that (aided by arms, disease and numbers) dispossessed us of our lands.

At the 2012 *Common Roots, Common Futures* international Indigenous governance conference convened in Tucson, Arizona, United Nations special rapporteur James Anaya identified three eras that aptly define our historic experience with settler-colonialism and our governance journey as Indigenous peoples: the first being exploration and colonisation; the second being the battle for rights recognition; and the third being the post-recognition implementation era in which we now find ourselves.[1]

This chapter deals with those eras and the governance challenges they posed to our First Nation in the context of the life, trials and legacy of an influential man among my own Gitxsan peoples of British Columbia (BC)—Delgamuukw (Albert Tait)—and the significant Canadian High Court decision in which he and the Gitxsan were the key protagonists: the *Delgamuukw (1997) Case*.[2]

That case was a culmination of many decades of advocacy by the Gitxsan to regain our land rights and rebuild our governance for that purpose. And Delgamuukw himself was one in a long line of leaders—men and women—who fought to transform Canadian First Nations' land claims and political advocacy into substantive rights and recognition. While Delgamuukw died before his case was handed down in the High Court of Canada in 1997, his 'rights recognition' legacy endures. The manifestation of his legacy, however, leaves us with what well may prove to be a larger and more important trial for Gitxsan and other Indigenous peoples in Canada and more widely: namely, the not insignificant challenge of transforming our rights into governing capabilities and practical outcomes so that we are effectively self-determining within our homelands once more, albeit in the context of today's reality.

CANADA: 1763–1867

The experience of First Nations in settler-colonial Canada was much the same as that experienced in Australia, Aotearoa-New Zealand and the United States, namely, one of progressive dispossession, marginalisation and erosion of our own governance systems. King George's 1763 Proclamation, which outlawed the private purchase of Native American land and reserved all the land in the Mississippi River watershed to Aboriginal nations, in effect recognised the rights of North American natives.[3] While the British applied the legal doctrine of *terra nullius* (purported to be land no one owns) to all its colonies, they abandoned the policy (for the most part) by the mid-eighteenth century in North America and did not apply it when colonising New Zealand (Banner 2005: 95).

A critical difference in Canada was the early treaty-making process. In eastern Canada, from 1701 to the early 1800s, the British negotiated what were referred to as 'Peace and Friendship Treaties' for the purpose of ending hostilities and encouraging cooperation between the British and Aboriginal peoples. Peace and Friendship Treaties did not require Aboriginal nations to surrender rights to their lands and resources nor did treaties negotiated after the time of confederation in 1867. After 1867, Canada went on to create treaty policy, established Treaty Commissioners and ratified treaty agreements. Eleven such treaties, known as the 'Numbered Treaties', were agreements with the government of Canada, administered by Canadian law, and are overseen today by the Minister of Aboriginal Affairs and Northern Development.[4]

The Rocky Mountains, however, hindered not only the westward march of explorers, fur traders and settlers to the Pacific Ocean but also came to represent an ideological barrier to the application of federal Aboriginal policy and treaty-making in BC. For two decades, treaty-making in BC followed in some respects the process that was taking place east of the Rockies. However, after Joseph Trutch replaced James Douglas as governor in the mid-1860s, an increasingly negative Aboriginal policy was established.

The Colony of Vancouver Island was created in 1849 with James Douglas (1803–1877) as governor.[5] Douglas applied practices consistent with those east of the Rocky Mountains, and he was aware of the Treaty of Waitangi concluded between Britain and the Maori people of New Zealand in 1840. The text he used in the treaties he negotiated with Vancouver Island tribes between 1850 and 1854 was taken from 'New Zealand precedents for purchasing Maori land' (Foster & Grove 2003: 51).

In the case of the Douglas treaties, the Aboriginal signatories and their descendants understood that they retained existing village sites and fields for their continued use, the 'liberty to hunt over unoccupied lands' and the right to 'carry on their fisheries as formerly' (Harris 2009: 140, 147). Contrary to current belief, the original text of the Douglas Treaties did not contain extinguishment language or the notion that an area of land was surrendered 'entirely and forever' in exchange for cash, clothing or blankets; such language was added later. The crown colonies of Vancouver Island and mainland BC became a single colony in 1866. In 1871, the colony joined confederation as the province of British Columbia. However, the Aboriginal land policy adopted in 1871 by BC's first Lieutenant Governor, Joseph Trutch (1826–1904), had all the hallmarks of Australia's *terra nullius* policy (Banner 2007: 223–24).

Born in England and a surveyor by profession, at age 22 Trutch made his way to the California gold fields in 1848–49. He worked in the western United States for about ten years and arrived in BC in 1859. Trutch was hostile to, and contemptuous of, Aboriginal people. In an 1850 letter to his wife regarding the Indians of Oregon, Trutch wrote, 'I think they are the ugliest and laziest creatures I ever saw, and we should as soon think of being afraid of our dogs as of them'.[6]

Trutch refused to recognise the legitimacy of the reserves established by his predecessor Governor Douglas and he had them re-surveyed in 1867, reducing their size by 91 per cent. Trutch's animosity towards Indians did not abate with continued exposure to other BC Aboriginal tribes. In 1870, referring to the Tsimshian at Metlakatla, near the mouth of the Skeena River, Trutch wrote:

> I have not yet met with a single Indian of pure blood whom I consider to have attained even the most glimmering perception of the Christian creed. (Fisher 1981:156)

Historian Robin Fisher summed up the Trutch legacy:

> In reality Trutch's views and actions left British Columbia, not only with growing Indian discontent, but with a legacy of litigation that in the long run was to

> cost the province more than extinguishing Indian title and laying out reasonable reserves would have done. In most areas of Canada, the Indian land question has been tied up in a neat European legal package called a treaty. In British Columbia by 1876, largely thanks to the influence of Trutch, it was still in the category of unfinished business. (Fisher 1981: 178)

The Aboriginal people of Canada east of the Rocky Mountains were little affected by colonial policy prior to, and long after, they had signed treaties with the British. But, eventually, settlers in increasing numbers began to take up Aboriginal lands with government consent and, as competition for resources ensued, the Aboriginal people were marginalised and subjected to enforced assimilation in residential schools. The transition west of the Rocky Mountains occurred later than in the east. For example, the Gitxsan and their neighbours continued to be self-determining in many respects after 1900, despite Canadian law banning their feasts and other so-called 'heathen practices' in the mid-1920s.

The name Joseph Trutch meant little to Albert Tait or to his parents and grandparents. Nevertheless, Trutch's dark legacy influenced BC Aboriginal policy for 130 years (from 1867 to 1997). Eventually, Albert Tait (Delgamuukw) and Alfred Joseph (Gisday Wa) would put an end to that policy.

THE RECOGNITION ERA (1901–1992)

Canada's Aboriginal people have been patient. They have spent more than 100 years trying to get recognition of their rights politically, but in vain, even though the courts had already considered the native title issue. In Ontario, for example, Indian title arose in the context of a company trying to secure a licence to log on treaty lands in 1888 (the resulting *St. Catherine's Milling and Lumber Co. v The Queen* was the first Indian title case in Canada). The company held a federal licence to log within Treaty No. 3. The province of Ontario challenged the federal government's right to grant a timber licence to the milling company. The case made its way through the Ontario courts, the Supreme Court and the British Privy Council.

The Privy Council decided that the province of Ontario could succeed in its claim if the Indian interest, which existed earlier in the land in question, were an interest less than the full fee simple interest of English property law. The Privy Council decided in favour of Ontario. The issue was that title had flowed to the province under s 109 of the *1867 British North America (BNA) Act* and that the treaty had extinguished Indian title (Elliott 1989: 57, 72). The idea that title flowed to the provinces under s 109 and that Treaty No. 3

extinguished Indian title was to become a crucial issue in British Columbia during the *Delgamuukw* case.

From the mid-nineteenth century onwards, BC's Aboriginal leaders struggled for years to gain political recognition of their Aboriginal rights. Despite almost 100 years of ongoing political efforts for recognition, it wasn't until the 1970s that frustrated Aboriginal peoples in Canada finally decided to take their valid concerns beyond the political arena, to the courts. By then, young leaders were becoming very political and publicly vocal. For example, it was against this background of generational leadership that in 1956, at age 15 years, I sat on the floor of a Vancouver hotel room listening to Native Brotherhood of BC (NBBC) leaders of the day (all of whom are now deceased) while they discussed Aboriginal issues.[7] They said, 'We need young people like you to go to school and get an education so you can help us settle the land question'. Today, we know the 'land question' as Aboriginal title and rights.

Organisations like the NBBC sprang up across Canada. The NBBC leadership believed in the Royal Proclamation of 1763 and trusted that the Queen of England could, and would, settle the land question. They had no reason to trust Canadian governments to do so. In 1959, the late Peter Kelly (1885–1966), Haida leader and BC Aboriginal rights activist, testified before a joint hearing of the Senate and House of Commons on Indian Affairs stating:

> But, gentlemen . . . so long as that title question is not dealt with, every Indian in British Columbia feels that he has been tricked, and he will never be satisfied . . . Let us say that it [will] be dealt with by the Supreme Court of Canada. (BC Historical Readings 204)

Nine years later, in 1968, the Nisga'a Nation in British Columbia decided to put title to the test. In *Calder v Attorney General of BC*, the Nisga'a sought a court declaration that they had Aboriginal title to their land, and that their title had not been terminated. The resulting 1973 decision in *Calder* did little to clarify the status of Aboriginal title, but it was significant, as David Elliott wrote, 'in its strong suggestion that Aboriginal title is not necessarily limited to the confines of the Royal Proclamation of 1763, but may be based on the concept of prior occupation of lands' (Elliott 1989: 75).

By 1975, the Calder case had forced the Canadian Government to implement a 'land claims policy' for the purpose of resolving the outstanding land claims that existed in non-treaty areas of Canada.[8] While any number of Aboriginal groups could get funding to conduct research in preparation for negotiations, the Canadian Government unilaterally stated at the time that it would actively negotiate with just six groups. One of these would be in British Columbia, with the Nisga'a Nation, resulting in the Nisga'a Treaty.

THE GENESIS OF THE DELGAMUUKW CASE

In BC, Gitxsan elders feared their Nisga'a neighbours would encroach on Gitxsan territory when settling their claim. For that reason, in 1975, nearly 100 Gitxsan elders met and instructed Gary Patsey, Alan Mason and me to develop a draft map showing the external boundaries of Gitxsan territory. Albert Tait (known also as *Delgamuukw*) was one of those elders. Two years later, on 7 November 1977, Gitxsan elders presented to the Canadian Government a draft map and statement of the claim we had prepared. Afterwards, the Gitxsan-Wet'suwet'en Tribal Council (GWTC) worked with Gitxsan and Wet'suwet'en elders to prepare for negotiations. By 1981, however, it was obvious that the Nisga'a claims process would take years to reach an agreement.[9] Negotiations were painfully slow because, consistent with Joseph Trutch's 110-year-old *terra nullius* policy, the government of the province of British Columbia refused at that stage to participate in land claims negotiations.

In the fall of 1981, a few days after, I was elected leader of the Gitxsan and Wet'suwet'en Nations, an alternate process presented itself.[10] Then-prime minister Pierre Trudeau decided to patriate the Canadian Constitution from Britain. Until 1982, Canada had been governed by a constitution that was a British law and could be changed only by an Act of the British Parliament with the consent of the Canadian Government. The Aboriginal people of Canada were incensed that the prime minister intended to patriate the constitution without involving Canada's First Peoples. Thousands of individuals and leaders from local, provincial and national Aboriginal organisations descended on Ottawa, the Canadian capital city, demanding that Aboriginal people be involved in the process. As a result, the prime minister and premiers relented. The prime minister scheduled four First Ministers Conferences with Canada's national Aboriginal leaders, to be held between 1983 and 1987.

The idea of including Aboriginal leaders in the First Ministers Conferences was unprecedented. However, it was clear by the close of the 1983 conference that Aboriginal expectations would not be met in the constitutional forum alone. Those of us involved in the process realised, first, that we needed to educate not only the First Ministers and their advisers but also ordinary Canadian citizens.[11] Second, we felt that another process was needed because the government lawyers and bureaucrats who were advising politicians in the First Ministers Conferences were also fighting us in the courts on fisheries, forestry and hunting-related issues.

The Gitxsan and Wet'suwet'en Nations decided to take the matter to court. On 23 October 1984, elders Delgamuukw (Albert Tait) and Gisday Wa (Alfred Joseph), accompanied by Wet'suwet'en leader, Victor Jim and me (as tribal council vice-president and president respectively), filed the Writ and Statement of Claim in the Smithers Court registry. A total of fifty-one plaintiffs stood up for the case: thirty-nine Gitxsan and twelve Wet'suwet'en. In the Writ and Statement of Claim, thirty-four of the final fifty-one potential plaintiffs (67%) had been born between 1890 and 1920.[12] These men and women had grown up on the land, speaking their languages (Gitxsanimx and Wet'suwet'en), and knew their histories, territories and laws. As leaders of the Tribal Council, we recognised that within a few short years, their on-the-land knowledge and legacy might be lost forever. This lent a sense of urgency to the case.

Lawyer Peter Grant, one of our early legal representatives in the case, recalls that there were lively discussions during a series of meetings among the elders about going to trial, with the Gitxsan and Wet'suwet'en sometimes meeting separately due to language differences.[13] Finally, Albert Tait spoke at the end of a lengthy Gitxsan meeting, summarising what he had heard and what he believed. The Gitxsan elders decided then that Albert would be the lead plaintiff for the Gitxsan. The Wet'suwet'en, during their deliberations chose Alfred Joseph (Gisday Wa) as their lead plaintiff, and all agreed that Delgamuukw (Albert Tait) would be the first-named plaintiff in the overall case.[14]

I began mapping and recording Gitxsan place names shortly after my family and I moved home to Hazelton in 1973, when I realised that many elders who were born and raised on the land were dying without passing on their knowledge (Sterritt 2016; Sterritt & Marsden 1998). The result was that, by 1987 when the trial began, we had recorded detailed territory and site information with more than 100 Gitxsan and Wet'suwet'en elders. We also gathered commissioned evidence from elders who were aged and frail and might not make it to trial.[15] Their evidence demonstrated the intimate relationship they had with their territories and, by extension, their knowledge of the collective comprising the Gitxsan and Wet'suwet'en Nations.

Unfortunately, believing that Albert Tait was healthy, we did not gather commissioned evidence from him. On a Sunday evening, four months before the trial was to commence, I phoned Albert to clarify some territories and place names he was familiar with. Fifteen minutes after our conversation ended, the phone rang. It was my sister who said, 'Neil. Albert is dead'.[16] I said, 'He can't be. I just finished talking to him and he was fine'. She said, 'Yes. He got up from his chair, went to the refrigerator and fell to the floor'. Albert Tait died on 18 January 1987 (four months before the case bearing his name would begin).

While Albert Tait was by no means the first Aboriginal person in our country to engage in the battle for recognition of our rights, his name is now synonymous in Canada with the achievement of a significant turning point in that lengthy struggle for recognition. For it was in the *Delgamuukw* case that the Supreme Court of Canada (1997) found that Aboriginal title at common law is protected in its full form by s 35(1) of the Canadian Constitution. So, who was this man? What can we learn from his personal and public 'trials' and what does his legacy hold for us as First Nations peoples across Canada and perhaps more widely?

ALBERT TAIT (1902–1987)

'Delgamuukw' is an ancient Gitxsan name meaning 'the talking copper'.[17] It has been passed on for generations and will continue to be held by one of Albert's great-nephews or nieces in the matriline, long into the future. It is both the name of a person and of a Gitxsan 'House' (an extended family), so it has important value for our collective identity and relationships.

Albert Tait was born on 16 May 1902. His first language was Gitxsanimx, and his education was a traditional one: he never attended a school and he was steeped in Gitxsan laws, culture and traditions. Albert was knowledgeable not only about his territories but also about the territories of many other Gitxsan hereditary chiefs. He grew up on the land, trapping, fishing, hunting and berry-picking. As an adult, Albert continued his traditional life but also became a man of many talents: a horseman and packer, carpenter and logger on the upper Skeena River, and a successful commercial fisherman at the Skeena Estuary in and around Prince Rupert, BC.[18] In many of these ways, Albert's life mirrored that of his fellow Gitxsan of the times.

I don't recall Albert being 'political' in the usual sense, but he was a wise man and listened carefully when others were speaking. He was also a patient man. After others had their say, he would speak, summarising what he had heard and only then offering his own considered opinion. As a leader, Albert Tait epitomised the Gitxsan saying: 'Sdinhl Xpaawhl Simoighet', that is, 'the chief's jaw is heavy, you don't flap your mouth and say nothing'. Albert Tait held the name Delgamuukw for 33 years, from 1954 until his death in 1987.

THE COURT TRIAL AND DECISION: *DELGAMUUKW V. BRITISH COLUMBIA*

The Gitxsan and Wet'suwet'en peoples, led by Delgamuukw (Albert Tait) and Gisday Wa (Alfred Joseph), claimed that they, their fellow plaintiffs and the people they represented,

- had a right to ownership and jurisdiction over their territories; and that
- the right of ownership and jurisdiction continues and has not been abandoned or lawfully extinguished.

The trial commenced on 11 May 1987. After a seemingly endless and stressful 318 days of evidence and 56 days of legal argument, the case concluded on 30 June 1990. As both a lay and an expert witness during the trial, I was on the stand for 33 days between mid-May and the end of October 1988.[19]

Chief Justice Allan McEachern rendered his decision on 8 March 1991, dismissing our claims to ownership and jurisdiction, concluding that Aboriginal customs ('if they could be described as laws') ceased to have any force after BC became a colony in 1858. The Chief Justice also found that any rights the Gitxsan and Wet'suwet'en had were extinguished by pre-confederation colonial land legislation.[20]

We appealed that decision to the BC Court of Appeal in 1993 with an amended claim in which Aboriginal title and self-government replaced ownership and jurisdiction and a communal claim by each nation replaced individual House territory claims. The BC Court of Appeal reversed the Supreme Court's extinguishment finding by rejecting the argument mounted by the government and accepted by the trial judge that certain land proclamations from the 1860s extinguished Aboriginal title. The Gitxsan and Wet'suwet'en chiefs, after extensive internal discussions and review of the Western legal meaning of 'aboriginal title', amended their claim to Aboriginal title while understanding that it encompassed their authority over the land and resources.[21]

Lawyers for the Gitxsan and Wet'suwet'en appeared before the Supreme Court of Canada on 16 and 17 June 1997. The Supreme Court handed down its decision on 11 December 1997, finding that Aboriginal title did encompass the rights of the Gitxsan and Wet'suwet'en chiefs, as the proper title holders, to make decisions over their Aboriginal title lands and resources.[22]

As a consequence of the successful appeal, Aboriginal title, therefore,

- is held by Aboriginal people in their traditional homelands;
- at common law is protected in its full form by s 35 (1);[23]
- is the right to exclusive use and occupation of land for a variety of purposes (subject to justifiable Crown interference, or purposes which would destroy the people's relationship to the land);[24]
- is a collective right held by all members of an Aboriginal nation as a whole (not by individual Aboriginal persons);[25] and
- is a *sui generis* right that 'arises from possession before the assertion of British Sovereignty'.[26]

The Supreme Court also found that the trial judge had made serious errors in his treatment of oral histories when he discounted the witnesses' evidence of personal knowledge on use of the land and in his treatment of territorial affidavits filed by the chiefs to establish House ownership of specific territories (Rush 1998).

Finally, the Court found that there is a fiduciary duty by federal and provincial governments to accommodate Aboriginal title when it is infringed and a duty to consult with Aboriginal nations in good faith. Specifically, consultation requires that,

- the Aboriginal nation be informed about the proposed infringing measures; and
- the nation be given full information on the effect of the proposed measure (Rush 1998: 186).

Interestingly, many Canadian court cases considered the Australian *Mabo* High Court case both before and after the 1997 *Delgamuukw* decision. Also, Indigenous and legal parties involved in the *Delgamuukw* case visited Australia in 1998 for the purpose of discussing its implications in Australia.

GOVERNANCE DURING THE RECOGNITION ERA

Our own internal governance late in this 'recognition' era (from about 1965 onwards) had much in common with North American protest movements. When a provincial game warden or federal conservation officer charged our people with hunting or fishing offences, rather than remain silent and allow our people to plead guilty in court, we hired lawyers and challenged the charges. If logging threatened an environmentally sensitive area, we blockaded the company. When a railroad was to be built into a previously pristine area, again, we set up a blockade.

Eventually, we became very effective at making ourselves heard, and we won some important cases. But equally it could be said that we were in reactive mode; that is, we were reacting to externally determined challenges and constraints posed by colonial governments. This mean that, in general, we had clear, albeit short-term, goals; broad community support, probably because we had a common focus (or foe); and governing institutions that may have lacked sophistication but worked well as oppositional modes of decision-making. It also meant that we built our credibility through protests and blockades, created uncertainty for government and industry, and grew increasingly effective politically and in the courts.

In that context, in June 1977, Bill Blackwater Senior[27] approached me while I was taking a Gitxsan art and carving course at 'Ksan.[28] He said, 'I have an office for you in Kispiox. We want you to set up our land claims office, and you can start tomorrow'. Although I had been a tribal council adviser since 1973, by accepting Bill's offer, I became the first full-time employee of the Gitxsan-Wet'suwet'en Tribal Council (GWTC). Later, from

1981 to 1987, I held the position of GWTC president. The creation of a land claims office was an intuitive strategic move on Bill's part. Within a month, we discovered that the Department of Fisheries and Oceans (DFO) had set up an undercover 'sting' operation and was charging Gitxsan and Wet'suwet'en fishermen (elders and otherwise) with selling food fish illegally. Those charged came to my office and complained. I discussed the situation with Bill Blackwater and other tribal council leaders. We decided to hire lawyers and fight the charges. A year later, the trial judge had acquitted all twenty persons. The DFO was stunned.

Over the years, we changed the Canadian Constitution. We went on to win major court cases. Some of our nations signed treaties, and the national and provincial governments began to devolve programmes and services to us. But what it took for us to be successful then wouldn't necessarily work in the future. We wanted self-government and got it. Now what were we going to do with it?

We had to make a huge shift into an implementation era: we had to become proactive governors, not reactive protestors. This shift in focus became most evident in the Yukon where, by the year 2000, many Yukon First Nations had negotiated treaties. There, the First Nations discovered that, as difficult and time-consuming as negotiating a treaty is, it was relatively 'easy' compared to successfully implementing the treaty. Securing lasting benefits from such court victories has proven to be similarly challenging for us in Canada and, I suspect, elsewhere in other countries for Indigenous peoples.

THE IMPLEMENTATION ERA (1992–2012): TRIALS OF ANOTHER TYPE

Nevertheless, in the early days of our court successes, there was optimism in Canada that First Nations would regain rights and real recognition, influenced in part by the 1993 treaty process and the 1997 *Delgamuukw* decision. First, the hope was that the cases would result in real change in our communities through the practical application of enlightened government legislation and policies.

Second, the hope was that the Indigenous leadership would be capable of building upon their court victories and assuming the renewed responsibilities that should accompany native title rights. We realise today that our optimism was unfounded. While the Supreme Court decision recognised our title and rights, subsequent government legislation and policies undermined it. Rather than enhance Indigenous self-determination, Canadian governments continued to obstruct it.[29] Among our own leadership ranks, the implementation era demanded new kinds of leadership skills and experience. While some leaders found it hard to adapt, others worked to transform Gitxsan understandings of leadership's requirements in this new era.

In 1990, the BC First Nations Summit (hereafter 'the Summit') established the BC Claims Task Force for the purpose of exploring options to address the land claims process. The Task Force included representatives of the Summit, British Columbia and Canada.[30] The 1991 Task Force Report recommended the creation of an independent body to oversee a 'made-in-BC' treaty process.[31] As a result, the BC Treaty Commission (BCTC) was established in 1992 as an independent body responsible for facilitating treaty negotiations among the governments of Canada, BC and BC's First Nations. The Treaty Commission and a six-stage treaty process were designed to advance negotiations and facilitate fair and durable treaties.[32]

In carrying out the recommendations of the BC Claims Task Force, the Treaty Commission has three roles: facilitation, funding, and public information and education. The Treaty Commission's primary role is to oversee the negotiation process to make sure that the parties are being effective and making progress in negotiations.[33]

The 1997 Supreme Court decision in *Delgamuukw* resulted in a range of responses across Canada, but its main impact would be felt in British Columbia, given that the province had refused to deal with Aboriginal title and rights since 1871. There was optimism among BC's Aboriginal peoples and anxiety and concern among industry and governments. In May 1998, the Summit held a business forum at which Aboriginal leaders recognised the *Delgamuukw* ruling could lead to partnerships between Aboriginal and non-Aboriginal communities. Later in the year, also recognising that implementing *Delgamuukw* would require a new level of governance skills among First Nations, Aboriginal leaders and the federal and provincial governments established a 'Capacity Panel' (Hurley 1998: 16). It appears that this Indigenous recognition of the need for governance capacity-building happened much sooner in Canada after the *Delgamuukw* decision than in Australia after *Mabo*. One result of the 'Capacity Panel' initiative was the creation in 2006 of the National Center for First Nations Governance (NCFNG). Several years later, an Institute for First Nations Data Sovereignty[34] was established in BC to promote and regain control over First Nations knowledge and data.

The BC Treaty Commission process marked its twentieth anniversary in 2012. But progress had been at a snail's pace, with only two finalised treaties to its credit since 1992: the Tsawwassen Treaty in 2009 and the Maa-nulth Treaty in 2011.[35] In her 2011 annual report, the Chief Commissioner Sophie Pierre told Indigenous leaders, the prime minister of Canada and the premier of BC: 'Get it done, or shut it down'.[36]

Between May 1993 and March 2018, the BC Treaty Commission had provided $730m (Canadian $567m loan funding and $163m in non-repayable contributions) in negotiation support funding to more than fifty BC First Nations. After twenty-five years, many BC First Nations were still in Stage 4 Agreement-in-Principle negotiations. BC lawyer Stuart Rush has argued that the Treaty Commission process is 'on the ropes because the federal/provincial governments provide minimal mandates and are dishonest regarding *Delgamuukw* directives'.[37]

As lawyer Louise Mandell argued, an important reason that treaties have not been concluded in BC is because government negotiation mandates remain out of alignment—not only with court cases with which Crown governments disagree but also with international norms and standards. This calls into question whether we are in a post-implementation phase at all: colonial doctrines continue to inform Canadian and provincial government litigation positions and the de facto political status quo remains one of government dominance, denial and delay in having the 'land question' resolved equitably.[38]

While government legislation and policies are obviously a large part of the problem, nevertheless, we must acknowledge that there are problems on the Aboriginal side too. Part of the problem is structural, by virtue of geography and circumstance. Many Canadian First Nation communities are small, remote and have limited economic potential.[39] For example, the average membership across all 617 First Nation communities in Canada is 1,260 persons, with about half the population residing off reserve in major cities.[40] This means the average number of members (adults and children) living in a First Nation community is about 600 persons. Of the 617 communities, 400 have less than 1,000 members (less than 500 if half live away), and 200 communities have less than 500 members (less than 250 if half live away). The median age of First Nation's members is 27 years (versus 40 years for non-Aboriginal Canadians).[41]

Even when Aboriginal organisations have economies of scale, they often lack formally educated members to run their institutions. This is the Inuit challenge for Nunavut self-government. The Inuit have 50,000 members and jurisdiction over 20,388,320 square kilometres of territory in Canada's north, but the Nunavut civil service is largely staffed by non-Inuit.[42]

Canadian journalist Jeffrey Simpson wrote that, 'The small population of most First Nations makes the ambition to have their own people staff their institutions difficult, or improbable'. Simpson further observed, 'There are huge geographic challenges—many [First Nations] reserves are isolated from larger population centers, [are] difficult to service and situated on land with limited economic potential'.[43] Simpson also points out that while the Inuit of Nunavut 'have the population [50,484 members] to make the claim of sovereignty a real one, the Nunavut's terrible disappointment is a lack of formally educated Inuit to run their own administration'.[44] Thus, when economies of scale do exist, other structural factors affect our ability to be truly self-determining.

As the demographics above reveal, too many of our communities are small, remote and lacking in the economies of scale to effectively deliver a broad range of services (i.e. schooling, health, policing, roads, housing, welfare, taxation, membership, justice, etc.). Finally, we often lack formally educated Indigenous people to run our institutions. These challenges of building internal capabilities among our nations are now taking on greater prominence as we assume weightier governing responsibilities arising from our treaty and court successes.

A NEW ERA OF GOVERNANCE BUILDING

It is arguable that Canada's modern-day treaty process has not met the 1998 expectations of Delgamuukw or his Indigenous peers. The question is, should we be surprised? Which leads us to ask another more fundamental question: Who is responsible for this outcome? Perhaps it's time we recognised that Canada's Indigenous policies are meant to contain and undermine native title and rights, not recognise and enable them. But equally, perhaps it's also time to recognise that our own reactive governance approach no longer suits the needs of our own people, or the demands of the times we live in.

That being the case, if we want self-government, then we have to exercise it ourselves and exercise it well. Arguably, however, many Canadian First Nations are currently finding it difficult to build and exercise effective governance over matters they have some authority over, let alone being able to take on greater governance responsibility for significantly expanded areas of jurisdiction. As stated earlier in this chapter, the success rate of treaty negotiations in BC has been dismal: just two treaties concluded in eighteen years out of the sixty being negotiated by 2010, and five more between 2010 and 2019. Consequently, in thinking about pathways for the future, I suggest there are two ways for Indigenous nations and our representative governments and organisations to begin the governance-rebuilding process: incrementally and comprehensively.

The Incremental Approach

In an incremental approach to self-government, a First Nation might select a single major project or area as its strategic priority (e.g., education, a business enterprise, housing) and focus its energy there by developing a business plan with logical targets, ensuring human and other resources are available to achieve the goal, and so forth. Mistakes may be made, but learning from those mistakes is an important part of the governance process. But once the First Nation has achieved its strategic priority, it can set another priority, pursue that one, achieve success and move on to yet another.

Any organisation, large or small, can take an incremental approach to self-government, but the incremental approach is especially suited to smaller organisations and First Nations. Successful examples of the incremental approach in British Columbia include the Osoyoos, Westbank and Squamish First Nations, along with the Nisga'a[45] and Haida Nations, and the Coastal First Nations (CFN).[46] Having participated in the negotiation and conclusion of the Maa-nulth Treaty, Huuay-aht First Nation citizen, Angela Wesley (see also chapter 7 of this volume) contends 'that you can't move into a comprehensive approach without already having done (or are well into) the incremental approach'.[47] Perhaps the reason Australia has produced so many agreements since its own *Native Title Act 1993* is that the native title claim mediation process allows for an incremental approach with multiple agreement-making outcomes along the way to the bigger ambition of getting a native title consent determination. By accident or design, it allows Indigenous Australian claimants to proceed at a more measured pace, with time to consider and negotiate their own chosen strategic objectives.

The underlying question in the incremental process, of course, is: Do we wish to be self-determining, and if so, when and how do we get there? Therefore, an additional consideration is whether the accumulated increments will add up to progressively expanding self-determination over the longer term, or simply become a series of administrative and service-delivery responsibilities with little jurisdictional weight.

The Comprehensive Approach

By contrast, Canada's modern-day treaty process is a classic example of a comprehensive approach to self-government, in which an extremely broad range of issues may be considered simultaneously. These might include, for example: a constitution and by-laws, duties and powers of governing bodies (a council, elders, a judicial council, youth), a membership code, election code, justice and law-making powers, relations with other governments (federal, provincial, municipal) and industry, wildlife management, capital works, education, housing, taxation and delegation of powers.

A comprehensive approach to self-government may be better suited to a large First Nation or to an alliance that represents a number of First Nations. Nevertheless, the process still requires experienced, capable leaders and resource people, and a genuine commitment to openness, transparency and setting strategic priorities. Continuity of good leadership through succession planning is also advantageous, as is the ability of leaders to sustain their energies on long-term strategic priorities.

Any First Nation lacking such qualities will struggle with the treaty process, and small First Nations are likely to have an especially difficult time.

Apart from ideological reasons, this perhaps is one of the main reasons why there has been such a lack of progress under the BC Treaty Commission process: it asks a lot of small First Nations with limited capacities to engage in massively demanding negotiations in search of comprehensive solutions.[48] The treaty process, in other words, is not a panacea or an instant solution to governance problems. On the contrary, it can bring underlying internal governance tensions and weaknesses to the foreground.

THE LEGACY OF DELGAMUUKW

If we expect to be self-determining, then perhaps it must be a new form of sovereignty that we strive to exercise. This will only occur if we become capable governors. Capable governance is the first step, self-government comes next, and out of that a renewed form of self-determination may ultimately follow. Indeed, it is arguable that if our First Nations today do not become better governors, then the very rights we fought so long to have recognised may be overturned, weakened and lost. The price of our rights must be eternal governance vigilance!

In 2012, Sir Mason Durie, an eminent New Zealand Maori leader, noted that progress and implementation have 'frequently been compromised by a lack of clarity around goals, insufficient human capability, inadequate resources, constitutional discouragement, and sets of relationships that have fragmented Maori resolve' (quoted in Smith 2012: 12). Sir Mason added that:

> Achieving a successful treaty or land claims negotiation often necessitates carrying out an entire restructuring of existing governance arrangements. What worked for people to get them through negotiations is not necessarily what will work to implement those (arrangements). Success propels people from thinking about past grievances to having to think about future need. (quoted in Smith 2012:15)

From the Gitxsan and broader BC experience, it is also clear how important it is to have input from as many members as possible and continue to do so. Nuu Chah Nulth leader, George Watts (1945–2005) was one of the more visionary Aboriginal leaders in British Columbia.[49] Not long before he died, Watts had this to say about nation-building and the treaty process:

> This treaty stuff is so complex and so intense, there is no one person that can do it, and the best thing you can do is have a good team. Every human being has an opinion that is worth something. You may think sometimes that you have all

> the ideas and then you go somewhere, and they bring out a new idea and you'll say, 'Yeah! That's a good idea.' And so, in my opinion the more ideas you get out on the table, the better chance our people will have of success.[50]

Clearly there will be no magic leap from 'rights-recognition' in the courts, to self-government or self-determination. We need to be practical and we need to begin with effective governance. But even that won't be easy, given the demographic, institutional and structural obstacles common in many First Nations communities. The size and remoteness of our communities; the chance of having and retaining experienced, educated Aboriginal people with capacity and skills; of being able to build organisations with economies of scale; and of having access to economic opportunities, all present significant challenges for governance-building. Nevertheless, we have to find innovative ways to meet this challenge, and perhaps eventually we will have to make some difficult decisions. How can we make a start? How can we build on the legacy left to us by great men such as Delgamuukw and his peers?

Unfortunately, many First Nations tend to take governance shortcuts. After gaining recognition of their rights and jurisdiction, they go directly to choosing and implementing projects rather than taking the time to build an enduring governance foundation. As a result of the many processes (political, legal, constitutional) where we have been successful over the last forty years, including the *Delgamuukw* decision, we are achieving the first step. But, if we want to be successful over a period of many years, during which time there may be changes in leaders and membership, we must develop stable institutions that will guarantee the continuity of our governance. That is the purpose of a properly designed constitution, by-laws and policies. A constitution also defines the distribution of powers between the members and their leaders. A corporate charter fulfils a similar purpose, but for a business enterprise. In other words, a governance-building phase is critical for the eventual success of Indigenous nations or groups. This will lead us to being more confidently able to identify our strategic priorities, and to choose projects based on those priorities, and implement them successfully.

A critical factor in each of these steps in building effective governance is communications, for effective implementation is directly related to the extent of support and engagement from our First Nation citizens. Angela Wesley, as chair of the Huu-ay-at Constitution committee, was instrumental in the development and community ratification of the Maa-nulth Treaty in BC. Angela explained that her nation,

> only began to get support for their work in the constitution rebuilding after one person made it their business to carry out thorough, informal and face-to-face discussions with all family members. That woman's efforts in knocking on doors and

> listening to people turned around many negative positions. [Angela emphasized:] It was only then that community trust, confidence and support for new ways of doing things were forthcoming. (quoted in Smith 2012: 16; see also this volume)

In fairness, a small First Nation with excellent leadership, a strong vision and strategic priorities can successfully negotiate and implement a treaty. The Tsawwassen First Nation, with just 325 members and a small land base is such a case. They had an exceptional leader in Chief Kim Baird, and a council and administration with depth of leadership and skills, along with a succession plan that brought in a capable young man as Baird's successor. Like the Maa-nulth, through good communications with all Tsawwassen First Nation members, excellent governance, superior negotiating skills and carefully chosen advisers, this tiny group nevertheless emphasises the importance of the steps outlined above that are needed for governance-building. Moreover, the Tsawwassen First Nation has unlimited access to economic opportunities, being strategically located at the Tsawwassen seaport within 25 kilometres of the city of Vancouver.

My experience with Yukon treaties, however, is that successfully negotiating a treaty, as difficult as that may be, is often 'easier' than implementing one. One of the main reasons for this is that governments tend to provide the financial resources needed to enable First Nations leaders to engage in the process, along with funds to hire professional advisers, but leave communities high and dry afterwards. Also, the BC treaty negotiations process is rich in funds and has become big business for those who are more interested in the process than they are in results. For example, a tribal administrator in British Columbia once told me that the treaty process does not meet his expectations for the following reasons:

- His communities lack the necessary level of sophistication and experience to negotiate and implement a treaty;
- Most communities have two-year terms of office, leading to a leadership continuity problem; and
- New leaders don't generally understand how the federal and provincial governments work (any more than the average Canadian citizen does), and their offices may not have the administrative capacity and records to enable new leaders to be brought up to speed on the nation's treaty files.

Similarly, Sacha McMeeking, a young Maori leader, has no illusions about this. She recently pointed out that

> there is an entire Indigenous generation of young people whose careers and involvement in Indigenous issues have occurred in [this] era—in the

> post-settlement, post-treaty and post-declaration of rights environment. (quoted in Smith 2012: 15)

Sacha and other young leaders like her not only have a 'different viewpoint on history and what's possible' than those of us who are the older generation of leaders and have been involved for many decades. They have good reason to be 'impatient and to expect proper implementation and practical outcomes' (quoted in Smith 2012: 15).

So, what should the enduring legacy of Delgamuukw the man be? Surely it is not just the trial outcomes but rather it must ensure better lives for his grandchildren and great grandchildren, and for all Indigenous peoples. If we are going to realise the hard work and legacy of such transformative leaders, then we have a responsibility to defend and build on the rights they helped win. The work of rebuilding or refashioning governance for a new 'implementation era' is precisely so that rights can be maintained and strengthened, and real outcomes delivered to (and by) a new generation of young Indigenous people.

How can we do that? How can we rebuild effective governance that will strengthen self-determination rather than undermine it? And deliver real outcomes that are proactive rather than reactive? What would a new kind of effective practical sovereignty look like? I believe Delgamuukw would expect us to do as he did: that is, focus on creating opportunities and lifestyle choices for our grandchildren, and their grandchildren. In doing so, individually as leaders and collectively as First Nations, we will need to:

1. Be strategic about choosing between incremental and comprehensive approaches to change. As First Nation leaders, we are flooded by the demands of government, industry, and our own people. We need to put such demands into perspective and we need to be both strategic and realistic about our resources and capacity. Given the size and remoteness of many of our communities, community leaders may wish to concentrate on as few as one or two achievable priorities, achieve success there, and then build on their success. In other words, seriously consider a strategic incremental approach. With continued success, community leaders can consider tackling a broader range of issues in a comprehensive approach.
2. Look at the phases and steps such as those that have been experienced by the Gitxsan and use them to develop a strategic approach to rebuilding our nation's governance and identifying priorities and the approach to be taken. The idea of strategic phases or steps is a useful tool for First Nation leaders and community members. They help us keep our goals and processes in perspective.

3. Ask the hard questions along the way to ensure that our governance solutions continue to work as we want them to. In other words, make sure we monitor and periodically review our checks and balances.
4. Ensure that the governance capacity and confidence of our people are being actively developed and continuously promoted, in parallel with implementing other strategic goals and agreements. Don't leave this till a crisis strikes.
5. But in addition, also make sure our community is behind our leadership and that our leadership is credible. There are countless stories told of leaders getting so far out in front of their members with a major project or treaty that when the time comes for community ratification it fails because the members are hearing about the details for the first time.
6. Look hard at genuine cultural solutions—adhere to culture, not cult.[51] We have survived as Aboriginal people because of our cultural institutions and values. Enduring cultural values require us to be respectful, inclusive, honest and accountable. Anyone who has a good idea, regardless of their status, is valuable to the community. Therefore, leaders who embrace cultural integrity work hard to unite all their citizens, not just those who support their ideas and goals.
7. Leaders must include their members in community planning and implementation. As George Watts said, credible leaders work hard to involve and unite the entire community or nation, as the case may be.
8. Make sure succession plans are in place and that young leaders can contribute their new ideas now, not later. Too often, charismatic leaders have been amazingly successful, but when they retire or fail in their leadership bid, the community falls apart. Leaders build for the future by mentoring youth who will carry on their good work long into the future.
9. Create genuine strategic alliances with other Aboriginal nations and with non-Aboriginal supporters. For example, shared decision-making is the norm on Haida Gwaii, thanks in part to the alliance they have with their fellow citizens. Non-native supporters can help compel governments to make systemic changes and implement Indigenous laws on the ground. Many people, not just Aboriginal peoples, want this to happen.

The Royal Proclamation of 1763 reflected international law, which has become part of the common law of Canada. Perhaps international law can close the circle compelling honourable Crown conduct in Canada and other settler-colonial states (see Australian Human Rights Commission 2012). But, given the lessons of our own histories, we should not wait. We need to do the hard work of getting our own 'governance houses' in order. That would constitute a proper honouring of the legacy of this extraordinary man. Delgamuukw would expect no less.

In conclusion, no matter what rights are achieved, community leaders and members have to be able to put their hard-won rights into practice in order to exercise them. British Columbia has had a modern treaty process that has experienced some valued success (with seven treaties signed), but with considerable wrangling (over content, land ownership, boundaries and membership). The costs have been high and ongoing.[52] For example, as Palmer wrote, 'In the ensuing 25 years, the [BC Treaty Commission] allocated about $730m in negotiation support to some 60 BC First Nations, [of which] $163m was in outright grants, the rest in loans repayable to the federal government'.[53] Meanwhile, as Palmer further noted, 'two-thirds of [BC's] 203 First Nations . . . have not chosen to join the [treaty] process in the first place'.[54] For example, it is arguable that the Gitxsan Nation is no closer to concluding a treaty today than they were when entering the treaty process in the mid-1990s, despite our 1997 Supreme Court victory.

The important lesson to be learned from this discussion is that leadership does make a difference, not just for securing rights but—even more importantly—for subsequently governing those rights. In other words, the leadership required to govern effectively may have to be different at different stages of the whole process. There may be a different kind of leadership and governance needed for the rights recognition battle and different leadership skills needed for the rights implementation phase. This means we need leaders who can grow and mature in their own skills and insights: who can be self-aware and able to adapt and who continue to keep the whole nation in their hearts.

So where do we go from here? Perhaps those of us who helped bring the Gitxsan Nation to this stage in our rights challenges need to reflect on how we got here. It is clear that Gitxsan Elders—men and women—steeped in Gitxsan history, culture and language during the mid-twentieth century recognised the need to involve youth with a balance of contemporary skills and experience to assist them in their quest. Today, nearly three-quarters of a century later, there are young Aboriginal men and women, many of them professionals in their own right, who must become involved and take us the rest of the way in our contemporary governance journey. They are, and must be, today's bridge to a successful future for each Aboriginal nation.

NOTES

1. James Anaya, UN Special Rapporteur on the Rights of Indigenous Peoples. Keynote presentation at the Common Roots, Common Futures conference, University of Tucson, Tucson, Arizona, 12 February 2012. Refer Chapter One of this publication.

2. The Gitxsan are an Indigenous nation comprising a total of about 7,000 people today, and have inhabited the upper Skeena and Nass River valleys in northwest British Columbia for at least 4,000 years.

3. The Proclamation set out the core elements of the relationship between First Nations and the Crown and established the recognition of First Nations rights in Canada. See www.aadnc-aandc.gc.ca.

4. The notion of extinguishment is an interpretation advanced by the Crown's governments in Canada based on the written text. The First Nations who concluded the numbered treaties did not understand 'surrender' and don't accept that the treaty accomplished this (Louise Mandell, pers comm., August 2012).

5. Shortly after colonisation in 1849, the British Government transferred Vancouver Island to the Hudson's Bay Company, at which time Chief Factor Douglas became governor of the colony. Originally, therefore, the 14 treaties Douglas negotiated were on behalf of the company, not Britain (Banner 2007: 204–05).

6. In 23 June 1850; see Joseph Trutch Papers, University of BC Library, folder A1.b.

7. These influential early leaders included people such as Johnny Clifton, Harold Sinclair, Guy Williams, Forest Walkem, Bill Roberts, Howard Wale, Walter Harris and others.

8. In the Yukon and Northwest Territories, northern Quebec and nearly all of British Columbia.

9. Almost two decades later, on 11 May 2000, the Nisga'a Final Agreement came into effect. It was BC's first modern-day land claims agreement under the 1970's comprehensive claims process. The Nisga'a Agreement has the status of a treaty under Canada's Constitution.

10. At the time, the elected councils of seven Gitxsan and Wet'suwet'en First Nations (i.e. band councils) elected the board of directors of the Gitxsan-Wet'suwet'en Tribal Council. I served six one-year terms as president. By 1990, the tribal council had adopted a more traditional process.

11. BC First Nations leaders included Edward John, Joe Mathias, George Watts, James Gosnell, Rod Robinson, Philip Paul, Wendy Grant-John, Rose Charlie, Jeanette Armstrong, Ardythe Cooper and many others from every province and territory in Canada.

12. For example, Gitluudaahlxw, Moses Morrison (1897–1985), died a year after the Writ was filed. Maxlaxleek, Johnny David (1890–1994) died before the Supreme Court decision in 1997.

13. Counsel for the plaintiffs included Stuart Rush, Peter Grant, Louise Mandell, Michael Jackson, Murray Adams, Stanley Gunther, Leslie Pinder, Michael Fleming and David Paterson.

14. See Monet and Wilson (1992), which features portraits, cartoons and text about the drama behind the three-year trial.

15. See Sterritt et al. (1998), which provides information about the nature of evidence presented during the trial.

16. For example, Shirley Muldon, whose husband, Earl Muldon, became *Delgamuukw* in 1991.

17. Copper shields were considered the ultimate symbol of wealth among northwest coast First Nations peoples, with some valued at a thousand Hudson's Bay blankets (Emmons 1991: 182).

18. Mule and horse pack trains arrived in the northwest in the 1860s, and before long, the Gitxsan adapted and became expert 'packers'.

19. The BC Provincial Government took the view that the case was brought by us as tribal council leaders, not by the hereditary chiefs. Also, having gained mapping skills while working in minerals exploration for thirteen years, and having worked with the hereditary chiefs throughout their territories, I qualified as a cartographer at trial.

20. The three periods of treaty-making in Canada are: Pre-Confederation Treaties during the colonial period (from the Royal Proclamation in 1763 to 1867); the Numbered Treaties (from 1871 to 1930); and modern-day treaties (from 1975 to the present).

21. Peter Grant, lawyer for the Plaintiffs (pers comm., June 2019).

22. Peter Grant, lawyer for the Plaintiffs (pers comm., June 2019).

23. *Delgamuukw v. British Columbia, [1998]* 1 CNLR 14 [SCC], para 133.

24. *Delgamuukw*, paras 117, 165, 128.

25. *Delgamuukw*, para 115.

26. *Delgamuukw*, para 114.

27. Bill Blackwater was then Chief Councillor of the Kispiox Band Council and a member of the Gitxsan-Wet'suwet'en Tribal Council.

28. The 'Ksan Association ran an Indian art course that taught northwest coast design, including the carving of rattles, masks, totem poles, the production of silk screen prints, and carving of silver and gold bracelets, pendants, and so on.

29. See Stephen Cornell, 'From rights to governance—and back: Transformations in Indigenous politics'. Invited lecture, Joseph A. Myers Center for Research on Native American Issues, University of California, Berkeley, 19 April. Unpublished public lecture.

30. Chief Joe Mathias (c. 1944–2000), Miles G. Richardson, Audrey Stewart, Murray Coolican, Grand Chief Edward John, Tony Sheridan and Allan Williams, QC (1922–2011).

31. See details at: www.bctreaty.ca/sites/default/files/BC_Claims_Task_Force_Report_1991.PDF.

32. The six stages are: 1. Statement of intent, 2. Confirm readiness, 3. Framework agreement, 4. Agreement-in-principle, 5. Final agreement, and 6. Treaty implementation.

33. See BC Treaty Commission (2019) website, available at www.bctreaty.ca (accessed 14 August 2019).

34. See University of British Columbia, Blockchain@UBC, available at blockchain.ubc.ca (accessed 14 August 2019).

35. Although Sliammon First Nation citizens had approved their treaty, the governments of Canada and British Columbia had yet to ratify it.

36. BC Treaty Commission Update, January 2012, available at www.bctreaty.ca.

37. Stuart Rush, also a lawyer on the *Delgamuukw* legal team (pers comm., May 2012).

38. Louise Mandell, another *Delgamuukw* lawyer (pers comm., 26 August 2012). See also *Williams v British Columbia*, 2012 BCCA 285.

39. The 2016 Canadian Census enumerated 1,673,785 Aboriginal persons. This included the Inuit (65,025 members), Metis (587,545) and First Nations (1,021,215) peoples. (Statistics Canada, available at www12.statcan.gc.ca.

40. BC Treaty Commission Update, January 2012, available at www.bctreaty.ca.

41. Human Resources and Skills Development Canada, *Canadians in Context: Aboriginal Population* 2011, available at (google: "*median age First Nations people 2011*").

42. The territory of Nunavut includes 20,388,320 square kilometres of land and 160,579 square miles of water (Wikipedia).

43. Jeffrey Simpson, *Globe and Mail*, 8 August 2009.

44. Jeffrey Simpson, *Globe and Mail*, 8 August 2009.

45. Nisga'a leaders successfully negotiated the 'School District 92 Nisga'a' on 1 January 1975. It was the first Aboriginal school district in British Columbia.

46. The CFN is an alliance of nine First Nations and the Haida Nation along the northwest coast of British Columbia in the area known as the Great Bear Rain Forest.

47. Angela Wesley, pers comm., 1 October 2012.

48. As of July 2012, two treaty 'tables' had concluded treaty negotiations with 58 tables at various stages of the six-stage process, as follows: Stage 2—six First Nations, Stage 3—two First Nations, Stage 4—forty-four First Nations, and Stage 5—six First Nations. However, the BC Treaty Commission's use of the term 'First Nation' is misleading, as some parties included in the figures are 'tribal entities' that represent a number of First Nations. Therefore, of 201 First Nations in BC, 116 are currently in the treaty process, not 58.

49. The Nuu Chanulth Nation territory includes St. George's Sound (later Nootka Sound), where Captain Cook spent from 29 March to 26 April 1779, before sailing north.

50. George Watts quoted in New Journey Productions, Maa Nulth Treaty Celebration Video Production, n.d., at 00:01:42, https://newjourney2011.wordpress.com.

51. Cult-like behaviour occurs where all teaching and guidance comes from the top. In such structures, governance can become vulnerable to leaders who are divisive and manipulative, and undermined by interpretations of 'culture' which are not only romanticised and unrealistic but also exploit 'culture' as a shield to deflect or stifle legitimate comment. Red flags include systemically weak governance, self-serving behaviour by leaders, and their rejection of all criticism as illegitimate.

52. There are currently nine First Nations in Final Stages negotiations, five in Advanced Agreement in Principle negotiations, 17 in Active Negotiations and 27 not currently negotiating a treaty (BC Treaty Negotiations Update, Overview 2017–2018: 27–9. www.bctreaty.ca.

53. Vaughn Palmer (2019, 22 March) *Feds forgive treaty loans, but will it revive painfully slow process,* available at Vpalmer@postmedia.com.

54. Vaughn Palmer (2019, 22 March).

References

Aboriginal and Torres Strait Islander Commission (ATSIC) and Australian Institute for Aboriginal and Torres Strait Islander Studies (AIATSIS). 2003. *Treaty: Let's Get It Right*. Canberra: Aboriginal Studies Press.

Aboriginal and Torres Strait Islander Healing Foundation. 2017. *Bringing Them Home 20 years on: An Action Plan for Healing*. Available at https://healingfoundation.org.au/app/uploads/2017/05/Bringing-Them-Home-20-years-on-FINAL-SCREEN-1.pdf.

Aboriginal First Nations. 2017. Uluru Statement from the Heart. Available at https://www.referendumcouncil.org.au/sites/default/files/2017-05/Uluru_Statement_From_The_Heart_0.PDF.

Abourezk, K. 2018. 'Tribes face obstacles at troubled Indian Health Service Facility'. Indianz.com, 18 July. Available at https://www.indianz.com/News/2018/07/16/tribes-face-obstacles-at-troubled-indian.asp.

Adams, A. 2000. The road not taken: How tribes choose between tribal and Indian Health Service management of health care resources. *American Indian Culture and Research Journal* 24(3), 21–38.

AIATSIS. (n.d.). The Barunga Statement. https://aiatsis.gov.au/collections/collections-online/digitised-collections/treaty/barunga-statement.

Aboriginal and Torres Strait Islander Commission (ATSIC). 2011. Agreements, Treaties and Negotiated Settlements Project. Available at https://www.atns.net.au/agreement.asp?EntityID=618.

Alfred, T. 2001. From sovereignty to freedom: Towards an Indigenous political discourse. *Indigenous Affairs* (3), 22–34. Copenhagen: International Work Group for Indigenous Affairs.

Alfred, T. 2009. *Peace, Power, Righteousness: An Indigenous Manifesto*. Oxford: Oxford University Press.

Alfred, T. and Corntassel, J. 2005. Being Indigenous: Resurgences against contemporary colonialism. *Government and Opposition* 40(4), 597–614.

Allen, L. 2012. 'Red Lake Nation Fishery Capitalizes on Wild-Caught Walleye'. *Indian Country Today Media Network*, 18 June. https://newsmaven.io/indiancountrytoday/archive/red-lake-nation-fishery-capitalizes-on-wild-caught-walleye-uRkVyWFcn0SIe8GVbmFgjg/.

American Indian Policy Review Commission. 1977. *Final Report*. Submitted to Congress 17 May. Available at: http://files.eric.ed.gov/fulltext/ED164229.pdf.

Anaya, J.S. 1991. Superpower attitudes toward Indigenous peoples and group rights. *American Society of International Law* 93(24–27), 251–260.

Anaya, J.S. 2008. 'Obervaciones del relator especial sobre la situation de derechos humanos y libertades funamentales de los Indigenes acerca del proceso de revision constitucional en la Ecuador', Special Report by the UN Special Rapporteur, 2008. Available at http://unsr.jamesanaya.org/list/special-reports.

Anaya, J.S. 2009. International norms on the right to consultation in relation to constitutional reform concerning Indigenous peoples in Chile. Special Report by the UN Special Rapporteur, 2009. Available at http://unsr.jamesanaya.org/list/special-reports.

Anaya, J.S. 2010. Statement by Professor James Anaya, Special Rapporteur on the situation of the human rights and fundamental freedoms of Indigenous people. Ninth Session of the United Nations Permanent Forum on Indigenous Issues, New York, 22 April 2010. Available at http://www.un.org/esa/socdev/unpfii/documents/statement%20by%20SR.pdf.

Anaya, J.S. 2011a. Measures needed to secure Indigenous and tribal peoples' land and related rights in Surinam. Special Report by the UN Special Rapporteur, 18 August 2011. Available at http://unsr.jamesanaya.org/list/special-reports.

Anaya, J.S. 2011b. Report of the Special Rapporteur on the rights of Indigenous peoples, Addendum: The situation of the Sami people in the Sápmi region of Norway, Sweden and Finland. Human Rights Council, 6 June 2011. Available at https://www.ohchr/Documents/Issues/IPeoples/SR/A-HRC-18-35-Add2_en.pdf .

Anaya, J.S. 2011c. Report of the Special Rapporteur on the rights of Indigenous peoples –The situation of Māori people in New Zealand. Available at http://unsr.jamesanaya.org/country-reports/the-situation-of-maori-people-in-new-zealand-2011.

Anaya, J.S. 2013a. Index of reports of the Special Rapporteur on the rights of Indigenous peoples, by theme and region, 6 September 2013. Available at http://unsr.jamesanaya.org/list/special-reports.

Anaya, J.S. 2013b. Report to the Human Rights Council. Study on extractive industries and Indigenous people, summary of activities. Available at http://unsr.jamesanaya.org/annual-reports/report-to-the-human-rights-council-a-hrc-24-41-2013.

Anaya, J.S. 2013c. Report to the General Assembly. Summary of activities. Identifying work methods and lessons learned. Factors that debilitate commitment to and action by states and other factors to implement the Declaration on the Rights of Indigenous Peoples. Available at http://unsr.jamesanaya.org/list/annual-reports-to-the-human-rights-council-and-general-assembly.

Anderson, D. 2006. 'Rebirth. Renewal. Red Lake'. *Minneapolis Star Tribune*, 7 May. Available at www.startribune.com.

Anderson, I., et al. 2016. 'Indigenous and tribal peoples' health'. *The Lancet-Lowitja Institute Global Collaboration* 388(10040), 131–57. DOI: 10.1016/S0140-6736(16)00345-7.

Anderson, K. and Perrin, C. 2007. The miserablest people in the world: Race, humanism and the Australian Aborigine. *The Australian Journal of Anthropology* 18(1), 18–39.

Anthony, T. 2010. 'Learning from ATSIC.' ABC News, 1 June. Available at www.abc.net.au/news/2010-01-06/27934.

'Aravind eye hospitals are social entrepreneurship companies'. 2019. *602 Communications*. Available at http://602communications.com/aravind-eye-hospitals-social-entrepreneurship-companies/.

Archibald, L. 2006. *Decolonization and healing: Indigenous experiences in the United States, New Zealand, Australia and Greenland*. Ottawa, Ontario: Aboriginal Healing Foundation.

Asch, M. (ed.). 1998. *Aboriginal and Treaty Rights in Canada*. Vancouver: UBC Press.

Atkinson, J. 2013. Trauma-informed services and trauma-specific care for Indigenous Australian children. Closing the Gap Clearinghouse, Resource Sheet 21. Available at https://earlytraumagrief.anu.edu.au/files/ctg-rs21.pdf.

Attwood, B. 2009. *Possession: Batman's Treaty and the Matter of History*. Carlton, Vic: Miegunyah Press.

Australian Broadcasting Corporation (ABC). 2018. 'SA Government decides not to go ahead with Aboriginal treaties.' ABC News, 8 June. Available at https://www.abc.net.au/news/2018-06-08/sa-govt-decides-not-to-go-ahead-with-aboriginal-treaty/9851166.

Australian Government. (n.d.). *Indigenous Peoples and cultures. Our People*. Available at https://www.australia.gov.au/about-australia/our-country/our-people.

Australian Government. 1991. *Royal Commission into Aboriginal Deaths in Custody, National Report*. Canberra: Australian Government. Available at http://www.austlii.edu.au/au/other/IndigLRes/rciadic/index.html.

Australian Government. 2019. *Northern Australia Agenda*. Department of Industry, Innovation and Science. Available at https://www.industry.gov.au/strategies-for-the-future/northern-australia-agenda.

Australian Human Rights Commission. 2012a. *Social Justice Report 2012*. Aboriginal and Torres Strait Islander Social Justice Commissioner. Available at https://www.humanrights.gov.au/sites/default/files/document/publication/social_justice_report_2012.pdf.

Australian Human Rights Commission. 2012b. *The Community Guide to the UN Declaration on the Rights of Indigenous Peoples*. Available at www.humanrights.gov.au.

Australian Human Rights Commission. 2019. *Close the Gap – 10 Year Review: 2018*. Available at https://www.humanrights.gov.au/our-work/aboriginal-and-torres-strait-islander-social-justice/publications/close-gap-10-year-review.

Australian Indigenous Governance Institute (AIGI). 2016. Canberra: Australia. Available at https://www.aigi.com.au/.

Australian Indigenous Governance Institute (AIGI). 2018. Canberra: Australia. Available at https://www.aigi.com.au/.

Australian Indigenous Governance Institute (AIGI). 2019. Indigenous Governance Toolkit. Available at http://toolkit.aigi.com.au/.

Australian Indigenous Governance Institute and Reconciliation Australia, 2018. 'Strong Governance Supporting Success: Stories and Analysis from the 2016 Indigenous Governance Awards'. Prepared by Wighton, Alice. Canberra, ACT. Available at http://toolkit.aigi.com.au/.

Australian Institute of Aboriginal and Torres Strait Islanders (AITSIS). (n.d.). The Barunga Statement. Available at https://aiatsis.gov.au/collections/collections-online/digitised-collections/treaty/barunga-statement.

Avery, C. 1918. 'Minnesota's Experiment in State Fishing'. *Transactions of the American Fisheries Society* 48(1), 57–64.

Awatere, S., Mika, J., Hudson, M., Pauling, C., Lambert, S. and Reid, J. 2017. Whakatipu rawa ma ngā uri whakatipu: Optimising the "Māori" in Māori economic development. *AlterNative: An International Journal of Indigenous Peoples* 13(2), 80–88.

Banner, S. 2005. Why terra nullius? Anthropology and property law in early Australia. *Law and History Review* 23(1), 95–132.

Banner, S. 2007. *Possessing the Pacific: Land, Settlers, and Indigenous People from Australia to Alaska.* Cambridge, MA: Harvard University Press.

Bardis, P. 1979. Social interaction and social processes. *Social Science* 54(3), 147–67.

The Barefoot College. (n.d.). The Barefoot Story. Available at https://www.barefootcollege.org/about/.

Bargh, M. 2013. Multiple sites of Māori political participation. *Australian Journal of Political Science* 48(4), 445–55. Available at https://doi.org/10.1080/10361146.2013.841123.

Bargh, M. 2016. Opportunities and complexities for Māori and mana whenua representation in local government. *Political Science* 68(2), 143–60. Available at https://doi.org/10.1177/0032318716671765.

Barr, L. and Reid, J. 2014. Centralized decentralization for tribal business development. *Journal of Enterprising Communities: People and Places in the Global Economy* 8(3), 217–32.

Barrett, M. 2014. Seki Sworn in as 6th Tribal Chairman of the Red Lake Nation. *Red Lake Nation News/Babaamaajimowinan* (Telling of news in different places), 3 July, p. 45.

Barsh, R and Trosper, L. 1975. Title I of the Indian Self-determination and Education Assistance Act of 1975. *American Indian Law Review* 3(2).

Batiwala, S. 2012. *Changing their World: Concepts and Practices of Women's Movements* (2nd ed.). Toronto: Association for Women's Rights in Development (AWID).

Battiliana, J., Lee, M., Walker, J. and Dorsey, C. 2012. In search of the hybrid ideal. *Stanford Social Innovation Review* 10(3), Summer.

Bauman, T., Smith, D., Quiggin, R., Keller, C. and Drieberg, L. 2015. *Building Aboriginal and Torres Strait Islander Governance: Current and Future Research and Practical Resource Needs*. Report for Australian Institute of Aboriginal and Torres Strait Islander Studies (AIATSIS) & Australian Indigenous Governance Institute. Canberra, ACT: AIATSIS. Available at https://aiatsis.gov.au/sites/default/files/products/research_outputs/bauman_building-indigenous-governance_web.pdf.

Begay, M., Cornell, C., Pryor, N. and Jorgensen, M. 2007. Rebuilding Native Nations: What do leaders do? In M. Jorgensen (ed.), *Rebuilding Native Nations: Strategies and Governance and Development*, pp. 275–295. Tucson: The University of Arizona Press.

Begay, M. Cornell, S., Jorgensen, M. and Kalt J. 2007. Development, Governance, Culture: What are they and what do they have to do with rebuilding Native Nations, In M. Jorgensen (ed.), *Rebuilding Native Nations: Strategies for Governance and Development.* Tucson: University of Arizona Press.

Behrendt, L. 2003. *Achieving Social Justice. Indigenous Rights and Australia's Future*. Sydney: Federation Press.

Berg, S. 2010. *Coming to Terms: Aboriginal Title in South Australia*. Adelaide: Wakefield Press.

Berry, A. 2009. Two forests under the big sky: Tribal v. federal management. In R. Meiners (ed.), *PERC Policy Series No. 45*, June. https://www.perc.org/wp-content/uploads/old/ps45.pdf.

Black Bear Casino Resort. (n.d.). Hope page. Available at http://www.blackbearcasinoresort.com/.

Blackshield, T. and Williams, G. 2010. *Australian Constitutional Law and Theory: Commentary and Materials* (5th ed.). Annandale, NSW: Federation Press.

Blaser M., Feit, H.A. and G. McRaie (eds). 2004. *In The Way of Development: Indigenous Peoples, Life Projects and Globalisation*. London: Zed Books Ltd.

Borch, M. 2001. Rethinking the origins of terra nullius. *Australian Historical Studies* 32(117), 222–39.

Borkholder, B.D., Edwards, A.J. and Olson, C.A. 2002. Biological, physical, and chemical characteristics of the Cloquet River from Indian Lake to Island Lake, 2000–2001. A Joint Report of the 1854 Authority and the Fond du Lac Division of Resource Management, Fond du Lac Division of Resource Management, Technical Report No. 36, August 2002. Available at http://www.1854treatyauthority.org/management/biological-resources/fisheries/reports.html?id=40&task=document.viewdoc.

Bowden, C. 2010. 'Native Lands'. *National Geographic* 218(2) August, 80–97.

Bowman, M. and Curry-Roper, J. 1982. *The Houma People of Louisiana: A Story of Indian Survival*. Houma, LA: United Houma Nation.

Boyd, T. 2011. 'Sauteed Walleye Fillets with Tarragon.' *Christian Science Monitor*, 24 May. https://www.csmonitor.com/The-Culture/Food/Stir-It-Up/2011/0524/Sauteed-walleye-fillets-with-tarragon.

Brennan, B. 'Call for investigation of numbers of Indigenous children in care'. *ABC News*, 31 January, audio file. Available at https://www.abc.net.au/radio/programs/am/call-for-investigation-into-number-indigenous-children-in-care/9377632.

Brennan, S., Behrendt, L., Strelein, L. and Williams, G. 2005. *Treaty*. Sydney: Federation Press.

Brenneman G.R., Handler, A.O., Kaufman, S.F. and Rhoades, E.R. 2000. Health status and clinical indicators. In E.R. Rhoades (ed.), *American Indian Health: Innovations in Health Care, Promotion, and Policy*, pp. 103–21. Baltimore, MD: Johns Hopkins University Press.

British Columbia Claims Task Force. 1991. *The Report of the British Columbia Claims Task Force*. Prepared for The First Nations of British Columbia, The Government of British Columbia and The Government of Canada. 28 June. Available at http://www.bctreaty.ca/sites/default/files/BC_Claims_Task_Force_Report_1991.pdf.

British Columbia Government. (n.d.). First Nations Negotiations. Available at http://www.treaties.gov.bc.ca/treaties_maa-nulth.html.

Broderstad, E.G. 2014. Implementing Indigenous self-determination: The case of the Sámi in Norway. In M. Woons (ed.), *Restoring Indigenous Self-Determination Theoretical and Practical Approaches*, pp. 72–79. Bristol: E-International Relations www.E-IR.info.

Brown, E., Hicks, S., and Jorgensen, M. 2002. *Imagining a New Future for American Indian Human Service Systems*. St. Louis, MO: Kathryn M. Buder Center for American Indian Studies, Washington University.

Bulloch, H. 2018. *In Pursuit of Progress. Narratives of Development on a Philippine Island*. Honolulu, Hawaii: University of Hawaii'i Press.

Burnie, R. 2019. 'Aboriginal Healers treat patients alongside doctors and nurses at Lyell McEwin Hospital'. *ABC News*, 20 February. Available at https://www.abc.net.au/news/2019-02-20/aboriginal-healers-treat-patients-alongside-doctors-and-nurses/10826666.

Bush Foundation. 2019. About us. Available at https://www.bushfoundation.org/about-us.

Bush Foundation, The Wilder Group. 2015. Lessons Learned from the Native Nations Initiative. Available at https://www.bushfoundation.org/learning/bush-papers/lessons-learned-native-nations-initiative.

Bush Foundation, Allen, C.L. 2018. Lessons from the Process of Creating the Native Governance Center. Available at https://www.bushfoundation.org/sites/default/files/public/32-3514_bush_foundation_whitepaper-v2.pdf.

Bylander, J. 2017. Designing a health system that works for the tribe. *Health Affairs* 36(4), 592–95.

Campbell, M., and Anaya, J.S. 2008. The case of the Maya villages of Belize: Reversing the trend of government neglect to secure Indigenous land rights. *Human Rights Law Review* 8(2), 377–99.

Carter, M. 2006. Greening the Ghetto. TED video. Available at https://www.ted.com/talks/majora_carter_s_tale_of_urban_renewal/transcript?language=en.

Cassidy, J. (n.d.). The stolen generations – Canada and Australia: The legacy of assimilation *Deakin Law Review* 11(1), 131–72.

Cassidy, J., Champagne, D., Torjenson, K.J. and Steiner, S. 2005. *Indigenous Peoples and the Modern State*. California: Altamira.

Castile, G. 1998. *Taking Charge. Native American Self-determination and Federal Indian Policy 1975 – 1993*. Tucson: University of Arizona.

Cawthorn, M. 2019. 'Role and function of a PBC'. Prescribed Body Corporate website. Available at https://www.nativetitle.org.au/learn/role-and-function-pbc/about-pbcs.

Central Land Council (CLC). 2013. Strong Aboriginal Governance, Report of the Tennant Creek Aboriginal Governance Summit, May 2013, CLC and Aboriginal Peak Organisations of the Northern Territory. Available at https://www.clc.org.au/files/pdf/APONT_Governance_Summit_2013_report.pdf.

Centre for First Nations Governance (CFNG). 2008. Principles to support effective governance. CFNG Discussion document. Available at http://www.fngovernance.org/publication_docs/Governance_Principles2008.pdf.

Cesar Chavez Foundation. 2016. What we do. Available at https://chavezfoundation.org/.

Champagne, D and Goldberg, C. 2012. *Captured Justice: Native Nations and Public Law 280*. Durham: Carolina Academic Press.

Chandler, M. and Lalonde, C. 2009. Cultural continuity as a moderator of suicide risk among Canada's First Nations. In Laurence J. Kirmayer and Gail Guthrie Valaskakis (eds), *Healing Traditions: The Mental Health of Aboriginal Peoples in Canada,* pp. 1–57. Vancouver: University of British Columbia Press.

Chapman, T. 2017. *Te Ao Māori: Trends and Insights*. Available at https://www.chapmantripp.com/Publication%20PDFs/2017%20Chapman%20Tripp%20Te%20Ao%20Maori%20-%20trends%20and%20insights%20E-VERSION.pdf.

Charles Sturt University. (n.d.). The Graduate certificate in Wiradjuri language, culture and heritage. Available at https://study.csu.edu.au/courses/teaching-education/graduate-certificate-wiradjuri-language-culture-heritage.

Charters, C. and Stavenhagen, R. 2009. The UN Declaration on the Rights of Indigenous Peoples: How it came to be and what it heralds. In C. Charters and R. Stavenhagen (eds), *Making the Declaration Work: The United Nations Declaration on the Rights of Indigenous Peoples*, pp. 1–14. International Work Group for Indigenous Affairs, Copenhagen 2009 Document No 127, New Jersey: Transaction Publishers. Available at http://www.internationalfunders.org/documents/MakingtheDeclarationWork.pdf.

Cheyne, C. M. and Tawhai, V. M. 2007. He wharemoa te rakau, ka mahue. Māori engagement with local government: Knowledge, experiences and recommendations. (A research project supported by the Royal Society of New Zealand Marsden Fund). Available at https://mro.massey.ac.nz/bitstream/handle/10179/7723/hwtrct.pdf?sequence=1&isAll owed=y.

Christensen, N. 2003. *Inuit in Cyberspace: Embedding Offline Identities Online*. Copenhagen: University of Copenhagen, Museum Tusclulanum Press.

Ciupa, K. 2017. The promise of rights: International Indigenous rights in the neoliberal era. In H. Brabazon (ed.), *Neoliberal Legality: Understanding the Role of Law in the Neoliberal Project*, pp. 140–66. London: Routledge.

Clarkson, G. 2006. Tribal bondage: Statutory shackles and regulatory restraints on tribal economic development. Paper #06-006, University of Michigan. Available at https://www.law.umich.edu/centersandprograms/lawandeconomics/abstracts/2006/Documents/06-006clarkson.pdf.

Clements, N., Clapton, J., and Chenoweth, L. 2010. Indigenous Australians and impaired decisionmaking capacity. *Australian Journal of Social Issues* 45(3), 383–93.

Commonwealth of Australia. 1991. *Royal Commission into Aboriginal Deaths in Custody, National Report.* Vol. 1. Canberra: Australian Government.

Commonwealth of Australia, 1997. *Bringing Them Home: The Stolen Children Report.* Canberra: Aboriginal and Torres Strait Islander Social Justice Commissioner, Human Rights Commission. Available at https://humanrights.gov.au/our-work/aboriginal-and-torres-strait-islander-social-justice/publications/bringing-them-home.

Commonwealth of Australia. 2019. *Australia's Faunal Extinction Crisis. Interim Report.* 3 April. Parliament House, Canberra: Senate Environment and Communications References Committee. Available at https://www.aph.gov.au/Parliamentary_Business/Committees/Senate/Environment_and_Communications/Faunalextinction/Interim_report.

Cooke, M., Mitrou, F., Lawrence, D., Guimond, E. and Beavon, D. 2007. Indigenous well-being in four countries: An application of the UNDP'S Human Development Index to Indigenous Peoples in Australia, Canada, New Zealand, and the United States. *BMC International Health Human Rights* 7, 9.

Cooper, D. 2001. Against the current: Social pathways and the pursuit of enduring change. *Feminist Legal Studies* 9(2), 119–48.

Cornell, S. 1988. *The Return of the Native: American Indian Political Resurgence.* New York: Oxford University Press.

Cornell, S. 2002. Nation-building and the treaty process. *Indigenous Law Bulletin* 5(17), 7.

Cornell, S. 2007a. Organizing Indigenous governance in Canada, Australia, and the United States. In J.P. White, S. Wingert, D. Beavon and P. Maxim (eds), *Aboriginal Policy Research: Moving Forward, Making a Difference* (vol. 4). Toronto: Thompson Educational Publishing.

Cornell, S. 2007b. Remaking the tools of governance: Colonial legacies, Indigenous solutions. In M. Jorgensen (ed.), *Rebuilding Native Nations: Strategies for Governance and Development*, pp. 57–77. Tucson: University of Arizona Press.

Cornell, S. 2012. From rights to governance – and back: Transformations in Indigenous politics. Invited lecture, Joseph A. Myers Center for Research on Native American Issues, University of California, Berkeley, 19 April.

Cornell, S. 2013. Reconstituting native nations: Colonial boundaries and institutional innovation in Canada, Australia, and the United States. In R. Walker, T. Jojola, and D. Natcher (eds), *Reclaiming Indigenous Planning*, pp. 35–59. Kingston, Ontario: McGill-Queen's University Press.

Cornell, S. 2015a. 'Wolves have a constitution': Continuities in Indigenous self-government. *The International Indigenous Policy Journal* 6(1), 16–31.

Cornell, S. 2015b. Processes of native nationhood: The Indigenous politics of self-government. *The International Indigenous Policy Journal* 6(4), 1–30.

Cornell, S. 2019. From rights to governance and back again: Indigenous political transformation in the CANZUS states. In W. Nikolakis, S. Cornell, H. Nelson, S. Pierre and G. Phillips (eds), *Reclaiming Indigenous Governance: Reflections and Insights from Australia, Canada, New Zealand, and the United States*, pp. 15–27. Tucson: University of Arizona Press.

Cornell, S., Begay, M., Kalt. J. and Jorgensen M. (eds), 2007. *Rebuilding Native Nations: Strategies for Governance and Development*. Tucson: University of Arizona Press.

Cornell, S., Curtis, C. and Jorgensen, M. 2004. The concept of governance and its implications for first nations. Native Nations Institute and The Harvard Project on American Indian Economic Development, Joint Occasional Papers on Native Affairs No. 2. Available at https://hpaied.org/sites/default/files/publications/The%20Concept%20of%20Governance%20and%20its%20Implications%20for%20First%20Nations.pdf.

Cornell, S. and Kalt, J.P. (eds). 1992. *What Can Tribes Do? Strategies and Institutions in American Indian Economic Development*. Los Angeles: American Indian Studies Center, UCLA. Available at https://hpaied.org/.

Cornell, S. and Kalt, J.P. 1995. Where does economic development really come from? Constitutional rule among the contemporary Sioux and Apache. *Economic Inquiry* 33(3), 402–26.

Cornell, S. and Kalt, J.P. 2000. Where's the glue? Institutional and cultural foundations of American Indian economic development. *The Journal of Socio-Economics* 29(5), 443–70.

Cornell, S. and Kalt, J.P. 2007. Two approaches to the development of Native nations: One works, the other doesn't. In M. Jorgensen (ed.), *Rebuilding Native Nations: Strategies for Governance and Development*, pp. 3–33. Tucson: University of Arizona.

Corntassel, J. 2012. Re-envisioning resurgence: Indigenous pathways to decolonization and sustainable self-determination. *Decolonization: Indigeneity, Education and Society* 1(1), 86–101.

Cosens, B. and Chaffin, B. 2016. Adaptive governance of water resources shared with Indigenous peoples. *Water* 8(3), 97. University of Idaho.

Coulthard, G.S. 2014. *Red Skin, White Masks: Rejecting the Colonial Politics of Recognition*. Minneapolis, MN: University of Minnesota Press.

Crepelle, A. 2018a. Standing Rock in the swamp: Oil, the environment, and the United Houma Nation's struggle for federal recognition. *Loyola Law Review* 64(141), 141–86. Available at https://dspace.loyno.edu/xmlui/handle/123456789/61?show=full.

Crepelle, A. 2018b. The United States first climate relocation: Recognition, relocation, and Indigenous rights at the Isle de Jean Charles. *Belmont Law Review* 6(1). Available at https://www.oxfordamerican.org/magazine/item/1816-goodbye-to-good-earth.

Curry-Roper, J. 1982. Houma blowguns and baskets in the Mississippi River Delta. *Journal of Cultural Geography* 2(2), 13–22.

Da Silveira. M. 2014. Human rights and social change in Angola. *Sur International Journal on Human Rights* 11(20), 212–212.

Dacin, M.T., Dacin, P.A., and Tracey, P. 2011. Social entrepreneurship: A critique and future directions. *Organization Science* 22(5), 1203.

Dahl, J. 2001. Self-government in Greenland. *Indigenous Affairs* 3, 34–41.

Davis, M. 2006. Treaty, yeah? The utility of a treaty to advancing reconciliation in Australia. *Alternative Law Journal* 31(3), 127–36.

Davis, M. and Langton, M. (eds). 2016. *It's Our Country: Indigenous Arguments for Constitutional Reform*. Melbourne: Melbourne University Press.

de la Sablonnière, R. 2017. Toward a psychology of social change: A typology of social change. *Frontiers in Psychology* 8, 397–397.

DeGagne, M. 2007. Towards an Aboriginal paradigm of healing: Addressing the legacy of residential schools. *Australasian Psychiatry* 15, 49–53.

DeMello, M. 2012. *Faces around the World: A Cultural Encyclopaedia of the Human Face*. ABC-CLIO.

Dixon, M. 2001. The unique role of tribes in the delivery of health services. In M. Dixon and Y. Roubideaux (eds), *Promises to Keep: Public Health Policy for American Indians and Alaska Natives in the 21st Century*. Washington, DC: American Public Health Association.

Dixon, M., Shelton, B., Roubideaux, Y., Mather, D. and Smith, C. 1998. *Tribal Perspectives on Indian Self-Determination and Self-Governance in Health Care Management*. Denver, CO: National Indian Health Board.

Dodson, M. 2012. Constitutional recognition of Indigenous Australians. *Papers on Parliament* 57, 11–22.

Dodson, M. and Smith, D.E. 2003. *Governance for Sustainable Development: Strategic Issues and Principles for Indigenous Australian Communities*. CAEPR Discussion Paper 250. Canberra, ACT: Centre for Australian Economic Policy Research (CAEPR), Australian National University.

Dodson, M., Bailey, P. and Wood, A. 2016. Australia and the international protection of Indigenous rights. In D.R. Rothwell and E. Crawford (eds), *International law in Australia*, pp. 139–64. Riverwood, NSW, Australia: Thomson Reuters.

Doherty, B., Haugh, H. and Lyon, F. 2014. Social enterprises as hybrid organizations: A review and research agenda. *International Journal of Management Reviews* 16(4), 417–36.

Dokken, B. 1999. 'The Big One that Got Away'. *Grand Forks Herald*, 6 February. Available at www.grandforkherald.com.

Dokken, B. 2000. 'A Tale of Two Lakes'. *Minnesota Conservation Volunteer* 63(369) March-April, 8–19.

Dokken, B. 2005. 'Red Lake Walleye Regulations Take Shape: Lower Limit, Protected Slot Expected to be Key Parts of DNR Plan'. *Grand Forks Herald*, 20 March, Section C (Outdoors), p. 10.

Dokken, B. 2009. 'Red Lake Recovery: Tribe to Resume Limited Netting'. *Grand Forks Herald*, 15 March. https://www.grandforksherald.com/sports/2093405-red-lake-recovery-tribe-resume-limited-netting.

Dokken, B. 2014. 'Red Lake 15 Years Later: Historic Agreement the Red Lake Band of Chippewa and Minnesota DNR Signed in April 1999 Produced Walleye Recovery'.

Bemidji Pioneer, 5 April. Available at https://www.bemidjipioneer.com/sports/2487169-red-lake-15-years-later-historic-agreement-red-lake-band-chippewa-and.

Dokken, B. 2016. 'Red Lake Walleye Make Comeback, but Not Without Pain'. *Twin Cities Pioneer Press*, 15 May. https://www.twincities.com/2016/05/13/red-lake-walleye-make-comeback-but-not-without-pain/.

Dolan, J. 2009. 'Do good things for the fish': Organizational innovation in tribal governance. Unpublished doctoral dissertation. Department of Sociology, University of Arizona, Tucson, AZ.

Dolan, J., Record, I., Jorgensen, M. and Briggs, E. 2015. The Red Lake Walleye Recovery Project. Cambridge, MA: Harvard Project on American Indian Economic Development.

Duarte, M.E. 2017. Connected activism: Indigenous uses of social media for shaping political change. *Australasian Journal of Information Systems* 21, 1–12.

Durie, M. 1999. Te Pae Māhutonga: A model for Māori health promotion. *Health Promotion Forum of New Zealand Newsletter* 49, 1–8.

Durie, Sir Mason, 2012. Towards Self-determination: Māori Pathways in Decade Two, Paper presented to the 'Common Roots, Common Futures Indigenous Governance Network' Workshop, University of Arizona, Tucson Arizona, 20–22 February 2012.

Duthu, B. 1997. The Houma Indians of Louisiana: The intersection of law and history in the federal acknowledgment process. *Louisiana History: The Journal of the Louisiana Historical Association* 38(4), 409–36. Available at https://www.jstor.org/stable/pdf/4233444.pdf?seq=1#page_scan_tab_contents.

Economic Commission for Latin America and the Caribbean (ECLAC). 2014. *Guaranteeing Indigenous Peoples Rights in Latin America. Progress in the Past Decade and Remaining Challenges*. Economic Commission for Latin America and the Caribbean, The Latin American and Caribbean Demographic Centre. Commissioned by United Nations Permanent Forum on Indigenous Issues (UNPFII) and the Continental Network of Indigenous Women of the Americas. Available at https://repositorio.cepal.org/bitstream/handle/11362/37051/4/S1420782_en.pdf.

Edwards, K., Morris, P and Red Thunder, S. 2009. *Exercising Sovereignty and Expanding Economic Opportunity through Tribal Land Management*. Washington, DC: Neighborworks America.

Elkin, A.P. 1938. *The Australian Aborigines: How to Understand Them*. Sydney: Angus & Robertson.

Elliott, D.W. 1989. Aboriginal title. In B.W. Morse (ed.), *Aboriginal Peoples and the Law*, Carleton: Carleton Library Series, Carleton University Press.

Elliott, M. 2017. Indigenous resurgence: The drive for renewed engagement and reciprocity in the turn away from the state. *Canadian Journal of Political Science* 51, 1–21.

Emmons, G.T. 1991. *The Tlingit Indians*. Washington: AMNH.

Encyclopaedia Britannica. 2019. White Australia policy. Available at https://www.britannica.com/event/White-Australia-Policy.

Encyclopaedia Britannica. (n.d.). Environmental costs. Available at https://www.encyclopedia.com/places/united-states-and-canada/us-political-geography/houma.

Enger, J. 2017. 'Fish Guts, Heritage Tomatoes: Red Lake Works to Feed Its Own.' *Minnesota Public Radio*, 12 September.

Environmental and Energy Study Institute. 2015. White House task force on climate preparedness and resilience: Recommended actions. Issue brief, April. Available at https://www.eesi.org/files/IssueBrief_White_House_Climate_Task_Force_Recommendations_040115.pdf.

Erickson, D.S. 2015. 'Mille Lacs Lake Problems: It's about the Fish.' *Mazina'igan: A Chronicle of the Lake Superior Ojibwe*, Fall.www.glifwc.org>mazinaigan.summer2007.

Escobar, A. 2008. *Territories of Difference. Place, Movements, Life, Redes*. London: Duke University Press.

Espey D.K., Jim, M.A., Cobb, N. et al. 2014. Leading causes of death and all-cause mortality in American Indians and Alaska Natives. *American Journal of Public Health* 104(3), 303–311.

Evans, L. 2011. *Power from Powerlessness: Tribal Governments, Institutional Niches, and American Federalism*. New York: Oxford University Press.

Evans, M.E. 2016. Navigating the territories of Indigenous leadership: Exploring the experiences and practices of Australian Indigenous arts leaders. *Leadership* 12(4), 470–90.

Expert Panel on Constitutional Recognition of Indigenous Australians, 2012. *Recognising Aboriginal and Torres Strait Islander Peoples in the Constitution: Report of the Expert Panel*. Canberra: Commonwealth of Australia.

Farmboy1. 2006. Red Lake restocking efforts. Forum post 5 May, In-depth Outdoors Upper Red Lake fishing forum. Available at https://www.in-depthoutdoors.com/community/forums/topic/ftlnorthernmn_328407/.

Feeney, M. 2009. Reclaiming the spirit of well being: Promising healing practices for Aboriginal and Torres Strait Islander people. Discussion paper for Stolen Generations Alliance. Available at http://earlytraumagrief.anu.edu.au/files/Feeney_HealingDiscussionPaper_2009-1.pdf.

Feir, D., Gillezeau, R. and Jones, M. 2018. The slaughter of the bison and reversal of fortunes on the Great Plains. Working Paper 2019-01, Center for Indian Country Development, Minneapolis Federal Reserve Bank. Minneapolis, Minnesota.

Ferguson, D. 2016. 'Tribal leaders move to cut out IHS middleman'. *Argus Leader*, 9 June. Available at https://www.argusleader.com/story/news/2016/06/09/ihs-rapid-city-hospital-no-longer-immediate-jeopardy/85642454/.

Ferrell, S.J. 2001. The concepts of self-determination and autonomy of Indigenous peoples in the draft United Nations Declaration on the Rights of Indigenous Peoples. *St. Thomas Law Review* 14(2), 259–70.

First Nations of Quebec and Labrador Health and Social Services Commission. 2015. Indigenous governance models and initiatives across Canada. First Nations in Quebec health and social services governance project. Available at http://www.cssspnql.com/docs/default-source/centre-de-documentation/css_1509_gouvern_mcgill_an_webf.pdf?sfvrsn=2; https://aifs.gov.au/cfca/publications/what-works-effective-indigenous-community-managed-programs-and-organisations/export.

Fischer, A. 1965. History and current status of the Houma Indians. *Midcontinent American Studies Journal* 6(149), 150–51.

Fisher, R. 1981. Joseph Trutch and Indian land policy. In W.P. Ward and R. McDonald (eds), *British Columbia Historical Readings*. Vancouver: Douglas & McIntyre Ltd.

Fitzsimmons, H. 2016. 'Victorian Government to begin talks with First Nations on Australia's first Indigenous treaty'. ABC *News* online, 26 February. Available at http://www.abc.net.au/news/2016-02-26/victoria-to-begin-talks-for-first-indigenous-treaty/7202492.

Fletcher, A and Christin, Z. 2015. The value of nature's benefits in the St Louis River Watershed. United States Environmental Protection Agency. Earth Economics, Tacoma, WA.

Fletcher, M. 2006. The iron cold of the Marshall trilogy. *North Dakota Law Review* 82(3), 627–96.

Fodder, T.A. (n.d.). Indigenous Governance Programs in America and New Zealand. The Māori and Indigenous Governance Centre. University of Waikato, NZ. Available at https://www.waikato.ac.nz/__data/assets/pdf_file/0010/211123/Indigenous-Governance-Programs-in-US-and-NZ-web-preview.pdf.

Fodder, T.A., Davis-Ngatai, P. and Jospeh, R. 2014. Retracing our steps: A Maori governance overview and literature review. The Maori and Indigenous Governance Centre, University of Waikato, NZ. Available at https://www.waikato.ac.nz/law/research/centre-for-maori-and-indigenous-governance/research-and-publications.

Fond du Lac Band of Lake Superior Chippewa. 2019a. Home page. Available at http://www.fdlrez.com.

Fond du Lac Band of Lake Superior Chippewa. 2019b. Tribal government. Available at https://www.leagle.com/decision/infco20130114091

Fond du Lac Casino. 2018. Home page. Available at http://www.fondduluthcasino.com/.

Fond du Lac Tribal Government. 2018. Onigamiinsing Dibaajimowinan Duluth's stories. Available at http://www.duluthstories.net/treaties.html.

Fond du Lac Tribal Government. 2019a. *Fond du Lac Band of Lake Superior Chippewa, Strategic Plan 2019–2025*. FDL Tribal Government. Available at: http://www.fdlrez.com/planning/downloads/2019FDLStrategicPlan.pdf.

Fond du Lac Tribal Government. 2019b. FDL Resource Management. Available at http://www.fdlrez.com/RM/index.htm.

Foster, H. and Grove, A. 2003. *BC Studies* 138/139, Summer, 51–84.

French, R. 1992. The race power: A constitutional chimera. In H.P Lee and G. Winterton (eds), *Australian Constitutional Perspectives*, 180. LBC.

Gallagher, J. 2019. Moment of Truth. Available at https://victreatyadvancement.org.au/sites/default/files/inline-files/Correspondence-%20Jill%20Gallagher.pdf (unofficial).

Gammage, B. 2012. *The Biggest Estate on Earth: How Aborigines Made Australia*. Sydney: Allen & Unwin.

Gaudet, M.G. and McDonald, J.C. (eds). 2003. *Mardi Gras, Gumbo, and Zydeco: Readings in Louisiana Culture*. Jackson, Louisiana: University Press of Mississippi, USA.

Gooda, M. 2014. *Social Justice and Native Title Report*. Canberra: Australian Human Rights Commission.

Goodman, J. 2010. Gulf oil spill threatens tribe's livelihood in Louisiana. *Miami Herald*, 1 June. Available at https://www.business-humanrights.org/en/documents/update-on-oil-spill-in-gulf-of-mexico.

Government Accountability Office. 2011. GAO 11-767 Report, 'Indian Health Services: Increase oversight needed to ensure accuracy of data used for estimating contract health service needs.' September. https://www.gao.gov/new.items/d11767.pdf.

Government of Canada. 2016. *British Columbia Treaty Commission Act*, SC 1995. Available at https://laws-lois.justice.gc.ca/eng/acts/b-8.5/FullText.html.

Government of Canada, British Columbia and First Nations Summit. 2016. *Multilateral engagement process to improve and expedite treaty negotiations*. Final draft, 17 March. Available at https://www.aadnc-aandc.gc.ca/DAM/DAM-INTER-HQ-LDC/STAGING/texte-text/bc_multiprop_1465303885525_eng.pdf.

Government of Canada, Indigenous and Northern Affairs. 2010. Comprehensive Community Planning for First Nations in British Columbia. Available at https://www.aadnc-aandc.gc.ca/eng/1100100021966/1100100021970.

Grant, S., and Rudder, J. 2010. *A New Wiradjuri Dictionary*. O'Connor, ACT: Restoration House.

Gunderson, D. 1998. 'Red Lake Walleye Fishing Ruined'. *Minnesota Public Radio*, 15 April.

Gustafson, B. 2009. *New Languages of the State: Indigenous Resurgence and the Politics of Knowledge in Bolivia*. London: Duke University Press.

Haga, C. 2006. 'A Long Year at Red Lake'. *Minneapolis Star Tribune*, 2 January. http://news.minnesota.publicradio.org/features/199804/15_gundersond_walleye-m/.

Haigh, N., Walker, J., Bacq, S. and Kickul, J. 2015. Hybrid organizations: Origins, strategies, impacts, and implications. *California Management Review* 57(3), 5–12.

Harfield, S.G., Davy, C., McArthur, A., Munn, Z., Brown, A. and Brown, N. 2018. Characteristics of Indigenous primary health care service delivery models: A systematic scoping review. *Global Health* 14, 1–12.

Harris, D., 2009. A court between: Aboriginal and treaty rights in the BC Court of Appeal. *BC Studies* 162, 140–47.

Harvard Project on American Indian Economic Development. 2000. *Honoring Nations: Tribal Governance Success Stories*. Cambridge, MA: John F. Kennedy School of Government, Harvard University.

Harvard Project on American Indian Economic Development. 2006. *Honoring Nations: Celebrating Excellence in Tribal Governance*. Cambridge, MA: John F. Kennedy School of Government, Harvard University.

Harvard Project on American Indian Economic Development. 2008a. Health. In HPAIED et al. (eds), *The State of the Native Nations: Conditions under U.S. Policies of Self-Determination*, Chapter 12. New York: Oxford University Press.

Harvard Project on American Indian Economic Development. 2008b. *Honoring Nations: Celebrating 10 Years of Excellence in Tribal Government*. Cambridge, MA: John F. Kennedy School of Government, Harvard University.

Harvard Project on American Indian Economic Development. 2015a. *Honoring Contributions in the Governance of American Indian Nations*. John F. Kennedy School of Government, Harvard University. Available at http://www.hpaied.org/honoring-nations/about-honoring-nations.

Harvard Project on American Indian Economic Development. 2015b. *Sovereignty Matters*. Available at https://hpaied.org.

Harvard Project on American Indian Economic Development. 2018. *Honouring Nations Awards*. Available at https://hpaied.org/honoring-nations.

Harvard Project on American Indian Economic Development. (n.d.). Available at https://hpaied.org/.

Hawthorne, B. 2007. Re: 4 fish bag limit on Red Lake possible. Forum post 8 March, Lake State Fishing discussion forum. Available at http://www.lakestatefishing.com/modules/newbb/viewtopic.php?post_id=30850.

Hayward, J. 2003a. Is local government a Treaty partner? In J. Hayward (ed.), *Local Government and the Treaty of Waitangi*, pp. 3–19. Melbourne: Oxford University Press.

Hayward, J. 2003b. *Local Government and the Treaty of Waitangi*. Melbourne: Oxford University Press.

Hemi, T. 2018. IMoko app to help teach kids importance of taking their meds. Available at http://www.maoritelevision.com/news/regional/imoko-app-help-teach-kids-importance-taking-their-meds.

Hemming, S., Rigney, D. and Berg, S. 2011. Ngarrindjeri futures: Negotiation, governance, environmental management. In S. Maddison and M. Briggs (eds), *Unsettling the Settler State: Creativity and Resistance in Indigenous Settler-State Governance*, pp. 98–113. Sydney: Federation Press.

Hemming, S., Rigney, D., Bignall, S., Berg, S. and Rigney, G. 2019. Indigenous nation building for environmental futures: Murrundi flows through Ngarrindjeri country. *Australasian Journal of Environmental Management* 26(3), 216–35.

Henderson, A. and Borrello, E. 2016. 'John Howard, Tony Abbott Lock in against Treaty with Indigenous Australians'. *ABC News*, 8 September. Available at www.abc.net.au/news/2016-09-08/conservatives-lock-in-against-treaty-with-indigenous-australians/7825298.

Henderson, W.B. 2018 [2006]. Indian Act. *The Canadian Encyclopaedia*. Available at https://www.thecanadianencyclopedia.ca/en/article/indian-act.

Henderson, W. and Parrott, Z., 2019. Indian Act. *The Canadian Encyclopaedia*. Available at https://www.thecanadianencyclopedia.ca/en/article/indian-act.

Hocking, R. 2018. 'Victorian Elders call for Clan-based treaties and more inclusion in process.' NITV News online, 14 May. Available at https://www.sbs.com.au/nitv/nitv-news/article/2018/05/14/victorian-elders-call-clan-based-treaties-and-more-inclusion-process.

Hotte, N., Nelson, H., Hawkins, T., Wyatt, S. and Kozak, R. 2018. Maintaining accountability between levels of governance in Indigenous economic development:

Examples from British Columbia, Canada. *Canadian Public Administration* 61(4), 1–27.

The Howard League. 2008. *The Howard League for Penal Reform*. Available at https://howardleague.org/wp-content/uploads/2016/05/Prison-work-and-social-enterprise.pdf.

Human Rights and Equal Opportunity Commission. 1997. *Report of the National Enquiry into the Separation of Aboriginal and Torres Strait Islander Children from Their Families*. Available at https://www.humanrights.gov.au/sites/default/files/content/pdf/social_justice/bringing_them_home_report.pdf.

Hunt, J. and Smith, D.E. 2006a. Building Indigenous community governance in Australia: Preliminary research findings. *CAEPR Working Paper No. 31*. Canberra: Centre for Aboriginal Economic Policy Research, The Australian National University.

Hunt, J. and Smith, D.E. 2006b. Report: Further key insights from the Indigenous Community Governance Project. Canberra: Centre for Aboriginal Economic Policy Research, The Australian National University.

Hunt, J. and Smith, D.E. 2011. Understanding and engaging with Indigenous governance. *Journal of Australian Indigenous Issues* 14(2–3), 30–53.

Hunt, J., Smith, D.E, Garling, S. and Sanders, W. (eds), 2008. *Contested Governance. Culture, Power and Institutions in Indigenous Australia*. Canberra, ACT: Australian National University Press.

Hurley, M.C. 2000. *Aboriginal Title: The Supreme Court of Canada Decision in Delgamuukw v. British Columbia*. Ontario, Canada: Parliamentary Research Branch, Library of Parliament.

Hutchins, N. 2015. Aboriginal Victoria to advance self-determination. Media release, 1 December. Available at https://www.premier.vic.gov.au/aboriginal-victoria-to-advance-self-determination/.

Huu-ay-aht First Nations. 2014. Constitution Act. Available at https://huuayaht.files.wordpress.com/2014/12/constitution-act-2011-official-consolidation.pdf.

Huu-ay-aht First Nations. 2017a. Report of the Social Services Panel. Huu-Ay-Aht First Nations Social Services Project: Safe, Healthy and Connected, Bringing Huu-ay-aht Children Home, 31 May. Available at https://huuayaht.files.wordpress.com/2017/06/2017-05-31-report-of-the-hfn-social-services-panel-01375005.pdf.

Huu-ay-aht First Nations. 2017b. Ancient Spirit, Modern Mind. Video. Available at https://www.youtube.com/watch?v=9nrji5O9d5g.

Huu-ay-aht First Nations. 2019. Legislation. Available at https://huuayaht.org/government/legislation/.

Huu-ay-aht First Nations. (n.d.)a. History. Available at https://huuayaht.org/about/history.

Huu-ay-aht First Nations. (n.d.)b. Mission. Available at https://huuayaht.org/about/mission/.

Huus, Kari. (n.d.). Houma and the Gulf oil spill. Manataka American Indian Council. Available at: www.manataka.org/page2187.html.

Iceman. 2006. Upper Red Lake meeting on 2006 harvesting. Forum post 26 January, Minnesota Fishing Forum. Available at http://myfishingpals.com/Minnesota-Fishi

ng-Forum.taf?_function=detail&ForumMasterThreads_uid1=851&start=1&ForumNumber=1.

Independent Māori Statutory Board. 2011. The Māori plan for Tāmaki Makaurau. Available at http://knowledgeauckland.org.nz/assets/publications/Māori-Plan-for-TamakiMakaurau-2012-IMSB.pdf.

International Court of Justice. 2019. Western Sahara. Available at https://www.icj-cij.org/en/case/61.

Ivison, D., 2018. 'Postcolonialism'. *Encyclopaedia Britannica*. Available at https://www.britannica.com/topic/postcolonialism.

Jack, I. 2014. 'Britain Took More out of India than It Put in – Could China Do the Same to Britain?' *The Guardian*, 20 June. Available at www.theguardian.com/commentisfree/2014/jun/20/britain-took-more-out-of-india.

Jett, S.C. 1983. Commentary 'Houma blowguns and baskets': Further observations. *Journal of Cultural Geography* 4(1), 126–28. Available at doi:10.1080/08873638309478589.

Joe, J. 2002. The rationing of healthcare and health disparity for the American Indians/Alaska Natives. In B.S. Smedley and A. Nelson (eds), *Unequal Treatment: Confronting Racial and Ethnic Disparities in Health Care*, p. 531. Washington, DC: National Academies Press.

John, S. 2015. Idle no more: Indigenous activism and feminism. *Theory in Action* 8(4), 38–54.

Johnson, E.A. and Rhoades, E.R. 2000. The history and organisation of Indian health services and systems. In E.R. Rhoades (ed.), *American Indian Health: Innovations in Health Care, Promotion, and Policy*. Baltimore, MD: Johns Hopkins University Press.

Johnson, J., T., Howitt, R., Cajete, G., Berkes, F., Paulani L., Louis, R. and Kliskey, A. 2016. Weaving Indigenous and sustainability sciences to diversify our methods. *Sustainability Science* 11(1), 1–11.

Joint Select Committee on Constitutional Recognition of Aboriginal and Torres Strait Islander Peoples. 2014. *Final Report*. Canberra: Parliament of the Commonwealth of Australia.

Joint Select Committee on Constitutional Recognition of Aboriginal and Torres Strait Islander Peoples. 2015. *Final Report*. Canberra: Parliament of the Commonwealth of Australia.

Joint Select Committee on Constitutional Recognition of Aboriginal and Torres Strait Islander Peoples, 2018. *Interim Report*. Canberra: Parliament of the Commonwealth of Australia .

Jonas, W. 2004. Statement on ATSIC, 16 April. Australian Human Rights Commission. Available at https://www.humanrights.gov.au/about/news/media-releases/statement-atsic.

Jones, R. 2000. Diagnosis in traditional Maori healing: A contemporary urban clinic. *Pacific Health Dialogue: Journal of Community Health and Clinical Medicine for the Pacific* 7(1), 17–24.

Jordan, J. 2005. Busted. Forum post 6 April, Indepth Outdoors. Available at https://www.in-depthoutdoors.com/community/forums/topic/ftlgeneral_193235/.

Jorgensen, M. (ed.). 2007. *Rebuilding Native Nations: Strategies for Governance and Development.* Tucson: University of Arizona Press.

Joseph, R.A. 2005. The government of themselves: Indigenous peoples' internal self-determination, effective self-governance and authentic representation. Unpublished doctoral dissertation. University of Waikato, Hamilton, New Zealand.

Jospeh, R., Tahan, A., Kilgour, J., Rakena, M. and Jeffries, T.P. (eds). 2016. Te Pai Tawhiti: Exploring the Horizons of Māori Economic Performance through Effective Collaboration. Centre for Maori and Indigenous Governance University of Waikato, NZ. Available at https://www.waikato.ac.nz/__data/assets/pdf_file/0006/322188/MAIN-FINAL-Te-Pai-Tawhiti-Report-Nov-11-2016.pdf.

Kalt, J.P. and Singer, J. 2004. Myths and realities of tribal sovereignty: The law and economics of Indian self-rule. RWP04-016. John F. Kennedy School of Government, Harvard University, Faculty Research Working Papers Series, Cambridge, Massachusetts.

Kawharu, I. H. 1968. Urban immigrants and "tāngata whenua". In E. Schwimmer (ed.), The Māori People in the Nineteen-Sixties, pp. 174–86. Auckland, New Zealand: Blackwood & Janet Paul.

Kawharu, M., Tapsell, P. and Woods, C. 2012. Maori entrepreneurial behaviour: Lachmannian insights. *Journal of Australian Indigenous Issues* 15(4), 62–75.

Keating, P. 1992. Transcript of Redfern Speech: Year for the World's Indigenous People. Delivered in Redfern Park by Prime Minister Paul Keating. ANTaR. Available at https://antar.org.au/sites/default/files/paul_keating_speech_transcript.pdf.

Klopotek, B. 2011. *Recognition Odysseys: Indigeneity, Race and Federal Tribal Recognition Policy in Three Louisiana Indian Communities (Narrating Native Histories).* Durham: Duke University Press.

Kniffen, F.B., Gregory, H.F. and Stokes, G.A. 1994. *The historic Indian Tribes of Louisiana, from 1542 to Present.* Baton Rouge, LA: LSU Press.

Kolpack, D. 2006. 'Walleye Fishing Set to Resume on Red Lake'. *Ojibwe News*, 5 May.

Kraker, D. 2013. 'New study suggests Fond du Lac band a big economic engine'. Statewide, MPR News. Blog post, 9 January. Available at https://blogs.mprnews.org/statewide/2013/01/new_study_suggests_fond_du_lac_band_a_big_economic_engine/.

Krakouer, J. 'The stolen generations never ended — they just morphed into child protection. *The Guardian*, IndigenousX, 17 October. Available at https://www.theguardian.com/commentisfree/2019/oct/17/the-stolen-generations-never-ended-they-just-morphed-into-child-protection.

Krawll, M.B. 1994. Understanding the role of healing in Aboriginal communities. Report to The Solicitor General of Canada, APC 10 CA. Available at https://www.publicsafety.gc.ca/cnt/rsrcs/pblctns/ndrstndng-hlng/index-en.aspx.

Krepps, M.B. and Caves, R.E. 1994. Bureaucrats and Indians: Principal agent relations and efficient management of tribal forest resources. *Journal of Economic Behavior and Organisation* 24(2), 133–51.

Kukutai T. 2011. Contemporary issues in Māori demography. In T. McIntosh and M. Mullholland (eds), *Māori and Social Issues*, pp. 11–48. Wellington, NZ: Huia.

Kunitz, S.J. 1996. The history and politics of US health care policy for American Indians and Alaskan Natives. *American Journal of Public Health* 86(10), 1464–73.

Langton, M., Mazel, O., Palmer, L. and Shain, K. (eds). 2008. *Settling with Indigenous People*. Sydney: Federation Press.

Larson, E., Johnson, Z. and Murphy, M. 2008. Emerging Indigenous governance: Ainu rights at the intersection of global norms and domestic institutions. *Alternatives: Global, Local, Political* 33(1), 53–82.

Lavarch, M. 2018. Mabo Lecture. 5 June 5. Available at https://aiatsis.gov.au/gallery/video/2018-mabo-lecture.

Lavoie, J.G., Forget, E.L., Prakash, T., Dahl, M., Martens, P. and O'Neil, J.D. 2010. Have investments in on-reserve health services and initiatives promoting community control improved First Nations' health in Manitoba? *Social Science & Medicine* 71(4), 717–24.

Leagle. 2017. *City of Duluth v Fond du Lac Band*. Available at https://www.leagle.com/decision/infco20130114091.

Leanui, P. 2000. Processes of decolonization. In M.A. Battiste (ed.), *Reclaiming Indigenous Voice and Vision*, pp. 79–88. Vancouver: UBC Press.

Lee, J.B. 2012. Marae a-kura: Tracing the birth of marae in schools. *SET: Research Information for Teachers* 2, 3.

Legal Information Institute. (n.d.). What are the criteria for acknowledgment as a federally recognized Indian tribe? Electronic Code of Federal Regulations, 25 CFR § 83.11. Available at https://www.law.cornell.edu/cfr/text/25/83.11.

Legislative Assembly, New South Wales. 1883. Protection of the Aborigines. Minute, 2 March. Available at https://aiatsis.gov.au/sites/default/files/catalogue_resources/91930.pdf.

Levine, H. B. 2001. Can a voluntary organisation be a treaty partner? The case of Te Whānau o Waipareira trust. *Social Policy Journal of New Zealand* 17, 161–70.

Liao Y., Tucker, P. and Giles, W.H. 2003. Health status of American Indians compared with other racial/ethnic minority populations – selected states, 2001–2002. *Morbidity and Mortality Weekly Report* 52(47), 1148–52.

Library of Congress. (n.d.). Louisiana as a Spanish colony. Available at https://www.loc.gov/collections/louisiana-european-explorations-and-the-louisiana-purchase/articles-and-essays/louisiana-as-a-spanish-colony/.

Lightfoot, S.R. 2020. The Pessimism traps of Indigenous resurgence. In T. Stevens and N. Michelsen (eds), *Pessimism in International Relations. Provocations, Possibilities, Politics*, pp.155–72. Palgrave Studies in International Relations Series. London: Palgrave Macmillan.

Local Government and Environment Committee. 2002. *Report of the Local Government Bill*. Wellington: New Zealand Government.

Local Government Commission. 2014. Draft proposal for reorganisation of local government in Wellington (Vol. 2). Available at https://www.nbr.co.nz/sites/default/files/4184558DA%20-%20Draft-ProposalWellington-Volume-2.pdf.

Logsdon, D.E. 2006. 'Contribution of Fry Stocking to the Recovery of the Walleye Population in the Red Lakes.' Investigational Report 535, Minnesota Department of Natural Resources, September.

Logsdon, Dale E., Anderson, C.S. and Miller, L.M. 2016. Contribution and performance of stocked Walleyes in the recovery of the Red Lakes, Minnesota Fishery. *North American Journal of Fisheries Management* 36, 828–43.

Lyon, F. and Sepulveda, L. 2009. Mapping social enterprises: Past approaches, challenges and future directions. *Social Enterprise Journal* 5(1), 83–94.

Macklem, P. 2017. The constitutional identity of Indigenous peoples in Canada: Status groups or federal actors? 21 April. Available at SSRN: https://ssrn.com/abstract=2956605 or http://dx.doi.org/10.2139/ssrn.2956605.

Mansell, M. 2016. *Treaty and Statehood: Aboriginal Self-determination.* Sydney: Federation Press.

Marimn Health. (n.d.). About us. Available at http://www.marimnhealth.org/about-us/.

Marks, K. 2018. 'Trick or Treaty. Will states address founding flaw?' *Griffith Review* 60. Available at https://griffithreview.com/articles/trick-or-treaty-state-redress-founding-flaw/.

Martin, R. L. and Osberg, S. 2007. Social entrepreneurship: The case for definition. *Stanford, CA: Stanford Social Innovation Review* 5(2), 28.

Matata-Sipu, Q. 2018. 'Māori women talk about the future of moko kauae'. Blog post, the Spinoff, 31 May. Available at https://thespinoff.co.nz/atea/31-05-2018/maori-women-talk-about-the-future-of-moko-kauae/.

McFarlane, P. 1993. *Brotherhood to Nationhood: George Manuel and the Making of the Modern Aboriginal Movement.* Toronto: Between the Lines Publishing.

McKenna, M. 2018. Moment of truth: History and Australia's future. *Quarterly Essay 69*. Melbourne: Black Inc.

McMeeking, S. 2019. Whānau Ora: Building Māori self-determination in Aotearoa New Zealand. In W. Nikolakis, S. Cornell and H.W. Nelson (eds), *Reclaiming Indigenous Governance: Reflections and Insights from Australia, Canada, New Zealand, and the United States*, pp. 155–71. Tucson: University of Arizona Press.

McMeeking, S., Grant, W. and Melrose, U. 2017. Insights on Māori social enterprise 2017 – Pakihi What Kaupapa. An unpublished report commissioned by Te Puni Kokiri (Ministry of Maori Development.

McMillan, L.J., Young, J. and Peters, M. 2013. Commentary: The 'idle no more' movement in eastern Canada. *Canadian Journal of Law and Society* 28(3), 429–31.

McMillan, M. 2018. Sovereignty. *Address at the Universities Australia Conference* Canberra 28 February–1 March. National Convention Centre, Canberra: Unpublished.

Mead, H. 2016. *Tikanga Māori (revised edition): Living by Māori Values.* Wellington, New Zealand: Huia NZ.

Mellish, L. 2013. Submission: Wellington your choice – Options for local governance. Available at http://www.gw.govt.nz/assets/About-GW-the-region/RegionalGovernance/Local-Government-Commission-Application/App9- Manawhenuaviews.PDF.

Metallic, A. and Chamberlin, A. 2006. Re-conceptualization of Mi'gmaq governance: Ta'n teliangweiasultigw, 'How a people best take care of each other.' Report prepared for Mi'gmawei Mawiomi Secretariat, 31 March. Available at http://www.aboutourland.ca/resources/reports/reconceptualization-mi%E2%80%99gmaq-governance.

Meyers, M.L. 1992. Red Lake Ojibwe. In H.E. Wright, B.C and N.E. Aaseng (eds), *Patterned Peatlands of Minnesota*, Minneapolis, MN: University of Minnesota Press.

Meuers, M.L. 2018. 'Statement/Clarification/Reminder on Red Lake Fishing Laws; Red Lake Nation is Sovereign, a Closed Reservation.' *Red Lake Nation News/ Babaamaajimowinan* (Telling of news in different places), 8 January.

Mikaere, A. 2003. *The Balance Destroyed: Consequences for Māori Women of The Colonisation of Tikanga Māori*. International Research Institute for Māori and Indigenous Education and Ani Mikaere, Auckland, New Zealand.

Miller, B.G. 1993. Presentation by Brenda Gedeon Miller, Listuguj Mi'gmaq First Nation Government, Restigouche, Quebec, 17 June. Royal Commission on Aboriginal Peoples, Transcriptions of Public Hearings and Round Table Discussions, 1992–1993. Available at http://digital.scaa.sk.ca/ourlegacy/solr?query=Repository%3A%22University%20of%20Saskatchewan%20Archives%22|Place%3A%22Canada!!Quebec!!Restigouche%22|Place%3A%22Canada%22|Subject%3A%22Royal%20Proclamation%20of%201763%22|Name%3A%22Gedeon%20Miller%2C%20Brenda%22&start=&rows=&mode=view&pos=0&page=1.

Miller, J.R. 2009. *Compact, Contract, Covenant: Aboriginal Treaty-Making in Canada*. Toronto: University of Toronto Press.

Miller, M.E. (ed.). 2006. *Forgotten Tribes: Unrecognised Indians and the Federal Acknowledgement Process*. Lincoln: University of Nebraska Press.

Minchew, R.D. 2017. 'Because colored means Negro' - The Houma Nation and its fight for Indigenous identity within a South Louisiana public school system, 1916–1963. Unpublished MA thesis. University of New Orleans, New Orleans. Available at https://scholarworks.uno.edu/td/2346.

Minnesota Department of Natural Resources. 2018. Upper Red Lake Walleye Regulations Announced for 2018 Open Water Season. News Release, 5 April.

Miron, M. 2006. 'Walleye Return: Federal, state, tribal collaborators celebrate in Red Lake'. *The Bemidji Pioneer*, 12 May.

Moberg, M. and Moberg, T.S. 2005. The United Houma Nation in the U.S. Congress: Corporations, Communities, and the Politics of Federal Acknowledgement. *Urban Anthropology and Studies of Cultural Systems and World Economic Development* 34(1), 85–124.

Monet, D. and Wilson, A. 1992. *Colonialism on Trial*. Gabriola Island, BC: New Society Publishers.

Montgomery, A.W., Dacin, P.A. and Dacin, M.T. 2012. Collective social entrepreneurship: Collaboratively shaping social good. *Journal of Business Ethics* 111(3), 375–88.

Mufwene, S.S. (n.d.). Mobilian jargon. *Encyclopaedia Britannica*. Available at https://www.britannica.com/topic/Mobilian-Jargon.

Murphy, M. 2008. Representing Indigenous self-determination. *University of Toronto Law Journal* 58(2), 185–216.

Murphy, M. 2014. Self-determination as a collective capability: The case of Indigenous peoples. *Journal of Human Development and Capabilities* 15(4), 320–34.

Museum of Australia. (n.d.). Documenting a democracy. Governor Phillip's Instructions 25 April 1787. www.foundingdocs.gov.au/resources/transcripts/nsw2_doc_1787.pdf.

Museum of Australian Democracy. (n.d.). Secret Instructions from Baron Ed. Hawke, Sir Piercy Brett and Lord C. Spencer to James Cook, 30 July 1768, 1. *Secret Instructions to Lieutenant Cook 30 July 1768 (GB)*. Museum of Australian Democracy. Available at https://www.foundingdocs.gov.au/item-sdid-67.html.

Nagel, J. 1997. *American Indian Ethnic Renewal: Red Power and the Resurgence of Identity and Culture*. New York: Oxford University Press.

National Commission on the BP Deepwater Horizon Oil Spill and Offshore Drilling. 2011. *Deep Water: The Gulf Oil Disaster and the Future of Offshore Drilling*. Report to the US President, 11 January. https://www.govinfo.gov/app/details/GPO-OILCOMMISSION/.

National Congress of Australia's First Peoples. 2019. A voice for Aboriginal and Torres Strait Islander Peoples. Available at https://nationalcongress.com.au/.

National Constitutional Convention. 2017. 'Uluru Statement from the Heart'. Referendum Council. Available at www.referendumcouncil.org.au/sites/default/files/2017-05/Uluru_Statement_From_The_Heart_0.PDF.

National Native Title Tribunal. 2017. *25 Years of Native Title Recognition*. Available at http://www.nntt.gov.au/Documents/Key%20native%20title%20cases.pdf.

National Native Title Tribunal. 2019. Current applications. Statistics. Available at http://www.nntt.gov.au/Pages/Statistics.aspx.

National Public Radio. 2010. 'Native American group hit hard by oil spill'. *Tell me more*, radio broadcast, 3 June. Transcript available at https://www.npr.org/templates/story/story.php?storyId=127405886?storyId=127405886.

National Tribal Budget Formulation Workgroup. 2018. *Recommendations on the Indian Health Service Fiscal Year 2020 Budget*. Available at https://www.nihb.org/docs/04122018/265620_NIHB%20IHS%20Budget%20Book_WEB.pdf.

Native Governance Center. (n.d.)a. Programs. Available at https://nativegov.org/programs/.

Native Governance Center. (n.d)b. Youth Rebuilders. Available at https://nativegov.org/youth-rebuilders/.

Native Nations Institute (NNI). 2019. Indigenous governance program. Available at https://igp.arizona.edu/.

Native Nations Institute (NNI). (n.d.). About us. Available at https://nni.arizona.edu/about-us.

Native Village of Kotzebue. 2019. Native Village of Kotzebue Environmental Program 1997–2019. Available at http://www.kotzebueira.org/programs/Native-Village-of-Kotzebue-Environmental-Program-February-2019.pdf.

New Journey Productions. 2011. Maa nulth Treaty Celebration. Video. Available at http://www.youtube.com/watch?v=EQeCOugKlJg.

News South Wales Government, Department of Aboriginal Affairs. (n.d.). Administering the NSW *Aboriginal Land Rights Act 1983*. Available at https://www.aboriginalaffairs.nsw.gov.au/land-rights/alra.

New Zealand Government. 2011. *The Future for New Zealanders: Māori*. Wellington: Statistics New Zealand.

Ng-A-Fook, N.A. 2006. Understanding an indigenous curriculum in Louisiana through listening to Houma oral histories. Doctoral dissertation. Louisiana State University, Baton Rouge. Available at https://digitalcommons.lsu.edu/gradschool_dissertations/2748.

Ngarrindjeri Nation. 2007. *Yarluwar-Ruwe Sea-Country Plan*. Ngarrindjeri Country: Ngarrindjeri Tendi. Available at https://www.mdba.gov.au/sites/default/files/pubs/sa-ngarrindjeri-nation-yarluwar-ruwe-plan-2006-rs.PDF.

Ngata, T. 2019. Wild West Festival denigrates Indigenous peoples. Blog post, 4 February. Available at https://leoniepihama.wordpress.com/2019/02/04/wild-west-festival-denigrates-indigenous-peoples/.

Nikolakis, W., Stephen C., Nelson, H.W., Pierre, S. and Phillips, G. (eds). 2019. *Reclaiming Indigenous Governance: Reflections and Insights from Australia, Canada, New Zealand, and the United States*. Tucson: University of Arizona Press.

Nikora, L.W., Rua, M. and Te Awekotuku, N. 2007. Renewal and resistance: Moko in contemporary New Zealand. *Journal of Community and Applied Social Psychology* 17(6), 477–89.

Niskanen, C. 2006. 'Tribe, Anglers Greet Return of Walleye'. *Pioneer Press*, 30 April.

Niskanen, C. 2011. Walleye Stocking Today. *Minnesota Conservation Volunteer* 74(436) May–June, 8–13.

Nixon, R. 1960. President Nixon, Special message on Indian affairs, July 8, 1970. Address to the Congress of the United States. Available at http://www.ncai.org/attachments/Consultation_IJaOfGZqlYSuxpPUqoSSWIaNTkEJEPXxKLzLcaOikifwWhGOLSA_12%20Nixon%20Self%20Determination%20Policy.pdf.

Noren, J., Kindig, D. and Sprenger, A. 1998. Challenges to Native American health care. *Public Health Reports* 113(1), 22–33.

Northern Territory Government, 2019. Aboriginal land and permits. Available at https://nt.gov.au/property/land/aboriginal-land-management/aboriginal-land-and-permits/land-council-roles-and-contacts.

Northland Fishing Tackle. 2016. 'Upper Red Lake, MN.' www.northlandtackle.com.

Norris, M.J. 2006. Aboriginal languages in Canada: Trends and perspectives on maintenance and revitalization. In J. P. White, S. Wingert, D. Beavon and P. Maxim (eds), *Aboriginal Policy Research: Moving Forward, Making a Difference*. Toronto: Thompson Educational Publishing.

Norris, M.J. 2003. From Generation to generation: Survival and Maintenance of Canada's Aboriginal Languages within Families, Communities and Cities. In *Maintaining the Links: Language, Identity and the Lands*. Proceedings of the

7th Conference of the Foundation for Endangered Languages, Broome, Western Australia: 22-24 September, 2003.

Nuu-chah-nulth Tribal Council. 2019. History. Available at https://nuuchahnulth.org/history.

Nyamba Buru Yawuru (NBY). 2016. *Annual Report, Yawuru PBC mabu buru. Mabu liyan.* Broome, WA: Nyamba Buru Yawuru. Available at https://www.yawuru.org.au/wp-content/uploads/2019/05/ANNUAL-REPORT-ONLINE-VERSION-2.pdf.

Nyamba Buru Yawuru (NBY). 2019a. Yawuru officially opens Liyan-Ngan Nyirrwa Cultural Wellbeing Centre. Media release, 24 June. Available at http://www.yawuru.org.au/wp-content/uploads/2019/06/MEDIA-RELEASE-YAWURU-OPENS-LIYAN-NGAN-CENTRE-24062019.pdf.

Nyamba Buru Yawuru (NBY). 2019b. Mabu buru: Health country. Available at http://www.yawuru.org.au/country.

O'Carroll, A.D. 2013. Virtual whanaungatanga. Māori utilising social networking sites to attain and maintain relationships. *AlterNative: International Journal of Indigenous People* 9(3), 230–45.

O'Fairchellaigh, C. 2018. Mining, development and Indigenous peoples, In S.K. Lodha (ed.), *Mining and Sustainable Development*, pp. 125–42. London: Routledge Taylor and Francis Group.

Office of Federal Acknowledgement. 1994. Summary under the criteria and evidence for proposed finding against Federal Acknowledgment of the United Houma Nation, Inc. Available at https://www.bia.gov/sites/bia.gov/files/assets/as-ia/ofa/petition/056_uhouma_LA/056_pf.pdf.

Office of Indian Affairs. 2008. Summary under the criteria for the amended proposed finding on the Biloxi, Chitimacha Confederation of Muskogees, Inc. 22 May. Available at https://www.bia.gov/sites/bia.gov/files/assets/as-ia/ofa/petition/056A_bccmsk_LA/056a_apf.pdf.

Office of Treaty Settlements. 2018. *Ka tika ā muri, ka tika ā mua. Healing the Past, Building a Future.* Available at https://www.govt.nz/assets/Documents/Red-Book Healing-the-past-building-a-future.pdf.

O'Neil, B. 2019. Decolonising the mind: working with transgenerational trauma and First Nations People, Judicial Officers Bulletin. *Judicial Commission of NSW Bulletin* 31(6), 54–58. Available at https://www.judcom.nsw.gov.au/wp-content/uploads/2019/11/decolonising-the-mind-article.pdf.

Oscar, J. 2018. Strong communities, strong kids, Speech by Social Justice Commissioner, Human Rights Commission, Sydney. Available at https://humanrights.gov.au/about/news/speeches/strong-communities-strong-kids-absec-biennial-conference.

Parliament of Australia. 2003. Make or break? A background to the ATSIC changes and the ATSIC Review. Current Issues Brief no. 29 2002–03. Available at https://www.aph.gov.au/About_Parliament/Parliamentary_Departments/Parliamentary_Library/Publications_Archive/CIB/cib0203/03cib29.

Parliament of Australia. 2018. Interim Report of the Joint Select Committee on Constitutional Recognition relating to Aboriginal and Torres Strait Islander Peoples. Available at https://www.aph.gov.au/Parliamentary_Business/Committee

s/Joint/Former_Committees/Constitutional_Recognition_2018/ConstRecognition/Interim_Report.

Parsons, L.S. and Lear, W.H. (eds). 1993. *Perspectives on Canadian Marine Fisheries Management.* National Research Council of Canada. Ottawa: NRC Research Press.

Pascoe, B. 2018. *Dark Emu.* Broome: Magabala Books, Australia.

Penehira, M. 2011. Mouri Tu, Mouri Moko, Mouri Ora! Moko as a wellbeing strategy. Unpublished doctoral dissertation, University of Waikato, Waikato, New Zealand.

PEP. 2018. PEP. Not just a program – A revolution. *Prison Entrepreneurship Program.* Available at https://www.pep.org/.

Peters, L. 2014. 10 Maya Angelou Quotes We'll Never Forget. Blog post, *Bustle*, 29 May. Available at https://www.bustle.com/articles/25986-10-maya-angelou-quotes-well-never-forget.

Petrie, H. 2013. *Chiefs of industry: Maori Tribal Enterprise in Early Colonial New Zealand.* Auckland: Auckland University Press.

Pfefferbaum, R.L., Pfefferbaum, B.R., Everett, R. and Strickland R.J. 1997. Providing for the health care needs of Native Americans: Policy, programs, procedures, and practices. *American Indian Law Review*, 211–58.

Pihama, L. 2005. Asserting Indigenous theories of change. In J. Barker (ed.), *Sovereignty Matters: Locations of Contestation and Possibility in Indigenous Struggles for Self-determination*, pp. 191–209. Series Editor Devon Abbott, Mihesuah: University of Nebraska Press, USA.

Pihama, L. 2016. Colonial naming reproduces historical trauma. Blog post, 19 February. Available at https:// https://tewhareporahou.wordpress.com/2016/02/19/colonial-naming-reproduces-historical-trauma/.

Pihama, L. 2018. Some reflections on Māori women and women's suffrage. Blog post, 19 October. Available at https://leoniepihama.wordpress.com/2018/10/19/some-reflections-on-maori-women-womens-suffrage/.

Pihama, L., Reynolds, P., Smith, C., Reid, J., Smith, L.T. and Nana, R.T. 2014. Positioning historical trauma theory within Aotearoa New Zealand. *AlterNative: An International Journal of Indigenous Peoples* 10(3), 248–62.

Postero, N. and Fabricant, N. 2019. Indigenous sovereignty and the new developmentalism in plurinational Bolivia, *Anthropological Theory*, February 2019. Available at https://journals.sagepub.com/doi/abs/10.1177/1463499618779735.

Pritchard, S. 2011. The 'race' power in Section 51(xvi) of the Constitution. *Australian Indigenous Law Review* 15(2), 44–57.

Productivity Commission. 2018. *Report on Government Services 2018*, Child protection Services and attachment tables. Chapter 16. Canberra, ACT: Productivity Commission. https://www.pc.gov.au/research/ongoing/report-on-government-services/2018/community-services/child-protection/rogs-2018-partf-chapter16.pdf.

Pulitano, E. 2012. *Indigenous Rights in the Age of the UN Declaration.* Cambridge, UK: Cambridge University Press.

Rainie, S.C., Jorgensen, M., Cornell, S. and Arsenault, J. 2015. The Changing landscape of health care provision to American Indian Nations. *American Indian Culture and Research Journal* 39(1), 1–24.

Read, P., Meyers, G. and Reece, B. (eds). 2013. *What good condition?: Reflections on an Australian Aboriginal Treaty 1986–2006*. Canberra: ANU Press.

Reconciliation Australia. 2017. About Us. History. Available at https://www.reconciliation.org.au/about-us/#our-history.

Record, I. (producer). 2010. *Return of the Red Lake Walleye*. Video recording. Tucson, AZ: Native Nations Institute, The University of Arizona.

Red Lake Department of Natural Resources and Project Preserve [producers]. 2008. *Maamakaadenbaagwad (it is amazing): The Miracle of the Walleye*. Video recording. Red Lake, MN: Red Lake Band of Chippewa Indians.

Red Lake Department of Natural Resources. 2016. 'Red Lake Walleye Population Remains Strong for 2016.' *Miskwaagamiiwi-zaaga'iganiig Aki-genawendamowaad* (Red Lake DNR newsletter) Biboon/Winter, 3.

Regan, P. 2010. *Unsettling the Settler Within: Indian Residential Schools, Truth Telling, and Reconciliation in Canada*. Vancouver: UBC Press.

Residential School History and Dialogue Centre (RSHDC). 2020. Achieving consistency between the United Nations Declaration on the Rights of Indigenous Peoples to the laws of British Columbia, Discussion Paper 1. In *Implementing UNDRIP in BC, Discussion Paper Series* by the RSHDC, University of British Columbia, Vancouver. Available at https://irshdc.ubc.ca/files/2020/03/UNDRIP_Article1_Consistency.pdf.

Reynolds, H. 1996. *Aboriginal Sovereignty: Three Nations, One Australia*. Sydney: Allen & Unwin.

Reynolds, H. 2013. *Forgotten War*. Sydney: University of New South Wales Press.

Rhoades E.R., D'Angelo, A.J. and Hurlburt, W.B. 1987. The Indian health service record of achievement. *Public Health Reports* 102(4), 356–60.

Rigney, D., Bignall, S. and Hemming, S. 2015. Negotiating Indigenous modernity: Kungun Ngarrindjeri Yunnan-listening to Ngarrindjeri speak. *AlterNative: An International Journal of Indigenous Peoples* 11(4), 334–49.

Rigney, D., Hemming, S. and Berg, S. 2008. Letters Patent, native title and the Crown in South Australia. In E. Johnston, M. Hinton and D. Rigney (eds), *Indigenous Australians and the Law*, pp. 161–78 (2nd ed.). London: Routledge.

Rivers, E. 2006. Red Lake: Back to the future. *Minnesota Conservation Volunteer* 69(406) May–June, 10–15.

Robbins, J.A. and Dewar, J. 2011. Traditional Indigenous approaches to healing and the modern welfare of traditional knowledge, spirituality and lands: A critical reflection on practices and policies taken from the Canadian Indigenous example. *The International Indigenous Policy Journal* 2(4).

Robertson, T. 2004. 'Red Lake Tribe Debates Future of Walleye Fishery'. *Minnesota Public Radio*, 9 August.

Robertson, T. 2006. 'Waskish Stakes a Future on Walleye'. *Minnesota Public Radio*, 12 May.

Robertson, T. 2008. 'Red Lake Tribe Resumes Commercial Fishing Industry'. *Minnesota Public Radio* 15 January.

Rorick, Isabel. (n.d.). A master spruce root weaver: S'it kwuns (Isabel Rorick). Interview by Emma Bonnemaison. Simon Fraser University, The Bill Reid Centre,

Online Exhibits, Spruce Root Weaving. Transcript available at https://www.sfu.ca/brc/online_exhibits/spruce-root-weaving/spruce-root-weaving.html.

Roubideaux, Yvette. 2002. *Current Issues in Indian Health Policy*. Tucson, AZ: Udall Center for Studies in Public Policy, The University of Arizona.

Royal Commission on Auckland Governance. 2009. Royal Commission on Auckland Governance, Vol. 1. Auckland: New Zealand Government.

Rudd, K. 2008. Apology to Australia's Indigenous Peoples. Speech to Parliament of Australia, House of Representatives, 13 February. Available at https://www.australia.gov.au/about-australia/our-country/our-people/apology-to-australias-indigenous-peoples.

Rush, S. 1998. Aboriginal title: The path to coexistence. In L. Strelein and K. Muir (eds), *Native Title in Perspective*, pp. 171–97. Canberra, ACT: Native Title Research Unit, AIATSIS.

Safina Center Seafood Analysts. 2017. 'Walleye, *Sander vitreus*: Minnesota/Red Lake, Handlines and Pole-Lines (Hand-Operated), Set Gillnets', 9 January. Seafood Watch, The Safina Center at Stony Brook University, Stony Brook, NY, and Monterey Bay Aquarium, Monterey, CA.

Santos, F.M. 2012. A positive theory of social entrepreneurship. *Journal of Business Ethics* 111(3), 335–51.

Scott, J. 1998. *Seeing Like a State: How Certain Schemes to Improve the Human Condition Have Failed*. New Haven, CT: Yale University Press.

Secretary of State, Louisiana. 2019. Louisiana Business Filings. Available at https://coraweb.sos.la.gov/commercialsearch/CommercialSearchDetails.aspx?CharterID=31214_B024B09EBC.

Seed-Pihama, J.E. 2017. Ko wai tō ingoa? The transformative potential of Māori names. Thesis for Doctor of Philosophy. University of Waikato, Hamilton, New Zealand. Available at https://hdl.handle.net/10289/11310.

Seidemann, R. 2009. Curious corners of Louisiana mineral law: Cemeteries, school lands, erosion, accretion, and other oddities. *The Tulane Environmental Law Journal* 23(1), 93–157.

Sen, A. 2004. *UN Human Development Report 2004: Chapter 1 Cultural Liberty and Human Development*. UN Human Development Reports. New York: United Nations Development Programme.

Sen, A. 2009. *The Idea of Justice*. Cambridge, MA: Belknap Press of Harvard University Press.

Simcosky, B. and Holmes, C. 2005. *Proud Nations: Celebrating Self-Governance*. Bellingham, WA: Self-Governance Communication and Education Project.

Simpson, L. 2008. Looking after Gdoo-naaganinaa: Precolonial Nishnaabeg diplomatic and treaty relationships. *Wicazo Sa Review*, 23(2), 29–42.

Singh, S., Bursey, D., Teal, C. and Curpen, R. 2019. British Columbia's UNDRIP legislation—A framework to advance reconciliation, The Canadian Bar Association Member Articles, December 06, 2019. Available at https://www.cba.org/Sections/Business-Law/Articles/2019/UNDRIP.

Smith, D. 2012. 'Upper Red Lake Comes Back from the Depths'. *Minneapolis Star Tribune*, 19 December.

Smith, D. 2015. 'Why Stocking Fish Isn't the Answer to Walleye Woes on Mille Lacs.' *Minneapolis Star Tribune*, 25 April.

Smith, D.E. 2004. From Gove to governance: Reshaping Indigenous governance in the Northern Territory. Discussion Paper 265/2004. Centre for Aboriginal Economic Policy Research. Canberra: Australian National University.

Smith, D.E. 2008. Cultures of governance and the governance of culture: Transforming and containing Indigenous institutions in West Arnhem Land. In J. Hunt, D.E. Smith, S. Garling and W. Sanders (eds), *Contested Governance: Culture, Power and Institutions in Indigenous Australia*, pp. 75–111. CAEPR Research Monograph No. 29. Canberra: Australian National University E Press.

Smith, D.E. 2012. Common Roots, Common Futures: Different Paths to Self-Determination: An International Conversation. Report on workshop proceedings, The University of Arizona, Tucson, USA, 20–22 February. Available at ww.aigi .com.au.

Smith, D.E. 2019. From little things, big things grow: Exercising incremental self-governance in Australia. In W. Nikolakis, S. Cornell, H.W. Nelson, S. Pierre and G. Phillips (eds), *Reclaiming Indigenous Governance: Reflections and Insights from Australia, Canada, New Zealand, and the United States*. Tucson: University of Arizona Press.

Smith, L.T. 1999. *Decolonizing Methodologies: Research and Indigenous Peoples*. London: Zed Books.

Smith, L.T. 2018. Blog post. Available at https://thespinoff.co.nz/atea/10-10-2018 /we-care-so-much-it-exhausts-us-a-Māori-educator-on-the-mountains-still-to-climb/.

Smith, M.L. 2017. 'Red Lake Indian Reservation Declares Public Health Emergency Over Drug Epidemic'. *Minneapolis Star Tribune*, 26 July.

South Africa. 1999. *Truth and Reconciliation Commission of South Africa Report*. Cape Town: Truth and Reconciliation Commission. Available at http://www.justice.gov.za/trc/report/.

South Australian Government. 2016. South Australian Aboriginal Regional Authorities Policy. Adelaide: SA Government (Aboriginal Affairs and Reconciliation). Available at https://statedevelopment.sa.gov.au/upload/aard/ara/ara-policy.pdf.

State of Victoria. 2018. Treaty legislation: The Advancing the Treaty Process with Aboriginal Victorians Act 2018 (Victoria). Aboriginal Victoria. Available at https ://www.vic.gov.au/aboriginalvictoria/treaty/treaty-legislation.html.

State of Victoria. (n.d.). What is a treaty? Aboriginal Victoria. Available at https://w. www.vic.gov.au/aboriginalvictoria/treaty/what-is-a-treaty.html.

Statistics Canada. 2016. *Census 2016*. Available at https://www12.statcan.gc.ca/ce nsus-recensement/2016/dp-pd/index-eng.cfm.

Statistics New Zealand. 2013. *Inside Wellington*. Available at http://archive.stats .govt.nz/browse_for_stats/snapshots-of-nz/infographics/insidewellington-infograp hic.aspx.

Steinman, E. 2005. Legitimizing American Indian sovereignty: Mobilizing the constitutive power of law through institutional entrepreneurship. *Law and Society Review* 39(4), 759–93.

Steinman, E. 2012. Settler colonial power and the American Indian sovereignty movement: Forms of domination, strategies of transformation. *American Journal of Sociology* 117(4), 1073–30.

Stenson, M. 2012. *The Treaty*. Auckland: Penguin Random House.

Sterritt, N. 2001. 'How did we get there: Settling the Aboriginal political-constitutional stage.' Unpublished paper presented to the Patriation Negotiations Conference, Edmonton, Alberta, Canada, pp. 1–15.

Sterritt, N.J. 2016. *Mapping My Way Home: A Gitxsan History*. Smithers, BC, Canada: Creekstone Press Ltd.

Sterritt, N.J., Marsden, S., Galois, R., Grant, P. and Overstall, R. 1998. *Tribal Boundaries in the Nass Watershed*. Vancouver: UBC Press.

Strelein, L. 2009. *Compromised Jurisprudence: Native Title Cases Since Mabo* (2nd ed.). Canberra, ACT: Aboriginal Studies Press.

Struthers, R. and Eschiti, V.S. 2004. The experience of Indigenous traditional healing and cancer. *Integrative Cancer Therapies* 3(1), 13–23.

Struthers, R., Eschiti, V.S. and Patchell, B. 2004. Traditional Indigenous healing: Part 1. *Complementary Therapies in Nursing and Midwifery* 10(3), 141–49.

Sullivan, P. and Oliver, K. 2007. Governance, Indigenous and non-Indigenous, as a social determinant of Aboriginal health. In I. Anderson, F. Baum and M. Bentley (eds), *Beyond Bandaids: Exploring the Underlying Social Determinants of Aboriginal Health*. Papers from the Social Determinants of Aboriginal Health workshop, Lowitja Institute, Adelaide, July 2004, pp. 181–90. Available at https://www.lowitja.org.au/page/services/resources/Cultural-and-social-determinants/social-determinants-of-health/Underlying-Social-Determinants-of-Aboriginal-Health.

Swanton, J.R. 1946. *Indians of the Southeastern United States*. Washington: United States Government Printing Office.

Swanton, J.R. 2010. *Indian Tribes of the Lower Mississippi Valley and Adjacent Coast of the Gulf of Mexico*. United States: Dover Publications.

Tatum, M.L., Jorgensen, M., Guss, M.E. and Deer, S. (eds). 2014. *Structuring Sovereignty: Constitutions of the Native Nations*. Los Angeles: University of California.

Taylor, J. 2019. Population and patterns of residence. In *The Macquarie Atlas of Indigenous Australia*, chapter 6. Sydney: Macquarie Library.

Te Awekotuku, N. and Nikora, W. 2007. *Mau moko: The world of Māori tattoo*. Auckland, New Zealand: Penguin.

Te One, A. 2018. Culture and governance. *International Indigenous Governance Conference*, Melbourne, Vic., 20 November. Available at http://www.aigi.com.au/indigneous-youth-in-governance-masterclass-2018/.

Te One, A. 2019. Mana Whenua, Mātaawaka, and local government. An examination of relationships between Māori and local government in Wellington and the Hutt Valley. Doctoral thesis. Canberra: The Australian National University, Canberra.

Te Rūnanga o Ngāi Tahu. 2006a. Ngāi Tahu Fund. Available at https://ngaitahu.iwi.nz/culture/ngai-tahu-fund/.

Te Rūnanga o Ngāi Tahu. 2006b. Whai Rawa: A pathway to prosperity for Ngāi Tahu Whānui. Available at https://whairawa.com/.

Te Rūnanga o Ngāi Tahu. 2013. *Ngāi Tahu 2025*. Available at https://ngaitahu.iwi.nz/wp-content/uploads/2013/06/NgaiTahu_20251.pdf.

Te Rūnanga o Ngāi Tahu. 2017. *Annual Report*. Available at https://ngaitahu.iwi.nz/investment/ngai-tahu-annual-reports/2017-annual-report/.

Te Rūnanga o Ngāi Tahu. 2018. *WE ARE Ngāi Tahu*. Available at https://ngaitahu.iwi.nz/wp-content/uploads/we-are-ngai-tahu.pdf.

Tester, J. 2012. Federal Recognition: Politics and Legal Relationship between Governments. Statement of Senator Jon Tester to the Hearing before the Committee on Indian Affairs, United States Senate, 112th Cong. 684, 12 July. Available at https://www.indian.senate.gov/sites/default/files/upload/files/CHRG-112shrg77947.pdf.

The Barefoot College. (n.d.). The Barefoot Story. Available at https://www.barefoot-college.org/about/.

Thomas, R. (Office of the Treaty Commissioner). 2017. *Talking Treaty*. Adelaide: Government of South Australia. Available at https://statedevelopment.sa.gov.au/upload/aboriginal-affairs/FinalTreatyCommissionerReport-170721.pdf?t=1518405482035.

Tiessen, M., Taylor, D.M. and Kirmayer, L.J. 2010. A key individual-to- community link: The impact of perceived collective control on Aboriginal youth well-being. *Pimatisiwin: A Journal of Aboriginal and Indigenous Community Health* 7(2), 241–67.

Tiller, V.E. 2005. *Tiller's Guide to Indian Country: Economic Profiles of American Indian Reservations*. Albuquerque, NM: BowArrow.

Tohunga Suppression Act 1907, No. 13: 2(1), New Zealand. Available at http://www.austlii.edu.au/nz/legis/hist_act/tsa19077ev1907n13353.pdf.

Toscano, N. 2016. 'Victoria begins talks about Australia's first-ever treaty with Indigenous people'. *The Age* online, 27 February. Available at https://www.theage.com.au/national/victoria/victoria-begins-talks-about-australias-firstever-treaty-with-indigenous-people-20160226-gn52f1.html.

Treacher, A. 2016. PATU Aotearoa take steps to fight obesity. Available at https://www.maoritelevision.com/news/sport/patu-aotearoa-take-steps-fight-obesity.

Treuer, A. 2012. *Rez Life: An Indian's Journey through Reservation Life*. New York: Atlantic Monthly Press.

Treuer, A. 2015. *Warrior Nation: A History of the Red Lake Ojibwe*. St. Paul: Minnesota Historical Society Press.

Trevorrow, G., Trevorrow, T. and Rigney, M. 2010. Preface. In S. Berg (ed.), *Coming to Terms: Aboriginal Title in South Australia*. Adelaide: Wakefield Press.

Trindade, A.A. 1976. Origin and historical development of the rule of exhaustion of local remedies in international law. *Revue Belge de Droit International / Belgian Review of International Law* 12(2), 499–527.

Trivedi, C. 2010. A social entrepreneurship bibliography. *The Journal of Entrepreneurship* 19(1), 81–5.

Trosper, R.L. 2003. Northwest coast indigenous institutions that supported resilience and sustainability. *Ecological Economics* 41, 329–44.

Trup, N. 2017. The Christchurch cafe Kākano reviving Maori cuisine. *The Guardian*. Available at https://www.theguardian.com/travel/2017/may/07/new-zealand-cafe-christchurch-kakano-reintroducing-maori-people-cuisine.

Tuck, E. and Yang, K.W. 2012. Decolonization is not a metaphor. *Decolonization: Indigeneity, Education and Society* 1(1), 1–40.

Tucker, B. 2013. 'Toxic, Childish, Poor and Pathetic. *The Guardian*, 20 March. Available at www.theguardian.com.au/story/1377269/toxic-childish-poor-and-pathetic/.

'Turnbull: We Are Committed to Doing Things with, Not to, Aboriginal People'. 2018. *The Mandarin*, 13 February. Available at www.themandarin.com.au/88266-turnbull-committed-doing-thing-with-aboriginal-people/.

United Houma Nations. 2012. Constitution. Available at https://unitedhoumanation.org/wp-content/uploads/2019/01/UHNConstitution.pdf.

United Houma Nations. 2019. Government. About Houma Nation. Available at https://unitedhoumanation.org/about/government/.

United Nations. 1969. Vienna Convention on the Law of Treaties (Article 7(2)(a)). No. 18232. Available at https://treaties.un.org/doc/publication/unts/volume%201155/volume-1155-i-18232-english.pdf.

United Nations. (n.d.). Declaration on the Rights of Indigenous Peoples. Available at https://www.un.org/development/desa/indigenouspeoples/declaration-on-the-rights-of-indigenous-peoples.html.

United Nations. (n.d.). The United Nations and Decolonization. Available at www.un.org/en/decolonization/specialcommittee.shtml.

United Nations Department of Economic and Social Affairs. 2019. *State of the World's Indigenous Peoples: Implementing the United Nations Declaration on the Rights of Indigenous Peoples*. New York: United Nations. Available athttps://social.un.org/unpfii/sowip-vol4-web.pdf.

United Nation Permanent Forum on Indigenous Issues (UNPFII). 2016. *Report of the Expert Group Meeting on Indigenous Peoples and Agenda 2030*, UN Permanent Forum on Indigenous Issues, 15th Session. Available at https://www.un.org/esa/socdev/unpfii/documents/2016/15th-session.

University of Arizona. (n.d.). What is Native Nation Building? Native Nations Institute. Available at http://nni.arizona.edu/index.php/programs-projects/what-native-nation-building.

University of Technology Sydney (UTS). 2019. Jumbunna Institute for Indigenous Education and Research. Available at jumbunna-institute-indigenous-education-and-research.

Upper Red Lake Association. 2019. Web page. Available at www.upperredlakeassn.com/index.html.

U.S. Census Bureau. 2012. Table 361. Largest Lakes in the United States. *Statistical Abstract of the United States*. Washington, DC: U.S. Census Bureau.

US Commission on Civil Rights. 2004. Broken promises: Evaluating the Native American health care system. Washington, DC: US Commission on Civil Rights.

US Department of Health and Human Services. 2014. Trends in Indian health, 2014 edition. Rockville, MD: Indian Health Service, US Department of Health and Human Services.

US Department of Health and Human Services. 2016. *Indian Health Service Fact Sheets: Tribal Self-Governance*, July. Available at https://www.ihs.gov/newsroom/factsheets/tribalselfgovernance/.

US Department of Health and Human Services. 2018. *Indian Health Service Fact Sheets: IHS Profile*, July. Available at https://www.ihs.gov/newsroom/factsheets/ihsprofile/.

US Department of Health and Human Services. (n.d.). Successful connections: Lasting partnerships. Rockville, MD: Indian Health Service, Office of Tribal Self-governance. Available at https://www.ihs.gov/selfgovernance/includes/themes/responsive2017/display_objects/documents/PocketFolderBrochure.pdf.

US Government, Office of the Press Secretary. 2009. The White House Native Tribal Nations Conference. Blog post, 5 November. Available at https://obamawhitehouse.archives.gov/blog/2009/11/05/white-house-tribal-nations-conference.

US Government, Office of the Press Secretary. 2013. Executive order on climate preparedness. Fact sheet, 1 November. Available at https://obamawhitehouse.archives.gov/the-press-office/2013/11/01/fact-sheet-executive-order-climate-preparedness.

van Oosten, J. and Deason, H. J. 1957. History of Red Lakes Fishery, 1971-38, with Observations on Population Status. Special Scientific Report, Fisheries No. 229. Washington, DC: Fish and Wildlife Service, U.S. Department of the Interior.

Veracini, L. 2011. Introducing: Settler colonial studies. *Settler Colonial Studies* 1(1), 1–12.

Vivian, A., Jorgensen, M., Reilly, A., McMillan, M., McRae, C. and McMinn, J. 2017. Indigenous self-government in the Australian federation. *Australian Indigenous Law Review* 20, 215.

Vivian, A., Jorgensen, M., Bell, D., Rigney, D., Cornell, S. and Hemming, S. 2017. Implementing a project within the Indigenous research paradigm: The example of nation building research. *Ngiya: Talk the Law*, 47–74.

Von Der Porten, S. 2012. Canadian indigenous governance literature: A review. *AlterNative: An International Journal of Indigenous Peoples* 8(1), 1–14.

Waitangi Tribunal. 1998. *Te Whanau o Waipareira Report*. Available at https://forms.justice.govt.nz/search/Documents/WT/wt_DOC_68641192/Wai%20414. Pdf.

Wakeling, S., Jorgensen, M., Michaelson, S. and Begay, M. 2001. Policing on American Indian Reservations. In X.F. Hartman and P. J. Kalt *A Report to the National Institute of Justice*, pp. 3–95. Washington, DC: National Institute of Justice, US Department of Justice. Available at Ncjrs.gov/pdffiles/nij/188095.pdf.

Walter Butler Company. 1978. *Peat Utilization and the Red Lake Indian Reservation.* St. Paul, MN: Minnesota Department of Natural Resources.

Walters, K. 2007. Indigenous perspectives in survey research: Conceptualising and measuring historical trauma, microaggressions, and colonial trauma response. *Mātauranga taketake: Traditional Knowledge. Indigenous Indicators of Well-being: Perspectives, Practices, Solutions*, pp. 27–44. Knowledge Exchange

Programme Of Ngā Pae o te Māramatanga, The National Institute of Research Excellence for Māori Development and Advancement, Auckland, New Zealand.

Walters, K., Mohammed, S.A., Evans-Campbell, T., Beltrán, R.E., Chae, D.H. and Duran, B. 2011. Bodies don't just tell stories, they tell histories: Embodiment of historical trauma among American Indians and Alaska Natives. *Du Bois Review: Social Science Research on Race* 8(1), 179–89.

Wellington City Council. 2017. Local governance statement 2016–2017. Available at https://wellington.govt.nz/~/media/your-council/structure-and-vision/files/local governance-statement.pdf?la=en.

Westbank First Nation. 2015. Community Plan. Available at https://www.wfn.ca/docs/wfn-community-plan.pdf.

Westbank First Nation. 2019. Website. Available at https://www.wfn.ca/.

Westmoreland, T. and Watson, K. 2006. Redeeming hollow promises: The case for mandatory spending on health care for American Indians and Alaska Natives. *American Journal of Public Health* 96(4), 600–605.

White, G. 2006. Indigenous governance in Melanesia. The Pacific Islands Development Program, East-West Center Department of Anthropology, University of Hawai'i. State, Society and Governance in Melanesia Project. Available at http://bellschool.anu.edu.au/sites/default/files/publications/attachments/2015-12/SSGM_IndigenousCustomaryGovernance_ResearchPaper_06_0.pdf.

Wild West Festival. 2019. Waimamaku. Facebook post, 4 February. Available at https://www.facebook.com/search/top/?q=waimamaku%20wild%20west%20festival&epa=SEARCH_BOX.

Wilkinson, C.F. 1996. Home Dance, the Hopi, and Black Mesa coal: Conquest and endurance in the American southwest. *BYU Law Review* 449, 456–58.

Williams, R.A. Jr. 1986. The algebra of federal Indian law: The hard trail of decolonizing and Americanizing the white man's Indian jurisprudence. *Wisconsin Law Review* 219.

Williams, R. A., Jr. 1999. *Linking Arms Together: American Indian Treaty Visions of Law and Peace, 1600–1800.* New York: Routledge.

Williams, W. (ed.). 2009. *Southeastern Indians since the Removal Era.* Athens, GA: University of Georgia Press, USA.

Wolfe, P. 2006. Settler colonialism and the elimination of the Native. *Journal of Genocide Research* 8(4), 387–409.

Women Empowering Women for Indigenous Nations. (n.d.). About WEWIN. Available at https://www.wewin04.org/about-wewin.

Wong C.A., Gachupin, F.C., Holman, R.C., et al. 2014. American Indian and Alaska Native infant and pediatric mortality, United States, 1999–2009. *American Journal of Public Health* 104(S3), S320–328.

Wood, A. 2016a. Constitutional recognition: A case for less Is more. In M. Davis and M. Langton (eds), *It's OurCcountry: Indigenous Arguments for MeaningfulCconstitutional Recognition and Reform*, pp. 104–13. Carlton, Victoria: Melbourne University Press.

Wood, A. 2016b. 'Is Australia ready to constitutionally recognise Indigenous peoples as equals?' In S. Young, J. Nielsen, and J. Patrick (eds), *Constitutional Recognition of First Peoples in Australia: Theories and Comparative Perspectives*, pp. 103–28. Annandale, NSW: Federation Press.

Wood, A. 2017. Confluence of the rivers: Constitutional recognition of Australia's First Peoples. In H. Devere, K. Te Maihāroa, and J.P. Synott (eds), *Peacebuilding and the Rights of Indigenous Peoples: Experiences and Strategies for the 21st Century*, pp. 89–104. Switzerland: Springer Press.

Yeh, C.J., Hunter, C.D., Madan-Bahel, A., Chiang, L. and Arora, A.K. 2004. Indigenous and interdependent perspectives of healing: Implications for counselling and research. *Journal of Counselling and Development* 82(4), 410–19.

York, G., 1990. *The Dispossessed, Life and Death in Native Canada*. London: Vintage UK Press.

Yunus, M. 2008. Creating a world without poverty: Social business and the future of capitalism. *Global Urban Development* 4(2), 16–41. Available at https://www.globalurban.org/GUDMag08Vol4Iss2/MagHome.htm.

Zillio, M. and Stueck, W. 2017. 'Trudeau Addresses Canada's Relationship with Indigenous Peoples in UN Speech.' *The Globe and Mail*, 20 September. Available at www.theglobeandmail.com/news/politics/trudeau-to-use-un-speech-to-recognize-canadas-relationship-with-indigenous-peoples/article36338926/.

Index

About the Authors

Diane Smith is a Research Fellow at the Centre for Aboriginal Economic Policy Research at the Australian Nation University. She is the Co-Founder and Chief Investigator of the Indigenous Community Governance Project, and current Co-Founder and Co-Lead Investigator of the Indigenous Governance of Development Project in Australia.

Stephen Cornell is Faculty Chair of the Native Nations Institute, Emeritus Professor of Sociology, and Emeritus Director of the Udall Center for Studies in Public Policy at the University of Arizona and Co-Founder and Co-Director of the Harvard Project on American Indian Economic Development.

Adam Delaney is a full-time PhD scholar with the Australian National University. His research project is on his people, the indigenous Motu Koita, and their governance in the National Capital District, Port Moresby, Papua New Guinea. Adam is an ex-diplomat, government official and private consultant. He has served on various international, Pacific regional and Australian advisory bodies and bureaus.

Alice Wighton is a Research Officer at the Centre for Aboriginal Economic Policy Research at the Australian Nation University, and previously at the Australian Indigenous Governance Institute, contributing to several projects, including on Indigenous regional decision-making, innovations in contemporary governance, and an audit of governance education and training for Indigenous people in Australia.

www.ingramcontent.com/pod-product-compliance
Lightning Source LLC
LaVergne TN
LVHW091532200926
848483LV00002B/380
* 9 7 8 1 5 3 8 1 4 3 6 3 6 *